SINKING OF THE TITANIC

EYEWITNESS ACCOUNTS

Edited by
Jay Henry Mowbray

DOVER PUBLICATIONS, INC.
Mineola, New York

Published in Canada by General Publishing Company, Ltd., 30 Lesmill Road, Don Mills, Toronto, Ontario.

Published in the United Kingdom by Constable and Company, Ltd., 3 The Lanchesters, 162–164 Fulham Palace Road, London W6 9ER.

Bibliographical Note

This Dover edition, first published in 1998, is an unabridged republication of *Sinking of the Titanic,* originally published by The Minter Company, Harrisburg, Pa., in 1912.

Library of Congress Cataloging-in-Publication Data

Mowbray, Jay Henry.
Sinking of the Titanic : eyewitness accounts / Jay Henry Mowbray. — Dover ed.
p. cm.
Originally published: Harrisburg, Pa. : Minter Co., 1912.
Includes index.
ISBN 0-486-40298-3 (pbk.)
1. Titanic (Steamship) 2. Shipwrecks—North Atlantic Ocean. I. Title.
G530.T6M7 1998
910'.91634—dc21 98-3690
CIP

Manufactured in the United States of America
Dover Publications, Inc.
31 East 2nd Street, Mineola, N.Y. 11501

PREFACE.

"WE are as near Heaven by sea as by land," cried Sir Humphrey Gilbert, ere his ship sank with him; and the hundreds who perished in the ocean within reach of the exultant welcome and the festal preparation of the shore have found Paradise as surely, and in giving "the last full measure of devotion" have gone as brave men would wish to go.

Sorrow that is too deep and strong for words clutches the heart-strings of humanity and the Nation mourns for the heroic dead, who were carried down into the sea with the crushed "Titanic." They faced death with high hearts, making the Supreme Sacrifice so that the women and the helpless little ones might live.

It is a heart-rending story, redeemed and ennobled by the heroism of the victims. Its details are appalling. The world is full of mournings for the dead. Nature has conquered again, destroying with ruthless hand the most marvelous ship that ever floated on the bosom of the deep.

It is the worst disaster that ever befell any vessel. It is the wrecking of a whole armada within one hull of steel, vaunted as unsinkable.

The sinking of the "Titanic" is an appalling catastrophe, in the contemplation of which any words that can be uttered are as futile as in the presence of the awful majesty of the Angel of Death.

The maiden trip of the newest, staunchest and greatest of the modern ocean greyhounds has thus apparently ended in the most appalling marine disaster ever recorded.

The first advices brought word of the safe removal of all the passengers and the possible success of the crew in their endeavor to bring the noblest ship afloat to shallow water. Another triumph of the wireless telegraph was hailed, and from both shores went up a paean of thanksgiving that the overwhelming loss was not of life but of things material, that, however valuable, are far less dear and can one day be replaced.

But now as a bolt from the blue, and as a forecast of the final mortal terrors of the Day of Judgment, comes the message that of 2300 souls aboard, but 700—chiefly women and children—have been saved.

All earthly concerns beside this calamity seem to fade into littleness and nothingness. The sole redeeming circumstance is that heroes met their death like men, and that human love was victorious over human terror, and mightier than Death and the open grave of the remorseless deep.

The one alleviating circumstance in this terrible tragedy is the fact that the men stood aside and insisted that the women and children should first have places in the boats.

There were men who were accustomed merely to pronounce a wish to have it gratified. For one of the humblest fishing smacks or a dory they could have given the price that was paid to build the immense ship that has become the most imposing mausoleum that ever housed the bones of men since the Pyramids rose from the desert sands.

But these men stood aside—one can see them—and gave place not merely to the delicate and the refined, but to the scared woman from the steerage with her toddler by her side, coming through the very gate of Death and out of the mouth of Hell to the imagined Eden of America.

To many of those who went it was harder to go than to stay there on the vessel gaping with its mortal wounds and ready to go down. It meant that tossing on the waters they must wait in suspense, hour after hour, even after the lights of the ship were engulfed in appalling darkness, hoping against hope for the miracle of a rescue dearer to them than their own lives.

It was the tradition of Anglo-Saxon heroism that was fulfilled in the frozen seas during the black hours of the night. The heroism was that of the women who went, as well as of the men who remained.

The sympathy of all the world will go out to the stricken survivors of the victims of a world-wide calamity.

INTRODUCTION.

HE human imagination is unequal to the reconstruction of the appalling scene of the disaster in the North Atlantic. No picture of the pen or of the painter's brush can adequately represent the magnitude of the calamity that has made the whole world kin.

How trivial in such an hour seem the ordinary affairs of civilized mankind—the minor ramifications of politics, the frenetic rivalry of candidates, the haggle of stock speculators. We are suddenly, by an awful visitation, made to see our human transactions in their true perspective, as small as they really are.

Man's pride is profoundly humbled: he must confess that the victory this time has gone to the blind, inexorable forces of nature, except in so far as the manifestation of the heroic virtues is concerned.

The ship that went to her final resting place two miles below the placid, unconfessing level of the sea represented all that science and art knew how to contribute to the expedition of traffic, to the comfort and enjoyment of voyagers.

She had 15 watertight steel compartments supposed to render her unsinkable. She was possessed of submarine signals with microphones, to tell the bridge by means of wires when shore or ship or any other object was at hand.

There was a collision bulkhead to safeguard the ship against the invasion of water amidships should the bow be torn away. In a word, the boat was as safe and sound as the shipbuilder could make it.

It was the pride of the owners and the commander that what has happened could not possibly occur. And yet the Titanic went down, and carried to their doom hundreds of passengers and men who intimately knew the sea and had faced every peril that the navigator meets.

In the hours between half-past 10 on Sunday night and half-past 2 Monday morning, while the ship still floated, what did the luxuries of their $10,000,000 castle on the ocean avail those who trod the eight steel decks, not knowing at what moment the whole glittering fabric might plunge with them—as it did plunge—to the unplumbed abyss below?

What was it, in those agonizing hours, to the men who remained aboard, or to the women and children placed in the boats, that there were three electric elevators, squash courts and Turkish baths, a hospital with an operating room, private promenade decks and Renaissance cabins? What is it to a man about to die to know that there is at hand a palm garden or a darkroom for photography, or the tapestry of an English castle or a dinner service of 10,000 pieces of silver and gold?

In that midnight crisis the one thing needful was not provided, where everything was supplied. The one inadequacy was—the lack of lifeboats.

In the supreme confidence of the tacit assumption that they never would be needed, the means of rescue—except in a pitably meagre insufficiency—was not at hand. There were apparently but 20 boats and rafts available, each capable of sustaining at most 60 persons.

Yet the ship was built to carry 2435 passengers and 860 in the crew—a total of 3295 persons.

Whatever the luxuriousness of the appointments, the magnificance of the carvings and the paintings that surfeited the eye, the amplitude of the space alloted for the promenade, it seems incredible no calculation was made for the rescue of at least 2000 of the possible floating population of the Titanic.

The result of the tragedy must be that aroused public opinion will compel the formulation of new and drastic regulations, alike by the British Board of Trade and by the Federal authorities, providing not merely for the adequate equipment of every ship with salvatory apparatus but for rigorous periodical inspection of the appliances and a constant drill of the crew.

Let there be an end of boasting about the supremacy of man to the immitigable laws and forces of nature. Let the grief of mankind be assuaged not in idle lamentation but in amelioration of the conditions that brought about the saddest episode in the history of ships at sea.

The particular line that owned and sent forth the vessel that has perished has been no more to blame than others that similarly ignored elemental precautions in favor of superfluous comforts, in a false sense of security.

When the last boatload of priceless human life swung away from the davits of the Titanic, it left behind on the decks of the doomed ship hundreds of men who knew that the vessel's mortal wound spelt Death for them also. But no cravens these men who went to their nameless graves, nor scourged as the galley slave to his dungeon.

Called suddenly from the ordinary pleasure of ship life and fancied security, they were in a moment confronted with the direct peril of the sea, and the absolute certainty that, while some could go to safety, many must remain.

It was the supreme test, for if a man lose his life he loses all. But, had the grim alternative thought to mock the cowardice of the breed, it was doomed to disappointment.

Silently these men stood aside. "Women first," the inexorable law of the sea, which one disobeys only to court everlasting ignominy,, undoubtedly had no place in their minds. "Women first," the common law of humanity, born of chivalry and the nobler spirit of self-sacrifice, prevailed.

They simply stood aside.

The first blush of poignant grief will pass from those who survive and were bereft. But always will they sense in its fullest meaning this greatest of all sacrifice. Ever must it remain as a reassuring knowledge of the love, and faithfulness, and courage, of the Man, and of his care for the weak.

"Greater love hath no man than this that a man lay down his life for his friend."

Hymn for Survivors of the Titanic.

By HALL CAINE;
The Great English Novelist.

[*To Tune of "God Our Help in Ages Past."*]

Lord of the everlasting hills,
  God of the boundless sea,
Help us through all the shocks of fate
  To keep our trust in Thee.

When nature's unrelenting arm
  Sweeps us like withes away,
Maker of man, be Thou our strength
  And our eternal stay.

When blind, insensate, heartless force
  Puts out our passing breath,
Make us to see Thy guiding light
  In darkness and in death.

Beneath the roll of soundless waves
  Our best and bravest lie;
Give us to feel their spirits live
  Immortal in the sky.

We are Thy children, frail and small,
  Formed of the lowly sod,
Comfort our bruised and bleeding souls,
  Father and Lord and God.

CONTENTS.

CHAPTER VI.

HOW SURVIVORS ESCAPED.

CHAPTER VII.

WOMAN'S THRILLING NARRATIVE.

CHAPTER VIII.

SURVIVORS' STIRRING STORIES.

CHAPTER IX.

HOW ASTOR WENT TO DEATH.

CHAPTER X.

NOTABLE WOMAN SAVED.

CHAPTER XI.

MAJOR BUTT, MARTYR TO DUTY.

CHAPTER XII.

MRS. ASTOR'S BRAVERY.

CHAPTER XIII.

LIFEBOATS BUNGLINGLY HANDLED.

CHAPTER XIV.

NOT LIKE BOURGOGNE DISASTER.

CHAPTER XV.

BOY'S DESPERATE FIGHT FOR LIFE.

CHAPTER XVI.

CARPATHIA TO THE RESCUE.

CHAPTER XVII.

REFUSED TO LEAVE HUSBAND.

GREAT MARINE DISASTERS FROM 1866 TO 1911.

Among the great marine disasters on record that have resulted in loss of lives and vessels are:

1866, Jan. 11.—Steamship London, on her way to Melbourne, foundered in the Bay of Biscay; 220 lives lost.

1866, Oct. 3.—Steamship Evening Star, from New York to New Orleans, foundered; about 250 lives lost.

1867, Oct. 29.—Royal Mail steamships Rhone and Wye and about 50 other vessels driven ashore and wrecked at St. Thomas, West Indies, by a hurricane; about 100 lives lost.

1870, —Indian Line steamship City of Boston left New York with 117 passengers and was never heard from.

1871, July 30.—Staten Island ferryboat Westfield exploded in New York hurricane; about 1000 lives lost.

1873, Jan. 22.—British steamship North Fleet sunk in collision off Dungeness; 300 lives lost.

1873, Nov. 23.—White Star liner Atlantic wrecked off Nova Scotia; 547 lives lost.

1873, Nov. 23.—French liner Ville du Havre, from New York to Havre, lost in collision with ship Lochearn; sank in 16 minutes; 110 lives lost.

1874, Dec. 26.—Immigrant vessel Cospatrick took fire and sank off Auckland; 476 lives lost.

1875, May 7.—Hamburg Mail steamship Schiller wrecked in fog on Sicily Isles; 200 lives lost.

1875, Nov. 4.—American steamship Pacific in collision 30 miles southwest of Cape Flattery; 236 lives lost.

1877, Nov. 24.—U. S. sloop of war Huron wrecked off North Carolina coast; 110 lives lost.

1878, Jan. 31.—Steamship Metropolis wrecked off North Carolina; 104 lives lost.

1878, March 24.—British training ship Eurydice, a frigate, foundered near the Isle of Wight; 300 lives lost.

1878, Sept. 3.—British iron steamship Princess Alice sunk in collision in the Thames; 700 lives lost.

1878, Dec. 18.—French steamship Byzantin sunk in collision in the Dardanelles with the British steamship Rinaldo; 210 lives lost.

1879, Dec. 2.—Steamship Borusia sunk off coast of Spain; 174 lives lost.

1880, Jan. 31.—British training ship Atlanta left Bermuda with 290 men and was never heard from.

1881, Aug. 30.—Steamship Teuton wrecked off the Cape of Good Hope; 200 lives lost.

1883, July 3.—Steamship Daphne turned turtle in the Clyde; 124 lives lost.

1884, Jan. 18.—American steamship City of Columbus wrecked off Gay Head Light, Mass.; 99 lives lost.

1884, April 19.—Bark Ponema and steamship State of Florida sank in mid-ocean after collision; 145 lives lost.

1884, July 23.—Spanish steamship Gijon and British steamship Lux in collision off Finistere; 150 lives lost.

1887, Jan. 29.—Steamship Kapunda in collision with bark Ada Melore off coast of Brazil; 300 lives lost.

1887, Nov. 15.—British steamship Wah Young caught fire between Canton and Hongkong; 400 lives lost.

1888, Sept. 13.—Italian steamship Sud America and steamship La France in collision near the Canary Islands; 89 lives lost.

1889, March 16.—U. S. warship Trenton, Vandalia and Lipsic and German ships Adler and Eber wrecked on Samoan Islands; 147 lives lost.

1890, Jan. 2.—Steamship Persia wrecked off Corsica; 130 lives lost.

1890, Feb. 17.—British steamship Duburg wrecked in China Sea; 400 lives lost.

1890, March 1.—British steamship Quetia foundered in Lorres Straits; 124 lives lost.

1890, Sept. 19.—Turkish frigate Ertogrul foundered off Japan; 540 lives lost.

1890, Dec. 27.—British steamship Shanghai burned in China Sea; 101 lives lost.

1891, March 17.—Anchor liner Utopia in collision with British steamship Anson off Gibraltar and sunk; 574 lives lost.

1891, April 16.—British ship St. Catharis wrecked off Caroline Island; 90 lives lost.

1892, Jan. 13.—Steamship Namehow wrecked in China Sea; 414 lives lost.

1892, Oct. 28.—Anchor liner Romania wrecked off Corsica; 113 lives lost.

1893, Feb. 8.—Anchor line Trinalria wrecked off Spain; 115 lives lost.

1893, June 22.—British battleship Pretoria sunk in collision with the Camperdown off Syria; 357 lives lost.

1894, Nov. 1.—Steamship Wairaro wrecked off New Zealand; 134 lives lost.

1894, June 25.—Steamship Norge wrecked on Rockall Reef in North Atlantic; nearly 600 lives lost.

1895, Jan. 30.—German steamship Elbe, sunk in collision with British steamship Grathie in North Sea; 335 lives lost.

1895, March 11.—Spanish cruiser Reina Regenta foundered in Atlantic at entrance to Mediterranean; 400 lives lost.

1898, July 2.—Steamship Bourgogne rammed British steel sailing vessel Cromartshire and sank rapidly; 571 lies lost.

1904, June 15.—General Slocum, excursion steamboat with 1400 persons aboard; took fire going through Hell Gate, East River; more than 1000 lives lost.

1905, Sept. 12.—Japanese warship Mikasa sunk after explosion in Sasebo harbor; 599 lives lost.

1907, Feb. 12.—Steamship Larchmont in collision with Harry Hamilton in Long Island Sound; 183 lives lost.

1907, Feb. 21.—English mail steamship Berlin wrecked off the Hook of Holland; 142 lives lost.

1907, Feb. 24.—Austrian Lloyd steamship Imperatrix, from Trieste to Bombay, wrecked on Cape of Crete and sunk; 137 lives lost.

1907, Jan.—British steamship Pengwern foundered in the North Sea; crew and 24 men lost.

1907, Jan.—Prinz Waldemar, Hamburg-American line, aground at Kingston, Jamaica, after earthquake; 3 lives lost.

1907, Feb.—French warship Jean Bart, sunk off coast of Morocco.

1907, March.—Steamship Congo sunk at mouth of Ems river by German steamship Nerissa; 7 lives lost.

1907, March.—French warship Jena, blown up at Toulon; 120 lives lost.

1907, July.—Steamship Columbia, sunk off Shelton Cove, California, in collision with steamship San Pedro; 50 lies lost.

1908, Feb. 3.—Steamship St. Cuthbert, bound from Antwerp to New York, burned at sea off Nova Scotia; 15 lives lost.

1908, April 25.—British cruiser Gladiator rammed by American liner St. Paul off Isle of Wight; 30 lives lost.

1908, July.—Chinese warship Ying King foundered; 300 lives lost.

1908, Aug. 24.—Steamship Folgenenden wrecked; 70 persons lost.

1908, Nov. 6.—Steamship Taish sunk in storm off Etoro Island; 150 lives lost.

1911, Feb. 2.—Steamship Abenton wrecked; 70 lives lost.

1911, April 23.—Steamship Asia ran aground; 40 lives lost.

1911, Sept. 5.—Steamship Tuscapel wrecked; 81 lives lost.

1911, Oct. 2.—Steamship Hatfield in collision and sunk; 207 lives lost.

1911, April 2.—Steamship Koombuna wrecked; 150 lives lost.

HUNDREDS WEEP AT MEMORIAL SERVICES HELD FOR "ARCHIE" BUTT.

Fifteen hundred sincere mourners for Major Archibald W. Butt, lost on the Titanic, wept unashamed at his home in Augusta, Georgia, on May 2, when President Taft called his former aid affectionately by his first name and choked with tears as he paid a personal tribute to the army officer.

It was at a monster memorial service for the soldier, where all Augusta paid homage to his memory. President Taft was the main speaker. He was deeply affected by the solemn ritual.

"If Archie could have selected a time to die he would have chosen the one God gave him," the President said, his voice broken with emotion.

"His life was spent in self-sacrifice, serving others. His forgetfulness of self had become a part of his nature.

"Everybody who knew him called him Archie.

"I couldn't prepare anything in advance to say here," the President continued. "I tried, but couldn't. He was too near me. He was loyal to my predecessor, Mr. Roosevelt, who selected him to be military aid, and to me he had become as a son or a brother."

Taft pictured a new side to Major Butt's character—his love for his mother.

"I think he never married because of that love for her who was taken from him two years ago," the President declared.

IN MEMORIAM
OF THE
STEAMSHIP
TITANIC'S
DEAD

TRIPLE SCREW STEAMER "TITANIC" WAS THE LARGEST AND FINEST VESSEL IN THE WORLD: 882½ FEET LONG, 45,000 TONS REGISTER, 92½ FEET WIDE

Life boats of the "Titanic" which would only hold one third of the passengers. All could have been saved had there been a sufficient number of boats. These few boats rescued all that were saved from this appalling disaster.

1 2 3 4 5 6 7 8 9

STEAMSHIP "TITANIC" SHOWING LENGTH AS COMPARED WITH HIGHEST BUILDINGS.

1	Bunker Hill Monument, Boston	221 Feet High	6	White Star Line's Triple Screw Steamer "TITANIC"	882½ Feet Long
2	Public Buildings, Philadelphia	534 Feet High	7	Cologne Cathedral, Cologne, Germany	516 Feet High
3	Washington Monument, Washington	555 Feet High	8	Grand Pyramid, Gizeh, Africa	451 Feet High
4	Metropolitan Tower, New York	700 Feet High	9	St. Peter's Church, Rome, Italy	448 Feet High
5	New Woolworth Building, New York	750 Feet High			

ENTRANCE HALL AND GRAND STAIRCASE OF THE "TITANIC."

A striking introduction to the wonders and beauty of the "Titanic" is the entrance hall and grand staircase in the forward section where one begins to realize for the first time the magnificence of this surpassing steamer. It is the largest and finest steamship in the world. It is indeed a floating palace.

CAPTAIN ROSTRON, OF THE "CARPATHIA," WHO RUSHED HIS SHIP TO THE RESCUE OF THE "TITANTIC'S" PASSENGERS AND BROUGHT THEM TO NEW YORK. THIS BOOK CONTAINS MANY THRILLING STORIES THAT WERE TOLD BY PASSENGERS WHILE ABOARD THIS RESCUE SHIP

WILLIAM T. STEAD OF LONDON, ENGLAND

EDITOR REVIEW OF REVIEWS, WHO STOOD BY CAPTAIN SMITH WHEN THE SHIP WAS SINKING AND WITHOUT TREPIDATION WENT TO A WATERY GRAVE

HUGE ICEBERG AS PHOTOGRAPHED ABOUT 100 MILES NORTH OF THE SCENE OF THE "TITANIC" DISASTER.

ISADORE STRAUSE.

THE NEW YORK MILLIONAIRE MERCHANT AND PHILANTHROPIST WHO LOST HIS LIFE ON THE GIANT TITANIC.

A TYPE OF MAGNIFICENT OCEAN GREY HOUND. THE STEAMSHIP "KAISERIN AUGUSTE VICTORIA" OF HAMBURG-AMERICAN LINE.

This steamer is 700 feet long, 77 feet wide and 54 feet deep. She has accommodations for 550 first-class passengers, 350 second-class, 300 third-class and 2300 steerage passengers, making altogether a floating city of 3500 population.

MAIN DINING ROOM, STEAMSHIP "KAISERIN AUGUSTE VICTORIA," OF THE HAMBURG-AMERICAN LINE.

It has promenade decks, large cabins with lower berths only, grand combination suites of rooms, and in addition to the grand dining saloon a perfectly equipped restaurant. Small tables have been provided in place of the long tables that have for many years been in use on steamships.

SEEKING INFORMATION ABOUT LOST RELATIVES AND FRIENDS AT THE OFFICE OF THE STEAMSHIP COMPANY.

EFFECT OF THE MIRAGE AS SEEN AMONG THE ICE FLOES.

THE SINKING "TITANIC" CARRYING HUNDREDS OF SOULS TO WATERY GRAVES BEFORE THE EYES OF TERRIFIED SURVIVORS IN LIFEBOATS. THIS AWFUL TRAGEDY SENT A MAGNIFICENT SHIP THAT WAS CALLED "UNSINKABLE" TO THE BOTTOM OF THE OCEAN AFTER RUNNING INTO AN ICEBERG

THESE BRIGHT LITTLE FRENCH CHILDREN WERE RESCUED FROM THE "TITANIC;" MISS HAYS, HERSELF A SURVIVOR, IS TAKING CARE OF THEM. THEY WERE COMING TO AMERICA WITH THEIR FATHER, WHO WENT DOWN WITH THE SHIP

SINKING OF THE "TITANIC." THERE WAS A MIGHTY ROAR WHEN THE SHIP WENT DOWN. THE BOW SANK FIRST, WITH STERN POISED IN THE AIR, WHEN SUDDENLY IT PLUNGED OUT OF SIGHT, CARRYING HUNDREDS OF SOULS TO ETERNITY

CHAPTER I.

FROM A DAY OF DELIGHT TO DEATH.

April 14, 1912, a Fateful Date—Lulled to False Security—Peaceful Sabbath Ends in Dire Disaster—Hopes Sink Beneath the Cruel and Treacherous Waves of the Atlantic—Man's Proudest Craft Crumbles Like an Eggshell.

The hands of the ship's clock pointed to 11.40. The beautiful day of April 14, 1912, rapidly was drawing to its close.

A solemn hush brooded over the ocean, the stillness broken only by the swish of the waters as they protested against being so rudely brushed aside by the mammoth creation of man. Then, too, the soft cadences of sacred music from the ship's orchestra sent their strains dancing o'er the billows to mingle with the star beam and intensify rather than mar the stillness.

Above, the stars and planets twinkled and glittered as they beam only in the rarified atmosphere of the far northern latitudes.

The day had been one of rare beauty. A soft and caressing breeze had kissed the sea and rocked the waves in a harmonious symphony against the steel-ribbed sides of the world's largest, greatest and most luxurious floating palace, the majestic Titanic, the newest addition to the trans-Atlantic fleet of the White Star Line of the International Navigation Company.

The star-sprinkled dome of heaven and the phosphorescent sea alike breathed forth peace, quiet and security.

Despite the lateness of the hour, aboard the Titanic all was animation. A few, to be sure, had wearied of Nature's marvels and had sought their slumber, but the gorgeous quarters of the first cabin and the scarcely less pretentious sections set apart for second class passengers were alike teeming with life and light.

Meanwhile, as they had for days past, the mighty engines of this monster of the sea pulsed and throbbed, while the rhythmic beat of the Titanic's great bronze-bladed propellors churned up a fast and steadily lengthening wake behind the speeded vessel.

"We'll break the record today," her officers laughed, and the passengers gleefully shared their mirth.

A record; a record!

And a record she made—but of death and destruction!

But who could know? And since no mortal could, why not eat, drink and be merry?

Britain's shores had been left behind far back across the waste of waters. America, the land of hope, was almost in sight ahead.

TALK OF HOME AND FRIENDS AND LIFE.

Small wonder that hundreds still strolled the Titanic's spotless, unsullied decks and talked of home and friends and life and joy and hope. Small wonder that other hundreds lounged at ease in her luxurious saloons and smoking rooms, while other scores of voyagers, their appetites whetted by the invigorating air, sat at a midnight supper to welcome the new week with a feast.

Why sleep when the wealth, the beauty, the brains, the aristocracy as well as the bone and sinew of a nation were all around one?

For, be it known, never before did ship carry so distinguished a company—a passenger list that reads like a Social Blue Book.

This maiden trip of the Titanic was an event that was to go down in history, they thought.

And so it will, but with tears on every page of the narrative and the wails of women and children in every syllable.

But since the future is unrolled only in God's own good time, how could they know?

Why wonder at their presence?

Was this not the first trip of the greatest triumph of marine architecture?

Had not the wealth and fashion of two continents so arranged their plans as to be numbered on its first passenger list?

Had not the hardy immigrant skimped and saved and schemed that he and his family should be carried to the Land of Promise aboard this greatest of all ships?

What mattered it to him that his place was in the steerage? Did not each pulsing throb of the Titanic's mighty engines bear him as far and as fast as though he, too, already held in his hand the millions he felt he was destined to win in this golden land of opportunity beyond the seas?

And so, from the loftiest promenade deck to the lowest stoke hole in the vitals of the ship peace and comfort and happiness reigned.

APPROACHING HOME AND FRIENDS.

To some the rapidly-nearing shores of America meant home—and friends. To others, opportunity—and work. Yet to all it meant the culmination of a voyage which, so far, had been one all-too-short holiday from the bustle and turmoil of a busy world.

"Man proposes, but God disposes!"

Never were truer words uttered, nor phrase more fitting to that fateful hour.

"In the midst of life we are in death."

Yet the soft breeze from the south still spread its balmy, salt-laden odors to delight their senses and to lull them to a feeling of complete security.

What was that?

A cold breath as from the fastnesses of the Frost King swept the steamer's decks.

A shiver of chill drove the wearied passengers below, but sent the ship's officers scurrying to their stations. The seaman, and the seaman alone, knew that that icy chill portended icebergs—and near at hand.

Besides, twice in the last few hours had the wireless ticked its warnings from passing vessels that the Titanic was in the vicinity of immense floes.

Why had the warning not been heeded?

Why had the ponderous engines continued to thunder with the might of a hundred thousand horses, and the ship to plunge forward into the night with the unchecked speed of an express train?

God knows!

The captain knew, but his lips are sealed in death as, a self-inflicted bullet in his brain, he lies in the cold embrace of the sea he had loved and had defied—too long.

THE LOOKOUT'S WARNING CRY.

Perhaps Bruce Ismay, the managing director of the line, who was on board—and survived when women drowned—also knows. Perhaps he will tell by whose orders those danger warnings were scoffed at and ignored.

Perhaps; perhaps!

The lookout uttered a sharp cry!

Too late!

One grinding crash and the Titanic had received its death blow. Man's proudest craft crumbled like an eggshell.

Ripped from stem to engine room by the great mass of ice she struck amidships, the Titanic's side was laid open as if by a gigantic can opener. She quickly listed to starboard and a shower of ice fell on to the forecastle deck.

Shortly before she sank she broke in two abaft the engine room, and as she disappeared beneath the water the expulsion of air or her boilers caused two explosions, which were plainly heard by the survivors adrift.

A moment more and the Titanic had gone to her doom with the fated hundreds grouped on the after deck. To the survivors they were visible to the last, and their cries and moans were pitiable.

The one alleviating circumstance in the otherwise unmitigable tragedy is the fact that the men stood aside and insisted that the women and the children should first have places in the boats.

There were men whose word of command swayed boards of directors, governed institutions, disposed of millions. They were accustomed merely to pronounce a wish to have it gratified.

Thousands "posted at their bidding;" the complexion of the market altered hue when they nodded; they bought what they wanted, and for one of the humblest fishing smacks or a dory they could have given the price that was paid to build and launch the ship that has become the most imposing mausoleum that ever housed the bones of men since the Pyramids rose from the desert sands.

But these men stood aside—one can see them—and gave place not merely to the delicate and the refined, but to the scared Czech woman from the steerage, with her baby at her breast; the Croatian with a toddler by her side, coming through the very gate of Death and out of the mouth of Hell to the imagined Eden of America.

HARDER TO GO THAN TO STAY.

To many of those who went it was harder to go than to stay there on the vessel gaping with its mortal wounds and ready to go down. It meant that tossing on the waters they must wait in suspense, hour after hour even after the lights of the ship were engulfed in appalling darkness, hoping against hope for the miracle of a rescue dearer to them than their own lives.

It was the tradition of Anglo-Saxon heroism that was fulfilled in the frozen seas during the black hours of that Sunday night. The heroism was that of the women who went, as well as of the men who remained.

The most adequate story of the terrible disaster is told by a trained newspaper man, who was on the Carpathia. He says:

Cause, responsibility and similar questions regarding the stupendous disaster will be taken up in time by the British marine authorities. No disposition has been shown by any survivor to question the courage of the crew, hundreds of whom saved others and gave their own lives with a heroism which equaled, but could not exceed, that of John Jacob Astor, Henry B. Harris, Jacques Futrelle and others in the long list of the first cabin missing.

Facts which I have established by inquiries on the Carpathia, as positively as they could be established in view of the silence of the few surviving officers, are:

That the Titanic's officers knew, several hours before the crash, of the possible nearness of icebergs.

That the Titanic's speed, nearly twenty-three knots an hour, was not slackened.

INSUFFICIENT LIFE-BOATS.

That the number of lifeboats on the Titanic was insufficient to accommodate much more than one-third of the passengers, to say nothing of the crew. Most members of the crew say there were sixteen lifeboats and two collapsibles; none say there were more than twenty boats in all. The 700 who escaped filled most of the sixteen lifeboats and the one collapsible which got away, to the limit of their capacity.

That the "women first" rule, in some cases, was applied to the extent of turning back men who were with their families, even though not enough women to fill the boats were at hand on that particular part of the deck. Some few boats were thus lowered without being completely filled, but most of these were soon filled with sailors and stewards, picked up out of the water, who helped man them.

That the bulkhead system, though probably working in the manner intended, availed only to delay the ship's sinking. The position and length of the ship's wound (on the starboard quarter) admitted icy water, which caused the boilers to explode, and these explosions practically broke the ship in two.

Had the ship struck the iceberg head-on, at whatever speed, and with whatever resultant shock, the bulkhead system of water-tight compartments would probably have saved the vessel. As one man expressed it, it was the "impossible" that happened when, with a shock unbelievably mild, the ship's side was torn for a length which made the bulkhead system ineffective.

The Titanic was 1799 miles from Queenstown and 1191 miles from New York, speeding for a maiden voyage record. The night was starlight, the sea glassy. Lights were out in most of the staterooms and only two or three congenial groups remained in the public rooms.

In the crows' nest, or lookout, and on the bridge, officers and members of the crew were at their places, awaiting relief at midnight from their two hours' watch.

At 11.45 came the sudden sound of two gongs, a warning of immediate danger.

The crash against the iceberg, which had been sighted at only a quarter of a mile, came almost simultaneously with the clink of the levers operated by those on the bridge, which stopped the engine and closed the watertight doors.

CAPTAIN SMITH ON THE BRIDGE.

Captain Smith was on the bridge a moment later, giving orders for the summoning of all on board and for the putting on of life preservers and the lowering of the lifeboats.

The first boats lowered contained more men passengers than the latter ones, as the men were on deck first, and not enough women were there to fill them.

When, a moment later, the rush of frightened women and crying children to the deck began, enforcement of the women-first rule became rigid. Officers loading some of the boats drew revolvers, but in most cases the men, both passengers and crew, behaved in a way trat called for no such restraint.

Revolver shots, heard by many persons shortly before the end of the Titanic caused many rumors. One was that Captain Smith shot himself, another was that First Officer Murdock ended his life. Smith, Murdock and Sixth Officer Moody are known to have been lost. The surviving officers, Lightoller, Pitman, Boxhall and Lowe, have made no statement.

Members of the crew discredit all reports of suicide, and

say Captain Smith remained on the bridge until just before the ship sank, leaping only after those on the decks had been washed away. It is also related that, when a cook later sought to pull him aboard a lifeboat, he exclaimed, "Let me go!" and, jerking away, went down.

What became of the men with life preservers? is a question asked since the disaster by many persons. The preservers did their work of supporting their wearers in the water until the ship went down. Many of those drawn into the vortex, despite the preservers, did not come up again. Dead bodies floated on the surface as the last boats moved away.

"NEARER MY GOD TO THEE."

To relate that the ship's string band gathered in the saloon, near the end, and played "Nearer, My God, To Thee," sounds like an attempt to give an added solemn color to a scene which was in itself the climax of solemnity. But various passengers and survivors of the crew agree in the declaration that they heard this music. To some of the hearers, with husbands among the dying men in the water, and at the ship's rail, the strain brought in thought the words

"So, by my woes I'll be
Nearer, My God, to Thee,
Nearer to Thee."

"Women and children first," was the order in the filling of the Titanic's lifeboats. How well that order was fulfilled, the list of missing first and second cabin passengers bears eloquent witness. "Mr." is before almost every name, and the contrast is but made stronger by the presence of a few names of women—Mrs. Isidor Straus, who chose death rather than to leave her husband's side; Mrs. Allison, who remained below with her husband and daughter, and others who, in various ways, were kept from entering the line of those to be saved.

To most of the passengers, the midnight crash against the ice mountain did not seem of terrific force. Many were so little disturbed by it that they hesitated to dress and put on life preservers, even when summoned by that hundering knocks and shouts of the stewards. Bridge players in the smoking room kept on with their game.

Once on deck, many hesitated to enter the swinging lifeboats. The glassy sea, the starlit sky, the absence, in the first few moments, of intense excitement, gave them the feeling that there was only some slight mishap—that those who got into the boats would have a chilly half-hour below, and might later be laughed at.

It was such a feeling as this, from all accounts, which caused John Jacob Astor and his wife to refuse the places offered them in the first boat, and to retire to the gymnasium. In the same way, H. J. Allison, Montreal banker, laughed at the warning, and his wife, reassured by him, took her time about dressing. They and their daughter did not reach the carpathia. Their son, less than two years old, was carried into a lifeboat by his nurse, and was taken in charge by Major Arthur Peuchen.

ADMIRATION AND CONFIDENCE.

The admiration felt by passengers and crew for the matchlessly appointed vessel was translated, in those first few moments, into a confidence which for some proved deadly.

In the loading of the first boat restrictions of sex were not made, and it seemed to the men who piled in beside the women that there would be boats enough for all. But the ship's officers knew better than this, and as the spreading fear caused an earnest advance toward the suspended craft, the order, "Women first!" was heard, and the men were pushed aside.

To the scenes of the next two hours on those decks and in the waters below, such adjectives as "dramatic" and "tragic" do but poor justice. With the knowledge of deadly peril gaining greater power each moment over those men and women, the nobility of the greater part, both among cabin passengers, officers, crew and steerage, asserted itself.

Isidor Straus, supporting his wife on her way to a lifeboat, was held back by an inexorable guard. Another officer strove to help her to a seat of safety, but she brushed away his arm and clung to her husband, crying, "I will not go without you."

Another woman took her place, and her form, clinging to her husband's, became part of a picture now drawn indelibly in many minds. Neither wife nor husband reached a place of safety.

Colonel Astor, holding his young wife's arm, stood decorously aside as the officers spoke to him, and Mrs. Astor and her maid were ushered to seats. Mrs. Henry B. Harris, parted in like manner from her husband, saw him last at the rail, beside Colonel Astor. Walter M. Clark, of Los Angeles, nephew of the Montana Senator, joined the line of men as his young wife, sobbing, was placed in one of the boats.

AN AGONIZING SEPARATION.

"Let him come! There is room!" cried Mrs. Emil Taussig as the men of the White Star Line motioned to her husband to leave her. It was with difficulty that he released her hold to permit her to be led to her place.

George D. Widener, who had been in Captain Smith's company a few moments after the crash, was another whose wife was parted from him and lowered a moment later to the surface of the calm sea.

Of Major Archie Butt, a favorite with his fellow tourists; of Charles M. Hayes, president of the Grand Trunk; of Benjamin Guggenheim and of William T. Stead, no one seems to know whether they tarried too long in their staterooms or whether they forebore to approach the fast filling boats, none of them was in the throng which, weary hours afterward, reached the Carpathia.

Simultaneously on all the upper decks of the ship the ropes creaked with the lowering of the boats. As they reached the water, those in the boats saw what those on the decks could not see—that the Titanic was listing rapidly to starboard, and that her stern was rising at a portentous angle. A rush of steerage men toward the boats was checked by officers with revolvers in hand.

Some of the boats, crowded too full to give rowers a chance, drifted for a time. None had provisions or water; there was lack of covering from the icy air, and the only lights were the still undimmed arcs and incandescents of the settling ship, save for one of the first boats. There a steward, who explained to the passengers that he had been shipwrecked twice before, appeared carrying three oranges and a green light.

That green light, many of the survivors says, was to the shipwrecked hundreds as the pillar of fire by night. Long after the ship had disappeared, and while confusing false lights danced about the boats, the green lantern kept them together on the course which led them to the Carpathia.

ECHOING SPLASH OF CHILLY WATERS.

As the end of the Titanic became manifestly but a matter of moments, the oarsmen pulled their boats away, and the chilling waters began to echo splash after splash as the passengers and sailors in life preservers leaped over and started swimming away to escape the expected suction.

Only the hardiest of constitutions could endure for more than a few moments such a numbing bath. The first vigorous strokes gave way to the heart-breaking cries of "Help! Help!" and stiffened forms were seen floating, the faces relaxed in death.

Revolver shots were heard in the ship's last moments. The first report spread among the boats was that Captain Smith had ended his life with a bullet. Then it was said that a mate had shot a steward who tried to push his way upon a boat against orders. None of these tales has been verified, and many of the crew say the captain, without a preserver, leaped in at the last and went down, refusing a cook's offered aid.

The last of the boats, a collapsible, was launched too late to get away, and was overturned by the ship's sinking. Some of those in it—all, say some witnesses—found safety on a raft or were picked up by lifeboats,

In the Marconi tower, almost to the last, the loud click of the sending instrument was heard over the waters. Who was receiving the message, those in the boats did not know, and they would least of all have supposed that a Mediterranean ship in the distant South Atlantic track would be their rescuer.

As the screams in the water multiplied, another sound was heard, strong and clear at first, then fainter in the distance. It was the melody of the hymn "Nearer, My God, to Thee," played by the string orchestra in the dining saloon. Some of those on the water started to sing the words, but grew silent as they realized that for the men who played the music was a sacrament soon to be consummated by death. The serene strains of the hymn and the frantic cries of the dying blended in a symphony of sorrow.

BOATS FOLLOW THE GREEN LIGHT.

Led by the green light, under the light of the stars, the boats drew away, and the bow, then the quarter, then the stacks and at last the stern of the marvel-ship of a few days before passed beneath the waters. The great force of the ship's sinking was unaided by any violence of the elements, and the suction, into so great as had been feared, rocked but mildly the group of boats now a quarter of a mile distant from it.

Sixteen boats were in the forlorn procession which entered on the terrible hours of rowing, drifting and suspense. Women wept for lost husbands and sons. Sailors sobbed for the ship which had been their pride. Men chocked back tears and sought to comfort the widowed. Perhaps, they said, other boats might have put off in another direction toward the last. They strove, though none too sure themselves, to convince the women of the certainty that a rescue ship would appear.

Early dawn brought no ship, but not long after 5 A. M. the Carpathia, far out of her path and making eighteen knots, instead of her wonted fifteen, showed her single red and black smokestack upon the horizon. In the joy of that moment, the heaviest griefs were forgotten.

Soon afterward Captain Rostrom and Chief Steward Hughes were welcoming the chilled and bedraggled arrivals over the Carpathia's side.

Terrible as were the San Francisco, Slocum and Iroquois disasters, they shrink to local events in comparison with this world-catastrophe.

True, there were others of greater qualifications and longer experience than I nearer the tragedy—but they, by every token of likelihood, have become a part of the tragedy. The honored—must I say lamented—Stead, the adroit Jacques Futrelle, what might they not tell were their hands able to hold pencil?

The silence of the Carpathia's engines, the piercing cold, the clamor of many voices in the companionways, caused me to dress hurriedly and awaken my wife at 5.40 A. M. Monday. Our stewardess, meeting me outside, pointed to a wailing host in the rear dining room and said, "From the Titanic. She's at the bottom of the ocean."

THE LAST OF THE LINE OF BOATS.

At the ship's side, a moment later, I saw the last of the line of boats discharge their loads, and saw women, some with cheap shawls about their heads, some with the costliest of fur cloaks, ascending the ship's side. And such joy as the first sight of our ship may have given them had disappeared from their faces, and there were tears and signs of faltering as the women were helped up the ladders or hoisted aboard in swings. For lack of room to put them, several of the Titanic's boats after unloading were set adrift.

At our north was a broad icefield, the length of hundreds of Carpathias. Around us on other sides were sharp and glistening peaks. One black berg, seen about 10 A. M., was said to be that which sunk the Titanic.

In his tiny house over the second cabin smoking room was Harold Cotton, the Marconi operator, a ruddy English youth, whose work at his post, on what seemed ordinary duty, until almost midnight, had probably saved the lives of the huddling hundreds below.

Already he was knitting his brows over the problem of handling the messages which were coming in batches from the purser's office. The haste with which these Marconigrams were prepared by their senders was needless, in view of the wait of two days and two nights for a long connection. "Safe" was the word with which most of the messages began; then, in many of them, came the words "——missing."

Dishevelled women, who the night before could have drawn thousands from husbands' letters of credit or from Titanic's safe, stood penniless before the Carpathia's purser, asking that their messages be forwarded—collect. Their messages were taken with the rest.

HOPE REVIVED BY SIGHT OF CATTLE BOAT.

The Californian, a cattle ship, came near us, and though it gave no sign of having any of the Titanic's refugees on board, its presence in the vicinity gave hope to many women who were encouraged in the belief hat the Californian might have picked up their loved ones.

Captain Rostrom's decision to abandon the Mediterranean course, begun the Thursday before, and to return to an American port, was soon known to the passengers. At first it was reported that Halifax or Boston would be the destination, but at noon the notice of the intended arrival at New York three days later was posted. At that time the Carpathia, at an increase over her usual moderate speed, was westward bound and her passengers were deferring their hopes of Gibraltar, Naples and Trieste, and were sharing their rooms with the newcomers. Few men of the Carpathia's passenger list slept in a bed in any of the nights that followed. They had the men of the Titanic lay in chairs on deck, on dining tables or smoking-room couches, or on the floors of the rooms which held their hand baggage and their curtained-off guests. The captain was the first to vacate his room, which was used as a hospital.

In the first cabin library, women of wealth and refinement mingled their grief and asked eagerly for news of the possible arrival of a belated boat, or a message from some other steamer telling of the safety of their husbands. Mrs. Henry B. Harris, wife of a New York theatrical manager, checked her tears long enough to beg that some message of hope be sent to her father-in-law. Mrs. Ella Thor, Miss Marie Young, Mrs. Emil Taussig and her daughter, Ruth; Mrs. Martin Rothschild, Mrs. William Augustus Spencer, Mrs. J. Stuart White and Mrs. Walter M. Clark were a few of those who lay back, exhausted, on the leather cushions and told in shuttering sentences of their experiences.

PROUD OF HER HUSBAND'S OARSMANSHIP.

Mrs. John Jacob Astor and the Countess of Rothes had been take nto staterooms soon after their arrival on shipboard. Those who talked with Mrs. Astor said she spoke often of her husband's ability as an oarsman and said he could save himself if he had a chance. That he could have had such a chance, she seemed hardly to hope.

To another stateroom a tall, dark man had been conducted, his head bowed, anguish in his face. He was Bruce Ismay, head of the International Mercantile Marine and chief owner of the Titanic and her sister ship, the Olympic. He has made the maiden voyage on each of his company's great ships. He remained in his room in a physician's care during the voyage back to New York. Captain Rostrom, his only caller, was not admitted to see him until Tuesday evening.

Before noon, at the captain's request, the first cabin passengers of the Titanic gathered in the saloon, and the passengers of other classes in corresponding places on the rescue ship. Then the collecting of names was begun by the purser and the stewards. A second table was served in both cabins for the new guests, and the Carpathia's second cabin, being better fitted than its first, the second class arrivals had to be sent to the steerage.

In the middle of the morning, the Carpathia passed near the spot, seamen said, where the Titanic went down. Only a few floating chairs marked the place. The ice peaks had changed their position. Which of those in sight, if any, caused the wreck was matter of conjecture.

Those of the refugees who had not lost relatives found subject for distress in the reflection that their money and jewels were at the bottom of the sea. Miss Edith L. Rosenbaum, writer for a fashion trade journal, mourned the loss of trunks containing robes from Paris and Tunis. Several of the late works of Philip Mock, miniature painter, were in his lost baggage, but the artist was not inclined to dwell on this mishap.

AN OBJECT OF PITYING SIGHS.

The child of the Montreal Allisons, bereft of both parents and carried by a nurse, was an object of pitying sighs in the saloon. In the second cabin, two French children engaged pitying attention. The two boys, four and two years old, who had lost their mother a year before and their father the night before, were children of beauty and intelligence, but were too abashed to answer any questions, even those put in their native tongue. Their surname is believed to be Hoffman. They are now in the care of Miss Margaret Hays, of 304 West Eighty-third street, New York.

Reminiscences of two bridge whist games of Sunday night in the smoking-room and the lounge room were exchanged by passengers who believed that the protracted games, a violation of the strict Sabbath rules of English vessels, saved their lives. Alfred Drachenstadt was leader in the smoking-room game, Miss Dorothy Gibson in the other.

Mrs. Jacques Futrelle, wife of the novelist, herself a writer of note, sat dry-eyed in the saloon, telling her friends that she had given up hope for her husband. She joined with the rest in inquiries as to the chances of rescue by another ship, and no one told her what soon came to be the fixed opinion of the men —that all those saved were on the Carpathia.

PHOTO. BY UNDERWOOD & UNDERWOOD, N. Y.

CAPTAIN SMITH, OF THE "TITANIC" WHO HEROICALLY DID ALL HE COULD TO SAVE WOMEN AND CHILDREN AND THEN LIKE THE TRUE HERO HE WAS WENT DOWN WITH HIS SHIP.

COL. JOHN JACOB ASTOR.

GRANDSON OF THE FOUNDER OF THE ASTOR FAMILY IN AMERICA, AFTER PUTTING HIS YOUNG BRIDE IN A LIFE BOAT HE REMAINED ON THE SHIP AND DIED AS A HERO.

PHOTO BY PAUL THOMPSON, N. Y.

CUNARD LINE STEAMSHIP "CARPATHIA," WHICH HEARD THE WIRELESS CALL OF DISTRESS AND WAS FIRST TO REACH THE SCENE OF THE DISASTER AND TAKE ON BOARD THE SURVIVORS WHO WERE FOUND IN THE LIFEBOATS

RESCUED PASSENGERS IN ONE OF THE "TITANIC'S" COLLAPSEABLE LIFE-BOATS WAITING TO BE TAKEN ABOARD THE CARPATHIA.

SCENE ON THE UPPER DECK OF THE "TITANIC," SHOWING LIFE BOATS AS THEY ARE CARRIED BY ALL STEAMSHIPS. ALL THE PASSENGERS COULD HAVE BEEN SAVED IF THIS SHIP HAD CARRIED THREE TIMES AS MANY LIFEBOATS.

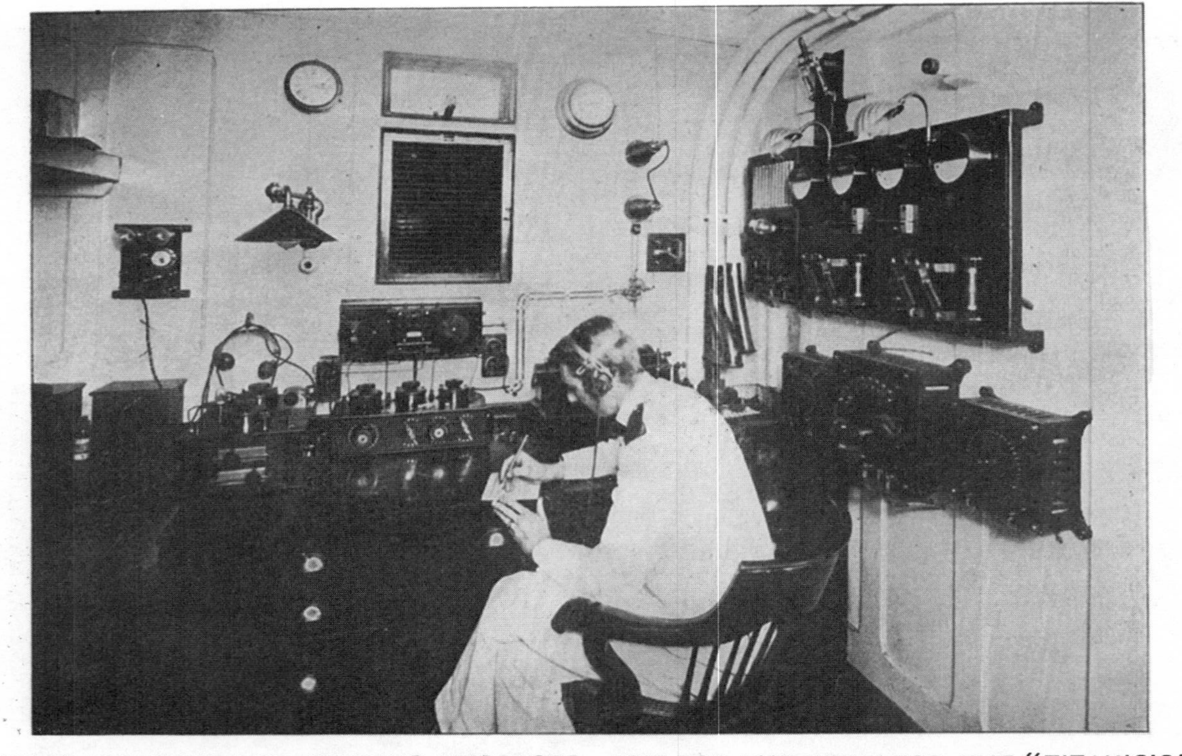

WIRELESS OPERATOR SENDING MESSAGES. BUT FOR THE WIRELESS, THE "TITANIC'S" PASSENGERS WOULD SURELY HAVE ALL BEEN LOST, AS THEY COULD NOT HAVE SURVIVED IN SMALL BOATS WITH ICE ALL AROUND THEM

MRS. JOHN JACOB ASTOR.

BRIDE OF COLONEL ASTOR WHO WENT DOWN WITH THE TITANIC.

MAJOR ARCHIBALD BUTT, THE FAMOUS MILITARY AIDE OF TWO PRESIDENTS — ROOSEVELT AND TAFT. HE BATTLED FOR THE RESCUE OF WOMEN AND CHILDREN UNTIL THE LAST LIFE BOAT HAD LEFT THE SHIP AND THEN WENT DOWN WITH THE "TITANIC" LIKE A TRUE HERO.

ONE OF THE DE LUXE ROOMS ON THE "TITANIC," SUCH AS WERE OCCUPIED BY JOHN JACOB ASTOR AND HIS BRIDE AND MANY OTHER MULTI-MILLIONAIRES WHO WENT DOWN WITH THE SHIP

PHOTO. BY UNDERWOOD & UNDERWOOD, N. Y.

VIEW OF THE PROMENADE DECK OF THE ILL-FATED WHITE STAR LINER "TITANIC." THIS DECK EXTENDS NEARLY THE WHOLE LENGTH OF THE SHIP, AND IS USED AS A PROMENADE FOR PASSENGERS.

PART OF THE MAGNIFICIENT CONCERT ROOM OF THE STEAMSHIP "TITANIC," WHERE WOMEN PASSENGERS SPENT MUCH OF THEIR TIME IN READING AND LISTENING TO THE MUSIC.

LUXURIOUSLY FURNISHED SMOKING ROOM OF THE "TITANIC," WHERE MEN SPENT MANY SOCIAL HOURS BEFORE GOING TO THEIR WATERY GRAVES

PHOTO BY PAUL THOMPSON, N. Y.

CAPTAIN SMITH OF THE "TITANIC," WHO SAVED MANY WOMEN AND CHILDREN, AND THEN, LIKE A TRUE HERO, WENT DOWN WITH HIS SHIP. THIS PICTURE ALSO SHOWS TWO OF HIS OFFICERS

PHOTO. BY UNDERWOOD & UNDERWOOD, N. Y.

INTERIOR OF CUNARD LINE PIER, ALL CLEARED OUT READY TO RECEIVE THE SURVIVORS OF THE "TITANIC," ON ARRIVAL OF THE "CARPATHIA," WHERE THEY WERE MET BY RELATIVES, PHYSICIANS, NURSES AND OTHERS.

PHOTO. BY UNDERWOOD & UNDERWOOD, N. Y.

A MOST REMARKABLE PHOTOGRAPH, TAKEN BY A PASSENGER ON THE "CARPATHIA," SHOWING MR. AND MRS. HARDER, A YOUNG HONEYMOON COUPLE. WHEN THE CRY CAME TO GET IN THE LIFE-BOATS, THEY, AS A LARK, THINKING THERE WAS NO DANGER, JUMPED IN THE FIRST BOAT LOWERED.

J. BRUCE ISMAY, WHITE STAR LINE MANAGER.

MR. ISMAY WAS ON THE "TITANIC" AND HAS BEEN SEVERELY CRITICISED FOR HIS ACTIONS IN CONNECTION WITH THIS GREAT CALAMITY.

"I feel better," Mrs. Futrelle said hours afterward, "for I can cry now."

Among the men, conversation centred on the accident and the responsibility for it. Many expressed the belief that the Titanic, in common with other vessels, had had warning of the ice packs, but that in the effort to establish a record on the maiden run sufficient heed had not been paid to the warnings. The failure of the safety compartments, said to have been closed from the bridge directly after the accident, was the occasion of amazement, and one theory offered was that the doors had, for some reason, not closed in the usual manner. Others contended that these devices are, at best, but time-savers, and said that without them the Titanic would have gone under before three boats could have been lowered.

THE OFFICERS' REQUIREMENTS DISCUSSED.

The requirement that the officers on the bridge should take temperatures of the water every fifteen minutes to indicate the approach of ice was also discussed.

As to the behavior of officers and crew, not a word of complaint was heard from the men. They were praised as worthy Britons and true seamen. In the same breath the survivors exalted the heroism of the missing men of the first cabin, who had stood calmly waiting for their turn—the turn which, because of scarcity of boats and shortness of time, never came for most of them.

"God knows I'm not proud to be here!" said a rich New York man. "I got on a boat when they were about to lower it and when, from delays below, there was no woman to take the vacant place. I don't think any man who was saved is deserving of censure, but I realize that, in contrast with those who went down, we may be viewed unfavorably." He showed a picture of his baby boy as he spoke.

As the day passed, the fore part of the ship assumed some degree of order and comfort, but the crowded second cabin and decks gave forth the incessant sound of lamentation. A bride of two months sat on the floor and moaned her widowhood. An Italian mother shrieked the name of her lost son.

A girl of seven wept over the loss of her Teddy Bear and two dolls, while her mother, with streaming eyes, dared not tell the child that her father was lost, too, and that the money for which their home in England had been sold had gone down with him. Other children clung to the necks of the fathers who, because carrying them, had been permitted to take the boats.

At 4 P. M. Monday the service for the dead was read by Father Roger Anderson, of the Episcopal Order of the Holy Cross, over the bodies of three seamen and one man, said to have been a cabin passenger, who were dead from exposure when received on this ship. Some of the Titanic's passengers turned away from the rail as the first of the weighted forms fell into the water.

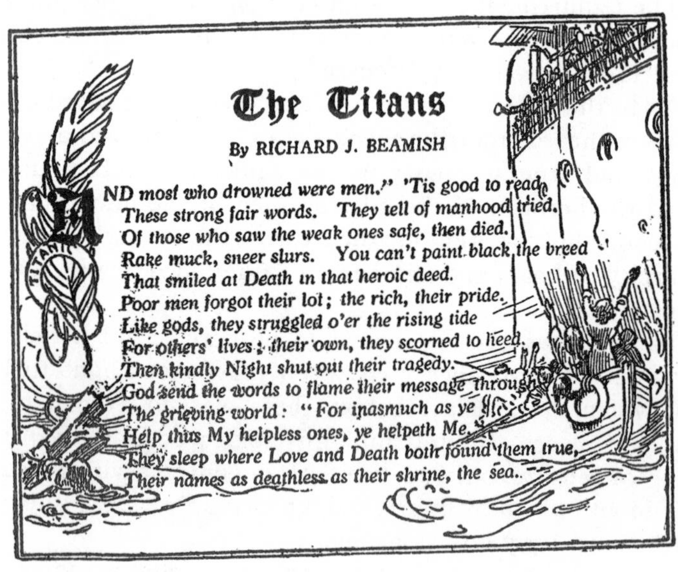

The Titans

By RICHARD J. BEAMISH

AND most who drowned were men." 'Tis good to read
These strong fair words. They tell of manhood tried.
Of those who saw the weak ones safe, then died.
Rake muck, sneer slurs. You can't paint black the breed
That smiled at Death in that heroic deed.
Poor men forgot their lot; the rich, their pride.
Like gods, they struggled o'er the rising tide
For others' lives; their own, they scorned to heed.
Then kindly Night shut out their tragedy.
God send the words to flame their message through
The grieving world: "For inasmuch as ye
Help thus My helpless ones, ye helpeth Me."
They sleep where Love and Death both found them true,
Their names as deathless as their shrine, the sea.

CHAPTER II.

HEART-RENDING SCENES ON CARPATHIA.

The Next Day—Caring for the Sick—Meeting of the Survivors—Personal Wireless Messages Given Precedence—Marconi's Appeal Fruitless—Quartermaster Tells Story.

The writer's narrative continues:

In the hospital and the public rooms lay, in blankets, several others who had been benumbed by the water. Mrs. Rosa Abbott, who was in the water for hours, was restored during the day. G. Wikeman, the Titanic's barber, who declared he was blown off the ship by the second of the two explosions after the crash, was treated for bruises. A passenger, who was thoroughly ducked before being picked up, caused much amusement on this ship, soon after the doctors were through with him, by demanding a bath.

Storekeeper Prentice, the last man off the Titanic to reach this ship, was also soon over the effects of his long swim in the icy waters, into which he leaped from the poop deck.

The physicians of the Carpathia were praised, as was Chief Steward Hughes, for work done in making the arrivals comfortable and averting serious illness.

Monday night on the Carpathia was one of rest. The wailing and sobbing of the day were hushed as the widows and orphans slept. Tuesday, save for the crowded condition of the ship, matters took somewhat their normal appearance.

Tuesday afternoon, in the saloon, a meeting of survivors was held and plans for a testimonial to the officers and crew of the Carpathia and the survivors of the Titanic's crew were discussed. It was decided that relief of the destitute should first be considered, and the chairman of the meeting, Samuel Goldenberg, appointed a committee consisting of I. G. Frauenthal,

Mrs. J. J. Brown, William Bushnell and George Stone to raise a fund. The first subscriptions were for $100 each, and the amounts were paid largely in travelers' checks or personal checks, cash being somewhat scarce among the refugees, who had kept their currency in the purser's safe.

Resolutions were adopted praising the Titanic's surviving officers and crew and the officers, crew and passengers of the Carpathia, and declaring that a memorial is needed for "those who in heroic self-sacrifice made possible the rescue of so many others." One speaker suggested that a memorial fund be raised by popular subscription, mentioning the "World" as a suitable medium. This and other suggestions were left to the committee to develop.

Rain and fog marked the Carpathia's homeward course, and those who were not seasick when New York was reached were none the less sick of the sea.

CAPTAIN ROSTROM'S RULE.

Captain Rostrom's rule that personal messages should take precedence of press messages was not relaxed, even when Tuesday a message from Guglielm Marconi himself asked the reason why press dispatches were not sent. The captain posted Marconi's message on the bulletin board, and beside it a bulletin stating that no press messages, except a bulletin to the Associated Press, had been sent. The implication was that none would be sent, and the most urgent and respectful appeals failed to change his determination, which, he seemed convinced, was in the best interest of the survivors and their friends.

My wife was my only active helper in a task which ten newspaper men could not have performed completely. Mr. S. V. Silverthorne, of St. Louis, aided greatly by lending me his first cabin passenger list, one of the few in existence.

Robert Hichens, one of the surviving quartermasters of the Titanic, the man who was on duty at the wheel when the ship struck the iceberg, told me the tale of the wreck on the Carpathia Thursday.

Save for the surviving fourth officer, Boxhall, whose lips are sealed, Hichens saw Sunday night's tragedy at closer range than any man now living.

In the hastily compiled list of surviving members of the crew, the names of Hichens and other quartermasters appear among the able-bodied seamen; but the star and anchor on the left sleeve of each distinguishes them in rank from the A. B.'s.

Hichens has followed the sea fifteen years and has a wife and two children in Southampton. His tale of the wreck, as he told it to me and as he expects to tell it to a Marine Court of Inquiry, is here given:

"I went on watch at eight o'clock Sunday night and stood by the man at the wheel until ten. At ten I took the wheel for two hours.

"On the bridge from ten o'clock on were First Officer Murdock, Fourth Officer Boxhall and Sixth Officer Moody. In the crow's nest (lookout tower) were Fleet and another man whose name I don't know.

SECOND OFFICER ON WATCH.

"Second Officer Lightoller, who was on watch while I stood by, carrying messages and the like, from eight to ten, sent me soon after eight to tell the carpenter to look out for the fresh water supply, as it might be in danger of freezing. The temperature was then 31 degrees. He gave the crow's nest a strict order to look out for small icebergs.

"Second Officer Lightoller was relieved by First Officer Murdock at ten, and I took the wheel then. At 11.40 three gongs sounded from the crow's nest, the signal for 'something right ahead.'

"At the same time one of the men in the nest telephoned to the bridge that there was a large iceberg right ahead. As Officer Murdock's hand was on the lever to stop the engines the crash came. He stopped the engines, then immediately by another lever closed the water-tight doors.

"The skipper (Captain Smith) came from the chart room on

to the bridge. His first words were 'Close the emergency doors.'

" 'They're already closed, sir,' Mr. Murdock replied.

" 'Send to the carpenter and tell him to sound the ship,' was the skipper's next order. The message was sent to the carpenter. The carpenter never came up to report. He was probably the first man on that ship to lose his life.

COLUMBIA AND BRITANNIA MOURN FOR THE "TITANIC'S" DEAD.

"The skipper looked at the commutator, which shows in what direction the ship is listing. He saw that she carried five degrees list to the starboard.

"The ship was then rapidly settling forward. All the steam sirens were blowing. By the skipper's orders, given in the next few minutes, the engines were put to work at pumping out the ship, distress signals were sent by Marconi and rockets were sent up from the bridge by Quartermaster Rowe. All hands were ordered on deck and life belts were sewed to the crew and to every passenger.

"The stewards and other hands helped the sailors in getting the boats out. The order 'women and children first' was given and enforced. There was no panic.

"I was at the wheel until 12.25. It was my duty to stay there until relieved. I was not relieved by anyone else, but was simply sent away by Second Officer Lightoller, who told me to take charge of a certain boat and load it with ladies.

"I did so, and there were thirty-two ladies, a sailor and myself in the boat when it was lowered, some time after 1 o'clock—I can't be sure of the time.

ALL BOATS BUT ONE GET AWAY SAFELY.

"The Titanic had sixteen lifeboats and two collapsible boats. All of them got away loaded, except that one of the collapsibles did not open properly and was used as a raft. Forty sailors and stewards who were floating in the water, got on this raft, and later had to abandon the raft, and were picked up by the different boats. Some others were floating about on chairs when picked up.

"Every boat, so far as I saw, was full when it was lowered, and every boat that set out reached the Carpathia. The green light on one of the boats helped to keep us together, but there were other lights. One was an electric flashlight that a gentleman had carried in his pocket.

"Our boat was 400 yards away when the ship went down. The suction nearby must have been terrific, but we were only rocked somewhat.

"I have told only what I know, and what I shall tell any marine court that may examine me."

G. Whiteman, of Palmyra, N. J., the Titanic's barber, was lowering boats on deck A, after the collision, and declares the officers on the bridge, one of them Second Officer Murdock, promptly worked the electrical apparatus for closing the watertight compartments. He believes the machinery was in some way so damaged by the crash that the front compartments failed to close tightly, although the rear ones were secure.

Whiteman's manner of escape was unique. He was blown off the deck by the second of the two explosions of the boilers, and was in the water more than two hours before he was picked up by a raft.

"The explosions," Whiteman said, "were caused by the rushing in of the icy water on the boilers. A bundle of deck chairs, roped together, was blown off the deck with me, and struck my back, injurying my spine, but it served as a temporary raft.

"The crew and passengers had faith in the bulkhead system to save the ship, and we were lowering a Benthon collapsible boat, all confident the ship would get through, when she took a terrific dip forward and the water rushed up and swept over the deck and into the engine rooms.

BLOWN FIFTEEN FEET.

"The bow went clean down, and I caught the pile of chairs as I was washed up against the rail. Then came the explosions and blew me fifteen feet.

"After the water had filled the forward compartments the ones at the stern could not save her. They did delay the ship's going down. If it wasn't for the compartments hardly any one could have got away.

"The water was too cold for me to swim and I was hardly more than one hundred feet away when the ship went down. The suction was not what one would expect and only rocked the water around me. I was picked up after two hours. I have done with the sea."

Whiteman was one of those who heard the ship's string band playing "Nearer, My God, to Thee" a few moments before she went down.

R. Norris Williams, a Philadelphia youth on his way home from England to take the Harvard entrance examinations, was one of the few saloon passengers at the rail excluded by the women-first order from the boats who was saved. His father, Duane Williams, was lost.

"There is much, and yet there is little, to tell of my experience," said young Williams. "My father and I had about given up our hope for life and were standing together, resolved to jump together and keep together if we could, so long as either of us lived. I had on my fur coat.

"The forward end, where we stood, was sinking rapidly, and before we could jump together the water washed my father over. Then, with the explosions, the ship seemed to break in two, and the forward end bounded up again for an instant. I leaped, but with dozens in the water between us my father was lost to me.

SWAM AND DRIFTED NEARLY TWO HOURS.

"I swam and drifted nearly two hours before I was pulled aboard the raft or collapsible boat which served for a time as a raft. Later, with the abandonment of the raft, I was taken aboard a boat."

Frederic K. Seward, who sat next to W. T. Stead at the Titanic's saloon table, told of the veteran English journalist's plans for his American visit. His immediate purpose was to aid in the New York campaign of the Men and Religion Forward Movement.

"Mr. Stead talked much of spiritualism, thought transference and the occult," said Seward. "He told a story of a mummy case in the British Museum which, he said, had had amazing adventures, but which punished with great calamities any person who wrote its story. He told of one person after another who, he said, had come to grief after writing the story, and added that, although he knew it, he would never write it. He did not say whether ill-luck attached to the mere telling of it."

Stead also told, Seward said, of a strange adventure of a young woman with an admirer in an English railroad coach, which was known to him as it happened, and which he afterward repeated to the young woman, amazing her by repeating everything correctly save for one small detail.

Had Harold Cotton, Marconi operator on the Carpathia, gone to bed Sunday night at his usual time, the Carpathia would have known nothing of the Titanic's plight, and the liftboats, without food or water, might have been the scenes of even greater tragedy than the great death ship itself.

The Carpathia, an easy going Mediterranean ship, has only one Marconi man, and when Cotton had not the receiver on his head the ship was out of communication with the world.

Cotton, an Englishman of twenty-one years, told me the morning after the wreck how he came to receive the Titanic's C Q D.

JUST ABOUT TO TURN IN WHEN CALLED BY C. Q. D.

"I was relaying a message to the Titanic Sunday night, shortly after 11 o'clock by my time," he said, "and told Phillips, the Titanic's Marconi man, that I had been doing quite a bit of work for him, and that if he had nothing else for me I would quit and turn in for the night. Just as I was about to take the receiver off my head came 'C Q D.' This was followed with 'We've hit something. Come at once.'

"I called a sailor and sent word to an officer, and a few minutes later the Captain turned the Carpathia, at eighteen knots, in the direction of the Titanic, which was sixty miles or more from us.

"Before I could tell the Titanic we were coming, came their 'S O S,' and the operator added 'I'm afraid we're gone.' I told him we were coming, and he went on sending out signals in every direction."

An assistant Marconi man from the Titanic, not on duty at the time of the wreck, was among the survivors and assisted Cotton in his work after Wednesday, having been laid up the two previous days by the shock of the chill he suffered in the water and by injuries to his legs.

He denied a report, generally circulated on this ship, that

Jack Binns, of Republic fame, was on the Titanic. He said Phillips, the Titanic's chief operator, was lost.

Mrs. Edward S. Robert, whose husband, a leading St. Louis attorney, died last December during her absence in England, and her daughter, Miss Georgette Madill, have been in close seclusion on the Carpathia since their rescue from the Titanic. They are accompanied by Mrs. Robert's maid.

S. V. Silverthorne, buyer for Nugent's, was one of three or four saloon passengers on the Titanic who saw the deadly iceberg just after the collision.

"I was in the smoking room reading near a bridge whist game at one of the tables," he said, "when the crash came. I said, 'We've hit something,' and went out on the starboard side to look. None of us was alarmed. It occurred to me that we might have bumped a whale, or at most, ran down some small craft.

ORDERED ON DECK AND TOLD TO GET INTO THE BOATS.

"I went back in the smoking room with the others. One of the bridge players had not left the smoking room at all and was waiting impatiently for the others to come back and resume the game. They returned and took up their hands and we were all about to settle down, when an officer ordered us on deck and told us to get into the boats, there not being enough women on deck to fill the first ones. We didn't like the idea of leaving the ship then, but did as we were told. Had we been in our rooms we would have had to stand aside, as other men did then."

Two orphan French boys, about two and four years old respectively, whose sur-name is believed to be Hoffman and who called each other Louis and Lolo, will be cared for by Miss Margaret Hays, of 304 W. 83d st., New York, while efforts will be made to find their relatives, to whom their father was thought to have been taking them. The elder boy has been ill with a fever for three days, the excitement, exposure and probably grief over the loss of his father having told on the little fellow. The other, too young to realize what has befallen him, played around the saloon or sat contentedly in the lap of one of his new made but devoted friends among the passengers.

The father, who is in the list of second cabin passengers as "Mr. Hoffman," is said to have told fellow-passengers on the Titanic the children's mother died recently.

Mrs. Sylvia Caldwell, of Bangkok, Siam, is happy in having her husband and little son. Since she was the last woman to embark, her husband was able to come with her.

Mrs. Esther Hart, whose husband was lost, was coming, with their daughter Eva, to visit Mr. Hart's sister in New York, then to go on to Winnipeg to make their home. They had sold the property at Ilford, Essex, England. All their money was lost when Mr. Hart went down with the Titanic.

Mrs. Lucy Ridsdale, of London, had said good-by to England and had started for Marietta, O., to make her home with her sisters. She was saved with the few clothes she wore. She had written letters telling of a "safe arrival and pleasant voyage" and had them ready to mail. They went down with the ship.

CHAPTER III.

BAND PLAYED TO THE LAST.

Suffering in the Lifeboats—Statement by Ismay—Would not Desert Husband—Thirty on Raft in Icy Water—Colonel Astor a Hero—Joked Over Collision—Officer Saves Many Lives.

But another account, compiled from various sources among the survivors gives somewhat varying angles and supplies quite a few missing details.

At the risk of a few slight repetitions it is given:

Of the great facts that stand out from the chaotic accounts of the tragedy, these are the most salient:

"The death list was increased rather than decreased. Six persons died after being rescued.

"The list of prominent persons lost stood as at first reported.

"Practically every woman and child, with the exception of those women who refused to leave their husbands, were saved. Among these last was Mrs. Isidor Straus.

The survivors in the lifeboats saw the lights on the stricken vessel glimmer to the last, heard her band playing and saw the doomed hundreds on her deck and heard their groans and cries when the vessel sank.

Accounts vary as to the extent of the disorder on board.

Not only was the Titanic tearing through the April night to her doom with every ounce of steam crowded on, but she was under orders from the general officers of the line to make all the speed of which she was capable.

This was the statement made by J. H. Moody, a quartermaster of the vessel and helmsman on the night of the disaster. He said the ship was making 21 knots an hour, and the officers were striving to live up to the orders to smash the records.

"It was close to midnight," said Moody, "and I was on the bridge with the second officer, who was in command. Suddenly he shouted 'Port your helm!' I did so, but it was too late. We struck the submerged portion of the berg."

"Of the many accounts given by the passengers most of them agreed that the shock when the Titanic struck the iceberg, although ripping her great sides like a giant can opener, did not greatly jar the entire vessel, for the blow was a glancing one along her side. The accounts also agree substantially that when the passengers were taken off on the lifeboats there was no serious panic and that many wished 'to remain on board the Titanic, believing her to be unsinkable.' "

EXPERIENCES OF PASSENGERS IN LIFE-BOATS.

The most distressing stories are those giving the experiences of the passengers in lifeboats. These tell not only of their own suffering, but give the harrowing details of how they saw the great hulk of the Titanic stand on end, stern uppermost for many minutes before plunging to the bottom. As this spectacle was witnessed by the groups of survivors in the boats, they plainly saw many of those whom they had just left behind leaping from the decks into the water.

J. Bruce Ismay, president of the International Mercantile Marine, owners of the White Star Line, who was among the seventy odd men saved; P. A. S. Franklin, vice president of the White Star Line, and United States Senator William Alden Smith, chairman of the Senate Investigating Committee, held a conference aboard the Carpathia soon after the passengers had come ashore.

After nearly an hour, Senator Smith came out of the cabin and said he had no authority to subpena witnesses at this time, but would begin an investigation into the cause of the loss of the Titanic at the Waldorf-Astoria Hotel the next day. He announced that Mr. Ismay had consented to appear at the hearing, and that Mr. Franklin and the four surviving officers of theTitanic would appear for examination by the Senate committee. He said the course the investigation would follow would be determined after the preliminary hearing.

Senator Smith was questioned as to the speed the Titanic was proceeding at when she crashed into the iceberg. He said he had asked Mr. Ismay, but declined to say what Mr. Ismay's reply was.

Bruce Ismay, chairman of the International Mercantile Marine, gave out the following prepared statement on the pier:

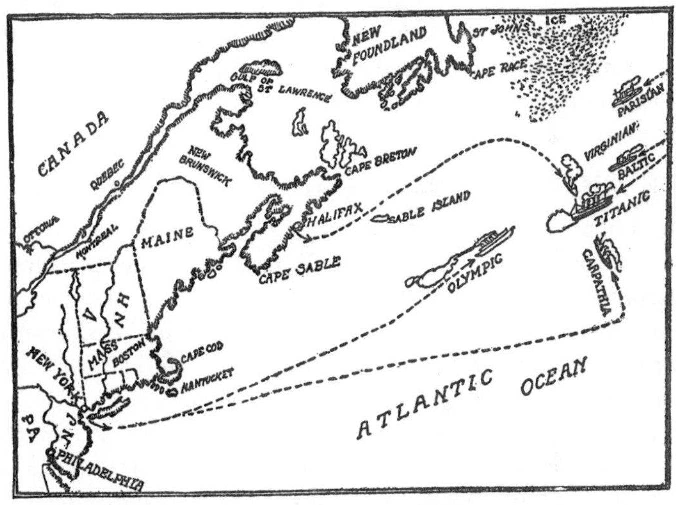

CHART OF THE NORTH ATLANTIC, SHOWING WHERE THE GREAT LINER "TITANIC" WENT DOWN.

"In the presence and under the shadows of a catastrophe so overwhelming my feelings are too deep for expression in words, and I can only say that the White Star Line officers and employes will do everything humanly possible to alleviate the suffering and sorrow of the relatives and friends of those who perished. The Titanic was the last word in shipbuilding. Every regulation prescribed by the British Board of Trade had been strictly complied with. The master, officers and crew were the most experienced and skillful in the British service.

"I am informed that a committee of the United States

Senate has been appointed to investigate the circumstances of the accident. I heartily welcome the most complete and exhaustive inquiry, and any aid that I can render is at the service of the public and of the Governments of both the United States and Great Britain. Under these circumstances I must defer making any further statement at this hour."

Mr. Ismay said informally before giving out his statement that he left the ship in one of the last boats, one of the collapsible boats on the port side. This statement, however, as will later appear, is scathingly denounced by several survivors as untrue.

"I do not know the speed at which the Titanic was going," said Mr. Ismay in reply to a question. "She hit the iceberg a glancing blow."

MR. ISMAY WILL MAKE A COMPLETE STATEMENT.

Mr. Ismay, after his interview with Senator Smith, said that he was desirous of sailing on the Carpathia the next afternoon. The Carpathia was scheduled to sail at 4 o'clock. Mr. Ismay assured the Senators, however, that he would make a complete statement of the catastrophe, and that if he could not finish in time for the sailing he would change his plans.

Mr. Ismay then went to his apartments at the Ritz-Carlton.

The arrival of the Carpathia brought a vast multitude of people to the Cunard docks. They filled the vast pier sheds, and, overflowing for blocks, crowded the nearby streets in a dense throng. Through it all the rain fell steadily, adding a funeral aspect to the scene. The landing of the survivors was attended with little excitement, the crowd standing in awe-like silence as the groups from the ship passed along. The docking actually began shortly after nine o'clock and the debarking of passengers was so quickly disposed of by the waiving of the usual formality that practically everything had been concluded by 10.30 o'clock. The crowds remained about the pier long after this, however, to get a glimpse of the rescuing steamer and to hear the harrowing stories which had been brought back by the ship.

Colonel Archibald Gracie, U. S. A., the last man saved,

went down with the vessel, but was picked up. He was met by his daughter, who had arrived from Washington, and his son-in-law, Paul H. Fabricius. Colonel Gracie told a remarkable story of personal hardship and denied emphatically the reports that there had been any panic on board. He praised in the highest terms the behavior of both the passengers and crew and paid a high tribute to the heroism of the women passengers.

Contrary to the general expectation, there was no jarring impact when the vessel struck, according to the army officer. He was in his berth when the vessel smashed into the submerged portion of the berg and was aroused by the jar. He looked at his watch, he said and found it was just midnight. The ship sank with him at 2.22 A. M. for his watch stopped at that hour.

WOULD NOT DESERT HER HUSBAND.

"Mrs. Isidor Straus," he said, "went to her death because she would not desert her husband. Although he pleaded with her to take her place in the boat, she steadfastly refused, and when the ship settled at the head the two were engulfed by the wave that swept her."

Colonel Gracie told of how he was driven to the topmost deck when the ship settled and was the sole survivor after the wave that swept her just before her final plunge.

"I jumped with the wave," said he, "just as I have often jumped with the breakers at the seashore. By great good fortune I managed to grasp the brass railing on the deck above, and I hung on by might and main. When the ship plunged down I was forced to let go and I was swirled around and around for what seemed to be an interminable time. Eventually I came to the surface, to find the sea a mass of tangled wreckage.

"Luckily I was unhurt and, casting about, managed to seize a wooden grating floating nearby. When I had recovered my breath I discovered a larger canvas and cork lifecraft which had floated up. A man, whose name I did not learn, was struggling toward it from some wreckage to which he had clung. I cast off and helped him to get on to the raft and we then began the work of rescuing those who had jumped into the sea and were floundering in the water.

"When dawn broke there were thirty of us on the raft, standing knee deep in the icy water and afraid to move lest the cranky craft be overturned. Several unfortunately, benumbed and half dead, besought us to save them and one or two made an effort to reach us.

"The hours that elapsed before we were picked up by the Carpathia were the longest and most terrible that I ever spent. Practically without any sensation of feeling, because of the icy water, we were almost dropping from fatigue. We were afraid to turn around to look to see whether we were seen by passing craft, and when some one who was facing astern passed the word that something that looked like a steamer was coming up one of the men became hysterical under the strain. The rest of us, too, were nearing the breaking point."

DENIES THAT ANY MEN WERE FIRED UPON.

Colonel Gracie denied with emphasis that any men were fired upon, and declared that only once was a revolver discharged.

"This was for the purpose of intimidating some steerage passengers," he said, "who had tumbled into a boat before it was prepared for launching. This shot was fired in the air, and when the foreigners were told that the next would be directed at them they promptly returned to the deck. There was no confusion and no panic."

"Before I retired," said Colonel Gracie, "I had a long chat with Charles H. Hays, president of the Grand Trunk Railroad. One of the last things Mr. Hays said was this: 'The White Star, the Cunard and the Hamburg-American lines are devoting their attention and ingenuity in vieing with the other to attain the supremacy in luxurious ships and in making speed records. The time will soon come when this will be checked by some appalling disaster.' Poor fellow, a few hours later he was dead."

"The conduct of Colonel Jacob Astor was deserving of the

highest praise," Colonel Gracie declared. "The millionarie New Yorker," he said, "devoted all his energies to saving his young bride, nee Miss Force, of New York, who was in delicate health.

"Colonel Astor helped us in our efforts to get her in the boat," said Colonel Gracie. "I lifted her into the boat, and as she took her place Colonel Astor requested permission of the officer to go with her for her own protection.

"'No, sir,' replied the officer, 'not a man shall go on a boat until the women are all off.' Colonel Astor then inquired the number of the boat, which was being lowered away, and turned to the work of clearing the other boats and in reassuring the frightened and nervous women.

"By this time the ship began to list frightfully to port. This became so dangerous that the second officer ordered every one to rush to starboard. This we did, and we found the crew trying to get a boat off in that quarter. Here I saw that last of John B. Thayer and George B. Widener, of Philadelphia."

SPEED KEPT UP DESPITE WARNINGS.

Colonel Gracie said that, despite the warnings of icebergs, no slowing down of speed was ordered by the commander of the Titanic. There were other warnings, too, he said. "In the 24 hours' run ending the 14th," he said, "the ship's run was 546 miles, and we were told that the next 24 hours would see even a better record posted.

No diminution of speed was indicated in the run and the engines kept up their steady running. When Sunday evening came we all noticed the increased cold, which gave plain warning that the ship was in close proximity to icebergs or icefields. The officers, I am credibly informed, had been advised by wireless from other ships of the presence of icebergs and dangerous floes in that vicinity. The sea was as smooth as glass, and the weather clear so that it seems that there was no occasion for fear."

"When the vessel struck," he continued, "the passengers were so little alarmed that they joked over the matter. The few that appeared on deck early had taken their time to dress properly and there was not the slightest indication of panic. Some of the fragments of ice had fallen on the deck and these were picked up and passed around by some of the facetious ones, who offered them as mementos of the occasion.

On the port side a glance over the side failed to show any evidence of damage and the vessel seemed to be on an even keel. James Clinch Smith and I, however, soon found the vessel was listing heavily. A few minutes later the officers ordered men and women to don life preservers."

E. Z. Taylor, of Philadelphia, one of the survivors, jumped into the sea just three minutes before the boat sank. He told a graphic story as he came from the Carpathia.

"I was eating when the boat struck the iceberg," he said. "There was an awful shock that made the boat tremble from stem to stern. I did not realize for some time what had happened. No one seemed to know the extent of the accident. We were told that an iceberg had been struck by the ship. I felt the boat rise, and it seemed to me that she was riding over the ice.

ROCKING OVER A VERITABLE SEA OF ICE.

"I ran out on the deck and then I could see ice. It was a veritable sea of ice and the boat was rocking over it. I should say that parts of the iceberg were eighty feet high, but it had been broken into sections, probably by our ship.

"I jumped into the ocean and was picked up by one of the boats. I never expected to see land again. I waited on board the boat until the lights went out. It seemed to me that the discipline on board was wonderful."

A young English woman who requested that her name be omitted told a thrilling story of her experience in one of the collapsible boats which had been manned by eight of the crew from the Titanic. The boat was in command of the fifth officer, H. Lowe, whose actions she described as saving the lives of many people. Before the lifeboat was launched he passed along the port deck of the steamer, commanding the people not to jump in the boats, and otherwise restraining them from swamping the craft. When the collapsible was launched Officer Lowe succeeded in putting up a mast and a small sail. He collected other boats together; in some cases the boats were short of adequate crews, and he directed an exchange by which each was adequately manned. He threw lines connecting the boats together, two by two, and all thus moved together. Later on he went back to the wreck with the crew of one of the boats and succeeded in picking up some of those who had jumped overboard and were swimming about. On his way back to the Carpathia he passed one of the collapsible boats, which was on the point of sinking with thirty passengers aboard, most of them in scant night-clothing. They were rescued just in the nick of time."

Among the first passengers off the Carpathia was Mrs. Paul Schabert, of Derby, Conn. She said that she had a stateroom on the port side and had sailed with her brother Phillip. Mrs. Schabert declared that her brother was saved because she refused to leave him.

IN THE GENERAL PANIC CAME THE CRY, "LADIES FIRST."

"It was a terrible experience," Mrs. Schabert added. "I was awakened by the shock of the collision and went out on deck. There was very little excitement and persons were coming from their rooms asking what had happened. Suddenly from the bridge came the cry 'ladies first.' This was the first inkling we had that the ship was in danger. I went back to my stateroom and dressed and then as I returned to the deck I heard the horrifying order that women must leave their husbands and brothers. I refused to leave my brother, and finally he was shoved into the boat with me.

"Mrs. Isidor Straus, who had a stateroom near me, and with whom I have frequently talked, declared that under no circumstances would she leave Mr. Straus. As we pushed away from the Titanic the ship started to go down and as she disappeared beneath the water Mr. and Mrs. Straus were standing arm in arm."

Mrs. D. W. Marvin, who was on a honeymoon trip with her husband, was almost prostrated when she reached the deck and learned that her husband had not been picked up by some other boat.

"My God, don't ask me too much," she said. "Tell me, have you any news from Dan? He grabbed me in his arms and knocked down men to get me into the boat. As I was put in the boat he cried. 'It's all right, little girl; you go and I will stay awhile, I'll put on a life preserver and jump off and follow your boat.' As our boat shoved off he threw a kiss at me and that is the last I saw of him."

Edward Beane, of Glasgow, Scotland, who, with his wife, occupied a stateroom in the second cabin, declared that fifteen minutes after the Titanic hit the iceberg there was an explosion in the engine room, which was followed in a few minutes by a second explosion.

FALSE REPORT OF PASSENGERS BEING SHOT.

"The stern of the boat floated for nearly an hour after the bow was submerged," said Mr. Beane, "and then went down. I heard a report that two steerage passengers were shot by the officers when they started to crowd in the boats, but later this was denied."

Max Frolicher-Stehli, who, with his wife and his daughter Margaret, was on the way to this city to visit a brother, said:

"My wife and two women entered one of the first boats lowered. Twelve men, including myself, were standing near and as there were no other women passengers waiting we were ordered to get in. The sea was calm. We were rowed by four seamen, one of whom was in charge.

"The order maintained on the Titanic was what I would call remarkable. There was very little pushing and in most cases it was the women who caused the commotion by insisting that their husbands go with them into the lifeboats. As a rule the men were very orderly. It was not until we had left the ship that many of the women showed fright. From that time on, however, they filled the air with shrieks."

The following statement issued by a committee of the surviving passengers was given the press on the arrival of the Carpathia.

"We, the undersigned surviving passengers from the S. S. Titanic, in order to forestall any sensational or exaggreated statements, deem it our duty to give the press a statement of facts which have come to our knowledge and which we believe to be true.

WARNING TOO LATE TO AVOID COLLISION.

"On Sunday, April 14, 1912, at about 11.40 P. M., on a cold, starlight night, in a smooth sea and with no moon, the ship struck an iceberg which had been reported to the bridge by the lookouts, but not early enough to avoid collision. Steps were taken to ascertain the damage and save passengers and ship. Orders were given to put on life belts and the boats were lowered. The ship sank at about 2.20 A. M. Monday and the usual distress signals were sent out by wireless and rockets fired at intervals from the ship. Fortunately the wireless message was received by the Cunard's S. S. Carpathia, at about 12 o'clock, and she arrived on the scene of the disaster at about 4 A. M. Monday.

"The officers and crew of the S. S. Carpathia had been preparing all night for the rescue and comfort of the survivors, and the last mentioned were received on board with the most touching care and kindness, every attention being given to all, irrespective of class. The passengers, officers and crew gave up gladly their staterooms, clothing and comforts for our benefit, all honor to them.

"On the boat at the time of the collision was: First class, 330; second class, 320; third class, 750; total, 1400; officers and crew, 940; total, 2340. Of the foregoing about the following were rescued by S. S. Carpathia:

"First class, 210; second class, 125; third class, 200; officers, 4; seamen, 39; stewards, 96; firemen, 71; total, 210 of the crew,

The net total of 745 saved was about 80 per cent. of the maximum capacity of the lifeboats.

"We feel it our duty to call the attention of the public to what we consider the inadequate supply of life-saving appliances provided for on modern passenger steamships, and recommend that immediate steps be taken to compel passenger steamers to carry sufficient boats to accommodate the maximum number of people carried on board.

"The following facts were observed and should be considered in this connection: The insufficiency of lifeboats, rafts, etc.; lack of trained seamen to man same (stokers, stewards, etc., are not efficient boat handlers); not enough officers to carry out emergency orders on the bridge and superintend the launching and control of lifeboats; absence of searchlights.

"The board of trade rules allow for entirely too many people in each boat to permit the same to be properly handled. On the Titanic the boat deck was about 75 feet above water, and consequently the passengers were required to embark before lowering boats, thus endangering the operation and preventing the taking on of the maximum number the boats would hold. Boats at all times to be properly equipped with provisions, water, lamps, compasses, lights, etc. Life-saving boat drills should be more frequent and thoroughly carried out; and officers should be armed at boat drills. Greater reduction in speed in fog and ice, as damage if collision actually occurs is liable to be less.

"In conclusion, we suggest that an international conference be called to recommend the passage of identical laws providing for the safety of all at sea, and we urge the United States Government to take the initiative as soon as possible."

The statement was signed by Samuel Goldenberg, chairman, and a committee of passengers.

CHAPTER IV.

NEGLECT CAUSED DISASTER.

Tardy Answer to Telephone Call—Lookout's Signals Not Answered—Ship Could Have Been Saved—Three Fatal Minutes—Ismay Accused—Women Help With Oars—Ship Broken in Two—Band Played Till Last.

The trifle of a telephone call hardly answered sent the Titanic to the bottom of the Atlantic, occasioned the greatest marine disaster in history and shocked all civilized nations.

This, at least, is the tale told by sailors of the ill-starred Titanic, brawny seamen who only lived to tell it because it happened in the line of their duty to help man the boats into which some of the Titanic's passengers were loaded.

But the telephone call that went unanswered for probably two or three minutes, none can tell the exact time, was sent by the lookout stationed forward to the first officer of the watch on the bridge of the great liner on the maiden voyage.

The lookout saw a towering "blue berg" looming up in the sea path of the Titanic, the latest and proudest product of marine architecture, and called the bridge on the ship's telephone.

When after the passing of those two or three fateful minutes an officer on the bridge of the Titanic lifted the telephone receiver from its hook to answer the lookout it was too late. The speeding liner, cleaving a calm sea under a star-studded sky, had reached the floating mountain of ice, which the theoretically "unsinkable" ship struck a crashing, if glancing, blow with her starboard bow.

Had the officer on the bridge, who was William T. Murdock, according to the account of the tragedy given by two of the Titanic's seamen, known how imperative was that call from the lookout man, whose name was given as Fleet, the man at the wheel of the world's newest and greatest transatlantic liner might have swerved the great ship sufficiently to avoid the berg altogether or at the worst would have probably struck the mass of ice with her stern and at much reduced speed.

For obvious reasons the identity of the sailormen who described the foundering of the Titanic cannot be divulged. As for the officer, who was alleged to have been a laggard in answering the lookout's telephone call, harsh criticism may be omitted.

Murdock, if the tale of the Titanic sailor be true, expiated his negligence, if negligence it was, by shooting himself within sight of all alleged victims huddled in lifeboats or struggling in the icy seas.

THE "UNWRITTEN LAW" OF THE SEA.

The revolver which the sailors say snuffed out Murdock's life was not the only weapon that rang out above the shrieks of the drowning. Officers of the Titanic, upon whom devolved the duty of seeing that the "unwritten law" of the sea—"women and children first"—was enforced, were, according to the recital of the members of the great liner's crew, forced to shoot frenzied male passengers, who, impelled by the fear of death, attempted to get into the lifeboats swinging from their davits.

The sailors' account of the terrific impact of the Titanic against the berg that crossed the path was as follows:

"It was 11.40 P. M. Sunday, April 14. Struck an iceberg. The berg was very dark and about 250 feet in height.

"The Titanic struck the berg a glancing blow on the starboard bow. The ship, which was traveling between twenty and twenty-three knots an hour, crashed into the berg at a point about forty feet back of the stem.

"The Titanic's bottom was torn away to about fore bridge. The tear was fully fifty feet in length and was below the water line."

Regarding the state of the sea and the character of the night the sailors declared:

"It was a perfect night, clear and starlight. The sea was

smooth. The temperature had dropped to freezing Sunday morning. We knew or believed that the cold was due to the nearness of bergs, but we had not even run against cake ice up to the time the ice mountain loomed up. The Titanic raced through a calm sea in which there was no ice into the berg which sank her."

Continuing, their joint account the two men of the Titanic's crew further said:

"The first officer of the watch was Murdock. He was on the bridge. Captain Smith may have been near at hand, but he was not visible to us who were about to wash down the decks. Hitchens, quartermaster, was at the wheel. Fleet was the outlook."

It is characteristic of sailors that they make no effort to learn the baptismal names of a ship's officers.

"Fleet reported the berg, but the telephone was not answered on the bridge at once. A few minutes afterwards the telephone call was answered, but it was too late.

THE SHIP HAD STRUCK.

"The ship had struck. Murdock, after the ship struck the berg, gave orders to put helm to starboard, afterwards he ordered the helm hard to port and the ship struck the berg again.

"Afterwards Murdock gave an order for the carpenter to sound the wells to learn how much water the ship was taking in. The carpenter came up and told Murdock the Titanic had seven feet of water in her in less than seven minutes."

Keeping on with their narrative the sailors, whose nerves had not been broken by their experiences declared:

"Then Captain Smith, who had put in an appearance, gave orders to get the boats ready.

"There was less than ten minutes between the time the Titanic first struck the berg and the second crash, both of which brought big pieces of ice showering down on the ship.

"Orders came to the crew to stand by the boats. The boats were got out. There were twenty-two boats all told."

At this juncture the sailors described without apparent prejudice or bitterness how J. Bruce Ismay, chairman of the Board of Directors of the White Star Line, was the first to leave the Titanic.

"Ismay," the sailors asserted, "with his two daughters and a millionaire, Sir Cosmo Duff-Gordon, and the latter's family, got into the first accident or emergency boats, which are about twenty-eight feet long, and were always ready for lowering under the bridge. The boat in which Ismay and Sir Cosmo left was manned by seven seamen. There were seventeen persons in the boat.

"This boat pulled away from the ship a half hour before any of the lifeboats were put into the water.

"There were thirteen first-class passengers and five sailors in the emergency boat. Both boats were away from the ship within ten or fifteen minutes of the ship's crashing into the berg."

FIRST BOATS TO GET AWAY.

Asked to explain how it was possible for two boats to be put over the ship's side into the water without being subjected to a rush on the part of the great ship's passengers, the Titanic seamen said: "Ismay and those who left in the two emergency boats occupied cabins de luxe. The two boats were swniging from davits ready for lowering. We have no idea who notified Mr. Ismay and his friends to make ready to leave the ship, but we do know that the boats in which they were got away first."

The sailors' seemingly unvarnished tale then went on as follows:

"It was perhaps a half hour before the first of the lifeboats was ready for lowering. Not a man was allowed in one of the lifeboats so far as we could see, only women and children. The boats were all thirty-six feet long and carried about sixty passengers. There were about thirty-five or forty passengers to a boat when they were lowered, but two sailors went in each boat. Besides the sixteen lifeboats and the two emergency boats, four collapsible boats, each with a carrying capacity of forty passengers, were put over the sides of the Titanic, every boat on the ship was put into the water.

"One of the collapsible boats filled with water. The women and children in the boat were mostly third-class passengers. The boat turned keel and nearly two score persons clung to it. Many of these were rescued by the lifeboats."

The spokesman for the sailors here asserted: "We want to make it plain that the officers and crew of the Titanic did their duty. Not a male passenger got into the lifeboats. During the early excitement men tried to force their way into the boats, but the officers shot them down with revolvers. I saw probably a half dozen men shot down as the lifeboat to which I was assigned was being filled. The men shot were left to die and sink on the upper deck of the Titanic."

The Titanic's sailors described how frail women, steeled by a desperate emergency, seized oars and labored with the seamen to get the lifeboats at a safe distance from the great liner, sinking deep and deeper under the weight of water.

WOMEN HELP WITH THE OARS.

"There were ten oars to each lifeboat," the sailors said. "The women seized the sweeps and helped us to get the boats clear of the ship. We got away about 100 yards from the ship and waited to see what would happen. The liner was sinking fast, but the lights continued to shine through the black night.

"The end came at 2.30 on Monday morning. The lights on the ship did not go out until ten minutes before the liner sank. The inrushing seas reaching the after fires produced an explosion, which sundered the big liner. The forward half of the Titanic dived gently down. The after part of the ship stood on end and then disappeared.

"The force of the explosion blew, it seemed to us watching from the lifeboats, scores of passengers and sailors into the air."

"That there were stout hearts on the Titanic, even in the last moments of an unprecedented catastrophe, that refused to quail was proven by the rough seamen's further testimony.

"The band on the promenade deck," they declared, "played 'Abide With Me' and 'Eternal Father, Strong to Save,' and other hymns as the ship sank."

The Titanic sank at 2.30, almost at the spot where she collided with the mountain of ice.

It was an hour later when the Carpathia was sighted by the thinly-clad occupants of the lifeboats and it was 4.30 before the first of the Titanic's passengers set foot on the deck of the Cunarder. It was 8 o'clock on Monday morning, April 15, before the last of the half-clad suffering passengers of the Titanic were taken aboard the Carpathia, a not difficult feat, as the sea continued smooth.

The Carpathia's run from the Newfoundland banks to New York was uneventful except for the burial at sea of five persons. Four of the five, according to the sailors, were consigned to the deep at about 4 P. M. on Monday, April 15. One of the four was a sailor, one a fireman and two male passengers of the third class.

TELEPHONE CALL DOUBTED.

The alleged negligence of Murdock, the first officer of the watch, who is blamed, as stated above, by some of the sailors for the wreck in not responding immediately to a telephone call from the lookout giving warning of the iceberg ahead, is doubted by a naval man who has had a long experience on transatlantic liners.

"I cannot help doubting, in fact, absolutely disbelieving, that an officer of the watch could be negligent in either responding to a call from the crow's-nest or even failing to discover anything in the course of his vessel as soon as the lookout. Especially considering the fact that the vessel had been warned of ice several times.

"The position of the senior officer of the watch is on the windward side of the bridge. He does not depend on the lookout, that man is only a check upon him. Usually any object in the course of the vessel is discovered by both at the same time. The lookout's signal was not a telephone call when I was on the seas, but a horn blast. Three blasts, object dead ahead; one blast, object on port bow; two blasts, object on starboard bow.

"That Murdock did not see the berg as soon as his lookout, seems improbable; that he did not see it immediately after his lookout, seems impossible; that he did not answer any signal from the lookout immediately is impossible, unless he was dead. Murdock knew his responsibility, and he wasn't shirking. He wouldn't have been on the watch, or on the Titanic, if he ever shirked.

"Could a vessel the size of the Titanic change its course sufficiently to avoid the berg within three minutes supposed to have elapsed during which Murdock didn't answer his lookout's call? It could. I never sailed a vessel the size of the Titanic, but I unhesitatingly say that the Titanic's course could be changed in considerably less than a mile. Why, by putting the wheel hard-a-port and stopping the engines on that side the vessel could be turned so quickly that it would list fifteen degrees in swinging around. I have steered a transatlantic liner in and out among fishing smacks and they are easier to hit than an iceberg."

QUESTIONED ABOUT CONDITIONS ON MOONLESS NIGHT.

Two other seafaring men of long experience, who have many nights sat in the crow's-nest of a liner and watched the course, were asked how far an iceberg the size of the one that the Titanic struck could be seen on a clear night without a moon, a condition on which all of the survivors seem to agree was present the night the Titanic was sunk.

One of these men said at least one mile, the other at least two miles. So the fact remains that Murdock was supposed to be on the bridge keeping a strict lookout and not depending on the crow's-nest; that he could have seen the iceberk when it was at least a mile from the vessel, and that the Titanic could have been easily turned sufficiently in her course to avoid the berg within a mile.

The surviving passengers are unanimous that the "unbelievable" happened. The voyage had been pleasant and uneventful, except for the fact that it was being made on the largest and most magnificent vessel that ever sailed and for the keen interest which the passengers took in the daily bulletins of the speed.

The Titanic had been making good time and all accounts agree that on the night of the disaster she was apparently going at her usual rate—of from 21 to 25 knots an hour.

J. H. Moody, the quartermaster, who was at the helm, said that the ship was making twenty-one and that the officers were under orders at the time to keep up speed in the hope of making a record passage.

These orders were being carried out in face of knowledge that the steamer was in the vicinity of great icebergs sweeping down from the north. That very afternoon, according to the record of the hyrographic officer, the Titanic had relayed to shore a wireless warning from the steamer Amerika that an unusual field of pack ice and bergs menaced navigation off the Banks.

OFFICERS CONFIDENT EVEN IN THE FACE OF DANGER.

But it was a "clear and starlight night," as all the survivors described the weather, and the great ship sped through the quiet seas with officers confident that even though an iceberg should be seen the vessel could be controlled in ample time, and the passengers rested in full confidence that their temporary quarters in the largest and most magnificent vessel ever constructed were as safe as their own homes.

This confidence is emphasized in the tales of nearly all the survivors that when the crash came there was almost no excitement. Many who felt anxious enough to go on deck to inquire what had happened were little perturbed when they learned that the ship had "only struck an iceberg." It appeared to be a glancing blow and at first there was no indication of a serious accident.

A group of men at cards in the smoking room sent one of their number to look out of the window, and when he came back with the announcement that the boat had grazed an iceberg, the party went on with the game. It was never finished.

The stoppage of the engines was noticed more than the collision, the effect being, as one survivor put it, like the stopping of a loud ticking clock.

The over-confident passengers were not brought to the slightest realization that the collision might mean serious danger until the call ran through the ship, "All passengers on deck with life-belts on."

Captain Smith, it is said, was not on the bridge when the collision occurred, but when hurriedly summoned by his first officer, he took charge of what seemed a hopeless situation in a manner which the passengers praise as calm, resolute and efficient to the highest degree.

One of the most stirring narratives of action and description of scenes that followed the collision was told by L. Beasley, a Cambridge University man, who was one of the surviving second cabin passengers.

THE CREWS ALLOTTED TO THE BOATS.

"The steamer lay just as if she were awaiting the order to go on again, when some trifling matter had been adjusted," he said. "But in a few minutes we saw the covers lifted from the boats, and the crews allotted to them standing by ready to lower them to the water.

"Presently we heard the order, 'All men stand back and all ladies retire to the next deck below'— the smoking room deck or 'B' deck. The men stood away and remained in absolute silence, leaning against the end railing or pacing slowly up and down.

"The boats were swung out and lowered from A deck. When they were to the level of B deck, where all the ladies were collected, the ladies got in quietly with the exception of some, who refused to leave their husbands. In some cases they were torn from them and pushed into the boats.

"All this time there was no trace of any disorder; no panic or rush for the boats, and no scenes of women sobbing hysterically. Everyone seemed to realize so slowly that there was imminent danger. When it was realized that we would be presently in the sea with nothing but our life-belts to support us until we were picked up by passing steamers, it was extraordinary how calm everyone was and how complete the self-control.

"One by one the boats were filled with women and children,

"Presently we heard the order, 'All men stand back and all lowered and rowed away into the night. Presently the word went around among the men, 'The men are to be put in boats on the starboard side.' I was on the port side and most of the men walked across the deck to see if this was so. Presently I heard the call, 'Any more ladies?'

"Looking over the side of the ship I saw boat No. 13 swinging level with B deck, half full of women. I saw no more come, and one of the crew said then: 'You'd better jump.' I dropped in and fell in the bottom as they cried 'lower away.' " ,

Beasely said that the lifeboat was nearly two miles away from the Titanic less than two hours later, when they made out that the great liner was sinking.

SHIP APPARENTLY BREAKS IN TWO.

Other survivors who were nearer to the sinking liner told of hearing the strains of "Nearer, My God, to Thee" played as the liner sank, and some of those in the lifeboats blended their voices in the melody. Suddenly there was a mighty roar and the ship, already half submerged, was seen to buckle and apparently break in two by the force of an explosion caused when the water reached the hot boilers.

The bow sank first and for fully five minutes the stern was poised almost vertically in the air, when suddenly it plunged out of sight.

With the last hope gone of seeing their loved ones alive, many women in the lifeboats seemed to be indifferent whether they were saved or not. They were nearly 1000 miles from land and had no knowledge that a ship of succor was speeding to them. Without provisions or water, there seemed little hope of surviving long in the bitter cold.

There were sixteen boats in the forlorn procession which entered upon the terrible hours of suspense.

The confidence that the big ship, on which they had started across the sea, was sure to bring them safely here was now turned to utter helplessness. But the shock of learning that their lives were in peril was hardly greater than the relief when, at dawn, a large steamer's stacks were seen on the horizon, and eager eyes soon made out that the vessel was making for the scene.

The rescue ship proved to be the Carpathia, which had received the Titanic's distress signals by wireless.

By 7 o'clock in the morning all the Titanic's sixteen boats had been picked up and their chilled and hungry occupants welcomed over the Carpathia's side. The Carpathia's passengers, who were bound for a Mediterranean cruise, showed every consideration for the stricken, and many gave up their cabins that the shipwrecked might be made comfortable.

The rescued were in all conditions of dress and undress, and the women on the Carpathia vied with one another in supplying missing garments.

On the four days' cruise back to New York many, who had realized that their experiences would be waited by an anxious world, put their narratives to paper while their nerves were still at a tension from the excitement of the disaster they had barely escaped.

CHAPTER V.

BELIEVED SHIP UNSINKABLE.

Shots and Hymn Mingle—Titanic Settled Slowly—Best Traditions Upheld by Passengers and Crew—Boiler Explosions Tore Ship Apart—Anguish in the Boats—Survivors Carried to Carpathia—Not Enough Provision Against Accident.

Outside of great naval battles no tragedy of the sea ever claimed so many victims as did the loss of the Titanic. The pitiful part of it is that all on board the Titanic might have been saved had there been a sufficient number of lifeboats aboard to accommodate the passengers and crew.

Only sixteen lifeboats were launched, one of these, a collapsible boat, the last to be launched, was overturned, but was used as a raft and served to save the lives of many men and women.

Many women went down with the ship—steerage women, unable to get to the upper decks where the boats were launched; maids, who were overlooked in the confusion; cabin passengers, who refused to desert their husbands, or who reached the decks after the last of the lifeboats was gone and the ship was settling for her final plunge to the bottom of the Atlantic.

Confidence in the ability of the Titanic to remain afloat led many of the passengers to death. The theory that the great ship was unsinkable remained with hundreds who had entrusted themselves to the gigantic hulk long after the officers knew that the vessel could not long remain above the surface.

That so many of the men passengers and members of the crew were saved, while such a large majority of females drowned was due to the fact that the women had not appeared about the lifeboats in sufficient numbers to fill them when whey they first were launched. Dozens of male survivors assert they were forced into the first boats lowered against their will by officers who insisted that the boats should go overboard filled to their capacity.

From a rather calm, well ordered sort of leaving of passengers over the side when the disaster was young the departure of survivors became a riot as the last boats were lowered and it was apparent that the Titanic would sink.

Steerage passengers fought their way to the upper decks and struggled with brutal ferocity against cabin passengers who were aimlessly trying to save themselves. Officers of the ship shot down men who sought to jump into already overcrowded boats. The sound of the pistol shots mingled with the strains of "Nearer, My God, to Thee," played by the ship's orchestra as the Titanic took her final plunge.

MURDOCK SHOOTS HIMSELF.

Murdock, the first officer, who was on the bridge in charge of the Titanic when she struck the iceberg, shot himself when convinced the vessel was doomed. The report that Captain Smith shot himself is contradicted by survivors, who say they saw him swept from the ship as she went down.

The Titanic settled into the sea gently. The greater part of her bulk was under water when she slipped beneath the waves. No trace of suction was felt by those in lifeboats only a few hundred yards away.

Colonel John Jacob Astor died a hero and went down with the ship. Had he leaped into the water as she made her final plunge, he might have been picked up by one of the lifeboats, but he remained on the deck and was swept under by the drawing power of the great bulk, bound for the bottom.

All the officers who died and most of the members of the crew upheld the traditions of heroism held sacred by seamen. They did their duty to the end and died with their ship. Not a man in the engine room was saved; not one of them was seen on deck after the collision. They remained at their posts, far down in the depths of the stricken vessel, until the waves closed over what was at once their pride and their burial casket.

A boiler explosion tore the Titanic apart shortly before she sank. This occurred when the sea water, which had been working its way through the forward compartments, invaded the fireroom. After the explosion the Titanic hung on the surface, upheld only by the water-tight compartments, which had not been touched by the collision.

Although the officers of the Titanic had been warned of the proximity of ice, she was steaming at the rate of twenty-three knots an hour when she met her end. The lookouts in the crow's nest saw an iceberg ahead and telephoned the bridge. The vessel swung slightly in response to her rudder, and the submerged part of the iceberg tore out her plates along the starboard quarters below the water.

COMPARTMENT WALL GIVES WAY.

Water rushed into several of the compartments. The ship listed to starboard. Captain Smith hurried to the bridge. It was thought the ship would float, until a shudder, that vibrated throughout the great frame, told that a compartment wall had given away. Then a definite order was given to man the lifeboats, and stewards were sent to instruct passengers to put on life preservers.

So thoroughly grounded was the belief of the cabin passengers that the Titanic was unsinkable that few of them took the accident seriously. Women in evening dress walked out of the magnificent saloons and joked about the situation. Passengers protested against getting into the lifeboats, although the ship was then sinking by the head.

Mr. and Mrs. H. J. Allison and their little daughter remained on the ship and were lost, after the infant son of the Allison family had been placed in a lifeboat in charge of a nurse.

Isidor Straus and his wife did not appear on deck until an order had been issued that only women and children should be allowed in the lifeboats. Mrs. Straus clung to her husband and refused to leave him. They died in each other's arms.

Those who escaped in the first lifeboats were disposed to

look on their experience as a lark. The sailors manning the oars pulled away from the Titanic. The sound of music floated over the starlit waves. The lights of the Titanic were burning.

Like simultaneous photographs of the same tragedy etched on the brains of 745 persons, survivors of the Titanic tell of their experiences and what they saw in those pitfully few hours between the great ship's impact on the iceberg and the appalling moment when she disappeared.

As the survivors came, half fainting, half hysterical, down the Carpathia's gang plank, they began to relate these narratives. Many of these were disjointed, fragmentary—a picture here, a frightful flash of recollection there, some bordered on hallucination, some were more connected as one of those who are now beginning to realize the horror through which they came. A few strangely enough, are calm and lucid. But every one thrills with some part of the awful truth as its narrator saw it.

INDIVIDUALLY CONFLICTING STORIES OF THE WRECK.

Each tale is like another view of the same many-sided shield. Sometimes they seem to contradict each other, but that is because those who witness such scenes see them as individuals. There is not a survivor but has something new and startling and dramatic to tell.

Taken altogether their accounts are a composite picture of 700 separate experiences.

The shock of the collision had barely jarred the ship. One man who was directing letters in his cabin kept on with his work until he felt a sudden shift in the position of the ship and rushed to the deck in time to leap into a lifeboat. Some of the passengers had returned to their berths.

Nothing occurred to indicate to the passengers aboard the Titanic or moving away from the ship in lifeboats that the vessel would not remain afloat until help should arrive, until the boilers exploded. Then the end was apparent to all.

Men with life-preservers strapped about their waists, jumped overboard by scores and some were picked up by boats which had not got far from the ship.

As the last three lifeboats were launched the restriction as to women and children was removed. It was a free-for-all then on the deck, where unskilled men, principally stewards, were trying to get the the cumberstone boats overboard. Nearly all those who took part in that struggle for life are dead. Those who survived are not anxious to talk about it.

Just before the Titanic disappeared from view men and women leaped from the stern. As the portion of vessel remaining above water swung up to an almost perpendicular position hundreds on the upper decks were thrown into the sea and were pulled down in the vortex. The biggest, most thrilling moments of the wreck were those last moments when the air-tight compartments in the after part of the Titanic were supporting the balance of the ship.

KEPT TOGETHER BY GREEN LIGHT.

None are alive to tell the tale of that short period. Toward 2 o'clock on Monday morning a green light aboard one of the lifeboats kept the fleet of craft carrying the survivors together. Through the hours until dawn the men in charge of the boats hovered about that green light. Occasionally bodies of men slipped by the lifeboats. A few men, more dead than alive, were pulled aboard the boats, that were now overcrowded.

The weather became bitterly cold and the survivors suffered physical pain as well as mental anguish. Benumbed by the extent of the catastrophe most of the women sat motionless in their places. The Carpathia appeared soon after dawn. Not until the big Cunarder was close by did the realization of what had happened reach the women survivors.

Many of them became temporarily insane. It was necessary to use force to place them in swings in which they were hoisted to the Carpathia's decks. The officers of the Carpathia knowing the Titanic had gone down, were prepared for an emergency. Passengers on the Cunarder gave their cabins to the Titanic sufferers. The captain surrendered his room for hospital purposes. Stewardesses were compelled to cut the clothing from some of the women who had jumped into the water and been picked up by the lifeboats.

Among the survivors picked up by the Carpathia were several babies. These little ones were tossed overboard by their parents and rescued by the boats. The identity of these orphans may never be determined. When the list of persons aboard the Carpathia was checked up it was found that among the survivors were thirty women who had been widowed by the disaster.

Nearly all these women, bereft of their life partners, were reassured by the hope that those who had been left behind had been picked up by another vessel until they reached New York. For some reason the impression prevailed on the Carpathia that the Californian had picked up a number of survivors floating in the sea upheld by life-preservers.

EVERY HUSBAND SAVED SAVES HIS WIFE.

As against the thirty widows stands the record of every married man who was saved. Each of these men saved his wife also. No wife was left on the Titanic by a husband who had reached a lifeboat.

Narratives of the various survivors, assembled in a consecutive narrative, makes one of the most thrilling tales of modern life. It is a narrative filled with heroism unparalleled—bravery and heroism performed by American business men. They were men of millions who had everything to live for and yet, in that crisis at sea, they worked coolly, steadfastly to save women and children. Then they went down with the White Star liner Titanic, the greatest ship afloat.

When the Carpathia came into port carrying the more than 700 survivors of the disaster, the curtain, which had hidden the story of the tragedy since the first word of it was flashed to a startled world, was drawn aside. Here is the real tale of the sinking of the Titanic.

The Titanic was athrob with the joy of life on Sunday night, when without warning, the great liner was jammed against a partly submerged iceberg. The blow, which was a glancing one, did not cause much of a jar and there were some on board who did not know that an accident had happened until later. The liner struck the berg on the starboard side amidships.

Only Captain E. J. Smith, the commander, realized that there might be grave danger, and even he did not regard the collision as fatal. Going to the wireless cabin in which Phillips, the operator, was in conversation with Cape Race on traffic matters, he gave orders to the wireless man to hold himself in readiness to flash out a distress signal.

At the time there was a great throng in the main saloon, where the ship's orchestra was giving a concert. Despite the bitterly cold weather, some of the passengers were taking advantage of the bright moonlight to stroll upon the decks. Survivors, who were upon the starboard side, said that the ice mountain which the vessel struck was at least 150 feet high where exposed

UNDER FULL HEAD OF STEAM.

At the time the ship was steaming ahead under nearly a full head of steam, at about twenty-one knots. If she had been going slowly the disaster probably would never have happened.

Acting under orders from Captain Smith, the ship's officers passed among the passengers, reassuring them as the rumor that the ship had struck spread.

"Keep cool; there is no danger," was the message which, repeated over and over, gradually became monotonous. The warning was hardly necessary for none, save the highest officers of the ship, who were in Captain Smith's confidence, knew the real gravity of the situation.

Captain Smith immediately went below and began an examination. This showed that quick action was necessary. Within fifteen minutes of his first warning the captain again entered the wireless cabin and told Phillips to flash the distress signal.

"Send the international call for help, so they will understand." Captain Smith said.

Bride, the assistant operator, who had been asleep, was standing at Phillips' side.

Some of the passengers who had been sleeping were aroused and left their berths. Many hastened on deck to get a glimpse of the berg, but, so swiftly was it moving in the gulf stream current, that, within twenty minutes after the vessel struck it, the ice mountain had disappeared from view. At 11.50 P. M., fifteen minutes after the collision, the first intimation of impending danger was given. Officers passed among the passengers warning them to put on life belts. The tarpaulins were cast off, the lifeboats and the life rafts and the davit guys loosened so that the boats could be swiftly swung over the side.

Members of the crew also donned life preservers; but, with studied forethought, Captain Smith ordered the principal officers not to don their belts. They were told, however, to be ready to do so in an emergency.

PHILLIPS POUNDS OUT THE S. O. S.

The ship soon had begun to list. The wireless masts were sputtering a blue streak of sparks. Phillips at his key pounded out one "S. O. S." call after another. He alternated between the "S. O. S." and the "C. Q. D." so that there might be no chance of the signal being misunderstood.

The first ship to respond to the Titanic was the Frankfurt; the second was the Carpathia. Phillips told the Carpathia's wireless man that the accident was serious and that the White Star liner was sinking by the head.

"We are putting about and coming to your aid," was the reply flashed by the Cunarder.

About 12.15 o'clock the officers began warning the women to get into the boats. Even at this time no one realized that there was any danger. Many of the women refused to get into the boats and had to be placed in them forcibly by the crew.

Colonel and Mrs. John Jacob Astor were walking upon the deck. They were approached by Captain H. D. Steffason, of the Swedish Embassy, at Washington. Captain Steffason advised Mrs. Astor to leave the ship. She demurred, saying there was no danger. Finally Colonel Astor said:

"Yes, my dear, it is better for you to go; I will follow in another boat after all the women have been taken off."

They kissed and parted. It was a beautiful parting.

Mrs. Washington Dodge, of San Francisco, wife of another prominent passenger, was asleep in her stateroom. She was aroused by her husband, who urged her to get in a boat. So certain were both that the measures were only precautionary and not necessary that they did not even kiss each other good-bye. Mr. Dodge embarked in another boat.

These incidents are given because they are typical. They show how little the passengers knew that they were standing at the brink of death.

THE GAP INCREASES.

The riven plates under the water increased the gap, allowing more and more water to pour into the hold. The steel frame had been buckled by the impact of the collision and water was rushing into the supposedly water-tight compartments around the doors. The dynamo supplying the ship's searchlight and the wireless outfit were put out of commission.

Officers hurried hither and thither, reporting to Captain Smith. This master mariner, hero of the White Star Line, knew that he was doomed to death by all the traditions of the sea, but did not flinch. He was the coolest man on board. As life boat after life boat was filled and swung over the side it pulled off some distance and stood by.

When the officers began to load the women of the steerage into the boats trouble started. Men refused to be separated from the wives. Families clamored to get into life boats together. The ship's officers had a hard time subduing some of the steerage passengers. The survivors say that some of the men of the steerage were shot by the ship's officers.

As the officers were loading the women of the first cabin list into the boat they came upon Mrs. Isador Straus, the elderly wife of the noted philanthropist. She started to get into a boat, but held back, waiting for her husband to follow. Mr. Straus tenderly took her in his arms, bade her farewell and explained that he must abide by the inexorable rule of the sea, which says women and children must be saved first.

"If you do not go I don't go," exclaimed the devoted wife. She clung to her husband's arm, and, despite his efforts and the efforts of officers to persuade her to get into one of the boats, she refused. The devoted couple went to death together.

While the vessel was going down the call for help was picked up and acknowledged by the White Star liners Olympic and Baltic. They turned their heads toward the Titanic, but were too far away to render aid.

STRAINS OF MUSIC DROWNS ALL CRIES.

The band, which had been playing incessantly in the main saloon, moved out to the open deck and the strains of music rose above the shouts of the officers and the cries of the passengers. By 1 o'clock even those who knew nothing of seamanship began to realize by the angle at which the giant liner careened that she was in grave danger. By this time more than half of the life boats had been sent away and they formed a ring in the darkness about the great vessel.

Excitement began to run high. Major A. W. Butt, U. S. A., military aide to President Taft; William T. Stead, the famous journalist; Colonel Astor, and others of the passengers volunteered their services to Captain Smith. They helped the officers hold back other male passengers who by this time had become thoroughly frightened.

As one of the lifeboats was being swung over the ship's side, a frantic mother who had been separated from her eight-year-old boy, cried out hysterically. Colonel Astor was standing by the boat, assisting the officers. The little boy, in fright and despair, stretched out his arms appealingly to his mother, but the officer in command of the boat said that it would not be safe for another to enter.

Colonel Astor, seeing a girl's hat lying upon the deck, stealthily placed it upon the boy's head. Lifting up the child, he called out: "Surely you will not leave a little girl behind." The ruse worked and the child was taken on board.

Up in the wireless room, Bride had placed a life preserver upon his companion, Phillips, while Phillips sat at his key. Upon returning from Captain Smith's cabin with a message, Bride saw a grimy stoker of gigantic proportions bending over Phillips removing the life belt. Phillips would not abandon his key for an instant to fight off the stoker. Bride is a little man (he was subsequently saved) but plucky. Drawing his revolver he shot down the intruder and the wireless work went on as though nothing had happened.

J. Bruce Ismay, managing director of the International Mercantile Marine Company, owners of the White Star Line, was sitting in the cafe chatting to some friends when the liner ran upon the berg. He was the first one informed by Captain Smith. Ismay rushed to the deck to look at the berg.

"THE SHIP CANNOT SINK."

"The ship cannot sink," was the reply which he gave, with smiling assurance, to all inquirers.

Nevertheless, there are survivors who say that Ismay was one of the passengers of the lifeboats which put off. They saw him enter the boat.

By 1.30 o'clock the great vessel, which only a short time before had been the marvel of the twentieth century, was a waterlogged hulk. Panic was steadily growing. The word had been passed around that the ship was doomed. The night continued calm. The sea was smooth. The moon was brilliant in the sky.

Into one of the last of the life boats that were launched two Chinamen, employed in the galley, had hidden themselves. They were stretched in the bottom of the boat, face downward, and made no sound. So excited were the women that they did not notice the presence of the Chinese until the boat had pulled off from the Titanic. Then the officer in charge drew his revolver and shot both to death. The bodies were tumbled overboard.

The weather was very cold and the sea was filled with floating ice. All were warned before getting into the boats to dress as warmly as possible. By the time the boats were filled the water had entered the engine-room and the ship was drifting helplessly. About 2 o'clock Captain Smith, who had been standing upon the bridge with a megaphone to his mouth, again went to the wireless cabin.

"Men," he said to Phillips and Bride, with a break in his voice, "you have done your full duty. You can do no more. Abandon your cabin, for it is now every man for himself."

Bride left the cabin, but Phillips still clung to his key. He perished. The saving of Bride, the second wireless man, was only one of a series of thrilling escapes. Wearing a life belt, Bride went upon deck. He saw a dozen men passengers tugging at a collapsible boat trying to work it to the edge of the deck.

BRIDE SWEPT OVERBOARD.

The wireless man went to their assistance and they had got it nearly to the point from which they could swing it over, when a wave rolled over the deck. Bride, who had hold of an oar lock, was swept overboard with the boat. The next thing he knew he was struggling in the water beneath the boat.

The icy water struck a chill through him. He realized that unless he got from beneath the boat he would drown. Diving deeply, he came up on the outside of the gunwale and grasped it. On every hand was wreckage of all kinds and struggling men who had been washed overboard by the submerging comber. Bride clung to the craft until he saw another boat near by. Exerting all his strength, he swam to this boat and was pulled in it more dead than alive.

By this time all the boats and life rafts had been taken from the ship. The boats were ringed about the ship from 150 feet to 1,000 yards distant. Their occupants could see the lights burning on the vessel which had settled low in the water.

Suddenly as they looked great billows of live sparks rose up through the four funnels. These were followed by billowing clouds of smoke and steam. The rush of water had reached the boiler rooms and the boilers had exploded. After this the great vessel sank more rapidly and within less than twenty minutes had plunged to her grave, two miles beneath the surface.

In the meantime, however, those upon the sinking ship, who knew that they had only a few hours at most to live, lived up to the most splendid example of Anglo-Saxon courage. As the ship sank lower those on board climbed higher, prolonging life to the last minute. Frenzied search was made of every part of the decks by those who hoped that the sailors had overlooked a life raft or small boat which might be used. Their search was vain.

Colonel Astor, Major Butt, C. M. Hays, W. M. Clark and other friends stood together. Astor and Butt were strong swimmers. When the water reached the ship's rail, Butt and Astor jumped and began swimming rapidly away. There was little suction despite the bulk of the foundering craft.

SHIP DISAPPEARS FROM VIEW.

There was a dreadful cry as the ship disappeared from view. Instantly the water was filled with hundreds of struggling men. The spot just above the grave of the liner was strewn with wreckage. Some tried to climb upon the ice cakes. But the cold air and the cold water soon numbed the fingers of the men in the water. Even the most powerful of the refugees soon gave out. Exhausted by their effort and numb from exposure they dropped one by one.

There are survivors, however, among them Dr. Henry J. Frauenthal, of this city, who said that they heard cries from the water for two hours after the Titanic sank. Amidst the acres and acres of wreckage hundreds of dead bodies floated. Many of them were among the first cabin passengers, still dressed in their evening clothes which they had worn when the ship struck the iceberg.

CHAPTER VI.

HOW SURVIVORS ESCAPED.

Managing Director Accused—Stoker Makes Direct Charge—Supported by Many Survivors—Tells about It—"Please Don't Knock"—Demanded Food—Brave Lot of Women—First Officer Shot Himself.

One man stands out in a most unenviable light amid the narratives of heroism and suffering attending the great Titanic sea tragedy. This man is J. Bruce Ismay, managing director of the White Star Line, who, according to accounts of survivors, made himself the exception to the rule of the sea, "Women first," in the struggle for life.

Some of these survivors say he jumped into the first life boat, others that he got into the third or fourth. However that may be, he is among the comparatively few men saved, and the manner of his escape aroused the wrath and criticism of many.

A woman with a baby was pushed to the side of the third boat, says one survivor. Ismay got out; he then climbed into the fourth boat. "I will man this boat," he said, and there was no one who said him nay.

"Mr. Ismay was in the first lifeboat that left the Titanic," declared William Jones, an eighteen-year-old stoker, who was called to man one of the lifeboats. Jones comes from Southampton, England, and this was his first ocean voyage. He left the Carpathia tottering. "There were three firemen in each boat," he said. "I don't know how many were killed in the boiler explosion which occurred after the last lifeboat had put off. I saw four boats, filled with first cabin passengers, sink. In the boat I was in, two women died from exposure. We were picked up about 8 o'clock."

Mrs. Lucien P. Smith, of Huntingdon, W. Va., daughter of Representative James Hughes, West Virginia, was in the third boat that was launched, and in that boat was Mrs. John Jacob Astor. "My niece saw Mr. Ismay leaving the boat. He was attended by several of the crew and every assistance was given him to get into the boat," says Mrs. Smith. "And when the Carpathia finally came along and rescued the shipwrecked passengers, some of the crew of the Carpathia, together with men of the Titanic, actually carried Mr. Ismay to spacious rooms that had been set aside for him. As soon as Mr. Ismay had been placed in this stateroom a sign was placed on the door: "Please don't knock."

MRS. W. J. CARDEZA'S NARRATIVE.

According to Mrs. W. J. Cardeza, of Philadelphia, who gave her narrative after she had arrived at the Ritz-Carlton with T. D. M. Cardeza, J. Bruce Ismay was not only safely seated in a lifeboat before it was filled, but he also selected the crew that rowed the boat. According to Mrs. Cardeza, Mr. Ismay knew that Mr. Cardeza was an expert oarsman and he beckoned him into the boat. Mr. Cardeza manned an oar until Mr. Ismay's boat was picked up about two hours later.

The White Star Line, through Ismay, disclaimed responsibility, saying that it was "an act of God." Ismay defended his action in taking to the lifeboat. He said that he took the last boat that left the ship. "Were there any women and children left on the Titanic when you entered the boat?" he was asked. The reply was, "I am sure I cannot say."

J. Bruce Ismay described to a reporter how the catastrophe occurred. "I was asleep in my cabin," said Mr. Ismay, "when the crash came. It woke me instantly. I experienced a sensation as if the big liner were sliding up on something.

"We struck a glancing blow, not head on, as some persons have supposed. The iceberg, so great was the force of the blow, tore the ship's plates half way back, I think, although I cannot say definitely. There was absolutely no disorder.

"I left in the last boat. I did not see the Titanic sink. I cannot remember how far away the lifeboat in which I was had been rowed from the ship when she sank."

Mr. Ismay began his interview by reading a prepared statement, to this effect:

"In the presence and under the shadow of so overwhelming a tragedy I am overcome with feelings too deep for words. The White Star Line will do everything humanly possible to alleviate the sufferings of the survivors and the relatives of those who were lost.

"The Titanic was the last word in ship building. Every British regulation had been complied with and her masters, officers and crew were the most experienced and skillful in the British service.

WELCOMES EXHAUSTIVE INQUIRY.

"I am informed that a committee of the United States Senate has been appointed to investigate the accident. I heartily welcome a most complete and exhaustive inquiry as the company has absolutely nothing to conceal and any aid that my associates or myself, our ship builders or navigators can render will be at the service of both the United States and the British Governments."

"How soon did she sink after she struck?" Mr. Ismay was asked. "Let me see, it was two hours and twenty-five minutes, I think. Yes, that is right."

"In other words, there would have been ample time to have taken everybody off if there had been enough lifeboats?" he was asked. "I do not want to talk about that now," was the reply.

"Did you go off in the first boat?" some one asked. "What do you mean?"

"Were you in the first boat that left the ship?" "No." he replied, slowly and firmly, "I was not. I was in the last boat. It was one of the forward boats."

"Did the captain tell you to get in the boat?" "No."

"What was the captain doing when you last saw him?" "He was standing on the bridge."

"It is not true that he committed suicide?" "No, I heard nothing of it."

Mr. Ismay was asked to explain the delay in the sending of the news of the wreck from the Carpathia. He said:

"I can't say anything about that now except that I sent the first telegram announcing what had happened to Mr. Franklin about 11 o'clock on the morning that we were picked up. I am told that that telegram did not reach its destination here until yesterday."

In response to requests for more details Mr. Ismay said: "I must refuse to say more until to-morrow, when I appear before the Congressional Committee."

"For God's sake, get me something to eat. I'm starved. I don't care what it costs or what it is. Bring it to me."

AN OFFICER'S COMPLETE ACCOUNT.

This was the first statement made by Ismay, a few minutes after he was landed on board the Carpathia. It is vouched for by an officer of the Carpathia. This officer gave one of the most complete accounts of what happened aboard the Carpathia from the time she received the Titanic's appeal for assistance until she landed the survivors at the Cunard line pier.

"Mr. Ismay reached the Carpathia in about the tenth lifeboat," said the officer. "I didn't know who he was, but afterward I heard the others of the crew discussing his desire to get something to eat the minute he put his foot on deck. The steward who waited on him, McGuire, from London, says Mr. Ismay came dashing into the dining room, and, throwing himself in a chair, said, 'Hurry, for God's sake, and get me something to eat; I'm starved. I don't care what it costs or what it is; bring it to me.'

"McGuire brought Mr. Ismay a load of stuff, and when he had finished it he handed McGuire a two-dollar bill. 'Your money is no good on this ship.' McGuire told him. 'Take it,' insisted Mr. Ismay, shoving the bill in McGuire's hand. 'I am well able to afford it. I will see to it that the boys of the Carpathia are well rewarded for this night's work.' This promise started McGuire making inquires as to the identity of the man he had waited on. Then we learned that he was Mr. Ismay. I did not see Mr. Ismay after the first few hours. He must have kept to his cabin.

"The Carpathia received her first appeal from the Titanic about midnight, According to an officer of the Titanic, that vessel struck the iceberg at twenty minutes to 12 o'clock and went down for keeps at nineteen minutes after 2 o'clock. I turned in on Sunday night a few minutes after 12 o'clock. I hadn't closed my eyes before a friend of the chief steward told me that Captain Rostron had ordered the chief steward to get out 3,000 blankets and to make preparations to care for that many extra persons. I jumped into my clothes and was informed of the Titanic. By that time the Carpathia was going at full speed in the direction of the Titanic.

THE CREW TOLD WHAT IS EXPECTED OF THEM.

"The entire crew of the Carpathia was assembled on deck and were told of what had happened. The chief steward, Harry Hughes, told them what was expected of them.

"'Every man to his post and let him do his full duty like a true Englishman,' he said. 'If the situation calls for it, let us add another glorious page to British history.'

"After that every man saluted and went to his post. There was no confusion. Everything was in readiness for the reception of the survivors before 2 o'clock. Only one or two of the passengers were on deck, one of them, Mr. Beachler, having been awakened by a friend, and the other because of inability to sleep. Many of the Carpathia's passengers slept all through the morning up to 10 o'clock, and had no idea of what was going on.

"We reached the scene of the collision about 4 o'clock. All was black and still but the mountain of ice just ahead told the story. A flare from one of the lifeboats some distance away was the first sign of life. We answered with a rocket, and then there was nothing to do but wait for daylight.

"The first lifeboat reached the Carpathia about half-past 5 o'clock in the morning, and the last of the sixteen boats was unloaded before 9 o'clock. Some of the lifeboats were only half filled, the first one having but two men and eleven women, when it had accommodations for at least forty. There were few men in the boats. The women were the gamest lot I have ever seen. Some of the men and women were in evening clothes, and others among those saved had nothing on but night clothes and raincoats.

IMAGINE THEIR HUSBANDS PICKED BY OTHER VESSELS.

"As soon as they were landed on the Carpathia many of the women became hysterical, but on the whole they behaved splendid. Men and women appeared to be stunned all day Monday, the full force of the disaster not reaching them until Tuesday night. After being wrapped up in blankets and given brandy and hot coffee, their first thoughts were for their husbands and those at home. Most of them imagined that their husbands had been picked up by other vessels and then began flooding the wireless rooms with messages. We knew that those who were not on board the Carpathia had gone down to death, and this belief was confirmed Monday afternoon when we received a wire from Mr. Marconi himself asking why no news had been sent.

"We knew that if any other vessel could by any chance have picked them up it would have communicated with land. After a while, when the survivors failed to get any answer to their queries, they grew so restless that Captain Rostron posted a notice that all private messages had been sent and that the wireless had not been used to give information to the press, as had been charged. Little by little it began to dawn on the women on board, and most of them guessed the worst before they reached here. I saw Mrs. John Jacob Astor when she was taken from the lifeboat. She was calm and collected. She kept to her stateroom all the time, leaving it only to attend a meeting of the survivors on Tuesday afternoon."

J. R. Moody was a quartermaster on the bridge beside First Officer Murdock when the Titanic struck the berg. "There is no way of telling the approach of a berg, and, besides, I do not intend to go into that now," said Moody. "We struck, and we paid dearly for it, and that is all there is to that now. We were running between twenty-two and twenty-three knots an hour.

WIRELESS TELEGRAPHIC APPARATUS.

It seemed incredible that much damage had been done at first, we struck so lightly. There was a little jar. Almost immediately, though, Captain Smith rushed to the bridge and took charge. Afterward I saw Murdock, standing on the first deck. I saw him raise his arm and shoot himself. He dropped where he stood.

"As far as Mr. Bruce Ismay goes, he was in the second boat that left the Titanic. The first boat swamped. I am sure of that, and Mr. Ismay was bundled into the second boat, regardless of his protests, to take charge of it in place of First Officer Murdock, who had shot himself.

"When the Titanic started to sink Captain Smith was on the

bridge. I saw him. The first lurch brought the bridge almost under water, and the captain was washed off. He clambered back, and must have been there another ten minutes. When the bridge sank slowly down and he was washed off for the second time, a boat tried to make back to him, but he waved for it to keep back. The last anybody saw of him he was fighting his way back to the Titanic. He drowned fighting to reach her."

"J. Bruce Ismay never showed himself once during the whole voyage and on the voyage on the Carpathia. We never saw him from the time the vessel took up the survivors until we reached the dock. Personally I do not think that Captain Smith was responsible for the high rate of speed at which the Titanic was traveling when the ship foundered. I kept a record during the voyage. From noon of Saturday to noon of Sunday the Titanic traveled 546 knots. I believe they were trying to break records. When the crash came the boat was traveling at top speed."

HENRY E. STENGEL'S STORY.

This was the statement which Henry E. Stengel gave early today at his residence, 1075 Broad st., Newark, N. J. Shaken with the horrors of the wreck and the nerve-racking voyage on the rescue ship Carpathia, Mr. Stengel spoke in stern terms of the recklessness which made the accident so appalling. Although it was near to midnight when he and his wife reached Newark, there were a hundred friends waiting to receive them, all of whom hung breathlessly on the recital of the perils which the two escaped.

Mr. Stengel and his wife had one of the most remarkable reunions of any persons on the ship. The two did not escape in the same boat. Mrs. Stengel being in the first launched, while her husband was in the very last boat from the starboard side. Mrs. Stengel looked many years older than when she left the other side a few weeks ago, and was even more emphatic than her husband in criticism of the shortcomings of the White Star officials.

"There was absolutely no water in our boat. We would have

died of thirst if rescue had not been near at hand," she said. "I understand it was the way in all the other lifeboats, few of which even had lanterns. I have heard that a couple of them were provided with bread at the last moment, but our boat was absolutely without any food."

Mrs. Stengel was worn by the constant strain which had been pressing upon her in the last five days. "This has been such a terrible worry that I feel as though I could never sleep again," she said. "Oh, it was horrible, horrible. Sometimes I think that I would have been better dead than to have so much to remember. You see when the crash first came no one realized the awful seriousness of the situation. It was a loud, grinding crash and it shook the boat like a leaf, but we had all become so filled with the idea that the Titanic was a creation greater than the seas that no one was terror-stricken. Some of the women screamed and children cried, but they told us it was all right and that nothing serious could happen.

DID NOT WANT TO LEAVE HER HUSBAND.

"I was just preparing for sleep when the crash came, and throwing on some clothes, I rushed on deck with my husband. In a short time we were told that the women would be sent in the boats. I did not want to leave my husband, but he laughed and told me that the boating was only temporary. There was very little confusion when we put off and the men in the first and second cabins were absolutely calm. Mr. Stengel kissed me and told me not to worry, that he would come in a later boat, unless it was decided to bring us back on the ship.

"For some reason no attention was paid to the men who were put in our boat. One of them was an undersized Chinaman and the other was an Oriental of some kind. When the lifeboat struck the water they crawled up in the bottom and began to moan and cry. They refused to take their places at the oars and first class women passengers had to man many of the rowlocks. Still none of us thought that the great Titanic would sink. We rowed two hundred yards away, as they had told us, watching the great ship. Then the lights began to go out and then came a terrible crash like dynamite.

"I heard a woman in the bow scream and then came three more terrific explosions. The boat gave a sudden lurch and then we saw the men jumping from the decks. Some of us prayed and I heard women curse, but the most terrible thing was the conduct of the Chinaman and the Oriental. They threw themselves about the boat in absolute fits and almost upset the boat. They were a menace during the whole night and in the morning when the light began to come in the east and when the women were exhausted from trying to man the oars, the two of them found some cigarettes and lay in the bottom of the boat and smoked while we tried to work the oars."

There is no survivor better qualified to tell of the last incidents aboard the vessel than Mr. Stegel is. He was one of the last three men to leave the boat. He is a man of scientific turn of mind and is in possession of some valuable data concerning the wreck.

LITTLE DISORDER ON BOARD.

"As my wife has told you, there was but little disorder on board after the crash," he said. "I realized the seriousness of the situation immediately, because I saw Captain Smith come out of the cabin. He was closely followed by Mr. and Mrs, George Widener, of Philadelphia.

" 'What is the outlook?' I heard Mr. Widener inquire. 'It is extremely serious, gentlemen,' he said. 'Please keep cool and do what you can to help us.'

Deck stewards rushed through the corridors rapping frantically on the doors of the occupied cabins. All were told that the danger was imminent. Some heeded and grasping the first clothing they could find, they rushed on deck. Others refused to come out. They would not believe there was danger.

On deck the boat crews were all at their posts. The big lifeboats had been shoved around ready to be put over the side. Women and children were picked up bodily and thrown into them. The rule of the sea, women and children first, was being enforced.

One after the other the boats went over the side. Then a cry was set up: "There are no more boats!" was the shout. Con-

sternation seized upon all that remained. They had believed there would be room for all. Uncontrollable terror seized many. They fought for the life belts. Some frantically tried to tear loose deck fittings hoping to make small rafts that would sustain them until help would come. But everything was bolted fast. Then, fearful that they would be dragged to death in the swirling suction that would follow, the men began to leap into the ice filled ocean.

They jumped in groups, seemingly to an agreed signal, according to the stories of the survivors tonight. Some who jumped were saved, coming up near lifeboats and being dragged into them by the occupants.

Slowly, steadily and majestically the liner sank. One deck after the other was submerged. Whether the boilers exploded is a question. Robert W. Daniel, a Philadelphia banker, says that when the icy water poured into the boiler room two separate explosions followed that tore the interior out of the liner. Others say they did not hear any explosions.

PISTOL SHOTS FIRED.

Pistol shots were fired. Some survivors say they were fired at men who tried to force women and children out of the way. No one who claimed to be an eye-witness to the shooting could be located. One account related in circumstantial detail that the captain and his first officer shot themselves, but Daniel and other passengers positively say they saw the white bearded, grizzled face of the veteran mariner over the top of the bridge just before the railing disappeared. They say that not until then did he jump into the ocean to drown in the suction that marked the last plunge of the Titanic.

The plight of the survivors in the boats was pitiful in the extreme. Few of the women or children had sufficient clothing, and they shivered in the bitter cold blasts that came from the great field of ice which surrounded them. The bergs and cakes of drift ice crashed and thundered bringing stark terror to the helpless victims.

Frail women aided with the heavy oars tearing their tender hands until the blood came. Few of the boats were fully manned, sailors had stood aside deliberately, refusing life that the women might have a chance for safety although their places were in the boats.

Daybreak found the little flotilla bobbing and tossing on the surface of the ocean. It was not known whether help was coming. Panic seized some of the occupants, some of the women tried to jump into the water, and had to be forcibly restrained. The babies, little tots, just old enough to realize their position, found themselves heroes. They set an example which moved their elders to tears as they told of it to-night. Some tried to comfort their stricken parents.

Finally, off in the distant horizon, a sailor in the leading boat, discerned smoke. "We are saved," went up the cry, and the rescue came just in time, for before the Carpathia had taken aboard the occupants of the last frail craft the waves were increasing in height, kicked up by the wind that had increased with the rising of the sun.

All were tenderly cared for on the Cunard liner. The regular passengers willingly gave up their cabins to their unfortunate refugees, medical aid was forthcoming, and nothing left undone that could relieve the distress.

DID NOT SEE ANY SHOTS FIRED.

"It was his face, more than anything else, which made me fearful," continued Mr. Stengel. "He looked like an old, old man. I heard him give instructions to his officers, and they took their stations at the boats. I did not see anyone shot during the whole wreck. They fired three shots in the air to show the steerage men that the guns were loaded, but I was on the boat almost to the last, and I didn't see anyone shot. The boat which saved me was not a regular lifeboat, but a light emergency boat. There was a great rush for it. By the time it was launched the first fear had subsided. It was the last to be lowered from the starboard side.

"The Titanic seemed to be floating safely, and a lot of people preferred it to the flimsy looking rowboats. A deckhand told me that there was a vacant place in it. There I found Sir Cosmo Duff-Gordon, Lady Duff-Gordon and their maid, Miss Francatelli. Just as the boat was being lowered Mr. A. L. Solomon jumped in. We had gone but a little way from the ship when the first boiler explosion came. It was followed in quick succession by three others, at intervals of about one second apart."

In the boat which harbored Mr. Stengel were three stokers and two members of the steerage. Mr. Stengel told graphically of the last plunges of the ship and its final sinking. He declared that there was a little eddy and no whirlpool when it sank. Many of the men on the Titanic jumped into sea before the decks were awash. In telling of the long night on the sea Mr. Stengel gave great credit to a member of the crew who had taken three green lanterns on board just as the small lifeboat was manned.

He said that it was the only beacon which the other lifeboats had for guidance, and said that without it many more would surely have been lost.

Mrs. Stengel spoke particularly of the calmness of the night.

"When the sun rose there was not a ripple on the water," she said. "It was as calm as a little lake in Connecticut. Words cannot express the wonderful terrible beauty of it all—but of course I couldn't appreciate it, because I thought my husband had gone down in the sea.

"The shout of 'land' ever uttered by an explorer was not half so joyful as the shout of 'ship!' which went up when the Carpathia appeared on the horizon that morning," she said. "The first dim lights which appeared were eagerly watched and when it was really identified as a ship, men and women broke down and wept."

The reunion of Mr. and Mrs. Stengel was on the Carpathia. Each was mourning the other as lost for more than an hour after they had been on the vessel, when they met on the promenade deck. Their separation and subsequent reunion was generally considered one of the most remarkable in the history of the wreck.

CHAPTER VII.

WOMAN'S THRILLING NARRATIVE.

Barber Says Good Word for Accused Shipowner—Claims He was a Witness—Saw the Whole Scene—Woman Tells Different Tale—Mrs. Carter's Thrilling Narrative—Barber's Story Differs From Ismay's Own.

J. Bruce Ismay, managing director of the White Star Line, who has been widely charged with cowardice in saving himself when the Titanic was wrecked, has found his first defender in the person of August H. Weikman, "commodore" barber of that company's fleet, who was chief ship's barber on the ill-fated vessel.

Weikman declares that he was a witness of the scene when Ismay left the vessel, and that he literally was thrown into the lifeboat by a seaman, who did not recognize him, and thought he was interfering with the work. He asserts that Ismay was striving valiantly to help in the work of launching the boats, and went overboard only under physical compulsion.

Weikman was accompanied to his home in Palmyra, N. J., by his brothers-in-law, A. H. and John Henricks, who tell of a vexatious experience in getting him off the Carpathia. Weikman was badly injured when he was blown off the ship by the explosion of the boilers.

A. H. Henricks charges that the custom officials refused him a pass to the pier because he wanted to get a member of the ship's crew, and the official said they were not bothering about the crew. The brothers finally made their way to the pier by running between double lines of automobiles. Weikman was brought off the Carpathia on a rolling chair too late to catch the special train which came to this city, and the Pennsylvania Railroad officials provided him with a berth free of charge.

"I was in my barber shop reading," said Weikman, "when I felt a slight jar and realized we had struck something. I went to the gymnasium to see whether others had noticed it. I found some of the men punching the bag, while Colonel Astor, Mr. Widener and a number of others were watching them.

"I had known Mr. Widener for some time, and I advised him to put on a life belt. He laughed at me.

"'What sense is there in that? This boat isn't going to sink,' he said to me. 'There is plenty of time. We're safer here than in a small boat, anyway.'

"Then came the order to man the boats and I went on deck to help. I saw Mr. Ismay at the rail, directing and helping the men. One of them did not recognize him and said: 'What are you interfering for? You get back out of the way.'

"GET BACK OR GO OVERBOARD."

"Another seaman warned the first man that he was speaking to the head of the line. 'I don't care who he is; he's got to get back or go overboard. We can't be bothered with him and his orders now,' was the reply. Mr. Ismay stuck to his place and continued giving orders and directing the men.

"The rule was observed of sending over four women and then a man to look after them. When four women had been put over, the seaman turned to Mr. Ismay and ordered him over the side. Mr. Ismay refused to go, when the seaman seized him, rushed him to the rail and hurled him over. I saw that myself, and I know that Mr. Ismay did not go of his own accord and that the charge of cowardice is unfair and untrue.

"While I was still helping at the boats there came an explosion from below-decks and the ship took an awful lunge, throwing everybody into a heap. I was hurled clear of the vessel's side and landed on top of a bundle of deck-chairs which was floating on the water. I was badly bruised and my back was sprained. My watch stopped at 1.50 A. M. and I believe it was at that time I was thrown into the water.

"While I lay floating on the bundle of chairs there came another terrific explosion and the ship seemed to split in two. There was a rain of wreckage and a big piece of timber fell on me, striking my lifebelt. I believe if it had not been for the belt I would have been killed. I floated for what I believe was about two hours. Then arms reached down and drew me aboard a life raft. The man who did this was a seaman named Brown, whose life I probably had saved two years ago by hurrying him to a hospital in England when he was taken ill suddenly.

"There were six persons on the raft and others were in the water up to their necks, hanging on to the edges of the raft. The raft was already awash, and we could not take them aboard. One by one, as they became chilled through, they bade us good-bye and sank. In the bottom of the raft was a man whom I had shaved that morning, and whom I had been told was worth $5,000,000. I did not know his name. He was dead.

PICKED UP BY THE CARPATHIA.

"And so we floated on the raft, bereft of hope and stupefied by the calamity, until picked up by the Carpathia. I was so badly injured they had to take me on board in a boatswain's chair."

The happiness of husbands at seeing their wives put in the way of safety from the Titanic was described by Mrs. Turrell Cavendish, daughter of Henry Siegel. She said: "I was with my husband in our stateroom when the accident happened. He awakened me, I remember it was midnight and told me something was the matter with the boat.

"My husband kissed me and put me into a boat, in which were twenty-three women. He told me to go and that he would stay on the ship with the other men. They were happy to see their wives lowered away in the boats. They kept telling us they would be all right because the ship could not sink.

"We were lowered into the water without any light, only one man tried to get into the boat. He was pushed back by a sailor. Most of the women in the boat I was in were in their bare feet. I can still see those husbands kissing their wives and telling them good-bye. I can see the sailors standing by so calm and brave. The sight of those good men who gave their lives for others will always be with me. Words can't tell the tale of their sacrifice.

"The hours we spent in that small boat after those heroic men went down were hours of torture. When we got on the Carpathia we were treated with the utmost consideration.

"I saw Mr. Ismay when he came on board. He was trembling from head to foot and kept saying, "I'm Ismay, I'm Ismay."

Immediately upon their disembarkation from the Carpathia Mr. and Mrs. William E. Carter, Miss Lucille Carter and William E. Carter, Jr., of Newport, Bryn Mawr, and 2116 Walnut street, Philadelphia, about whom so much anxiety was felt for the first twenty-four hours after the news of the Titanic disaster reached the mainland, went in taxicabs to the home of William Dickerman, at 89 Madison avenue. Mr. Dickerman is a brother-in-law of Mr. Carter.

IT WAS LIFE OR DEATH.

"I kissed my husband good-bye and as he stood on the deck I went down the side to a lifeboat. There were no seamen there. It was life or death. I took an oar and started to row," said Mrs. Carter, who was formerly Miss Lucille Polk, of Baltimore, when seen later at the Madison avenue house.

Mrs. Carter had just come from the ship, and the tears were still in her eyes; glad tears from the welcome she had received from her relatives, among whom was Anderson Polk, who had come to New York to meet her. She told of being roused from her sleep at fourteen minutes of twelve on Sunday night by the sudden crash, of rushing out on the deck to find the chaos of destruction quickly from itself into the decisive action of brave men about to face their death.

Clasping her hands tightly she told how the men had stood back or else helped to lower away the lifeboats, and then, kissing their wives, bade them a good-bye which they thought would be forever. In brief words, tensely spoken, she told of going into the lifeboat and taking an oar. At ten minutes past 1 o'clock there was a sudden explosion and the giant hulk of the Titanic blew up, rearing in the water like a spurred horse and then sinking beneath the waves.

She had to pull hard with her oars in the desperate attempt which the poorly manned lifeboat had to make to keep from being sucked down with the diving Titanic. After minutes of work with the desperation of death, they made their way out of the suction and were saved. It was not until she was taken aboard the Carpathia that she met her husband, saved because he had to man an oar in another lifeboat.

DID NOT ANTICIPATE TROUBLE.

"We had a pleasant voyage from England," began Mrs. Carter. "The ship behaved splendidly, and we did not anticipate any trouble at all. I had retired on Sunday night, an hour before we struck the iceberg. The men were in the cabin smoking. Most of them were in the smoking-room when the ship hit.

"The first I knew of the accident was a tremendous thump which nearly threw me out of my berth. I realized that something must have happened, and feared that it was a bad accident. A moment later my husband came down to the stateroom and told me that we had struck an iceberg.

"There was no confusion. I dressed myself hurriedly and went on deck with my children. The ship was badly damaged. The officers thought at first that she would not sink and we were told to be calm. But it was not long before we knew that the ship could not long stand the strain of the water which was pouring into the bow and bearing the ship down on her forward part.

"Then came the time when we knew that it must either be the lifeboats or stay on the ship and sink with her. The seamen began to lower away the lifeboats. One after another they released whatever machinery held them and they dropped into the ocean. There was ice all about us and the night being comparatively clear we could see the floes around us when we peered down over the side of the ship.

"When the boats had been lowered then it was that the time of parting came. There was no excitement. Every one of the men whose wives or women folk were with them took them to the side of the ship where a lifeboat was waiting and kissed them over the side.

"Major Archibald Butt remained on board and went down with the ship. Colonel Astor also went down with the ship. Mrs. Astor was in my boat. The Colonel took her to the side and kissed her and saw her over the side.

"When I went over the side with my children and got in the boat there were no seamen in it. Then came a few men, but there were oars with no one to use them. The boat had been filled with passengers and there was nothing else for me to do but to take an oar.

WARNED TO PULL AWAY FROM SHIP.

"We could see now that the time of the ship had come. She was sinking and we were warned by the cries from the men above to pull away from the ship quickly. Mrs. Thayer, wife of the vice president of the Pennsylvania Railroad, was in my boat, and she, too, took an oar.

"It was cold and we had no time to clothe ourselves with warm overcoats. The rowing warmed me. We started to pull away from the ship. We could see the dim outlines of the decks above, but we could not recognize anybody.

"We had pulled our lifeboat away from the Titanic for a distance of about a city block, that is about all, I should say—when the Titanic seemed to shake to pieces. The ship had struck about fourteen minutes to 12. It was ten minutes past 1 when we saw her lunge.

"She had exploded. There was a rumbling noise within her, then she gave a lurch and started to go down. We realized what it meant. That the sinking ship would suck us under with her. It was a moment later that the suction struck us. It was all we could do to keep from being caught, so strong was the drag down that followed the Titanic.

"But we pulled away at last, after straining as hard as we could at the oars. Then we were alone in the boat, and it seemed darker. We remained in the boat all night waiting for daylight to come. It came at last, and when it broke over the sea we saw ice floes all about it.

"It was about 8.30 o'clock when the Carpathia came into sight. I can't tell how I felt when I saw her. I had believed that my husband had gone down on the ship. It was not until after we were taken over the side of the Carpathia that I saw him.

"Mr. Carter had been compelled to take an oar in a lifeboat that was not sufficiently manned. That is how he came to be saved. All of the men waited for the women to go first. Mr. Carter was among the number. When he put me into a lifeboat he stayed back, and I had thought when I saw the ship blow up and sink that he had gone down with her.

DOES NOT DESERVE CRITICISM.

"Mr. Ismay does not deserve any criticism for being saved. He was another of those who had to man an oar in a lifeboat, so as to get the boats out of danger by being sucked under by the sinking Titanic."

Three French survivors, Fernand Oment, Pierre Marechal, son of the well-known French Admiral, and Paul Chevre, the sculptor, conjointly cabled to the "Matin" a graphic narrative of the disaster to the Titanic, in which they repeatedly insist that more lives could have been saved if the passengers had not had such dogged faith that the Titanic was unsinkable. Several boats, they declared, could have carried double the number.

The three Frenchmen say that they were playing bridge with a Philadelphian when a great, crunching mass of ice packed up against the port holes. As they rushed on deck there was much confusion, but this quickly died down. One of the officers when questioned by a woman passenger humorously replied:

"Do not be afraid. We are merely cutting a whale in two."

Presently the captain appeared to become somewhat nervous and ordered all to put on life preservers. The boats were then lowered, but only a few people stirred and several of the boats put off half empty, one with only fifteen persons in it.

When the Frenchmen's boat rowed off for half a mile the Titanic presented a fairylike picture illuminated from stem to stern. Then suddenly the lights began to go out and the stern reared up high in the air. An immense clamor rose on all sides, and during an hour anguished cries rang out.

It was, say the narrators, like a great chorus chanting a refrain of death with wild obstinacy. Sometimes the cries died out and then the tragic chorus began again more terribly and more despairingly.

The narrative continues:

"Those shrieks pursued us and haunted us as we pulled away in the night. Then one by one the cries ceased, and only the noise of the sea remained. The Titanic was engulfed almost without a murmur. Her stern quivered in a final spasm and then disappeared."

The Frenchmen and their companions suffered bitterly from the cold. They cried out to attract attention, and a German baron, who was with them, emptied his revolver in the air. When finally the Carpathia appeared a feeble hurrah went up from the small boats, every one of which moved as swiftly as possible toward the liner.

The Frenchmen related tragic incidents as they were leaving the sides of the Titanic. After all the boats had been launched many of the passengers who had stayed behind too long tried to embark on a collapsible raft, which worked badly. Fifty persons climbed onto the raft, which was half filled with water.

One after another the passengers on the raft were drowned, or perished with the cold. When a body was found in the way it was thrown overboard, and only fifteen of the fifty who had taken refuge on the raft were saved by the Carpathia.

CHAPTER VIII.

SURVIVORS' STIRRING STORIES.

Survivors' Stirring Stories—How Young Thayer Was Saved—His Father, Second Vice President of the Pennsylvania Railroad, Drowned—Mrs. Straus' Pathetic Death—Black Coward Shot—Countless Aids in Rowing Boat.

Standing at the rail of the main deck of the ill-fated Titanic, Arthur Ryerson, of Gray's lane, Haverford, Pa., waved encouragement to his wife as the lifeboat in which she and her three children—John, Emily and Susan—had been placed with his assistance glided away from the doomed ship. A few minutes later, after the lifeboat with his loved ones had passed beyond the range of his vision, Mr. Ryerson met death in the icy water into which the crushed ship plunged.

It is now known that Mr. Ryerson might have found a place in one of the first lifeboats to be lowered, but made no effort to leave the ship's deck after assuring himself that his wife and children would be saved.

It was not until the Carpathia reached her dock that relatives who were on hand to meet the survivors of the Ryerson family knew that little "Jack" Ryerson was among the rescued. Day by day since the first tidings of the accident to the Titanic were published, "Jack" had been placed among the missing.

Perhaps of all those who came up from the Carpathia with the impress of the tragedy upon them, the homecoming of Mrs. Ryerson was peculiarly sad.

While motoring with J. Lewis Hoffman, of Radnor, Pa., on the Main Line, on Monday a week before, Arthur L. Ryerson, her son, was killed. His parents abandoned their plans for a summer pleasure trip through Europe and took passage on the first home-bound ship, which happened to be the Titanic, to attend the funeral of their son. And now upon one tragedy a second presses.

Upon leaving the Carpathia Mrs. Ryerson, almost too exhausted and weak to tell of her experiences, was taken in a taxicab to the Hotel Belmont. With her were her son "Jack" and her two daughters, Miss Emily and Miss Susan Ryerson.

The young women were hysterical with grief as they walked up from the dock, and the little lad who had witnessed such sights of horror and tragedy clung to his mother's hand, wide eyed and sorrowful.

Mrs. Ryerson said that she and her husband were asleep in their staterooms, as were their children, when the terrible grating crash came and the ship foundered.

The women threw kimonos over their night gowns and rushed barefooted to the deck. Master Ryerson's nurse caught up a few articles of the little boy's clothing and almost as soon as the party reached the deck they were numbered off into boats and lowered into the sea.

HARROWING AND TERRIBLE.

Mrs. John M. Brown, whose husband was formerly a well-known Philadelphian, but now lives in Boston, described her experience on the Titanic as the "most harrowing and terrible that any living soul could undergo."

"Oh, it was heart-rending to see those brave men die," Mrs. Brown said, half-sobbingly, after she had left the pier in a taxicab brought by her husband.

Mr. Brown, for his part, said the days of agony which he had experienced, when the lists of Titanic survivors were altered, diminished and published incomplete, leaving him indecisive as to his wife's fate, was almost on a par what she had undergone.

In contradiction to several other statements, Mrs. Brown declared that she saw no signs of panic or disorder on the Titanic and did not know until later that there had been shooting on board the vessel.

"I was in my berth when the crash came," Mrs. Brown said,

"and after the first shock when I knew instinctively that the vessel was sinking I was comparatively calm.

"I had hardly reached deck when an officer called to me to enter a lifeboat. I did so, and saw the huge liner split in half, with a pang almost as keen as if I had seen somebody die."

Mrs. Brown said that John B. Thayer, Jr., after jumping from the deck of the liner, clad only in pajamas, swam through cakes of floating ice to a broken raft. He was picked up by the boat of which Mrs. Brown was an occupant.

Mrs. Brown said that it was about two hours after the Titanic sank that their boat came within sight of an object bobbing up and down in the cakes of ice, about fifty yards away.

Nearing, they made out the form of a boy clinging with one leg and both arms wrapped around the piece of wreckage. Young Thayer uttered feeble cries as they pulled alongside.

LAD PULLED INTO LIFE-BOAT.

The lad was pulled into the already crowded lifeboat exhausted. With a weak, faint smile, Mrs. Brown said, the lad collapsed.

Women, who were not rowing or assisting in maneuvering the boat, by vigorous rubbing soon brought Thayer to consciousness and shared part of their scanty attire to keep him from dying from exposure. In the meantime the boat bobbed about on the waves like a top, frequently striking cakes of ice.

Mrs. Brown said for several hours more they battled with the sea before help arrived.

"It was a blessed sight when all saw the Carpathia heading in our din," she declared. "We had hopes that a ship would come to our rescue and all on board prayed for safe deliverance.

"No one can realize our feeling of gratitude when the Carpathia hoved into sight. With increased energy the men, aided by the women, pulled on the oars. We were soon taken aboard. Young Thayer was hurried into the hospital on board the boat and was given stimulants and revived.

"Three survivors died soon after; they were buried at sea.

Mrs. Brown said that Mrs. John Jacob Astor, the wife of Colonel John Jacob Astor, who proved himself a hero, was also an occupant of her boat.

"Mrs. Astor was frantic when she learned that her husband had gone with the Titanic, but between sobs said he died a hero," Mrs. Brown said.

"The colonel kissed her and pushing his bride to the side of the ship told her to hurry to the lifeboats awaiting below.

"Mrs. Astor refused to listen to her husband's entreaties until he assured her that he would follow on the next boat, although all the time he knew that he would sink."

"The following horrors have never left me, day or night," Mrs. Brown continued.

DEAD BODIES OF BRAVE MEN.

"I saw dead bodies of brave men float past the lifeboats. I heard the death cries of women and saw the terrible desolation of the wreck by dawn."

In the boat with Mrs. Brown were her two sisters, Mrs. Robert Cornell, wife of Judge Robert Cornell, and Mrs. S. P. Appleton.

They followed each other down the long, roughly constructed rope ladder, a distance of more than fifty feet, into the tenth lifeboat. All were thinly clad. They had retired for the night and were tumbled from their berths when the crash came.

When the Titanic sank and the first news came of the disaster, there appeared in the list of first cabin passengers the name of "Washington Logue." Until J. Washington Logue, of Philadelphia, could be found to explain that he was not on the high seas, many of his friends feared that he had been on the Titanic.

When he landed from the Carpathia, Washington Dodge, of San Francisco, was told how his name had been confused in the wireless reports from the Olympic. He said he congratulated Mr. Logue on having been no closer to disaster than this.

Mr. Dodge, who is a millionaire; Mrs. Dodge and their four-year-old son, Washington Dodge, Jr., were among the first to land on the dock from the Cunarder. Mr. Dodge carried a life preserver of the Titanic as a memento.

"Nearly all the passengers had retired when the crash came, about twenty minutes passed 10 o'clock," said Mr. Dodge. "The liner was struck on the starboard side, near the bow. The bow, it seemed, withstood the crash, but water rushed into several compartments at the same time."

"There was complete order among the passengers and crew. We really didn't think there was any danger. We were assured that the ship would float and that there were plenty vessels in the reach of wireless to come to our aid if that should become necessary.

"Then the sinking of the Titanic by the head began and the crew was ordered to man the boats. There was no panic. The officers told the men to stand back and they obeyed. A few men were ordered into the boats. Two men who attempted to rush beyond the restraint line were shot down by an officer who then turned the revolver on himself. I could see Mrs. Isador Straus. She clung to her husband and refused to leave him.

FLOATED FOR FOUR HOURS.

"We floated for four hours until we were picked up. Mr. Ismay left the Titanic on a small boat.

"I did not see the iceberg. When we got into the boat she was gone.

"As the Titanic went down, Major Archibald Butt was standing on the deck. I saw him."

The body of one black coward, a member of the Titanic's crew, lies alone in the wireless "coop" on the highest deck of the shadowy bulk of what was once the world's greatest ship two miles down in the dark of unplumbed ocean depths. There is a bullet hole in the back of his skull.

This man was shot bv Harold Bride, the second wireless man aboard the Titanic, and assistant to the heroic Phillips, chief operator, who lost his life. Bride shot him from behind just at the instant that the coward was about to plunge a knife into

Phillips' back and rob him of the life preserver which was strapped under his arm pits. He died instantly and Phillips, all unconscious at that instant that Bride was saving his life, had but a brief little quarter of an hour added to his span by the act of his assistant, and then went down to death.

This grim bit of tragedy, only a little interlude in the whole terrible procession of horror aboard the sinking boat, occurred high above the heads of the doomed men and women who waited death in the bleak galleys of the decks.

"I had to do it," was the way Bride put it.

"I could not let that coward die a decent sailor's death, so I shot him down and left him alone there in the wireless coop to go down with the hulk of the ship. He is there yet, the only one in the wireless room where Phillips, a real hero, worked madly to save the lives of two thousand and more people."

NEW YORK PHYSICIAN'S ESCAPE.

Miss Alice Farnan Leader, a New York physician, escaped from the Titanic on the same boat which carried the Countess Rothes.

"The Countess is an expert oarswoman," said Dr. Leader, "and thoroughly at home on the water. She took command of our boat, when it was found that the seamen who had been placed at the oars could not row skilfully. Several of the women took their places with the Countess at the oars and rowed in turns while the weak and unskilled stewards sat quietly in one end of the boat."

"The men were the heroes," said Mrs. Churchill Candee, of Washington, one of the survivors, "and among the bravest and most heroic, as I recall, were Mr. Widener, Mr. Thayer and Colonel Astor. They thought only of the saving of the women and went down with the Titanic, martyrs to their manhood.

"I saw Mr. and Mrs. Isador Straus on the deck of the Titanic as I was lowered into one of the lifeboats. Mrs. Straus refused to leave the ship unless her husband could accompany her. They were on the top deck, and I heard her say she would not leave her husband. She went down with him as she had lived and traveled with him. Life without him did not concern her, seemingly. 'I've always stayed with my husband, so why should I leave him now? I'll die with him,' I heard her say.

"Captain Smith, I think, sacrificed safety in a treacherous ice field for speed. He was trying to make 570 miles for the day, I heard. The captain, who had stood waist deep on the deck of the Titanic as she sank, jumped as the ship went down, but he was drowned. All of the men had bravely faced their doom for the women and children.

"The ship settled slowly, the lights going out deck after deck as the water reached them. The final plunge, however, was sudden and accompanied by explosions, the effect of which was a horrible sight. Victims standing on the upper deck toward the stern were hurled into the air and fell into the treacherous ice-covered sea. Some were rescued, but most of them perished. I cannot help recalling again that Mr. Widener and Mr. Thayer and Colonel Astor died manfully.

TWO DISTINCT SHOCKS.

"The ice pack which we encountered," explained Mrs. Candee, "was fifty-six miles long, I have since heard. When we collided with the mountainous mass it was nearly midnight Sunday. There were two distinct shocks, each shaking the ship violently, but fear did not spread among the passengers immediately. They seemed not to realize what had happened, but the captain and other officers did not endeavor to minimize the danger.

"The first thing I recall was one of the crew appearing with pieces of ice in his hands. He said he had gathered them from the bow of the boat. Some of the passengers were inclined to believe he was joking. But soon the situation dawned on all of us. The lifeboats were ordered lowered and manned and the word went around that women and children were to be taken off first. The men stood back as we descended to the frail craft or assisted us to disembark. I now recall that huge Woolner Bjornstrom was among the heroic men."

"The Philadelphia women behaved heroically."

This was the way Mrs. Walter B. Stephenson, of Haverford, a survivor of the wreck of the fated Titanic, began her brief but graphic account of the disaster at her home in Haverford, which she reached on the special train that brought Mrs. John B. Thayer and others over from New York.

Worn by hours of terrible uncertainty on the frail lifeboats in the open sea, almost distracted by the ordeal of waiting for news of those left behind on the big liner, Mrs. Stephenson bore herself as did the women whom she described heroically indeed.

She told how John B. Thayer, Jr., fell overboard when the boats were launched, and how he was saved from the death that his father met, by the crew of the lifeboat. She described tersely, to linger sadly as she finished with the words, "But we never saw Mr. Thayer, Sr., at all."

OCCUPANTS OF THE SAME BOAT.

Mrs. Thayer, Mrs. J. Boulton Earnshaw, of Mt. Airy, and Mrs. George D. Widener were occupants of the same boat that carried Mrs. Stephenson to safety, and, like Mrs. Stephenson, they witnessed the final plunge of the Titanic.

"We were far off," said Mrs. Stephenson, "but we could see a huge dark mass behind us. Then it disappeared." That was all she could tell of the fate of those left on board.

"Then it disappeared," she paused and her voice choked. "We weren't sure but what we might have been mistaken. A lingering hope remained until long after the Carpathia picked us up. Then the wireless told the terrible tidings. We were the sole survivors."

Mrs. Stephenson wore the same dress that she hastily donned when the crash occurred. It was a simple gown of dark texture, showing the wear in its crumpled shape. Over it she had managed to throw a cape, and to the covering she clung, as if yet fearful of the icy blasts of the Northern Ocean.

Conveyed in a taxicab to the Pennsylvania Railroad Station from the Cunard wharf, Mrs. Stephenson alighted, hastened across the train shed and into a waiting elevator. She walked unaided. Relatives who had rushed from Philadelphia to convey her in safety, were solicitous for her welfare, but she assured them that she was well.

"And she is well," said T. DeWitt Cuyler, a director of the Pennsylvania Railroad who met the train. "She has borne up remarkably under the strain."

"I was wakened in my cabin by the shock," Mrs. Stephenson began. "It was nearly 12 o'clock, but I cannot be sure. The shock was great, but not as great as the one I experienced in the San Francisco earthquake. I was staying in the St. Francis Hotel at the time of the earthquake. Even this terrible disaster cannot shake the memory of that night from my mind.

ASSURANCE OF NO IMMEDIATE DANGER.

"I rose hastily from my berth and was about to hasten to the deck when my maid assured me that there was no immediate danger and that I would have time to dress. I put on this dress that I am wearing and threw a cape around my shoulders. Then I went on deck.

"Scarcely had I gotten out in the air when an officer ordered me to don a life belt. I returned to the cabin to buckle one around me. When I returned I heard the order to man the lifeboats. There was no disorder. The crew was under perfect discipline. Quickly and without any excitement I was lifted into a lifeboat. Beside me I found Mrs. Thayer, Mrs. Earnshaw and Mrs. Widener. Like myself they had no clothing except what they wore.

"John B. Thayer, Jr., was with us. As the boat was lowered by the davits, he slipped and fell into the water; luckily he wore a life belt and was kept afloat until a sailor lifted him safely aboard. We never saw Mr. Thayer, Sr., at all.

"As the boat pushed off from the ship Mrs. Widener collapsed. She was finally revived. The Philadelphia women behaved heroically. They stood up splendidly under the suspense, which was terrible. The sailors rowed our boat some distance away. We thought we saw the Titanic sink, but we couldn't be sure. Behind us we could see a dark shape. Then it disappeared. We despaired of any others being saved, but some hope remained until long after the Carpathia had picked us up. Then the wireless told the sad tale.

WAIFS FROM TITANIC RESTORED TO MOTHER'S ARMS.

Lola and Momon, the little waifs of the Titanic disaster, snatched from the sea and kept for a month in a big, strange land, were clasped in the arms of their mother Mme. Marcelle Navratil, who arrived in New York, on May 16, from France on the White Star liner Oceanic.

Hurrying down the gangplank, after kindly customs officials had facilitated her landing, Mme. Navratil, who is an Italian, 24 years old, of remarkable beauty, rushed to Miss Margaret Hays, the rescuer of the two little boys, who, with her father, was waiting on the pier. They took her in a cab to the Children's Society rooms, and there she was reunited with her children.

The little boys, four and two years old, were thrust into one of the last of the lifeboats to leave the sinking Titanic by an excited Frenchmen, who asked that they be cared for. A steward told him he could not enter the boat and he said he did not want to, but must save his boys.

Arriving in New York on the Carpathia, Miss Hays at first could learn nothing of the children's identity, and she planned to care for them. Then developed another chapter of the weird story of the disaster in the ice fields. The Frenchman's body was recovered and taken to Halifax, where it was found that he was booked on the passenger list under the name of "Hoffman."

Cable messages to France brought the information that Mme. Narvatil's husband, from whom she was separated, had kidnapped her children and said he was going to America. He often used the name "Hoffman." Photographs of the boys were sent to Mme. Navratil in France, and she identified them as her children.

CHAPTER IX.

HOW ASTOR WENT TO DEATH.

How Astor Went to Death—"I Resign Myself to My Fate," He Said—Kissed Wife Fond Farewell—Lifted Cap to Wife as Boat Left Ship—Crushed to Death By Ice—Famous Novelist's Daughter Hears of His Death—Philadelphia Millionaires' Heroism—Last to See Widener Alive—Major Butt Dies a Soldier's Death.

The heroism of the majority of the men who went down to death with the Titanic has been told over and over again. How John Jacob Astor kissed his wife and saluted death as he looked squarely into its face; the devotion of Mrs. Isidor Straus to her aged husband and the willingness with which she went to her doom with his loving arms pressed tenderly around her, the tales of life sacrificed that women might be saved brought some need of comfort to the stricken.

G. A. Brayton, of Los Angeles, Cal., says: "John Jacob Astor went to one of the officers and told them who he was, and asked to go in the lifeboat with his wife. The officer told him he could not go in the lifeboat. Astor then kissed his wife goodbye and she was put in the lifeboat. Astor said: 'I resign myself to my fate' and saluted in farewell."

"Colonel Astor and Major Archibald Butt died together on the bridge of the ill-fated ship," said Dr. Washington Dodge, of San Francisco, one of the survivors. "I saw them standing there side by side. I was in one of the last boats, and I could not mistake them. Earlier during the desperate struggle to get the boats cleared I had seen them both at work quieting passengers and helping the officers maintain order.

"A few minutes before the last I saw Colonel Astor help

his wife, who appeared ill, into a boat, and I saw him wave his hand to her and smile as the boat pulled away."

Before the lifeboats left the ship, not far from the woman who would not let her husband meet death alone, Colonel Astor stood supporting the figure of his young bride, says another survivor. A boat was being filled with women. Colonel Astor helped his wife to a place in it. The boat was not filled, and there seemed no more women near it. Quietly the Colonel turned to the second officer, who was superintending the loading.

"May I go with my wife? She is ill," he asked. The officer nodded. The man of millions got into the boat. The crew were about to cast off the falls. Suddenly the Colonel sprang to his feet, shouting to them to wait. He had seen a woman running toward the boat. Leaping over the rail, he helped her to the place he had occupied.

TRIED TO CLIMB FROM THE BOAT.

Mrs. Astor screamed and tried to climb from the boat. The Colonel restrained her. He bent and tenderly patted her shoulder.

"The ladies first, dear heart," he was heard to say.

Then quietly he saluted the second officer and turned to help in lowering more boats.

Miss Margaret Hayes gave another version of the manner in which Colonel Astor met his death: "Colonel Astor, with his wife, came out on deck as I was being assisted into a lifeboat," said Miss Hayes, "and both got into another boat. Colonel Astor had his arms about his wife and assisted her into the boat. At the time there were no women waiting to get into the boats, and the ship's officer at that point invited Colonel Astor to get into the boat with his wife. The Colonel, after looking around and seeing no women, got into the boat, and his wife threw her arms about him.

"The boat in which Colonel Astor and his wife were sitting was about to be lowered when a woman came running out of the companionway. Raising his hand, Colonel Astor stopped the preparations to lower his boat and, stepping out, assisted the woman into the seat he had occupied.

"Mrs. Astor cried out, and wanted to get out of the boat with her husband, but the Colonel patted her on the back and said something in a low tone of voice."

A nephew of Senator Clark, of Butte, Montana, said Astor stood by the after rail looking after the lifeboats until the Titanic went down.

Brayton says: "Captain Smith stood on the bridge until he was washed off by a wave. He swam back, stood on the bridge again and was there when the Titanic went to the bottom." Brayton says that Henry B. Harris, the theatrical manager, tried to get on a lifeboat with his wife, but the second officer held him back with a gun. A third-class passenger who tried to climb in the boats was shot and killed by a steward. This was the only shooting on board I know of."

Another account of Captain Smith's death is as follows:

CAPTAIN SMITH DIED A HERO.

Captain Smith died a hero's death. He went to the bottom of the ocean without effort to save himself. His last acts were to place a five-year-old child on the last lifeboat in reach, then cast his life belt to the ice ridden waters and resign to the fate that tradition down the ages observed as a strict law.

It was left to a fireman of the Titanic to tell the tale of the death of Captain Smith and the last message he left behind him. This man had gone down with the vessel and was clinging to a piece of wreckage about half an hour before he finally joined several members of the Titanic's company on the bottom of a boat which was floating among other wreckage.

Harry Senior, the fireman, with his eight or nine companions in distress, had just managed to get a firm hold on the upturned boat, when they saw the Titanic rearing preparatory to her final plunge. At that moment, according to the fireman's tale, Captain Smith jumped into the sea from the promenade deck of the Titanic with an infant clutched tenderly in his arms.

It only took a few strokes to bring him to the upturned lifeboat, where a dozen hands were stretched out to take the little child from his arms and drag him to safety.

"Captain Smith was dragged on the upturned boat," said the fireman. "He had on a life buoy and a life preserver. He clung there a moment and then he slid off again. For a second time he was dragged from the icy water. Then he took off his life preserver, tossed the life buoy on the inky waters and slipped into the water again with the words: 'I will follow the ship.' "

At that time there was only a circle of troubled water and some wreckage to show the spot where the biggest of all ocean steamers had sunk out of sight.

"No," said the stoker, as he waved a sandwich above his head, holding a glass of beer in the other hand, "Captain Smith never shot himself. I saw what he did. He went down with that ship. I'll stake my life on that."

THE SAME STORY REPEATED.

Oddly enough, a Swedish stoker and survivor, named Oscar Ingstrom, at another hotel in the same vicinity, gave to one of the most prominent Swedish newspaper men in New York City practically the same tale that Senior told.

Wilson Potter, whose mother, Mrs. Thomas Potter, Jr., of Mt. Airy, Pa., was one of the survivors, told how she had urged Colonel Astor and his wife to leave the Titanic before the vessel went down.

"My mother was one of the first to leave the Titanic," he said. "As the lifeboats were filling up, she called to Colonel and Mrs. Astor to come aboard. Mrs. Astor waved her off, exclaiming, 'We are safer here than in that little boat,'

"Hundreds of other passengers thought the same way. So much so, that the first lifeboat, which my mother boarded, was large enough to hold forty persons besides the crew; still only ten came along. All were of the opinion that the Titanic would remain afloat until aid came from another steamer."

Mr. Potter also related another version of how J. B. Thayer, Jr., and his mother were rescued.

"As the crash came Mrs. Thayer fainted. Young Mr. Thayer carried her to one of the lifeboats. As she was lifted in father and son lost their hold and fell between the sinkingsteamer and the lifeboat.

"After struggling in the water for several minutes Young Mr. Thayer was picked up by a raft. Two hours later the raft was found by the Carpathia."

A third remarkable escape as related by Mr. Potter was that of Richard Norris Williams.

"Mr. Williams remained on the stern of the Titanic," said Mr. Potter. "He says the stern of the boat went down, then came up. As it started to go down a second time Mr. Williams says he dived off and swam to a raft, which was picked up two hours later by the Carpathia."

UTTERLY EXHAUSTED FROM HER EXPERIENCE.

When utterly exhausted from her experience, Mrs. John Jacob Astor was declared by Nicholas Biddle, a trustee of the Astor estate, to be in no danger whatever. Her physicians, however, have given orders that neither Mrs. Astor nor her maid, who was saved with her, be permitted to talk about the disaster.

On landing from the Carpathia, the young bride, widowed by the Titanic's sinking, told members of her family what she could recall of the circumstances of the disaster. Of how Colonel Astor met his death, she has no definite conception. She recalled, she thought, that in the confusion, as she was about to be put into one of the boats, the Colonel was standing by her side. After that, as Mr. Biddle recounted her narrative, she had no very clear recollection of the happenings until the boats were well clear of the sinking steamer.

Mrs. Astor, it appears, left in one of the last boats which got away from the ship. It was her belief that all the women who wished to go had been taken off. Her impression was that the boat she left in had room for at least fifteen more persons.

The men, for some reason, which, as she recalled it, she could not and does not now understand, did not seem to be at all anxious to leave the ship. Almost every one seemed dazed.

"I hope he is alive somewhere. Yes, I cannot think anything else," the young woman said of her husband to her father as she left the latter to go to the Astor home, according to some who overheard her parting remarks.

The chief steerage steward of the Titanic, who came in on the Carpathia, says that he saw John Jacob Astor standing by the life ladder as the passengers were being embarked. His wife was beside him, the steward said. The Colonel left her to go to the purser's office for a moment, and that was the last he saw of him.

WRITER GOES DOWN WITH THE SHIP.

Mrs. May Futrelle, whose husband, Jacques Futrelle, the writer, went down with the ship, was met here by her daughter, Miss Virginia Futrelle, who was brought to New York from the Convent of Notre Dame in Baltimore.

Miss Futrelle had been told that her father had been picked up by another steamer. Mrs. Charles Copeland, of Boston, a sister of the writer, who also met Mrs. Futrelle, was under the same impression.

"I am so happy that father is safe, too," declared Miss Futrelle, as her mother clapsed her in her arms. It was some time before Mrs. Futrelle could compose herself.

"Where is Jack?" Miss Copeland asked.

Mrs. Futrelle, afraid to let her daughter know the truth, said: "Oh! he is on another ship."

Mrs. Copeland guessed the truth and became hysterical. Then the writer's daughter broke down.

"Jack died like a hero," Mrs. Futrelle said, when the party became composed. "He was in the smoking-room when the crash came—the noise of the smash was terrific—and I was going to bed. I was hurled from my feet by the impact. I hardly found myself when Jack came rushing into the stateroom.

"The boat is going down, get dressed at once!" he shouted. When we reached the deck everything was in the wildest confusion. The screams of women and the shrill orders of the officers were drowned intermittently by the tremendous vibrations of the Titanic's bass foghorn.

"The behavior of the men was magnificent. They stood back without murmuring and urged the women and children into the lifeboats. A few cowards tried to scramble into the boats, but they were quickly thrown back by the others. Let me say now that the only men who were saved were those who sneaked into the lifeboats or were picked up after the Titanic sank.

"I did not want to leave Jack, but he assured me that there were boats enough for all and that he would be rescued later.

LIFTED INTO A LIFE-BOAT AND KISSED.

"Hurry up, May, you're keeping the others waiting," were his last words, as he lifted me into a lifeboat and kissed me good-bye. I was in one of the last lifeboats to leave the ship. We had not put out many minutes when the Titanic disappeared. I almost thought, as I saw her sink beneath the water, that I could see Jack, standing where I had left him and waving at me."

Mrs. Futrelle said she saw the parting of Colonel John Jacob Astor and his young bride. Mrs. Astor was frantic. Her husband had to jump into the lifeboat four times and tell her that he would be rescued later. After the fourth time, Mrs. Futrelle said, he jumped back on the deck of the sinking ship and the lifeboat bearing his bride made off.

George D. Widener and his son, Harry Elkins Widener, lost in the wreck of the Titanic, died the death of heroes. They stood back that the weaker might have a chance of being saved.

Mrs. Widener, one of the last women to leave the ship, fought to die with her husband and her son. She would have succeeded probably had not sailors literally torn her from her husband and forced her on to a life-raft.

As she descended the ladder at the ship's side, compelled to leave despite her frantic, despairing pleas, she called to Mr. Widener and to her son pitifully:

"Oh, my God!" she cried. "Good-bye! George! Harry! Good-bye! Good-bye! Oh, God! this is awful!" And that was the last she saw of her husband and of her son, who waved a brave farewell as she disappeared down the ladder.

Mr. Widener, according to James B. McGough, 708 West York street, Philadelphia, a buyer for the Gimbel store, one of those rescued, was as calm and collected, except at the time of the final parting from his wife, as though he were "taking a walk on Broad street."

HELPED WOMEN AND CHILDREN.

The financier's son, too, was calm. The two men helped the women and the children to make their escape, but always stood back themselves when a boat or raft was launched. As soon as the vessel had struck the iceberg Mr. and Mrs. Widener had sought out Captain Smith.

"What is the outlook?" Mr. Widener was heard to inquire.

"It is extremely serious," was the quick reply. "Please keep cool and do what you can to help us." And this is what Mr. Widener did.

Mr. McGough, when he returned to his home, contributed to the several versions of the escape of John B. Thayer, Jr., son of John B. Thayer, second vice president of the Pennsylvania Railroad, who was lost. One version was that the boy jumped from the Titanic just as she sank, and that he swam about among big cakes of ice until taken aboard a lifeboat.

Mr. McGough in his account of the lad's rescue says the boy jumped as the vessel sank, but that he alighted near a life-raft, to which, half frozen, he clung until taken aboard a boat.

Another statement by Mr. McGough was that when a man, presumably an Associated Press correspondent, boarded the

Carpathia off Cape Cod, and tried to wireless a message ashore a ship officer seized it and threw it into the ocean.

Several weeks ago Mr. McGough was sent abroad on a purchasing trip for his firm. With him were J. D. Flynn, of New York, formerly of Philadelphia, and N. P. Calderhead, also a former Philadelphian.

When the gang plank was thrown down from the Carpathia, Mr. McGough was the first passenger from the ill-starred Titanic to land, waiting for him were his wife, Mrs. Mary McGough, and his three brothers, Philip A., Thomas and Andrew McGough, all of 252 South Seventh street, Philadelphia. His wife saw him first. Stretching out her arms, she threw herself from the police lines toward him, and in a moment he had her clasped in his embace.

SENDS A MESSAGE TO HIS MOTHER.

Afterward he rushed through the crowd and took a motor car to the home of a relative. Thence he went to the Imperial Hotel. From the hotel he sent a message to his mother at 252 South Seventh street.

"I am here, safe," the message read.

"The collision which caused the loss of the Titanic," Mr. McGough said, "occurred about 11.40 o'clock. I had an outer state-room on the side toward the iceberg against which the ship crashed. Flynn who occupied the room with me, had just gone to bed. Calderhead was in bed in a stateroom adjoining.

"When the crash came, I ran to the porthole. I saw the ice pressed close against the side of the ship. Chunks of it were ground off, and they fell into the window. I happened to glance at my watch, and it showed me exactly the hour.

"I knew that something was seriously wrong, and hastily got into my clothes. I took time, also, to get my watch and money. Flynn, in the meantime, had run over to Calderhead's stateroom and had awakened him. When I had dressed I ran outside.

"I saw the iceberg. The boat deck stood about ninety feet

out of the water and the berg towered above us for at least fifty feet. I judge the berg stood between 140 and 150 feet out of the water.

"Many of the women on board, I am sure, did not leave their staterooms at once. They stayed there, at least for a time. I believe that many of them did not awaken to their danger until near the last.

"One statement I want to correct, the lights did not go out, at least not while I was on board. When I ran to the deck I heard Captain Smith order that the air chambers be examined. An effort was made to work the doors closing the compartments, but to no avail. When the ship ran upon the iceberg, the sharp-pointed berg cut through both thicknesses of the bottom and left it in such a position that it filled rapidly.

MIGHT HAVE PERISHED.

"I remember that it was a beautiful night. There was no wind and the sea was calm. But for this it is certain that when the boats were launched most all of us would have perished in the ice-covered sea. At first the captain ordered the hatches over the steerage fastened down. This was to prevent the hysterical passengers in that part of the ship rushing to the deck and increasing the panic. Before we left, however, those passengers were released.

"Two sailors were put into each of the boats. When the boats were lowered the women hung back. They feared to go down the long, steep ladder to the water. Seeing them hesitate, I cried: 'Someone has to be first,' and started down the ladder.

"I had hardly starteld before I regretted I had not waited on deck. But I feel if I had not led the way the women would not have started and the death list would have been much larger. Flynn and Calderhead led the way into other boats.

"It was only a short time before the boat was filled. We had fifty-five in our boat, nearly all of them women. We had entered the craft so hastily that we did not take time to get a light.

"For a time we bobbed about on the ocean. Then we started to row slowly away. I shall never forget the screams that flowed over the ocean toward us from the sinking ship. At the end there was a mad rush and scramble.

"It was fearfully hard on the women. Few of them were completely dressed. Some wore only their night gowns, with some light wrapper or kimono over them. The air was pitilessly cold.

"There were so few men in the boat the women had to row. This was good for some of them, as it kept their blood in circulation, but even then it was the most severe experience for them imaginable. Some of them were half-crazed with grief or terror. Several became ill from the exposure.

"I saw Mr. Widener just before I left, and afterward, while we were rowing away from the vessel I had a good glimpse of him. He appeared as calm and collected as though he were taking a walk on Broad st. When the rush for the boats began he and his son Harry, stood back.

SHIP GOES DOWN AT 2.30 O'CLOCK.

"At the end sailors had to tear Mrs. Widener from him, and she went down the ladder, calling to him pitifully. The ship went down at 2.20 o'clock exactly. The front end went down gradually. We saw no men shot, but just before the finish we heard several shots.

"I was told that Captain Smith or one of the officers shot himself on the bridge just before the Titanic went under. I heard also that several men had been killed as they made a final rush for the boats, trying to cut off the women and children.

"While we were floating around the sailors set off some redfire, which illuminated the ocean for miles around. This was a signal of distress. Unfortunately there was no one near enough to answer in time.

"John B. Thayer, Jr., was saved after he had gone down with the ship. Just as the vessel took the plunge he leaped over the side. He struck out for a life raft and reached it. There he clung for several hours until, half-frozen, he was taken into one of the boats which was a trifle less crowded than the others.

"For six hours we bobbed around in the ocean. We rowed over to a boat that was provided with a light, and tied the two small craft together. Finally daylight came, and the sun rose in a clear sky. There we were, a little fleet, alone in the limitless ocean, with the ice cakes tossing about on all sides.

"It was after 8 o'clock in the morning when we saw the masts of a steamship coming up over the horizon. It was the most blessed sight our eyes ever saw. It meant an end to the physical suffering, a relief to the strain under which we had been laboring. Many broke down when they saw it.

"The ship, of course, was the Carpathia. While it was hurrying toward us the crew and passengers had made the most generous preparations for us. When they took us on board they had blankets, clothing, food and warm liquids all ready. Their physicians were ready to care for the sick. The passengers gave up their warm beds to us.

BUMPED INTO FLOATING BODIES.

"During the time we were in the water we bumped frequently into the bodies that floated about us. A great many of the men jumped into the water before the boat sank, and they were their bodies that we struck."

D. H. Bishop, a rich lumber man of Dowagaic, Mich., who with his wife, was returning from a bridal trip to Egypt, is the last person known to have seen George D. Widener alive. Mr. Bishop said:

"My wife and I had just retired when we heard the jar and felt a decided tilt of the ship. I got up and started to investigate, but soon became reassured and went back to bed. A few minutes later we heard calls to put on life belts.

"My wife felt very alarmed and kneeled to pray. She said she knew we would be lost, though at that time there was no reason to think so, and she remarked: 'What is the use bothering with jewelry if we are going to die?' Accordingly she left in her stateroom jewelry worth about $11,000, but strangely enough insisted upon me running back and getting her muff.

"As we came up the stairway we met Captain Smith and Colonel John Jacob Astor talking hurriedly. What they said I do not know. When we got on deck there were not more than fifty people there and no one seemed excited and no one appeared to want to get into the lifeboats, though urged to do so. Mrs. Bishop and I were literally lifted into the first lifeboat.

"At that time I observed Mr. and Mrs. Widener, and I saw the former leave his wife as she was getting into the lifeboat and, accompanied by his son, go toward the stairway. I did not see them again, as our lifeboat with only twenty-eight persons in it and only half-manned, was lowered over the side at that moment. An instant later there was an apparent rush for the lifeboats and as we rowed away they came over the side with great rapidity.

"Before we were a hundred yards away men were jumping overboard, and when we were a mile away the ship went down with cries from the men and women aboard that were heart-rending.

"There is nothing to say concerning the blame, except that I do know that icebergs were known to be in our vicinity and that it was the subject of much talk that the Titanic was out for a record. Captain Smith was dining with J. Bruce Ismay, managing director of the White Star Line, and of course was not on the bridge. It was rumored on the Carpathia that Captain Smith tried to save himself in a lifeboat at the last minute, but of this I know nothing.

CHAPTER X.

NOTABLE WOMAN SAVED.

Praises Captain and Crew—Bids President of Grand Trunk Railway Good-bye—In Water for Six Hours— Saved by Cake of Ice—Boats not Filled, she says—Millionaire Died to Save Wife's Maid—Heroic Sacrifice of Railroad Official.

From William E. Carter, Bryn Mawr, Pa., who, with his wife and two children, Lucille and William E. Carter, Jr., was saved from the wreck of the Titanic, it was learned today that the three women probably most notable among the survivors were in the same lifeboat. They were Mrs. John Jacob Astor, Mrs. George D. Widener and Mrs. John B. Thayer. In the same boat were Mrs. Carter and her two children.

Colonel Astor, Mr. Thayer, Mr. Widener and Mr. Carter separated as soon as the ladies were safely in the lifeboats, and Mr. Carter never saw the three men again.

Mr. Carter was a passenger on the lifeboat in which J. Bruce Ismay, managing director of the White Star Line, made his escape from the sinking liner. Mr. Carter declared that the boat was the last to leave the starboard side of the Titanic and was nearly the last which left the vessel.

When entered by Mr. Carter and Mr. Ismay the boat was occupied entirely by women of the third cabin. Every woman on the starboard side of the vessel had been sent off in lifeboats when Mr. Ismay and he got into the boat, Mr. Carter said.

Mr. Carter and his family were staying for a few days at the home of his brother-in-law, William C. Dickerman, 809 Madison ave., New York. Mr. Carter expressed the greatest admiration for the discipline maintained by the officers of the Titanic, and voiced the opinion that Mr. Ismay should not be held open to criticism.

"If there had been another woman to go, neither Mr. Ismay nor myself would have gotten into the boat. There can be no criticism of Mr. Ismay's action."

In describing his experience Mr. Carter said he had urged Harry Elkins Widener to go with him to the starboard side of the vessel. Young Mr. Widener, thinking that there was no immediate danger, remarked that he would take his chances on the vessel.

Mr. Carter said he was in the smoking room of the Titanic when the crash came. "I was talking to Major Butt, Clarence Moore and Harry Widener," he explained. "It was just seventeen minutes to 12 o'clock.

"Although there was quite a jar, I thought the trouble was slight. I believe it was the immense size of the Titanic which brought many of the passengers to believe there was no danger. I went on deck to see what had happened. Almost as I reached the deck the engines were stopped.

VESSEL LISTS TO PORT.

"I hurried down to see about my family and found they were all in bed. Just then the vessel listed a little to port, and I told my wife and children they had better get up and dress.

"Just then orders were issued for everyone to get on life preservers. When we came out on the deck boats were being lowered. Mrs. Carter and the children got into the fourth or fifth boat with Mrs. Astor, Mrs. Widener and Mrs. Thayer.

"After I got my family into the boat and saw it pushed off the Titanic listed more and more to one side. I decided that I had better look out for myself and went up to a deck on the starboard side. In the meantime a good many boats were getting off.

"There were no women on the starboard side when I reached there except one collapsible raft load of third-class women passengers. Mr. Ismay and myself got into the boat, which was either the last or the next to the last to leave the Titanic.

"As we left the ship the lights went out and the Titanic

started to go down. The crash had ripped up the side and the water rushing into the boiler-room caused the boilers to explode.

"We were a good distance off when we saw the Titanic dip and disappear. We stayed in the boat until about 5 o'clock, Mr. Ismay and myself pulling on the oars with three members of the crew practically all the time.

"Never in my life have I seen such splendid discipline as was maintained by Captain Smith and his men. There was no panic and the order was splendid.

"Before I left Harry Widener I urged him to come with me to the starboard side of the ship, and it was then he told me he would take his chances on the vessel. He had on a life belt, as did every other passenger, many of whom stayed in the smoking room playing bridge.

MR. WIDENER PARTED FROM HIS WIFE.

"I saw Colonel Astor place his wife in the same boat that I put my family in, and at the same time Mr. Widener parted from his wife and Mr. Thayer put Mrs. Thayer in the boat. I did not see the men again."

Major Arthur Puechen, a wealthy resident of Toronto, Canada, was the last man on the Titanic to say goodbye to Charles M. Hays, president of the Grand Trunk Pacific Railway, who lost his life.

After assisting members of the crew in filling up the first five boats, Major Puechen who is an experienced yachtsman, was assigned by the second mate to take charge of boat No. 6. Major Puechen said he declined to accept such a post, not desiring to have any preference over any of his fellow passengers.

Captain Smith, wishing an experienced boatsman on boat No. 6, directed the second officer to give the Major a written order to take charge of it. Major Puechen displayed this order to some of his friends last night, so as to make it plain that it was at the demand of the ship's officers that he undertook the assignment.

Just as the Major was about to leave in the lifeboat, his old friend, Charles M. Hays, of the Grand Trunk, came up and said goodbye. Mr. Hays had no idea, according to Major Puechen that the ship would sink as soon as it did, but believed that help would be at hand sufficient to care for all before the vessel went down.

Mr. Hays remarked to the Major that the ship could not possibly sink within eight hours, and that long before then everybody would be taken off safely. Mr. Hays expressed no fear that he would be lost by remaining on board the ship.

Peter D. Daly, of New York, jumped from the deck of the Titanic after it was announced that there were only boats enough for the women and children. As he saw the ship settling gradually he swam away with all his might to prevent being carried down with the suction of the sinking liner.

PICKED UP BY CARPATHIA.

"For six hours I beat the water with hands and feet to keep warm," he said. "Then I was picked up by one of the Carpathia's boats, which was cruising around looking for survivors. I was numb from the cold, after a fight which I can scarcely bear to discuss.

"Even after I recovered from the chill and shock, I was practically prostrated by the nervous strain, and every mention of the disaster sends a shiver through me.

"There was no violent impact when the vessel collided with the ice. I rushed to the deck from my cabin, got a life preserver and, when things began to look serious, threw myself into the water. The boat had already begun to settle."

A huge cake of ice was the means of aiding Emile Portaluppi, of Aricgabo, Italy, in escaping death when the Titanic went down. Portaluppi, a second class passenger, was awakened by the explosion of one of the boilers of the ship. He hurried to the deck, strapped a life preserver around him and leaped into the sea. With the aid of the preserver and by holding to a cake of ice he managed to keep afloat until one of the lifeboats picked him up. There were thirty-five people in the boat when he was hauled aboard.

Mrs. Lucine P. Smith, of Huntington, W. Va., daughter of Representative James P. Hughes, of West Virginia, a bride of about eight weeks, whose husband was lost in the wreck, gave her experience through the medium of her uncle, Dr. J. H. Vincent, of Huntington, West Virginia.

"The women were shoved into the lifeboats," said Dr. Vincent. "The crew did not wait until the lifeboat was filled before they lowered it. As a matter of fact there were but twenty-six people in the boat, mostly all women, when an officer gave instructions to lower it. Mr. Smith was standing alongside the boat when it was lowered. There was plenty of room for more people to get into the lifeboats, the capacity being fifty.

APPEALS TO CAPTAIN WERE IGNORED.

"Mrs. Smith implored Captain Smith to allow her husband in the boat, but her repeated appeals, however, were ignored. This lifeboat was permitted to be lowered with but one sailor in it and he was drunk. His condition was such that he could not row the boat and therefore the women had to do the best they could in rowing about the icy waters.

"As the boat swung out from the side it was evident that the three men knew absolutely nothing about rowing and Mrs. Kenyon said she and another woman seized the oars and helped the sailors to pull clear. Gradually the small boat was worked away from the Titanic. The boat had gone quite a distance when suddenly all heard a terrific explosion and in the glare which followed they saw the body of a man hurled from the bridge high in the air. Then darkness fell. At 6.30 the boat was picked up by the Carpathia."

Mrs. Elizabeth Dyker, of Westhaven, Conn., a bride whose husband perished, lost besides her husband all her worldly possessions.

"When the crash came," said Mrs. Dyker, "I met Adolph on deck. He had a satchel in which were two gold watches, two diamond rings, a sapphire necklace and two hundred crowns. He couldn't go in the boat with me but grabbed a life preserver and said he would try to save himself. That was the last I saw of him. When the life boat came alongside the Carpathia one of the men in it threw my satchel to the deck. I have not seen it since."

Kate Mullin, of County Longford, Ireland, told of how stewards had tried to keep back the steerage women. She said she saw scores of men and women jump overboard and drown.

Bunar Tonglin, a Swede, was saved in the next to the last boat which left the Titanic. Before getting into the boat he placed two hysterical women in another boat. Then he heard a cry, and, looking up, saw a woman standing on the upper deck. The woman, he said, dropped from her arms her baby, which Tonglin caught, and gave to one of the women he had put in the boat. Then he got into his own boat, which was lowered, and shortly afterwards came the two explosions, and the plunge downward of the Titanic. Tonglin declared that he had seen numerous persons leap from the decks of the Titanic and drown.

HELPS HIS WIFE TO A PLACE IN THE BOAT.

Mrs. Fred R. Kenyon, of Southington, Conn., was one of the Titanic's survivors. Her husband went down with the vessel rather than take the place of a woman in a boat. Mrs. Kenyon said that when the call was given for the women to take places near the boat davits, in readiness to be placed in the boats as they were swung off, Mr. Kenyon was by her side. When it came her turn to enter the boat, Mr. Kenyon helped his wife to a place and kissed her goodbye. Mrs. Kenyon said she asked him to come with her, and he replied: "I would not with all those women and children waiting to get off."

In an instant Mr. Kenyon had stepped back and other women took their places and the boat swung clear and dropped to the water. In the boat Mrs. Kenyon said there were one sailor and three men who had been ordered in because they said they could row.

Mrs. John B. Thayer, whose husband, the second vice-president of the Pennsylvania Railroad, went down with the Titanic, after heroically standing aside to allow his wife's maid to take his place in the lifeboat, and whose young son, John B. Thayer, Jr., was pulled abord a lifeboat after being thrown from the giant liner just before she sank, seemed too dazed by what she had gone through to realize the awful enormity of the tragedy when she reached her home at Haverford, Pa.,

After reaching the Thayer home Mrs. Thayer was put to bed and the greatest precautions were taken to see that neither she nor young "Jack" Thayer was disturbed. Detectives from the Pennsylvania Railroad, assisted by two members of the Lower Merion police force, guarded the house both front and rear. All callers were told that both Mrs. Thayer and her son were too much overcome by their heartbreaking experience to see any one.

DIED TO SAVE WIFE'S MAID.

Mrs. Thayer, young John B. Thayer, junior no longer, Miss Eustis, a sister of Mrs. Walter B. Stephenson, of Haverford, and Margaret Fleming, Mrs. Thayer's maid, for whose safety Mr. Thayer sacrificed his own life, all arrived at the Haverford Station at 12.30 o'clock. They had made the trip from Jersey City in a special train consisting of an engine, baggage car and Pullman, with two day coaches to add the necessary weight to make the train ride easily. The special left the Pennsylvania Station at 10.16 and drew up at the Haverford Station just two hours and fourteen minutes later.

Harry C. Thayer, of Merion, a brother of Mr. Thayer, met his sister-in-law and nephew at the New York pier where the Carpathia docked, together with Dr. R. G. Gamble, of Haverford, the Thayers' family physician. Mrs. Thayer, though seemingly composed, is really in a very serious condition, according to Dr. Gamble. Her hours of exposure in an open boat, her uncertainty as to the fate of her son, whom she saw jump overboard, just before the Titanic sank, carrying her husband to a watery grave, was more than any woman could be expected to bear.

Eight or ten friends and relatives of the Thayer family, together with Captain Donaghy, of the Lower Merion police department, and a squad of his men, were awaiting the special train at the Haverford Station. A big limousine automobile was also on hand with the motor running, ready to whisk the party to the Thayer home, "Redwood," just back of the Merion Cricket Club.

As the train slowed up, the relatives and friends formed a double line opposite the Pullman car. The moment the train stopped, Mrs. Thayer was helped down the steps and to the automobile. Wearing heavy brown furs, a dark hat with a half veil, Mrs. Thayer looked dazed and walked as one asleep, as she was assisted into the motor car. Her son, young "Jack" Thayer, was at her side, with Miss Eustis and the maid, Margaret Fleming, bringing up the rear. The boy, a husky youngster, looked little the worse for his experiences and bore himself in manly fashion.

TOO OVERCOME TO BE QUESTIONED.

There was a clang of the motor car door, a crashing bang as the gears were shoved into place and the machine was off at top speed for the Thayer residence. Dr. Gamble, whose car was also in waiting, acted as spokesman for all. Mrs. Thayer, he said, was too overcome to be questioned, but he had gleaned from young "Jack" Thayer and from Margaret Fleming, the maid, a few details that brought out in vivid relief the quiet heroism of Mr. Thayer.

The son, also had proven, himself in the critical moment. Shortly after the Titanic crashed into the iceberg, said the doctor, Mr. Thayer had collected his wife, his son and his wife's maid and gotten them in line for a lifeboat. Realizing that there was not enough room for the men, Mr. Thayer forced his wife and her maid into the boat and then tried to get his son in also.

The lad, however, refused to desert his father. Stepping back, he made room for some one else, said to have been a grown man, and grasping his father's hand, said he "guessed he would stick by dad." Before Mr. Thayer could protest or forcibly place his son in the lifeboat, it had been launched and the opportunity was gone.

A few seconds before the Titanic sank, however, Mr. Thayer seemed to grasp the fact that the end was near. Picking up the boy he threw him into the sea. "Swim to a boat, my boy." he said.

Young Thayer, taken by surprise, had no chance to object. Before he knew what had happened, he was struggling in the icy waters of the ocean. Striking out, the lad swam to a lifeboat, said Mr. Gamble, but was beaten off by some of those aboard, as the boat was already overcrowded.

But the pluck that has made so many Thayers famous as athletes in many branches of sport was deeply implanted in young "Jack" Thayer. Turning from the lifeboat from which he had been beaten off, he swam to another. Once again he was fended away with a long oar. And all this time Mrs. Thayer, safe in another boat, watched her son struggle for life, too overcome with horrow to even scream.

NOT AS MUCH SUCTION AS EXPECTED.

A few seconds later the Titanic went down. There was a swirling of the waters, though not as much suction as had been expected. To save himself from the tug of the indraw waters, young Thayer grasped a floating cake of ice. To this he clung until another boat, filled with people of more kindly hearts, came by and pulled him aboard.

In this boat was Miss Brown, a friend of the boy's mother. She took charge of him until they were taken on board the Carpathia. Mrs. Thayer had not seen the rescue of her son. She had fainted, it is said, but revived a few moments later and did yeoman service at the oars. Other survivors in her boat spoke in the highest terms of her calm courage, which served to keep up the spirits of the women, half frozen from the bitter cold, insufficiently clad and bereft of their loved ones. Taking an oar, without waiting to be asked, she used every ounce of her strength for long hours before the Carpathia arrived, aiding the few sailors aboard to keep the boat's head to the sea and to dodge the myriads of ice cakes.

The exercise, however, served to keep her warm, and when she was lifted to the deck of the Carpathia she did not need hospital treatment. Her son, however, was in bad shape when he was rescued. His clothing was frozen to his body and he was exhausted from his battle with the ice-filled sea. Restoratives and hot water bottles in the Carpathia's hospital brought him around in time, however, and the moment he was able to stand on his feet he rushed through the ship, seeking his mother. That was a joyful reunion for both, but particularly for Mrs. Thayer, as she had given her son up for lost.

STAYED ON BOARD UNTIL SHE SANK.

Broken in spirits, bowed with grief, Mrs. Thayer stepped off the Carpathia at New York with the other few hundreds of survivors last night. With her was her young son, John B. Thayer, Jr., who stayed on board the vessel until she sank to share his father's fate, but who proved more fortunate than the railroad magnate, and was saved. She was heavily veiled and was supported by the son, who seemed, with his experience, to have aged twice his sixteen years.

Awaiting her arrival was a special train, sent by officers of the Pennsylvania Railroad for her arrival. One of the cars was that in which she and Mr. Thayer frequently had taken trips together. It was in this car that she rode to Philadelphia, the last time she ever will enter it.

Every arrangement had been made for the care and comfort of Mrs. Thayer. Immediately upon her arrival at the pier where the rescue ship, Carpathia, docked, relatives and representatives of the railroad were ready to receive her.

A motor car had beeen held in readiness and when she disembarked from the vessel, leaning upon the arm of her young son, she was led silently to it. They were the first of the Philadelphia survivors to arrive at the Pennsylvania station. It was exactly 10 o'clock when the car in which she and her son had ridden, pulled up outside the great building erected when her husband was one of the directing heads of the road. With her was Dr. Neidermeier, the station physician, who had been sent to take care of her during the short time she stayed in New York. Tenderly he lifted Mrs. Thayer to the pavement and then led her inside and across the central floor toward the train.

Garments had been brought from her home for Mrs. Thayer, to take the place of those which she had worn when, scantily clad, she bade her husband good-bye and climbed down the ladder of the Titanic to the waiting lifeboats. But the widow was too worn physically and too greatly bowed down with grief to make the change. She wore a thin raincoat which reached nearly to the ground. Its folds were wrinkled. A heavy veil completely covered her head, crushing down her hat.

MET AT THE CUNARD PIER.

Following her from the cab came her son and Henry Thayer, a brother of the former railroad man. Dr. Gamble, the family physician, and Mr. Norris, a relative of Mrs. Thayer, were also in the party which had met her at the Cunard pier.

As the widow of their former chief passed them, the employes of the railroad stopped and removed their hats. T. DeWitt Cuyler, a director of the Pennsylvania Railroad, saw her coming and stepped toward her. As he did so, Dr. Neidermeier quicky grasped his arm and drew him to one side where Mrs. Thayer would not hear.

"Mr. Thayer is dead," the physician whispered silently. Mr. Cuyler gripped the doctor's hand and then, his face working violently, he turned quickly away.

It was only a few minutes after Mrs. Thayer had stepped on board the car that the train started for Philadelphia. It left the station at 10.19 o'clock.

"I was with father," said "Jack" Thayer, speaking for himself of his experience. "They wanted me to go into a boat, but I wanted to stay with him. Men and women kept calling to me to hurry and jump in a boat, but it wasn't any use. I knew what

I was doing. It didn't seem to be anything to be afraid about. Some of the men were laughing. Nobody appeared to be excited. We had struck with a smash and then we seemed to slide off backwards from the big field of ice. It was cold, but we didn't mind that.

"The boats were put off without much fuss. Mother was put into one of the boats. As I said, she wanted me to go with her. But I said I guessed I would stick with dad. After awhile I felt the ship tipping toward the front. The next thing I knew somebody gave me a push and I was in the water. Down, down, down, I went, ever so far. It seemed as if I never would stop. I couldn't breathe. Then I shot up through the water just as fast as I went down. I had just time to take a long, deep breath when a wave went over me.

"When I came to the surface a second time I swam to a boat. They wouldn't take me in. Then I tried another. Same result. Finally, when I was growing weak, I bumped against something. I found it was an overturned lifeboat. It was a struggle to pull myself upon it, but I did it after a while. My, it was cold! I never suffered so much in my life. All around were the icebergs.

"I could see boats on all sides. I must have shouted, because my throat was all raw and sore, but nobody seemed to notice. I guess they all were shouting, too. Every part of me ached with the cold. I thought I was going to die. It seemed as if I couldn't stand it any longer.

"The time was so long and I was so weak. Then I just couldn't feel anything any more. I knew if I stayed there I would freeze. A boat came by and I swam to it. They took me aboard. The next thing I remember clearly was when the boat from the Carpathia came and I was taken into it and wrapped up in the coats of the men. They told me I was more than three hours on that raft and in that open boat. It seemed more like three years to me."

CHAPTER XI.

MAJOR BUTT, MARTYR TO DUTY.

Major Butt Martyr to Duty—Woman's Soul-Stirring Tribute—Died Like a Soldier—Was the Man of the Hour—Assisted Captain and Officers in Saving Women—Cool as if on Dress Parade—Robert M. Daniel Tells of Disaster and Death of Heroes—Tiny Waifs of the Sea.

Captain E. J. Smith, the commander of the Titanic, was a guest at a banquet which was being given by W. Bruce Ismay, managing director of the White Star Line, when the big steamer plunged into that fated iceberg, according to Robert M. Daniel, member of the banking firm of Hillard-Smith, Daniel & Co., 328 Chestnut street, Philadelphia.

The fourth officer was in charge of the vessel, said Mr. Daniel, when seen at the Waldorf-Astoria in New York, to which hotel he went immediately after landing from the Carpathia, accompanied by his mother and younger brother, who had come up from their home in Virginia to meet him.

"We were about fifty miles ahead of our schedule at the time the accident happened," said Mr. Daniel, "and were running at about a twenty-mile-an-hour rate. Everybody on board had been talking all along about how we were trying to beat the Olympic's record for the Western trip and many pools were made on each day's run.

"I was asleep in my berth when the collision came and so cannot tell how we happened to hit that berg or what occurred immediately afterwards. I got up and looked out of my stateroom door, but all seemed to be quiet and I went back to bed again.

"A little later I heard some one crying that the boats were being manned and I got frightened. So I wrapped an overcoat about me and went on deck. On the way I grabbed a life belt and tied it on.

"The boat had already sunk so far down that the lower decks were awash. I didn't waste any time in thinking. I just jumped overboard. I clung to the same overturned lifeboat that young John B. Thayer, Jr., swam to later and saw him jump from the Titanic. It looked to me as though his father pushed him off and jumped after him, but the boat sank so soon afterwards and things were so mixed up that I couldn't be sure about that.

"A boat came by after a while that was full of women. They were frightened and seeing me, pulled me aboard, saying they needed a man to take charge. I did my best to cheer them up, but it was a poor effort and didn't succeed very well. Still I kept them busy with one thing and another and so helped pass the weary hours until we were picked up by the Carpathia."

JUMPED AS THE LINER WAS GOING DOWN.

Mr. Daniel stated with emphasis that Colonel John Jacob Astor stayed on the Titanic until the last second, then jumped just as the liner was going down, and he did not see the millionaire again.

Captain Smith also stuck to the bridge, until the ship sank, said Mr. Daniel, when the skipper also jumped, but disappeared below the waves and apparently never came up again.

"I spoke to the fourth officer just before I went to my cabin," said Mr. Daniel, "and he told me he was in charge while the captain was at dinner. Then I remembered I had heard Ismay was giving a banquet.

"The fourth officer said the skipper was coming up 'pretty soon' to relieve him," added Mr. Daniel.

On the Carpathia, Mr. Daniel said, were nineteen women who had been made widows by the Titanic disaster. Six of them were young brides who were returning on the steamship from honeymoon trips on the Continent. None of them, he said, was able to obtain from the passengers of the Carpathia mourning garb.

While on the Carpathia Mr. Daniel proved of cosiderable assistance to the wireless operator. He is an amateur student of wireless telegraphy. Following the disaster the operator on the Carpathia was compelled to work night and day.

While the operator was engaged in the arduous task of sending to shore the long list of those who had been snatched from the sea, Mr. Daniel went into the operating room. He found the operator on the verge of collapse, and, volunteering his services, sent a large part of the list himself.

Mr. Daniel denied that all the lifeboats and collapsible rafts launched from the Titanic had been picked up by the Carpathia.

"Only twelve boats were picked up," he said, "while there were half a dozen more that drifted away in other directions. There has been no storm, and I don't see why they should not have been located by some other vessel."

"FRANKFURT" MUCH NEARER THAN CARPATHIA.

A German steamer, the "Frankfurt," was thirty-five miles nearer to the Titanic than was the Carpathia at the time of the accident, but for some reason would not come to the assistance of the stricken liner, Mr. Daniel said.

Asked if any women had been left aboard the Titanic he said: "Only those women who positively refused to leave their husbands and who could not be forced into lifeboats for lack of time.

"One of the most remarkable features of this horrible affair is the length of time that elapsed after the collision before the seriousness of the situation dawned on the passengers. The officers assured everybody that there was no danger, and we all had such confidence in the Titanic that it didn't occur to anybody that she might sink."

As to the reports that many persons had been shot to prevent them from rushing the lifeboats, Mr. Daniel said several shots had been fired in the air to frighten the steerage passengers and keep them in order, but that he did not know or hear of anyone being hit by a bullet.

Mrs. John Jacob Astor, said Mr. Daniel, had been confined to her stateroom under the doctor's care during her stay on the Carpathia. "I did not lay eyes on her nor on Bruce Ismay. He stuck close to his cabin and I don't think he came on deck once during the trip on the Carpathia."

Even when the passengers finally realized that the Titanic was doomed, there was no disorder, according to Mr. Daniel. The crew's discipline was perfect and the women were placed in the boats quietly and without confusion. It was only after the ship had gone down, he added, and the women awoke to the fact that their husbands, brothers, sons and sweethearts, who had told them they would follow "in other boats," had sunk to their death, that there was any hysteria.

THE CRIES WERE HEART-RENDING.

"Then the cries were awful to listen to; some of the women screamed all the time. For four straight hours they kept at it. First from one boat, then from another. It was heart-rending."

Asked why the Carpathia had refused to answer the wireless messages relayed to her, Mr. Daniel answered that so many land stations were trying to get the vessel that the air was full of cross currents, and it was almost impossible to catch any one message meant for the rescue ship, let alone trying to reply to any of them.

While Mr. Daniel was talking to the newspaper men on the pier, just after landing from the Carpathia, a man ran up and, showing him two newspaper photographs, asked if he remembered the face.

"It's my brother, Mr. White, of California," said the man. "Is he on board the Carpathia?"

"I don't think so," answered Mr. Daniel. "I remember meeting this gentleman on board the Titanic, but I have not seen him since." Mr. White's brother grabbed the photographs and rushed away.

Many of the men, said Mr. Daniel, refused to jump from the Titanic until the ship was actually disappearing beneath the waves.

"They seemed to think they were safer on board," he said, "and by waiting too long lost their chance of being saved, for they were probably carried down by the suction. Howard B. Case, of New York, was one who declined to jump. C. Duane Williams was another. He was washed overboard, but his son, Richard Norris Williams, jumped and was saved."

Mr. Daniel was in the water or on a cake of ice nearly an hour before he was pulled aboard a lifeboat. He had nothing to keep him from freezing save a light overcoat over his pajamas. While on the Carpathia he slept on the floor of the dining saloon and was so weak when he landed that he could hardly move.

When in Philadelphia, Mr. Daniel makes his home at the Southern Club, though he is a native of Richmond, Va., where his mother and brother live.

CRAWLED ON TO CAKE OF ICE.

"When I finally went on deck," said Mr. Daniel, "the water already was up to my ankles. I saw the women and some of the men taking to the boats. A short distance away was a big cake of ice. I jumped for it and crawled on it.

"John B. Thayer, Jr., came to the same ice cake later, after the Titanic sank. Then a boat passed near and he swam to it and was pulled aboard. A half hour afterwards another boat came by and I was pulled aboard.

"It seemed a long time before we saw the masts of the Carpathia, but when the straight masts and the blur of smoke from her funnels were outlined against the horizon, we realized that it meant rescue for all of us. When the boat finally reached us, the men in the boat did what they could to help the women to the vessel, but most of us were almost helpless from the cold and exposure.

"I cannot pretend to explain the accident. All I can say is that we knew for five hours before the accident that there were ice fields about. I saw Colonel Astor after I was on the raft. He was still on deck. The water was washing about his knees. He made no effort to get into a boat.

"The last I saw of Major Butt," Mr. Daniel added, "he was playing bridge whist with Clarence Moore, of Washington, formerly of Philadelphia, and widely known as a horse show exhibitor, and two other men. This was just before I went to my cabin.

"When I came on deck again, I did not see him. I have no doubt he met his death as a soldier should."

Major Archibald Butt, U. S. A., military aid to President Taft, who lost his life on the Titanic, met his death in a manner that fully justified the President's estimation of him as expressed in the eulogy given out at the White House, in which the President tenderly referred to his late aide as a man "gentle and considerate," and as one who was "every inch a soldier."

GRAVITY OF THE TITANIC'S CONDITION.

From the moment the Titanic climbed to her death on the jagged shelf of the great iceberg until the last boatload of women and children, and some men, was lowered, Major Butt was to all intents and purposes an officer not only of the American Army, but of the British mercantile marine. He was among the first to realize the gravity of the Titanic's condition, and he immediately forgot self and went to the assistance of the sorely taxed skipper and junior officers of the sinking liner.

From the moment that Captain Smith let it be known to his officers and a few of the men passengers that the Titanic was doomed, Major Butt was an officer of the Titanic. He was here and there and everywhere, giving words of encouragement to weeping women and children, and uttering when necessary commands to keep the weak-kneed men from giving in and rendering the awful situation even more terrible.

That this was the manner in which Major Butt met death is certain.

Captain Charles E. Crain, of the Twenty-seventh United

States Infantry was a passenger on the Carpathia, and when he learned that Major Butt was among the dead, he made it his duty to get the true tale of his comrade's death.

"Naturally," said Captain Crain, "I was deeply concerned in the fate of Major Butt, for he was not only a fellow-officer of the army, but also a personal friend of many years' standing. I questioned those of the survivors who were in a condition to talk, and from them I learned that Butt, when the Titanic struck, took his position with the officers and from the moment that the order to man the lifeboats was given until the last one was dropped into the sea, he aided in the maintenance of discipline and the placing of the women and children in the boats.

AS COOL AS THE ICEBERG.

"Butt, I was told was as cool as the iceberg that had doomed the ship, and not once did he lose control of himself. In the presence of death he was the same gallant, courteous officer that the American people had learned to know so well as a result of his constant attendance upon President Taft. There was never any chance of Butt getting into any of those lifeboats.

"He knew his time was at hand, and he was ready to meet it as a man should, and I and all of the others who cherish his memory are glad that he faced the situation that way, which was the only possible way a man of his calibre could face it."

Mrs. Henry B. Harris, of Washington, a survivor of the Titanic, said:

"I saw Major Butt just before they put me into a collapsible raft with ever so many women from the steerage. Mr Millet's little smile, which played on his lips all through the voyage, had gone, but when I was put in the boat I saw him wave his hand to a woman in another boat.

"But, oh, this whole world should rise in praise of Major Butt. That man's conduct will remain in my memory forever; the way he showed some of the other men how to behave when women and children were suffering that awful mental fear that came when we had to be huddled in those boats. Major Butt was near me, and I know very nearly everything he did.

"When the order to take to the boats came he became as one in supreme command. You would have thought he was at a White House Reception, so cool and calm was he. A dozen or so women became hysterical all at once as something connected with a lifeboat went wrong. Major Butt stepped to them and said: 'Really you must not act like that; we are all going to see you through this thing.'

"He helped the sailors rearrange the rope or chain that had gone wrong and lifted some of the women in with gallantry. His was the manner we associate with the word aristocrat.

MAJOR BUTT A MAN TO BE FEARED.

"When the time came for it, he was a man to be feared. In one of the earlier boats fifty women, it seemed, were about to be lowered when a man, suddenly panic-stricken, ran to the stern of it. Major Butt shot one arm out, caught him by the neck and pulled him backward like a pillow. His head cracked against a rail and he was stunned.

" 'Sorry,' said Major Butt; 'women will be attended to first or I'll break every bone in your body.'

"The boats were lowered away, one by one, and as I stood by my husband he said to me: 'Thank God for Archie Butt.' Perhaps Major Butt heard it, for he turned his face toward us for a second.

"Just at that time a young man was arguing to get into a lifeboat, and Butt had hold of the lad by the arm like a big brother and appeared to be telling him to keep his head.

"I was one of three first cabin women in our collapsible boat, the rest were steerage people. Major Butt helped those poor frightened peolple so wonderfully, tenderly, and yet with such cool and manly firmness. He was a soldier to the last."

"If anything should happen to me, tell my wife in New York that I've done my best in doing my duty."

This was the last message of Benjamin Guggenheim, of

the famous banking family, dictated to a steward only a short while before the banker sank to his death with the Titanic.

It was was not until several days later that the message was received by Mrs. Guggenheim.

It was delivered by James Etches, assistant steward in the first cabin of the Titanic, to whom Mr. Guggenheim communicated it. Etches appeared at the St. Regis Hotel and inquired for Mrs Benjamin Guggenheim. He said that he had a message from Benjamin Guggenheim, and that it had to be delivered in person.

Mrs. Guggenheim was in the care of Daniel Guggenheim, whose apartments are at the St. Regis. The steward was admitted, but was not permitted to see Mrs. Guggenheim, who is prostrated with grief. He insisted that he must see her personally, but finally consented to transmit the message through her brother-in-law.

TOGETHER ALMOST TO THE END.

"We were together almost to the end," said the steward. "I was saved. He went down with the ship. But that isn't what I want to tell Mrs. Guggenheim."

"Then the steward produced a piece of paper. He had written the message on it, he said, to be certain that it would be correct. The message was as given.

"That's all he said," added the steward, "there wasn't time for more."

Little by little Mr. Guggenheim got the account of his brother's death from the steward. It was the first definite news that he had received of his brother.

"Mr. Guggenheim was one of my charges," said the steward anew. "He had his secretary with him. His name was Giglio, I believe, an Armenian, about twenty-four years old. Both died like men.

"When the crash came I awakened them and told them to get dressed. A few minutes later I went into their rooms and helped them to get ready. I put a life preserver on Mr. Guggenheim. He said it hurt him in the back. There was plenty of time and I took it off, adjusted it, and then put it on him again. It was all right this time.

"They wanted to get out on deck with only a few clothes on, but I pulled a heavy sweater over Mr. Guggenheim's life belt, and then they both went out. They stayed together and I could see what they were doing. They were going from one lifeboat to another helping the women and children.

"Mr. Guggenheim would shout out, 'Women first,' and he was of great assistance to the officers.

"Things weren't so bad at first, but when I saw Mr. Guggenheim about three quarters of an hour after the crash there was great excitement. What surprised me was that both Mr. Guggenheim and his secretary were dressed in their evening clothes. They had deliberately taken off their sweaters, and as nearly as I can remember they wore no life belts at all.

" 'What's that for?' I asked.

" 'We've dressed up in our best,' replied Mr. Guggenheim, 'and are prepared to go down like gentlemen.' It was then he told me about the message to his wife and that is what I have come here for.

"Well, shortly after the last few boats were lowered and I was ordered by the deck officer to man an oar, I waved good-bye to Mr. Guggenheim, and that was the last I saw of him and his secretary."

CHAPTER XII.

MRS. ASTOR'S BRAVERY.

Showed Wonderful Fortitude in the Hour of Peril—Sailors in Lifeboat Tell Of Her Heroism—Pleaded To Remain With Husband—Change Clothes to Embark—Seamen Confirm Murdock's Suicide—One Heartless Fiend—Williams Killed as Funnel Fell.

Narratives of the remarkable heroism of Colonel John Jacob Astor and the patient fortitude of Mrs. Astor under conditions that tried the self-control of the hardiest, continue to come to light.

The narrative of the dreadful suspense which in a short time changed her from a radiant bride to a sorrowing widow was told by a friend of the family.

At the same time survivors who occupied lifeboat No. 4, in which Mrs. Astor and her maid escaped, told of how Mrs. Astor had helped calm the other women and had even offered fellow sufferers portions of her slender stock of clothing.

"Mrs Astor was the bravest little woman I ever met," said Jack Foley, who, with his mate, Sam Parks, pulled an oar in boat No. 4.

"Colonel Astor was a man all through, if there ever was one," continued Foley. "You see, it took us some time to launch boat No. 4. After we had all the women and the children in the boat we discovered that we couldn't launch her until we removed the sounding spar several decks below.

"So Sam and I got down and chopped the spar away. We were some time doing this, as we had to hunt for an ax.

"We finally got the spar away and launched the boat. That is why boat No. 4 was the last boat to be launched. The others had a free way below it and could be put in the water at once.

"While waiting up there Mrs. Astor several times wanted to leave the boat. Mr. Astor kept telling the good little woman that he was sure to be saved and that it was her duty to go.

"She stretched out her arms just as though she was pleading with him to let her get out of the boat and take her place with him. Mr. Astor picked up a heavy steamer shawl and wrapped it about her shoulders.

"After pulling those eight men into the boat I was pretty wet and was shivering. Mrs. Astor threw the shawl about my shoulders and said that I needed it more than she did. I told her that I would get warmed up after pulling a while at the oar and would have no use for it.

WHIMPERING WITH COLD.

"I put the shawl back on her lap. Sitting next to Mrs. Astor was a Swedish woman with a little girl that I should take to be three or four years old. The little girl was whimpering with the cold.

"Mrs. Astor took the shawl and threw it about the shoulders of this woman, who thanked her in some foreign lingo. Then the steerage woman kissed her little girl and took her into her arms and wrapped the shawl about her.

"When the explosion occurred aboard the ship Mrs. Astor made some kind of a sound, but I couldn't understand whether she said anything or merely sobbed. She turned her head away from the direction of the vessel."

So little was the impact felt at the time of the collision that Mrs. Astor thought the crash was the result of some mishap in the kitchen and paid no attention to it until the engines stopped.

Then, realizing that something was wrong, she inquired of her steward the cause. He informed her that a slight accident had happened, and that the captain had ordered the women to the lifeboats, but he added that this was only a precautionary measure, and that they would all be back soon again on the ship.

Mrs. Astor then entered her stateroom and changed her dress, preparatory to leaving the Titanic for one of the lifeboats in company with her maid.

As she left the room the steward told her he would lock up her suite so that nobody would enter it during her absence, for he thought everybody would soon return.

Colonel Astor accompanied his wife and her maid to lifeboat No. 4. When he attempted to enter it he was pushed back by the sailor in charge, and was told that no men were permitted in it.

"But," said Colonel Astor, "there are no more women to be taken in, and there is plenty of room."

"That makes no difference," replied the man; "the orders are no men, so you cannot get in."

There was no use arguing, Colonel and Mrs. Astor thought, so, waving her adieu, he called out:

"Good-bye, Madeleine."

TITANIC GOING DOWN TO HER DOOM.

Lifeboat No. 4 did not go far before she returned to the place which soon after became the Titanic's grave. The great "unsinkable" ship was already going fast to her doom, and fear that the suction from the sinking vessel would draw down the little lifeboat made its sailors once more turn away from the wreck and seek safety, with its handful of women and its empty seats.

When the Carpathia hove in sight two sailors in lifeboat No. 4 were dead. The watch of one, which a woman looked at, had stopped at 2.15 o'clock.

In the roster of the Titanic's heroes the name of Robbins should appear. He was Colonel Astor's old butler, and, like the Colonel's valet, always traveled with him. He is numbered among the Titanic's dead.

Faithful unto death was Kitty, Colonel Astor's Airedale terrier and constant companion. On land or sea, Kitty was never far from her master's heels, and the two were familiar figures on 5th avenue.

When the crash came Robbins went below and brought Kitty up on deck. There, the most faithful of friends, she stood beside her master while the sea embraced them, and she now shares his grave.

Reports that a number of men—probably steerage passengers—on the Titanic who tried to rush the lifeboats and preempt the places of women and chidlren were unceremoniously shot were confirmed by Jack Williams and William French, able seamen, survivors of the Titanic's crew.

THE FIRST STAMPEDE.

"When the first of the 56-foot lifeboats were being filled," explained Williams, "the first stampede of panic-stricken men occurred. Within a dozen feet of where I stood I saw fully ten men throw themselves into the boats already crowded with women and children.

"These men were dragged back and hurled sprawling across the deck. Six of them, screaming with fear, struggled to their feet and made a second attempt to rush the boats.

"About ten shots sounded in quick succession. The six cowardly men were stopped in their tracks, stagged and collapsed one after another. At least two of them vainly attempted to creep toward the boats again. The others lay quite still. This scene of bloodshed served its purpose. In that particular section of the deck there was no further attempt to violate the 'women and children first' rule."

"Were any of these men from the first or second cabins?" Williams was asked.

Williams, a medium-sized, stockily-built, blond-haired man of thirty-six passed the query on to his sailor chum French, who replied:

"It was hard to tell. All of them were so scantily dressed. In the semi-darkness and prevailing excitement faces left no distinct impression with me. I should say that most, if not all of them, were from the steerage.

"Other men passengers who in a general way resembled these same men were among a score or so who jumped from the upper decks into the boats occupied by women and children, after the order had been given to lower boats. These men were not shot. They were tossed by the officers and crew of the boat into the sea ,where most of them perished, as they deserved to.

"The report that First Officer Murdock and not Captain Smith, shot himself on the bridge just as the forward section of the Titanic sank is true. I still have before me the picture of Mr. Murdock standing on the bridge as the waters surged up about him, placing the pistol to his head and disappearing as the shot that ended his life rang out."

EMERGENCY BOATS MADE READY.

"French and I," said Williams, "stood by as the two emergency boats—those that are always kept ready for rescue purposes at sea—were made ready. These boats were only twenty-six feet long, while the regular lifeboats are about fifty-six feet in length.

"It was in the first of these emergency boats that Mr. Ismay put off. This boat and emergency boat No. 2 were launched with first class passengers less than a half hour after the collision.

"A lot had been printed in the papers about the heroism of the officers, but little has been said of the bravery of the men below the decks. I was told that seventeen enginemen who were drowned side by side got down on their knees on the platform of the engine room and prayed until the water surged up to their necks.

"Then they stood up clasped hands so as to form a circle and died together. All of these men helped rake the fires out from ten of the forward boilers after the crash. This delayed the explosion and undoubtedly permitted the ship to remain afloat nearly an hour longer, and thus saved hundreds of lives."

Mrs. John C. Hogeboom, her sister, Miss Cornelia T. Andrews, and their niece, Miss Gretchen F. Longley, of Hudson, N. Y., were at the home of Mrs Arthur E. Flack, in East Orange, N. J., where Miss Andrews told how she and her aunts waited for the fourth lifeboat because there was not room for the three of them in the first three boats launched.

"And when we finally did get into a boat," continued Miss Andrews, "we found that our miserable men companions could not row and had only said they could because they wanted to save themselves. Finally I had to take an oar with one of the able seamen in the boat.

"Alongside of us was a sailor, who lighted a cigarette and flung the match carelessly among us women. Several women in the boat screamed, fearing they would be set on fire. The sailor replied: 'We are going to hell anyway and we might as well be cremated now as them."

At this point Mrs. Hogeboom interrupted and said:

BETTER PUT ON LIFE PRESERVERS.

"A little after 12 we heard commotion in the corridor and we made more inquiries, and they told us we had better put on life preservers. We had only five minutes to get ready. We put our fur coats right on over our night dresses and rushed on deck.

"One lifeboat was already full, but there was no panic. The discipline in a way was good. No one hurried and no one crowded. We waited for the fourth boat and were slowly lowered seventy-five feet to the water. The men made no effort to get into the boat. As we pulled away we saw them all standing in an unbroken line on the deck.

"There they stood—Major Butt, Colonel Astor waving a farewell to his wife; Mr. Thayer, Mr. Case, Mr. Clarence Moore, Mr. Widener, all multi-millionaires, and hundreds of other men bravely smiling at us all. Never have I seen such chivalry and fortitude. Such courage in the face of fate horrible to contemplate filled us even then with wonder and admiration.

"Before our boat was lowered they called to some miserable specimens of humanity and said: 'Can you row?' and for the purpose of getting in they answered 'Yes.' But upon pulling out we found we had a Chinese and an American, neither of whom knew how to row. So there we were in mid-ocean with one able-bodied seaman.

"Then my niece took one oar and assisted the seaman and some of the other women rowed on the other side. We then pulled out about a mile as we feared the suction should the ship do down.

"Scarcely any of the lifeboats were properly manned. Two, filled with women and children, capsized before our eyes. The collapsible boats were only temporarily useful. They soon partially filled with water. In one boat eighteen or twenty persons sat in water above their knees for six hours.

EIGHT MEN THROWN OVERBOARD.

"Eight men in this boat were overcome, died and were thrown overboard. Two women were in this boat. One succumbed after a few hours and one was saved.

"The accident was entirely the result of carelessness and lack of necessary equipment. There were boats for only one-third of the passengers—there were no searchlights—the lifeboats were not supplied with food or safety appliances—there were no lanterns on the lifeboats—there was no way to raise sails, as we had no one who understood managing a sailboat."

Mrs. Hogeboom explained that the new equipment of masts and sails in the boats was carefully wrapped and bound with twine. The men undertook to unfasten them, but found it necessary to cut the ropes. They had no knives, and in their frenzy they went about asking the ill-clad women if they had knives. The sails were never hoisted.

According to Richard Norris Williams, Jr., his father, C. Duane Williams, was killed, not drowned, in the Titanic wreck.

The son, who, with his father, was on his way to visit Richard Norris Williams, his uncle, 8124 St. Martin's lane, Chestnut Hill, Pa., says his father was crushed to death by a falling funnel.

His account of the tragedy was given through Mrs. Alexander Williams, daughter-in-law of Richard Norris Williams.

"Richard told us," she said, "that he and his father had been watching the Titanic's lifeboats lowered and filled with women, The water was up to their waists and the ship was about at her last.

"Suddenly one of the great funnels fell. Richard sprang aside, trying to drag his father after him. But Mr. Williams was caught under the funnel. A moment later the funnel was swept overboard, and the decks were cleared of water. Mr. Williams, the father, had disappeared.

SWAM THROUGH THE ICE.

"Richard sprang overboard and swam through the ice to a life raft. He was pulled aboard. There were five other men there and one woman. Occasionally they were swept off into the sea, even the woman, but they always managed to climb back. Finally those on the raft were picked up by a Titanic lifeboat, and later were saved by the Carpathia."

Young Mr. Williams said he didn't see J. Bruce Ismay, managing director of the White Star Line, after the iceberg was struck. He didn't know the Wideners or other Philadelphians aboard when he saw them.

Young Mr. Williams and his father were on their way here from Geneva, Switzerland. The young man was met at the pier in New York when the Carpathia docked by G. Heide Norris, a cousin. Together they went to the Waldorf-Astoria, where they remained for a few days.

The Rev. P. M. A. Hoque, a Catholic priest of St. Cesaire, Canada, who was a passenger on the Carpathia, told of finding the boats containing the survivors. He said:

"Every woman and child, as if by instinct, put the loops around their bodies and drew them taut. Some of the women climbed the ladders. To others chairs were lowered and in these they were lowered and in these they were lifted aboard.

"Not a word was spoken by any one of the rescued or the rescuers. Everybody was too be-numbed by horror to speak. It was a time for action and not words.

"Not a tear dimmed the eyes of one of the hundreds we got on deck. The women were less excited than the men. Apparently they all had drained their tear ducts dry, for every eye was red and swollen."

One of the most interesting accounts of the Titanic disaster which has come to light is in a letter written on board the Carpathia by Dr. Alice Leeder, of New York, one of the survivors, after she had been transferred to the Carpathia in a lifeboat.

The letter is a personal communication addressed to Mrs. Sarah Babcock, 2033 Walnut st., Philadelphia. By the wavering of the handwriting one can readily realize the state of mind in which it was written.

DR. LEEDER'S LETTER.

In the letter Dr. Leeder said there was no panic on board the Titanic, and that everyone who had to meet death met it with composure. She speaks of the generosity and kindness shown by the crew and passengers of the Carpathia in their treatment of the survivors. Following is the letter:

"Royal Mail Steamship Carpathia,

Wednesday, April 16.

"My Dear Mrs. Babcock:

"We have been through a most terrible experience—the Titanic and above a thousand souls sunk on Monday about 3 o'clock in the morning. Margaret and I are safe, although we have lost everything. One of our party, also, Mr. Kenyon, was lost. He was such a charming man—so honorable and good.

"I sat talking to him a little before the accident—and a little later he was dead. His wife is crushed by the blow. I can say one thing, nothing could part me from my husband in time of danger.

"After floating about for four hours we were taken on board the steamer that was bound for Naples—but she is now taking us to New York.

"It is terrible to see the people who have lost their families and friends—one lady has lost $15,000 worth of clothing, and no one has saved anything. Many of the passengers have only their night clothes with coats over them.

"I shall never forget the sight of that beautiful boat as she went down, the orchestra playing to the last, the lights burning until they were extinguished by the waves. It sounds so unreal, like a scene on the stage. We were hit by an iceberg.

"We were in the midst of a field of ice; towers of ice; fantastic shapes of ice! It is all photographed on my mind. There was no panic. Everyone met death with composure—as one said the passengers were a set of thoroughbreds.

"We are moving slowly toward New York. Everyone on this boat is so kind to us. Clothing and all the necessaries are at our convenience. I am attired in my old blue serge, a steamer hat; truth to tell, I am a sorry looking object to land in New York.

"This is rather a mixed up epistle, but please pardon lack of clearness of expression. If you want me, some time I will come to Philadelphia for a day or two in the future.

"With dear love,
"ALICE J. LEEDER."

Two handsome little boys, tiny waifs of the sea, are one of the mysteries of the Titanic disaster. These small boys were rescued as the big liner was foundering. Miss Hays, who has them in charge, said:

"These two beautiful children speak French fluently, and they know what their first names are, but they do not know their last names. They are 'Louis,' four and a half years old, I should say, and 'Lump,' a year younger.

"They were rescued from the Titanic and brought to the Carpathia where I was taken in another boat. Nobody knows who they are. There was but one man in the second class cabin who had two children with him, and that was a Mr. Hoffmann, but no one knows any more about him than that. Whether these are his children or not, we do not know.

"We in the first cabin used to see them and greatly admired them for their beauty and sweet ways.

"When they were brought on board the Carpathia there were no New York people except myself, who had not lost friends, I was the only one in a position to befriend them, and I went to the committee of passengers we had on board and offered to take them to my home.

"They gladly gave them to me because it meant that otherwise some society would grab them and they might be separated and never reunited.

"I think that the boys are French, but perhaps Swiss, French or Alsatian. I have tried them in Italian, German and English, but they cannot understand. Louis, the oldest, is brown eyed, with curly brown hair, very regular teeth and has no scar or mark on his body that would identify him. Both are well bred. The little fellow is just like his brother, but a year younger. Both have very long, curling lashes.

"When they got up this morning they asked first thing for a bath, and at breakfast placed their napkins under their chins themselves. Louis came aboard wrapped in a blanket that a sailor had given him. The other boy had a little blue coat with white collar. Louis's French is not a patois and he has a very large vocabulary.

I shall keep them till they are identified and make every effort to find out who they are. Any one who can help me will win my thanks and the thanks doubtless of some poor, stricken relatives. It seems almost impossible that these boys can fail to be identified in this day and generation."

CHAPTER XIII.

LIFEBOATS BUNGLINGLY HANDLED.

Widow of College Founder Scores Management for Lack of Drill—First Thought Damage was Slight—Aid May Have Been Near—No Oil in Life Lamps—Hudson, N. Y., Woman's Pathetic Recital—A. A. Dick, of New York, Talks.

The urgent need of lifeboat drills on the trans-Atlantic liners was touched upon by Mrs. William R. Bucknell, widow of the founder of Bucknell University, and herself one of the survivors of the disaster, in the course of a graphic account of the wreck of the Titanic given by her at the home of her son-in-law, Samuel P. Wetherill, Jr., at 23d and Spruce sts., Philadelphia.

Mrs. Bucknell said that not only were the passengers on the Titanic absolutely unfamiliar with the life saving equipment of the vessel, but that the equipment was inadequate and even faulty.

The lifeboats were bunglingly fastened to their davits, she said, and many of the collapsibles were too stiff to open and thus useless for service.

To her the greatest crime was the "unpreparedness" of the lifeboat equipment. Mrs. Bucknell declared one of the boats was launched with the plug out of the bottom, and afterwards sank, the occupants fortunately being rescued by the Titanic's fifth officer.

The lifeboat in which she was placed by Captain Smith, she declared, was manned only by a steward and three ordinary seamen. And none of the men, she declared, knew how to row.

Mrs. Bucknell also said that she had not seen a lifeboat drill while she was aboard the Titanic, and diligent inquiry among those rescued, after they were safely aboard the Carpathia, failed to develop any knowledge on their part of such drills ever having been held.

Mrs. Bucknell said that the only provisions aboard her lifeboat was a basket full of bread. She saw no water, although she said that two small casks beneath one of the seats may have contained water.

"The lifeboats were so bunglingly fastened to the davits in the first place that it was hard work to get them free." said Mrs. Bucknell.

"Half the collapsible boats were so stiff that they could not be opened and were useless. Those that were not already opened and ready for use were unavailable, also, for none on board seemed to understand how they worked. Hundreds more could have been saved if these collapsible boats had worked properly.

LIFEBOAT BEGINS TO FILL.

"One of the lifeboats had a big hole in the bottom. A plug had fallen out, I believe. When it was loaded and lowered over the side into the sea it began to fill at once. At this point the fifth officer proved himself a hero. Women in the leaking boat were screaming with fright and tearing off their clothing in wild and fruitless efforts to plug up the hole.

"The boat filled to the gunwhales before any were saved. The brave fifth officer to my knowledge rescued nineteen of the women in this boat, some of whom had fallen over the side into the sea. It was finally hauled alongside and replugged, loaded and relaunched.

"I was asleep in my cabin when the crash came," said Mrs. Bucknell, beginning her account of the disaster. "I cannot explain just what the noise was like, except that it was horrible and sounded like a mixture of thunder and explosions.

"In a moment there was a roaring sound and I knew that something serious was the matter. The corridors filled rapidly with frightened passengers and then the stewards and officers came, reassuring us with the announcement that everything was all right and that only a small hole had been stove in the bow.

"As I stepped out of my stateroom I saw lying before me on the floor a number of fragments of ice as big as my fists. More was crumbled about the porthole, and it flashed over me at once just what had happened.

" 'We have hit an iceberg,' I said to my maid, 'get dressed at once.'

"We hurried into our clothes, and I took the precaution to get fully dressed. So did my maid. I even thought to wrap myself in my warm fur coat, for even then I felt sure we would have to take to the boats. Something told me the damage was greater than we had been told.

"My fears were realized a few minutes later when a steward walked briskly down the corridor, calling to the passengers who had retired again to hurry into their clothes and get on deck at once. I could see by this man's drawn and haggard face that something dreadful had happened.

WOULD NOT BE SEPARATED.

"There was very little confusion on the deck. Once a group of men shouted that they would not be separated from their wives if it became necessary to take to the boats and made a rush to find accommodations for themselves. The captain seemed to straighten out his shoulders and his face was set with determination.

" 'Get back there, you cowards,' he roared. 'Behave yourself like men. Look at these women. Can you not be as brave as they?"

"The men fell back, and from that moment there seemed to be a spirit of resignation all over the ship. Husbands and wives clasped each other and burst into tears. Then a few minutes later came the order for the women and children to take to the boats.

"I did not hear an outcry from the women or the men. Wives left their husbands' side and without a word were led to the boats. One little Spanish girl, a bride, was the only exception.

She wept bitterly, and it was almost necessary to drag her into the boat. Her husband went down with the ship.

"The last person I remember seeing was Colonel Astor. When he had been told by the captain that it would be impossible for the husbands to take to the boats with their wives, he took Mrs. Astor by the arm and they walked quietly away to the other side of the vessel. As we pulled away I saw him leaning tenderly over her, evidently whispering words of comfort.

"There were thirty-five persons in the boats in which the captain placed me. Three of these were ordinary seamen, supposed to manage the boat, and a steward.

"One of these men seemed to think that we should not start from the sinking ship until it could be learned whether the other boats would accommodate the rest of the women. He seemed to think that more could be crowded into ours, if necessary.

"'I would rather go back and go down with the ship than leave under these circumstances,' he cried.

ORDERED TO PULL FOR THE LIGHT.

"The captain shouted to him to obey orders and to pull for a little light that could be just discerned miles in the distance. I do not know what this little light was. It may have been a passing fishing vessel, which, of course, could not know our predicament. Anyway, we never reached it.

"We rowed all night. I took an oar and sat beside the Countess de Rothes. Her maid had an oar and so did mine. The air was freezing cold, and it was not long before the only man that appeared to know anything about rowing commenced to complain that his hands were freezing.

"A woman back of him handed him a shawl from about her shoulders.

"As we rowed we looked back at the lights of the Titanic. There was not a sound from her, only the lights began to get lower and lower, and finally she sank. Then we heard a muffled explosion and a dull roar caused by the great suction of water.

"There was not a drop of water on our boat. The last minute before our boat was launched Captain Smith threw a bag of bread aboard. I took the precaution of taking a good drink of water before we started, so I suffered no inconvenience from thirst.

"Another thing that I must not forget to mention, it is but additional proof of my charge that the Titanic was poorly equipped. The lamp on our boat was nearly devoid of oil.

" 'For God's sake, keep that wick turned down low, or you will be in complete darkness,' we were told on leaving. It wasn't long before these words proved true, and before daylight we were dependent on a cane one of the women had brought along, which contained a tiny electric lamp.

FOUGHT THEIR WAY THROUGH THE DARKNESS.

"With this little glow worm we fought our way through the darkness. I rowed for an hour straight ahead. Then I rested and some one else took my place. Then I grasped the oars again. I have had lots of experience in this form of exercise, and at my place in the Adirondacks am at it continually, so, contrary to stories that have been written, I did not blister my hands.

"I want to say right here that I did not manage the boat. I helped row it and that's all.

"We had rowed about ten miles when looking over Countess Rothe's oar I spied a faint light to the rear.

" 'What's that light?' I almost screamed.

"One of the sailors looked where I indicated and said: 'It's a ship—I can tell by the lights on her masthead.'

"As we passed over the spot where the Titanic had gone down we saw nothing but a sheet of yellow scum and a solitary log. There was not a body, not a thing to indicate that there had been a wreck. The sun was shining brightly then, and we were near to the Carpathia."

Mrs. K. T. Andrews, of Hudson, N. Y., a first class passenger on the Titanic, said:

"When our boat was away from the Titanic there was an explosion and the Titanic seemed to break in two. Then she sank, bow first. Just before this, I saw Mr. Astor, Mr. Thayer and Mr. Case standing on deck. They were smiling and as we went off they waved their hands."

Thomas Whitley, a waiter on the Titanic, who was sent to a hospital with a factured leg, was asleep five decks below the main saloon deck. He ran upstairs and saw the iceberg towering high above the forward deck of the Titanic.

"It looked like a giant mountain of glass," said Whitely. "I saw that we were in for it. Almost immediately I heard that stokehold No. 11 was filling with water and that the ship was doomed. The water-tight doors had been closed, but the officers, fearing that there might be an explosion below decks, called for volunteers to go below to draw the fires.

COULD ALMOST FEEL THE WATER RUSHING IN.

Twenty men stepped forward almost immediately and started down. To permit them to enter the hold it was necessary for the doors to be opened again, and after that one could almost feel the water rushing in. It was but a few minutes later when all hands were ordered on deck with lifebelts. It was then known for a certain fact that the ship was doomed."

Charles Williams, the racquet coach at Harrow, Eng., who is the professional champion of the world and was coming to New York to defend his title, said he was in the smoking-room when the boat struck. He rushed out, saw the iceberg, which seemed to loom above the deck over a hundred feet. It broke up amidship and floated away.

He jumped from the boat deck on the starboard side as far away from the steamer as possible. He was nine hours in the small boat, standing in water to his knees. He said the sailors conducted themselves admirably."

A. A. Dick, of New York, said:

"Everybody in the first and second cabin behaved splendidly. The members of the crew also behaved magnificently. But some men in the third class, presumably passengers, were shot by some of the officers. Who these men were we do not know. There was a rush for the lifeboats.

"It was fully an hour after the boats struck that the lifeboats were launched. This was due to the fact that those aboard had not the slightest idea that the ship would sink."

George Rheims, of 417 Fifth avenue, New York, was on the Titanic with his brother-in-law, Joseph Holland Loring, of London. He said no one seemed to know for twenty minutes after the boat struck that anything had happened. Many of the passengers stood round for an hour with their life belts on, he said, and saw people getting in the boats.

When all the boats had gone, he added, he shook hands with his brother-in-law, who would not jump, and leaped over the side of the boat.

BOAT HALF UNDER WATER.

He swam for a quarter of an hour and reached a boat and climbed in. He found the boat, with eighteen occupants, half under water. The people were in water up to their knees. Seven of them, he said, died during the night.

The sufferings of the Titanic's passengers when taken off the lifeboats by the Carpathia were told by John Kuhl, of Omaha, Neb., who was a passenger on the latter vessel. Many of the women, he said, were scantily clad and all were suffering from the cold. Four died on the Carpathia as a result of the exposure.

"In spite of the suffering and the crowded condition of the boats," said Mr. Kuhl, "the utmost heroism was displayed by all of the unfortunates. When they were lifted to the deck of the Carpathia many of the women broke down completely, and there were many touching scenes. Many of the women were incoherent and several were almost insane."

Of all the heroes who went to their death when the Titanic dived to its ocean grave, none, in the opinion of Miss Hilda Slater, a passenger in the last boat to put off, deserved greater credit that the members of the vessel's orchestra.

According to Miss Slater, the orchestra played until the

last. When the vessel took its final plunge the strains of a lively air mingled gruesomely with the cries of those who realized that they were face to face with death.

Mrs. Edgar J. Meyer, of New York, said:

"It was a clear and star-lit night. When the ship struck we were in our cabin. I was afraid and made my husband promise if there was trouble he would not make me leave him. We walked around the deck a while.

"An officer came up and cried: 'All women into the lifeboats.' My husband and I discussed it—and the officer said: 'You must obey orders.' We went down into the cabin and we decided on account of our baby to part. He helped me put on warm things.

"I got into a boat, but there were no sailors aboard. An English girl and I rowed for four hours and a half. Then we were picked up at 6 o'clock in the morning."

THERE WAS TWO EXPLOSIONS.

Hugh Wellner, a son of Thomas Wellner, R. A., of London, says there were two explosions before the Titanic made her dive into the sea. Wellner believes he was the last person to leave the Titanic.

Mrs. Alexander T. Compton and her daughter, Miss Alice Compton, of New Orleans, two of the Titanic's rescued, reached New York completely prostrated over the loss of Mrs. Compton's son, Alexander, who went down with the big liner.

"When we waved good-bye to my son," said Mrs. Compton, "we did not realize the great danger, but thought we were only being sent out in the boats as a precautionary measure. When Captain Smith handed us life preservers he said cheerily: 'They will keep you warm if you do not have to use them.' Then the crew began clearing the boats and putting the women into them. My daughter and I were lifted in the boat commanded by the fifth officer. There was a moan of agony and anguish from those in our boat when the Titanic sank, and we insisted that the officer head back for the place where the Titanic had disappeared.

"We found one man with a life preserver on him struggling in the cold water, and for a moment I thought that he was my son."

That all possible means were taken to prevent the male passengers on board the Titanic from going away in lifeboats and allowing the women and children to perish is the tale told by Miss Lily Bentham, of Rochester, N. Y., a second class passenger, who said she saw shots fired at men who endeavored to get away.

Miss Bentham was in a hysterical condition when the Carpathia landed, and was unable to give a full account of what happened, but Mrs. W. J. Douton, a fellow passenger, who also comes from Rochester, and who lost her husband, told about what took place.

PACKED LIKE SARDINES IN THE BOAT.

"I had not been in bed half an hour," said Mrs. Douton, "when the steward rushed down to our cabin and told us to put on our clothes and come upon deck. We were thrown into lifeboats and packed like sardines. As soon as the men passengers tried to get to the boats they were shot at.

"I don't know who did the shooting. We rowed frantically away from the ship and were tied to four other boats. I arose and saw the ship sinking.

"The band was playing 'Nearer, My God, to Thee.' There was a baby in the boat with one of the women. The baby's hands had been cut off. I think it was still alive. The mother did not give it up. During the night, when waiting for the Carpathia, four of the crew died in the boat and were thrown overboard.

"It was bitter cold, and we had to wait until 8 o'clock in the morning before being taken off by the lifeboats of the Carpathia."

John R. Joyce, a banker of Carslbad, N. M., a passenger on the Carpathia, said: "When the Carpathia reached the scene of the wreck we saw eighteen boats and one raft on the water. The Carpathia picked them all up. Four persons on the raft were dead. They were buried at sea on our way back to New York. A survivor told me that some of the Titanic's passengers jumped for the lifeboats, missed them and were drowned. I heard nothing of Major Butt."

Mrs. Dickinson Bishop, of Detroit, declared that she was the first woman in the first boat. "We floated around a half mile or so from the scene of the disaster for four hours before we were picked up by the Carpathia," she said.

"I was in bed when the crash came. I was not much alarmed, but decided to dress and go on deck. By the time I was dressed everything seemed quiet, and I lay down in my berth again, assured that there was no danger. I rose again at the summons of a stewardess. There were very few passengers on the deck when I reached there.

DISCIPLINE WAS PERFECT.

"There was no panic and the discipline of the Titanic's crew was perfect. My husband joined me on the Carpathia, and we knelt together and thanked God for our preservation."

That the stokers of the Titanic were the first to realize the seriousness of the accident and came rushing pell mell to the upper decks for safety was the tale related by one of the survivors to John R. Joyce, a passenger aboard the Carpathia, who hails from Carlsbad, N. M.

"Soon after the crash," said Mr. Joyce, "I was told that about a dozen stokers came scrambling to the upper decks. They were whispering excitedly and edging their way cautiously toward one of the lifeboats. Suddenly and without consulting any of the officers of the ship they climbed into the lifeboat and were off before any others of the crew were the wiser."

George Biorden, of California, had this to say:

"I was beside Henry B. Harris, the theatrical manager, when he bade his wife bood-bye. Both started toward the side of the boat where a lifeboat was being lowered.

"Mr. Harris was told it was the rule for women to leave the boat first. 'Yes, I know, I will stay,' Harris said. Shortly after the lifeboats left a man jumped overboard. Other men followed. It was like sheep following a leader.

"Captain Smith was washed from the bridge into the ocean. He swam to where a baby was drowning and carried it in his arms while he swam to a lifeboat, which was manned by officers of the Titanic. He surrendered the baby to them and swam back to the steamer.

"About the time Captain Smith got back there was an explosion. The entire ship trembled. I had secured a life preserver and jumped over. I struck a piece of ice but was not injured.

"I swam about sixty yards from the steamer when there was a series of explosions. I looked back and saw the Titanic go down, bow first. Hundreds of persons were in the water at the time. When the great steamer went down they shrieked hysterically."

MRS. PAUL SCHABERT'S STORY.

Mrs. Paul Schabert, of Derby, Conn., said:

"I was in stateroom No. 28, on the port side and was asleep at the time of the collision. The shock awoke me, but there seemed no excitement and people were walking about in orderly fashion, many stateroom doors being opened simply to permit inquiries as to the cause of the shock.

"Then in the midst of all this quiet, came the startling cry of 'Ladies first,' and it was the first intimation of danger that we had. Many of us, however, went back to our staterooms to dress, and did it in rather leisurely fashion, until the order was passed that women must leave their husbands, brothers and other male relations and take to the lifeboats.

"By this time the ship's orchestra had been ordered to play as the lifeboats were sent away from the Titanic's side. I refused to leave unless my brother also was permitted to go with me.

"I stood aside and saw about a dozen boats rowed away and

several times officers of the boat tried to persuade me to go along. When the next to the last lifeboat was ready to leave, there was not another woman in sight and the word was passed that I might take Philip with me.

"The Titanic sank about 1.50 o'clock Monday morning, and it was 6 o'clock the same morning that the Carpathia put in an appearance and we were picked up. We were probably a mile from the Titanic's grave when taken aboard the Carpathia."

C. H. Romaine, Georgetown, Ky., tells his story as follows:

"I had just retired for the night when the Titanic crashed to its doom. The jar was so slight that not much attention was paid to it. Before going on deck I was told that there was not the slightest danger.

"Forty-five minutes afterwards we were told that the vessel was sinking. Men, women and children were gathered together on deck. Men stood aside to let the women and children take their places in the boats. The men who remained behind were confident that the Titanic would float for hours. I was commanded to row in one of the first boats that left the ship.

"We passed out of sight of the Titanic before she sank, but distinctly heard the explosion."

CHAPTER XIV.

NOT LIKE BOURGOGNE DISASTER.

Lone Woman Survivor Makes Comparison—Does Not Like "Law of the Sea"—Families First, It Should Be, She Says—Husband Greeted Like the Hero He Was—Privations and Horror Hasten Death.

Whenever men speak of tragedies of the sea, the story of La Bourgogne, the French Line steamship, which was sunk in collision with the British ship Cormartyshire, is always recalled. The conduct of the French sailors upon that occasion is held up as a shining example of what the behavior of a crew should not be. It even appears more reprehensible in the light of comparison with the heroism and noble sacrifices of the male passengers and crew who went down with the Titanic.

There were 584 persons drowned in the wreck, and only one woman was saved. She was saved by her husband, who seems to have been the only man in all that great company who showed his manhood in the face of that overwhelming disaster.

This hero was Adrien Lacasse, a young French teacher, of Plainfield, N. J. He died three years ago in New York, pneumonia being given as the immediate cause of death. His friends know that the horrors through which he had gone so weakened his constitution that he could not withstand the illness.

Mrs. Victoire Lacasse is living quietly in this city with her son Robert, who was born after the disaster.

Time has not erased the lines left by the tragedy in her face, and only a glance at that sad, patient face tells the story of her suffering.

Since the news of the wreck of the Titanic came she has not dared to remain alone with her thoughts, but has always had some friend near her when it was possible, and when it was not has found comfort in talking to them over the telephone.

Mrs. Lacasse has written the story of the Bourgogne. She has taken occasion in this story to protest against the "rule of the sea" which provides for "women and children first."

On the contrary, she believes that it should be "families first," and says that she would rather have gone down with her husband than have been saved without him. Mrs. Lacasse's story follows:

I have read only the headlines about the wreck of the Titanic. That is all that I had to read. The rest I know. I can see all the things that happened aboard the big funeral ship as vividly as if I had been aboard her when she collided head-on with the iceberg.

WENT DOWN OFF SABLE ISLAND.

I can even picture the ocean, the day and all the surroundings, because, as many will recall, it was just off Sable Island that La Bourgogne went to her grave on July 4, 1898, the same day that all America was rejoicing over its victory in the Spanish-American War.

I have the most heartfelt sympathy for the bereaved, unfortunate survivors of this last terrible wreck. It has always seemed to me a great mistake to compel women and children to be saved first. How much better it would be to save entire families than to have so many widows and children.

I know that I should have preferred going down with my husband to being saved without him. The women and children from the Titanic, who have just passed through this ordeal of being separated from their husbands and fathers, stepping into little boats and looking back on their loved ones for the last time, must feel just as I do.

Why should the rule of the sea supersede the marriage vow, "until death do us part."

The story of La Bourgogne has been told and retold so often, and there have been so many different versions of the wreck, that I do not believe that the public understands the truth yet. For one thing, I think too much stress has been laid upon the alleged brutality of the crew.

While it is undoubtedly true that they were untrained and undisciplined, and were not at their proper stations, I don't believe that they fought back the women and children with their knives. It was the men in the steerage who did these things.

We boarded La Bourgogne on Saturday, July 2, from New York. The steamship was bound for Havre. My husband, who, I may mention, had served ten years in the French navy, wanted to spend the summer months with his parents.

The first two days we had beautiful weather. Sunday night I could not sleep, recalling the stories of the passengers as I did. At one o'clock on Monday morning I awakened my husband, telling him that I heard a foghorn.

THERE WAS NOTHING TO FEAR.

He laughed and tried to comfort me by saying that we had a good boat and that Captain Deloncle was a good captain and there was nothing to fear. I insisted and told him that I would not to go to sleep unless he went up on deck to make certain that everything was all right.

My husband dressed himself and went up on deck. He did not come down to our cabin again until half-past four and then he threw himself, all dressed, upon the bed. I called to him again that I heard the foghorn, which had been blowing all that time. He went to the port hole to look out.

He had hardly done so when the crash came and he was thrown violently on his back. He was on his feet in a minute, and half dragged me out of bed. Then he put a life preserver on me and another on himself.

Then we both went on deck, my husband taking several other life preservers with him and leaving them on the deck for others. Some men from the steerage saw us and evidently thought that we had the best life preservers, because they came at us with their knives. I screamed and they went away.

Meanwhile some sailors and passengers were trying to launch boats on the other side of the ship. My husband tried to help them, but there was no use. The ship was listing too much.

I cannot describe much of what happened on board after this, as my husband cried to me to close my eyes if I would keep my senses. I do remember hearing the captain shouting orders, but I don't believe they were being obeyed. We ran to the stern and climbed aboard a raft.

Immediately after this the raft slipped from under us into the water and left us hanging on the rail of the steamer. Then we both fell into the water backwards. My husband swam to the raft with me. He climbed on it first and then dragged me up after him.

EVERYONE FIGHTING EVERYONE ELSE.

We were the first people on the raft, but it wasn't long before we were surrounded by the men from the boats. Everyone was fighting everyone else to get on the raft and to keep the others from getting on.

It was more horrible than the most realistic nightmare. About twenty men had managed to get on our raft, which was built to hold ten.

The buoys of the raft were already under water and the raft was nearly sinking. An old man swam to us. The men shouted to push him off if he tried to get on, but my husband wouldn't do it and pulled him on board.

He was a Mr. Achard, of Baltimore, and had lost his wife, his son and his daughter in the wreck.

We were drifting helplessly around, no one knowing what to do, when my husband said that there must be a pair of oars on the raft. He felt underneath and found a pair, so the men were able to row out of danger.

The ship first went down up to the stern, but righted up.

Then the bow arose above the water almost like a porpoise. The ship went slowly down. We saw the captain on his bridge.

We saw the water come up and up until it almost reached him. Then we heard a pistol shot. Many people thought that he had shot himself, but it was simply his last call for help. He went down with his boat.

It had been just forty minutes after the collision that La Bourgogne took her final dive. Then suddenly men, women and children, some of them still alive, were spouted out like sticks in a boiling volume. Those poor creatures, those who had the strength, would swim to the rafts and beg to be taken aboard, and, being denied, turn and disappear into the ocean.

Presently the sun broke through the heavy fog and the great curtain lifted. The surface of the ocean, which had been disturbed by great swells, became as calm as a millpond. It was a beautiful summer's day. There was nothing to indicate that a great tragedy had just been enacted on these waters.

NEARLY AN HOUR BEFORE RELIEF CAME.

Our men pulled at the oars and after some hours we came in sight of the Cromartyshire. There were two boats from La Bourgogne tied to her stern, but it was nearly an hour before they sent a boat for us. When they did I would not get into one and they towed us to the side, where I was helped aboard.

When wireless telegraphy was discovered I thought that great wrecks would be impossible, but the fate of the Titanic has shown us differently. We must rely upon lifeboats and life preservers. I think every person should learn how to put on a life preserver when he goes on board a vessel. He can not learn when the ship starts to sink. My husband said that nearly all could have been saved from La Bourgogne if they had put on life belts and kept cool.

Adrien Lacasse was greeted as a returning hero. On his trip through Canada to this city, he was besieged by people who wanted to see him and shake hands with him. He pulled down the shade of the window in his car to avoid notoriety. The crowds shook hands with an American woman, who sat behind him, believing that she was Mrs. Lacasse.

Mothers named their babies after him, and from all corners of the earth came letters of praise. He was a hero because he kept cool, and was the only man who did. The heroes of the Titanic can not be counted. They all kept their heads, so far as is known, but their only reward was the knowledge that they had not been cowards in the face of death.

Standing in a circle in the engine room of the Titanic as she went down, with hands clasping those of their comrades and all praying, the gallant thirty-three engine men of the wounded vessel met their death.

The tragic story of their bravery in the face of what they must have known was certain death was told by Thomas Hardy, chief steward of the Titanic, as he left for England, a passenger on board the Red Star Line steamship Lapland.

SCENE THAT HARDY WITNESSED.

His voice breaking with emotion, Hardy told the story of the scene that he and other stewards witnessed from the galleries overlooking the engine room.

"When the order that every man should take his post, as the vessel was sinking, was sent through the Titanic," said Hardy, "there were eleven men on duty in the hold.

"The twenty others, without the least hesitancy, came hurrying to their posts beside the engines and dynamos. They must have known as well as Captain Smith that the Titanic was going down, for when they arrived in the engine room the water was rising over the floor. There was nothing for them to do but to keep the dynamos running.

"Not one of them moved to quit their posts and not one would have dared to, even they had been willing, in the face of the stern men who had chosen to die there. Yet they could be of no use, for the Titanic was going down then.

"The water was rising about them when I looked down from a gallery. I saw the little circle of Chief Engineer Bell and sixteen of his men standing there in the water with their lips moving in prayer. I pray that I may never see the like of it again; it was real heroism."

Perhaps one of the clearest stories of the disaster was told by Albert Smith, steward of the Titanic. Smith was one of the number of six members of the crew of the sunken liner who manned boat No 11, which carried fifty women and no men other than the half dozen necessary to row it to safety.

"From the time that the first boat pushed off," he said, "until ten minutes before the Titanic sank, the band was playing. They played light music, waltzes and popular airs at first.

"The last thing they played was 'Nearer, My God, to Thee.' The voices of the men on board joining in the singing came perfectly clear over the water. It was so horrible it was unbelieveable. You kept thinking you would wake up.

"I saw First Officer Murdock, of the Titanic, shoot himself. It was Murdock who was on the bridge when the ship struck.

DID NOT THINK IT SERIOUS.

"I was in my bunk when the crash came. It was not much of a shock. Of course, I knew something had happened, but it never dawned on me there was anything serious.

"I threw on a few clothes, hurriedly, though according to drill, and went to boat No. 11, which was my place in case of emergency. I stood there until one of the officers came by and said there was no danger and that the men might return to their bunks. I was partly undressed again when the second call came.

"I went back to my post at No. 11 and we prepared to lower the small boats. We had made 565 miles during the day and the Titanic was running at the rate of twenty-three knots an hour when she struck. My boat station was on the promenade deck. I want to say right here that there was no confusion or panic while the boats were being filled.

"As a matter of fact, there was no particular rush for the boats, because it did not enter the heads of any at first that the Titanic could actually sink.

"Many believed it was safer to stay on board the big liner, even wounded as she was, than to trust themselves to the boats. When we had filled our boat we lowered. We had about fifty women with us, which crowded our small craft, so that we were only able to man our oars very slowly and clumsily. In consequence of this we were not more than a half mile from the Titanic when she sunk.

"We saw her plainly all the time, and whatever anybody else may say, believe me, her lights were gleaming until about five minutes before she went down. The night was clear and cold and calm and so bright that the many stars were reflected in the sea.

"We put off into a field of small ice. The berg we had struck was plainly visible. The Titanic struck a large, jagged, submerged portion of the berg, on the port side; as she slowly slid back and away from the mountain of ice it passed her on the starboard side and went slowly on its way.

IT WAS APPALLING.

"As I say, we rowed slowly because of our heavy cargo. The Titanic settled slowly at first. When she got going, though, she went rapidly. It was appalling. I do not think any of us really believed until her final lurch that she would actually sink.

"She started to go down bow first. She dove like that until her propeller was out of water. Everybody rushed to the stern of the boat. You could see them climbing and clinging to the higher places. Suddenly the Titanic gave a frightful lurch. Hundreds of those on the stern were flung into the air.

"They looked like a swarm of bees; little and black. Then the Titanic broke, snapped in the middle and the boilers blew up and the engines dropped out with a frightful noise. She sank practically in two pieces, broken directly in half. There was little or no swirl or intake. I do not think any of the boats were drawn down.

"Murdock stood on the promenade deck when the last boat pushed off. Captain Smith had taken charge of the bridge. Murdock put a pistol to his right temple and fired. I saw him do it. And I saw him drop.

"Now I have just one dollar and twenty-five cents left tied up in a corner of my handkerchief. I was going to take that to cable one word. It will cost me one dollar to cable "Safe," but I have a mother who is walking the streets of London waiting for that one word."

The survivors of the Titanic are still paying a tribute without precedent to the bravery of the men and women of the wrecked liner, steerage passenger, stoker and millionaire.

Major Archibald Butt, U. S. A., military aide to President Taft, met his death in a manner that fully justified the President's estimation of him as expressed in the eulogy given out at the White House, in which the President tenderly referred to his late aide as a man "gentle and considerate," and as one who was "every inch a soldier."

MAJOR BUTT AN OFFICER OF THE TITANIC.

From the moment that Captain Smith let it be known to his officers and a few of the men passengers that the Titanic was doomed, Major Butt was an officer of the Titanic.

He was here and there and everywhere, giving words of encouragement to weeping women and children, and uttering, when necessary, commands to keep weak-kneed men from giving in and rendering the awful situation even more terrible.

That this was the manner in which Major Butt met death is certain. Captain Charles E. Crain, of the Twenty-seventh United States Infantry, was a passenger on the Carpathia, and when he learned that Major Butt was among the dead, he made it his duty to get the true tale of his comrade's death.

"Naturally," said Captain Crain, "I was deeply concerned in the fate of Major Butt, for he was not only a fellow-officer of the army; but also a personal friend of many years' standing.

"I questioned those of the survivors who were in a condition to talk, and from them I learned that Butt, when the Titanic struck, took his position with the officers and from the moment that the order to man the lifeboats was given until the last one was dropped into the sea, he aided in the maintenance of discipline and the placing of the women and children in the boats.

"Butt, I was told, was as cool as the iceberg that had doomed the ship, and not once did he lose control of himself. In the presence of death he was the same gallant, courteous officer that the American people had learned to know so well as a result of his constant attendance upon President Taft.

"There was never any chance of Butt getting into any of those lifeboats. He knew his time was at hand, and he was ready to meet it as a man should, and I and all of the others who cherish his memory are glad that he faced the situation that way, which was the only possible way a man of his calibre could face it."

"This is a man's game, and I will play it to the end," was the word that Benjamin Guggenheim, the millionaire smelter magnate, sent to his wife from the ill-fated Titanic.

NO CHANCE OF ESCAPING.

The message was delivered to the stricken widow by John Johnson, the room steward, to whom it was given. Guggenheim, Johnson said, realized almost from the beginning that there was no chance of escaping. He sent for Johnson, who he knew was an expert swimmer, and for his secretary, and asked them if they should be saved to get word to Mrs. Guggenheim.

"Tell her, Johnson," the steward relates, "that I played the game straight and that no woman was left on board this ship because Benjamin Guggenheim was a coward. Tell her that my last thoughts were of her and the girls."

Guggenheim, according to Johnson, lit a cigar and sauntered up to the boat deck to help load the lifeboats. He afterward returned to the main deck and was engulfed with the ship.

"Mr. Guggenheim was one of my charges," said the steward anew. "He had his secretary with him. His name was Giglio, I believe, an Armenian, about twenty-four years old. Both died like men.

"When the crash came I awakened them and told them to get dressed. A few minutes later I went into their rooms and helped them to get ready. I put a life preserver on Mr. Guggenheim. He said it hurt him in the back. There was plenty of time and I took it off, adjusted it, and then put it on him again. It was all right this time.

"They wanted to get out on deck with only a few clothes on, but I pulled a heavy sweater over Mr. Guggenheim's lifebelt, and then they both went out.

"They stayed together and I could see what they were doing. They were going from one lifeboat to another helping the women and children. Mr. Guggenheim would shout out, 'Women first,' and he was of great assistance to the officers.

THERE WAS GREAT EXCITEMENT.

"Things weren't so bad at first, but when I saw Mr. Guggenheim about three-quarters of an hour after the crash there was great excitement. What surprised me was that both Mr. Guggenheim and his secretary were dressed in their evening clothes. They had deliberately taken off their sweaters, and as nearly as I can remember they wore no lifebelts at all.

" 'What's that for?' I asked.

" 'We've dressed up in our best,' replied Mr. Guggenheim, 'and are prepared to go down like gentlemen.' It was then he told me about the message to his wife and that is what I have come here for.

"Well, shortly after the last few boats were lowered and I was ordered by the deck officer to man an oar, I waved good-bye to Mr. Guggenheim, and that was the last I saw of him and his secretary."

Taking refuge on the bridge of the ill-fated Titanic, two little children remained by the side of Captain Smith until that portion of the big ship had been swept by water. Survivors of the crew who went down with the Titanic, but were saved by clinging to an over turned lifeboat, told of their gallant commander's effort to save the life of one of the children. He died a sailor's death, and the little girl who had intrusted her life to his care died with him.

"He held the little girl under one arm," said James McGann, a fireman, "as he jumped into the sea and endeavored to reach the nearest lifeboat with the child. I took the other child into my arms as I was swept from the bridge deck. When I plunged into the cold water I was compelled to release my hold on the child, and I am satisfied that the same thing happened to Captain Smith.

"I had gone to the bridge deck to assist in lowering a collapsible boat. The water was then coming over the bridge, and we were unable to launch the boat properly. It was overturned and was used as a life raft, some thirty or more of us, mostly firemen, clinging to it. Captain Smith looked as though he was trying to keep back the tears as he thought of the doomed ship.

EVERY MAN FOR HIMSELF.

"He turned to the men lowering the boat and shouted: 'Well, boys, it's every man for himself.' He then took one of the children standing by him on the bridge and jumped into the sea. He endeavored to reach the overturned boat, but did not succeed. That was the last I saw of Captain Smith."

Other graphic accounts of the final plunge of the Titanic were related by two Englishmen, survivors by the merest chance. One of them struggled for hours to hold himself afloat on an overturned collapsible lifeboat, to one end of which John B. Thayer, Jr., of Philadelphia, whose father perished, hung until rescued.

The men give their names as A. H. Barkworth, justice of the peace of East Riding, Yorkshire, England, and W. J. Mellors, of Christ Church Terrace, Chelsea, London. The latter, a young man, had started for this country with his savings to seek his fortune, and lost all but his life.

Mellors says Captain Smith, of the Titanic, did not commit suicide. The captain jumped from the bridge, Mellors declares, and he heard him say to his officers and crew: "You have done your duty, boys. Now every man for himself."

Mellors and Barkworth, both declare there were three distinct explosions before the Titanic broke in two, and bow section first, and stern part last, settled with her human cargo into the sea.

Her four whistles kept up a deafening blast until the explosions, declare the men. The death cries from the shrill throats of the blatant steam screechers beside the smokestacks so rent the air that conversation among the passengers was possible only when one yelled into the ear of a fellow unfortunate.

"I did not know the Thayer family well," declared Mr. Barkworth, "but I had met young Thayer, a clean-cut chap, and his father on the trip. I did not see Mr. Thayer throw his son from the ship, but the lad and I struggled in the water for several hours endeavoring to hold afloat by grabbing to the sides and end of an overturned lifeboat.

KEPT AFLOAT BY FUR OVERCOAT.

"I consider my fur overcoat helped to keep me afloat. I had a life preserver under it, under my arms, but it would not have held me up so well out of the water but for the coat. The fur of the coat seemed not to get wet through and retained a certain amount of air that added to buoyancy. I shall never part with it.

"The testimony of J. Bruce Ismay, managing director of the White Star Line, that he had not heard explosions before the Titanic settled, indicates that he must have gotten some distance from her in his lifeboat.

"There were three distinct explosions and the ship broke in the centre. The bow settled headlong first and the stern last. I was looking toward her from the raft to which young Thayer and I had clung.

"I thought I was doomed to go down with the rest. I stood on the deck, awaiting my fate, fearing to jump from the ship. Then came a grinding noise, followed by two others, and I was hurled into the deep. Great waves engulfed me, but I was not drawn toward the ship, so that I believe there was little suction. I swam about for more than one hour before I was picked up by a boat."

Confirming the statements made by J. Bruce Ismay, managing director of the White Star Line, before the Senatorial Investigating Committee in New York, William E. Carter, of Philadelphia, who was saved, together with his wife and two children, declared that J. Bruce Ismay had not acted like a coward but instead had aided in placing women and children in the boats and had gotten into the last one himself only after he had failed to find any more women after calling for several minutes.

Mr. Carter related his experience on the Titanic from the time the ship struck the mountain of ice until he left the ill-fated vessel on the last lifeboat a short time before she went to her doom.

UNJUST TO MR. ISMAY.

Mr. Carter declared that the statements which have been made by many persons regarding Mr. Ismay's conduct were an injustice to him and added that the head of the White Star Line felt extremely sad following the collision and the subsequent sinking of the world's largest steamer.

He said that while the lifeboat containing himself and Ismay was moving away from the Titanic, Ismay rowed with two seamen and himself until they sighted the Carpathia.

One of the most interesting statements made by Mr. Carter was that a short time before he left the ship he spoke to Harry E. Widener and advised him to get into one of the boats if he could. Mr. Widener replied: "I think I'll stick to the big ship, Billy, and take a chance."

Relating his experiences, Mr. Carter said: "I was in the smoking room for several hours prior to the collision with Major Archie Butt, Colonel Gracie, Harry Widener, Mr. Thayer, Clarence Moore, of Washington; William Dulles and several other men.

At exactly seventeen minutes to 12 o'clock we felt a jar and left the room to see what the trouble was outside. We were told that the ship had struck an iceberg. Many of the men were in the card room, and after learning what had happened returned to their games.

The officers informed us that the accident was not a serious one, and there was little excitement at the time. However, I went to the lower deck, where Mrs. Carter and my two children were sleeping. I awoke my wife and told her what had occurred and advised her to dress and take the children to the deck.

"I then returned to the upper deck and found that the crew were lowereing lifeboats containing women and children. When Mrs Carter and the children came up I had them placed in one of the boats, which also contained Mrs. Astor, Mrs. Widener, Mrs. Thayer and several other women.

WATER POURING INTO THE SHIP.

"I believed at the time that they would all return to the steamer in a short time, feeling certain that there was no danger. A few minutes later, however, I learned that water was pouring into the ship and that she was in a serious condition. I saw Harry Widener and walked to where he was standing on the port side of the Titanic. An order had been given before the boats were launched to put on lifebelts, and I had adjusted one around myself.

"I said to Mr. Widener, 'Come on, Harry, let us go to the starboard side and see if there is any chance to get in one of the boats.' He replied, 'I think I'll stick to the big ship, Billy, and take a chance.' I left him there and went to the starboard side of A deck.

There I saw Mr. Ismay and several officers filling the boats with women. I aided them in the work, and as the last boat was being filled we looked around for more women.

"The women that were in the boat were from the steerage with their children. I guess there were about 40 of them. Mr. Ismay and myself and several of the officers walked up and down the deck crying, 'Are there any more women here?' We called for several minutes and got no answer.

"One of the officers then declared that if we wanted to we could get into the boat if we took the place of seamen. He gave us this preference because we were among the first-class passengers.

"Mr Ismay called again and after we got no reply we got into the lifeboat. We took the oars and rowed with the two seamen. We were about a mile away from the Titanic when she went down. It seemed to me that it was less than a half hour.

All the women were clad in thin clothes while I was in my evening clothes, withtout a hat, and had on a pair of slippers. The night was a dark one despite the fact that the stars were out. I looked around just as the Titanic went down, being attracted by the explosions. Mr. Ismay did not turn and look but instead was very quiet, pulling on the oars.

THE CARPATHIA SIGHTED.

"I don't know how long we were in the boat. It seemed to be several hours before we sighted the Carpathia. One of the women saw the steamer with her lights standing out in the darkness. We then started toward her. All this time I was fearing for my family, not knowing how they fared after leaving the Titanic in the lifeboat.

"We reached the side of the Titanic before dawn and were taken aboard and given food and warmed. I do not know what became of Mr. Ismay, for I saw my wife and children and hurried toward them. I can tell you I was happy at that moment.

"On board the Carpathia we were taken care of excellently and treated fine by the officers and passengers. As we were among the first taken aboard we were given a little room. My wife and little girl slept in the bunk, while I slept on the floor. It was a terrible experience and one I never want to go through again.

"It was my intention, if I could not get into one of the boats, to leap from the hurricane deck and swim to one of the boats.

"During the trip across I did not see any lifeboat drills, but this may have been due to the fact that the members of the crew were new to the boat and the fact that the officers thought her perfectly safe. I believe that many more could have been saved if there had been more boats.

"The men seemed to think that there was no immediate danger, and I myself did not know whether to get into the boat with Mr. Ismay or not until he said, 'Come on, you might as well get aboard.'

"I desire to correct what has been said about him. He was perfectly cool and collected and aided a great deal in keeping the women from the steerage quiet. I will probably be called before the Senatorial investigating committee, and I can only say that Mr. Ismay only left the boat after he saw there were no more women on the deck.

"He called and so did I and we found none. I heard no shooting while I was on the Titanic, but do not know what happened after I left on the last boat."

"Billy" Carter, his ten-year-old son, told of his experience after he was awakened by his mother and dressed.

"Mamma woke me just after it happened," he said "and papa hurried to our rooms. While mamma and sister were dressing I got dressed as quickly as I could. She told me to be a brave boy, and we all went to the upper deck.

"All the women were on one side and the men on the other. The officers held revolvers in their hands. We were placed in one of the boats and rowed around for an awful long time until everybody began to worry and think we would not be picked up. Mamma helped to row our boat, and in the morning we sighted the big ship Carpathia and were taken on board. I felt cold, but we soon got warm and got something to eat. Then a short time later papa came on board."

CHAPTER XV.

BOY'S DESPERATE FIGHT FOR LIFE.

Plunged Into Icy Sea—Did Not See Berg—Parted From Parents —Saw Many Jump Overboard—Leaped Into Ocean—Eight Year Old Boy's Narrative—Was "Very Quiet After He Was In Boat"—Another Lad Tells How He Saw His Uncle Die.

John B. Thayer, the seventeen-year-old son of Mrs. John B. Thayer, gave a thrilling account of the sinking of the Titanic in which his father lost his life.

Mrs. Thayer was saved in one of the lifeboats, while her son was rescued after a most exciting experience on an upturned boat, upon which he clambered after struggling on the icy water for some time.

According to Thayer's account there was an explosion as the Titanic sank, this explosion forcing him a considerable distance and probably saving him from being drawn in by the suction as the steamer went down. His statement follows:

"Father was in bed and mother and myself were about to get into bed. There was no great shock. I was on my feeet at the time, and I do not think it was enough to throw anyone down.

"I put on an overcoat and rushed up on 'A' deck on the port side. I saw nothing there. I then went forward to the bow to see if I could see any signs of ice. The only ice I saw was on the well deck.

"I could not see very far ahead, having just come out of a brilliantly lighted room. I then went down to our room and my father and mother came on deck with me, to the starboard side of 'A' deck. We could not see anything there. Father thought he saw small pieces of ice floating around, but I could not see any myself. There was no big berg.

"We walked around to the port side and the ship had then a fair list to port. We stayed there looking over the side for about five minutes. The list seemed very slowly to be increasing. We then went down to our rooms on 'C' deck, all of us dressed quickly, putting on all our clothes.

"We all put on life preservers, including the maid, and over these we put our overcoats. Then we hurried up on deck and walked around, looking out at different places until the women were all ordered to collect on the port side. Father and I said good-bye to mother at the top of the stairs on 'A' deck on the port side and we went to the the starboard side.

"As at this time we had no idea the boat would sink, we walked around 'A' deck and then went to 'B' deck. Then we thought we would go back to see if mother had gotten off safely, and went to the port side of 'A' deck. We met the chief of the main dining saloon and he told us that mother had not yet taken a boat and he took us to her.

FATHER LOST SIGHT OF FOREVER.

"Father and mother went ahead and I followed. They went down to 'B' deck, and a crowd got in front of me and I was not able to catch them, and lost sight of them. As soon as I could get through the crowd I tried to find them on 'B' deck, but without success. That is the last time I saw my father.

"This was about one-half hour before she sank. I then went to the starboard side, thinking that father and mother must have gotten off in a boat. All of this time I was with a fellow named Milton C. Long, of New York, whom I had just met that evening.

"On the starboard side the boats were getting away quickly. Some boats were already off in a distance. We thought of getting into one of the boats, the last boat to go on the forward part of the starboard side, but there seemed to be such a crowd around I thought it unwise to make any attempt to get into it.

"He and I stood by the davits of one of the boats that had left. I did not notice anybody that I knew, except Mr. Lindley, whom I had also just met that evening. I lost sight of him in a few minutes. Long and I then stood by the rail just a little aft of the captain's bridge.

"The list to the port had been growing greater all the time. About this time the people began jumping from the stern.

"I thought of jumping myself, but was afraid of being stunned on hitting the water. Three times I made up my mind to jump out and slide down the davit ropes and try to make the boats that were lying off from the ship, but each time Long got hold of me and told me to wait a while.

"He then sat down and I stood up waiting to see what would happen. Even then we thought she might possibly stay afloat.

"I got a sight on a rope between the davits and a star and noticed that she was gradually sinking. About this time she straightened up on an even keel and started to go down fairly fast at an angle of about thirty degrees.

SAYS GOOD-BYE TO EACH OTHER.

"As she started to sink we left the davits and went back and stood by the rail about even with the second funnel. Long and myself said good-bye to each other and jumped up on the rail. He put his legs over and held on a minute and asked me if I was coming.

"I told him I would be with him in a minute. He did not jump clear, but slid down the side of the ship. I never saw him again.

"About five seconds after he jumped I jumped out, feet first. I was clear of the ship, bent down, and as I came up I was pushed away from the ship by some force. I came up facing the ship, and one of the funnels seemed to be lifted off and fell towards me, about 15 yards away, with a mass of sparks and steam coming out of it.

"I saw the ship in a sort of a red glare, and it seemed to me that she broke in two just in front of the third funnel. At this time I was sucked down, and as I came up I was pushed out again and twisted around by a large wave, coming up in the midst of a great deal of small wreckage.

"As I pushed it from around my head my hand touched the cork fender of an overturned lifeboat. I looked up, saw some men on the top and asked them to give me a hand. One of them, who was a stoker, helped me up. In a short time the bottom was covered with about 25 or 30 men.

"When I got on this I was facing the ship. The stern then seemed to rise in the air and stopped at about an angle of 60 degrees. It seemed to hold there for a time and then, with a hissing sound, it shot right down out of sight with people jumping from the stern.

"The stern either pivoted around towards our boat or we were sucked towards it, and as we only had one oar we could not keep away. There did not seem to be very much suction and most of us managed to stay on the bottom of our boat.

"We were then right in the midst of fairly large wreckage, with people swimming all around us. The sea was very calm and we kept the boat pretty steady, but every now and then a wave would wash over it.

SANG A HYMN AND SAID THE LORD'S PRAYER.

"The assistant wireless operator was right next to me, holding on to me and kneeling in the water. We all sang a hymn and said the Lord's prayer, and then waited for dawn to come.

"As often as we saw the other boats in a distance we would yell 'Ship ahoy!' but they could not distinguish our cries from any others so we all gave it up, thinking it useless. It was very cold and none of us were able to move around to keep warm, the water washing over her almost all the time.

"Towards dawn the wind sprang up roughing up the water and making it difficult to keep the boat balanced. The wireless man raised our hopes a great deal by telling us that the Carpathia would be up in about three hours. About three thirty or four o'clock some men on our boat on the bow sighted her mast lights.

"I could not see them as I was sitting down with a man kneeling on my leg. He finally got up and I stood up. We had the second officer, Mr. Lightholler, on board. We had an officer's whistle and whistled for the boats in the distance to come up and take us off.

"It took about an hour and a half for the boats to draw near. Two boats came up. The first took half and the other took the balance, including myself.

"We had great difficulty about this time in balancing the boat, as the men would lean too far, but were all taken aboard the already crowded boat and in about a half or three-quarters of an hour later we were picked up by the Carpathia.

"I have noticed second officer Lightholeer's statement that 'J. B. Thayer was on our overturned boat,' which would give the impression that it was father, when he really meant it was I, as he only learned my name in subsequent conversation on the Carpathia and did not know I was 'Junior.'"

Little Arthur Olsen, eight years old, said that America was a pretty good place, and that he was going to like it.

TOOK CARE OF HIM IN THE LIFEBOAT.

Arthur came to that conclusion because so many people had been good to him. First there was Fritzjof Madsen, one of the survivors, who took care of him in the lifeboat.

Then Miss Jean Campbell gave him hot coffee and sandwiches and propped him comfortably against some clothing while she busied herself with others.

Mrs. William K. Vanderbilt, Jr., next appeared with two nice, big men, put him in a taxi with Miss Campbell and sent him to a hot bath and bed at the Lisa Day Nursery, No. 458 West Twentieth street, New York. And the next morning Miss Florence Hayden taught him kindergarten songs and dances with her class.

Later Arthur's stepmother, Mrs. Esther Olson of No. 978 Hart street, Brooklyn, appeared and clasped him in her arms. Her husband, Arthur's father, Charlie Olsen, perished in the wreck.

Mrs. Olsen had never seen Arthur, because after Charlie

Oslen's first wife died in Trondhjem, Norway, leaving the little baby Arthur, he had come to America, where he married again.

A while ago Olsen crossed to see about the settlement of an estate and to bring his son home. He and the boy were in the steerage of the Titanic.

Arthur is a sturdy, quiet-faced little chap with red hair, freckles and a ready smile. He speaks only Norwegian, but Mrs. Olsen translated for him when he told his story.

"I was with papa on the boat," said the youngster timidly, "and then something was the matter. Papa said I should hurry up and go into the boat and be a good boy. We had a friend, Fritzjof Madsen, with us from our town, and he told me to go too.

"The ship was kind of shivering and everybody was running around. We kept getting quite close down to the water, and the water was quiet, like a lake.

THE LAST BOY SAW OF PAPA.

"Then I got into a boat and that was all I saw of papa. I saw a lot of people floating around drowning or trying to snatch at our boat. Then all of a sudden I saw Mr. Madsen swimming next to the boat and he was pulled in. He took good care of me.

"In our boat everybody was crying and sighing. I kept very quiet. One man got very crazy, then cried just like a little baby. Another man jumped right into the sea and he was gone.

"It was awful cold in the boat, but I was dressed warm, like we dress in Norway. I had to put on my clothes, when my papa told me to on the big ship. I couldn't talk to anybody, because I don't understand the language. Only Mr. Madsen talked to me and told me not to be afraid, and I wasn't afraid. Mr. Madsen was shivering in his wet clothes, but he got all right after the Carpathia came."

A bright-faced boy of eight walked up and down in front of Blake's Star Hotel at No. 57 Clarkson street, New York, the day after the Carpathia arrived. He was Marshall Drew of Greenport, L. I., one of the survivors of the Titanic.

"It all seems just like the bad dreams that I used to have," he confided. "I never want to go to England again. I went over there with my uncle and aunt, Mr. and Mrs. James Drew, to visit my grandpa. We had a good time in England and started back on the Titanic.

"The night of the wreck my aunt woke me and said she was going to dress me and take me out on deck. I was sleepy and didn't want to get up. I could hear funny noises all over the ship and sometimes a woman talking loud out in the corridor. My aunt didn't pay any attention to what I said but hurried me into my clothes and rushed me with her up to the deck.

"There every one was running about. Some of the men were laughing and saying there was no danger. They were taking all the women and hurrying them into the boats along with the children. We could not see what for. I thought at first that we had got home.

WAS HURRIED INTO A BOAT.

"Aunt Lulu put me into the boat and then stood back with Uncle James, and in a moment some one had hurried her into the boat, too, and we went down the side, Uncle James waving his hand at us and Aunt Lulu standing up and looking at him.

"Then the boat pulled away from the ship and there was a lot of talk and screaming. We were a long time on the water and were finally picked up by the Carpathia."

Marshall and his aunt were saved. They were met at the pier by his grandfather, Mr. Henry P. Christian, of Greenport, and with his aunt were taken to the hotel along with other survivors of the second cabin.

Miss Emily Rugg, 20 years old, of the Isle of Guernsey, England, told a graphic story of the sinking.

Miss Rugg, who was one of the second class passengers, was met in New York by her uncle, F. W. Queripel, a grocer. The young woman was on her way to visit relatives.

She was asleep when the ship struck the berg, and the jar aroused her. Looking out she saw a mass of ice. Throwing a coat about her, she went on deck and saw lifeboats being lowered.

Returning to the cabin, she dressed, and then went to an adjoining cabin and aroused two women friends.

Following this Miss Rugg ran up on deck and was taken in charge by some of the crew, who dragged her toward a lifeboat. She was lifted into the third from the last which left the ship.

She said that there seemed to be nearly seventy-five persons in the boat and that it was very much crowded. In the meantime a panic had started among those who remained on board the Titanic.

An Italian jumped from the steerage deck and fell into a lifeboat, landing upon a woman who had a baby in her arms.

Miss Rugg saw the Titanic go down and declares but for the horror of it all, it might have been termed one of the grandest sights she ever saw.

SHIP TAKES ITS FINAL PLUNGE.

The boat seemed to have broken in half, and with all the lights burning brightly, the stern arose into the air, the lights being extinguished as it did so. A moment later the ship plunged beneath the surface.

Karl H. Behr, the well known tennis player, who went to Australia in 1910 with the American team, was one of the Titanic survivors.

He was graduated from Yale in 1906 and later from Columbia, where he took a law degree. This is his statement of his experiences on the night of the disaster.

"We were a party of four, Mr. and Mrs. R. L. Beckwith, Mrs. Beckwith's daughter, Miss Helen W. Newsom, and myself. Mr. Beckwith and I had stayed up in the smoking room. We left just before it closed for the night.

"I went to my stateroom and only partly undressed when I felt a distinct jar run through the whole vessel, which quivered all over. It was distinct enough for me to be certain that we had hit something. I dressed again immediately, my first thought and purpose being to reach my party at once."

Mr. Behr told of assembling his party and added:

"I knew exactly where the lifeboats were, so Miss Newsom and I and Mr. and Mrs. Beckwith went to the top deck. We waited quietly while the first boat filled and was lowered. It appeared to me to be quite full.

"We then went to the second boat, which was quite full. Mr. Ismay was directing its launching. When Mrs. Beckwith came to the edge of the lifeboat, which was hanging over the sides, she asked Mr. Ismay before attempting to get in whether her men could go with her, and I heard him reply quietly, 'Why certainly, madam.' We then got into the boat.

"After we were in the boat we heard Mr. Ismay calling out and asking if there were any more passengers to go in the boat.

THE LAST PASSENGERS ON TOP DECK.

"There were none, and we must have waited at least three minutes or more before he ordered an officer into the boat and two or three more of the crew who were alone on deck and under perfect control. We were evidently the last passengers on the top deck, as we could see no others.

"Most fortunately for us, when we left the ship everything was handled in perfect discipline, Mr. Ismay launching our lifeboat in a most splendid fashion, with absolute coolness, making sure that all passengers were on board and that our crew was complete. What happened later we know little about.

"As far as I am concerned I saw no signs of a panic and not one person in our boat lost his head, nor do I know of a single person being left behind on the top deck."

George A. Harder, of No. 117 Eightth avenue, Brooklyn, who with his bride was saved from the Titanic, told at his home a graphic story of his experience.

"When the crash came my wife and I were in our stateroom, about to retire," said Harder. "Suddenly there came what seemed like a low, long groan at the ship's bottom. It did not sound like a collision.

"Taking my wife by the arm, I rushed to the deck. Passengers were already swarming there, asking what had happened.

"I heard an officer order a carpenter below to ascertain the damage. He never returned. That the officers already knew the ship was likely to founder was evident from the fact that one lifeboat containing among others Karl M. Behr, the Brooklyn tennis player, had been launched. Persons on our side of the boat—the starboard side—were climbing into a second boat.

"It was a bitter cold night. The stars were bright and their rays were reflected in the surrounding sea, which was as smooth as glass. Farther and farther we drifted away in the lifeboat, leaving behind us the doomed ship.

BLOWN TO SAFETY BY EXPLOSION.

"Suddenly there sounded from the Titanic the strains of 'The Star-Spangled Banner.' As I glanced back at the mighty vessel in the glare of her lights I saw Col. Archibald Gracie clinging to a brass rail near one of the forward funnels. I afterward learned the explosion of the boilers blew him out of the vortex of the sucked in water to calmer water, where he was rescued.

"Gradually the distance between the Titanic and our lifeboat increased. Her lights continued to gleam, her band to play. Two hours later, as she loomed a dark mass on the horizon, her lights suddenly went out. Then across the water, mingling with the strains of 'Nearer, My God, to Thee,' came the distressing cries of those about to die.

"Out of the jumble of foreign tongues could be distinguished the shrieks of steerage women who were grouped at the aft end of the boat. And above all the sounds, like a benediction, sounded that hymn. It was nameless anguish to us to sit in that open boat and realize our helplessness to aid those about to die. We forgot our own losses, our own sufferings. Only a few of us dared to look at the mighty ship as, bow first, she plunged beneath the surface."

Harder denied that many passengers were shot. He said

he knows three Italians were killed, but by whom he does not know.

Police Magistrate Robert C. Cornell, whose wife and her two sisters, Mrs. Edward Appleton and Mrs. John Murray Brown, of Denver, were among those rescued from the Titanic, told her story.

"Mrs. Cornell," said the Magistrate, "is of the same opinion as many others of the survivors, that many of the lifeboats left the side of the Titanic before they had nearly their capacity.

"Mrs. Cornell, with Mrs. Appleton, was assigned a place in the second boat. This boat when it was lowered contained twenty-three persons and she says there was room for at least seventeen more without overcrowding. In fact, all of the boats, my wife says, could have carried many more passengers with safety.

"There were three oars in the boat in which my wife and Mrs. Appleton were put, and no food or water or covering of any sort to keep out the cold. The crew of this boat consisted of one sailor and one petty officer.

"When the boat was lowered an Italian was seen struggling in the water and he was picked up. The three men then each took an oar and did the best they could.

"Mrs. Cornell and her sister, who have a slight knowledge of rowing, took turns at the oars, as did the other women in the boat, and after drifting about in the sea for about four hours were picked up by the Carpathia.

"Miss Edith Evans, a niece of Mrs. Cornell and her sisters were traveling with them, and she and Mrs. Brown were assigned to places in one of the boats which left after the one in which Mrs. Cornell and Mrs. Appleton were placed.

"When this boat was about to be lowered it was found that it contained one more passenger than it could carry. Then the question came as to who should leave.

"Miss Evans, a handsome girl of twenty-five, said to Mrs. Brown that she had children at home and should be the one to remain. Miss Evans left the boat saying she would take a chance of getting in a boat later.

CHAPTER XVI.

CARPATHIA TO THE RESCUE.

Cunarder's Race to Titanic's Aid—Captain Rostrom's Unvarnished but Dramatic Report—Knot in Operator's Shoelace Saved Hundreds of Lives—Was About to Retire, but Slight Delay Enabled Him to Hear Message—Icebergs Defied in Desperate Rush.

Before the Carpathia sailed once again on her sadly interrupted voyage to the Mediterranean, Captain A. H. Rostrom made public the report he has sent to the Cunard Company telling an unvarnished tale of the rescue of the Titanic survivors. The report written on the regular stationery of the Carpathia, reads:

R. M. S. Carpathia,
April 19, 1912.

General Manager Cunard Steamship Company, Ltd., Liverpool.

Sir: I beg to report that at 12.34 A. M. on the 15th inst. I was informed of urgent distress message from Titanic, with her position. I immediately ordered ship turned around and put in course for that position; we being then fifty-eight miles S. 42 E. (T) from her. Had heads of all departments called and issued what I considered the necessary orders to be in preparation for any emergency.

At 2.40 A. M., saw flare half a point on port bow, taking this for granted to be ship. Shortly after we sighted our first iceberg (I had previosuly had lookouts doubled, knowing that Titanic had struck ice, and so took every care and precaution).

We soon found ourselves in a field of bergs, large and small, and had to alter course several times to clear bergs; weather fine and clear, light airs, calm sea, beautifully clear night, though dark.

We stopped at 4 A. M., thus doing distance in three hours and a half, picking up the first boat at 4.10 A. M.; boat in charge of an officer and he reported to me that Titanic had foundered.

At 8.30 A. M. last boat picked up. All survivors aboard and all boats accounted for, viz fifteen lifeboats alongside, one lifeboat abandoned, two Berthon boats alongside (saw one bottom upward among wreckage) and according to second officer not been launched, it having got jammed, making sixteen lifeboats and four Berthon boats accounted for.

By the time we had cleared first boat it was breaking day, and we could distinguish the other boats all within an area of four miles. We also saw that we were surrounded by icebergs, large and small, and three miles to the N. W. of us a huge field of drift ice with large and small bergs in it, the ice field trending from N. W. round by W. and S. to S. E., as far as we could see either way.

PROMPT IN RESCUE WORK.

At 8 A. M. the Leyland S. S. California came up. I gave him the principal news and asked him to search and I would proceed to New York; at 8.50 proceeded full speed. While searching over vicinity of disaster and while we were getting people aboard I gave orders to get spare hands along and swing in all our boats, disconnect the falls and hoist us as many Titanic boats as possible in our davits; also, get some on fo'castle deck by derricks. We got thirteen lifeboats, six on forward deck and seven in davits.

After getting all survivors aboard and while searching I got a clergyman to offer a short prayer of thankfulness for those saved and also a short burial service for those lost

Before deciding definitely where to make for I conferred with Mr. Ismay, and though he told me to do what I thought best I informed him, taking everything into consideration. I considered New York best.

I knew we should require more provisions, clean linen, blankets and so forth, even if we went to the Azores.

As most of the passengers saved were women and children, and they were very hysterical, and not knowing what medical attention they might require, thought it best to go to New York; also thought it would be better for Mr. Ismay to get to New York or England as soon as possible and knowing that I should be out of wireless communication with anything very soon if I proceeded to the Azores.

Again, passengers were all hysterical about ice, and pointed out to Mr. Ismay the possibility of seeing ice if we went to Halifax. Then I knew from the gravity of the disaster that it would be desirable to keep in touch with land stations all we could.

THE MAJORITY OF THE WOMEN LOSE THEIR HUSBANDS.

I am pleased to say that all survivors have been very plucky. The majority of the women, first, second and third classes lost their husbands, and considering all have been wonderfully well. Tuesday our doctor reported all survivors physically well.

Our first class passengers have behaved splendidly, giving up the cabins quite voluntarily and supplying the ladies with clothes and so forth. We all turned out of our cabins to give them up to survivors, saloons, smokerooms, library and so forth also being used for sleeping accommodations. Our crew also turned out to let the crew of the Titanic take their quarters.

I am pleased to state that owing to preparations made for the comfort of the survivors none are the worse for exposure and so forth.

I beg to specially mention how willingly and cheerfully the whole of the ship's company have behaved throughout, receiving the highest praise from everybody, and I can assure you, that I am very proud to have such a ship's company under my command.

We have experienced very great difficulty in transmitting news, also names of survivors. Our wireless is very poor, and again, we have had so many interruptions from other ships, and also messages from shore (principally press, which we ignored). I gave instructions to send first all official messages, then names of passengers, then survivors' private messages, and the last press messages, as I considered the three first items most important and necessary.

We had haze early Tuesday morning for several hours; again more or less all Wednesday from 5.30 A. M. to 5 P. M. Strong south-southwesterly winds and clear weather Tuesday with moderate rough sea.

Bearing the survivors of the ill-fated Titanic and with them the first detailed news of the most terrible catastrophe of the sea, the steamship Carpathia, vessel of woe, bore up through the narrows of the harbor of New York, and tied up at the Cunard pier whence it had sailed less than a week before.

LIKE A FUNERAL SHIP.

Silently as a funeral ship the Carpathia sped. Passengers and crew lined the upper decks. From portholes peered the faces of scores.

But no cheer such as usually comes at the end of a cruise was heard. The lights shone brilliantly from every port and from the upper decks, but the big vessel moved silently, almost spectral in its appearance.

There was all the speed at the vessel's command in its approach. Moving in from the open sea, the liner turned its prow up the channel toward the spot where the reflection in the sky showed the presence of the great city.

At full speed she bore northward between the twinkling lights on shore. There were sick on board and their condition did not permit of delay.

To the dismal souls on board, the weather must have seemed peculiarly fitting.

All day the vessel had raced before a half a gale which beat fiercely against her prow as her course was changing northward.

The rain fell heavily and was blown in gusts that defied protecting shelter.

Spray flew from the waves and was thrown in showers as high as the top of the huge bulwarks.

Such good headway had the Carpathia made, that she docked fully two hours before it had been expected. All day heavy fog had hung over the lower bay and it was reported that the weather was heavy and thick outside.

Officers of the Cunard and White Star Lines, from their offices on Lower Broadway, informed the anxious hundreds who appealed for information that the boat would not be in until probably one or two o'clock in the morning. Tug skippers, shipping men and the weatherwise made wagers among themselves, over the time the Carpathia would arrive. There were many who predicted confidently that the sorrow-laden liner would not be able to come up the channel before the dawn.

CARPATHIA'S WELCOME RETURN.

At 6 o'clock in the morning the wireless flashed to the shore that the Carpathia was abreast of the Nantucket light ship. This is 187 miles from Ambrose Light, at the entrance to the Channel. The Carpathia is rated as a thirteen knot boat, and it was not believed port would be reached until at least 11 o'clock at night.

But a favorable wind beat upon the ship that was bringing home the griefstricken women who had sailed so joyously on the Titanic. The gale that beat the waves, also hurried the ship on the last leg to port. It seemed that Captain Rostrom, in command, anticipating possibly that fog might make dangerous a trip up the channel in the night, had wished to avoid the scores of tugs that he knew would be sent to meet him.

In consequence, the first word that came from Fire Island Light was vague and uncertain. They knew only that a great vessel, lighted from stem to stern, was approaching the harbor, but whether it was the Carpathia, the Mauretania or some other liner, could not be ascertained.

But when the vessel came opposite Ambrose Light, there was no longer any doubt. From Sandy Hook to Quarantine and to all the stations up the channel the word was flashed that the Carpathia was coming. From the Battery to the Bronx the news spread and sent thousands hurrying toward the great Cunard docks.

Then the tugs began snorting and steaming as they pushed the large hulk around in midstream. Slowly she yielded until headed straight toward the slip.

The slow process was accomplished while a dozen other tugs pressed their noses against the sides, and those on board tried vainly to get some connected descriptions of the great catastrophe that stunned the peoples of two continents.

Their efforts were largely futile. The passengers were too far away for their voices to carry well. The crew, acting under instructions, which, rightly or wrongly, have been credited by persons here to the desires of J. Bruce Ismay, the White Star Line chief, who escaped in one of the boats from the Titanic, refused to give any information they may have procured.

While the ship was being docked, the photographers on the tugs were active. Flash after flash shot across the water as the camera men took their pictures.

Finally the Carpathia was fast at her dock, and the gangways were lowered to let the sorrow-laden survivors ashore to receive the welcome that awaited them.

CHAPTER XVII.

REFUSED TO LEAVE HUSBAND.

"Where You Are I Shall Be," Said Mrs. Isidor Straus—He Begged Her in Vain to Enter the Waiting Lifeboat—Women Row Lifeboats—Stokers no Oarsmen—Crazed Men Rescued—Collapsible Boats Failed to Work.

The story of how Mrs. Isidor Straus, wife of the New York merchant, met death with her husband on the Titanic rather than be separated from him, was rendered complete when Miss Ellen Bird, maid to Mrs. Straus, told how the self-sacrifice of Mrs. Straus made it possible for her to escape a watery grave.

Miss Bird also supplied details of the appealing scenes between Mrs. Straus and her husband when the elderly though heroic woman brushed aside three opportunities to be saved, declaring to solicitous passengers that death in her husband's arms was more to be desired than life without him.

Miss Bird's narrative was repeated by Sylvester Byrnes, general manager of R. H. Macy & Co. He said:

"When the Titanic struck the iceberg Mr. and Mrs. Straus were walking arm in arm on the upperdeck. Although assured by the officers that there was no immediate cause for alarm, Mrs. Straus, with her husband, hurried to the stateroom of her maid, cautioning Miss Bird to dress hurriedly and as comfortably as she could, because the passengers might have to take to the lifeboats. Then Mr. and Mrs. Straus returned to the deck, where, shortly after, they were joined by Miss Bird.

"Mr. Straus stepped aside when the first boat was being filled, explaining that he could not go until all the women and children had been given places. 'Where you are, Papa, I shall be,' spoke up Mrs. Straus, rejecting all entreaties to enter the boat.

"Mr. Straus vainly attempted to persuade his wife to enter the second boat, assuring her that eventually he would find a place after all the women and children had been taken off.

"Miss Bird, who was making her first trip across, having been engaged in London by Mrs. Straus, joined other passengers in urging Mrs. Straus to enter the boat, but she clung closer to her husband and repeated previous declarations that unless Mr. Straus accompanied her she would remain behind. Mr. Straus only shook his head.

"One after another the boats were lowered. Finally that in which Mrs. John Jacob Astor was rescued was made ready. 'Here is a place for you, Mrs. Straus!' cried Mrs. Astor. Mrs. Straus only shrank closer to her husband.

"Several passengers, at least two of them being women, attempted to force Mrs. Straus into the boat, but she cried out against separation from her husband and ordered her maid, Miss Bird, to take the place beside Mrs. Astor.

" 'You go,' said Mrs. Straus to the maid. I must stay with my husband.'

CLASPED IN EACH OTHERS ARMS.

"Seeing it was useless to argue with Mrs. Straus, several men passengers lifted Miss Bird into the boat, which was lowered with all haste. As this boat and two others, comprising the last to leave the vessel, glided across the waters into the black night the last glimpse caught of Mr. and Mrs. Straus showed them standing on the deck, clasped in each other's arms, weeping."

Mr. and Mrs. C. E. Henry Stengel, of Newark, N. J., received the congratulations of friends on their rescue in their home at Broad street and Lincoln Park.

Mr. and Mrs. Stengel left the Titanic in different boats. Mr. Stengel first saw his wife safely aboard one boat, then assisted other women to leave. As a small boat, half full, was being lowered, Mr. Stengel says he asked the officer in charge if he should come aboard.

"He replied, 'Sure, come on in,' said Mr. Stengel.

"I jumped and was rolled along the bottom of the boat. The

man in charge said, 'That's the funniest drop I have seen in a long while.'

"Every one in the boat was laughing. There was no real thought of danger among the passengers, and we all expected to return to the steamer within a few hours.

"In our boat was Sir Cosmo and Lady Duff-Gordon, Miss Francatolla, A. L. Solomon, three stokers and two sailors. We tried to keep near the other boats, but, finding it hard to do so, tied three of the boats together.

An officer on one of the boats had provided himself with some blue fire, and so when the Carpathia arrived at the scene we were the second or third boat to be picked up.

"I cannot tell the time of events. For a long time after we left the Titanic her lights were all burning, and we were trying to keep as close as possible to her. She settled so slowly that I did not notice anything unusual, until suddenly all the lights of the steamer went out.

CAPTAIN KEEPS EVERY BODY IN GOOD SPIRITS.

"Then I realized that every one was in danger. I saw the captain twice after the collision with the iceberg. His face showed great anxiety, but his words were so reassuring that every one kept in good spirits."

Mrs. Stengel said:

"When the shock came I was retiring. At first I was not going to leave the stateroom, but we heard some loud talking, and Mr. Stengel urged me to go. I put on a coat and tied a veil over my head. He put on his trousers and wore a coat. As we reached the deck a loud order was given of 'Women and children into the lifeboats!' There did not appear to be any danger, but my husband insisted I should get into one of the boats. He walked away and I could see him assisting other women into boats.

"Suddenly our boat was lowered. I could still see my husband, and waved my veil, and he waved a handkerchief. Our boat was crowded with women. There were three stokers and one officer.

The stokers knew nothing about the use of oars, and we women took the oars.

"We stayed close by another boat in which three Chinamen had been found lying face down at the bottom of the boat. They could not be made to do anything. There was little alarm. The band was playing on the steamer and most every one wished to get back.

"Suddenly the lights on the steamer went out, and then we realized what had happened. At first several of the boats kept together, as there was something in the distance that appeared to be a light. We all tried to get to the light, but after an hour or so found that it was simply some light reflection from the tip of an iceberg.

"Just before leaving the steamer I saw Col. Astor. He was with his wife, and was insisting that she get into a lifeboat that was being filled. She seemed to resist, and Mr. Astor picked her up and put her in a seat. He was smiling all the time. There was some difficulty in the next boat, and Col. Astor was laughing as he helped several women into the boat.

ALL THE MEN ACTED CALMLY AND CHEERFULLY.

"All the men among the passengers, so far as I could see, acted calmly, cheerfully, masterfully. Among the stokers and others who were sent to man the lifeboats there were many cowards."

Mrs. Emily Richards, who with her mother and her two children was on the Titanic, journeying from Penzance, Cornwall, to join her husband in Akron, O., said:

"I had put the children in bed and had gone to bed myself. We had been making good time all day, the ship rushing through the sea at a tremendous rate, and the air on deck was cold and crisp. I didn't hear the collision, for I was asleep. But my mother came and shook me.

" 'There is surely danger,' said mamma. 'Something has gone wrong.'

"So we put on our slippers and outside coats and got the children into theirs and went on deck. We had on our night gowns under our coats. As we went up the stairway some one was shouting down in a calm voice: 'Everybody put on their life preservers before coming on deck!'

"We went back and put them on, assuring each other that it was nothing. When we got on deck we were told to pass through the dining room to a ladder that was placed against the side of the cabins and led to the upper deck.

"We were put through the portholes into the boats, and the boat I was in had a foot of water in it. As soon as we were in we were told to sit down on the bottom. In that position we were so low that we could not see out over the gunwale.

"Once the boat had started away some of the women stood up, and the seamen, with their hands full with the oars, simply put their feet on them and forced them back into the sitting position.

"We had not got far away by the time the ship went down, and after that there were men floating in the water all around, and seven of them were picked up by us in the hours that followed between that and daybreak.

MAD WITH EXPOSURE.

"Some of these seven were already mad with exposure, and babbled gibberish, and kept trying to get up and overturn the boat. The other men had to sit upon them to hold them down.

"Two of the men picked up were so overcome with the cold of the water that they died before we reached the Carpathia, and their dead bodies were taken aboard. One woman, who spoke a tongue none of us could understand, was picked up by the boat and believed that her children were lost.

"She was entirely mad. When her children were brought to her on the Carpathia she was wild with joy, and lay down on the children on the floor, trying to cover them with her body, like a wild beast protecting its young, and they had to take her children away from her for the time to save them from being suffocated."

Miss Caroline Bonnell, of Youngstown, O., one of the survivors, said that passengers who got into lifeboats were led to believe that a steamship was near and that the lives of all would be saved.

Miss Bonnell and her aunt, Miss Lily Bonnell, of London, England, were traveling with George D. Wick, an iron and steel manufacturer of Youngstown, his wife and daughter, Mary Natalie Wick. The women were saved. Mr. Wick went down with the ship. Like hundreds of others, he stood aside to give the women and children first chance.

"Miss Wick and I occupied a stateroom together," said Miss Bonnell. "We were awakened shortly before midnight by a sudden shock, a grinding concussion. Miss Wick arose and looked out of the stateroom window. She saw some men playfully throwing particles of ice at one another, and realized that we had struck an iceberg.

"She and I dressed, not hastily, for we were not greatly alarmed, and went on deck.

"There we found a number of passengers. Naturally they were all somewhat nervous, but there was nothing approaching a panic. The other members of our party also had come on deck, and we formed a little group by ourselves.

HAD NO IDEA THE SHIP WAS SINKING.

"We were told to put on life belts, and obeyed. Then the sailors began to launch the lifeboats. Still we were not alarmed. We had no doubt that all on board would be saved. In fact, we had no idea that the ship was sinking and believed that the resort to the lifeboats was merely a precaution.

"Mr. Wick kissed his wife good-by, and our boat, the first on that side of the ship, was lowered to the sea. There were about twenty-five women in the boat, with two sailors and a steward to row. These were the only men. The boat would have held many more.

"As the boat was being loaded the officer in charge pointed out a light that glowed dimly in the distance on the surface of the sea and directed our sailors to row to that, land their passengers and return to the Titanic for more.

"As we were rowed away we saw that the great liner was settling. We kept our boat pointed toward the light to which we were to row. As a matter of fact, there were two lights—one red and the other white. Sailormen on the Carpathia told us subsequently that the lights might have been those of a fishing boat caught in the ice and drifting with it—but who can tell?

"After a while our sailors ceased rowing, saying it was of no use to keep on. Then we women tried to row, with the double light our objective. We rowed and rowed, but did not seem to gain on the light, which, like a will-o'-the-wisp, seemed ever to evade us. Finally we gave up and sat huddled in the lifeboat.

"Some of the women complained of the cold, but the members of our own party did not suffer, being provided with plenty of wraps.

"From the distance of a mile or more we heard the explosion and saw the Titanic go down. The lights did not go out all at once. As the ship slowly settled the rows of lights, one after another, winked out, disappearing beneath the surface. Finally the ship plunged down, bow first, and the stern slipped beneath the waves.

HAD HOPED ALL ON BOARD WOULD BE SAVED.

"Even then we had hoped that all on board might be saved. It was only after we had been taken aboard the Carpathia, and somehow few of us there were compared with the great company aboard the Titanic, that we got the first glimmer of the appalling reality."

"I never dreamed that it was serious," said Alfred White, one of the two oilers from the engine room who were saved by being picked up.

"I was on the whale deck in the bow calling the watch that was to relieve me when the ice first came aboard. It was a black berg that we struck—that is, it was composed of black ice. It could not be seen at all at night.

"The striking opened seams below the water line, but did not even scratch the paint above the line. I know that because I was one of those who helped make an examination over the side with a lantern.

"I went down into the light engine room, where my station was, at 12.40 o'clock. We even made coffee, showing that there wasn't much thought of danger. An hour later I was still working around the light engines. I heard the chief engineer tell one of his subordinates that No. 6 bulkhead had given away.

"At that time things began to look bad, for the Titanic was far down by the bow. I was told to go up and see how things were going, and made my way up through the dummy funnel to the bridge deck.

"By that time all the boats had left the ship and yet every one in the engine room was at his post. I was near the captain and heard him say: 'Well, boys, I guess it's every man for himself now.'

"I slipped down some loose boat falls and dropped into the water. There was a boat not far away, which later picked me up. There were five firemen in her as a crew, forty-nine women and sixteen children. There was no officer.

"THE MILLIONAIRES BOAT."

"During the six hours we were afloat we were near what we boys later called the millionaries' boat. That lifeboat had only sixteen passengers in her. When all were put aboard the Carpathia the six men who were the crew of that millionaires' boat each got £5. Those who had worked harder saving second-class passengers didn't get a cent."

White then told of the way in which the children from the open boats were swung aboard the Carpathia in sacks, while the women were hoisted up in rope swings.

"Near the boat in which I was," White went on, "were two collapsible boats which had failed to work and were not better than rafts. They had thirty-two men clinging to them who were later picked up by the lifeboats.

"The other two collapsible boats which had about sixty persons in them deposited what women they carried in the regular lifeboats and went to the scene of the sinking.

"From the water were picked up perhaps fifty of the crew who had floated off when she sank or else who had jumped before. The second officer was picked up, too, and took command of a boat.

"Now, about the sinking itself. There was some sort of an explosion just about 2 o'clock, or shortly after I had gone overboard.

It was not until this explosion, the nature of which I do not know, that the lights went out. They had been fed by steam from oil boilers.

"The explosion caused a break in the ship just aft of the third funnel. The forward section went down bow first. The after part then seemed almost to right itself, and we thought she might keep afloat.

"But it wasn't long before the propellers shot out of the water, and down she went. A steward who stood on the poop deck had the ship go down under him. He was picked up later, and his watch was found to have stopped at 2.20 A. M., so we knew that that was the time she foundered. There was no apparent suction when she foundered.

CONTINUALLY BUMPED INTO DEAD BODIES.

While we were cruising about the place our oars continually bumped into dead bodies, wearing life belts. Some of the bodies were of the half-naked stokers. They were killed by the shock. We knew that the temperature of the water had been 28 degrees at 11 o'clock the same evening. While we were waiting for the boat to go down we heard some fifteen or twenty shots from the rail of the ship. We only surmised what they were."

There was a fireman who told of a woman in the boat which he helped man who started up "Pull for the Shore" and "Nearer My God, to Thee" after his boat had left the wreck. This kept up all night until the Carpathia arrived.

Laurence Beasley, a Cambridge University man, who was a second-cabin passenger on the Titanic, amplified his previous account while visiting the White Star offices. After describing events immediately following the collision with the iceberg and his departure in a lifeboat, Mr. Beasley is quoted as saying:

"We drifted away easily as the oars were got out, and headed directly away from the ship. Our crew seemed to be mostly cooks in white jackets, two at an oar, with a stoker at the tiller, who had been elected captain. He told us he had been at sea twenty-six years and had never yet seen such a calm night on the Atlantic.

"As we rowed away from the Titanic we looked back from time to time to watch her, and a more striking spectacle it was not possible for any one to see. In the distance she looked an enormous length, her great bulk outlined in black against the starry sky, every porthole and saloon blazing with light. It was impossible to think anything could be wrong with such a leviathan, were it not for that ominous tilt downward in the bows where the water was by now up to the lowest row of portholes.

SHIP'S END ONLY A QUESTION OF MINUTES.

"About 2 A. M., as near as I can remember, we observed her settling very rapidly, with the bows and the bridge completely under water, and concluded it was now only a question of minutes before she went, and so it proved. She slowly tilted straight on end, with the stern vertically upward, and, as she did, the light in the cabins and saloons, which had not flickered for a moment since we left, died out, came on again for a single flash, and finally went out altogether. At the same time the machinery roared down through the vessel with a rattle and a groaning that could be heard for miles, the weirdest sound, surely, that could be heard in the middle of the ocean a thousand miles away from land.

"But this was not quite the end. To our amazement, she remained in that upright position for a time which I estimate at five minutes; others in the boat say less, but it was certainly some minutes while we watched at least one hundred and fifty feet of the Titanic towering up above the level of the sea and looming black against the sky.

"Then, with a quiet, slanting dive, she disappeared beneath the waters. And there was left to us the gently heaving sea, the boat filled to standing room with men and women in every conceivable condition of dress and undress; above, the perfect sky of brilliant stars, with not a cloud in the sky, all tempered with a bitter cold that made us all long to be one of the crew who toiled away with the oars and kept themselves warm thereby—a curious, deadening, bitter cold unlike anything we had felt before.

"And then, with all these, there fell on the ear the most appalling noise that ever human ear listened to—the cries of hundreds of our fellow-beings struggling in the icy-cold water, crying for help with a cry that we knew could not be answered. We longed to return and pick up some of those swimming, but this would have meant swamping our boat and further loss of the lives of all of us. We tried to sing to keep the women from hearing the cries, and rowed hard to get away from the scene of the wreck.

"We kept a lookout for lights, and several times it was shouted that steamers' lights were seen. Presently, now down on the horizon, we saw a light that slowly resolved itself into a double light, and we watched eagerly to see if the two would separate and so prove to be only two of our boats. To our joy they moved as one, and round we swung the boat and headed for her.

"The steersman shouted: 'Now, boys, sing!' and for the first time the boat broke into song, 'Row for the Shore, Sailors,' and for the first time tears came to the eyes of us all as we realized that safety was at hand. Our rescuer showed up rapidly, and as she swung around we saw her cabins all alight, and knew she must be a large steamship. She was now motionless and we had to row to her. Just them day broke—a beautiful, quiet dawn. We were received with a welcome that was overwhelming in its warmth."

CHAPTER XVIII.

LADY DUFF-GORDON'S EXPERIENCES.

Says it was as if Giant Hand had Pushed Ship Down—Realistic Picture of Titanic's Death Plunge—The Long, Dreary Wait—Man at Wheel Tells of Crash—Told by Phone "Iceberg Ahead" Just as Ship Struck—Saw Captain on Bridge.

Almost frenzied by the memory of the disaster through which they had passed many of the survivors were unable for days even to discuss all the details of the Titanic horror.

One of the best accounts was given by Lady Duff-Gordon, wife of Sir Cosmo Duff-Gordon, who dictated it. Her tale shows that the Titanic was near icebergs before she went to bed on the night of the disaster.

Here is her story, as well as that of others:

"I was asleep. The night was perfectly clear. We had watched for some time the fields of ice. There was one just before I went below to retire. I noticed among the fields of ice a number of large bergs.

"There was one which one of the officers pointed out to me. He said that it must have been 100 feet high and seemed to be miles long. It was away off in the distance. I went to my bedroom and retired.

"I was awakened by a long grinding sort of shock. It was not a tremendous crash, but more as though some one had drawn a giant finger all along the side of the boat.

"I awakened my husband and told him that I thought we had struck something. There was no excitement that I could hear, but my husband went up on deck. He returned and told me that we had hit some ice, apparently a big berg, but that there seemed to be no danger. We went on deck.

"No one, apparently, thought there was any danger. We watched a number of women and children and some men going into the lifeboats. At last one of the officers came to me and said, 'Lady Gordon, you had better go in one of the boats.'

"I said to my husband: 'Well, we might as well take the boat, although I think it will be only a little pleasure excursion until morning.

"The boat was the twelfth or thirteenth to be launched. It was the captain's special boat. There was still no excitement. Five stokers got in and two Americans—A. L. Solomon, of New York, and L. Stengel, of Newark. Besides these there were two of the crew, Sir Cosmo, myself and a Miss Frank, an English girl.

"There were a number of other passengers, mostly men, standing near by and they joked with us because we were going out on the ocean. "The ship can't sink," said one of them. "You will get your death of cold out there in the ice."

CRUISED AMONG ICE FOR TWO HOURS.

"We were slung off and the stokers began to row us away. We cruised around among the ice for two hours. Sir Cosmo had looked at his watch when we went off. It was exactly 12.15 A. M., and I should think fifteen minutes after the boat struck. It did not seem to be very cold. There was no excitement aboard the Titanic.

"Suddenly I had seen the Titanic give a curious shiver. The night was perfectly clear. There was no fog, and I think we were a thousand feet away. Everything could be clearly seen. There were no lights on the boats except a few lanterns which had been lighted by those on board.

"Almost immediately after the boat gave this shiver we heard several pistol shots and a great screaming arose from the decks.

"Then the boat's stern lifted in the air and there was a tremendous explosion. Then the Titanic dropped back again. The awful screaming continued. Ten minutes after this there was another explosion. The whole forward part of the great liner dropped down under the waves. The stern rose a hundred feet, almost perpendicularly. The boat stood up like an enormous black finger against the sky. The screaming was agonizing. I never heard such a continued chorus of utter despair and agony.

"Then there was another great explosion and the great stern of the Titanic sank as though a great hand was pushing it gently down under the waves. As it went, the screaming of the poor souls left on board seemed to grow louder. It took the Titanic but a short time to sink after that last explosion. It went down slowly without a ripple.

"We had heard the danger of suction when one of these great liners sink. There was no such thing about the sinking of the Titanic. The amazing part of it all to me as I sat there in the boat, looking at this monster being, was that it all could be accomplished so gently.

"Then began the real agonies of the night. Up to that time no one in our boat, and I imagine no one in any of the other boats, had really thought that the Titanic was going to sink. For a moment a silence seemed to hang over everything, and then from the water about where the Titanic had been arose a bedlam of shrieks and cries. There were women and men clinging to the bits of wreckage in the icy water.

AN AWFUL CHORUS OF SHRIEKS.

"It was at least an hour before the last shrieks died out. I remember next the very last cry was that of a man who had been calling loudly: 'My God! My God!' He cried monotonously, in a dull, hopeless way. For an entire hour there had been an awful chorus of shrieks gradually dying into a hopeless moan until this last cry that I spoke of. Then all was silent. When the awful silence came we waited gloomily in the boats throughout the rest of the night.

"At last morning came. On one side of us was the ice floes and the big bergs, and on the other side we were horrified to see a school of tremendous whales. Then, as the mist lifted, we caught sight of the Carpathia looming up in the distance and headed straight for us.

"We were too numbed by the cold and horror of that awful night to cheer or even utter a sound. We just gazed at one another and remained speechless. Indeed, there seemed to be no one among us who cared much what happened.

"Those in the other boats seemed to have suffered more than we had. We, it seemed, had been miraculously lucky. In one of the boats was a woman whose clothing was frozen to her body.

"The men on the Carpathia had to chop it off before she could be taken to a warm room. Several of the stokers and sailors who had manned the boats had been frozen to death, and they lay stiff and lifeless in the bottom of the boats, while the women and children were lifted to the Carpathia.

"I did not see Captain Smith after I was put into the small boat, but others told me that when the Titanic went down Captain Smith was seen swimming in the icy water. He picked up a baby that was floating on a mass of wreckage and swam with it to one of the small boats. He lifted the baby into the boat, but the child was dead.

"The women in the boat, according to the story told me, wanted the captain to get into the boat with them, but he refused, saying: 'No, there is a big piece of wreckage over here, and I shall stick to that. We are bound to be rescued soon.' Nothing more was seen of Captain Smith.

FIFTEEN BRIDES LOSE THEIR HUSBANDS.

"There was an absolute calm and silence on the Carpathia. There were hundreds of women who had lost their husbands, and among them fifteen brides. Few of these had been married more than five or six months. No one cared to talk. The gloom was awful. I buried myself in my cabin and did not come on deck again."

From Robert Hichens, quartermaster at the wheel of the Titanic when the great vessel crashed into the iceberg, and then in command of one of the boats which left the steamship before it went down, have come details of the terrible sight at sea which could have been known to perhaps no other person.

And standing out in memory of this young Cornishman are shrieks and groans that went up from the dark hulk of the giant steamship before she sank.

Hichens, a type of young Englishman who follows the sea, had for years been on the troopship Dongolo, running to Bombay, and thought himself fortunate when he obtained his berth as quartermaster of the Titanic, the greatest and largest of all steamships. He told in their sequence the events of the night and morning of April 14 and 15.

It was in his boat that Mrs. John Jacob Astor took her place, after Col. Astor had kissed her good-by, and handed her a flask of brandy, then taking his place in the line of men, some of whom realized even then that the steamship was doomed. And his last sight as his boat was lowered was of Captain Smith, standing on the bridge, giving his orders as calmly as if he were directing her entrance into a harbor.

He told of how the officers stood with revolvers drawn, to enforce, if the emergency should arise, that rule of the sea of women first; but the emergency did not arise, and the men stood back or helped the women to their seats.

A SEAMAN'S NARRATIVE.

In the way of a seaman, he told the narrative of the night spent in the little boat, comforting as best he could the women who did not realize as he did that some of them had looked upon their loved ones for the last time.

"My watch was from 8 to 12 o'clock," said Hichens. "From 8 to 10 o'clock I was the stand-by man, and from 10 to 11 o'clock I had the wheel. When I was at the stand-by it was very dark, and, while it was not dark, there was a haze. I cannot say about the weather conditions after 10 o'clock, for I went into the wheelhouse, which is enclosed.

"The second officer was the junior watch officer from 8 to 10 o'clock, and at 8 o'clock he sent me to the carpenter with orders for him to look after the fresh water, as it was going to freeze.

"The thermometer then read 31½ degrees, but so far as could be seen there was no ice in sight. The next order was from the second officer for the deck engineer to turn the steam on in the wheelhouse, as it was getting much colder. Then the second officer, Mr. Loteheller, told me to telephone the lookout in the crow's nest.

" 'Tell them,' he said, 'to keep a sharp and strict lookout for small ice until daylight and to pass the word along to the other lookout men.'

"I took the wheel at 10 o'clock, and Mr. Murdock, the first officer, took the watch. It was 20 minutes to 12 and I was steering when there were the three gongs from the lookout, which indicated that some object was ahead.

"Almost instantly, it could not have been more than four or five seconds, when the lookout men called down on the telephone, 'Iceberg ahead!' Hardly had the words come to me when there was a crash.

"I ain't likely to forget, sir, how the crash came. There was a light grating on the port bow, then a heavy crash on the port bow, then a heavy crash on the starboard side. I could hear the engines stop, and the lever closing the watertight emergency doors.

TITANIC SETTLES IN THE WATER.

"Mr. Murdock was the senior officer of the watch, and with him on the bridge were Mr. Buxtell, the fourth officer, and Mr. Moody, the sixth officer. The Titanic listed, perhaps, five degrees, to the starboard, and then began to settle in the water. I stood attention at the wheel from the time of the crash until 20 minutes after 12, and had no chance to see what the captain did."

Mrs. Potter, Mrs. Earnshaw and Mrs. Stephenson had spoken freely of the accident to the conductor of the train which took them home.

"From the descriptions of the scene that followed the accident given to me by the three ladies," said the conductor, "it seems utterly impossible to tell adequately of the suffering and hardship brought about by the catastrophe. It all happened so suddenly, without a moment to make the least preparation.

"Most of the passengers had gone to bed. The day had been clear, and nearly everybody spent the afternoon and evening on the decks and between 10 and 10.30 o'clock the steamer chairs, smoking rooms and cafes were gradually vacated. The sea was perfectly calm, and least expected was the crash which was the sounding note of the Titanic's doom.

" 'I was in the first lifeboat that was lowered,' Mrs. Potter told me. 'The jar, which tumbled nearly everyone from his berth, was followed by a wild scramble to the decks. Women in night clothes, over which were thrown coats, ran distractedly in all directions. Men almost crazed with excitement, tore madly about trying to gather together families and relatives, and the confusion was increased by the orders shouted by the ship's officers to the crew to make ready the lifeboats.

" 'Colonel and Mrs. John Jacob Astor were standing near me when I got into the boat. They did not attempt to leave the ship, and the last time I saw them together was when they, embracing each other, watched the first boat lowered.

" 'I was placed in the boat with Mrs. Thayer. From the boat we could see 'Jack' Thayer jump from the ship. His mother saw him struggling in the water. We cried to him to swim to our boat. He tried twice to get into a lifeboat near him, and both times he was pushed away by persons in it. We saw him swim to an icecake on which were thirty men. Only ten of them were saved.

SUFFERED FROM EXPOSURE.

" 'In our boat were about twenty persons, most of them women, who suffered intensely from the exposure. Their scanty clothes were no protection from the water and ice. Mrs. Thayer rowed us for more than two hours. She battled with the waves which threatened to overturn us, and worked as valiantly as any experienced seaman could have done. To her, for the most part, we owe our lives.

" 'We did not meet with Mrs. Thayer's son until we had been on the Carpathia for twenty-four hours. He had been picked up from a raft and placed in the ship's hospital. As soon as he was able to get about he ran hurriedly through the Carpathia, and there was a happy meeting when he there saw his mother.

" 'While the accommodations on the Carpathia were not very comfortable, the passengers of the Titanic who were rescued by that vessel were well treated, and feel grateful to the officers and passengers.' "

The eight musicians who went down in the Titanic and who

were playing "Nearer My God to Thee" when all the boats had gone, were under the leadership of Bandmaster Hartley, who was transferred from the Mauretania to take up his duties on the largest steamer of the White Star Line. Under his direction were John Hume, violinist; Herbert Taylor, pianist; Fred Clark, bass viol; George Woodward, cellist, and Messrs. Brailey, Krins and Breicoux, who played when the others were off duty.

On the Celtic were John S. Carr and Louis Cross, cellist and bass viol of the orchestra on that steamship. When they got shore leave they told something about the men on the Titanic, with whom they had made many voyages. They also were acquainted with the conditions under which the men lived on the Titanic, and gave a graphic idea of the manner in which they must have responded when the call of duty came.

A MAN WITH A HIGH SENSE OF DUTY.

"Some were already in bed and some were probably smoking when the ship hit the iceberg," said John S. Carr. "The Titanic had a special lounging and smoking room, with the sleeping rooms opening off it. It was so late that they all must have been there when the first shock came. Bandmaster Hartley was a man with the highest sort of a sense of duty.

"I don't suppose he waited to be sent for, but after finding how dangerous the situation was he probably called his men together and began playing. I know that he often said that music was a bigger weapon for stopping disorder that anything on earth. He knew the value of the weapon he had, and I think he proved his point."

"The thing that hits me hardest," said Louis Cross, "is the loss of Happy Jock Hume, who was one of the violinists. Hume was the life of every ship he ever played on and was beloved by every one from cabin boys to captains on the White Star Line. He was a young Scotchman, not over 21, and came of a musical family.

"His father and his grandfather before him had been violinists and makers of musical instruments. The name is well known in Scotland because of it. His real first name was John, but the Scotch nickname stuck to him.and it was as Jock Hume that he was known to every one on the White Star Line, even when he sailed as bandmaster.

"Over in Dumfries, Scotland, I happen to know there's a sweet young girl hoping against hope. Jock was to have been married the next time that he made the trip across the ocean. He was a young man of exceptional musical ability. If he had lived, I believe he would not long have remained a member of a ship's orchestra. He studied a great deal, although he could pick up without trouble difficult composition which would have taken others long to learn.

"The odd part of it is that Jock Hume's mother had a premonition that something would happen to him on this trip. He was on the sister ship Olympic a few months ago when, on her maiden voyage, she collided with the warship Hawk. There was a rent torn in the side of the Olympic at that time and she had to be towed back to Belfast.

A MOTHER'S FATEFUL DREAM.

"Young Hume went back to his home in Dumfries to spend the time until she should be repaired, and when his mother heard of the accident she begged him not to go back to life on the sea. He told numbers of persons in Liverpool about it. Mrs. Hume had a dream of some sort, and said she was sure no good would come of it if he went back.

"Jock had his eye on going in for concert music sooner or later, but he laughed at his mother's fears and took the chance to go on the Titanic. He was known on many ships and had friends in New York. Last winter he got to know Americans who were wintering at the Constant Springs Hotel in Kingston, Jamaica.

"He had been bandmaster on the Carmania, of the Cunard Line, and had played with the orchestra of the Majestic, the California, of the Anchor Line, and the Megantic, of the White Star Company, which plies between Liverpool and Montreal.

"Hume was a light hearted, fine tempered young fellow with curly blond hair, a light complexion and a pleasant smile. He was the life of every ship he ever sailed on and was full of fun. He is mourned by every man who knew him.

"Another thing of which we are all talking is that Fred Clark, the bass viol of the Titanic, should have gone down on his first trip across the Atlantic. Clark was well known in concert in Scotland, and had never shipped before. The White Star people were particularly anxious to have good music on the first trip of the Titanic, and offered him good pay to make just one trip. As the winter concert season had closed, he finally accepted.

"He was 34 years of age and was not married, but had a widowed mother. He was a well set-up man of a little over medium height, with black hair, dark complexion, and a high forehead. Clark was jolly company and of optimistic temperament. Just before he sailed a number of persons were joking with him about his finally going to sea, and he said:

" 'Well, you know it would be just my luck to go down with the ship. I've kept away from it so long it might finish me on this trip.' Then he laughed cheerily and all his friends joined in. They all considered the Titanic as safe as a hotel.

THE BOAT'S MUSICIANS.

"Herbert Taylor, the pianist, was considered a master of his instrument. He was a man of an intellectual turn of mind, with a thin studious face. He was married, and his home was in London. About Woodward, the 'cello, I can tell you but little. His home was in Leeds. The other three men—Brailey, Krins and Breicoux—made up the trio which played in the second cabin and in the restaurant. They had been playing together for some time, but neither Carr nor myself shipped with them on any voyage.

"It's a mistake from the technical point of view to call a steamer's orchestra a band," said Carr. "The term is a survival of the days when they really had a brass band on board. On all the big steamships now the music is given by men who are thorough masters of their instruments. The Titanic orchestra was considered one of the finest which was ever boated when the ship put out from the other side, and I think the way the men finished up showed that they had about as good stuff inside as any who went down in the Atlantic."

H. E. Steffanson, of New York, another survivor who leaped into the sea and was picked up, declared that he saw the iceberg before the collision.

"It seemed to me that the berg, a mile away, I should say, was about 80 feet out of the water. The ice that showed clear of the water was not what we struck. After the collision I saw ice all over the sea. When we hit the berg we seemed to slide up on it. I could feel the boat jumping and pounding, and I realized that we were on the ice, but I thought we would weather it. I saw the captain only once after the collision. He was telling the men to get the women and children into the boats. I thought then that it was only for precaution, and it was long after the boats had left that I felt the steamer sinking.

"I waited on the upper deck until about 2 o'clock. I took a look below and saw that the Titanic was doomed. Then I jumped into the ocean and within five minutes I was picked up."

DISCIPLINE DESCRIBED AS PERFECT.

Steffanson also described the discipline upon the boat as perfect. Many women, as well as men, he said, declined to leave the Titanic, believing she was safe.

Miss Cornelia Andrews, of Hudson, N. Y., was one of the first to be put into a lifeboat.

"I saw the Titanic sink," she said. "I saw her blow up. Our little boat was a mile away when the end came, but the night was clear and the ship loomed up plainly, even at that distance. As our boat put off I saw Mr. and Mrs. Astor standing on the deck. As we pulled away they waved their hands and smiled at us. We were in the open boat about four hours before we were picked up."

E. W. Beans, a second-cabin passenger, was picked up after swimming in the icy water for twenty minutes. He, too, jumped into the sea after the boats were lowered.

"I heard a shot fired," said Beans, "just before I jumped. Afterward I was told a steerage passenger had been shot while trying to leap into a lifeboat filled with women and children."

How the wireless operator on the Carpathia, by putting in an extra ten minutes on duty, was a means of saving 745 lives was told by Dr. J. F. Kemp, the Carpathia's physician.

"Our wireless operator," said Dr. Kemp, "was about to retire Sunday night when he said, jokingly: 'I guess I'll wait just ten minutes, then turn in.'

"It was in the next ten minutes that the Titanic's call for help came. Had the wireless man not waited, there would have been no survivors."

"The iceberg that sank the Titanic looked to be as big as the Rock of Gibraltar," said Thomas Brown, one of the stewards of the Carpathia, in describing what he saw when the crew of his ship picked up the survivors from the Titanic. Brown left the Carpathia a few minutes after she was docked and he gave a vivid description of the work of the rescue.

"There were 2,341 persons aboard the Titanic, counting officers and crew," said the steward. "Seven hundred and ten persons were saved; so the list of those who drowned numbers 1,631 persons.

A CLEAR S. O. S. SIGNAL.

"I had turned in for the night when Main, our wireless operator, caught the 'S. O. S.' signal of distress. He told me it was the clearest signal of any sort he ever received. The minute he got the message he hastened to Captain Rostrom and said, 'Captain, the Titanic is sinking; she struck an iceberg.' Captain Rostrom did not believe it. 'Here it comes again, Captain,' said the operator.

"That was all the captain needed to get our crew into action; he sounded the bell for the watchman, and sent him to order all hands on deck.

"I doubt if any passengers on the Carpathia knew of the tragedy until Jones, the first mate, sounded the emergency gong after the watchman had summoned the crew.

"A few minutes after we got the signal for help we were ready for action. The 'S. O. S.' reached us shortly after midnight. We were then 56 miles away from the Titanic. Our engineer turned about and put on full speed, and we reached the Titanic about 3.30 o'clock Monday morning.

"While the Carpathia was speeding toward the doomed ship Captain Rostrom summoned the higher officers together, and said he would hold every man responsible for the work assigned to him.

"He told Main to answer the Titanic and tell Captain Smith that we were making for his ship, full steam ahead.

"Phillips, the operators of the Titanic, evidently did not get our reply, or, if he did receive it, he could not answer us in any way. Captain Rostrom told Mrs. Smith, the stewardess, to prepare for any emergency. He told me to get coffee, sandwiches and other food ready for the survivors.

"On our way to the Titanic the captain went below and told the engineer that he must get to the Titanic before she sank. I doubt if Captain Rostrom ever got as much speed out of the Carpathia as he did on the way to the Titanic.

"Long before the Carpathia got near the scene of the wreck our boats were ready to be lowered into the water.

PROMPTNESS IN HANDLING LIFEBOATS.

"Two men were stationed at each boat, and I and Thomas McKenna, seaman, were in charge of boat No. 1. We have sixteen boats on the ship, and they were hanging suspended from the davits within fifteen minutes after we received the 'S. O. S.' call for help.

"I must not forget the women who were on the Carpathia. They were the most self-sacrificing women I ever saw. Their fortitude under the distressing circumstances was so remarkable that each one ought to be rewarded for the work she did after the survivors were lifted aboard the Carpathia.

"As we got near the scene of the wreck the barometer dropped considerably. It became cold—bitter cold. We did not see the icebergs then, but Captain Rostrom said that we were nearing them. Suddenly, as the iceberg loomed up ahead of our ship, Captain Rostrom ran to the pilot house and took charge of the helm.

"The night was clear and starlight, but we did not see an iceberg until the Carpathia was within a half mile of it. Of course, we had ample time to steer clear of the floes.

"At 3.30 o'clock our vessel plunged into a sea of open ice. I believe there must have been thirty or forty icebergs in the water around the Carpathia. Captain Rostrom took his ship safely through the floe and suddenly we heard a shriek. It was faint at first and then it became louder.

" 'The women and children, get them first,' Captain Rostrom shouted to the crew on the boat deck who were awaiting the signal to cut loose lifeboats. Our searchlight was trained on the sea ahead and the boats filled with the shipwrecked passengers stood out in bold relief.

"I shall never forget the sight. There were many boats from the Titanic loaded with women and children wedged among the ice. Even before we got up to the first boat from the Titanic we could see the iceberg which sank her. It looked to be as big as the Rock of Gibraltar. It towered high in the air and it moved very slowly.

AVOIDS CRASHING INTO SHIPWRECKED PASSENGERS.

"I believe it was over 500 feet high, and we can judge by its size by recalling that seven-eighths of an iceberg is submerged. Within fifty yards of the boats in the water Captain Rostrom gave the signal to reverse the engines so our ship would not crash into the shipwrecked passengers.

" 'Ready men—go,' shouted the captain to me, and McKenna loosened the rope and our boat dropped into the water. We tugged away at the oars with all our strength. We shoved our boat alongside of boat No. 13 from the Titanic. It was filled with passengers. I believe there were about fifteen children in it.

"Poor little things! Some were benumbed with cold; others were apparently lifeless, and several moaned piteously. The women in the boat were scantily clad. Their clothing was grotesque. They had on wraps, night robes, silk shawls over their heads and men's coats around them. Many had no shoes, and all of them suffered from the cold.

"McKenna and I tied a hawser to the boat and then rowed back to the Carpathia. Harris, the bos'n's mate, and another member of the crew helped us to lift the unfortunate ones from the boat. Some had to be carried up the ladder to the boat deck of the Carpathia.

"A few could walk, but the majority were so benumbed that they could neither speak nor walk.

"As fast as others of our crew could get the Titanic's boats they were dragged toward the side of the Carpathia. We rescued twenty boatloads of passengers—710 in all. Our ship resembled a hospital on our way back to New York, for a number of the women and children were ill.

"The three physicians on the Carpathia told me as we were going up the bay that there were sixteen patients for the hospital as soon as the Carpathia docked."

From a little porthole on the side of the Carpathia a woman passenger told how the wireless call from the wrecked Titanic sent the Cunard liner racing to the rescue; how the fainting, hysterical survivors were taken from the lifeboats, and of the nerve-wrecking scenes that followed on board the rescue ship.

A NARRATIVE ON THE TUG BOAT REYNOLDS.

The narrative was told to persons on the tug boat Reynolds as the latter sped side by side with the Carpathia as she moved up the North river to her berth at the Cunard pier. The woman thrust her head through the porthole of the liner in response to megaphone calls shouted from the Reynolds.

"What's the trouble now?" she asked.

"Tell us about the wreck of the Titanic. Who are you?"

"Miss Peterson, of Passaic, N. J.," was the answer. She was a passenger on the Carpathia.

The captain of the Reynolds, William Bennett, turned his craft closer to the Carpathia, so those on the tug could get within speaking distance.

"It's almost too horrible to speak about," began Miss Peterson. "It seems like a dream. I was asleep in my berth. I had walked along the promenade deck until about 10 o'clock and had gone to my room and fallen asleep. Suddenly I heard a deep blast from the horns. I awoke startled.

"Then came another blast. The lights were turned on all over the ship. I heard the officers and crew running up and down the decks. I dressed hurriedly, thinking something was wrong on the Carpathia. I hastened to the deck. It was about 2 o'clock in the morning and the stars were shining brightly overhead.

"I met Captain Rostrom and asked what was the trouble. 'The Titanic has struck an iceberg and is sinking. Great God, men,' he shouted, turning to his officers, 'get ready to save these poor souls. There must be 2,500 on board.'

"Before the captain had told us of the wreck the Carpathia was being turned around toward the Titanic. I went on the boat deck and met many of our passengers. I heard the wireless buzz, and I knew the operator was trying to talk to the Titanic. I tried to get below to see the wireless instrument and operator, but I was told to go on deck again. The operator was clad only in his trousers and undershirt.

"Captain Rostrom said: 'Can't you get her?' 'No,' replied the operator, 'she doesn't answer.'

" 'She's going down,' said Captain Rostrom, and he ordered the engineer to put on full speed.

SPEEDED FASTER THAN USUAL.

"I don't know how fast we went, but the speed of the Carpathia at that time was greater by far than the way we had been traveling on our way across the ocean. You can imagine the excitement aboard the Carpathia. Everyone was dressed and on deck before we got to the Titanic, or rather what was left of her.

"I guess it was about 3.30 o'clock when we got near the boats of the Titanic. The Carpathia had all her boats hanging on the davits and Captain Rostrom was ready. I heard women scream as the Carpathia approached the Titanic's boats. I shrieked with them because every one was saying, 'Oh, oh, it's awful, awful.' I saw the first boat of the Titanic taken from the water.

"I saw the icebergs all around the boats. I wonder now how they kept afloat. Before the Carpathia had slackened speed much a lifeboat from our ship was in the water and the men were pushing toward the other boats.

"They tied a rope to the Titanic's boats and then moved back to the Carpathia and the first boatload of survivors were taken from the water only a few minutes after we saw it.

"There were about fifty women and children in it; some had fainted and lay motionless. Others were screaming and were hysterical. There were no men in the boat and none of the survivors were dressed properly.

"They had on night robes, furs, evening gowns, anything they could find. Some were almost frozen. A little girl, they called her Emily, was shrieking, 'Oh, mama, mama, I'm sick. Oh, mama, mama!'

"Her mother could not comfort her, because she collapsed as soon as she was lifted to the deck of the Carpathia. All the women on our boat got their heavy clothing and threw it around the survivors. Captain Rostrom told us to take them to our staterooms, and we did all we could to make them comfortable.

NEARLY ALL BOATS TAKEN FROM WATER.

"I did not go on deck again until an hour or more had passed; by that time the crew of the Carpathia had taken nearly all the boats from the water. I saw three loads of passengers taken from the boats and the mate of the Carpathia said there were about 800 saved. Captain Rostrom had tears in his eyes while he was directing the work of rescue.

"We were here, there, everywhere it seemed all at once. We got a few men aboard, but they were not taken from the lifeboats. It was women and children first.

"Our ship was a hospital ship on April 15. All the women on our boat offered to give up their staterooms and the captain ordered many of the survivors placed in our berths.

"The doctors had more than they could do to care for the sick. Women fainted one after the other. Mrs. Astor was unconscious at times. She called for her husband time and again, and so we dared not tell her that Colonel Astor was not aboard."

A steward from the Carpathia told the following tale of the rescue of the Titanic's passengers and crew to a group of his mates:

"It was between quarter after and half after 1 o'clock, ship's time, Monday morning," he said, "when all the stewards were mustered and Chief Steward Highes told us that a wireless had just come in that the Titanic had hit an iceberg and probably would need help. He urged us to turn right in and get ready for a ship's load of people. The Carpathia turned in the direction the wireless had called from.

"We got hot coffee ready and laid out blankets and made sandwiches and everything like that. It seemed as if every passenger on the boat knew about the trouble and turned out. Captain Rostrom had shut off the hot water all over the ship and turned every ounce of heat into steam, and the old boat was as excited as any of us.

"After we got things ready we went out on deck. It was a glorious morning— no swell in the sea, but bitter cold. The ship's lights were on full blaze and we were there in the middle of a sea of ice—the finest sight I ever saw.

COMPARATIVELY EMPTY BOAT WITHOUT WOMEN.

"Just as it was about half day and dark we came upon a boat. There were eighteen men in it and it was in charge of an officer. There were no women in the boat, and it was not more than one-third filled. All of the men were able to come up the Jacob's ladder on the Carpathia, which we threw over the port side. Every one of them was given some brandy or hot black coffee. After they were all on board we pulled up their boat.

"It was bright morning by now and all around the Carpathia, here and there, about a quarter mile apart, were more boats. These were fuller than the first and there were women in all of them. The women were hoisted up in bo'suns chairs, and the men who could do so climbed the Jacob's ladder. Some of the men, however, had to be hauled up, especially the firemen. There was a whole batch of firemen saved. They were nearly naked. They had jumped overboard and swam after the boats, it turned out, and they were almost frozen stiff.

"The women were dressed, and the funny thing about it is only five of them had to be taken to the hospital. Both the men's hospitals were filled—twenty-four beds in all. We got twelve boatloads,

I think, inside of a little more than an hour. Then, between quarter after and half after 8 o'clock, we got the last two boats—crowded to the guards and almost all women.

"After we got the last boatload aboard the Californian came alongside and the captains arranged that we should make straight for New York and the Californian would look around for more boats. We circled round and round, though, and we saw all kinds of wreckage. There was not a person on a stick of it and we did not get sight of another soul.

"While we were pulling in the boatloads of women we saved were quiet enough and not making any trouble at all. But when it seemed sure we would not find any more persons alive then bedlam came.

"I hope I never go through it again. The way those women took on for the folks they had lost was awful and we could not do anything to quiet them until they cried themselves out.

"There were five Chinamen in the boats and not a soul knew where they came from. No one saw them get into the boats; but there they were—wherever they came from.

"The fellows from the crew of the Titanic told us that lots more of them could have got away, only no one would believe that their ship could sink."

CHAPTER XIX.

SENATORS HEAR STARTLING STORIES.

Senators Hear Startling Stories—Probing Committee Took Prompt Action—Special Investigation to Forestall Spiriting Away of Witnesses—Prominent Persons on Stand—Carpathia's Captain and Head of White Star Line Chief Witnesses—Inventor of Wireless Telegraphy Also Testifies.

Managing Director of the White Star Line, J. Bruce Ismay; Captain Rostrom, of the Carpathia; Guglielmo Marconi, inventor of wireless; the second officer of the Titanic and others testified before the Senate committee which was investigating the disaster that caused the loss of more than 1600 lives when the Titanic hit an iceberg.

Mr. Ismay was visibly nervous when he took the stand to testify in the Waldorf-Astoria, where the hearings were being held.

Several times he avoided direct answers by saying: "I know nothing about it." Little if any light was thrown on the sea tragedy by his testimony.

That the Titanic's rate of speed was approximately 26½ land miles was brought out from his lips.

He was not sure in just what boat he left the Titanic, nor was he sure how long he remained on the liner after she struck.

He added, however, that before he entered a lifeboat he had been told that there were no more women on the deck, and he denied that there had been any censorship of messages from the Carpathia.

The seriousness of the inquiry by the Senate investigating committee in the Titanic disaster was disclosed when Senator Smith, of Michigan, the chairman, at first flatly refused to let any of the officers or the 200 odd members of the crew of the sunken steamship get beyond the jurisdiction of the United States Government. The men were all to have sailed on the steamer Lapland.

Later it was settled that the greater part of the crew would be permitted to sail on this steamer, but that the twelve men and four officers among the survivors now under subpena, together with Mr. Ismay, would not be allowed to depart.

Captain Rostrom told a simple, apparently straightforward story, thrilling from its very simplicity and the sailorman quality of the narrative.

He answered questions direct and gave the first authoritative tale of the hearing of the appeal for help, the rush to aid the sinking liner and the sighting of the ship's boats and picking them up, the preparations made, while the Carpathia was being urged along under every ounce of steam its boilers could make, to provide for the reception of the survivors on board.

CAPTAIN ROSTROM'S DENIAL.

Captain Rostrom denied emphatically there was any intention on his part to disregard the inquiry made by the President of the United States or that any censorship was exercised over wireless messages by any person other than himself.

Charles W. Lightholder, second officer of the Titanic and senior surviving officer of the ship, told of what preceded the sinking of the Titanic, what happened while women were taken away in boats as brave men stood by, and what happened when the Titanic took her last dip. It was a story of heroism, told quietly and calmly.

Lightholder said that tests of the water had been made for ice. It was part of the routine. Water was taken from the side of the ship in canvas buckets and the temperature learned by putting a thermometer in it.

As the second officer of the ship, Lightholder said he had been in charge of it on Sunday when the Titanic struck, from 6 o'clock in the evening until 10, or inside of two hours before the collision.

He would not admit that the tests were being made solely for the purpose of searching for information as to icebergs.

It was part of the routine of the ship. The tests were made for routing purposes and other purposes. The water was not much above freezing.

The witness said that he did not know what the tests of the water that day showed. No reports had been made to him. He did not think it necessary that night, when he was on the bridge in charge, to make tests for the purpose of finding out if the Titanic was in the vicinity of icebergs.

ICEBERGS REPORTED.

"Did you know that the Amerika had reported to the Titanic the location of icebergs in that neighborhood?" asked Senator Smith.

"I heard of the message, but I didn't know that it was the Amerika."

"Did you get from Captain Smith that night any information about the icebergs?"

"Not that night,' said Lightholder. "I think it was in the afternoon, about 1 o'clock. I was on the bridge, having relieved First Officer Murdock, who had gone to lunch."

Captain Smith, he said, told him of the wireless message from the Amerika about the icebergs. Lightholder said he couldn't recall just what position the ship was in then, but he could work it out on the chart.

When Chief Officer Murdock returned to the bridge, Lightholder said, he told him exactly the information Captain Smith had communicated to him.

"What did Murdock say?" asked Senator Smith. "All right," replied Lightholder.

"So the chief officer of the ship was fully advised by you that you were in proximity to icebergs?" he was asked. "Yes, sir."

"How fast was the boat going at that time?" "Between 21½ and 22 knots."

"Was that her maximum speed?" "So far as we knew," said Lightholder, "she could go faster than that if pushed. We understood that that was not her maximum speed."

"During your voyage, did you know you were in the vicinity of ice?" Senator Smith asked. "I knew some had been reported."

He said the ship was not in proximity to icebergs Saturday or Sunday, although he knew the ship would be near ice on Sunday night. The witness said he knew nothing of the Amerika and the Titanic talking by wireless about icebergs.

Senator Smith asked if he sought to send any wireless messages from the Titanic after she struck. He said not.

MR. ISMAY'S REMARKS.

Turning to the subject of lifeboats, Mr. Ismay said he heard the captain give the order to lower the boats. "I then left the bridge." Three boats, he said, he saw lowered and filled. In his own boat were four members of the crew and forty-five passengers.

"Was there any jostling or attempt by men to get into the boats?" asked Senator Smith. "I saw none."

"How were the women selected?" "We picked the women and children as they stood nearest the rail."

Representative Hughes handed Senator Smith a note, and then the chairman told Mr. Ismay that it was reported that the second lifeboat left without its full complement of oarsmen, and from 11.30 until 7.30 women were forced to row the boat. "I know nothing about it."

Representative Hughes' daughter was in this boat and was assigned to watch the cork in the boat and, if it came out, to use her finger as a stopper.

Then Senator Smith asked the circumstances under which he left the boat. "The boat was being filled," began Mr. Ismay. "The officers called out to know if there were any more women to go. There were none. No passengers were on the deck. So as the boat was being lowered I got into it."

"The ship was sinking?" asked Senator Smith. "The boat was sinking," almost whispered Mr. Ismay.

"Was there any attempt to lower the boats of the Carpathia to take on passengers after you went aboard her?" asked Senator Smith. "There were no passengers there to take on," said Mr. Ismay.

He said he saw no liferafts in the sea.

"How many lifeboats were there on the Titanic?" "Twenty altogether, I think," said Mr. Ismay, "sixteen collapsible and four wooden boats." Whether the boats were taken on board the Carpathia or not he did not know.

"It has been suggested," Senator Smith continued, "that two of the lifeboats sank as soon as lowered. Do you know anything about that?" "I do not. I never heard of it, and I think all the lifeboats were accounted for."

NO INDICATIONS OF TITANIC'S BREAKING.

"When you last saw her were there indications that the Titanic had broken in two?" "No, there was no such indication."

"How long after you left her was it that you looked back for the last time?" "It may have been ten minutes or a half hour. I am not sure. Impossible for me to tell."

"Was there confusion apparent on the Titanic when you looked back?" "I didn't see any. All I saw was the green light the last time I looked."

"After you left Captain Smith on the bridge did you see him again?" "I did not."

"Did you have any message from him?" "None."

"How many wireless operators were there on the Titanic?" "I presume there were two. One is always on watch."

"Did they survive?" "I have been told one did, but I do not know whether it is true or not."

Mr. Ismay was asked what he had on when he got into the

lifeboat. "A pair of slippers, a pair of pajamas, a suit of clothes and an overcoat."

Captain Rostrom, of the Carpathia, followed Mr. Ismay. He told Mr. Smith that he had been captain of the Carpathia since last January, but that he had been a seaman twenty-seven years.

The captain told in detail of the arrangements made to prepare the lifeboats and the ship for the receipt of the survivors.

Arriving at the zone of the accident, Captain Rostrom testified, he saw an iceberg straight ahead of him and, stopping at 4 A. M., ten minutes later he picked up the first lifeboat. The officer sang out he had only one seaman on board and was having difficulty in manning his boat.

ICEBERGS ON EVERY SIDE.

"By the time I got the boat aboard day was breaking," said the captain. "In a radius of four miles I saw all the other lifeboats. On all sides of us were icebergs; some twenty, some were 150 to 200 feet high, and numerous small icebergs or 'growlers.' Wreckage was strewn about us. At 8.30 all the Titanic's survivors were aboard."

Then, with tears filling his eyes, Captain Rostrom said he called the purser. "I told him," said Captain Rostrom, "I wanted to hold a service of prayer—thanksgiving for the living and a funeral service for the dead.

"I went to Mr. Ismay. He told me to take full charge. An Episcopal clergyman was found among the passengers, and he conducted the services."

As the prayers were being said, Captain Rostrom testified, he was on the bridge searching for survivors. He told of talking with the California, which had arrived. As he searched the sea, one body with a life preserver on floated by.

The man was dead, probably a member of the crew, the captain said. The body was not picked up, the officer explaining, "because the survivors of the Titanic were in no condition then to see a body brought aboard."

"But I must say," declared Captain Rostrom with positiveness, "every one of the survivors behaved magnificently. They sat in the boats until the order came for them to mount the ladder in turn, and then came up."

Asked about the lifeboats, Captain Rostrom said he found one among the wreckage in the sea. Several of the lifeboats brought in on the Carpathia to New York, he said, were lowered last night and hauled away by tenders, he knew not where.

Captain Rostrom said that the Carpathia had twenty lifeboats of her own, in accordance with the British regulations.

"Wouldn't that indicate that the regulations are out of date, your ship being much smaller than the Titanic, which also carried twenty lifeboats?" Senator Smith asked. "No. The Titanic was supposed to be a lifeboat herself."

Captain Rostrom then explained that it was for the good of the shipwrecked people that he brought his ship to New York instead of going to Halifax.

WOMEN AT THE OARS.

At Representative Hughes' suggestion, Captain Rostrom was asked further about the lifeboat with one officer and one seaman in it. This was the boat from which the Representative's daughter was rescued. At least two women were rowing in this boat. In another lifeboat he saw women at the oars, but how many he could not tell.

In discussing the strength of the Carpathia's wireless, Captain Rostrom said the Carpathia was only 58 miles from the Titanic when the call for help came. "Our wireless operator was not on duty," said Captain Rostrom, "but as he was undressing he had his apparatus to his ear. Ten minutes later he would have been in bed and we never would have heard."

Mr. Marconi took the stand as soon as the hearing was resumed for the afternoon. He said he was the chairman of the British Marconi Company. Under instructions of the company, he said operators must take their orders from the captain of the ship on which they are employed.

"Do the regulations prescribe whether one or two operators should be aboard the ocean vessels?" "Yes, on ships like the Titanic and Olympic two are carried," said Mr. Marconi. "The Carpathia, a smaller boat, carries one. The Carpathia's wireless apparatus is a short-distance equipment. The maximum efficiency of the Carpathia's wireless, I should say, was 200 miles. The wireless equipment on the Titanic was available 500 miles during the daytime and 1000 miles at night."

"Do you consider that the Titanic was equipped with the latest improved wireless apparatus?" "Yes, I should say that it had the very best."

Charles Herbert Lightholder, second officer of the Titanic, followed Mr. Marconi on the stand. Mr. Lightholder said he understood the maximum speed of the Titanic, as shown by its trial tests, to have been 22½ to 23 knots. Senator Smith asked if the rule requiring life-saving apparatus to be in each room for each passenger was complied with.

LIFE-SAVING EQUIPMENT INSPECTED.

"Everything was complete," said Lightholder. Sixteen lifeboats, of which four were collapsible, were on the Titanic, he added. During the tests, he said, Captain Clark, of the British Board of Trade, was aboard the Titanic to inspect its life-saving equipment.

"How thorough are these captains of the Board of Trade in inspecting ships?" asked Senator Smith. "Captain Clark is so thorough that we called him a nuisance."

Lightholder said he was in the sea with a lifebelt on one hour and a half.

"What time did you leave the ship?" "I didn't leave it."

"Did it leave you?" "Yes, sir."

"Where were you when the Titanic sank?" "In the officers' quarters."

"Were all the lifeboats gone then?" "All but one. I was about fifteen feet from it. It was hanging in the tackle, and they were trying to get it over the bulwarks the last time I saw it.

The first officer, Mr. Murdock, who lost his life, was managing the tackle."

The last boat, a flat collapsible, to put off was the one on top the officers' quarters, Lightholder said. Men jumped upon it on deck and waited for the water to float it off. Once at sea, it upset. The forward funnel fell into the water, just missing the raft, and overturning it. The funnel probably killed persons in the water.

"This was the boat I eventually got on," declared Lightholder. "No one was on it when I reached it. Later about thirty men clambered out of the water on to it. All had on life preservers."

DIED AND SLIPPED OFF INTO THE WATER.

"Did any passengers get on?" asked Senator Smith. "J. B. Thayer, the second Marconi operator and Colonel Gracie I recall," said the witness. "All the rest were firemen taken out of the water. Two of these died that night and slipped off into the water. I think the senior Marconi operator did that."

"Did you see any attempt to get women to go who would not?" "Yes."

"Why would they not go?" "I hadn't time to learn."

"Did any ask for their family to go?" "Yes, one or two."

"Did any families go?" "No."

In the first boat to put off, Lightholder said, he put twenty to twenty-five. Two seamen were placed in it. The officer said he could spare no more and that the fact that women rowed did not show the boat was not fully equipped.

At that time he did not believe the danger was great. Two seamen placed in the boat he said were selected by him, but he could not recall who they were.

"The third boat?" "By the time I came to the third boat—all these on the portside—I began to realize that the situation was serious and I began to take chances."

"How long did all the work of loading and lowering a lifeboat take?" "It was difficult to say, but I think about fifteen or twenty minutes."

"How many passengers did the third boat contain?" "I filled it up as full as I dared, sir, then lowered it; about thirty-five, I think. The women and children couldn't have stood quieter if they'd been in church."

In loading the fourth lifeboat Lightholder said he was running short of seamen. "I put two seamen in and one jumped out. That was the first boat I had to put a man passenger in. He was standing nearby and said he would go if I needed him.

"I said, 'Are you a sailor?' and he replied that he was a yachtsman. Then I told him that if he was sailor enough to get out over the bulwarks to the lifeboat to go ahead. He did and proved himself afterward to be a very brave man."

"Who was he—did you know him?" "I didn't know him then, but afterward I looked him up. He was Major Peuchen, of Toronto."

"Had you ever seen him before?" "Never."

DIFFICULTY IN FINDING WOMEN.

Of the fifth boat Lightholder had no particular recollection. "The last boat I put out, my sixth boat," he said, "we had difficulty finding women. I called for women and none were on deck. The men began to get in—and then women appeared. As rapidly as they did the men passengers got out of the boats again.

"The boat's deck was only ten feet from the water when I lowered the sixth boat. When we lowered the first the distance to the water was 70 feet." All told, Lightholder testified, 210 members of the crew were saved.

Lightholder declared he stood on top the officers' quarters and as the ship dived he faced forward and dived also. "I was sucked against a blower and held there," testified the officer.

"Head above water?" "No, sir. A terrific gust came up the blower—the boilers must have exploded—and I was blown clear."

"How far were you blown?" "Barely clear. I was sucked down again; this time on the 'fidley' grating."

"Did anyone else have a similar experience?" "Yes, Colonel Gracie."

"How did you get loose?" "I don't know, maybe another explosion. All I know is we came up by a boat."

"Were there any watertight compartments on that ship?" the Senator asked. "Certainly, forty or fifty."

Thomas Cottam, 21 years old, of Liverpool, the Marconi operator on the Carpathia, was the first witness at the evening session.

He denied himself some glory by saying he had no stated hours for labor on the Carpathia. Previous witnesses had testified he was not "on duty" when he received the Titanic's signal for help.

UNCERTAIN AS TO THE KIND OF WORK.

He was decidedly uncertain whether he was required to work at night, finally saying it depended on whether he had commercial or ship's business to get off.

"What were you doing last Sunday evening about 10 o'clock?" asked Senator Smith. "Receiving news from Cape Cod," said Cottam. He said he had also been "sending a lot of messages for the Titanic."

"Had you closed your station for the night?" "No."

"What do you do when you close your station?" "Switch the storage battery out," said Cottam.

"Does that prevent receiving or sending messages?" the Senator continued. "No."

"Does it lessen the likelihood of your getting a signal of any kind?" "No, not in the least," Cottam replied.

"You say the Carpathia wireless instruments would send a message about 250 miles with accuracy?" "Yes, sir."

"Was there any thunder or lightning Sunday night?" "No, it was clear."

"Well, how did you happen to catch the Titanic message of

distress?" "I was looking out for a confirmation by the steamer Parisian of a previous message from the Parisian—a message that came some time in the afternoon."

"Did you hear the captain of the Carpathia testify here today?" "No."

"He said you were about to retire and caught this Titanic distress message rather providentially?" "Yes, sir."

"How far had you got along in your arrangement to retire? Had you taken off your clothes?" "Yes, my coat."

"Did you have any instruments then?" "Yes, the telephones were on my head. I was waiting for the Parisian's answer. I had just called it."

"How long would you have waited?" "Several minutes."

"Would you have retired pretty soon, you think?" "Yes."

"Well, when you got the distress message from the Titanic Sunday night, how did you get it?" "I called the Titanic myself, sir."

SENDING MESSAGES TO THE TITANIC.

"Who told you to call the Titanic?" "No one, sir. I did it of my own free will. I asked the Titanic operator if he was aware that Cape Cod had been sending messages for the Titanic."

"What was the answer?" "'Come at once' was the message, sir," said Cottam.

"Was that all of it?" "No, the operator said, I think, 'come at once—this is a distress message. C. Q. D.'" Cottam testified.

When word of the Titanic's distress was received, Operator Cottam said he immediately sent them the position of the Carpathia and added that they would hurry to the rescue.

"Get any reply to that?" asked Senator Smith. "Yes, sir; immediately. They acknowledged receipt of it."

The witness said the next communication with the Titanic was four minutes later, when he confirmed the position of both vessels. At this juncture the Frankfurt, of the North German Lloyd Line, broke in on the communication, having heard the

Titanic's call for help. Later the steamship Olympic also replied.

"What did you do then?" asked Senator Smith. "I called the attention of the Titanic to the Olympic's efforts to raise it," answered the witness. "The Titanic replied it could not hear because of the rush of air and the noise made by the escaping steam."

Immediately after telling the Titanic of the Olympic's attempt to get in communication with her, the former, the witness said, sought the Olympic's aid, reporting that it was "head down" and giving its position. The Baltic broke in at this time, but its efforts to reach the Titanic were without avail.

"I was in communication with the Titanic at regular intervals until the final message," said Cottam. "This was 'come quick; our engine room is filling up to the boilers.' "

"What was your condition?" asked Senator Smith. "I was desperately tired. I was worked out," answered Cottom, who was then excused.

The committee adjourned at 10.20 o'clock to meet at 10 o'clock the next morning.

CHAPTER XX.

SURVIVING OPERATOR'S EXPERIENCES.

Surviving Operator's Experiences—Tells Senator How He Escaped—Tale of Suffering and Death—Managing Director's Flight Balked—Long Hours and Low Wages for Wireless Men—Refused Help from Frankfurt—Called Its Operator a Fool—Laxity of Wireless—Denies Sending "Saved" Message—Gave Warning of Ice.

With J. Bruce Ismay, managing director, and P. A. S. Franklin, general manager of the White Star Line, Harold Thomas Cottam, wireless operator on the Carpathia; Harold Bride, surviving operator of the Titanic, the five surviving officers from the ill-fated ship and thirty of her seamen in the custody of the sergeant-at-arms of the United States Senate, Senator Smith, of Michigan, and Francis G. Newlands, of Nevada, brought their investigation of the greatest sea horror of modern times to a close so far as New York was concerned.

When the men of the Titanic, British seamen, had been heard under oath by the committee they were allowed to return to their homes, where they were subject to the call of their own government.

"We must hear the Englishmen first," said Chairman Smith, a few minutes before he and Senator Newlands left shortly after midnight for Washington, "because they need to get back home as soon as possible. We will be able to get the Americans whenever we want them."

It had been suggested to Chairman Smith that the British Government might offer objections to the keeping of British seamen in this country under the circumstances.

"I am proceeding," said Mr. Smith, "just as if there was not the slightest possibility of such a protest. Should one come we will deal with it at that time."

The committee had in mind the drafting of important legislation as the result of its hearing. Regulation of the use of the air by wireless operators so as to prevent interference in times of wreck at sea is one law that seemed almost sure to be enacted. Another was legislation requiring not only American, but all foreign vessels using American ports to be equipped with enough lifeboats to take off every passenger and every member of the ship's crew if need be. Patrol of the steamship lanes for icebergs was another.

It seemed likewise not at all unlikely that the committee would recommend and Congress enact a law requiring ships, at least those under American registry, to carry two operators so that one may be on duty while the other sleeps. The President seemed likely to be asked by a joint resolution of Congress to open negotiations with foreign powers to establish a new and much more southerly steamship lane across the Atlantic by international agreement.

SENATE TO PROBE FALSE MESSAGE.

It developed that the Senate Committee intended to make one of the most important features of its probing work and examination in the false messages that were given out by the White Star Line office in New York on Monday when it was said that the Titanic had struck an iceberg, but that she was in tow of the Virginian, which was taking her to Halifax and that all on board were safe.

Incident to the sudden close of the hearing was the story of Harold S. Bride, the second and only surviving wireless operator of the Titanic. His tale was one of suffering and of death.

He told of the final plunge of the vessel to its ocean burial. It's captain's end also was revealed. He leaped from the bridge when the waters were closing over his ship.

In connection with the transfer of the hearing to Washington it was intimated that the power of the Senate on federal territory would be undisputed in getting at the real facts and no question of State rights could arise to interfere.

Throughout the hearing, also, officials of the White Star Line had portrayed the dangers of sailors' boarding houses in New York as a reason why those detained by the committee should be allowed to sail on the Lapland, which left today.

Throughout the hearing Wireless Operator Bride, crippled as a result of his experiences and seated in an invalid's chair, told his story of the last moments of the Titanic.

His narrative, drawn from him piecemeal by Senator Smith, of Michigan, chairman of the committee held enthralled the committee and the audience.

When his ordeal was ended he was almost on the verge of collapse.

THE LAXITY OF THE WIRELESS

Another phase of the laxity of the wireless, so far as man is concerned, was developed by the chairman. He drew from the witness an acknowledgment that on Sunday evening Bride was sitting, the telephonic apparatus strapped to his ears, adjusting his accounts, while the steamship Californian, seeking to warn the Titanic that icebergs were invading the lanes of ocean travel, called incessantly.

Bride said he heard the call but did not answer because he was "busy."

It was not until a half hour later that the Californian, striving to reach the steamship Baltic, reached also the Titanic, whereupon the warning that three huge icebergs had been sighted, was noted by Bride and verbally communicated to the liner's captain.

"At this time, however, neither of us worried a bit. When we heard the confusion on deck I went out to investigate and when I returned I found Mr. Phillips sending out a "C. Q. D." call, giving our position.

"We raised the Frankfurt first and then the Carpathia and the Baltic. As I have said, we did not try for the Frankfurt for any length of time, but concentrated our messages on the Carpathia, which had answered that she was rushing to our aid."

"From time to time either Mr. Phillips or I would go on deck to observe the situation. The last time I went on deck I found the passengers running around in confusion and there was almost a panic.

"They were seeking lifebelts. All of the large lifeboats were gone, but there was one liferaft remaining. It had been lashed on the top of the quarters on the boat deck. A number of men were striving to launch it.

"I went back to the wireless cabin then. Mr. Phillips was striving to send out a final 'C. Q. D.' call. The power was so low that we could not tell exactly whether it was being carried or not, for we were in a closed cabin and we could not hear the crackle of the wireless at the mast.

BOTH CARED FOR A WOMAN

Phillips kept on sending, however, while I buckled on his lifebelt and put on my own. Then we both cared for a woman who had fainted and who had been brought into our cabin.

"Then, about ten minutes before the ship sank, Captain Smith gave word for every one to look to his own safety. I sprang to aid the men struggling to launch the liferaft and we had succeeded in getting it to the edge of the boat when a giant wave carried it away.

"I went with it and found myself underneath. Struggling through an eternity, I finally emerged and was swimming one hundred and fifty feet from the Titanic when she went down. I felt no suction as the vessel plunged.

"I did not see Mr. Ismay at all. Captain Smith stuck to the bridge and, turning, I saw him jump just as the vessel glided into the depthts. He had not donned a life belt, so far as I could see, and went down with the ship."

The witness showed so plainly the mental and physical strain under which he was laboring that both Senators Newlands and Reed urged Senator Smith to excuse him. After a few more interrogations Senator Smith did so.

"I regret extremely having had to subject you to such an ordeal," he said, addressing Bride, "because of your condition. I would have avoided it, if possible, but the committee thanks you most heartily for the forbearance you have shown and the frankness of your testimony."

Senator Smith then called what he evidently expected to be one of the most important witnesses, Harold S. Bride, the sole surviving wireless operator of the Titanic.

Crippled as a result of his experiences, he was wheeled in an invalid's chair to the table where the committee sat.

"Contrary to the usual procedure," said Senator Smith, rising in his place, "I must place you under oath. Raise your right hand."

SENATE REPEATS THE OATH.

The witness, hand uplifted, listened while the Senator repeated the oath. Then he bowed in assent. Bride said he was a native of London, was 22 years old and had learned his profession in a British school of telegraphy.

"What practical experience have you had?" asked Senator Smith.

"I have crossed to the States three times and to Brazil twice," said Bride.

Bride remembered receiving and sending messages relative to the speed of the Titanic on its trial tests. After leaving Southampton on the Titanic's fatal trip he could not remember receiving or sending any messages for Ismay. Senator Smith asked particularly about messages on Sunday.

"I don't remember, sir," said Bride. "There was so much business Sunday."

He was asked if Captain Smith received or sent any messages Sunday.

"No, sir," was the reply.

"How do you know he did not?"

"Because I see the messages Mr. Philips takes when they are made up."

"Were those for Sunday made up?"

"No, they never were."

After testifying he made no permanent record of the iceberg warnings, Bride insisted he gave the memorandum of the warning to the officer on the watch. The name of the officer he could not tell.

"I know the officers by sight but not by name," he said. He did not inform Captain Smith.

Bride said he was in bed when the impact came. He was not alarmed at the collision and remained in bed about ten minutes. He saw Phillipps in the operating room.

"He told me he thought the boat had been injuried in some way and he expected it would have to go back to the builders." said Bride.

BETTER SEND OUT A CALL FOR ASSISTANCE.

The witness said that according to arrangement he relieved Phillipps. "Immediately the captain came in and said we had better send out a call for assistance," testified Bride. "Phillipps asked if he wanted to send a distress call. The captain said he did. I could read what Phillipps sent—C. Q. D."

"How soon did he get a reply?"

"As far as I know, immediately. I could not hear what he received, however."

The witness told of having intercepted a message from the Californian intended for the Baltic, which told of the presence ot three huge icebergs in the vicinity of the former vessel.

"I gave the message to the captain personally," he said.

Bride did not take down the message and could not give its precise form. "The Californian was seeking out the Baltic, and I merely noted that it was an ice report and told the captain," he said.

Under a fire of questions Bride acknowledged that a half hour previously, or at 4.30 Sunday afternoon, he was working on his accounts in the wireless room when he heard the Californian trying to raise the Titanic. He did not respond, he said, because, he was "busy."

"You had the telephone apparatus at your ear?" inquired Senator Smith, in surprise.

"Yes, sir."

"And you did not respond to the call?"

"No, sir."

"Then a half hour later on, about five hours before the disaster, you took the message when it was intended for another vessel, the Baltic?"

"Yes, sir."

In an effort to determine whether the signal "C. Q. D." might not have been misunderstood by passing ships Senator Smith called upon Mr. Marconi.

MEANING OF DIFFERENT CALLS.

"The C. Q.," said Mr. Marconi, "is an international signal which meant that all stations should cease sending except the one using the call. The 'D' was added to indicate danger. The call, however, now has been superseded by the universal call, 'S. O. S."

Senator Smith then resumed the direct examination of Bride, who has said the North German Lloyd was the first to answer the Titanic's distress signal.

"Have you heard it said that the Frankfurt was the ship nearest to the Titanic?" the senator asked.

"Yes, sir; Mr. Phillipps told me that."

"How did he know?"

"By the strength of the signals," said the witness, who added that the Carpathia answered shortly after.

The witness said that twenty minutes later the Frankfurt operator interrupted to ask "what was the matter?"

"What did you reply?" the senator inquired.

"Mr. Phillipps said he was a fool and told him to keep out."

There was no further effort to get the Frankfurt's position.

Time after time Senator Smith asked in varying forms why the Titanic did not explain in detail its condition to the Frankfurt.

"Any operator receiving C. Q. D. and the position of the ship, if he is on the job," said Bride, "would tell the captain at once."

"Ask him if it would have taken longer to have sent 'You are a fool, keep out,' than 'we are sinking?' " suggested Senator Reed.

"Was your object in dismissing the somewhat tardy inquiry of the Frankfurt due to your desire to hang on to a certainty, the Carpathia?" inquired Senator Smith.

The witness said it was. "But under the circumstances could you not with propriety send a detailed message to the Frankfurt?" Senator Smith insisted.

"I did not think we could under the circumstances."

BRIDE INTERROGATED.

"Would you still make the same reply if you were told that the Frankfurt was twenty miles nearer to you than the Carpathia?"

Bride replied that the Carpathia was then on its way with its lifeboats ready.

Mr. Marconi testified to the distress signals and said the Frankfurt was equipped with Marconi wireless. He said the receipts of the signals C. Q. D. by the Frankfurt's operator should have been all sufficient to send the Frankfurt to the immediate rescue.

Under questioning by Senator Smith Bride said that undoubtedly the Frankfurt received all of the urgent appeals for help sent subsequently to the Carpathia.

"Why did you not send the messages to the Frankfurt as well as to the Carpathia?" asked Senator Smith.

"He would not have understood."

The witness said that before leaving the cabin ten minutes before the ship went down Phillipps sent out a final C. Q. D.

There was no response, Bride saying the spark was then so weak that it probably did not carry.

When Bride and Phillipps stepped out on the beat deck he said they found persons rushing around in confusion. They were seeking life belts.

"There were no big lifeboats aboard at that time," said Bride. "There was a life raft over the officers quarters, which later was lost over the side."

The witness then told of his experience in following with a small boat beneath which he nearly was drowned before he could extricate himself. With a number of other survivors he clambored on the overturned boat.

"One of these was Phillipps," said the witness. "He died on the way to the Carpathia and was buried later at sea."

When Bride gained the bottom of the boat he found between 35 and 40 men already there.

THE LAST MAN ABOARD.

"I was the last man invited aboard," said Bride.

"Did any others seek to get on?"

"Yes, sir, dozens. We couldn't take them."

The witness said he did not see J. Bruce Ismay, and that the last he saw of Captain Smith he was in the act of jumping from the bridge just as the ship went down. He said he was swimming within 150 feet of the ship when it went down and that he felt no suction.

Long before the hearing was resumed in the afternoon crowds besieged the Waldorf-Astoria rooms, but few who had not been sought by the committee were admitted.

C. P. Neil, commissioner of labor of the Department of Commerce and Labor, and Representatives Levy and Livingston, of New York, were among the visitors.

Senators Smith and Newlands conferred after luncheon for more than an hour, and it was nearly 4 o'clock when they reached the committee room.

"Is Mr. Bride, the operator of the Titanic, here?" Senator

Smith asked of Mr. Marconi and Mr. Sammis, of the Marconi Company.

They told him that Mr. Bride had been sent to a physician, but could be brought back later. The senator said he wanted to ask the operator several additional questions, but could postpone them.

The second officer of the Titanic, C. H. Lightoller, was called by Senator Smith, but was not present, and the third officer of the Titanic, Herbert John Pittman, took the stand.

"Do you know of your own knowledge whether the Titanic's ship's log was preserved or taken from the Titanic?" asked Senator Smith.

"I do not."

After the hearing adjourned Senator Smith made a statement to the press in which he explained the intentions of the committee. He said:

"The object of the committee in coming to New York coincidental with the arrival of the Carpathia was prompted by the desire to avail itself of first-hand information from the active participants in this sad affair. Our course has been guided solely by this purpose—to obtain accurate information without delay."

CHAPTER XXI.

THE FUNERAL SHIP AND ITS DEAD.

116 Buried at Sea—Nearly All Sailors—No Prominent Men Buried—No Bullet Wounds Found—Halifax's Bells Toll For Dead—Astor's Body Identified—Death Ship's Voyage —The Captain's Story—Canon Hind's Narrative.

The cable ship Mackay-Bennett which had been sent out to recover as many as possible of the Titanic's dead, reached her pier in the dockyard at Halifax, Nova Scotia, the nearest port, at 9.30 on the morning of April 30, almost exactly two weeks after the disaster.

Down the gangway to the pier in the sunlight of a perfect April day they carried 190 of those who had started forth on the maiden voyage of the biggest ship afloat.

In her quest the Mackay-Bennett had found 306 of the Titanic's dead, but only 190 were brought to shore. The rest, the 116, were buried at sea. And 57 of those 116 were among the identified dead.

Of those who were brought to shore, 60 lay unnamed at the curling rink on the edge of the town. It was believed that the 60 were all members of the Titanic's crew, but the slender hope that their own dead might be among them sent many to the rink.

One of the sixty was a little baby girl. Five of them were women, but none of the women that were found were from the first cabin passengers. There was no hope that the body of Mrs. Straus was among them. There was practically no hope that Major Butt was among the unnamed sixty. The quest of the Mackay-Bennett bore greater results than were anticipated, and Capt. Lardner believed that his ship recovered about all of those who did not go down in the Titanic.

The search was continued over five days, sometimes with

the ship drifting without success amid miles and miles of wreckage, tables, chairs, doors, pillows, scattered fragments of the luxury that was the White Star liner Titanic.

At other times the bodies were found close together, and once they saw more than a hundred that looked to the wondering crew of the Mackay-Bennett like a flock of sea gulls in the fog, so strangely did the ends of the life belts rise and fall with the rise and fall of the waves.

Those whose dead the Mackay-Bennett brought to shore came forward with their claims, and from the middle of the afternoon the rest of the day was filled with the steps of identification and the signing of many papers.

The first to be claimed was John Jacob Astor and for his death was issued the first "accidental drowning" death certificate of the hundreds who lost their lives in the wreck of the Titanic.

Vincent Astor and Nicholas Biddle started for New York with the body the next night.

THE BODY OF ISADORE STRAUS IDENTIFIED.

The second identified was Isidor Straus. The start for New York was made early the next morning. Three went on the same night. These were George E. Graham, Milton C. Long, and C. C. Jones. Lawrence Millett has identified his father.

Friends quickly took charge of the bodies of E. H. Kent, W. D. Douglass, Timothy McCarty, George Rosenshine, E. C. Ostby, E. G. Crosby, William C. Porter, A. O. Holverson, Emil Brandies, Thomas McCafferty, Wykoff Vanderhoef, and A. S. Nicholson.

Sharp and distinct in all the tidings the Mackay-Bennett brought to shore the fact stands out that fifty-seven of those who were identified on board were recommitted to the sea. Of the 190 identified dead that were recovered from the scene of the Titanic wreck only 130 were brought to Halifax.

This news, which was given out almost immediately after the death ship reached her pier, was a confirmation of the suspicion that in the last few days had seized upon the colony of those waiting here to claim their dead.

Yet it came as a deep, a stirring surprise. It stunned the White Star men who have had to direct the work from Halifax.

They had been confidently posting the names of the recovered as the wireless brought the news in from the Atlantic. When the suspicion arose that some of the identified might have been buried at sea the White Star people said that they did not know, but they were working on the assumption that Capt. Lardner would bring them all to port, and that only the unidentifiable had been recommitted to the sea.

THE UNNAMED DEAD.

Then they learned that the Mackay-Bennett had brought in sixty unidentified. The hallway of the curling rink where the dead were removed from the cable ship was thronged all afternoon with friends and relatives eager beyond expression to see those unnamed dead, but the attention of the embalmers was turned to those already identified, for whom the claimants were waiting. For the most part the unidentified could not be viewed until the next morning.

One of them was thought to be Arthur White, a member of the Titanic's crew.

The suspense was acute. Yet those who were most anxious for the morrow to come knew that hope was of the slenderest. They knew that the nameless sixty were almost all members of the crew. Capt. Lardner said that he was sure of it. He knew it by the clothes they wore.

As to the fifty-seven identified dead that were buried at sea, the whole colony was stirred by pity that it had to be, and not a few wonder if it really had to be, a wonder fed by the talk of some of the embalmers. Yet few were immediately concerned, most of those in Halifax were waiting for men who sailed first cabin of the Titanic. It appears that only one of these was among the ones who were buried at sea. This was Frederick Sutton, of

Philadelphia. The large majority were either members of the Titanic's crew or steerage passengers.

Of the 116 that Capt. Lardner thought best to return to the sea, he explained that the unidentified seemed unidentifiable, that the identified were too mutilated to bring to shore.

"Let me say first of all," he announced when the reporters gathered around him, "that I was commissioned to bring aboard all the bodies found floating, but owing to the unanticipated number of bodies found, owing to the bad weather and other conditions it was impossible to carry out instructions, so some were committed to the deep after service, conducted by Canon Hind."

Capt. Lardner explained that neither he nor any of his people had dreamed that so many of the Titanic's dead would be found floating on the surface of the Atlantic.

ONLY 106 BODIES PRESRRVED.

It was more than his embalmer could handle, for, although the material for embalming seventy bodies, which was all that Halifax sent out with the Mackay-Bennett, was supplemented at sea by materials borrowed from the Minia, the number of dead so preserved for the return to shore was only 106.

He did not know how long he would have to stay at his grim work on the scene of the wreck. He did not know how long bad weather would impede the homeward voyage.

He did not know how long he could safely carry the multitude of dead. It seemed best to recommit some to the sea, and so on three different days 116 were weighted down and dropped over the edge of the ship into the Atlantic.

Then rose the question as to why some were picked for burial at sea and others left on board to be brought home to the waiting families on shore. The reporters put the question to the Captain, and he answered it:

"No prominent man was recommitted to the deep. It seemed best to embalm as quickly as possible in those cases where large property might be involved. It seemed best to be sure to bring back to land the dead where the death might give rise to such questions as large insurance and inheritance and all the litigation.

"Most of those who were buried out there were members of the Titanic's crew. The man who lives by the sea ought to be satisfied to be buried at sea. I think it is the best place. For my own part I should be contented to be committed to the deep."

To emphasize the uncertainty of the task he directed, Capt. Lardner pointed silently to the forward hold, where an hour before those on the pier had seen the dead lying side by side on the floor, each in the wrapping of tarpaulin.

"They were ready for burial," the Captain said. "We had the weights in them, for we didn't know when we should have to give them up."

A FEW MORE BODIES RECOVERED.

To those who hoped to find their own among the unidentified in the curling ring to-morrow Capt. Lardner held out little encouragement except the prospect that the quest of the Minia may result in a few more bodies being recovered. He believed that his own ship gathered in most of those who were kept afloat by the lifebelts.

Almost all of the rest, in his opinion, went down with the rush of waters that closed over the Titanic, driving them down in the hatchways and holding the dead imprisoned in the great wreck.

Survivors told of many pistol shots heard in those dark moments when the last lifeboats were putting off, and though the pier on the night the Carpathia landed was astir with rumors of men shot down as they fought to save their lives, not one of the bodies that were recovered yesterday had any pistol shots, according to Capt. Lardner and the members of his crew.

The mutilations which marked so many were broken arms and legs and crushed skulls, where the living on the Titanic were swept against the stanchions by the onrush of the sea.

The little repair shop on the Mackay-Bennett was a treasure

house when she came to port. Fifteen thousand dollars in money was found on the recovered bodies and jewelry that will be worth a king's ransom. One of the crew related his experience with one dead man whose pockets he turned inside out only to have seventeen diamonds roll out in every direction upon the littered deck.

It was a little after 9.30 that the Mackay-Bennett was sighted by those waiting for her since the break of day. For it was in the chill of 6 o'clock on a Canadian Spring morning that the people began to assemble on the pier in the dockyard.

They were undertakers for the most part, mingling with the newspaper men who hurried to and fro between the water's edge and the little bell tent set up a few yards back to guard the wires that were to flash the news to the ends of the continent.

WATCH FOR MEN WITH CAMERAS.

The dockyard was patrolled by twenty members of the crew and four petty officers from H. M. C. S. Niobe and by a squad of men from the Dominion police, who were instructed to keep out all without passes countersigned by the commandant, and who were particularly vigilant in the watch for men with cameras.

Just as the death ship reached her pier, and in the midst of the eager movement forward to learn what news she brought from the scene of the Titanic's wreck, a little tug was spotted near by, and Commander Martin, in charge of the dockyard, scented a moving picture man.

In a very few moments he was putting out for the tug in the little patrol launch. Again a few moments and he was standing on the pier with a complacent smile on his face.

"I have the films," he said in explanation, so the privacy was guarded.

The friends and relatives of those who were lost when the great liner went down were urged not to assume the ordeal of meeting the Mackay-Bennett. Almost without exception they followed this advice, and only a scattering few could be seen among those waiting on the pier.

In all the crowd of men, officials, undertakers, and newspaper men, there was just one woman, solitary, spare, clasping her heavy black shawl tightly around her.

This was Eliza Lurette, for more than thirty years in the service of Mrs. William August Spencer, who was waiting at her home on East Eighty-sixth Street, New York, while Miss Lurette had journeyed to Halifax to seek the body of Mr. Spencer, who went down with the Titanic.

So the crowd that waited on the pier was made up almost entirely of men who had impersonal business there, and the air was full of the chatter of conjecture and preparation.

Then, warned by the tolling of the bells up in the town, a hush fell upon the waiting people. The gray clouds that had overcast the sky parted, and the sun shone brilliantly on the rippling water of the harbor as the Mackay-Bennett drew alongside her pier.

THE DEAD LAY EVERYWHERE.

Capt. Lardner could be seen upon the bridge. The crew hung over the sides, joyously alive and glad to be home. But in every part of the ship the dead lay. High on the poop deck coffins and rough shells were piled and piled.

Dead men in tarpaulins lined the flooring of the cable-wells both fore and aft, so that there was hardly room for a foot to be put down. And in the forward hold dead men were piled one upon another, their eyes closed as in sleep, and over them all a great tarpaulin was stretched. Those that pressed forward to see were sickened and turned back.

The business of moment was to discharge that freight, and this was done with all possible dispatch.

The uncoffined dead were carried down in stretchers, placed in the rough shells that were piled upon the pier, and one by one driven up the slope and into the town in the long line of hearses and black undertaker's wagons that had been gathered from every quarter. It was speedily done, but quietly and without irreverent haste.

For two hours this business proceeded before anyone could go upon the pier and the sounds were like the hum of a small factory. There were the muffled orders, the shuffling and tramping of feet, the scraping as of packing boxes drawn across the rough flooring and the eternal hammering that echoed all along the coal sheds.

Two hours it was before any one could go on board, and then came another hour when the coffins were swung down from the deck and piled up on the wharf ready for the removal that took until well into the middle of the afternoon.

Few of the relatives were allowed to pass beyond the cordon that stretched all about the pier at which the dead were landed.

One of the first to get through the lines and the first of all the waiting crowd to make his way aboard after the ship reached her pier was Capt. Richard Roberts, of the Astor yacht, who was filled with a great concern at the news that had come from the Widener party.

NOT MR. WIDENER.

For long before the Mackay-Bennett reached her pier it was established as definitely as it may ever be established that the man who was picked up at sea for George D. Widener was not Mr. Widener, but his man-servant Edward Keating.

Although the name was sent in by wireless, a later examination of the dead man's clothing and effects proved that it was Keating's body. A letter in the pocket was addressed to Widener, but the coat was labeled "E. K." and the garments were of an inferior quality. Identification by features was out of the question, for the dead man had been struck by some spar or bit of wreckage, and the face was mutilated past recognition. He was buried at sea, and the news sent on to the waiting family.

Young Mr. Widener, who had been waiting here for a week with a private car to carry the body of his father home to Philadelphia, had heard of the uncertainty, and in a fever of impatience he met the Mackay-Bennett at Quarantine, went over the effects with Captain Lardner, and was satisfied that it was Keating whose body was found and who was later committed to the deep.

The haunting fear that this same error might have been made in the case of Colonel Astor had possession of the whole Astor party and grew acute as the Widener story went out. That was what sent Captain Roberts hurrying to the ship. He was admitted and saw for himself. The coffin top was removed on board.

The plain gold ring with the two little diamonds set deep, the gold buckle on the belt that Colonel Astor always wore, and a sum amounting to nearly $3000 in the pockets settled the uncertainty. Twenty minutes after he had boarded the ship Captain Roberts was hurrying through the crowd to reach the nearest telephone that he might speed the news to waiting Vincent Astor.

QUESTIONS OF IDENTITY.

Beyond these two cases the questions of identity were taken up at the Mayflower Curling Rink at the edge of the town, where the line of hearses had been trundling since the Mackay-Bennett landed. As they passed the crowds were hushed, men bowed their heads, and officers saluted.

At the rink the great main floor was given over to the coffins and shells containing the identified dead, and as soon as the embalmers had done their work the friends and relatives came forward and claimed their own.

Upstairs in the large, bare room the packets of clothing were distributed in rows upon the floor.

There the oak chests of the Provincial Cashier were opened for the sorting of the canvas bags that contained the valuables, the letters and the identifying trinkets of the dead. It was all very systematic. It was all very much businesslike, and while a lunch counter served refreshments to the weary workers, and while the Intercolonial set up a desk for railway tickets, the Medical Examiner was busy issuing death certificates, and the Registrar was issuing burial permits, all to the accompanying click, click of several typewriters.

A satisfactory arrangement was reached as to the disposition of the personal effects. A man would claim his dead, take the number, make his way to the representatives of the Provincial Secretary, and there claim the contents of the little canvas bag by making affidavit that he was the duly authorized representative of the executor or next of kin.

The little crimson tickets that are the death certificates were printed for the tragedies of every day in the year. Their formal points and dimensions seemed hopelessly inadequate for even the briefest statement of the tragedy of the Titanic.

CERTIFICATE FOR THE DEAD.

The first body claimed and removed from the rink was that of John Jacob Astor. The certificate, the first issued for one of the Titanic dead, reads:

> Name of deceased—John Jacob Astor. Sex—M. Age—47. Date of death—April 15, 1912. Residence, street, etc.—840 Fifth Av., N. Y. C. Occupation—Gentleman. Married. Cause—Accidental drowning. S. S. Titanic at sea. Length of illness—Suddenly. Name of physician in attendance.

Such details as these filled the day.

After the greater part of the Titanic's dead had been shifted from the Mackay-Bennett to the pier, Captain Lardner descended to the dining saloon, and with the reporters from all over the country gathered around the table, he opened the ship's log and, slowly tracing his fingers over the terse entries, he told them the story of the death ship's voyage.

Lardner is English by birth and accent, and tall and square of build, with a full brown beard and eyes of unusual keenness.

"We left Halifax," he began, "shortly after noon on Wednesday, April 17, but fog and bad weather delayed us on the run out, and we did not get there till Saturday night at 8 o'clock.

"We asked all ships to report to us if they passed any wreckage or bodies, and on Saturday at noon we received a communication from the German mailboat steamship Rhein to the effect that in latitude 42.1. N. longitude 49.13, she had passed wreckage and bodies.

"The course was shaped for that position. Later in the afternoon we spoke to the German steamship Bremen, and they reported having passed three large icebergs and some bodies in 42 N. 49.20 W.

"We arrived on the scene at 8 o'clock Saturday evening, and then we stopped and let the ship drift. It was in the middle of the watch that some of the wreckage and a few bodiese were sighted.

"At daylight the boats were lowered, and though there was a heavy sea running at the time, fifty-one bodies were recovered

The Rev. Canon K. C. Hinds, rector of All Saints' Cathedral, who officiated at the burial of 116 bodies, the greatest number consigned to the ocean at one time, tells the story of the Mackay-Bennett's trip as follows:

OUR JOURNEY SLOW.

We left Halifax shortly after noon on April 17, and had not proceeded far when fog set in so that our journey was slow. We reached the vicinity of the wreckage on Saturday evening. Early on Sunday morning the search for bodies began, when the captain and other officers of the ship kept a lookout from the bridge.

Soon the command was given "Stand by the boat!" and a little later the lifeboat was lowered and the work begun of picking up the bodies as they were pointed out in the water to the crew.

Through the day some fifty were picked up. All were carefully examined and their effects placed in separate bags, all bodies and bags being numbered.

It was deemed wise that some of them should be buried. At 8 P. M. the ship's bell was tolled to indicate all was in readiness for the service. Standing on the bow of the ship as she rocked to and fro, one gazed at the starry heavens and across the boundless deep, and to his mind the psalmist's words came with mighty force:

"Whither shall I go then from Thy spirit, or whither shall I go then from Thy presence? If I ascend up to heaven Thou art there, I make my bed in the grave, Thou art there also. If I take the wings of the morning and dwell in the uttermost part of the sea, even there shall Thy hand lead me, and Thy right hand shall hold me."

In the solemn stillness of the early night, the words of that unequaled burial office rang across the waters: "I am the resurrection and the life, saith the Lord. He that believeth in Me shall never die."

When the time of committal came these words were used over each body:

COMMIT HIS BODY TO THE DEEP.

"Forasmuch as it hath pleased Almighty God to take upto Himself the soul of our dear brother departed, we, therefore, commit his body to the deep to be turned to corruption, looking for the resurrection of the body (when the seas shall give up her dead) and the life of the world to come, through Jesus Christ Our Lord, who shall change our vile body, that it may be like unto His glorious body, according to the mighty working whereby He is able to subdue all things to Himself."

The prayers from the burial servicee were said, the hymn "Jesus, Lover of My Soul," sung and the blessing given.

Any one attending a burial at sea will most surely lose the common impression of the awfulness of a grave in the mighty deep. The wild Atlantic may rage and toss, the shipwrecked mariners cry for mercy, but far below in the calm untroubled depth they rest in peace.

On Monday the work began again early in the morning, and another day was spent in searching and picking up the floating bodies and at night a number were buried. On Tuesday the work was still the same until the afternoon, when the fog set in, and continued all day Wednesday.

Wednesday was partly spent in examining bodies, and at noon a number were committed to the deep. Thursday came in fine and from early morning until evening the work went on.

During the day word came that the cable ship Minia was on her way to help and would be near us at midnight.

"Early on Friday some more bodies were picked up. The captain then felt we had covered the ground fairly well and decided to start on our homeward way at noon. After receiving some supplies from the Minia we bid good-bye and proceeded on our way.

"The Mackay-Bennett succeeded in finding 306 bodies, of which 116 were buried at sea, and one could not help feeling, as we steamed homeward, that of those bodies we had on board it would be well if the greater number of them were resting in the deep.

"It is to be noted how earnestly and reverently all the work was done and how nobly the crew acquitted themselves during a work of several days which meant a hard and trying strain on mind and body.

"What seems a very regrettable fact is that in chartering the Mackay-Bennett for this work the White Star Company did not send an official agent to accompany the steamer in her search for the bodies.

CHAPTER XXII.

INQUIRY BY UNITED STATES SENATE.

Loading at the Rail—Inadequate Life-saving Appliances—No Extra Lookout—Searchlights Blinding—Wireless Rivals Not All Aroused—Went to Death in Sleep—Scratch Seamen—Cries of Agony—A Pitiful Story—Senators Ascertain Pertinent Facts—Much Good Accomplished.

What has been accomplished by the Senatorial inquiry into the loss of the Titanic with sixteen hundred lives?

For more than a week of the two that have elapsed since the Titanic made a record on her maiden voyage—a record never paralleled in marine history for its horrors, its sacrifice of life and material property—an earnest body of United States Senators has been at work conscientiously striving to uncover the facts, not alone for the purpose of placing the responsibility for what has now become one of the most heartrending chapters of all ocean history, but also in the hope of framing remedial legislation looking to the prevention of its recurrence.

To attempt to draw conclusions as to the value of the work of a committee which is yet upon the threshold of its task would be presumptuous, but it is not too soon to present and formulate some of the pertinent facts which its researches have established in the light of sworn evidence.

Any attempt at systematic analysis of the facts deduced from the many thousand of pages of testimony already taken naturally divided itself into two departments:

Were the Titanic's equipment and her general state of preparedness such as to justify the broad claims made in her behalf before the crisis arose, that she represented the acme of human possibility not only in ocean going comfort and speed but also in safety at sea?

Were the personnel and discipline of her officers and crew of such a standard that, after the supreme crisis confronted them, they utilized to the best advantage such facilities for the safeguarding and preservation of life as remained at their disposal?

With ten thousand families on both sides of the Atlantic mourning the untimely death of relatives and friends who went down into the depths from the decks of a brand new ship, widely proclaimed the greatest and the safest that ever ploughed the sea, these are, after all, the most pertinent questions that may be asked by a sorrowing world as it looks to the future rather than the past.

LIFE-SAVING APPARATUS INADEQUATE.

It has been demonstrated—and frankly conceded by the company's managers and officers in the light of after knowledge—that the Titanic's life-saving appliances were woefully inadequate to the safeguarding of even one-half her complement of passengers and crew. On the day after the disaster was known to the world it was shown that the ship's equipment of lifeboats complied with the requirements of the English Board of Trade, but that those requirements were so obsolete and antiquated that they dated back to 1898 and were drafted to provide for vessels of less than one-quarter the gross tonnage of the mammoth craft of 46,000 tons of displacement.

The Titanic carried on her boat deck—sometimes referred to as her sun deck—fourteen of the largest regulation size lifeboats, seven on her port side and seven on the starboard. Each of these had a carrying capacity, according to the Board of Trade's established method of computation, of 65.5 persons. Their aggregate capacity when afloat, therefore, was 917. The ship carried, in addition, four of the so-called collapsible boats and two others known as emergency boats—comparatively small craft employed in occasional duty—as when a man falls overboard.

The combined capacity of these six when afloat was hardly more than sufficient to care for two hundred persons. At the most liberal estimate, therefore, the entire equipment of boats aboard the great White Star liner might have afforded refuge, in the most favorable conditions, to less than 1,200 persons, or not quite half the number actually aboard the ship, on her maiden voyage.

In stating the lifeboat capacity the term "when afloat" has been used advisedly. One of the points which each of the Titanic's surviving officers has emphasized in evidence is the vast difference between loading with its human freight a boat that has been already placed in the water and loading one "at the rail," from a deck seventy feet above the water, with the subsequent perils of lowering it by means of the tackles sustaining its weight from bow and stern. Several of the officers have said that, in lowering loaded boats from the rail of the Titanic's boat deck, they would consider it unwise and even dangerous to fill the boats to more than one-half their rated capacity.

All the lifeboats that went away from the Titanic were loaded and lowered from the rail. Some of the smaller collapsible and emergency boats did not get away at all until the ship was so low in the water that they were simply pushed overboard, and one of them went over bottom up.

BOAT CARRIES 58 PERSONS.

Harold G. Lowe, the fifth officer, commanded a boat which carried fifty-eight persons aboard. This, so far as is known, is the largest number of passengers carried in any of the lifeboats. Mr. Lowe testified that as his craft was lowered away from the davits he feared momentarily that, as a result of the tremendous strain upon her structure, she would buckle amidships and break before she reached the sustaining surface of the water, dropping all into the sea. "Had one more person leaped aboard her amidships as she was going down past the other decks," he said, "it might well have proved to be the last straw."

Mr. Lowe feared this might happen, as he saw steerage passengers "glaring at the boat" as it was lowered past the decks whereon they stood. It was for that reason, he explained to the investigating committee, that he discharged his revolver three times into the air as he and his boatload were dropping past the three lower decks. His purpose, he said, was to show that he was armed and to prevent any effort to overload the craft beyond a point which he already considered perilous.

C. H. Lightoller, second officer and ranking surviving officer of the Titanic, expressed the opinion that, in filling lifeboats from the Titanic's boat deck, "at the rail," it was involving serious risk to load them to more than half their rated capacity for filling while afloat. H. G. Boxhall, fourth officer, expressed a like view, but added that in an extreme emergency one man might take more chances than another.

In view of these expert opinions, it will be seen that, when it came to loading the Titanic's passengers into lifeboats "from the rail," the actual life-saving capacity of her available equipment was far less than the one thousand or eleven hundred that might have been carefully packed away into boats already resting safely on the surface of a calm sea.

A PUZZLING QUERY.

And this consideration naturally suggests the query, Why were the Titanic's lifeboats all loaded "from the rail" of the topmost deck, at a point fully seventy feet above the sea? Why were they not lowered empty, or with only the necessary officers or crew aboard, and then filled with their quota of passengers, either from some lower deck, or else after they had reached the sustaining surface of the water?

It is evident that course was contemplated. Three of the surviving officers have testified that the available force of seamen was depleted after the ship struck, because a detail of men had been sent below to open up the gangway doors, for the purpose of embarking the passengers into the ilfeboats from those outlets. There is nothing in evidence as yet to show that this purpose was ever accomplished, or to reveal the fate of the men sent to do the work.

Whether the men were unable or incompetent to force open the gangway doors, from which the lowered boats might easily have been filled, as the sea was as smooth as a mill pond; whether these outlets were jammed as a result of collision with the berg, or stuck because the ship's mechanisms were new, has not been revealed and may never be known.

Certain it is that all the lifeboats were loaded "from the rail," and their safe capacity was thereby reduced one-half in the judgment of the officers to whom their command was entrusted.

The inadequacy of the Titanic's lifeboat appliances is not disputed. Steamship companies are already vying with one another to correct in this respect the admitted shortcomings of the past. The sole excuse offered is that collision bulkheads, watertight compartments and other like devices have been regarded until now as making the marvelous vessels of the present day "their own best lifeboats." The Titanic and many of her sister ships of the ocean fleets have been called "unsinkable." They were generally believed to be so, and it is only since this greatest of disasters has shattered many illusions that marine engineers have confessed ruefully that the unsinkable ship has never yet been launched.

PERILS MINIMIZED.

Since the day of the watertight compartment and of the wireless telegraph sea perils have been so minimized that in the most extreme of likely emergencies the function of the lifeboat had come to be regarded as that of an ocean ferry capable of transferring passengers safely and leisurely from an imperilled vessel to another standing by and co-operating in the task.

That was all the lifeboat had to do when the Republic sank. That was all they had to do years ago, when the Missouri, under Captain Hamilton Murrell's expert management, took off a thousand persons from a foundering ship without the loss of a single life. So it had come to be believed that the lifeboats would never be called upon to do more than that, and least of all in the case of the Titanic, latest and most superb of all the vessels built by man since the world began.

So deep rooted was this conviction in the minds of seagoing men that when Senator Smith, of Michigan, chairman of the investigating committee, asked one of the surviving officers: "What was the purpose of the Titanic carrying her fourteen full-size lifeboats?"

he naively replied: "To comply, I suppose, with the regulations of the London Board of Trade."

There has been no evidence to indicate that the Titanic lacked the proper number of life jackets, or life belts—one for every person aboard the ship—and it has not been proven that these life belts were not new and of proper quality and strength. Major Peuchen, of Toronto, one of the surviving passengers, however, in the course of his testimony, made two significant comments. He said that when the Carpathia, on the morning after the disaster, steamed through a lot of the Titanic's floating wreckage, he was surprised to note great quantities of broken bits of cork, such as are used in life preservers. He was astonished also that he did not see a larger number of floating bodies.

"I have always supposed," said Major Peuchen, who is an experienced yachtsman, "that a life preserver in good condition would sustain a dead body as well as a live one."

STEAMING AT 21 KNOTS.

It has been demonstrated by ample evidence that at the time the Titanic hit the iceberg she was steaming at the undiminished speed of twenty-one knots an hour into a zone littered with icebergs and floating ice fields, warning of which her officers had received hours before by wireless from several other ships, including the Amerika, of the Hamburg-American Line. When day broke on Monday, according to Mr. Lane, at least twenty icebergs surrounded the Carpathia, the largest of which was 150 feet high. They were within a six-mile radius.

In the chart room, tucked into the corner of a frame above the table where the navigating officers of the Titanic did their mathematical work, was a written memorandum of the latitude and longitude wherein two large icebergs had been reported directly in the track. Mr. Boxhall had worked out this position under Captain Smith's instructions. Mr. Lightoller, the second officer, was familiar with it, and when his watch ended at 10 o'clock Sunday night and he surrendered the post on the bridge to the first officer, Mr.

Murdock, the remark was made that they would probably "be getting up into the ice during Mr. Murdock's watch."

Despite all this the Titanic was rushing on, driving at railroad speed toward the port of New York and "a record for a maiden voyage."

It was a cloudless and starlit night with no sea running. No extra lookout was posted in the "ship's eyes," the most advanced position on the vessel's deck. Up in the crow's nest Fleet and Lee, both experienced lookouts, were keeping a sharp watch forward. They had been duly warned of ice by the pair of lookouts whom they had relieved.

UNAIDED BY SEA GLASSES.

But the men in the crow's nest had to depend entirely upon the vision of the naked eye. They had no glass to aid them. Fleet had occupied a similar post of responsibility four years on the Oceanic without mishap. His testimony before the committee was that he never before had been without the aid of a glass. He had a pair of binoculars when the ship made her trial trip from Belfast, but they had been mislaid, and when the Titanic steamed out from Southampton he asked Mr. Lightoller for another pair and was told that there was no glass for him. Fleet's warning was too late to prevent the impact. His testimony was that with a glass he would have reported the berg in time to have prevented the ship striking it.

When Quartermaster Hitchens came on watch at 10 o'clock the weather had grown so cold that he, experienced seaman that he was, immediately thought of icebergs, though it was no part of his duty to look out for them. The thermometer showed thirty-one degrees, and the first orders he received were to notify the ship's carpenter to look to his fresh-water supply because of the freezing weather, and to turn on the steam-heating apparatus in the officers' quarters.

Still no extra lookout was placed and the men in the crow's nest were straining their tired eyes ahead without the help of a lens.

Captain Arthur Rostrom, of the Carpathia, testified that when he was rushing his ship to the aid of the stricken Titanic, taking unusual chances because he knew lives were at stake, he placed a double watch on duty.

Each of the surviving officers, when he was questioned as to the Titanic's speed at a time when the proximity of dangerous ice was definitely reported and clearly indicated by the drop in temperature, said that it was "not customary" to slacken speed at such times, provided the weather was clear. The custom is, they said, "to go ahead and depend upon the lookouts in the crow's nest and the watch on the bridge to 'pick up' the ice in time to avoid hitting it."

Mr. Lowe, the fifth officer, who was crossing the Atlantic for the first time in his life, most of his fourteen years' experience at sea having been in the southern and eastern oceans, yawned wearily in the face of the examiner as he admitted that he had never heard that icebergs were common off the Banks of Newfoundland and that the fact would not have interested him if he had. He did not know that the Titanic was following what is known as "the southern track," and when he was asked, ventured the guess that she was on the northerly one. .

MIGHT HAVE BEEN SAVED BY SEARCHLIGHT.

Questions framed by Senator Smith several times have suggested that the use of a searchlight might have saved the Titanic. War ships of all nations make the searchlight a part of their regular equipment, as is well known. The Titanic's surviving officers agreed that it has not been commonly used by vessels of the merchant marine. Some of them conceded that in the conditions surrounding the Titanic its use on a clear night might have revealed the iceberg in time to have saved the ship. Major Peuchen, of Toronto, said emphatically that it would have done so.

Mr. Lightoller, however, pointed out that, while the searchlight is often a useful device for those who stand behind it, its rays invariably blind those upon whom they are trained. Should the use of searchlights become general upon merchant vessels, he thought, it would be a matter for careful consideration, experiment and regulation.

The Senatorial inquiry has indicated that the single lifeboat drill upon the Titanic had been a rather perfunctory performance; there had been neither a boat drill nor a fire drill from the time the great ship left Southampton until she struck the iceberg. While she lay in harbor before starting on her maiden voyage, and with her port side against the company pier, two of her lifeboats had been lowered away from her starboard side, manned by a junior or a warrant officer and a crew of four men each, who rowed them around a few minutes and then returned to the ship.

There had also been an inspection in the home port to see whether the lifeboats contained all the gear specified by the Board of Trade regulations and Officer Boxhall testified that they did. Yet, when the emergency came, many of the boats were found to contain no lights, while others lacked extra oars, biscuits and other specified requisites.

UTILITY OF WATER-TIGHT COMPARTMENTS DOUBTED.

The Titanic's loss has completely exploded the fallacy that watertight compartments, of which the big ship had fifteen in her main divisions, can save a vessel from foundering after having sustained a raking blow, tearing and ripping out her plates from thirty feet aft of the bow almost to midships.

Mr. Lightoller expressed the belief under oath that the starboard side of the Titanic had been pierced through compartments 1, 2, 3 and probably 4, numbering from the collision bulkhead toward the midship section. The testimony of Quartermaster Hitchins showed that the vessel filled so fast that when the captain looked at the commutator five minutes after the ship struck, the Titanic showed a list of five degrees to starboard. Rushing water drove the clerks out of the mail room before they could save their letter bags.

One reform that is likely to take shape early as a result of the Senatorial investigation is a more thorough regulation of wireless telegraphy both in shore stations and on ships at sea. Interference by irresponsible operators will probably be checked by governmental action, and the whole subject may come up for uniform international regulation in the Berlin conference.

It is conceded that on all ships the receiving apparatus of the wireless instruments should be manned at all hours of the day and night, just as are the ship's bridge and the engine rooms. The Senate inquiry has showed that had the death call of the Titanic gone out five minutes later it would never have reached the Carpathia, whose one wireless operator was about to retire for the night when he heard the signal that took the Cunarder to the rescue of the seven hundred who survived.

There has been shown, too, grave need of some cure for the jealousies and rivalries between competing systems of wireless. To the Frankfurt, which was one of the nearest, if not the nearest, of the several ships to the sinking Titanic, her operator sent the curt message, "Shut up!" From the Californian the operator refused to take a message, which proved to be an ice warning, because "he was busy with his accounts." With the sanction of high officers of their company wireless operators have suppressed vital public information for the purpose of commercializing their exclusive knowledge for personal profit.

So much for the Titanic's boasted equipment—or the lack of it. There remains to be summarized the evidence adduced as to the personnel and discipline, as these were indicated by what occurred after the ship confronted the direst of all emergencies.

The Titanic was expected to make a record on her maiden voyage. She made one unapproached in ocean annals; one which, it is hoped, may long stand unparalleled.

LIST OF TITANIC PASSENGERS MISSING AND RESCUED

The following passengers on the Titanic were lost:

FIRST CABIN

A

Anderson, Harry.
Allison, H. J.
Allison, Mrs. and maid.
Allison, Miss.
Andrews, Thomas.
Artagavoytia, Mr. Ramon.
Astor, Col. J. J., and servant.
Anderson, Walker.

B

Beattie, T.
Brandies, E.
Mrs. William Bucknell's maid.
Baumann, J.
Baxter, Mr. and Mrs. Quigg.
Bjornstrom, H.
Birnbaum, Jacob.
Blackwell, S. W.
Borebank, J. J.
Bowden, Miss.
Brady, John B.
Brewe, Arthur J.
Butt, Major A.

C

Clark, Walter M.
Clifford, George Q.
Colley, E. P.
Cardeza, T. D. M., servant of.
Cardeza, Mrs. J. W., maid of.
Carlson, Frank.
Case, Howard B.
Cavendish, W. Tyrrell.
Corran, F. M.
Corran, J. P.
Chaffee, H. I.
Chisholm, Robert.
Compton, A. T.
Crafton, John B.
Crosby, Edward G.
Cumings, John Bradley.

D

Davidson, Thornton.
Dulles, William C.
Douglas, W. D.
Nurse of Douglas, Master, R.

E.

Eustis, Miss E. M. may be reported saved as Miss Ellis.
Evans, Miss E.

F.

Fortune, Mark.
Foreman, B. L.
Fortune, Clarles.
Franklin, T. P.
Futrelle, J.

G.

Gee, Arthur
Goldenberg, E. L.
Goldschmidt, G. B.
Greenfield, G. B.
Giglio, Victor
Guggenheim, Benjamin.

H.

Servant of Harper Henry S.
Hays, Charles M.
Maid of Hays, Mrs. Charles M.
Head, Christopher.
Hilliard, H. H.
Hopkins, W. F.
Hogenheim, Mrs. A.
Harris, Henry B.
Harp, Mr. and Mrs. Charles M.
Harp, Miss Margaret, and maid.
Hoyt, W. F.
Holverson, A. M.

I.

Isham, Miss A. E.
Servant of J. Bruce Ismay.

J.

Julian, H. F.
Jones C. C.

K.

Kent, Edward A.
Kenyon, Mr. and Mrs. F. R., (may be reported saved as Kenchen and Kennyman
Kimball, Mr. and Mrs. E. N., (may be reported saved as Mr. and Mrs. E. Kimberley).
Klober, Herman.

L.

Lambert, Williams.
Lawrence, Arthur.
Long, Milton.
Longley, Miss G. F.
Lewy, E. G.
Lindsholm, J., (may be reported saved as Mrs. Sigrid Lindstrom).
Loring, J. H.
Lingrey, Edward.

M.

Maguire, J. E.
McCaffry, T.
McCaffry, T., Jr.
McCarthy, T., Jr.
Marvin, D. W.
Middleton, J. C.
Millett, Frank D.
Minahan, Dr. and Mrs.
Marechal, Pierre.
Meyer, Edgar J.
Molson, H. M.
Moore, C., servant.

N.

Natsch, Charles.
Newall, Miss T.
Nicholson, A. S.

O.

Ovies, S.
Ostby, E. C.
Ornout, Alfred T.

P.

Parr, M. H. W.
Pears, Mr. and Mrs. Thomas.
Penasco, Mr. Victor.
Partner, M. A.
Payne, V.
Pond, Florence, and maid.
Porter, Walter.

R.

Reuchlin, J.
Maid of Robert, Mrs. E.
Roebling, Washington A., 2d.
Rood, Hugh R.
Roes, J. Hugo.
Maid of Countess Rothes.
Rothschild, M.
Rowe, Arthur.
Ryerson, A.

S.

Shutes, Miss E. W. (probably reported saved as Miss Shutter).
Maid of Mrs. George Stone.
Straus, Mr. and Mrs. Isidor.
Silvey, William B.
Maid of Mrs. D. C. Spedden.
Spedden, Master D., and nurse.
Spencer, W. A.
Stead, W. T.
Stehli, Mr. and Mrs. Max Frolisher.
Sutton, Frederick.
Smart, John M.
Smith, Clinch.
Smith, R. W.
Stewart, A. A. (may be reported saved as Frederick Stewart.
Smith L. P.

T.

Taussig, Mrs. Emil.
Maid of Mrs. Thayer.
Thayer, John B.
Thorne, C.

V.

Vanderhoof, Wyckoff.

W.

Walker, W. A.
Warren, F. M.
White, Percival A.
White, Richard F.
Widener, G. D. and servant.
Widener, Harry.
Wood, Mr. and Mrs. Frank P.
Weir, J.
Wick, George D.
Williams, Duane.
Wright, George.

SECOND CABIN

A.

Abelson, Samson.
Andrew, Frank.
Ashby, John.
Aldsworth, C.
Andrew Edgar.

B.

Beacken, James H.
Brown, Mrs.
Banfield, Fred.
Beight, Nail.
Braily, Bandsman.
Breicoux, Bandsman.
Bailey, Percy.
Bainbridge, C. R.
Byles, the Rev Thomas
Beauchamp, H. J.
Beesley, Lawrence.
Berg, Miss E.
Benthan, I.
Bateman, Robert J.
Butler, Reginald.
Botsford, Hull.
Bowener, Solomon.
Berriman, William.

C

Clarke, Charles.
Clark, Bandsman.
Corey, Mrs.
Carter, the Rev. Ernest
Carter Mrs.
Coleridge, Reginald.
Chapman, Charles.
Cunningham, Alfred
Campbell, William.
Collyer, Harvey.
Corbett, Mrs. Irene.
Chapman, John R.
Chapman, Mrs. E.
Colander, Erie.
Cotterill, Harry.
Charles, William (probably reported saved as William Charles).

D.

Deacon, Percy.
Davis Charles, (may be reported saved as John Davies).
Debben, William.
De Brits, Jose.
Danborny, H.
Drew, James.
Drew, Master M.
David, Master J. W.
Duran, Miss A.
Dounton, W. J.
Del Vario, S.
Del Vario, Mrs.

E.

Enander, Ingar.
Eitmiller, G. F.

F.

Frost, A.
Fynnery, Md.
Faunthrope, M.
Fillbroock, C.
Funk, Annie.
Fahlsthom, A.
Fox, Stanley N.

G.

Greenberg, S.
Giles, Ralph.
Gaskell, Alfred.
Gillespie, William.
Gilbert, William.
Gall, Harry.
Gall, S.
Gill, John.
Giles, Edgar.
Giles, Fred.
Gale, Harry.
Gale, Phadruch.
Garvey, Lawrence.

H.

Hickman, Leonard.
Hickman, Lewis.
Hume, bandsman.
Hickman, Stanley.
Hood, Ambrose.
Hodges, Henry P.
Hart, Benjamin.
Harris, Walter.
Harper, John.
Harper, Nina.
Harbeck, W. H.
Hoffman, Mr.
Hoffman, Child.
Hoffman, Child.
Herman, Mrs. S.
Howard, B.
Howard, Mrs. E. T.
Hale Reginald.
Hamatainen, Anna, and infant son (probably reported saved as Anna Hamilton).
Hilunen, M.
Hunt, George.

J.

Jacobson, Mr.
Jacobson, Mrs.
Jacobson, Sydney.
Jeffery, Clifford.
Jeffery, Ernest.
Jenkin, Stephen.
Jarvis, John D.

K.

Keane, Daniel.
Kirkland, Rev. C.
Karnes, Mrs. F. G.
Kaynaldo, Miss.
Krillner, J. H.
Krins, bandsman.
Knight, R.
Karines, Mrs.
Kantar, Selna.
Kantar, Mrs. (probably reported saved as Miriam Kanton).

L.

Lengam, John.
Levy, P. J.
Lahtigan, William.
Lauch, Charles.
Leyson, R. W. N.
Laroche, Joseph.
Lamb, J. J.

M.

McKane, Peter.
Milling, Jacob.
Mantville, Joseph.
Malachard, Noll, (may be reported saved as Mme. Melicard).
Moraweck, Dr.
Mangiovacci, E.
McCrea, Arthur G.
McCrie, James M.
McKane, Peter D.
Mudd, Thomas.
Mack, Mary.
Marshall, Henry.
Mayberg, Frank H.
Meyer, August.
Myles, Thomas.
Mitchell, Henry.
Matthews, W. J.

N.

Nessen, Israel.
Nichols, Joseph C.
Norman, Robert D.
Nasser, Nicholas, (may be reported saved as Mrs. Nasser).

O.

Otteo, Richard.

P.

Phillips, Robert,
Ponesell, Martin (may be reported saved as M. F. Pososons).
Pain, Dr. Alfred.
Parkes, Frank.
Pengelly, F.
Pernot, Rene.
Peruschitz, the Rev.
Parker, Clifford.
Pulbaum, Frank.

R.

Rogers, Getina (probably reported saved as Miss Eliza Rogers).
Renouf, Peter E.
Rogers, Harry.
Reeves, David.

S.

Slemen, R. J.
Sjoberg, Hayden.
Slatter, Miss H. M.
Stanton, Ward.
Sinkkonen, Anna (probably reported saved as Anna Sinkkanea).
Sword, Hans K.
Stokes, Philip J.
Sharp, Percival.
Sedgwick, Mr.
Smith, Augustus.
Sweet, George.
Sjostedt, Ernst.

T.

Toomey, Ellen, may be reported saved as Ellen Formery.
Taylor, Bandsman.
Turpin, William J.
Turpin, Mrs. Dorothy.
Turner, John H.
Trouneansky, M.
Tervan, Mrs. A.
Trant, Mrs. Jesse (probably reported saved as Mrs. Jesse Traut).

V.

Veale, James.

W.

Wilhelm, Charles (probably reported saved as Charles Williams.
Watson, E.
Woodward, Benjamin
Woodward, Bandsman.
Ware, William C.
Weiss, Leopold.
Wheadon, Edward.
Ware, John J.

Ware, Mrs.. (may be reported saved as Miss Florence Mare).
West, E. Arthur.
Wheeler, Edwin.
Wenman, Samuel.

THIRD CLASS—S

A.

Allum, Owen.
Alexander, William.
Adams, J.
Alfred, Evan.
Allen, William.
Akar, Nourealain.
Assad, Said.
Alice, Agnes.
Aks, Tilly.
Attala, Malakka.
Ayont, Bancura.
Ahmed, Ali.
Alhomaki, Ilmari.
Ali, Willliam.
Anders, Gustafson.
Assam, Ali.
Asin, Adola.
Anderson, Albert.
Anderson, Ida.
Anderson, Thor.
Aronson, Ernest.
Ahlin, Johanna.
Anderson, Anders, and family.
Anderson, Carl.
Anderson, Samuel.
Andressen, Paul.
Augustan, Albert.
Abelsett, Glai.
Adelseth, Karen.
Adolf, Humblin.
Anderson, Erna.
Angheloff, Minko.
Arnold, Josef.
Arnold, Josephine.
Asplund, Johan.

B.

Braun, Lewis.
Braun, Owen.
Bowen, David.
Beavan, W.
Bachini, Zabour.
Belmentoy, Hassef.
Badt, Mohamet.
Betros, Yazbeck.
Barry, —
Bucklely, Katherine.
Burke, Jeremiah.
Barton, David.
Brocklebank, William.
Bostandyeff, Cuentche.
Bensons, John.
Billiard, A. and two children.
Bontos, Hanna.
Baccos, Boulos.
Bexrous, Tannous.
Burke, John.
Burke, Katherine.
Burke, Mary.
Burns, Mary.
Berglind, Ivar.
Balkic, Cerin.
Brobek, Carl.
Backstrom, Karl.
Berglund, Hans.
Bjorkland, Ernest.

C.

Can, Ernest.
Crease, Earnest.
Cohett, Gurshon.
Coutts, Winnie, and two children.
Cribb, John.
Cribb, Alice C.
Catavelas, Vassilios.
Caram, Catherine.
Cannavan, P.
Carr, Jenny.
Chartens, David.
Conlin, Thomas.
Celloti, Francesco.
Christman, Emil.
Caxon, Daniel.
Corn, Harry.
Carver, A.
Cook, Jacob.
Chip, Chang.
Chanini, Georges.
Chronopolous, Demetris
Connaghton, M.
Connors, P.
Carls, Anderson.
Carlsson, August.
Coelhe, Domingo.
Carlson, Carl.
Coleff, Sotie.
Coleff, Peye.
Cor. Ivan, and family.
Calic, Manda.
Calic, Peter.
Cheskosics, Luka.
Cacic, Gego.
Cacic, Luka.
Cacis, Taria.
Carlson, Julius.
Crescovic, Maria.

D.

Dugemin, Joseph.
Dean, Bertram.
Dorkings, Edward.
Dennis, Samuel.
Dennis, William.
Drazenovic, Josef.
Daher, Shedid.
Daly, Eugene.
Dwar, Frank.
Davies, John.
Dowdell, E.
Davison, Thomas.
Davison, Mary.
Dwyer, Tillie.
Dakic, Branko.
Danoff, Yoto.
Dantchoff, Christo.
Denkoff, Mitto.
Dintcheff, Valtcho.
Dedalic, Regzo.
Dahlberg, Gerda.
Demossemacker, Emma
Demossemacher, Guillaume.
Dimic, Jovan.
Dahl, Mauritz.
Dahl, Charles.
Drapkin, Jennie.
Donahue, Bert.
Doyle, Ellen.
Dalbom, Ernst. and family.
Dyker, Adolph.
Dyker, Elizabeth.

E.

Everett, Thomas.
Empuel, Ethel.
Elsbury, James.
Elias, Joseph.
Elias, Hanna.
Elias, Foofa.
Emmett, Thomas.
Ecimosic, Joso.
Edwardson, Gustave.
Eklund, Hans.
Ekstrom, Johan.

F.

Ford, Arthur.
Ford, Margaret, and family.
Franklin, Charles.
Foo, Cheong.
Farrell, James.
Flynn, James.
Flynn, John.
Foley, Joseph.
Foley, William.
Finote, Lingi.
Fischer, Eberhard.

G.

Goodwin, F., and family.
Goldsmith, Frank, and family.
Guest, Frank.
Green, George.
Garfirth, John.
Gillinski, Leslie.
Gheorgeff, Stano.
Ghemat, Emar.
Gerios, Youssef.
Gerios, Assaf.
Ghalil, Saal.
Gallagher, Martin.
Ganavan, Mary.
Glinagh, Katie.
Glynn, Mary.
Gronnestad, Daniel.
Gustafsch, Gideon.
Goldsmith, Nathan.
Goncalves, Mancel.
Gustafson, Johan.
Graf, Elin.
Gustafson, Alfred.

H.

Hyman, Abraham.
Harknett, Alice.
Hane, Youssef, and 2 children.
Haggendon, Kate.
Haggerty, Nora.
Hart, Henry.
Howard, May.
Harmer, Abraham.
Hachini, Najib.
Helene, Eugene.
Healy, Nora.
Henery, Della.
Hemming, Nora.
Hansen, Claus.
Hansen, Fanny.
Heininan, Wendis.
Hervonen, Helga and child.
Haas, Alaisa.
Hakkurainen, Elin.
Hakkurainen, Pekka.
Hankomen, Eluna.
Hansen, Henry.
Hendekovic, Ignaz.
Hickkinen, Laina.
Holm, John.
Hadman, Oscar.
Haglund, Conrad.
Haglund, Invald.
Henriksson, Jenny.
Hillstrom, Hilda.
Holten, Johan.

I.

Ing, Hen.
Iemenen, Manta.
Ilmakangas, Pista.
Ilmakangas, Ida.
Ilieff, Kriste.
Ilieff, Ylio.
Ivanoff, Kanie.

J.

Johnson, A., and family.
Jamila, Nicola, and child.
Jenymin, Annie.
Johnstone, W.
Joseph, Mary.
Jeannasr, Hanna.
Johannessen, Berdt.
Johannessen, Elias.
Johansen, Nils.
Johanson, Oscar.
Johansson, Gustav.
Jonkoff, Lazar.
Johnson, Elis, and family.
Johnson, Jakob.
Johnsson, Nils.

Jansen, Carl.
Jardin, Jose.
Jansen, Hans.
Johansson, Eric.
Jussila, Eric.
Jutel, Henry.
Johnsson, Carl.
Jusila, Kathina.
Juslia, Maria.

K.

Keefe, Arthur.
Kassen, Houssein.
Karum, Franz, and child.
Kelly, Anna.
Kelly, James.
Kennedy, John.
Kerane, Andy.
Kelley, James.
Keeni, Fahim.
Khalil, Lahia.
Kiernan, Philip.
Kiernan, John.
Kilgannon, Theodore.
Kakic, Tido.
Karajis, Milan.
Karkson, Einar.
Kalvig, Johannes.
King, Vincenz, and family.
Kallio, Nikolai.
Karlson, Nils.
Klasson, Klara, and two children.

L.

Lovell, John.
Lob, William.
Lobb, Cordelia.
Lester, James.
Lithman, Simon.
Leonard, I.
Lemberopolous, P.
Lakarian, Orsen.
Lane, Patrick.
Lennon, Dennis.
Lam, Ah.
Lam. Len.
Lang, Fang.
Ling, Lee.
Lockyer, Edward.
Latife, Maria.
Lennon, Mary.
Linehan, Michael.
Leinenen, Antti.
Lindell, Edward.
Lindell, Elin.
Lindqvist, Vine.
Larson, Viktor.
Lefebre, Frances and family.
Lindblom, August.
Lulic, Nicola.
Lundal, Hans.
Lundstrom, Jan.
Lyntakoff, Stanka.
Landegren, Aurora.
Laitinen, Sofia.
Larsson, Bengt.
Lasson, Edward.
Lindahl, Anna.
Lundin, Olga.
Linehan, Michael.

M.

Moore, Leonard.
Mackay, George.
Meek, Annie.
Mikalsen, Sander.
Miles, Frank.
Miles, Frederick.
Morley, William.
McNamee, Neal.
McNamee, Ellen.
Meanwell, Marian.
Meo, Alfonso.
Maisner, Simon.
Murdlin, Joseph.
Moor, Belle.
Moor, Meier.
Maria, Joseph.
Mantour, Mousea.
Moncarek, Omine, and two children.
McElroy, Michael.
McGowan, Katherine.
McMahon —.
McMahon, Martin.
Madigan, Maggie.
Manion, Margaret.
Mechan, John.
Mocklare, Ellis.
Moran, James.
Mulvihill, Bertha.
Murphy, Kate.
Mikahen, John.
Melkebuk, Philomen.
Merms, Leon.
Midtsjo, Carl.
Myhrman, Oliver.
Myster, Anna.
Makinen, Kale.
Mustafa, Nasr.
Mike, Anna.
Mustmans, Fatina.
Martin, Johan.
Malinoff, Nicola.
McCoy, Bridget.
Markoff, Martin.
Marinko, Dimitri.
Mineff, Ivan.
Minkoff, Iazar.
Mirko, Dika.
Mitkoff, Nitto.
Moen, Sigurd.

N.

Nancarror, William.
Nomagh, Robert.
Nakle, Trotik.
Nosworthy, Richard.
Naughton, Hannah.
Norel, Manseur.
Niels, —.
Nillson, Herta.
Nyoven, Johan.
Naidenoff, Penke.
Nankoff, Minko.
Nedelic, Petroff.
Nenkoff, Christe.
Nilson, August.
Nirva, Isak.
Nandewalle, Nestor.

O.

O'Brien, Dennis.
O'Brien, Hanna.
O'Brien, Thomas.
O'Donnell, Patrick
Odele, Catherine.
O'Connoy, Patrick.
O'Neill, Bridget.
Olsen, Carl.
Olsen, Ole.
Olson, Elin.
Olson, John.
Ortin, Amin.
Odahl, Martin.
Olman, Velin.
Olsen, Henry.
Olman, Mara.
Olsen, Elide.
Orescovic, Teko.

P.

Pedruzzi, Joseph.
Perkin, John.
Pearce, Ernest.
Peacock, Treesteall, and two children.
Potchett, George.
Peterson, Marius.
Peters, Katie.
Paulsson, Alma, and family.
Panula, Mari, and family.
Pekonami, E.
Peltomaki, Miheldi.
Pacruic, Mate.
Pacruic, Tamo.
Pastche, Petroff.
Pletcharsky, Vasil.
Palovic, Vtefo.
Petranec, Matilda.
Person, Ernest.
Pasic, Jacob.
Planks, Jules.
Peterson, Ellen.
Peterson, Olaf.
Peterson, Wohn.

R.

Rouse, Richard.
Rush, Alfred.
Rogers, William.
Reynolds, Harold.
Riordan, Hannah.
Ryan, Edward.
Rainch, Razi.
Roufoul, Aposetun.
Read, James.
Robins, Alexander.
Robins, Charity.
Risian, Samuel.
Risian, Emma.
Runnestvet, Kristian.
Randeff, Alexandre.
Rintamaki, Matti.
Rosblon, Helen, and family.
Ridegain, Charles.

S.

Sadowitz, Harry.
Saundercock, W.
Shellark, Frederick.
Sage, John and family.
Sawyer, Frederick.
Spinner, Henry.
Shorney, Charles.
Sarkis, Lahound.
Sultani, Meme.
Stankovic, Javan.
Salini, Antoni.
Seman, Betros.
Sadlier, Matt.
Scanlon, James.
Shaughnessay, P.
Simmons, John.
Serota, Maurice.
Sommerton, F.
Slocovski, Selmen.
Sutchall, Henry.
Sather, Simon.
Storey, T.
Spector, Woolf.
Sirayman, Peter.
Samaan, Jouseef.
Saiide, Barbara.
Saad, Divo.
Sarkis, Madiresian.
Shine, Ellen.
Sullivan, Bridget.
Salander, Carl.
Sepelelanaker, Alfons.
Skog, William and family.
Solvang, Lena.
Strangberg, Ida.
Strilik, Ivan.
Salonen, Ferner.
Sivic, Husen.
Svenson, Ola.
Svenst, —.
Sandman, Mohan.
Saljilsvick, Anna.
Schelp, Peter.
Sihvola, Antti.
Slabenoff, Peter.
Staneff, Ivan.
Stoytcho, Mikoff.
Stoytehoff, Illa.
Sydcoff, Todor.
Sandstrom, Agnes and two children.
Sheerlinch, Joan.
Smiljanik, Mile.
Strom, Elma, and child.
Svensson, John.
Swensson, Edwin.

T.

Tobin, Roger.
Thomson, Alex.
Theobald, Thomas
Tomlin, Ernest.
Thorneycroft, P.
Thorneycroft, F.
Torber, Ernest.
Trembisky, Berk.
Tiley, Edward.
Tamini, Hilion.
Tannans, Daper.
Thomas, John.
Thomas, Charles.
Thomas, Tannous.
Tumin, Thomas, and infant.
Tikkanen, Juho.
Tonglin, Gunner.
Turoin, Stefan.
Turgo, Anna.
Tedoreff, Ialie.

U.

Usher, Haulmer.
Uzelas, Jose.

V.

Vander and family.
Vereuysse, Victor.
Vjoblon, Anna.
Vaclens, Adulle.
Vandersteen, Leo.
Vanimps, Jacob, and family.
Vatdevehde, Josep.

W.

Williams, Harry.
Williams, Leslie.
Ware, Frederick.
Warren, Charles.
Waika, Said.
Wazli, Jousef.
Wiseman, Philip.
Werber, James.
Windelor, Einar.
Weller, Edward.
Wennerstrom, August.
Wendal, Olaf.
Wistrom, Hans.
Wiklund, Jacob.
Wiklund, Carl.
Wenzel, Zinhart.
Wirz, Albert.
Wittewrongel, Camille.

Y.

Youssef, Brahim.
Yalsevac, Ivan.

Z.

Zakarian, Mapri.
Zievens, Rene.
Zimmerman, Leo.

OFFICIAL LIST OF PASSENGERS RESCUED.

The following is the official list of passengers rescued by the Carpathia and taken to New York :

FIRST CABIN

A.

Anderson, Harry.
Appleton, Mrs. E. W.
Alison, Master, and nurse.
Allison, maid of.
Andrews, Miss K. T. (Miss Cornelia I.?)
Allen, Miss E. W.
Astor, Mrs. John Jacob, and maid.
Aubert, Mrs. N., and maid.

B.

Behr, Karl.
Bucknell, Mrs. William and maid.
Barkworth, Mr. A. H.
Bowerman, Miss E.
Brown, Mrs. J. J.
Burns, Miss C. M.
Bishop, Mr. and Mrs. D. (Mr. and Mrs. Dickinson Bisley).
Blank, Mr. H.
Baxter, Mrs. Jas.
Brayton, Geo. A.
Bonnell, Miss Caroline.
Bonnell, Miss Eliz.
Brown, Mrs. J. Murray.
Bowen, Miss Grace I.
Beckwith, Mr. and Mrs. R. L.

C.

Cardeza, Mrs. J. W., and maid.
Cassebere, Mrs. H. A., Jr.
Clarke, Mrs. W. M.
Chibnail, Mrs. H.
Crosby, Mrs. E. G.
Crosby, Miss H.
Cardell, Mrs. Churchill.
Calderhead, E. P.
Cavendish, Mrs. Turrell, and maid.
Chaffee, Mrs. H. L.
Cardeza, Mr. Thos.
Cummings, Mrs. J. B.
Chevre, Mr. Paul.
Cherry, Miss Gladys.
Chambers, Mr. and Mrs. N. C.
Carter, Mr. and Mrs. W. F.
Carter, Miss Lucille P.
Carter, Master Wm. T.
Cornell, Mrs. Robt. C.

D.

Douglass, Mrs. Fred C.
De Villiers, Mme.
Daly, Mr. P. D.
Daniel, Mr. Robt. W.
Davidson, Mrs. Thornton.
Douglass, Mrs. Walter, and maid.
Dodge, Mr. Washington.
Dodge, Mrs. Washington, and son.
Dick, Mr. and Mrs. A. A.
Drachstedt, Mr. A.
Duff-Gordon, Sir Cosmo.
Duff-Gordon, Lady.

E.

Endress, Miss Caroline (Mrs.?)
Earnshaw, Mrs. Boulton.
Eustis, Miss Eliz. M.

F.

Flegenheim, Miss Antoinette.
Francatelli, Miss M.
Flynn, Mr. J. I.
Fortune, Miss Alice.
Fortune, Miss Ethel.
Fortune, Mrs. Mark,
Fortune, Miss Mabel.
Fraunethal, Mr. and Mrs. Hy. W.
Frauenthal, Mr. and Mrs. I. G.
Frolicher, Mr. and Max.
Frolicher, Miss Margaret.
Futrelle, Mrs. Jacques.

G.

Gracie, Col. Archibald.
Graham, Mrs. Wm.
Graham, Miss.
Gibson, Miss Dorothy.
Goldenberg, Mr. and Mrs. Samuel.
Greenfield, Mrs. Lee D
Greenfield, Mr. W. B.
Gibson, Mrs. Leonard.

H.

Haven, Mr. H.
Nippach, Mrs. Ida S.
Hippach, Miss Jean
Harris, Mrs. H. B.
Holverson, Mrs. Alex.
Hogebloom, Mrs. J. C.
Hawksford, Mr. W. L.
Harper, Mrs. H. S.
Harper, Mr. Henry S., and manservant.
Hoyt, Mr. and Mrs. Fred M.
Harder, Mr. and Mrs. George.
Hays, Mrs. Chas. M.
Hays, Miss Margaret B

I.

Ismay, Mr. J. Bruce.

K.

Kimball, Mr. and Mrs. E. M.
Kenyon, Mrs. F. A.
Krenchen, Miss Emile. (F. R. ?)

L.

Longley, Miss G. F.
Leader, Mrs. F. A.
Lines, Mrs. Ernest.
Lines, Miss Mary C.
Lindstrom, Mrs. Sigfrid.

M.

Meyer, Mrs. E. G.
Madill, Miss G. A.
Maloney, Mrs. R. (Marvin?), Mrs. D. W.
Marechell, Pierre, Mr.
Minahan, Mrs. Wm. E.
Minahan, Miss Daisy.
Mock, Mr. Philip E.
McGough, Mr. Jas.

N.

Newell, Miss Marjorie (Miss Alice?).
Newell, Miss Madeline.
Newson, Miss Helen M.

O.

Ostby, Miss Helen.
Ormond, Mr. F.

P.

Penasco, Mrs. Joseph, (Victor?).
Potter, Mrs. Thos. J.
Peuchen, Major Arthur
Pears, Mrs. Thomas.
Perrcault, Mrs. A.

R.

Rothschild, Mrs. Marton.
Rosenbaum, Miss Edith
Rheims, Mr. George.
Rothes, Countess of.
Roberts, Mrs. E. S.
Rolmane, Mr. C.
Ryerson, Mr. J. B.
Ryerson, S. R., Miss
Ryerson, Miss Emily.
Ryerson, Mrs. Arthur.

S.

Stone, Mrs. Geo. M. and maid.
Seward, Mr. Fred. K.
Shutes, Miss E.
Sloper, Mr. Wm. T.
Swift, Mrs. F. Joel.
Schaber, Mrs. Paul.
Spedden, Robert Douglass.
Snyder, Mr. and Mrs. John.
Silverhorn, Mr. R. Spencer.
Saalfeld, Mr. Adolf.
Smith, Mrs. Lucien P.,
Stephenson, Mrs. W. B.
Solomon, Mr. Abraham.
Silvey, Mrs. Wm. B.
Stengle, Mr. and Mrs., C. E. H.
Spencer, Mrs. W. A. and maid.
Slayter, Miss Hilda.
Spedden, Mr. and Mrs. F. O.
Straus's, maid of

T.

Thayer, Mrs. J. B., and maid.
Thayer, J. B., Jr.
Taussig, Miss Ruth.
Taussig, Mrs. E.
Taylor, E. Z.
Taylor, Mrs. E.
Tucker, Gilbert M., Jr.
Thorne, Mrs. Gertrude

W.

Woolner, Hy.
Williams, Rich. M., Jr.
Warren, Mrs. F. M.
Wilson, Miss Helen A.
Willard, Miss C.
Wick, Mrs. George.
Wick, Miss Mary.
Widener, Mrs. George D., and maid.
White, Mrs. J. Stewart, and maid.
Widener, Valet G.

Y.

Young, Miss Marie G.

SECOND CABIN

Angle, Mrs.
Abelson, Mrs. Hanna.
Abbott, Mrs. Rosa.
Argenia, Mrs. Genovia, and two children.

Balls, Mrs Ada E.
Bass, Miss Kate.
Becker, Mrs. A. O., and three children.
Beane, Mr. Edward.
Beane, Mrs.
Brown, Mildred.
Brown, Mrs. Elizabeth
Bentham, Lillian W.
Bystron, Karolina.
Bryhl, Dagmar,
Beesley, Mr. L.

Clark, Mrs. Ada.
Cameron, Miss Clara.
Caldwell, Albert F.
Caldwell, Mrs Sylvan.
Caldwell, Infant Alden
Christy, Alice,
Christy, Julia,
Collet, Stuart (Mr.).
Collyer, Mrs. Charlotte
Collyer, Miss Marjorie
Doling, Mrs. Ada.
Doling, Miss Elsie
Drew, Mrs. Lulu and child.
Davis, Mrs. Agnes.
Davis, Miss Mary.
Davis, John M.
Duran, Florentine.
Duran, Miss A.

Faunthorpe, Mrs. Lizz.

Garside, Ethel.

Hart, Mrs. (Esther).
Hart, Child, (Eva)
Harris, George.
Hewlett, Mrs. Mary.
Harper, Nana.
Hold, Mrs. A.
Hosno, Mr. Masabumi.
Hocking, Mrs. and daughter.
Herman, Mrs. Jane
Herman, Miss Kate,
Herman, Miss Alice
Hamlia, Mrs. H. and child.
Hoffman, Lolo.
Hoffman, Lues.
Ilett, Bertha.

Jacobson, Mrs. Amy.
Jerman, Mrs. M.

Keane, Miss Nora A.
Kelly, Mrs. F.
Kemton, Mirriam.
Leitch, Jessie,
Laroche, Mrs.
Laroche, Miss Simmome.
Laroche, Miss Louise.
Lehman, Bertha.
Lauch, Mrs. A.
Lamore, Amelia.

Mellinger, Eliz.
Mellinger, Child.
Marshall, Mrs. Kate.
Mallet, Mrs.
Mallett, Master R. E.
Mellers, W. J.
Mussa or Nesser, Mrs.

Nye, Elizabeth.

Oxenham, Thomas.

Phillips, Alice.
Pallas, Mrs. Emilio (?)
Padro, Mr. Julian.
Pinsky, Rosa.
Portaluppi, Emilio.
Parish, Mrs. David.
Quick, Mrs. Jane.
Quick, Miss Vera.
Quick, Miss Phyllis.

Rinaldo, Mrs. Emcarmacion.
Ridsdale, Lucy.
Renouf, Mrs. Lily.
Rugg, Miss Emily.
Richards, Emily, and two children.
Rogers, Miss Selina.

Sincock, Miss Maude.
Smith, Miss Marion.
Silven, Lylle.
Simpson, Alma.

Toney, Miss.
Trent, Mrs. Jessie.
Trout, Miss E.

Williams, C. Chas.
Weitz, Mrs. (Mathilda)
Webber, Miss Susie.
Wright, Miss Marion.
Watt, Mrs. Bessie.
Watt, Miss Bertha.
West, Mrs.
West, Miss Constance.
West, Miss Barbara.
Wells, Addie.
Wells, Miss.
Wells, Master.
Ware, Mrs. Florence.
Whilems, Chas.
Water, Nellie.
Woolcroft, Nellie.

THIRD CLASS STEERAGE

Anderson, Emma.
Aks, Leah.
Aks, Fily.
Abrahamson, August.
Asplund, John.
Abelseth, Olaus.
Abelseth, Koran.
Asplund, Selina.
Asplund, William.
Asplund, Felix.
Assay, Marion.
Ajul, Bemora.
Anderson, Carla.

Brien, Hanno O.
Buckley, Daniel.
Bradley, Bridget.
Badman, Emily.
Bockstrom, Mary.
Bolos, Monthora.
Bakline, Latifa.
Bakline, Marie.
Bakline, Eugene.
Bakline, Helena.

Coutts, Winnie.
Coutts, William.
Coutts, Veville.
Carr, Ellen.
Colier, Gosham,
Cribb, Laura.
Cassen, Nassef.
Connelly Kate.

Dorkings, Edward.
Driscoll, Bridget.
Daly, Eugene.
Devincy, Margaret.
Draplin, Jennie.
Dean, Ettie.
Dean, Bertram.
Dean, Gladys.
Davidson, Mary.
Dahl, Charles.
Daly, Marcella.
Dardell, Elizabeth.
Dyker, Elizabeth.
Darawich, Hassin.
Darawich, George.
Darawich, Marian.
Dugennon, Joseph.

Emanuel, Ethel.

Fastaman, David.
Frithjof, Mathesen.
Fatnai, Ermaculmam.

Glynn, Mary.
Goldsmith, Emily.
Goldsmith, Frank.
Gallinagh, Kate.
Gunner Tonjlon.

Hyman, Abraham.
Howard, Mary.
Hokkarmer, Ellen.
Hermen, Hilda.
Hanson, Jenny.
Hedman, Oscar.
Hamann, Merris.
Hillsbrom, Hilda.
Hakanen, Line.
Hankonen, Elena.

Jelscrac, Ivar.
Jermyn, Annie.
Johansen, Oscar.
Joseph, Katherine.
Joseph, Mary.
Jenson, Carl.
Johanson, Berendt.
Johanson, Oscar L.
Johnson, Alice.
Johnsen, Eleanora.
Johnsen, Harold.
Joseph, Mary.
Jousef, Shanin.
John, Borah.
Janson, Carl.
Jonsila, Eric.
Kelly, Annie.

Kelly, Mary.
Kockoven, Erichan.
Kennedy, John.
Kink, Anton.
Kink, Louisa.
Kink, Louisa.
Kurum, Franz.
Kurum, Anna.
Karlson, Einac.
Lindin, Olga.
Lundstrom, Imric.
Lundegren, Aurora.
Lulu, Newlin.

Mulder, Theodor De.
Moran, Bertha.
Madigan. Maggie.
Mechlane, Ellen.
McDermott, Delia.
Marion, Margaret.
Murphy, Maggie.
Murphy, Kate.
Moor, Neuna.
Moor, Belle.
Mulvehill, Bertha.
McCoy, Bernard.
Mullen, Kate.
Murphy, Norah.
Midtago, Carl.
Moss, Albert.
Messenacker, Arcina.
Monbarck, Annie.
Monbarck, Gurio.
Monbarck, Halim.

McCormack, Thos.
McCoy, Agnes.
McCarthy, Kate.
McCoy, Alice.
McGovan, Mary.
McGovan, Annie.
Nelson, Bertha.
Nzsten, Annan.
Nelson, Helmina.
Nicola, Jancole.
Nicola, Elias.
Neckard, Said.
Neckard, Wodar.
Neckard, Marim.
Nigel, Joseph.
Niskanan, John.

O'Dwyer, Nellie.
O'Keefe, Patrick.
O'Leary, Norah.
Olsen, Archer.
Olman. Vilm.
Osman, Mara.

Person, Ernes.

Ryan, Edward.
Reardon, Hannah.
Roth, Sarah.

Schurlich, Jane.
Sap, Jules.
Sunderland, Victor.

Shina, Ellen.
Smyth, Julian.
Stanley, Amig.
Sevenson, Servin.
Sundman, Julian.
Sjoblom, Annie.
Sandstrom, Agnes.
Sandstrom, Margaret.
Sandstrom, Beatrice.
Salkjclsock, Anna.
Scunda, Famimi.
Scunda, Assed.
Strand, Jahs.

Thornycroft, Florence.
Treunbisky, Buk.
Turnqu, Wm. H.
Turgen, Ann.
Turkala, Hevig.

Vagie, Adele Jane.
Winnerstrom, Amy E.
Wilkes, Ellen.
Yeslick. Salamy.
Zuni, Fabim.

Luigi, Finoli.
Ah Lam.
Bing Lee
Tang Lang.
Hee Lang.
Chip Chang.
Foo Chang.
Stachelm, Mr. Max.
Simonius, Mr. Alfon-

A CATALOG OF SELECTED

DOVER BOOKS

IN ALL FIELDS OF INTEREST

A CATALOG OF SELECTED DOVER BOOKS IN ALL FIELDS OF INTEREST

STICKLEY CRAFTSMAN FURNITURE CATALOGS, Gustav Stickley and L. & J. G. Stickley. Beautiful, functional furniture in two authentic catalogs from 1910. 594 illustrations, including 277 photos, show settles, rockers, armchairs, reclining chairs, bookcases, desks, tables. 183pp. 6½ x 9¼. 23838-5 Pa. $9.95

AMERICAN LOCOMOTIVES IN HISTORIC PHOTOGRAPHS: 1858 to 1949, Ron Ziel (ed.). A rare collection of 126 meticulously detailed official photographs, called "builder portraits," of American locomotives that majestically chronicle the rise of steam locomotive power in America. Introduction. Detailed captions. xi + 129pp. 9 x 12. 27393-8 Pa. $12.95

AMERICA'S LIGHTHOUSES: An Illustrated History, Francis Ross Holland, Jr. Delightfully written, profusely illustrated fact-filled survey of over 200 American lighthouses since 1716. History, anecdotes, technological advances, more. 240pp. 8 x 10¾. 25576-X Pa. $12.95

TOWARDS A NEW ARCHITECTURE, Le Corbusier. Pioneering manifesto by founder of "International School." Technical and aesthetic theories, views of industry, economics, relation of form to function, "mass-production split" and much more. Profusely illustrated. 320pp. 6⅛ x 9¼. (USO) 25023-7 Pa. $9.95

HOW THE OTHER HALF LIVES, Jacob Riis. Famous journalistic record, exposing poverty and degradation of New York slums around 1900, by major social reformer. 100 striking and influential photographs. 233pp. 10 x 7⅞. 22012-5 Pa. $10.95

FRUIT KEY AND TWIG KEY TO TREES AND SHRUBS, William M. Harlow. One of the handiest and most widely used identification aids. Fruit key covers 120 deciduous and evergreen species; twig key 160 deciduous species. Easily used. Over 300 photographs. 126pp. 5⅜ x 8½. 20511-8 Pa. $3.95

COMMON BIRD SONGS, Dr. Donald J. Borror. Songs of 60 most common U.S. birds: robins, sparrows, cardinals, bluejays, finches, more–arranged in order of increasing complexity. Up to 9 variations of songs of each species. Cassette and manual 99911-4 $8.95

ORCHIDS AS HOUSE PLANTS, Rebecca Tyson Northen. Grow cattleyas and many other kinds of orchids–in a window, in a case, or under artificial light. 63 illustrations. 148pp. 5⅜ x 8½. 23261-1 Pa. $4.95

MONSTER MAZES, Dave Phillips. Masterful mazes at four levels of difficulty. Avoid deadly perils and evil creatures to find magical treasures. Solutions for all 32 exciting illustrated puzzles. 48pp. 8¼ x 11. 26005-4 Pa. $2.95

MOZART'S DON GIOVANNI (DOVER OPERA LIBRETTO SERIES), Wolfgang Amadeus Mozart. Introduced and translated by Ellen H. Bleiler. Standard Italian libretto, with complete English translation. Convenient and thoroughly portable–an ideal companion for reading along with a recording or the performance itself. Introduction. List of characters. Plot summary. 121pp. 5¼ x 8½. 24944-1 Pa. $2.95

TECHNICAL MANUAL AND DICTIONARY OF CLASSICAL BALLET, Gail Grant. Defines, explains, comments on steps, movements, poses and concepts. 15-page pictorial section. Basic book for student, viewer. 127pp. 5⅜ x 8½. 21843-0 Pa. $4.95

BRASS INSTRUMENTS: Their History and Development, Anthony Baines. Authoritative, updated survey of the evolution of trumpets, trombones, bugles, cornets, French horns, tubas and other brass wind instruments. Over 140 illustrations and 48 music examples. Corrected and updated by author. New preface. Bibliography. 320pp. 5⅜ x 8½. 27574-4 Pa. $9.95

HOLLYWOOD GLAMOR PORTRAITS, John Kobal (ed.). 145 photos from 1926-49. Harlow, Gable, Bogart, Bacall; 94 stars in all. Full background on photographers, technical aspects. 160pp. 8⅜ x 11¼. 23352-9 Pa. $12.95

MAX AND MORITZ, Wilhelm Busch. Great humor classic in both German and English. Also 10 other works: "Cat and Mouse," "Plisch and Plumm," etc. 216pp. 5⅜ x 8½. 20181-3 Pa. $6.95

THE RAVEN AND OTHER FAVORITE POEMS, Edgar Allan Poe. Over 40 of the author's most memorable poems: "The Bells," "Ulalume," "Israfel," "To Helen," "The Conqueror Worm," "Eldorado," "Annabel Lee," many more. Alphabetic lists of titles and first lines. 64pp. 5³⁄₁₆ x 8¼. 26685-0 Pa. $1.00

PERSONAL MEMOIRS OF U. S. GRANT, Ulysses Simpson Grant. Intelligent, deeply moving firsthand account of Civil War campaigns, considered by many the finest military memoirs ever written. Includes letters, historic photographs, maps and more. 528pp. 6⅛ x 9¼. 28587-1 Pa. $11.95

AMULETS AND SUPERSTITIONS, E. A. Wallis Budge. Comprehensive discourse on origin, powers of amulets in many ancient cultures: Arab, Persian Babylonian, Assyrian, Egyptian, Gnostic, Hebrew, Phoenician, Syriac, etc. Covers cross, swastika, crucifix, seals, rings, stones, etc. 584pp. 5⅜ x 8½. 23573-4 Pa. $12.95

RUSSIAN STORIES/PYCCKNE PACCKA3bl: A Dual-Language Book, edited by Gleb Struve. Twelve tales by such masters as Chekhov, Tolstoy, Dostoevsky, Pushkin, others. Excellent word-for-word English translations on facing pages, plus teaching and study aids, Russian/English vocabulary, biographical/critical introductions, more. 416pp. 5⅜ x 8½. 26244-8 Pa. $8.95

PHILADELPHIA THEN AND NOW: 60 Sites Photographed in the Past and Present, Kenneth Finkel and Susan Oyama. Rare photographs of City Hall, Logan Square, Independence Hall, Betsy Ross House, other landmarks juxtaposed with contemporary views. Captures changing face of historic city. Introduction. Captions. 128pp. 8¼ x 11. 25790-8 Pa. $9.95

AIA ARCHITECTURAL GUIDE TO NASSAU AND SUFFOLK COUNTIES, LONG ISLAND, The American Institute of Architects, Long Island Chapter, and the Society for the Preservation of Long Island Antiquities. Comprehensive, well-researched and generously illustrated volume brings to life over three centuries of Long Island's great architectural heritage. More than 240 photographs with authoritative, extensively detailed captions. 176pp. 8¼ x 11. 26946-9 Pa. $14.95

NORTH AMERICAN INDIAN LIFE: Customs and Traditions of 23 Tribes, Elsie Clews Parsons (ed.). 27 fictionalized essays by noted anthropologists examine religion, customs, government, additional facets of life among the Winnebago, Crow, Zuni, Eskimo, other tribes. 480pp. 6⅛ x 9¼. 27377-6 Pa. $10.95

FRANK LLOYD WRIGHT'S HOLLYHOCK HOUSE, Donald Hoffmann. Lavishly illustrated, carefully documented study of one of Wright's most controversial residential designs. Over 120 photographs, floor plans, elevations, etc. Detailed perceptive text by noted Wright scholar. Index. 128pp. 9¼ x 10¾. 27133-1 Pa. $11.95

THE MALE AND FEMALE FIGURE IN MOTION: 60 Classic Photographic Sequences, Eadweard Muybridge. 60 true-action photographs of men and women walking, running, climbing, bending, turning, etc., reproduced from rare 19th-century masterpiece. vi + 121pp. 9 x 12. 24745-7 Pa. $10.95

1001 QUESTIONS ANSWERED ABOUT THE SEASHORE, N. J. Berrill and Jacquelyn Berrill. Queries answered about dolphins, sea snails, sponges, starfish, fishes, shore birds, many others. Covers appearance, breeding, growth, feeding, much more. 305pp. 5¼ x 8¼. 23366-9 Pa. $8.95

GUIDE TO OWL WATCHING IN NORTH AMERICA, Donald S. Heintzelman. Superb guide offers complete data and descriptions of 19 species: barn owl, screech owl, snowy owl, many more. Expert coverage of owl-watching equipment, conservation, migrations and invasions, etc. Guide to observing sites. 84 illustrations. xiii + 193pp. 5⅜ x 8½. 27344-X Pa. $8.95

MEDICINAL AND OTHER USES OF NORTH AMERICAN PLANTS: A Historical Survey with Special Reference to the Eastern Indian Tribes, Charlotte Erichsen-Brown. Chronological historical citations document 500 years of usage of plants, trees, shrubs native to eastern Canada, northeastern U.S. Also complete identifying information. 343 illustrations. 544pp. 6½ x 9¼. 25951-X Pa. $12.95

STORYBOOK MAZES, Dave Phillips. 23 stories and mazes on two-page spreads: Wizard of Oz, Treasure Island, Robin Hood, etc. Solutions. 64pp. 8¼ x 11. 23628-5 Pa. $2.95

NEGRO FOLK MUSIC, U.S.A., Harold Courlander. Noted folklorist's scholarly yet readable analysis of rich and varied musical tradition. Includes authentic versions of over 40 folk songs. Valuable bibliography and discography. xi + 324pp. 5⅜ x 8½. 27350-4 Pa. $9.95

MOVIE-STAR PORTRAITS OF THE FORTIES, John Kobal (ed.). 163 glamor, studio photos of 106 stars of the 1940s: Rita Hayworth, Ava Gardner, Marlon Brando, Clark Gable, many more. 176pp. 8⅜ x 11¼. 23546-7 Pa. $12.95

BENCHLEY LOST AND FOUND, Robert Benchley. Finest humor from early 30s, about pet peeves, child psychologists, post office and others. Mostly unavailable elsewhere. 73 illustrations by Peter Arno and others. 183pp. 5⅜ x 8½. 22410-4 Pa. $6.95

YEKL and THE IMPORTED BRIDEGROOM AND OTHER STORIES OF YIDDISH NEW YORK, Abraham Cahan. Film Hester Street based on Yekl (1896). Novel, other stories among first about Jewish immigrants on N.Y.'s East Side. 240pp. 5⅜ x 8½. 22427-9 Pa. $6.95

SELECTED POEMS, Walt Whitman. Generous sampling from *Leaves of Grass*. Twenty-four poems include "I Hear America Singing," "Song of the Open Road," "I Sing the Body Electric," "When Lilacs Last in the Dooryard Bloom'd," "O Captain! My Captain!"–all reprinted from an authoritative edition. Lists of titles and first lines. 128pp. 5$^{3}/_{16}$ x 8¼. 26878-0 Pa. $1.00

THE BEST TALES OF HOFFMANN, E. T. A. Hoffmann. 10 of Hoffmann's most important stories: "Nutcracker and the King of Mice," "The Golden Flowerpot," etc. 458pp. 5⅜ x 8½. 21793-0 Pa. $9.95

FROM FETISH TO GOD IN ANCIENT EGYPT, E. A. Wallis Budge. Rich detailed survey of Egyptian conception of "God" and gods, magic, cult of animals, Osiris, more. Also, superb English translations of hymns and legends. 240 illustrations. 545pp. 5⅜ x 8½. 25803-3 Pa. $13.95

FRENCH STORIES/CONTES FRANÇAIS: A Dual-Language Book, Wallace Fowlie. Ten stories by French masters, Voltaire to Camus: "Micromegas" by Voltaire; "The Atheist's Mass" by Balzac; "Minuet" by de Maupassant; "The Guest" by Camus, six more. Excellent English translations on facing pages. Also French-English vocabulary list, exercises, more. 352pp. 5⅜ x 8½. 26443-2 Pa. $8.95

CHICAGO AT THE TURN OF THE CENTURY IN PHOTOGRAPHS: 122 Historic Views from the Collections of the Chicago Historical Society, Larry A. Viskochil. Rare large-format prints offer detailed views of City Hall, State Street, the Loop, Hull House, Union Station, many other landmarks, circa 1904-1913. Introduction. Captions. Maps. 144pp. 9⅜ x 12¼. 24656-6 Pa. $12.95

OLD BROOKLYN IN EARLY PHOTOGRAPHS, 1865-1929, William Lee Younger. Luna Park, Gravesend race track, construction of Grand Army Plaza, moving of Hotel Brighton, etc. 157 previously unpublished photographs. 165pp. 8⅞ x 11¾. 23587-4 Pa. $13.95

THE MYTHS OF THE NORTH AMERICAN INDIANS, Lewis Spence. Rich anthology of the myths and legends of the Algonquins, Iroquois, Pawnees and Sioux, prefaced by an extensive historical and ethnological commentary. 36 illustrations. 480pp. 5⅜ x 8½. 25967-6 Pa. $8.95

AN ENCYCLOPEDIA OF BATTLES: Accounts of Over 1,560 Battles from 1479 B.C. to the Present, David Eggenberger. Essential details of every major battle in recorded history from the first battle of Megiddo in 1479 B.C. to Grenada in 1984. List of Battle Maps. New Appendix covering the years 1967-1984. Index. 99 illustrations. 544pp. 6½ x 9¼. 24913-1 Pa. $14.95

SAILING ALONE AROUND THE WORLD, Captain Joshua Slocum. First man to sail around the world, alone, in small boat. One of great feats of seamanship told in delightful manner. 67 illustrations. 294pp. 5⅜ x 8½. 20326-3 Pa. $5.95

ANARCHISM AND OTHER ESSAYS, Emma Goldman. Powerful, penetrating, prophetic essays on direct action, role of minorities, prison reform, puritan hypocrisy, violence, etc. 271pp. 5⅜ x 8½. 22484-8 Pa. $6.95

MYTHS OF THE HINDUS AND BUDDHISTS, Ananda K. Coomaraswamy and Sister Nivedita. Great stories of the epics; deeds of Krishna, Shiva, taken from puranas, Vedas, folk tales; etc. 32 illustrations. 400pp. 5⅜ x 8½. 21759-0 Pa. $10.95

BEYOND PSYCHOLOGY, Otto Rank. Fear of death, desire of immortality, nature of sexuality, social organization, creativity, according to Rankian system. 291pp. 5⅜ x 8½. 20485-5 Pa. $8.95

A THEOLOGICO-POLITICAL TREATISE, Benedict Spinoza. Also contains unfinished Political Treatise. Great classic on religious liberty, theory of government on common consent. R. Elwes translation. Total of 421pp. 5⅜ x 8½. 20249-6 Pa. $9.95

MY BONDAGE AND MY FREEDOM, Frederick Douglass. Born a slave, Douglass became outspoken force in antislavery movement. The best of Douglass' autobiographies. Graphic description of slave life. 464pp. 5⅜ x 8½. 22457-0 Pa. $8.95

FOLLOWING THE EQUATOR: A Journey Around the World, Mark Twain. Fascinating humorous account of 1897 voyage to Hawaii, Australia, India, New Zealand, etc. Ironic, bemused reports on peoples, customs, climate, flora and fauna, politics, much more. 197 illustrations. 720pp. 5⅜ x 8½. 26113-1 Pa. $15.95

THE PEOPLE CALLED SHAKERS, Edward D. Andrews. Definitive study of Shakers: origins, beliefs, practices, dances, social organization, furniture and crafts, etc. 33 illustrations. 351pp. 5⅜ x 8½. 21081-2 Pa. $8.95

THE MYTHS OF GREECE AND ROME, H. A. Guerber. A classic of mythology, generously illustrated, long prized for its simple, graphic, accurate retelling of the principal myths of Greece and Rome, and for its commentary on their origins and significance. With 64 illustrations by Michelangelo, Raphael, Titian, Rubens, Canova, Bernini and others. 480pp. 5⅜ x 8½. 27584-1 Pa. $9.95

PSYCHOLOGY OF MUSIC, Carl E. Seashore. Classic work discusses music as a medium from psychological viewpoint. Clear treatment of physical acoustics, auditory apparatus, sound perception, development of musical skills, nature of musical feeling, host of other topics. 88 figures. 408pp. 5⅜ x 8½. 21851-1 Pa. $10.95

THE PHILOSOPHY OF HISTORY, Georg W. Hegel. Great classic of Western thought develops concept that history is not chance but rational process, the evolution of freedom. 457pp. 5⅜ x 8½. 20112-0 Pa. $9.95

THE BOOK OF TEA, Kakuzo Okakura. Minor classic of the Orient: entertaining, charming explanation, interpretation of traditional Japanese culture in terms of tea ceremony. 94pp. 5⅜ x 8½. 20070-1 Pa. $3.95

LIFE IN ANCIENT EGYPT, Adolf Erman. Fullest, most thorough, detailed older account with much not in more recent books, domestic life, religion, magic, medicine, commerce, much more. Many illustrations reproduce tomb paintings, carvings, hieroglyphs, etc. 597pp. 5⅜ x 8½. 22632-8 Pa. $11.95

SUNDIALS, Their Theory and Construction, Albert Waugh. Far and away the best, most thorough coverage of ideas, mathematics concerned, types, construction, adjusting anywhere. Simple, nontechnical treatment allows even children to build several of these dials. Over 100 illustrations. 230pp. 5⅜ x 8½. 22947-5 Pa. $7.95

DYNAMICS OF FLUIDS IN POROUS MEDIA, Jacob Bear. For advanced students of ground water hydrology, soil mechanics and physics, drainage and irrigation engineering, and more. 335 illustrations. Exercises, with answers. 784pp. 6⅛ x 9¼. 65675-6 Pa. $19.95

SONGS OF EXPERIENCE: Facsimile Reproduction with 26 Plates in Full Color, William Blake. 26 full-color plates from a rare 1826 edition. Includes "TheTyger," "London," "Holy Thursday," and other poems. Printed text of poems. 48pp. 5¼ x 7. 24636-1 Pa. $4.95

OLD-TIME VIGNETTES IN FULL COLOR, Carol Belanger Grafton (ed.). Over 390 charming, often sentimental illustrations, selected from archives of Victorian graphics–pretty women posing, children playing, food, flowers, kittens and puppies, smiling cherubs, birds and butterflies, much more. All copyright-free. 48pp. 9¼ x 12¼. 27269-9 Pa. $7.95

PERSPECTIVE FOR ARTISTS, Rex Vicat Cole. Depth, perspective of sky and sea, shadows, much more, not usually covered. 391 diagrams, 81 reproductions of drawings and paintings. 279pp. 5⅜ x 8½. 22487-2 Pa. $7.95

DRAWING THE LIVING FIGURE, Joseph Sheppard. Innovative approach to artistic anatomy focuses on specifics of surface anatomy, rather than muscles and bones. Over 170 drawings of live models in front, back and side views, and in widely varying poses. Accompanying diagrams. 177 illustrations. Introduction. Index. 144pp. 8⅜ x11¼. 26723-7 Pa. $8.95

GOTHIC AND OLD ENGLISH ALPHABETS: 100 Complete Fonts, Dan X. Solo. Add power, elegance to posters, signs, other graphics with 100 stunning copyright-free alphabets: Blackstone, Dolbey, Germania, 97 more–including many lower-case, numerals, punctuation marks. 104pp. 8⅛ x 11. 24695-7 Pa. $8.95

HOW TO DO BEADWORK, Mary White. Fundamental book on craft from simple projects to five-bead chains and woven works. 106 illustrations. 142pp. 5⅜ x 8. 20697-1 Pa. $4.95

THE BOOK OF WOOD CARVING, Charles Marshall Sayers. Finest book for beginners discusses fundamentals and offers 34 designs. "Absolutely first rate . . . well thought out and well executed."–E. J. Tangerman. 118pp. 7¾ x 10⅝. 23654-4 Pa. $6.95

ILLUSTRATED CATALOG OF CIVIL WAR MILITARY GOODS: Union Army Weapons, Insignia, Uniform Accessories, and Other Equipment, Schuyler, Hartley, and Graham. Rare, profusely illustrated 1846 catalog includes Union Army uniform and dress regulations, arms and ammunition, coats, insignia, flags, swords, rifles, etc. 226 illustrations. 160pp. 9 x 12. 24939-5 Pa. $10.95

WOMEN'S FASHIONS OF THE EARLY 1900s: An Unabridged Republication of "New York Fashions, 1909," National Cloak & Suit Co. Rare catalog of mail-order fashions documents women's and children's clothing styles shortly after the turn of the century. Captions offer full descriptions, prices. Invaluable resource for fashion, costume historians. Approximately 725 illustrations. 128pp. 8⅜ x 11¼. 27276-1 Pa. $11.95

THE 1912 AND 1915 GUSTAV STICKLEY FURNITURE CATALOGS, Gustav Stickley. With over 200 detailed illustrations and descriptions, these two catalogs are essential reading and reference materials and identification guides for Stickley furniture. Captions cite materials, dimensions and prices. 112pp. 6½ x 9¼. 26676-1 Pa. $9.95

EARLY AMERICAN LOCOMOTIVES, John H. White, Jr. Finest locomotive engravings from early 19th century: historical (1804–74), main-line (after 1870), special, foreign, etc. 147 plates. 142pp. 11⅜ x 8¼. 22772-3 Pa. $10.95

THE TALL SHIPS OF TODAY IN PHOTOGRAPHS, Frank O. Braynard. Lavishly illustrated tribute to nearly 100 majestic contemporary sailing vessels: Amerigo Vespucci, Clearwater, Constitution, Eagle, Mayflower, Sea Cloud, Victory, many more. Authoritative captions provide statistics, background on each ship. 190 black-and-white photographs and illustrations. Introduction. 128pp. 8⅞ x 11¾. 27163-3 Pa. $13.95

EARLY NINETEENTH-CENTURY CRAFTS AND TRADES, Peter Stockham (ed.). Extremely rare 1807 volume describes to youngsters the crafts and trades of the day: brickmaker, weaver, dressmaker, bookbinder, ropemaker, saddler, many more. Quaint prose, charming illustrations for each craft. 20 black-and-white line illustrations. 192pp. 4⅝ x 6. 27293-1 Pa. $4.95

VICTORIAN FASHIONS AND COSTUMES FROM HARPER'S BAZAR, 1867–1898, Stella Blum (ed.). Day costumes, evening wear, sports clothes, shoes, hats, other accessories in over 1,000 detailed engravings. 320pp. 9⅜ x 12¼. 22990-4 Pa. $14.95

GUSTAV STICKLEY, THE CRAFTSMAN, Mary Ann Smith. Superb study surveys broad scope of Stickley's achievement, especially in architecture. Design philosophy, rise and fall of the Craftsman empire, descriptions and floor plans for many Craftsman houses, more. 86 black-and-white halftones. 31 line illustrations. Introduction 208pp. 6½ x 9¼. 27210-9 Pa. $9.95

THE LONG ISLAND RAIL ROAD IN EARLY PHOTOGRAPHS, Ron Ziel. Over 220 rare photos, informative text document origin (1844) and development of rail service on Long Island. Vintage views of early trains, locomotives, stations, passengers, crews, much more. Captions. 8⅞ x 11¾. 26301-0 Pa. $13.95

THE BOOK OF OLD SHIPS: From Egyptian Galleys to Clipper Ships, Henry B. Culver. Superb, authoritative history of sailing vessels, with 80 magnificent line illustrations. Galley, bark, caravel, longship, whaler, many more. Detailed, informative text on each vessel by noted naval historian. Introduction. 256pp. 5⅜ x 8½. 27332-6 Pa. $7.95

TEN BOOKS ON ARCHITECTURE, Vitruvius. The most important book ever written on architecture. Early Roman aesthetics, technology, classical orders, site selection, all other aspects. Morgan translation. 331pp. 5⅜ x 8½. 20645-9 Pa. $8.95

THE HUMAN FIGURE IN MOTION, Eadweard Muybridge. More than 4,500 stopped-action photos, in action series, showing undraped men, women, children jumping, lying down, throwing, sitting, wrestling, carrying, etc. 390pp. 7⅞ x 10⅝. 20204-6 Clothbd. $25.95

TREES OF THE EASTERN AND CENTRAL UNITED STATES AND CANADA, William M. Harlow. Best one-volume guide to 140 trees. Full descriptions, woodlore, range, etc. Over 600 illustrations. Handy size. 288pp. 4½ x 6⅜. 20395-6 Pa. $6.95

SONGS OF WESTERN BIRDS, Dr. Donald J. Borror. Complete song and call repertoire of 60 western species, including flycatchers, juncoes, cactus wrens, many more–includes fully illustrated booklet. Cassette and manual 99913-0 $8.95

GROWING AND USING HERBS AND SPICES, Milo Miloradovich. Versatile handbook provides all the information needed for cultivation and use of all the herbs and spices available in North America. 4 illustrations. Index. Glossary. 236pp. 5⅜ x 8½. 25058-X Pa. $6.95

BIG BOOK OF MAZES AND LABYRINTHS, Walter Shepherd. 50 mazes and labyrinths in all–classical, solid, ripple, and more–in one great volume. Perfect inexpensive puzzler for clever youngsters. Full solutions. 112pp. 8⅛ x 11. 22951-3 Pa. $4.95

PIANO TUNING, J. Cree Fischer. Clearest, best book for beginner, amateur. Simple repairs, raising dropped notes, tuning by easy method of flattened fifths. No previous skills needed. 4 illustrations. 201pp. 5⅜ x 8½. 23267-0 Pa. $6.95

A SOURCE BOOK IN THEATRICAL HISTORY, A. M. Nagler. Contemporary observers on acting, directing, make-up, costuming, stage props, machinery, scene design, from Ancient Greece to Chekhov. 611pp. 5⅜ x 8½. 20515-0 Pa. $12.95

THE COMPLETE NONSENSE OF EDWARD LEAR, Edward Lear. All nonsense limericks, zany alphabets, Owl and Pussycat, songs, nonsense botany, etc., illustrated by Lear. Total of 320pp. 5⅜ x 8½. (USO) 20167-8 Pa. $6.95

VICTORIAN PARLOUR POETRY: An Annotated Anthology, Michael R. Turner. 117 gems by Longfellow, Tennyson, Browning, many lesser-known poets. "The Village Blacksmith," "Curfew Must Not Ring Tonight," "Only a Baby Small," dozens more, often difficult to find elsewhere. Index of poets, titles, first lines. xxiii + 325pp. 5⅝ x 8¼. 27044-0 Pa. $8.95

DUBLINERS, James Joyce. Fifteen stories offer vivid, tightly focused observations of the lives of Dublin's poorer classes. At least one, "The Dead," is considered a masterpiece. Reprinted complete and unabridged from standard edition. 160pp. 5$\frac{3}{16}$ x 8¼. 26870-5 Pa. $1.00

THE HAUNTED MONASTERY and THE CHINESE MAZE MURDERS, Robert van Gulik. Two full novels by van Gulik, set in 7th-century China, continue adventures of Judge Dee and his companions. An evil Taoist monastery, seemingly supernatural events; overgrown topiary maze hides strange crimes. 27 illustrations. 328pp. 5⅜ x 8½. 23502-5 Pa. $8.95

THE BOOK OF THE SACRED MAGIC OF ABRAMELIN THE MAGE, translated by S. MacGregor Mathers. Medieval manuscript of ceremonial magic. Basic document in Aleister Crowley, Golden Dawn groups. 268pp. 5⅜ x 8½. 23211-5 Pa. $8.95

NEW RUSSIAN-ENGLISH AND ENGLISH-RUSSIAN DICTIONARY, M. A. O'Brien. This is a remarkably handy Russian dictionary, containing a surprising amount of information, including over 70,000 entries. 366pp. 4½ x 6⅛. 20208-9 Pa. $9.95

HISTORIC HOMES OF THE AMERICAN PRESIDENTS, Second, Revised Edition, Irvin Haas. A traveler's guide to American Presidential homes, most open to the public, depicting and describing homes occupied by every American President from George Washington to George Bush. With visiting hours, admission charges, travel routes. 175 photographs. Index. 160pp. 8¼ x 11. 26751-2 Pa. $11.95

NEW YORK IN THE FORTIES, Andreas Feininger. 162 brilliant photographs by the well-known photographer, formerly with *Life* magazine. Commuters, shoppers, Times Square at night, much else from city at its peak. Captions by John von Hartz. 181pp. 9¼ x 10¾. 23585-8 Pa. $12.95

INDIAN SIGN LANGUAGE, William Tomkins. Over 525 signs developed by Sioux and other tribes. Written instructions and diagrams. Also 290 pictographs. 111pp. 6⅛ x 9¼. 22029-X Pa. $3.95

ANATOMY: A Complete Guide for Artists, Joseph Sheppard. A master of figure drawing shows artists how to render human anatomy convincingly. Over 460 illustrations. 224pp. 8⅜ x 11¼. 27279-6 Pa. $10.95

MEDIEVAL CALLIGRAPHY: Its History and Technique, Marc Drogin. Spirited history, comprehensive instruction manual covers 13 styles (ca. 4th century thru 15th). Excellent photographs; directions for duplicating medieval techniques with modern tools. 224pp. 8⅜ x 11¼. 26142-5 Pa. $12.95

DRIED FLOWERS: How to Prepare Them, Sarah Whitlock and Martha Rankin. Complete instructions on how to use silica gel, meal and borax, perlite aggregate, sand and borax, glycerine and water to create attractive permanent flower arrangements. 12 illustrations. 32pp. 5⅜ x 8½. 21802-3 Pa. $1.00

EASY-TO-MAKE BIRD FEEDERS FOR WOODWORKERS, Scott D. Campbell. Detailed, simple-to-use guide for designing, constructing, caring for and using feeders. Text, illustrations for 12 classic and contemporary designs. 96pp. 5⅜ x 8½. 25847-5 Pa. $2.95

SCOTTISH WONDER TALES FROM MYTH AND LEGEND, Donald A. Mackenzie. 16 lively tales tell of giants rumbling down mountainsides, of a magic wand that turns stone pillars into warriors, of gods and goddesses, evil hags, powerful forces and more. 240pp. 5⅜ x 8½. 29677-6 Pa. $6.95

THE HISTORY OF UNDERCLOTHES, C. Willett Cunnington and Phyllis Cunnington. Fascinating, well-documented survey covering six centuries of English undergarments, enhanced with over 100 illustrations: 12th-century laced-up bodice, footed long drawers (1795), 19th-century bustles, 19th-century corsets for men, Victorian "bust improvers," much more. 272pp. 5⅝ x 8¼. 27124-2 Pa. $9.95

ARTS AND CRAFTS FURNITURE: The Complete Brooks Catalog of 1912, Brooks Manufacturing Co. Photos and detailed descriptions of more than 150 now very collectible furniture designs from the Arts and Crafts movement depict davenports, settees, buffets, desks, tables, chairs, bedsteads, dressers and more, all built of solid, quarter-sawed oak. Invaluable for students and enthusiasts of antiques, Americana and the decorative arts. 80pp. 6½ x 9¼. 27471-3 Pa. $8.95

HOW WE INVENTED THE AIRPLANE: An Illustrated History, Orville Wright. Fascinating firsthand account covers early experiments, construction of planes and motors, first flights, much more. Introduction and commentary by Fred C. Kelly. 76 photographs. 96pp. 8¼ x 11. 25662-6 Pa. $8.95

THE ARTS OF THE SAILOR: Knotting, Splicing and Ropework, Hervey Garrett Smith. Indispensable shipboard reference covers tools, basic knots and useful hitches; handsewing and canvas work, more. Over 100 illustrations. Delightful reading for sea lovers. 256pp. 5⅜ x 8½. 26440-8 Pa. $7.95

FRANK LLOYD WRIGHT'S FALLINGWATER: The House and Its History, Second, Revised Edition, Donald Hoffmann. A total revision–both in text and illustrations–of the standard document on Fallingwater, the boldest, most personal architectural statement of Wright's mature years, updated with valuable new material from the recently opened Frank Lloyd Wright Archives. "Fascinating"–*The New York Times*. 116 illustrations. 128pp. 9¼ x 10¾. 27430-6 Pa. $11.95

PHOTOGRAPHIC SKETCHBOOK OF THE CIVIL WAR, Alexander Gardner. 100 photos taken on field during the Civil War. Famous shots of Manassas Harper's Ferry, Lincoln, Richmond, slave pens, etc. 244pp. 10⅝ x 8¼. 22731-6 Pa. $9.95

FIVE ACRES AND INDEPENDENCE, Maurice G. Kains. Great back-to-the-land classic explains basics of self-sufficient farming. The one book to get. 95 illustrations. 397pp. 5⅜ x 8½. 20974-1 Pa. $7.95

SONGS OF EASTERN BIRDS, Dr. Donald J. Borror. Songs and calls of 60 species most common to eastern U.S.: warblers, woodpeckers, flycatchers, thrushes, larks, many more in high-quality recording. Cassette and manual 99912-2 $9.95

A MODERN HERBAL, Margaret Grieve. Much the fullest, most exact, most useful compilation of herbal material. Gigantic alphabetical encyclopedia, from aconite to zedoary, gives botanical information, medical properties, folklore, economic uses, much else. Indispensable to serious reader. 161 illustrations. 888pp. 6½ x 9¼. 2-vol. set. (USO) Vol. I: 22798-7 Pa. $9.95
Vol. II: 22799-5 Pa. $9.95

HIDDEN TREASURE MAZE BOOK, Dave Phillips. Solve 34 challenging mazes accompanied by heroic tales of adventure. Evil dragons, people-eating plants, blood-thirsty giants, many more dangerous adversaries lurk at every twist and turn. 34 mazes, stories, solutions. 48pp. 8¼ x 11. 24566-7 Pa. $2.95

LETTERS OF W. A. MOZART, Wolfgang A. Mozart. Remarkable letters show bawdy wit, humor, imagination, musical insights, contemporary musical world; includes some letters from Leopold Mozart. 276pp. 5⅜ x 8½. 22859-2 Pa. $7.95

BASIC PRINCIPLES OF CLASSICAL BALLET, Agrippina Vaganova. Great Russian theoretician, teacher explains methods for teaching classical ballet. 118 illustrations. 175pp. 5⅜ x 8½. 22036-2 Pa. $5.95

THE JUMPING FROG, Mark Twain. Revenge edition. The original story of The Celebrated Jumping Frog of Calaveras County, a hapless French translation, and Twain's hilarious "retranslation" from the French. 12 illustrations. 66pp. 5⅜ x 8½. 22686-7 Pa. $3.95

BEST REMEMBERED POEMS, Martin Gardner (ed.). The 126 poems in this superb collection of 19th- and 20th-century British and American verse range from Shelley's "To a Skylark" to the impassioned "Renascence" of Edna St. Vincent Millay and to Edward Lear's whimsical "The Owl and the Pussycat." 224pp. 5⅜ x 8½. 27165-X Pa. $4.95

COMPLETE SONNETS, William Shakespeare. Over 150 exquisite poems deal with love, friendship, the tyranny of time, beauty's evanescence, death and other themes in language of remarkable power, precision and beauty. Glossary of archaic terms. 80pp. 5$\frac{3}{16}$ x 8¼. 26686-9 Pa. $1.00

BODIES IN A BOOKSHOP, R. T. Campbell. Challenging mystery of blackmail and murder with ingenious plot and superbly drawn characters. In the best tradition of British suspense fiction. 192pp. 5⅜ x 8½. 24720-1 Pa. $6.95

AUTOBIOGRAPHY: The Story of My Experiments with Truth, Mohandas K. Gandhi. Boyhood, legal studies, purification, the growth of the Satyagraha (nonviolent protest) movement. Critical, inspiring work of the man responsible for the freedom of India. 480pp. 5⅜ x 8½. (USO) 24593-4 Pa. $8.95

CELTIC MYTHS AND LEGENDS, T. W. Rolleston. Masterful retelling of Irish and Welsh stories and tales. Cuchulain, King Arthur, Deirdre, the Grail, many more. First paperback edition. 58 full-page illustrations. 512pp. 5⅜ x 8½. 26507-2 Pa. $9.95

THE PRINCIPLES OF PSYCHOLOGY, William James. Famous long course complete, unabridged. Stream of thought, time perception, memory, experimental methods; great work decades ahead of its time. 94 figures. 1,391pp. 5⅜ x 8½. 2-vol. set.
Vol. I: 20381-6 Pa. $12.95
Vol. II: 20382-4 Pa. $12.95

THE WORLD AS WILL AND REPRESENTATION, Arthur Schopenhauer. Definitive English translation of Schopenhauer's life work, correcting more than 1,000 errors, omissions in earlier translations. Translated by E. F. J. Payne. Total of 1,269pp. 5⅜ x 8½. 2-vol. set. Vol. 1: 21761-2 Pa. $11.95
Vol. 2: 21762-0 Pa. $12.95

MAGIC AND MYSTERY IN TIBET, Madame Alexandra David-Neel. Experiences among lamas, magicians, sages, sorcerers, Bonpa wizards. A true psychic discovery. 32 illustrations. 321pp. 5⅜ x 8½. (USO) 22682-4 Pa. $8.95

THE EGYPTIAN BOOK OF THE DEAD, E. A. Wallis Budge. Complete reproduction of Ani's papyrus, finest ever found. Full hieroglyphic text, interlinear transliteration, word-for-word translation, smooth translation. 533pp. 6½ x 9¼.
21866-X Pa. $10.95

MATHEMATICS FOR THE NONMATHEMATICIAN, Morris Kline. Detailed, college-level treatment of mathematics in cultural and historical context, with numerous exercises. Recommended Reading Lists. Tables. Numerous figures. 641pp. 5⅜ x 8½.
24823-2 Pa. $11.95

THEORY OF WING SECTIONS: Including a Summary of Airfoil Data, Ira H. Abbott and A. E. von Doenhoff. Concise compilation of subsonic aerodynamic characteristics of NACA wing sections, plus description of theory. 350pp. of tables. 693pp. 5⅜ x 8½. 60586-8 Pa. $14.95

THE RIME OF THE ANCIENT MARINER, Gustave Doré, S. T. Coleridge. Doré's finest work; 34 plates capture moods, subtleties of poem. Flawless full-size reproductions printed on facing pages with authoritative text of poem. "Beautiful. Simply beautiful."–*Publisher's Weekly*. 77pp. 9¼ x 12. 22305-1 Pa. $6.95

NORTH AMERICAN INDIAN DESIGNS FOR ARTISTS AND CRAFTSPEOPLE, Eva Wilson. Over 360 authentic copyright-free designs adapted from Navajo blankets, Hopi pottery, Sioux buffalo hides, more. Geometrics, symbolic figures, plant and animal motifs, etc. 128pp. 8⅜ x 11. (EUK) 25341-4 Pa. $8.95

SCULPTURE: Principles and Practice, Louis Slobodkin. Step-by-step approach to clay, plaster, metals, stone; classical and modern. 253 drawings, photos. 255pp. 8⅛ x 11.
22960-2 Pa. $11.95

2017 WILLA Literary Award Winner in Contemporary Fiction

Short-listed for the ASLE Environmental Creative Book Award

"Moore's writing is dreamy and rhythmic, lulling as the sea, which murmurs in the background of her story. A prize-winning nature writer who resides in Oregon and spends summers on Chichagof Island, Moore doesn't hold back when it comes to description, and the Southeast Alaska landscape breathes around every page, every character . . . This is a remarkable book, a remarkable story, and if at times the landscape threatens to eclipse the characters, so be it. Because this is also a funny book, with characters so odd and funny, so lovable and flawed that one can't help but think of Steinbeck's *Cannery Row*."

—*Alaska Dispatch News*

"In *Piano Tide*, Kathleen Dean Moore has given us a an action adventure, a lesson in the natural history of Southeast Alaska, and a cast of unforgettable backwoods characters. As Pacific tides rise and fall, almost engulfing the hamlet called Good River Harbor, we witness humans as well as bears, salmon, and the forest itself, fighting to survive amid forces of man-made destruction and nature's renewal. *Piano Tide* is a fine read, sure to join the ranks of Ed Abbey's *Monkey Wrench Gang* on the eco/thriller bookshelf."

—Annick Smith, author of
Crossing the Plains with Bruno and *Homestead*

"*Piano Tide* captures with remarkable perception the beauty of Alaska, the environmental conflicts that tear at and unite communities, and the interconnectedness of all things. You'll be swept into this world as if by a turning tide, and you will love the characters—human and otherwise—you find there. Moore writes from deep knowledge and empathy, with an open heart."

—Nancy Lord, author of *Fishcamp, Beluga Days*, and
Early Warming, and former Alaska Writer Laureate

"I think Kathleen Dean Moore can do anything—including write a savagely funny and deeply insightful novel of the tidepool and rainforest country she knows so well!"

—Bill McKibben

"*Piano Tide* is a rare beauty, a novel whose deeply flawed characters are written with compassion and insight; a book vibrating with drama and lyrical prose side-by-side with hard-hitting questions that ask how earth—and all life on earth—will survive uncompromising capitalism. Moore introduces the philosophical 'Problem of Unnecessary Beauty'—why beauty in nature sometimes thrives for no apparent reason. But *Piano Tide* is a necessary beauty. You may read it in one sitting; but when you turn that last page, you'll want to stand up for the things we share: this earth, this life, this wild and enduring hope."

—BK Loren, author of *Theft* and *Animal, Mineral, Radical*

"With *Piano Tide*, Kathleen Dean Moore proves herself the rare writer at home in both the novel and nonfiction. Her debut novel evokes Alaska's silvery bears and clouds as vividly as her beloved nature writing, with beguiling characters bound by tide and moral compromise in a fishing village at the end of the world. Moore's story will have you rooting for not only piano-toting Nora, but an entire landscape and all its life. Masterfully told and full of heart, *Piano Tide* is one of those books you can't stop thinking about for days after you've turned the final page."

—Cynthia Barnett, author of
Rain: A Natural and Cultural History

PIANO TIDE

A NOVEL

KATHLEEN DEAN MOORE

COUNTERPOINT | BERKELEY

Library of Congress Cataloging-in-Publication Data is Available

Cover design by Kelly Winton
Interior design by Sabrina Plomitallo-González, Neuwirth & Associates

Paperback ISBN: 978-1-61902-572-1

COUNTERPOINT
2560 Ninth Street, Suite 318
Berkeley, CA 94710
www.counterpointpress.com

Printed in the United States of America
Distributed by Publishers Group West

3 5 7 9 10 8 6 4 2

For the damp-haired children
and for the young of all beings in Southeast Alaska,
who deserve an enduring way of life.

CONTENTS

PERSONAE

Lillian Mary Shaddy. b. 1943, Seattle, WA.
Owner/operator, Good River Harbor Bath 'n' Bar, Good River Harbor, AK.

Christopher "Tick" McIver. b. 1970, Skagway, AK.
Carpenter, Good River Products, Inc. Good River Harbor, AK.
Wife: Annie Klawon. Sons: Davy and Tommy McIver.

Nora Montgomery. b. 1973. Birthplace unknown.
Writer, Alaska Marine Highway.

Axel Hagerman. b. 1960, Good River Harbor, AK.
President and CEO, Good River Products, Inc.
Wife: Rebecca Hagerman. Daughter: Meredith Hagerman.

David "Davy" McIver. b. 1995, Good River Harbor, AK.
Father: Tick McIver. Mother: Annie Klawon.

Thomas "Tommy" McIver. b. 2002, Good River Harbor, AK.
Father: Tick McIver. Mother: Annie Klawon.

Howard Fowler. b. 1965, San Mateo, CA.
Surveyor, communications manager, and assistant production supervisor,
Good River Products, Inc. Good River Harbor, AK.
Wife: Jennifer Fowler. Daughter: Taylor Fowler.

Kenny Isaacson. b. 1950, Chicago, IL.

Meredith Hagerman. b. 1995, Juneau, AK.
Father: Axel Hagerman. Mother: Rebecca Hagerman.

Rebecca Hagerman. b. 1960, Bar Harbor, ME. Housewife.
Husband: Axel Hagerman.
Daughter: Meredith Hagerman.

Annie Klawon. b. 1970, Ketchikan, AK.
Husband: Christopher McIver.
Sons: Davy and Tommy McIver.

≋

EACH OF THE characters in this book is a creation of the author's imagination. None of them are real people—not even remotely. The author just stood at her little desk and made them up. It will do no good, and probably a lot of harm, to look crosswise at a character, wondering if you have met him or her. You have not.

Not only that. None of the places are factual, and it will do no good to check for them on a map. The author has ranged widely over Oregon and the Pacific Northwest, doing her best to remember a muskeg here, a boat dock there, a sinking skiff in another place, a piling topped with fireweed, a clamflat, a dump. From these glass shards of memory and imagination, Good River Harbor is created.

PRELUDE

HEAVY OVERCAST. RAIN. Wind twenty knots from the southeast. The ferry plowed through the Fairweather Narrows, crowded on both sides by palisades of hemlocks and Sitka spruce. Their branches shredded the fog. A woman in a yellow slicker leaned over the rail, watching until the ship was safely past the buoy that marked a hidden shoal. Hard on the port side, so close it threw spray onto the deck, a creek poured over the broken face of a hanging glacier and twisted down an avalanche chute to the sea. In the black muck beside the creek mouth, skunk cabbage unfurled giant leaves. A bear had been through—probably night before last—trampling the skunk cabbage to dig around the roots, probing into sour mud with lips curled back and teeth reaching tentative as fingertips. Dark water had collected in the sinkholes of its front paws. To starboard, the mountains climbed up and up toward snowfields and granite crags. For three long hours, there was no evidence of humanity except for the buoys and range-markers that led the ferry along the silver sea-path between forested rocks.

So green as to be almost black at first, the forest eventually gave way to lighter green patches along the water, as if a shark had leapt up with pointed teeth to scrape away the trees, leaving only an understory of salmonberry thickets and Sitka alders—dog-hair alders, grown up thick as hairs on a dog's back after the forest was cut to stumps. Some of the cuts were bare to the mud. This, at last, was evidence of human industry. And now the town of Good River Harbor came into view at the base of the mountains.

From the distance, Good River Harbor looked like a string of gulls flying along the water below the mountain range, or a rim of barnacles just uncovered by the tide. One thing it did not look like was a town, but the town fathers could be forgiven for that. The wilderness was desperately steep; the only place to put a building was on a tidal flat that flooded twice a day. So the worthy fathers raised a boardwalk fifteen feet above high tide, a long wooden pier parallel to shore, and along its length, built their houses on pilings. Even the school and the post office were built on a rickety thicket of stilts and piers. The town couldn't be distinguished from the docks, or the docks from the town—almost everything was either tied to a dock or built on it, almost everything grew a thick beard of barnacles and blue mussels. The only structures on actual ground were the remains of an old cannery site on one end of town, the dump on the other, and a little empty cabin at Green Cove. There were no cars, but there were plenty of wheelbarrows and bikes, and a row of beached boats, some more deeply filled with greening rainwater than others, and fine skiffs and seiners nosing into the dock like suckling puppies.

The town of Good River Harbor did not have a real harbor. In fact, it didn't even have a river, and if it had, it wouldn't have been a good one, wandering through the intertidal muck. The town was named after Basil Everett Good, who arrived in 1910 with everything he owned under canvas tarps in a wooden canoe. He aimed to make a living digging clams and selling them to fishermen who happened by. He built a cabin over a stream that drained a ravine and made out all right, until he realized that the real money was not in clams after all, but in salmon. So he signed up to crew on a passing seiner and, for the proverbial bottle of whiskey, traded his cabin to a crew member who was sick of the North Pacific seas.

The town grew and shrank like the tides, as it sold and then exhausted the abundance of the land. In order of date expunged: (1) ancient yellow cedars draped in old-man's beard, (2) Sitka spruce trees six feet across, (3) sweet, feathery hemlocks three hundred years old, (4) king salmon a yard long and fat as dogs, (5) herring dripping yellow eggs, (6) cross-eyed halibut as big as the fishermen's skiffs. The sawmill closed after loggers high-graded the forest and clear-cut all the slopes accessible to logging barges. The cannery closed when the fish could not be counted on. Only forty to fifty people lived in Good River Harbor when the ferry pulled in, not counting the tourists and gunkholers, and a random seiner and his crew—maybe a dozen more souls a day.

The ferry bumped hard into the pilings, shifting the joints of the old timbers. The woman in the yellow raincoat gripped the railing. Deckhands grabbed the lines with boathooks and looped them over the bollards. Old winches cranked the boat to the dock, and the hands wrapped the lines tight over the drum. Bolts clanked and chains rumbled to lower the ferry ramp to the wharf. When the ramp hit the gangway, gulls squawked and shot into the air, as if they had been pinched.

PART ONE
PINK-SALMON TIDE

See here, the urgency of a pink salmon finally coming home. See here, salmon polished to such a sheen that even under an overcast sky the sun reflects on their flanks. They've been gone a year, chasing herring under storm-blue seas. Now they are almost home, so close they can taste it. As they circle at the mouth of the Kis'utch River, their backs darken and their tail stems flush pink. Their flanks streak with white, as if someone had grabbed them before the paint was dry. The backs of the big males grow humped. Their teeth grow long.

On the surge of the flood-tide, the fish throw themselves over the sandbar and press up the stream. In their eagerness to be home, they shoulder each other out of the way, flapping their bodies over gravel bars, swimming sometimes through water so shallow that their humps carve air. Bears wade into them. They toss fish out of the creek to eat later, or they bite out the hump or the fatty brain. More salmon press through bloodied water, like an invading army marching over its own dead.

June 15

HIGH TIDE		LOW TIDE	
2:58 am	18.9	9:28 am	-4.0
4:03 pm	16.6	9:47 pm	1.3

As the ferry pushed into the pilings, Lillian Mary Shaddy spread a plastic grocery bag on the bench at the top of the gangway and lowered herself to sitting. She elbowed a big-bearded man, who moved his bulk over to give her room.

"Who's the woman in the yellow raincoat?" she asked, not expecting an answer.

The woman at the rail of the ferry looked like everybody else in Good River Harbor—baseball cap, wet hair, slicker open in the rain, XtraTuf boots. But the way she was looking around, snapping her head to port, starboard—that would make her somebody new. She wasn't a tourist. A tourist would be running up and down the railing, taking pictures. She wasn't somebody's visitor, because she wasn't waving at anybody and nobody was waving at her. But she wasn't frantically checking her ticket either, so she had planned to come to odd little Good River Harbor.

Lillian tugged her raincoat closed and searched behind her for the belt. No yellow rain slicker for her. Lillian wore a regular department-store raincoat, the kind women wore in Seattle. Carefully, she tied the belt in a square knot that perched like a chipmunk in the cozy place between her bosom and her belly. She adjusted the clear plastic rain bonnet over her hair, which was that day a color called mahogany, and settled her back against the bench. On that damp morning, Lillian felt as groany-jointed as the old ferry, but it's not attractive to complain, and she didn't. She lit a cigarette instead. Smoking in the rain is one of the arts a lady acquires in Southeast Alaska, learning to hold the cigarette between her thumb and forefinger, while the rest of her fingers make a nice little tent. She leaned forward through the smoke to study the new arrival.

The woman's ponytail was knotted up and stuck through the hole in her baseball cap. Sticking out like that, it was as black and wind-smoothed as a crow's tail, and she was skittish as a crow, in fact. But she was tall and long-legged, more like a great blue heron. Whatever kind of bird she was, Lillian was not prepared to say. By this time, the new woman was down on the cargo deck, standing next to a big dog, a pile of totes, and an object wrapped in a blue tarp—a really big object, big enough to be a refrigerator or a shower stall. Lillian took a thoughtful drag on her cigarette and exhaled a long, slow river of smoke.

"The plot thickens," she said to the big man sitting next to her and elbowed him again. He scooted himself even farther away. "Hey, Tick, how about you wander down and introduce yourself. Pretend you're the chamber of commerce. Tell her welcome or something. Or pretend you're a moving company. That's good. Help her with that thing, whatever it is, and find out where's she's going." Honest to God, Lillian thought but did not say, you'd think some people had no sense of curiosity.

Tick McIver was big enough to be a moving company, but he didn't exactly look like a welcoming committee. Lillian had told him a dozen times that he should clean up a little bit—for his own good. Trim that awful orange beard. The thing looked like a stray cat sleeping on his chest. Get rid of those rubber overalls that come barely to the top of his boots. But he protested. He said he cut his overalls off because they're too short anyway, him so tall, and this way they're not always underwater, and he liked his beard, kept his chest warm and scared mice away. And that baseball cap, she'd told him, it looks like it spent the night in the bilge. Well, that's because it spent lots of nights in the bilge, he'd said back.

Tick sighed, hoisted himself to standing, and walked down the gangway to the cargo deck.

TICK WALKED A circle around the new woman's cargo. Somebody who knew knots had tied that tarp up—a single trucker's hitch, no nonsense.

"Whatcha got there?" he asked. Months later, he would think about this time, knowing what he didn't know back then—that he hadn't asked the most important question.

From the gangway, he had thought she looked like a bird. But close up, her face looked more like a fish. Not in a bad way. But her eyes were big and sort of bulgy, and they were golden as a quillback rockfish. That caught Tick by surprise, the big gold eyes. Her face was wide, sculpin-like, and open in a nice kind of way, and when she smiled, she blinked reflexively, as if her eyes and her mouth were connected by the plate of her cheeks, as are the eyes and mouth of a cod. Youngish. Maybe thirty, maybe thirty-five, although now that Tick was forty, he thought everybody was young.

She had a dog with her, a big one, part German shepherd maybe, maybe some golden retriever. The dog strolled around on the cargo deck, sniffing the backsides of every town dog, nosing up to every kid on the deck, looking for a nuzzle or a hug. When the ferry whistle gave a warning blast to signal imminent departure, the dog galloped back to the woman, panicked as a colt. She hushed it with a hand gesture. It sat beside her, whining.

The whistle motivated the woman too. She reached over, yanked the rope's bitter end, and pulled it off the tarp. The tarp thundered as she dragged it to the deck. Under the tarp was an upright piano.

Tick lifted off his baseball cap, smudged the blackflies on his forehead, and settled the cap more firmly on his head. "That looks like a piano," he said. He glanced up the gangway to Lillian, who gave him a big thumbs-up. The new woman laughed, splitting her face with a grin.

"Yep. It's a piano all right. Can *you* help me get it to the Green Cove cabin?"

"It takes a good high tide to move a piano," Tick protested, even though he knew that this tide *was* high, a sixteen-footer, high enough to bend the sedges, flattening them in a swirl, as if a bear had wallowed there. High enough to hoist the windrow of rock-wrack another yard up the beach. High enough to launch mussel shells like double-end dories. High enough, Tick knew, to float a boat over the intertidal rocks and bring it right up to the rock ledge at the Green Cove cabin.

"Yeah, I could move a piano, if we did it now, at the peak of the tide," he finally said. "It can be done." Although he was still a young man, he wasn't a man to leap to conclusions. He was capable of leaping to *action* if needed—if, for example, his boat was on fire. But men of the sea are wary of conclusions. "But why?" he asked. It was a reasonable question under the circumstances, but still, in retrospect, not the right one.

"Because this ferry is about to sail off to whatever godforsaken place it goes next, and I don't want my piano to sail with it, and because I bet you're the one who can do it."

The ferry was in fact about to sail off to Bean Point, which *was* a gloomy godforsaken place in Tick's opinion, and he knew that the people had moved out of that little D-log cabin at Green Cove. He knew of a nice granite shelf slanting up from the beach to the yard, where he had offloaded the logs for that very cabin. He could do this.

He walked across the cargo deck and returned with a four-wheel dolly. He fixed up a lever from a block of wood and a two-by-four and he pried that piano up. He put the woman on the pry bar, and he bent down to slide the dolly underneath. Tick was strong, and easy around water and big things, and before long, he and the woman were edging the piano down the gangway. Couple of turns around piano and post, and Tick had the rope slipping around a piling, and the woman was hanging on to the far end, and Tick had that piano tiptoeing down the ferry ramp like a drunk crossing a log.

A damp-headed boy ran ahead of them, shoving gearboxes and buckets out of the way. The town dogs ran along behind. Then the piano was on the dock, swaying a little. Tick gave the piano a pat and walked down the dock toward the *Annie K.*

Tick had two boats in the harbor—a little skiff and the *Annie K*, a twenty-six-foot landing craft left over from World War II. The *Annie K* was a bucket of a boat, and people compared it unfavorably to their own boats until they needed it, and who doesn't need a landing craft when they have a load of lumber to move, and who doesn't have an inconvenient load of lumber on occasion? With the flat bow that lowers on a winch, landing crafts always leak, but it was dry enough to move a piano, and that is what Tick was going to do. At least the rain had stopped. At least he had the tide on his side. He didn't want to be dragging a load that size over wet rocks, slipping on the rock-wrack.

Casting off his lines, Tick cranked on the engine. He pointed the bow of the boat toward the wharf where the piano and the woman threw long reflections across the harbor. Everything a tide can lift was floating on the polished water. Cork net-floats, a two-by-four, a bloated rockfish—they were all bobbing round down there on the reflection of the town, boats floating upside down and right side up, kids riding down the dock in orange life jackets, reflected upside down on the water beside a floating beer can and tangled kelp.

The challenge of moving a big object by boat brings in the men, faster even than an ancient halibut laid out gasping on the dock. Seemed like every man in Good River Harbor was striding down the ramp. Every one of them started giving directions, pointing here, pointing there, bossing things, even though it didn't look like anybody needed bossing, least of all the piano woman. She stood aside while at least three men stood there on the dock and waved the *Annie K* in. Tick pulled the pins that held the bow closed and engaged the winch. Chains clanked through the guides, the old hinges trumpeted, and the apron of the boat lowered like a castle gate over a moat, bridging the boat and the dock. With men giving hand signals—this way, that way, stop, go, *stop*—they jockeyed the piano around a tight angle and rolled it onto the *Annie K*'s bow. Its sudden weight lowered the bow, and all the reflections bent and rolled. The yellow-coated men shredded into yellow lines that bounced around the breakwall.

The piano secured, the dog and gear totes loaded, the new woman aboard, Tick backed out the boat, and the *Annie K* headed northwest out the harbor, heading for the Green Cove cabin. As he left, he saw the kids and the men and the dogs all headed northwest too, pounding up the boardwalk, then bouncing down the ramp to the trail to the cove. Tick was going to need them, and in Good River Harbor, where men were needed, they would go.

He turned on his depth-sounder and steered wide around Green Point. No doubt the rocks were safely submerged on a tide this high, but he was a careful man with a boat and not one to be taking chances. As he tipped up his cap, his eyes rested on the woman who stood beside her piano on the foredeck. With one boot braced on the bow, she leaned forward into the wind.

That woman doesn't look like a fish or a bird, Tick decided. She looks like George Washington crossing the Delaware. "*Row, men, row, damn the ice floes.*" He considered the similarity. Yep, they could be identical twins, if Washington had worn a yellow slicker, and if George Washington had a strand of dark hair stuck to his cheek by blowing rain.

He poked his head out of the wheelhouse and yelled into the weather. "I'm Tick McIver. Actually Christopher, but nobody could handle a word that big, so they called me . . . just . . . Tick. Not because I stick to things like a tick. But things stick to *me*. Even bad luck follows me around like a grinning . . . dog."

His speech ended in a mutter and he bent over the wheel, his neck flushing.

"I'm Nora," said George Washington.

Tick did not speak for the rest of the trip.

Out at Nora's cabin, there was a great deal of dragging around of sheets of plywood. There was a great deal of throwing straps around trees to hold the winch. There was a great deal of cranking. Kids in boots, soggy dogs, men with beards. One may make fun, but these people are very, very good at this sort of thing, and they would get the job done with no delay, no crushed fingers, and not that many beers.

"Up she goes, easy, easy."

"Pull to her starboard side."

"She's turning, she's turning. The bitch got a mind of her own. Kick that wheel."

"Hey, Tick, you got any more rope on that tub?"

"Easy. Easy."

"Barney, you damn dog, let go of that rope. C'mon, this is not a game. Christ."

When the piano rolled off the boat on that grand and momentous piano tide, the assembled town cheered. When it rolled up the ramp onto the porch of the cabin, they cheered again. Then somebody figured out the piano wouldn't fit through the front door. All the discussion and laughter then, the men measuring with the span of their hands, dogs barking at the uproar. Being practical people, the men began calculating how much trouble it would be to pry out the doorframe and chain saw a bigger opening.

But Nora just shoved the piano up under the porch roof, tight against the wall, and toweled it down, pulled a case of beer out of a tote, and threw a welcoming party for herself and her dog, whom she introduced as Chum. Standing at the piano, because she had no chair, Nora picked out a semblance of "Amazing Grace." It was awful. She winced and grimaced and even the piano seemed to shudder. Hard to know why a person who couldn't play the piano any better than that would haul it all the way out to the bush, but there are people who just love to carry around a guitar case, so who knows and nobody cared. They all wanted to play her piano under the hemlocks, even people who hadn't touched a key since they were kids. Pretty much all they knew was "Chopsticks." So the kids and the dogs danced to "Chopsticks."

Tick put a can of beer in each pocket and headed back to the harbor, shoving the *Annie K* away from the beach with an oar. On a falling tide, you can't hold a boat on shore. The tide will drop right out from under you, grounding you, and there you will sit on the mud and rocks for about ten hours, looking stupid.

IN THE MORNING, sunlit yellow fog sagged on the roofs of Good River Harbor and invisible ravens clonked and muttered from the hidden spars. Tick McIver sat on the step of his house on the boardwalk, drinking a second cup of coffee.

Tick was a big man, although he never meant to be and denied responsibility—heavy head, powerful shoulders, meaty hands, beard big and orange. The beard was rumpled, but soon enough he would rummage his fingers through the fur and get it all arranged. His hair he wore in one orange braid down the length of his back. He was big, but he wasn't fat, any more than a tree trunk is fat even if your arms can't reach around it.

That particular morning, he was giving serious thought to seeing what was wrong with the carburetor on his Evinrude, so he'd put on the dirtier of his two denim work shirts and a huge pair of Carhartt overalls. The overalls stopped short of his ankles, their rolled hems having been sawn off with a pocketknife. Logging or fishing or banging nails, you want your overalls to rip when they catch on a snag or an oarlock or a spike in a board. Tick hadn't got around yet to putting on his boots for the day. So when he unbent his knees and extended his legs across the boardwalk, the fog formed droplets of dew on his woolen socks and on two stripes of white skin stuck with orange hairs.

Tick cupped a hand over his eyes to shield his headache from the light and squinted in the direction of his big feet. He lived right there on the boardwalk, and the whole town had to walk past his door to get anywhere at all, so Tick wasn't surprised when another pair of feet showed up next to his. Rubber boots and a woman's long legs. He had to crane his neck to look at her, she had stopped so close to him. All he had was a silhouette in fog so bright it hurt his eyes. Still, he could see she was tall. Her raincoat flapped off her shoulders and her hair flopped out the hole in the back of her baseball cap. So it was that new woman. He remembered from the piano party that the dog's name was Chum, but that morning Tick fumbled to remember the woman's name.

"Hey, Tick," she said, smiling and blinking at Tick. "Pretty day."

Chum sniffed at Tick's socks.

"Yep. Pretty as a calendar picture," he managed to say back.

Nora sat down beside him. "Mind?"

Tick didn't know if he minded or not. He didn't know this woman who was now leaning her back on his railing and stretching her legs out beside his.

"It's really pretty until you look at those mountainsides that have been cut to mud," she said. But that's all she said, which was good, because he'd been one of the guys who hauled the choker up and down the mountain, yarding out the logs, and of course that's not pretty, the stickers and the sweat. She didn't like the mud, she should have tried dodging trees in that muck. That was a pretty big silence then. The woman just sat there and bounced her fist up and down against her thigh.

"Sorry," she eventually said. "When will I learn to keep my mouth shut?"

Tick didn't know, so he didn't say. Instead, he lifted his beard and scratched his neck. This woman, she just sat there thinking and pounding her leg.

"What the hell," she finally said. "What's the harm?" She turned to Tick, who didn't know the answer to that one either. "Who's the boss of the logging outfit here?"

Tick knew that one, sure enough. "That would be Axel Hagerman, CEO of Good River Products, Inc. Office right there. Axel'll be coming along pretty soon, eight o'clock sharp."

Later, he might have wished he hadn't said that, but it wasn't like Axel was some kind of secret agent, and at the time, he was just being nice to somebody new in town. There is never anything wrong with being nice.

Sure enough, pretty soon along came the president of Good River Products, carrying a workman's lunch box in one hand and a briefcase in the other. That was in fact Axel Hagerman. Axel was a polyp of a man—small, soft, white, roundish now, but capable of many shapes. Just a fuzz of pale hair on his head, hardly more than a baby. He covered his body with the snappiest nautical blues. Navy blue polyester pants, navy blue bowling jacket with the GR Products logo. Under his jacket, his shirt collar was white—white of all things, in Good River Harbor. Indoors and out, he wore a Greek fisherman's hat with a patent leather bill, also navy blue, also emblazoned GR PRODUCTS.

As soon as Axel hit the turn to his office, the new woman jumped to her feet, ran after him, and started in talking. Tick hunched down so he could see between the railings of his porch.

"You're Axel Hagerman, head of Good River Products," she said, as if he didn't already know.

"President and CEO," Axel said, and stuck out his hand. Tick didn't think there was anything wrong with that. She was new to town and Axel was polite to strangers. All the same, he felt the hair prick up on his neck.

She shook his hand, not up and down, but sort of side to side, like his arm was a tiller.

"Nora Montgomery," she said.

So that was her name, or at least what she said. Her ponytail bobbed up and down when she said it, and she reached around to grab her hair.

The way she yanked, it looked like she was trying to stop a runaway horse. That probably would be a good idea, Tick was thinking.

"I've just come in on the ferry," she said. "Got a good view of the logging operation in the old growth this side of the Fairweather Narrows. That outfit is logging too close to the creek." She looked Axel in the eye and he looked at her, and it was like two people bonked heads, you could almost hear it.

"Tick says it's Good River Products running that show," she said, "and maybe you know something about that, being the president and CEO."

Oh god. Tick slumped down behind his railing and buried his face in his hands. Why didn't she keep him out of it?

Axel didn't say anything, but he grew a little taller and stiffer. The hems of his pants lifted off the tops of his shoes.

"There's a pink-salmon run in that stream," she said.

Tick crawled toward his door. He didn't want to see what was going to happen next. Nora raised her voice and lit into Axel again.

"You want fish, you've got to keep deep shade on that water. Warming ocean, they'll need that cool place. And the mud. If you keep cutting those mountainsides, mud's going to suffocate the fish."

Bucked up against his door, Tick groaned. Just on and on, she was explaining it like a professor, like she thought Axel would want to know. She should have had a blackboard, and she could have drawn a bunch of fish floating belly-up with their tongues hanging out and big *X*'s across their eyes. And she could have pointed at them with a long stick, for emphasis.

"And if that salmon run dies off," she said, "what will the seiners do? And who gets the blame?"

Her voice was calm, like a friendly old professor encouraging a stupid student, but it was loud enough to wake the moldering salmon. Tick wished she would shut up. Those aren't the kinds of things you say to a man like Axel.

But Axel just stood there. He stood there in his office clothes, looking at her. The man seemed surprised, and who wouldn't be, yelled at by a woman in town just one week—a week—and they had probably not even said hello more than three times. Crazy, she was saying these things to him—the big, the only, employer in town, living here all his life. That's what Tick would have told her. But Axel didn't say a thing. Not a word.

Instead, Axel turned around, walked down the gangway into his toolshed, pulled out a chain saw with a forty-eight-inch bar. He grabbed a wedge and maul and his ear protectors and walked up the boardwalk and down the ramp to the Green Cove trail toward Nora's cabin. Nora sort of jumped along after him, still lecturing about fish. Tick snuck along behind, tree to tree, to see what would happen next. Nora's dog, Chum, ran ahead, wagging his tail. That was a dumb dog, if he couldn't sniff the air and know that trouble was coming.

Axel stood there in the forest not ten feet from Nora's cabin and looked all around. That was old stuff in there, three-hundred-year-old spruces and hemlocks. He was eyeballing them, moving around, looking at them with a professional's gaze, tipping his head back to assess the overstory. He picked out a hemlock that must have been three feet across, a couple hundred years old. Carefully, he put his ear-cup hearing protectors on over his cap and adjusted them just right.

"What do you think you are doing? Get away from my cabin."

Good thing Axel couldn't hear Nora anymore, yammering in a voice that got higher and higher. He leaned over and ripped the chainsaw's cord. The motor started on the first pull. That says a lot about a man, when his chain saw starts on the first pull.

Chum took one look at Nora's face and stiffened up. He started growling, way low. Nora grabbed him by the collar. Axel revved a couple of times and pressed the bar against the tree. Blue smoke and wood chips flew out. Nora trotted in circles round the hemlock.

"Stop that."

The chain saw roared in response.

"That's not your tree. Stop right now."

Blat.

"That's a felony. Don't do that. You have no right. What's the matter with you? That's a grandmother tree."

Grandmother tree, oh man. Tick groaned. But Axel acted like he hadn't heard her, which of course, he hadn't, and he just kept working. Chum lunged and barked. The chain saw snarled. In no time, Axel had carved a notch a third of the way through the trunk.

Chum threw himself forward with so much force he would have dislocated the shoulder of a lesser woman.

There was nothing for Nora to do but run around shouting. The last time Tick had ever seen anybody act like that, it was a mother merganser, and an eagle was rocketing down, talons open. It snatched one chick off the water, then came back for another one and the next one, until they were all gone and the mother merganser was circling an empty space on the bay, whistling soft.

All this time, Axel didn't say a word. He just did his work. Once the notch was cut, he walked around the tree and made a cut halfway through the trunk a few inches above the notch.

Finally he turned around, and courteous as a gentleman, he said to Nora, "If I were you, I would back off."

She shouted, "Like hell! Just stop it. Stop."

But she dragged the dog back a few yards. Axel drove the wedge into the cut, smacked it one good one, and that tree swayed on its base, then slowly tipped. It shivered, cracked its length. Picking up speed, it whomped through the air and slammed onto Nora's trail with a thud that set her piano humming.

Axel shut off the engine.

The two of them stood there in the sudden quiet, listening to the piano's trembling chord. They stood there in a gentle rain of pollen and hemlock needles.

Then Axel brushed the sawdust off his good pants, took off his ear protectors and his cap, swiped his hand over his high forehead, replaced the cap, straightened his jacket, picked up his chain saw, and walked up the trail toward his office.

NORA SLUMPED ONTO the stump. "God damn you, Nora," she said quietly. "What's the matter with you? Why can't you leave it alone?"

Tick couldn't help her there, but oh man, this was trouble. All his working life, Tick had worked for Axel when he had a job to do. He didn't think Axel should have done that, but she shouldn't have chewed him out, and Tick didn't dare take sides.

What Nora didn't know was that there was no future in getting crossways with Axel. Tick and Axel had grown up together in this little town, and didn't Tick know. Axel was ten years older than Tick, so he turned into a man and left school when Tick was still learning block letters. But little boys in a one-room school watch the older boys out the side of their eyes.

When Axel was a boy, he lived with old Mr. and Mrs. Hagerman on their fishing boat. It was a steel seiner, but it wasn't fishing because Mr. Hagerman bunged up his back and couldn't do the work. The boat was their house, tied to the dock with rope thicker than a boy's arm and never once untied. On school days, Axel climbed backward off the boat with his lunch box, walked up the gangway, and went to school. Kids would have made fun of Axel, living in a steel box with a straggle-haired woman and a humpback man like in some evil fairy tale, but they were afraid of him. Not because he was big. He wasn't big. He was small and lumpy. But he was tough.

Everybody said Mr. and Mrs. Hagerman weren't Axel's mom and dad, but they took care of him and they probably loved him. Nobody knew Axel's real mom and dad. They were just passing through when he was born, everybody said, and they drowned when he was a newborn baby. Mrs. Hagerman was babysitting Axel then, so she took him in and raised him up. Mrs. Hagerman died before Axel got out of school, and Mr. Hagerman got sent to the Pioneer Home in Sitka. So Axel lived in that cold, steel seiner by himself through the year he was sixteen, but here's the thing.

In that year, he fixed up that old boat, got the diesels running, took apart the winches and pullers, oiled them, and put them back together again, spiffed it all up, painted the decks, mended the nets. And the very month he graduated from school, he hired a crew of grown men, drove an axe blade through the crusted ropes, and went seining for pink salmon. All along, the kid had had a plan. He came back with money in his pocket, and the crew members had money in their pockets, and he started dating the cutest girl in the school, Rebecca Schmidt, who was sixteen too. Then all the boys in the school wanted to work for Axel, including Tick. They cleaned his fish, they cut his logs, they scraped his barnacles off his boats—whatever he had going.

So cleaning up after Axel was nothing new to Tick. And Lord knows there was a dandy cleanup job waiting to be done out at Nora's. He didn't think there would be anything wrong with helping her make that tree into a pile of firewood. But Tick waited until Axel had time to get back in his office. Then he trotted into town the back way, scurried around to his shed to dig out his splitting maul. He picked up his chain saw and a jerry can of gas. He stuck the bar oil in his pocket and rounded up his kids.

All morning, Tick and Nora were out there limbing that tree and bucking it up into rounds. Heavy work with a tree that old, all its years grown tight, layer around layer, a sapling encased in summer winter summer winter like layers of varnish, all those years since the one year when a fleck of a seed blew into the moss on a deadfall's back and the first British man-o'-war explored the dreadful coast—that many years old. Heavy air, fog and sawdust and pollen. Blackflies moved in, and the soft flies they called little bastards.

As Tick worked, he shook his head at Nora and muttered nonstop, "Oh man, aw man, you shouldn't be even breathing ideas like that. It's okay to make a mistake first time you're in town, and you learned a quick lesson, that's for sure. Axel shouldn't of done it, I don't think." The chain saw roared over his words, drowned them in blue smoke. "But you shouldn't of said what you said. No good to come here, just out of the blue, and start a war—especially not with Axel. Nobody's asking me, so I can't say yes or no, good or bad, but it's dangerous to cross Axel, and it's good you learned early. Axel didn't need to do that. Okay. Okay. But you can't even be thinking that I might go against him. I got kids, two kids. I got a wife. I got troubles already, and nobody needs yours. Aw man. You'll have yourself a couple winters' worth of stovewood after it dries, which you were going to have to put by anyway, so maybe Axel did you a favor. If it doesn't start something. Which it probably has," but then the chain saw popped and died, and he fell silent.

Tick tied a thick overhand knot in his beard and tucked it down his shirt. He poured chain saw gas into the tank. He grabbed a beer from

Nora's tote and poured it down his throat. Refueled, the man and the machine roared and mumbled along the tree, dropping rounds, and the piano danced spasmodically, humming away. Teamed up with Tick's older boy, Davy, Nora split the rounds and threw the cordwood into a pile by the back door. Tick's little guy, Tommy, ran around throwing branches into a big burn pile, but then he must have gotten tired of working, because he just ran around.

LILLIAN MARY SHADDY unlaced her sneakers and pushed her stocking feet into old galoshes. She tugged her raincoat on over her apron, flipped off the lights, and stepped out of the Good River Harbor Bath 'n' Bar. She would sit for a while, watch the night come on, let the swelling in her ankles go down, see what she could see. Humming, sometimes letting the words break out, Lillian sat and watched. *And I'll show you a young man with many reasons why, there but for fortune . . .* She pulled a foot out of a boot and rubbed it thoughtfully. *Show me the whiskey stains on the floor.* She wasn't spying on anybody, and she wasn't a gossip. She was definitely not watching for Axel Hagerman, although his house was directly across the boardwalk from the bar. The truth was that when you own the town's only bathhouse and bar, it's your business to keep track of everybody's business. People coming and going in this little town rustle up against each other like the tide, and things get rearranged. Crabs flip on their backs, kelp ties itself in knots, sand fleas snap like sprung springs, and sometimes a stinking murrelet washes in, tangled in fishing line. It's good to keep an eye on a falling tide.

Especially now, with this new woman washed up into town. Already everybody was talking about how she insulted Axel. Poor guy, just trying to make a living. She was trouble. Lillian would reserve judgment until she met her. But that new woman was trouble. Lillian lit a cigarette and held it at arm's length, watching the tip glow in the damp and endless dusk.

And here came Axel Hagerman, home late from the office of Good River Products, Inc. Reaching under her plastic rain hat, Lillian patted her hair into place. She squashed her cigarette out in a pot of blue pansies and twirled it between her fingers to let the last of the tobacco fall onto the soil. Streetlights shone cones of cold light one after another down the boardwalk. As Axel made his way toward home, passing from one light to another, his pale head blinked on and off, marking his progress like landing lights. His shoulders were soft, and his briefcase and lunch pail hung heavy. Under each streetlight, his shadow puddled at his feet.

Lillian flicked open her lighter and drew sharply on a new cigarette.

"Evening," she said.

The unexpected flash on sucked-in cheeks must have startled Axel, because he spun to face her.

"Oh. Evening," he said, and pumped himself straighter.

That's better, Lillian thought. He's a good man.

"How are you, Axel?" she said, smiling smoke.

He paused, as if he were thinking about how he was exactly. Then, without answering, he made a leaning right turn into his gangway and entered the comfort of his house and marriage.

A small wave on the ebbing tide sucked out, took its time to push back into the light thrown from Axel's bedroom window, out and again in. Sucking out, returning, out, and again in, the wave wove a slick rope of kelp, eelgrass, sedge straw, feathers black and torn. The abandoned exoskeleton of a crab rolled end-over-end up and down the beach, losing legs, one after another, water sucking out, pressing in. The water took the crusty legs and offered them back again, carrying them in the line of white foam at the slow lip of the wave. Lillian took her time too, watching the tide, her thoughts fading and returning.

The light went out in Axel's bedroom, and the wave made its way out and in, unseen. Lillian knew these sounds. A tumble of pebbles, down, a flight of pebbles, up. She knew the smells of the evening too—sweet pansies, gooey salt of the rock-wrack, woodsmoke, kerosene lamps, maybe somewhere under the wharf a starfish, dissolved and stinking, maybe a downdraft from mountain snowfields and hemlocks. She breathed them every night. In and out. Now, she heard a woman's soft cry. A man's grunt. Lillian looked up sharply, then turned away. The rhythmic bump and bump, pushing white foam into the dark of it, the cries and the grunts, repeated, repeated.

The lightbulb hanging from a cord over Axel's doorway swung in the rhythm of their lovemaking. Lillian closed her eyes. Axel's wife was giving him a sweet gift tonight, and would you call a man a bad man who takes what is given? The earth gives, man takes. Would you call a man a bad man who takes what mother earth holds out to him in her smooth and stony hand?

THE WIND PICKED UP as night came on, and rain began to fall. Nora flicked on a headlamp and walked onto her porch to watch the squall. Rain came down hard, hitting the alder leaves with such force that they spun on their stems as if they had been slapped. Water rebounded from the alders, from the green platter leaves of the devil's club, from the sword ferns, pinging on the windrows of beer cans left from the party. Wind blew rain hard onto the porch, making tiny craters in the sawdust on Nora's piano.

She did what she could in the storm. Balanced on a round of old hemlock, she drove nails into the beams of the porch roof. There was the devil to pay in that wind, to get the grommets of the blue tarp hung up on the nails, and get the nails hammered flat. The tarp worked hard against her, thundering in the gusts, wrapping around her body until she was soaked to the skin. She chased a bottom corner of the tarp, pulled it tight to the edge of the porch floor, and nailed it down. The tarp slapped and billowed like a loose jib. She grabbed the other corner. Once that was nailed down, the tarp was trimmed neat into the wind and she had created a blue shelter for the piano. Noisy in there, though—the drubbing rain and thrashing wind. Nora dragged the hemlock round over to the piano and sat there, warming her hands in her armpits.

She wanted to play. She wanted to be back in her cabin in the hills above Bellingham, practicing the piano, even if the logging trucks sprayed mud on her window as they carried heavy loads down to the mill, even if their jack-brakes brayed with contempt. She wanted to be backstage with that excitement in her stomach and, in her ears, the song of every instrument in the orchestra converging on A. But there was no going back.

Nora shook out her hands. Was it possible that, in the noise of this storm, she could risk it? Who would hear her? She experimentally played an A-minor chord. It frightened her, the sound of it. There was safety in silence. She knew this, and she wouldn't shed tears over it. Lord knows, the piano was wet enough. She had left herself no choice. Whatever life she lived now would be lived like music—as dependent on discord as it is on concord—finding the energy of it, its beauty, in waves of tension and release, regret and grace, loneliness and . . . and what? Doesn't everything yearn to be called back in? Doesn't everyone long to be part of some whole, some home? She lifted her hands over the keyboard.

If a man had walked through the rain into Nora's clearing that night, all he would have heard was rain popping on alder leaves. All he would have smelled was broken hemlock. He would have been puzzled to see a soft blue glow from Nora's porch and in that glow, the silhouette of a seated woman whose hands flew over the keyboard, suspended in space like angels, making no sound at all.

June 25

HIGH TIDE		LOW TIDE	
0.10 am	16.7	6:44 am	-1.2
1:16 pm	14.3	6:51 pm	3.2

The drone of the outboard motor echoed over the Kis'utch clamflats on the far side of the inlet, as Davy aimed his dad's skiff toward the shore. When he killed the engine, the uproar of the waterfall grew loud again, then came the grind of his hull on gravel as his boat kissed the flat.

"Hey-up," Davy hollered, as he stepped onto the sandflat. He was only a fifteen-year-old kid, but he knew you've got to be polite to a brown bear, let it know you're coming. And you can't just sing out a one-note "hey-up," because your voice might be tuned to the river or the wind, and a bear won't hear it. You've got to pitch it low and squeal up the whole octave, like calling a pig. "Hey-yuuup." And Davy knew not to say, "Hi Bear" or "Bear-anything," because if the bear thinks you're calling it, it will probably come. Bears are very polite.

"No reason to be afraid of bears, as long as you're respectful," Davy told Nora. He held the boat steady as she reached out one long leg, then the other. "Don't want to scare you, but I don't want to lead you into a bear either." That would be a bad start to his new career as a wilderness guide.

When you split wood together all afternoon, lifting that maul over your head and cracking it down maybe ten thousand times each in that stuttery syncopated duet, you get to know a person, and by the time Davy and Nora had split Axel's tree into firewood, they were buddies. He said he would take her to the best place in the whole world, the place across the inlet where the Kis'utch River falls down the mountain into the little pool. A place where the pink salmon come home to spawn. The most beautiful place in the whole world, he told her, a place his mom said was sacred, but he didn't know about that. Nora said she wanted very much to see such a place. So she hired him as a wilderness guide, twenty dollars a day.

"I never guided," he said, "but I've been across the inlet a million times, goose hunting, clamming, whatever, so I'm your man."

"Yep," said Nora, "you're my man." She was nice. "And five dollars extra for boat gas."

"We'll take my dad's skiff, not his landing craft. No point in using all the gas it takes to push that barge around. And we need to go on a rising tide," he told her, "so we don't strand the boat." He wasn't sure how much Nora already knew about boats and water, because sometimes Outsiders can be super dumb.

"You're the expert," Nora had said.

Davy was big Tick McIver and Annie Klawon's boy, born and bred in Good River Harbor. He got his mom's straight black hair, which relieved him, since the alternative was his dad's flaming orange. He'd been growing it long, but so far, his hair only got down to about his chin. To keep it out of his eyes, he walked with his head turned about twenty degrees off-course, and he spent a lot of time throwing hair out of his face by jerking his head. Davy was a lanky kid—legs grown faster than his brain, his dad said, and he better slow down growing and let his brain catch up. One of his dad's dumb jokes.

Davy went to school at the Good River Harbor School, where there were two other people in his grade—Axel's daughter Meredith, who was smart and beautiful, and Curtis Daley, who was a jerk. The food Davy ate came from Good River Harbor or it came in on the barge. So he was made of the Kis'utch country—hot and salty goose breast and clam fritters and thimbleberry jam. Of course, he had seen snowstorms in his years and once drought in the summer, and smoky air. But except for those, most days were cloudy and cool—fifty-five maybe, which was two degrees warmer than the Japanese Current that followed the coast. Whether he was walking on the boardwalk or sitting in school, he was always on the water, or at least the water was always underneath him, as much as if he were in a boat. And even though he had worn a raincoat and rubber boots most every day of his life, he was often wet, because the Kis'utch Mountains were the first place the winds made landfall after they crossed the Pacific, and that meant rain. So Davy was made of the Kis'utch that way too—wet and made of water, like a jellyfish.

By the time he was five, he could tell the burrow of a geoduck from a butter clam's by the shape of its hole in the sand, and the difference between a merganser and a loon by the speed of its wings. When he was ten, he was strong enough on the pull cord to start an outboard motor. When he was eleven, he could sometimes get a chain saw going, although chainsaws are tricky. When he was twelve, he shot his first deer. When he was fourteen, he rode on a bus in Seattle with his mom. And the next great event, at age fifteen: his first paying job as a wilderness guide for Nora Montgomery.

While Davy was tilting up the engine, Nora grabbed the anchor, carried it up the mudflat and dropped it behind a log. She had on her yellow raincoat and Davy's hip boots. They smucked into the mud, but that didn't slow her down. Clams squirted in front of her, high as her shoulders, which were high. Every time a clam squirted, Nora laughed. That turned out to be a lot of laughing. She waded into the middle channel of the river and stood there, her arms raised, her face to the sky. Everything was shining from the rain—the mudslicks, the stranded kelp, her raincoat, even Nora's broad cheeks, holding up her big shiny eyes and big shiny smile. Davy stared at her, wondering.

She breathed in noisily.

"Smell the rock-wrack, Davy," she said. "Smell the salt and the cedar."

She made Davy nervous, standing in the creek. It's slippery on algae. Davy thought he should warn her, maybe say something like, "Be careful here, Nora." He practiced in his mind, and then he said it, "Be careful here Nora." But she was out of the river and walking up the mudflat toward the beach rye at the high-tide line. She spooked three eagles off a stranded log and stopped to watch them fly. Davy was glad she stopped, because if eagles were waiting there for the salmon, so were bears.

"Hey-uuuuup," he shouted, and listened for anything moving in the bush.

They followed a bear trail through the beach rye. Bears walk in the same track forever, so they make a good trail, about a foot wide, a foot deep. Davy knew he should be singing. His mom said, "Always be singing." But he wasn't sure which would be more embarrassing—a wilderness guide singing at the top of his lungs or his client surprising a bear. Davy showed

Nora the indentations where bears stepped in their own footprints, going upstream and downstream all their lives.

"Sort of like me," he said, "walking up and down the same boardwalk all my life."

"Be glad for that," she told him. "Could be lots worse." Nora poked with her toe at a pile of bear droppings.

"Sedge," he said. "That's a hungry bear, impatient for the salmon, probably angry at the wait."

"I *come on the sloop John B*," Davy sang out. "*My grandfather and me*." Probably it's okay for a wilderness guide to sing, he decided, if it's sort of a manly song, like his dad sings, not like his mom.

They came out of the grass onto the gravel bank where Davy's mom picks beach peas. There's a dike made out of river stones that goes almost across the river.

"An old fish weir. That's wonderful," Nora whispered, and she knelt on the rocks. "How old?"

Davy never could understand why people would whisper in bear country. Here he was, trying to make as much noise as he could, and she was whispering. And actually, Davy didn't know how old the weir was.

"Ten thousand years," he said.

His mom had told him the People made the weir, piling on cobbles and building the weir back up whenever a flood washed it out. Jimmy Pete fished it every year until he died, but that was before Davy was born. He fished on the pink-salmon tide, when the high tide floods over the weir, bringing salmon. Then the ebb tide leaks out between the stones, trapping the fish. Jimmy Pete gathered them in baskets and took them to town. Davy's dad remembered getting fish from Jimmy Pete.

Before long, they lost the bear trail in a mess of corn lilies and cow parsnip higher than Davy's head. Nora moved fast, but following her was easy as tracking a bear. He could see the bush moving around her, and she left a big fat trail of crushed plants and that sharp smell of the broken parsnips. She should stay closer.

"*Round Nassau Town we did roam, drinkin' all night*."

They waded through the meadow, back into the thimbleberries and blind turns. They hardly got back into the bush before they walked right onto a clearing where bears had chewed out the skunk cabbage roots, battering them into the muck, and scuffed up the parsnips.

"Bear kitchen," he told her. "*Got into a fight. Oh, I feel so broke up.*"

In a few more steps, they burst through the last of the parsnip's stickery stink-smelling leaves and swarming white petals onto a muskeg filled with wildflowers. Nora leaned to cup a spiky blue flower in her palm.

"That's *jelch-tache*," Davy said. "It means 'raven's odor.' Smell it."

"Smells like an onion," she said, but Davy knew ravens didn't smell like onions, that's for sure.

"They smell like crap and armpits."

Nora guffawed. "I didn't know that," and she skied down the muddy bank and started walking up the river, with Davy following along behind.

Around the next curve, Nora stopped short. There, in front of her, was the side of the mountain, a glistening green wall of ferns and moss-covered rocks. The Kis'utch River dropped through them, combed into a thousand silver threads. Where the water came to earth, it changed from silver into lavender bubbles that dove into a black pool draped with lady ferns. The light was dim and green, latticed with hemlock, saturated with the splash of the stream. Water eddied through the pool, there, cold and clear, and flowed through a freestone pond where the salmon came to spawn.

The current pushed against Nora's boots. Rain dripped off the bill of her cap. Davy walked up beside her and flicked his hair out of his face. She was quiet for so long, Davy thought maybe she didn't like it. When she did talk, he could hardly hear her, it was so noisy by the waterfall. But he won't forget what she said, because she was crying and it didn't make any sense.

What she said was, "Maybe I'm finally home too." Then she reached over and hugged him by the neck and rumpled his hair, like he'd seen her do to her dog. He thought it probably made her dog happier than it made him.

They were following their track back through the corn lilies, almost to the weir, when they heard the grumble of an engine. Davy jerked his head up, listening, and pulled the hair out of his eyes. Nora crouched like a wary raven. Now Davy could see the plane and he was really surprised, because it was Charlie's charter, and Charlie watches the weather. He wouldn't be bringing a plane under a ceiling this low unless it was really important to somebody. Davy listened as Charlie brought the floatplane over the tide-flat, took a hard turn upriver, and flew straight toward Jimmy Pete's weir. Davy ducked without thinking, the plane was that low. It throttled down and kept on course. When he was starting to think Charlie was going to hit the waterfall, the plane banked hard and flew out over the inlet, buzzing them again on the way out. Davy could tell from the engine noise that Charlie was bringing it into the mouth of the river. He hoped Charlie saw the anchor line on his skiff.

Davy listened for the *slapslapslap* as the plane landed, the falling pitch of the engine, the rev when the plane taxied toward shore. It was quiet then.

"I don't know," he answered, although Nora hadn't asked the question. "Either this is a rich tourist or it's Axel—the only people with enough money to charter a plane."

He looked toward Nora, but she wasn't there.

SHE WASN'T HARD to track, but he pushed through a lot of devil's club and elderberry before Davy found Nora, crouched under the low, sweeping arms of a hemlock. She'd taken off her yellow raincoat and was sitting on it with her knees in the air. For once, she was not grinning.

"Okay, wilderness guide," she said before he could ask a single question. "Find me the back way out of here."

He led her away from the river, up a blueberry slope into an open spruce forest carpeted in moss. Once they had angled so far that they could no longer hear the river, he circled them back around and broke trail through tangled alder, crawling over windfall, placing their boots carefully on musky duff mined with squirrel dens. Whenever he called out for bears, she shushed him. They were weaving now under cover of alders toward the soft rustling sound of the sea and its bright smell. That's when he felt he could finally ask her what they were running from. But what came out of Davy's mouth was not a question.

"Shit," he said. He swiveled to face into an onrushing noise—a galloping horse, a war drum, a falling cedar, tearing branches off all the trees in its path, the thudding vibration of the hollow duff, and Davy could see the bear, thundering straight at them, slapping away willows the way a skiff slaps waves.

"HEY-UUUUP," Davy shouted. He flapped his arms over his head.

To Nora, "Come close to me, spread your jacket, make yourself big, stand your ground."

And to the bear, "HEY, HEY, HEY."

The bear was so close, Davy could see rims of white around his eyes.

He could hear him pant.

"Back away slowly," Davy muttered, and took a first slow step back as the bear charged. Davy tripped on a log and fell flat on his backside.

That's how they were, as the bear pounded past them and disappeared into the brush—Davy sitting stupid on the ground, Nora standing beside him flapping her jacket like the wing nubbins of a nestling crow.

After that, they stayed just inside the screen of alders where the forest gave way to the beach, moving now toward the sound of the river. They were climbing on broken mussel shells across a rock outcrop when they heard a man's voice.

Axel. It's not a hard voice to recognize, kind of sharp around the edges. Davy didn't know if he was doing something wrong or something Axel would think was bad. He didn't even know what he was supposed to be afraid of. But he knew he didn't want Axel to catch him out there guiding for Nora. He couldn't think of anything wrong with guiding Nora, whoever she was, but if there was anything wrong with it, Axel would figure it out. Axel did that, figure things out that are bad. This was a worry, especially if your dad wanted to work for him. And especially if you were a dumb kid secretly in love with Axel's smart and beautiful daughter.

Davy looked out from behind the curtain of leaves. There were two men on the beach, talking. Charlie was standing on the float of his seaplane anchored at the mouth of the river, right next to Davy's boat.

"We're not going anywhere," Davy said.

Nora considered. "You're going to have to go talk to those guys. Find out who they are and what they want. If they're okay, just signal me and I'll come. If they're not, then launch your boat and come get me at the end of the beach."

"Okay about what, Nora?" Davy didn't know why he was suddenly frightened. "What's going on?"

≈≈≈

AXEL DIDN'T SEEM a bit surprised to see Davy, and why would he be surprised, with Davy's skiff anchored right there on the beach. Axel had on his good pants, stuck into the tops of his XtraTufs, and his slick jacket with the zipper pockets to hold his cash, and the same old GR Products watchman's cap. He was about the only guy without a beard in Good River Harbor. In fact, he didn't seem to have any hair at all, any more than a melted candle has hair. Davy's dad said he was the only guy without a beer gut too, and you can't trust a guy who's gutless—another one of his dad's bad jokes.

But Davy didn't feel like laughing. He felt sick.

"What are you doing here, Davy?" said Axel, as if there was something wrong with that.

"Guiding," said Davy, and just about fainted with horror at what he'd said. Because, sure enough, Axel said back, "Guiding who?"

Davy looked around wildly.

"Nobody, I guess," he said.

There was a man with Axel. "Best kind of client," he said. But then he was off and talking.

"Hey, you should have been here a little while ago. Came on a huge bear. Man, did we ever scare it. Said, 'Boo,' and the big guy hightailed it out of here, like he was shot from a cannon. Probably didn't stop running for a mile. Guess he knows who's in charge." And the man began to chuckle, *heh heh heh heh,* with a sound like an outboard running out of gas.

Davy looked at the man closely. He was nobody he had ever seen before. With short gray hair, tight skin, big ears, the guy's head was a dog's head, smooth and long and gray. He was carrying a daypack and a big surveyor's tape, and he had on XtraTufs, but here's what threw Davy. The guy was wearing a white office shirt, the kind he'd seen in advertisements for photocopiers, and he had on a long diagonally striped tie. Davy stared. It's the first tie he had ever seen in real life. Once he'd seen a tourist in a bow tie, but not like this. Just above his pocket the shirt said, FOWLER'S SURVEYORS. The guy's sleeves were rolled up, and the hair on his forearms was the same gray dog's hair.

"This is Davy McIver, from Good River Harbor," Axel said, and Davy wondered how Axel could make a guy's own name sound like a knife in the leg.

"Meet Howard Fowler, a surveyor from Seattle. Got him on a project here."

"Jesus Christ," said Howard Fowler.

He was staring up the beach. They all turned to look.

The bear stood broadside on a thick drift-log, not thirty yards away. His back was arched and the rough fur on his shoulders flared, a bear of monstrous size. He swung his immense head side to side, slinging strings of drool. The sound he made was the exhalation of a coming storm, that low and elemental, huffing with unmistakable menace.

"Jeezus Kee-rist," Fowler repeated himself.

"I am lord of this beach and all its salmon and sows," Davy translated in a low voice, as he backed slowly away. "I am the biggest bear and the baddest bear, and you are peewees. Get out of here before I get mad."

"Looks like that bear changed his mind about who's in charge," Axel observed.

Howard Fowler stripped off his pack and started rummaging around.

"Got bear spray and flares." Must have been under his raincoat there, somewhere, not there by the water bottle. He unzipped another pocket. Not there.

"Jeezus. Jeezus. Jeezus."

"Forget it, Fowler," Axel growled. "Come in close to us and back away."

Shoulder to shoulder, they drew away, backing carefully over a tangle of kelp, backing carefully over a sand shingle pocked with clam-siphon holes, backing through a patch of sea asparagus, and then stepping carefully into the river. They pivoted like a marching band and waded downstream. The current slid off their boots, eddying behind them, as they stepped over the algae-pinked rocks and sea urchins to the mouth of the creek. Howard lofted himself into the floatplane, Axel climbed in after him, and Charlie flew them back to town.

≈≈≈

NORA LEANED BACK in the bow-seat with both arms hanging over the gunwales and her big boots propped on the front bench seat. "Jeezus. Jeezus. Jeezus," she squeaked again, her face split by a great big grin. She sure was cheery, now she knew there was nothing to be afraid of. The boat puttered back toward Good River Harbor. "Those two guys flailing out to their hips to get in the seaplane, and flopping like salmon onto the floats."

Davy wasn't laughing. Tucked neatly behind a log on the Kis'utch beach was the anchor from his dad's boat. He'd had to cast off the anchor line and leave the anchor there, rather than walk back up that bear's beach to fetch it.

Davy dropped his voice into Tick's growl. "*If you're old enough to use my equipment, you're old enough to take care of* it. My dad has only said that about twenty thousand times." His head drooped behind a screen of black hair.

"Hey, wilderness guide," Nora said, sitting up to swack his shoulder. "You did a darned good job showing me the wildlife, finding us a route. You're a pro."

"Should of known the salmon were coming in. Should of known that old bear would be back to play king of the mountain." He tossed his hair out of his face. "But Nora, what were you so afraid of on that seaplane?"

She grinned. "Nothing, turns out. Nothing at all."

Davy slowed the skiff, giving his mind time to work, but for all the extra time, it didn't get much done. So he said, "Tide's high, flooding up under the houses. We could float right up under there. Guides do this in Seattle," he said, perking up. "Put rich tourists on a boat and tour the town."

The putter of the outboard echoed in the sudden dark under the library, and the smell of seaweed and creosote floated thick on black water. There was a constant pock and patter as moisture dropped from the stringers. Metal plates dripped stalagmites of murky minerals and salt. Davy and Nora raised their hoods. He gave her a good tour, steering in and out under the pilings all the way to the end of town, where the docks gave way to a rocky cliff and a boulder beach. That's where the old cannery used to be, but the site had been abandoned for years.

Nothing remained of the cannery but a couple of pilings and a big cedar water tank on a ledge halfway up the cliff. That's where they'd stored rainwater for the fish processing—a round, above-ground cistern sort of thing, thirty feet across easy, probably fifteen feet high. People in Good River Harbor were proud of the tank, a work of art, they said, made out of cedar staves bound with steel rods, like an enormous barrel. Tight enough to hold water, still tight after all these years. It used to have a pointed roof like a witch's hat, but that blew off ages ago. Then moss grew on the rim of the tank and black stains ran down the edges of the staves. A tiny rivulet dripped from a pipe into the top of the tank, and another pipe leaked water out the bottom. There was a wooden floor, Davy knew, but it was covered deep in spruce needles and duff.

Curtis was over there throwing rocks at the empty tank. Idling just offshore, Davy yelled *hey* but said he couldn't come throw rocks because he was working as a guide. Then he cut the engine and they just floated.

"The stones bonking against the cistern sound just like the mallet hitting a wooden temple bell," Nora said.

Another rock bounced off the wall. The tank clonked. A raven answered, *clonk*. "Bull's-eye," shouted dumb Curtis.

"Funny, my mom talks about bells too. 'When it's quiet, you can hear the Earth ring.' That's what she said."

Nora stared at him.

"That was a long time ago when she said that, after I told her how empty our house is when she's off in Seattle, and how quiet it is at night. Listen, she said, because the Earth rings like a bell. But maybe not like a cistern. I don't know.

"But wooee, that cistern isn't going to be empty for long. Axel still owns the cannery site, so he can do whatever he wants there."

"What now?" Nora slumped in the bow.

"My secret girlfriend, Meredith, said that Axel was going to let her mom make the tank into a little community garden—a walled garden with its own little creek flowing through it. Whoever wants to, can grow things there, even high school kids. No deer, no slugs, but piles of flowers or kale, rhubarb, whatever.

"See, that's the kind of person Meredith is," Davy told Nora. "She shares." And he was off—nothing can stop a man from talking about the woman he loves, while his skiff drifts under a rotting wharf and pivots on a pile of floating kelp.

"Like when the teacher decided to teach us justice. Mrs. Brenner had this big chocolate bar—huge. And she said one person would get the chocolate, but the class had to decide who would get it and then why, and no fair avoiding the problem by just dividing it up. So we were stumped."

"Mmm," Nora agreed.

"Finally that jerk Curtis grabbed it, said he gets it because he's hungriest, but we made him give it back. Then we just sat there, looking at the candy and being mad at Mrs. Brenner for setting us up, wishing she would just take her dumb chocolate and go away. Meredith was pretty sad, but all of a sudden, she says, 'Give the candy to me.' Curtis is like, 'What? Your dad's rich. You can get candy whenever you want.' But Meredith is all 'No, no, give it to me. I want it,' and she took it. She said, 'It's mine now, right? And I can do whatever I want with it, right?' That was right. So she unwrapped it, divided it into parts, and gave us all chocolate."

Davy grinned. "See what I mean? She's so nice."

Nora stared at Davy with her mouth gaping. "Davy!" she barked. "Think! How did she get the candy in the first place?" But then she clamped her mouth shut tight as a cod.

"And smart," he added, smiling to himself. "And beautiful."

He yanked the cord on the outboard and steered the boat under the houses and the clanking old Quonset hut. He told her, "That's my house," and showed her the window to his and Tommy's bedroom, tacked on and stuck up on pilings.

"That's wonderful," she said. "Like the crew's quarters on a boat."

"If so, that boat's kind of washed up on the rocks and stove in," he said, and then he was ashamed. But in fact, Davy wasn't altogether sure the town makes a good impression when you see it from below like that. It's sort of an embarrassment, poking around under the buildings, like looking up somebody's skirt. All the pilings are crappy with barnacles and blue mussels, with popweed caught up in them and scraps of line, and there's seaweed dripping off the cross-bracing. Everybody hangs junk there, not just Tick's family—crab pots they're going to fix up and broken oars. Davy wished his dad would get rid of the bike that's been hanging off their back porch for a hundred years, all rusted and the tires rotting off. Tick said he might make something of it, but he said that about everything.

"I've been here all my life," Davy told Nora. "I walk up to my door on the boardwalk, step over that pile of stovewood and the tote with all the boots and halibut jigs, and I'm home. There's the table with the red-checked plastic tablecloth. There's Tommy and Dad. There's never any question. Summer's summer. Winter's dark. School or not school. It's just where I am. I wonder what it's like to be away from home, or even not to know where home is."

Nora didn't answer. Maybe she hadn't heard him, or maybe she was wondering too. So Davy ran her in and out of the docks, right up under the bows of the big boats. The seiners were in, with the guys winching up their nets, coiling the lines, checking for rips. They're all going someplace—into harbor, onto the fishing ground, back out again. But still, they know where their home harbor is. They've got it written on their transom, in case they need to check. But most of the boats at the docks weren't going anywhere. They just sat there under blue tarps, riding lower and lower in the water. Because somebody's going to fix them up sometime and sail somewhere. But why would you? Where else would you go?

All the way out to Nora's cabin on Green Point, there was only the grinding of the outboard. Davy wanted to ask Nora where she came from, but she talked over him, kind of absentminded.

"I'm glad for you, that you have a place," she said. "This spring, I put my piano on the ferry and made myself a promise. Where I go next, I'm staying. The weight of this piano is the only anchor I'll ever have. I'm going to haul this piano up over rocks somewhere, get it fouled in some place I'll never get it out of, and then figure a way to stay. I just want to lead a normal life."

Something about that last sentence came out sort of wet.

Davy cringed. He was going to get in bad enough trouble because he'd left his dad's anchor on the beach. But he didn't do it on purpose; the bear made him do it. He would be doomed if he fouled an anchor on purpose. But he hoped Nora stayed. She was nice. Weird, but nice. So was Chum.

"What are you going to do for money?" he asked her.

"I don't need much money. Sometimes I write stuff for cruise ship pamphlets or ferries. Little pieces about bears or salmon, that kind of thing."

"Well, then, why didn't you just stay home where you were?"

Nora took off her baseball cap, caught up her hair in a ponytail, put back on the cap, pulled her hair through the hole, pulled it to both sides to tighten it all up, tugged down on the brim.

"Do you know what it means to burn your bridges?"

"Sure." Did she think he was an idiot?

"That's what I did."

"Oh jeez," he said. He'd have to run away from home too, if he set fire to a bridge.

"Jeezus. Jeezus. Jeezus," Nora said, and grinned.

HIGH TIDE OR low, hungry or not, but usually hungry, the father and sons of the McIver family always ate dinner at 6:30 p.m. Alaska time—big Tick, and Davy and Tommy—in a tiny kitchen propped on pilings. In her rented room in Seattle, the boys' mother, Annie Klawon, always ate at 7:30 p.m. Pacific time, which is the same time. That way the whole family sat down together for supper, even though Annie had to live in Seattle to work at that insurance place. It holds families together, she always said, to have supper together. Davy once told his mom he didn't know if that counted as "together," with them in Good River Harbor and her being a secretary in Seattle. That made her cry, but she said they had to do it just in case it worked. There's lots of things you do, she said, just in case they work.

Supper for the Good River Harbor McIvers that night was potatoes and venison. Tick tucked his great beard into his collar to keep from setting himself on fire, put on massive mitts, and fished the potatoes and Dutch oven out of the woodstove. They waited just a minute to make sure their mom was seated, then they held hands round the table, little Tommy grabbing however much of Tick's hand he could hold in one of his.

"It's good to be together again," they said in unison. It was a prayer, it was a blessing, it was gratitude, it was relief to count noses at the end of the day and find them all accounted for. Bigger than hope, it was faith in the strength of the circle, the cycle of coming and going and always returning, it was the magic fact that a circle has no end.

"Cha cha cha," Davy taunted, as he always did, to make up for holding hands with his dad and little brother.

They set to.

At 6:45 Alaska time, they were full and the pot was empty.

"Okay, you guys do the dishes," said Tick, which was not that big a deal—a rinse with hot water from the teakettle and a good rub on a towel. "I'm gonna go work on the boat, clean it up for when your mom comes home." He pulled out his beard, gave it a flap, and angled his mass out the kitchen door.

"I'm going to work on the boat" meant "I'm heading to Lillian's," which meant that Davy had to stay home and put Tommy to bed. Six years old, and he wouldn't go to sleep unless somebody lay down beside him—usually Davy. Then, when Tommy fell asleep, Davy had to get up without creaking the bed or bumping his head on the upper bunk, which was where he slept. When it was blowing and the waves broke on the pilings under their room, Davy sometimes fell asleep too and didn't wake up until dark. But he wouldn't fall asleep that night, because he had a lot to think about, especially how he would advertise his wilderness guide business, which had already earned twenty dollars in one day, plus gas money.

Davy tucked the blankets around Tommy's shoulders, like his mom did, and lay down beside his little brother. Pretty soon, their mom would be singing them a song, back in Seattle. Tommy lay still to hear her voice, which he sometimes said he could. Davy, on the other hand, knew it was just the wind in the long lines on the boats, but it would be cruel to say that to Tommy. And anyway, sometimes Davy thought he could hear her too, her singing, even sometimes the words maybe.

He listened with Tommy. At calm dusk, he heard the snick of tide through eelgrass and the hum of a skiff far away and vanishing. In the forest, varied thrushes whistled. So softly the sound came through the woods, it echoed the silver whisper of Tommy breathing as he slept. From across the channel, the Kis'utch falls murmured like a nursing bear. Now and then a raven clonked. The tide licked a last few pebbles and quietly fell into its own bed.

After Annie Klawon's song was finished, Davy told her about his day, about how Nora gave him a twenty-dollar bill and a five-dollar bill. Or if he didn't tell her, at least he thought hard in his mom's direction, knowing that she turned her face to the north each night and listened. It wasn't really telling her about his day, he was old enough to know, but who else would he tell?

When Tommy cried out in his sleep, Davy reached over to put a hand on his back like his mom did, just the weight of it, so Tommy would know he wasn't adrift. Low tide was breathing whispery now, all the slips and sighs. A moving tide was splashy as a river. A high tide was so still that if you listened, maybe you could hear the vibration of the sea, a shimmering that was almost sound. A low tide was as quiet as it could make itself, pretending to be asleep. Davy listened, but what he heard was men laughing over at Lillian's.

June 26

HIGH TIDE		LOW TIDE	
0:52 am	16.9 ft	7:25 am	-1.6
1:57 pm	14.7 ft	7:33 pm	3.0

For every flood tide, there is an ebb. This Lillian knew. For every pebble beach concealed, there is a mussel bed revealed. For every taking, there must be a giving. This is the way of the world.

The flood-tide was ebbing when Lillian propped open the door of the Good River Harbor Bath 'n' Bar and lit up the open sign. Drawn by alcohol's own gravitational force, or maybe just by habit or boredom, or by the sucking force of loneliness, men began to move in her direction. Lillian watched them come. Four fishermen on a seiner hung rubber overalls by their suspenders on the wall of the pilothouse and strode up the wharf. "I'm heading to the harbor," big Tick called to his boys. He shoved a screwdriver and a Vise-Grip into his capacious back pocket and walked down to his boat. He glared at it, then turned around and walked the gangway toward Lillian's. Gunkholers on the party deck of the sailing vessel *Penury* drained their martini glasses and headed for the bar. To get there, they all walked past the gangway that led to the cabin of a man named Kenny Isaacson, who would soon be showing signs of thirst.

"GETTING ON TIME for a drink," Kenny informed Ranger. He spun his wheelchair toward the door.

Ranger trotted ahead of him and nosed into the streak of light on the doorsill.

"You thirsty yellow dog," Kenny said, and gave Ranger a fond swat on the rear end. Kenny tugged a pine-squirrel fur hat down over his ears, ran his hand over the braids on his chin, pulled on leather fingerless gloves, and they were ready to go.

Kenny had shown up in town about twenty-five years before. Nobody knew where he'd come from, or what he was all about. Not even Lillian knew, although she had ventured to ask him more than once. He moved into a broken-down cabin right there on the boardwalk, and after a while, he was just part of the town—a sort of sullen and fierce part of town. Townspeople tolerated him, even though they might have been a little put off by his manner and his fur hats. But the little boys worshipped him. He taught them to tie a dental-floss noose around the neck of a horsefly and take it for a walk, like a flying dog. He taught the kids to set miniature snares to catch mice and mink, and when they did, he made the skins into hats and wore them every day. They loved him the way little boys love belches, although they were afraid of him, and they followed him at a distance like blackflies follow the smell of sweat.

And tourists *loved* Kenny, even though they pretended not to see him. He was a tourist attraction all right, sitting there scowling in a wheelchair. He flew an American flag from the back of his chair and a rainbow whirligig off the armrest. Rain or shine, he wore a camouflage poncho and those ridiculous fur hats, and if that wasn't a sight—a guy in a house-mouse hat with tails hanging down beside each ear. He braided his chin-hair into tight little braids with rubber bands to hold the bitter ends. Lillian had told him a hundred times, "Just shave. Is that so hard? What are you hiding back there under the bullrushes? You're a handsome guy, got a good jaw and nice skin, like a rock-face after a landslide, storm-polished like that, but who can see you under that hat?"

"Har," he always said, as if he were some kind of pirate, and that's the backstory the little boys gave him, that he was a fierce pirate—maybe even Jack Sparrow—who marauded over the seven seas until he got his legs cracked by cannon fire from a British man-o'-war and had to come to Good River Harbor, wearing a disguise that fooled no one. Little boys know things like that.

As he wheeled down his pier onto the boardwalk, men were roaming around the door to Lillian's Bath 'n' Bar like dogs on the scent. Even over the rumble of his wheels, Kenny could hear them yapping. With his arms crossed over his orange beard, big Tick was leaning against Lillian's chalkboard menu. His huge denim shirt erased more of the menu every time he disagreed with somebody. Already he was down to *ish and chips*. Another argument, and there'd be nothing left to eat but *ips*.

"Har."

"Mighty fine weather," Tick shouted. He leaned over to scratch the sweet spot between Ranger's ears.

Weather wasn't as crappy as it usually was—Kenny agreed with Tick about that—rain finally letting up, sun rolling sideways along the mountains. The guys had apparently been down to see the pile of sawdust and stovewood at the new woman Nora's cabin. That mess was all they could talk about.

"D'ya see that huge hemlock Axel felled?" Tick shouted, and dropped a big hand on Kenny's shoulder. Kenny could never figure out why people think that if you can't walk, you probably can't hear.

"Nah," Kenny shouted back. "But I don't have to see bear shit to know it's there—and it sounds like that Nora woman has made a steaming hell of a pile."

But they stopped talking and got real interested in the clouds, because along came Nora. She was wearing her yellow raincoat and jeans with some kind of tool stuck in her back pocket. Trotting along behind was her dog, Chum.

Kenny called in Ranger. The dog backed up and sat by Kenny's wheel, thumping his stump-tail.

"Don't need any dry-humping today," Kenny warned him. Ranger thumped even harder.

Kenny studied Nora's dog. Chum seemed like a good dog, an overgrown shepherd maybe mixed up with some golden retriever, and that was one point for Nora—that she had a good big dog. Chum ran up to Tick and the rest of the rabble. They all reached down to pat him and scratch him behind the ears. Then he ran back to Nora. He pushed his nose between her legs and shoved his way through, rubbing against her jeans. He ran around and nuzzled in again, pressing his shoulders into her legs and whining until she spread her knees. Nora laughed, leaning over him, rubbing her knuckles into his ribs, fluffing his backside, telling him how much she loved him.

"Tick, look at me," Kenny demanded. "Tell me if my eyes are bugging out like I got smacked on the back of the head with a two-by-four."

Tick's cheeks flushed as bright as his beard. Chum pushed between Nora's thighs again. She sat on his back while he squirmed through and came around to lick her mouth. Kenny grimaced. He could see all those guys trying not to lick their own chops, no different from dogs. Kenny and Ranger followed Nora into the bar and soon enough, Chum wandered in too, and so did Tick, and the half-pint town dog everybody called Lucky, because she was the luckiest Chihuahua that ever decided to chase a bear out of town.

Everybody stopped at the door to pry off their XtraTufs. Lillian insisted on this. Hers wasn't any ordinary bar. It was a bath-and-bar, a place of cleanliness and worth. Brown boots lined up as close to the wall as teenage boys on a dance floor. Everybody hung their raincoats on hooks by the woodstove.

A couple of gunkholer-tourists crowded in, laughing too loud, tripping over Lucky. "Oops. Sorry." Kenny cut his wheels in front of them and growled in their general direction. Just because they own a fancy sailboat doesn't mean they own the place. Kenny could do without tourists, because he didn't like being a tourist attraction himself. There were plenty of nice little houses on the boardwalk, but his was the one they wanted a picture of. Kenny thought that was perverse, being singled out because you're broken down. His cabin was the original—adze-squared spruce logs, fishtail joints, glacier clay in the cracks, fireweed blooming in the gutter, moss on the roof. The door was sort of askew because the front beam gave way, but who needs a square door as long as it opens?

Kenny made his cabin nice, sticking stuff in the window boxes, like plastic flowers and pinwheels, an eagle feather, whatever. Some of the tourists stole his decorations, and some put new things in. A Cleveland Indians pennant showed up one week. But it burned Kenny's butt when some kids on an eco-cruise stole his SOLITARY POOR NASTY BRUTISH AND SHORT needlepoint. Stole it right off his wall. It had taken him a couple of months to stitch it just right. So he wired down his HAYDUKE LIVES sign. Didn't want it hanging in some damn dorm room at Yale.

Shooting pictures of his house was bad enough. But when tourists took pictures of Kenny, he thought that was out of line. They walked by, staring away from him and his wheelchair-o-rama—which was still a kind of staring. Then they came back again, and Kenny could see the little digital cameras they were holding by their sides.

"Philistine," he would mutter. "I'd rather have my busted-up body than your busted-up soul." Muttering always made the tourists rear back and walk away fast, which cracked Kenny up. His shoulders would jiggle up and down under his poncho, as he tried not to laugh out loud, and that scared the tourists even worse. And if he was really ready for a joke, he would put on a biblical voice and shout out something he remembered from way back, and then wouldn't the tourists scuttle. "*And men go abroad to admire the mighty waves of the sea and the circuits of the stars*," Kenny trumpeted, "*yet pass over the mystery of themselves without a thought*." Saying the truth in a big voice always makes people think you are nuts. And nutcases scare tourists half to death.

"If it's tourist season, why don't we shoot 'em?" That's what Tick said, and Kenny thought that would be justified. Greatest good for the greatest number.

Once a couple of tourists standing on the dock asked, "How far above sea level are we here?" Course, they didn't ask Kenny. They asked Davy McIver, thinking a teenager's going to know more than a cripple. Poor kid didn't know what to say, he's so polite. Kenny thought he should have said, "Take a step backward and you'll find out." But he said, "Two feet at high tide." Straight as an arrow, that kid.

Sometimes they even ask his dog their questions, so they don't have to talk to a guy under a camo poncho in a wheelchair, just because he's flying a flag and wearing a mouse-skin cap complete with tails. "Does anybody here know where the post office is, hum?" they croon, holding Ranger's snout or scratching him between the eyes. "Dog ain't tellin'," Kenny always said. Made them skitter. Made him laugh.

Lillian hummed over to Kenny's table, gave it a swipe with a rag, and handed him a whiskey. "She's fast, that fat old lady," Kenny said to Tick. "'Whiskey on the rocks. Comin' right up. Quarter for the jukebox. Yes-sirree. Rum and Coke, light on the Coke, and a bag of jalapeno chips.'

Faster she serves them, the faster they drink them, the faster coins fall into the till. Har."

Tick cringed behind his big beard. "Be nice," he whispered.

"Nice." Kenny considered. "How's this? Isn't it too bad that her feet hurt, trundling around like a tub in a gale, and whose feet wouldn't be sore, if they had to hold up that barge all day?"

"I said, be nice. If she heard you talking, she'd unlatch your brake and roll you right off the wharf. Besides, can't you see she's trying to be pretty?"

While Kenny watched Lillian over the slosh of his whiskey, a stranger opened the door. He peeked into a bar probably darker than he expected, but made up his mind and came in. He walked up to the bar and hung one butt cheek on the stool. Kenny had never seen him before. Big ears, gray hair short like a Weimaraner. Murmurs rolled across the room.

"That guy is wearing a button-down shirt and a goddamn tie."

"Is that a noose around that guy's neck?"

"Anybody here need any car insurance?"

Lillian yawled on over.

"I give townies and gunkholers the two things they can't get along without."

Kenny had heard Lillian say this a thousand times, and she always said it fast, as if she were trying to get all their questions over with, so she could ask her own.

"Whiskey is one. A bath is the other. Whiskey in this room. Showers and washing machines in the back. Been here forever, the first place to go up on the boardwalk after the sawmill went in. Been here through the lumber mill, through the cannery, and I'll be here when they figure out the next thing they can sell. Don't miss anything much to speak of, and I don't speak of it.

"Who are you, stranger?"

Kenny swung his chair around so he could hear the answer. But before the guy could catch his breath, Nora sang out from all the way across the room, "Hey, you're the surveyor with Axel over at the Kis'utch River." She sashayed right over and sat next to the surveyor at the bar. Chum crowded in between them. And then the whole room was quiet except for the tourists who kept on guffawing, and then they were quiet too, looking around embarrassed.

Kenny knew that every time a surveyor came to town, another chunk got bitten out of the forest and shipped off to Japan or someplace. Some families got some pocket change, dad working in the woods. Or somebody had to jack up their cabin and drag it off what had suddenly become someone else's land. Or a beach got bulldozed and a dock went in. A surveyor always means winners and losers, usually means money. You don't know. Might be good. Might be bad. Almost certainly smelled of Axel. But what's he gonna take next? Kenny wondered. What have they got over at the Kis'utch River that he could sell? Nothing there but water.

"What's the project?" Nora asked, sweet as can be.

"Axel Hagerman's gonna dam up the Kis'utch River at the old weir, build a big holding tank and a deepwater dock."

"The old weir? Jimmy Pete's weir?"

Every back straightened a little, but Ranger was the only one who raised his head.

"Yup. Then he'll bring in tankers to load up the freshwater from the Kis'utch River to bottle in Japan. Sell it back to California—Good River Glacier Water."

If the surveyor heard Kenny fart, he didn't show it.

"That Axel Hagerman thinks big and he thinks ahead. The more global warming heats things up, the more people will pay for good clean water, and the faster that glacier's gonna melt into money. He's gonna make a killing on this."

The surveyor paused, looked around, waiting for acclamation or even interest. He found neither. Tick leaned way down to scratch his ankle. Kenny fingered his braids. Oblivious as usual, the tourists elbowed each other and snuck more pictures of the stocking feet and dogs under the tables. Kenny watched Nora to see what she would say, but she just looked sort of pop-eyed at the surveyor. Sometimes she can look like a rockfish, Kenny thought, bulgy gold eyes and wide smile from gill plate to gill plate. The surveyor centered his butt on the barstool.

"Can a guy get a drink around here?" he asked.

But evidently, a guy can't. Not right away, anyhow.

"Damming up the Kis'utch?" Nora said, a little too loudly.

The surveyor nodded, not quite so sure.

"There's salmon spawning in that river," she told him.

Chum's ears stood up. He looked at Nora and whined. Then he jumped up with his front paws on her legs and stuck his nose under her elbow, trying to pry up her arm.

"It's okay, baby," she said, and reached down to rumple his rump.

"Good old Nora," Kenny said under his breath. "Gonna start up some trouble again." He sat by himself, laughing silently. His shoulders jerked up and down, until gradually they stilled, the way waves will quiet over time. Waves settle. When all the jittering sinks away, still water glazes over, hard as glass.

DAVY ROLLED TO the edge of Tommy's bed, paused, rolled out onto the floor, and quietly stood up. Tommy lay still, curled into a gently breathing ball. Stepping only on the boards he'd screwed tighter last week, Davy made his way into the kitchen and closed the bedroom door. He didn't need Tommy waking up in the middle of this project. He retrieved the clamshell he'd been saving under the stovewood and found a piece of paper and a pencil. *Dear* . . . Should he write *dearest*? *Dear Meredith, I am a wilderness guide now. I earned twenty-five dollars* . . . It was actually twenty, but with five more, that made twenty-five, so that was not a lie. *I earned twenty-five dollars today. So I guess I'm not as worthless as you thought. You know where to find me.* Should he write *love, Davy*? *Your secret very good friend,* he wrote. Okay, so that was good. He read it again and folded it into a careful wad that he tucked into the clamshell. He closed the lid, looking around for string. There was a tie string hanging from the bottom of his Dad's raincoat. He cut it off and wrapped it securely around the clam. It was yellow. Looked good, like *tie a yellow ribbon round the old oak tree.*

He wasn't supposed to leave home when Tommy was asleep, but what was home, really? Not just these three little rooms held up by posts and luck. His bedroom was connected to the pier and then the boardwalk and then the gangway to Meredith's house. Good River Harbor was home. Staying home wasn't his problem. His problem was that he had to get this clam to a place exactly between his dad, at Lillian's, and Axel, at home. His dad wouldn't come out of the bar until he needed to pee off the end of the outhouse pier, which wouldn't be for a long time, knowing his bladder. With Axel, he just had to take his chances. In winter, this would be easy, but in June, God, it hardly ever got dark. If Meredith wasn't hiding from him, it would be easy to get her a message. Ordinary people just hang out on the boardwalk and talk. But Meredith was, like, not around, and Davy figured her dad had told her to stay away from the riffraff, which he supposed he had been, but was not any more, since he now had money. He grabbed up a fishing pole to give himself an excuse to be on the dock and set out.

A couple of tourists wobbled out of the bar and headed to the harbor. Davy quickly turned into Kenny's gangway and dropped a fishing lure into the last place anyone would expect fish, the eddy where Kenny emptied his pee can and slop jar. When the tourists had passed, he reeled in and walked the last few yards toward Meredith's house. There was no delaying now. A quick glance into the bar, where he saw his dad's broad back and braid, a quick glance at Axel's, where there was no motion to be seen, Davy trotted to the front door, pawed around in the pile of boots for the smallest one—M.A.H., it said—and dropped in the clam. He turned to leave.

The door opened, almost knocking him off the pier.

"Just a minute, big guy."

Damn.

"Thought I'd do a little fishing . . ."

Axel reached around in the boot until he found the clam. He held it the way he would hold a stinking thing, pinched between his thumb and fleshy forefinger. He untied the bow, unfolded the note, moved it arm's length to read. The white of the paper flashed on his white face. He refolded the paper and put it back in the clam.

"I'll say this once."

Davy flipped his head to hide his face behind a screen of hair.

"Look at me."

"Yes, sir."

"You stay away from my daughter, Mr. Big Shot. If I catch you two together, it won't be you who pays the price. It will be your no-good father."

Axel retied the yellow cord and held the clamshell over the water. Opening his hand, he dropped it in the sea. Two fat bubbles, and the clam was gone.

HOWARD ROLLED UP the sleeves on his surveyor's shirt and loosened his tie. His eyes scanned the room. At the bar, a huge orange-bearded guy twisted an empty beer can into a lump and called for another. Four boys from a seiner leaned on their elbows talking in low tones, looking over their shoulders. The rude guy in the fur hat had rolled himself to a table in the back. Every beefy hand that wasn't holding a drink was under the table scratching a dog. The woman Nora wandered the length of the bar like an overgrown puppy herself, nosing up into conversations, grinning an enormous grin. Looked like she knew everybody and apparently the names of all their dogs and children and whether they liked her to drape a long arm over their shoulders or just nudge into their backs.

Lillian pried open a bottle of beer for Howard.

"Here you go, Mr. Surveyor." As soon as she shoved it across the bar, she eased herself off her feet into a chair. Her body melted over the sides of the seat. With the palm of her hand, she pushed the sweat off her forehead, lifting a fringe of bangs into the air. For some reason, her hair was maroon, her eyelids were green, and she had a rosy spot on each cheek. She wasn't looking at him.

Even though the bar was crowded and everybody was talking, nobody was talking to Howard Fowler, Surveyor. He took the beer from Lillian and found a table by himself in the corner. A crowded bar is a lonelier place than the most isolated forest tract he'd ever been in. Better to be by yourself than butt to butt on barstools with people who've known each other for twenty years. Howard had surveyed his fair share of mountains like these, laying out timber buys up and down the West Coast, keeping ahead of the logging camps, and he'd breathed his fair share of the smoke and Clorox smell of bars like Lillian's. When he came home from a trip like this, Jennifer always wrinkled her pretty nose and told him to go straight to the basement, empty his suitcase into the washer, and head for the shower. "You smell like a thirty-nine-dollar-a-night highway motel," she would say, and that was about right. His own house back in Bellevue smelled of new carpet and crayons.

A rack of split spruce barricaded the corner Howard had chosen. It was dark and warm back there. Faces flashed into view when the woodstove kicked up, then fell back into shadow. Raincoats steamed. Dogs snored. Howard drank up the Foster's without setting down the bottle.

"Soon's I knew it, I heard this crashing down the mountain, like a boulder bouncing and falling."

Howard turned toward the voice.

"Sure enough, it's a sow and she's tearing down at me, ripping out the alders, spraying dirt. I go, 'Lordy!' I swing up my shotgun and shoot from the hip. That bear died two feet from my poor gut." The guy's buddies hooted, and he patted his belly, letting his fat cells know they were safe with him.

"Bear tall enough to look in a second-story window."

"The hell."

Another guy looked deep into his drink. "Yeah, so I was riding my bike down the trail, minding my own business, came around a corner and rode right between a sow and her cub. Ah crap, I was thinking. She came after me, snarling and snapping. I lifted up my bike like it was a shield and every time she charged at me, she got a mouthful of Schwinn. Course, then I tripped over backward, and it was a bike sandwich—me, the bike, and the bear. I closed my eyes, sure I was dead, and when I squinted one eye open, the bear was gone. I laid there for a while, thinking am I dead in heaven or are those just the most beautiful clouds I ever seen? Then I wheeled my gimpy, bear-bent bike to the edge of the channel and pitched it in."

"If you'd a been dead, Erwin, those clouds would have been on fire."

Howard laughed along with everybody else.

He leaned back in his chair, starting to enjoy that dark corner, eavesdropping on the town liars. But sure enough—it didn't take five minutes before the huge guy with an orange beard sat himself down at Howard's table and plunked down two glasses of hooch.

"Stay in this town long enough and you'll learn to love R and R," the guy said, and Howard laughed, even though he didn't know what the guy was talking about. "Rich and Rare," the man said, lifting his glass. "Rotgut and Rumble." He pushed a glass toward Howard and stretched his legs under the table. His socks stuck out the other side, gray wool socks with a red stripe, Wigwams. This boot business was a phenomenon Howard had seen from Ketchikan to Barrow. Like everybody else, this man had left his boots at the door. There was a big lineup of them there, each one identical to all the others. Impossible to know how they tell one pair from another. Of course, if the boots are all the same, maybe it doesn't matter which ones a man brings home from the bar.

"Tick McIver," the guy said, and nodded his head. "Just here for a nip. My big guy is putting my little guy to bed."

"Howard Fowler," Howard said, and Tick laughed. He reached across the table to offer a big, bent-up hand.

"So how's the surveying business, Howie?"

"Fine," Howard said.

"Where you from?"

"Bellevue, Washington."

Tick pulled his chair closer to the table. He had a fuzzy reddish braid down the center of his back and, under a huge beard, a denim shirt with the cuffs cut off, like all these guys who work around water or the woods.

"So what do you do in this town?" Howard said, though he didn't really care.

Tick leaned his chair back on two legs.

"I just try to keep my boys fed," he said. "I'm Tick McIver, Halibut Slimer. Holder of the world's record for best job done on the worst job in the world. Got my rubber overalls and a disposable plastic apron, and bloody rubber gloves."

Howard had worked out of Valdez. He'd heard what a halibut slimer does for a living and didn't really want to hear it again. But what can you do when you're drinking a slimer's whiskey? Howard threw back the whiskey, which was way better than the beer.

"I stand at the conveyor belt with an ulu in my hand. Always noisy in there, storm winds banging the Quonset hut around.

"A gutted halibut skids down the belt, big as a picnic table. I lift the roof of ribs and look right into the hole where its heart used to be. Whatever guts are left, I scrape at, scratching off pieces of kidney and liver and gonads. I flick the pieces into a tray. They got a hose spraying cold water nonstop. Axel—that's the boss—he comes around, presses his face into the cavern, looking for crap, presses his face into mine, yells, 'Keep up the good work.' I told you, I'm a good slimer."

"Congratulations," Howard said, hoping that was the end of the conversation.

"The liver is the worst, Howie. Sticks to the backbone like paint.

"My job is to make the corpse look good. That's my job. Trim around its head, not hurting those bulgy eyes. Smooth the edges of the throat wound. Cut out the anus—people don't like their fish to have an asshole. I give it all a quick spray to knock off the bloody globs, rub it down with the rubber glove to slick off the slime, shove it down the rollers, reach for the next.

"But here's the thing." Tick leaned across the table, pulling in his feet. "Some of those fish are as old as I am. They grow a foot every ten years, so anything over four feet has just about got me beat. All the big old halibut are females. When I get one of them, I trim up the slit in her throat nice and sweet, give her an extra pat, and tell her that she's done a hell of a lot more with her life than I have with mine."

Howard looked away.

"I did a good job. Then Axel fired me. Closed down the line. 'Hard to find halibut any more, he said, like the fish were hiding behind rocks. Like the fish were playing goddamn hide-and-seek. They mined them out, that's what. Fished 'em till they caught them all. Then what? Then what, Howie?"

He stared at Howard like he knew and wouldn't say.

"Then what?"

Howard didn't know then what. He didn't care then what. What was, he was thinking he needed to pee.

"Where's the bathroom?"

Tick swung his beard toward the front door. So Howard wove between the tables and out the door and sure enough, there was an outhouse on the end of a narrow pier. He held on to both railings and made his way out. No point in taking chances. Fifty percent of the guys who drown, drown with their fly open. That's a fact. Inside the outhouse, he stared down the hole. The tide was swaying down there, seaweed floating by, everything striped with light from between the planks. A big fish jumped straight up, and Howard jumped too, spraying the wall.

When he got back, Lillian was standing there, looking at the empty glasses. Tick was looking at them too, like he was blaming them for something.

"Two more," Howard said, before he could stop himself. Tick nodded approval and started right in where he'd left off.

"Hard to know what to do in a little town without a job. I asked Axel, but he didn't need any help closing down the fish-packing plant. By now, I got Davy and Tommy, my two boys, and Annie Klawon. Annie's my wife."

Interesting name, Howard thought. Haida? Tlingit? He wondered where she was, and why Tick would be drinking alone.

"So I decided I'd scout for stray logs. Towed 'em into town and cut 'em to rounds and split them for shakes. But then everybody had all the shakes they needed, and have you ever tried towing a fifty-foot log, waves knocking the log around? It'll jerk your boat under, sink your stern, and then you're a goner. And Axel was saying those were his logs, saying I was a rustler. It wasn't worth the trouble, fighting about that. You don't win a fight with Axel."

Without lifting his elbows off the table, Tick reached across his face to scratch the far side of his beard.

"Then there wasn't nothing for me to do. Set chokers for Axel's logging outfit for a couple of months, built them some splash-dams to move logs on a flood, then they moved on. All the easy timber was gone, mined that out too. I'd of gone back to work at the mill, pulling plywood, but that's been shut down for years. I poached a lot of deer this winter."

Just saying it outright like that—poached a lot of deer this winter—made him laugh. "Poached a lot of deer this winter," Tick said again, choking he was laughing so hard.

"Finally you're telling the truth," somebody yelled from another table. Tick stopped laughing.

"I wish Annie wouldn't of went. She knew I'd think of something. I told her I was thinking I could be a hunting guide, bring in some dudes, show 'em how to find deer or bear, make a lot of money, set up a lodge."

He paused, staring into the fire.

"That was it for her. She emptied her closet into a tote and hauled off on the next ferry. 'If you're not going to earn a living, I will,' she told me. She moved to Seattle, got a job at an insurance company, sends money for the boys. 'Don't send *me* any money,' I told her. 'I got money in the bank.' Seattle. God. Damn. You can get run over by a bus in Seattle."

Tick sat there for a long time, turning his glass in his hands, round and round, so intent on turning that glass you'd think he was making it out of clay.

"I want her to come home."

Howard cleared his throat, sucked at his empty glass. He didn't know if he should buy Tick another drink, in hopes that he'd fall asleep with his forehead on the table. But a man could go bust buying drinks for every drunk in this dead-end town.

"So anyway, maybe I'll be a surveyor. Any money in that? What's Axel pay you?"

Not much, Howard could have told him. That's a fact. And if he's going to be a surveyor, he better get the hell out of this kind of place, where every boundary line goes straight up a mountain through some alder hell or blow-down Sitka spruce or bear daybed, and the land's rebounding so fast now the glaciers are gone, beaches won't hold still long enough to pound in a stake. And it's not like *he* was home snuggling with his wife or watching TV with his little girl, instead of drinking with a deadbeat in a town that looks like if you cut it loose, it'd drift out with the tide.

"How about this new water-bottling plant or whatever it is—Axel's latest scheme? Any jobs in that?"

"I don't know. Axel will probably hire outside. He says he's got a piss-poor local labor pool in Good River Harbor."

Howard knew he shouldn't have said it before he even got done saying it. The words sailed out into a room gone dead quiet, the way a room will do at just the wrong time. He cast around desperately for a way to take it back. Nobody looked at him, but nobody was saying anything either. Just kind of studying the labels on their beers.

But Tick didn't seem to have heard him. He was staring up at the ceiling, sort of smiling with half his mouth, so Howard looked up too. Any diversion was a good diversion. It was a high bead-board ceiling, glistening amber from decades of cigarette smoke. A couple of long florescent light fixtures hung askew, and over the bar was an old ship's bell, surely rescued from a wreck. Brass, with a short bell rope. Howard looked around, and suddenly everybody was watching him, and it seemed like everybody was sort of wistful about the bell.

"That's an old ship's bell, washed in on a board one blasted winter storm, same storm as washed up a poor fisherman's body. The rope got torn short. Nobody's tall enough to ring that bell," Tick said, and bent his head in sorrow. "But Lillian promises that if anybody can make that bell ring, it's free drinks all around."

Lillian nodded her head in agreement, grimacing. She was probably thinking how much it would cost her, if that bell dinked. The crowd rumbled.

"Go for it, stranger," somebody shouted. The fire dropped in the woodstove and the thrust-forward faces flashed on and off. Shadows danced around, swaying against the cases of beer. By the door, all those empty boots looked like they wanted to go home, get some sleep. But ringing a bell didn't seem so hard. It was a high ceiling, but Howard was a tall man, still agile enough, leaping over blowdown for a living. If he stood on the bar, he'd be most of the way there. He could get a big soup spoon or something from Lillian and reach it up and smack the bell. Take their minds off the jobs they weren't going to get. Show them how it's done. Buy everybody a beer without spending a cent. Seemed like something Tick could have done himself, if he'd had the gumption.

Lillian produced a soup ladle, and Howard clambered up on the bar. The bar was shaky, and the air up there was hot. He had to squint his eyes against the smoke. But he got up there all right, and he reached as high as he could, which turned out to be high enough. People crowded around, cheering. He was balanced to give the spoon a mighty swing, when a half dozen guys grabbed hold of his pants and pulled them down.

"Shit." There he was, standing on the bar in his jockey shorts with his pants around his ankles. A big cheer went up, and he knew he'd been cooked by the oldest trick in the bar. Tick danced around, bent over yowling, and the dogs howled, like it was the greatest joke in the universe, to pants a stranger in your hometown, pulling down his pants just when he was reaching up with both hands, trying to ring the bell.

So he didn't get the bell rung, but Howard did get a free drink, thanks to Lillian. She handed him a beer and patted him on the head.

"Harder than you'd think," she said, "making the bells ring around this place. And don't I know that as well as anybody in this town."

Then she handed out beers as fast as people could crowd in and grab them. This seemed to call for a party, and what was Howard supposed to do? His dark room above the Good River Harbor library, its small window and narrow bed—nobody there but him, no sound but the oddly traffic sound of the Kis'utch River falling down the mountain—that was sounding awful good. But you can't just go to your room after you get pantsed. Howard was sure there was some manhood rule against that. So he got back in line and grabbed another free beer. There was probably a rule against that too, but Lillian was puffing and sweating like a tugboat, working too hard to see who was lining up behind her.

"Come sit with us, stranger," somebody yelled. Howard headed over. Nora got up from the table as soon as Howard arrived.

"Take my chair," she said. "Come on, Lillian. I'll hand out the beer. You sing us a song."

"A song, Lilly, a song," the crowd echoed. Howard looked around wildly, not wanting to be the punch line for another practical joke.

Lillian straightened up and wiped her forehead on the inside of her elbow. She put her hands on her hips and surveyed the murmuring crowd.

"I already gave you free beer," she said. "Why should I give you a free song?" She untied her apron and folded it neatly on the bar. With her thumb and forefinger, she arranged a row of curls across her forehead. People sat down wherever they stood. If there was a chair nearby, they sat in a chair. If not, they sat on the floor or a bottom step or a cardboard box of Fritos. Simultaneously, all the dogs stood up. Cigarette smoke was a blue sky at the ceiling. The chatter drained away. Howard steeled himself for whatever was coming next in this crazy place. And Lillian began to sing.

Oh my, but you have a pretty face
You favor a girl that I knew
I imagine that she's still in Tennessee
And by God I should be there too.
I've got a sadness too sad to be true.

Howard stared. There was no end of surprises in this town. The woman sang like an angel. This woman, Lillian, swayed there on her swollen ankles and broken-back shoes and sang the words so beautifully, so . . . Howard thought . . . so significantly, she could have been an archangel singing the coming of Christ. Tick looked proudly at Howard and smiled. Then he leaned back and listened with his eyes closed. The golden pools of Nora's eyes filled with tears.

Howard fumbled for his wallet and laid a twenty on the table. He wanted to be alone, where he could feel what he was feeling. It was eleven o'clock in Bellevue and Jennifer would be checking to be sure the front door was locked, and he had just been pantsed in the bar of an angel with maroon hair. All he wanted was to close the door to his little room, where he could be alone and understand how alone he really was. As Howard passed through the door, Tick was gravely waltzing through the bar with the guy who almost got his gut bitten out by a bear.

WITH BOTH BLACK-GLOVED hands, Kenny pushed slowly away from the table. The seiners managed to scoot their chairs out of the way without looking at him. He maneuvered around the bar and rolled onto the boardwalk. Ranger followed him out.

Rain had started up again. Dusk was finally falling, and the rings on the water do-si-doed in the yellow glow from Lillian's windows. Kenny didn't really want to go home to that black box of a cabin. But he sure didn't want to sit in a crowded bar. On the shadowed boardwalk, though, he felt safe. He would see people coming before they saw him. The tide was coming in under the planks, striped with light. A school of holy-cross jellyfish paraded by. The crosses in their transparent backs glowed as if they'd been blessed. Kenny watched them pulse through the water. Give me a jellyfish any day, he thought. A jellyfish doesn't have a brain at all, and it's smarter than that pack of tourists all put together. And somebody told him a jellyfish can have sex with itself, which is a point in favor of tentacles.

A fish jumped somewhere out in the dark.

Kenny rolled to the railing and looked down. Another fish jumped. Something deep flashed silver. A fish showing its side? Is there a school of fish circling down there? He backed up and pulled in sideways to get closer to the railing.

Somebody was coming up behind him. The boardwalk bounced with each step, and then there was Nora standing next to him. She braced her palms on the rail and leaned over the water. Another fish jumped.

"Pinks," she said in a quiet voice.

It was the first word she had ever spoken to Kenny. Or maybe she was talking to the fish.

"They've come home," she said. He didn't look at her face to see if she was waiting for some response, but he couldn't have thought of one anyway. The reflected yellow light flickered on her jeans. Starting in the place where the jeans puckered into her boots, the light rode up and down her legs, rocking like the water. He felt the heat of her legs on his face and he backed away a little, the way he backs away from a woodstove once it gets cranking.

In a black mass, the fish moved slowly through the water. Glints of white sides flashed back at the streetlights, then disappeared. Sometimes a fish jumped clear of the water and slapped on its side, splashing. Carefully not looking at Nora, Kenny watched the fish for a long time, while their dogs sniffed each other's asses and Kenny tried not to notice that she was there.

Before long, the channel would be crazy with salmon at the mouth of every creek. The seiners would move out before dawn to be in place when the season opened. Then the fish-eating killer whales would infiltrate, squadrons of five or six, with fins sticking out of the water, tall as a man. There would be sea lions hanging offshore, blowing bubbles and farting. Already there were humpback whales, following schools of herring. Kenny would hear their blows rising through the floorboards of his cabin, grunts and sighs like lovers behind pasteboard walls in cheap motels.

Kenny turned and rolled home. That night, like every night, he lowered himself onto his cot, pulled his woolen blankets to his chin. As he listened to the humpbacks breathing, he wrapped his thighs around his blanket. He thought about the sex life of weightless, sighing mammals, what that would be like, floating, rolling, holding a great barnacle-warted beast in his fleshy fins.

June 30

HIGH TIDE		LOW TIDE	
3:21am	16.1ft	9:45am	-1.1ft
4:14pm	14.9ft	10.1pm	3.1ft

Lillian held a spoon in one fist like a dagger. With the other fist, she held down a salmon carcass that kept slipping off her cutting board. Grinning head on one end, tail on the other, and in between just a spine and a bunch of ribs—there's not a lot to hold on to. She adjusted her grip, taking hold of the backbone where it emerged from the skull. She scraped the spoon hard down the length of a rib, collecting a spoonful of beautiful pink flesh. She knocked the meat off into a bowl, then applied her spoon to the next rib. There would be rich hot creamy salmon chowder at the Bath 'n' Bar tonight, which meant a good crowd for a foggy afternoon.

When Lillian had opened her front door that morning, she had found a blue plastic tote on her doorstep. Ravens hopped around it, jabbing it with heavy beaks. Lillian snapped a dish towel at them, and they hopped away, clonking and grumbling. But as soon as she opened the lid, they were back again, leaping up as well as a raven can leap and stumbling over her slippers. Inside the tote were what remained of three big king salmon and two silvers after their fillets had been removed. The guys from the seiners often caught kings and silvers in their pink-salmon purse seines. It's illegal to sell bycatch, but nothing says you can't slice off a couple of fillets for dinner and give away what's left, especially if you give them to Good River Harbor's goddess of salmon chowder.

Lillian lifted her short curls with the back of her hand, which gave the carcass a chance to slide off the cutting board. "Screw it," she said. She reached for her ice pick and drove it through the fish's eye.

That's when the door opened and Axel slid in. Howard followed him, walking as if his shoulders were tied to his knees, never once looking at the bell on the ceiling above the bar.

"Thought we might talk here," Axel said.

"What," Lillian answered, "your own kitchen table catch fire?"

"You might say." Axel threw a conspiratorial look at Howard. "My sweet wife, Rebecca, is a little riled up today. She thinks it might be better if we met someplace other than home for a while, and Meredith's working in my office."

Lillian washed her hands and poured them coffee. She couldn't remember the last time Axel had sat at her table. Neither man looked up when she put the coffee in front of them.

"I've got a new project, Howard," Axel said. "And I want you to be in charge of it. I'll promote you to assistant production supervisor. How does that sound?"

Howard grinned and leaned forward.

"Set aside work on the Kis'utch River water project for a while," Axel was saying. "Might be a good time to let that one simmer down. There will be time for that. The river's not going anywhere.

"This one is a better idea, and we can move fast on it, have money rolling in before fall. So let's sketch out plans for a bear zoo. Timetable too."

Howard nodded. "Bear zoo. That's a good one." He straightened his tie and pulled a little spiral notebook out of his shirt pocket. He held the pencil over the page. "Bear zoo. Where exactly, and what bear?"

"In that old cedar cistern halfway up the cliff above where the old cannery used to be. Not too big, but big enough to hold a bear or two." Axel poked a short finger at Howard. "And as for the bear, you can leave that to old Axel." Fondly, Axel stroked the top of his head.

"Full moon was last night, which means we'll get good high tides next couple of nights, highest tomorrow midnight. Probably have a half ton of lumber to off-load at the bear zoo site. We need to get that organized and loaded onto the barge to deliver at the midnight tide. A seventeen-foot tide will float the barge almost to the base of the cistern, and the boys can off-load there. Save a lot of hauling over slippery rocks.

"First thing today, you go over and hire Tick McIver as a carpenter."

Howard started to write that down in his spiral notebook but stopped with the pencil in the air.

Axel chuckled. “Tick’ll be glad to get on any job I’ve got going,” he said. “Besides, if I give Tick something, he’s got something I can take away.”

Axel lowered his voice. “It’s just a little thing with his scruffy son. First rule of human resource management—give ’em what they want. Then you own them.”

Howard, clearly baffled, wrote down the instructions.

“Get him to stage the lumber on the ledge next to the cistern. Sure don’t want to wait another month. Want to get cracking on this so I can have tourists there yet this summer.” Axel rubbed his furzy head as if he were buffing its shine.

“This might be the best idea I’ve ever had—making the old water tank into a zoo for wild brown bears. Sometimes I think I’m a genius.”

Axel laughed out loud, and Howard joined him. *Heh heh heh*, the same dying motor. Lillian swung her head quickly toward them and just as quickly back to her work.

“Call the eco-tour boats today. I’ll give you contact names. Tell them this will be the best tourist attraction in Southeast, work out a good price for them to tie to our new dock. Get a half dozen of them to sign on, won’t that be a pot of money, four hundred tourists a day lined up to see grizzlies up close and personal. Refreshment stand, two bucks a Coke.”

Howard jotted notes in his little notebook, flipped over to a clean page, and waited.

“Hey,” Howard said, as if he’d just thought of it. “I’m really sorry I jumped the gun on telling people about the water-bottling project. I didn’t know it was a secret . . .”

“I already told you, never mind.” Axel interrupted him. “This sorry-stuff is getting tiresome. Yeah, you made a mistake, and yeah, you’re a schmuck, and yeah, I hadn’t planned on breaking the news about the water project for another couple of months. Leave it alone.” Axel leaned back in his chair.

“If a person’s fast on his feet, he can make a glitch work for him, and if I’m anything, I’m fast on my feet. Let Nora fuss about logging next to the creeks or the Kis’utch water project across the channel. I’ll be moving ahead on the old cistern out at the cannery site.”

Axel raised his coffee cup and clinked Howard's cup. Howard managed a smile.

"That's the thing: You look for opportunities in every direction. If something exists, it can be sold. It just happens that what I'm thinking of selling this week isn't water. It's bears. Water can wait." He chuckled.

"We're going to need a good name for the tank where we keep the bears. Some name that brings in the tourists."

"The Bear Zoo?"

"The Bear Palace?"

"Hagerman's Bear Palace?"

"Good River Harbor Bear Palace?"

"That's good. Classy. 'Bring your kids to see wild Alaskan brown bears. Feed wild Alaskan grizzlies. See a threatened species before it's gone.' Mmm. I like that one. Write that down, Howard. That can be the guts of your advertising campaign. People adore threatened species, and if it's endangered, all the better."

Lillian yanked the ice pick out of the last salmon's head and dropped the skeleton into her compost bucket. She started in chopping onions, but that made so much noise she couldn't overhear anything. She decided that peeling potatoes was a better idea. There was quiet in the Bath 'n' Bar then, except for the squink of the potato peeler and the scratch of Howard's pen. Axel looked around the bar, pointing his nose at the stacked firewood, the smoky light, the neat piles of cigarette cartons. Lillian followed his glance, hoping he liked her place. Axel shook his head.

"I don't know why my sweet wife's tail is in such a knot, Howard. Everything I do, I do for her—for Rebecca. Everything she has, she has because of me. And that goes for the people in this town too. How do they think they're going to eat, if it isn't for Good River Products? Money grows on trees. I told Rebecca that. Money grows on trees. But it doesn't just rain down on you. You have to be smart. You have to work hard to get it out. And aren't I smart enough, and don't I work hard? I'm the guy who figures out how to capitalize undeveloped resources. Then I hire people, and they get paid. 'But sweetheart, you can't squeeze blood out of a turnip,' I told Rebecca. That's what set her off. I thought it was a good joke."

Howard laughed weakly. Lillian smiled too, trusting that the humor would later become apparent.

"Rebecca wanted the old cannery's water tank to be a community garden, of all things. A garden that the whole town would share. For free. Jesus, Howard, I bring her milk crates for her flower gardens. I stack up tires higher than the tide so she can plant rhubarb. I nail gutters to all the railings on our gangway and porches so she can plant flowers. I bring her home a tote-load of fish heads for fertilizer each spring. I help her haul the very best dirt all the way from her special bend in the Kis'utch River. In buckets. On a skiff. The whole damn house is blooming. Bees own the place. Hummingbirds are going to carry us away. I am a very nice man about gardens."

Lillian knew that was true. Their house was buried in flowers.

"But that evidently is not enough for Rebecca." Axel banged his coffee cup down on the table. He reconsidered, picked it up, and set it down gently. Lillian walked over to swipe a rag at what he had spilled and top off his cup.

"Heat yours up?" she asked Howard, but Howard was staring at Axel.

"I love her, Howard. I love it when she's happy and humming. I know she lives for her summer gardens, because winter almost kills her, that darkness, and ice on the shrouds and electric lines. I would do anything for her. But does a good husband have to sit and all the time hear about *compost?*"

Poor Howard. His head shook, no, and then his head shook, yes, and then it just rolled around a little bit and came to a stop. He held on to his tie for dear life. Lillian wiped her hands on a towel and leaned against the counter. Some days, her heart wept for Axel. Other days, her foot itched to kick his behind. Some things he knew really well. On other things, he was ignorant as a child. It was sad. He wasn't a bad man. He was just clueless, and was that his fault? The greatest mystery in all of Good River Harbor was how two people so utterly different as Axel and Rebecca could love each other.

The parents of Axel's wife, Rebecca, were hippies, honest-to-God hippies. They were gentle people who moved to the bush so they could live in true harmony with the land. Rebecca was a flower child of flower children, a tiny baby cradled on her mother's back in a shawl printed with sunflowers and forget-me-nots. Even back then, her hair was soft and her eyes disappeared into her smile. There was always a flower tied in her hair, a sprig of fireweed or blueberry bells right there in the wave on top of her head. She was so beautiful it made a person ache to hold such a child. Back then, even Lillian—who never let anyone touch her—sat Rebecca on her lap and cradled her in the sun. Without her own child, it was a comfort to her. She taught little Rebecca to sing "*you shall have a fishie on a white dishie*," even though Rebecca had never tasted fish in her beautiful two years.

Rebecca's parents vowed that they would take only what was given to them by the good Earth and kill nothing that breathed. That makes it hard to live in Alaska, even if you believe that plants don't breathe. Rebecca's mother tended a big garden—spinach and rhubarb, zucchini—and gathered spruce tips and huckleberries, salmonberries, currants. For his part, her father went out in search of the perfect piece of wood. Damned if he didn't find it the first year, a Sitka spruce trunk maybe four feet across and thirty feet long. It had soaked in saltwater for upward of fifty years, part of an old fish trap, before it finally washed to shore.

He cut the spruce into big blocks and stacked them in their cabin. Now and then he would take his band saw and saw off a thin sheet of wood that he would sell to a guitar maker—Martin, Gibson, Taylor. His wood was famous around the world; men journeyed all the way to Good River Harbor to buy a piece of this wood. Half their little cabin was spruce blocks. The other half was a simple kitchen and a dance floor, because Rebecca's father not only supplied wood for guitars, but also played them. When the family wasn't dancing, they rolled out mats to sleep on, all in a pile, like puppies.

So there was money for whole-wheat flour and beans and honey, and sometimes oranges from Outside. Rebecca was raised on good, thick, seed-studded bread and salmonberry jelly. The harmony didn't last, of course. The mother was the one who got restless first and shipped out to Nepal. So Rebecca lived with her dad. When Rebecca was in high school, she seemed to be hungry for something else, maybe something even more nourishing than bread. For a while, she and Lillian sat together in the evenings, struggling through the *Tao Te Ching*. But there was nothing in there that Rebecca hadn't already learned from living in the coming and going of strong tides.

Then Axel came home from his first fishing season, just sixteen, but confident as a man. People called him "successful," and maybe that was the right word. And oh, he wooed Rebecca, the prettiest, sweetest girl in the whole town. He had brought her dried cherries from the Pike Place Market and Brie so ripe it melted onto the paper and fresh corn on the cob—food she had never seen before. Over a beach fire at Green Point, Axel roasted the corn and fed her soft cheese and cherries. And she did love him, not because of the gifts he had brought, but because he had brought them. Because he knew her well enough to know what would delight her, and because he wanted her so desperately to be glad. That was his way, Axel: to decide what he wanted and then figure out how to get it, but that was a good thing, because kindness was the only way to win Rebecca. So that is how they lived, Axel trying to make Rebecca glad, and Rebecca being glad in fact, and loving him in return.

Outside the window of Lillian's bar, the fog had torn into shreds that tangled in the masts. A single beam of sunlight somehow managed to find its way to the back of Axel's lowered head, where it lit his bare neck like a saint's. When he spoke again, Axel spoke with Rebecca's soft, slow voice. His voice was so quiet that Lillian had to come out from behind the bar to restock the packets of ketchup on the tables.

"Rebecca thought the water tank would make the world's most beautiful raised-bed garden. 'The walls will keep out the bears and the deer and the slugs,' she said.

"'Everybody can compost there,' she said, 'and not worry about bears getting into the fish heads,'" Axel crooned.

"'We won't have to chop up our kitchen garbage and dump it out to sea anymore,' she said. She loved this idea.

"'The whole town could raise Nootka roses and honeysuckle, turn the cistern into heaven.'

"I've never seen her so excited, Howard. That's when I had to tell her it didn't pencil out. I told her, you can't make any money on a community garden. Can't squeeze blood out of a turnip."

Axel chuckled. Howard winced. Lillian put more ketchup packets in the little bowl on their table.

"But God, it was just a joke!

"If we put bears in the old cistern, it's going to turn a profit within a year, I told her, guaranteed, but she said she didn't care.

"I hate it when she tries to cry and talk at the same time, that little face all hiccups and sobs. She better get control of herself and learn which side her bread is buttered on. And that goes for the rest of the people in this town. Nora Montgomery and that innocent little 'What are your plans for cutting at Fairweather Bay?' garbage. And Tick better be careful, pulling off your pants in the bar and then asking me for a job. Cutting up stovewood for Nora Montgomery, honeying up to her, and then thinking I should give him a job. And if he doesn't keep his kid Davy away from Meredith, I'll ruin them both. He better figure out his bread and butter too. He's got to know there's other people in this town can hammer a nail." Axel took a deep breath, looked to Howard for an understanding nod, got it, and plowed on.

"It isn't easy making good when you're an orphan, when your own mom and dad drown the week after you're born. Yeah, so the Hagermans took me in, and the Hagermans were good people, but it's not like I was born lucky. Hell no. I call that born out of luck. I made my luck, and I'm a better man for it."

Lillian turned away. It pained her that Axel felt orphaned. But she had learned that Axel was right: You run out of luck, you have no choice but to make yourself some more. You make it out of whatever you have at hand. What she couldn't decide was whether there's only so much luck in the world, so when you make it for yourself, you have to take the ingredients from somebody else. She wondered what had she taken from Axel.

She walked over to refill his coffee.

"It isn't easy when people lean on you," Axel went on, not noticing the coffee. "It isn't easy juggling all these balls. Because some of them fall. Nobody wants to tell a guy there's no job left, nothing left to catch or cut or can. But stuff runs out or costs too much to get. You got to keep thinking of new ideas. And you got to know how to make those ideas work. Do a good job of it, have the right kind of brains, you make money.

Some of the money goes to the guy with the brains, but you give most of the money away to the mindless people who work for you. So now Rebecca acts like that's some kind of evil, and sometimes I think, okay.

"Okay, I'll tell her.

"Okay. Have it your way. I'll stop working so hard. See how you eat then. See how long this family sticks together. See how long this town lasts. I'm serious. Who's the one who cares about his family? Who's the one who cares about this town? Who's the one working his tail off to hold things together? And who's the one his own wife despises? How fair is that? This town owes me, and I collect my debts."

Axel stopped to catch his breath. The gusts of his words had pumped up his face, but now it deflated—slowly, like dough poked with a wooden spoon. Behind the counter, the potato water was boiling furiously. The windows had steamed up and moisture beaded on the ship's bell above the bar. Lillian bustled back to turn down the heat. She stirred the potatoes and pulled the salt pork out of the cooler. Soon it was crackling in the bottom of her biggest soup pot. The room was thick with steam and old cigarette smoke and the smell of pork sizzling in its own fat. Axel walked over to open the door.

Howard was saying nothing. He scratched behind his ear. Then he turned another page around the spiral in his little notebook and picked up his pencil.

"What else you got for me, Axel?"

Axel took a deep breath and looked at him with an expression that might have been gratitude.

"Right. Right. We have a job to do. Bear project is going to take a lot of lumber, the way we have it designed. Hope I have enough fir under tarps by the Quonset. Here, make a list of what I need from you." At the top of the new page, Howard wrote, *Things to Do for the Bear Tourist Attraction*, and made notes as Axel spun off the questions.

"We'll need a dock, but I think we can use the pilings from the old cannery dock. Check on that. A floating dock, and a ramp going up to the cistern. Better put railings on that. It's a long way down to those rocks. Don't want to lose some tourist's kid. On that ledge next to the cistern, a pavilion with a welcome sign and some educational kiosks. You sketch it all out.

"Check on the required number of outhouses. That would be a state reg, I would think.

"Check with Mark Custer. See how soon we'll get the check for our rural economic development grant.

"And—do this quietly—find out how the Alaska Department of Fish and Game permits problem bears."

"Quietly," Howard repeated, flushing. "Can do."

"Check with the Feds to see if we can get mitigation funds for habitat restoration inside the tank."

Howard put down his pen. "Habitat restoration?" he asked. "On the inside of a moldy water tank?"

Axel beamed. "There's money everywhere if you know where to look," he said. The Feds love to give out money to restore habitats, and what habitat more needs to be restored than the inside of a cannery's old water cistern?" But then he stopped short and considered.

"Now there's a brilliant idea. I could give Rebecca the Feds' money and get *her* to restore a bear habitat inside the tank. That's better than my plan to dump in some construction site debris. She can have all the fireweed and thimbleberries she would ever want. Turnips, for all I care. Compost. Geraniums. Whatever. Bears won't care.

"See, Howard, you've got to be fast on your feet. Sometimes I think I'm a genius—a little slow on the uptake, but a genius. Would have saved Rebecca a lot of crying if I'd thought of this yesterday.

"Okay, so here's the angle on your story. Write it up and get it out. Good River Harbor's famous gardener, the lovely Rebecca Hagerman, will create an ecosystem in the cistern, in a project that will save doomed bears. Perfect. A bear figures out he can get food in town, starts hanging around the dump, killing dogs—that's a dead bear. But we'll rescue the problem bears and put them in the pit. Fish and Game will love us. Tourists on the eco-tours will love us. Eco-freaks will love us. Maybe Rebecca—I don't know. It won't be a Bear Palace. That was a mistake—sounds too much like a circus. It'll be a Bear *Shelter*, like a homeless shelter, only the bears can't leave to go hang out on the street corners, boozing and begging."

Axel stood up to put on his Good River Products hat and jacket.

"Oh, and another thing for your list," he told Howard. "You'll have to be the one to tell Rebecca she gets to make the habitat in the bear pit. She's not talking to me."

As soon as they left, Lillian turned the stove to simmer and crossed to the mirror. Axel has her eyes, she thought, shiny blue, although his were closer together than hers. "Ah," she scolded her reflection. "Don't go there."

But she did let herself wonder if he got his business sense from her. One good tree is seventy-three years of winter rains or 1,060 board feet of lumber or 208 two-by-fours or 6,890 rolls of toilet paper. One good tree is a year of community college classes learning small engine repair; it's a new room on the house for the baby, already grown a beating heart the size of a raisin. One good tree is food on the table or control over a man otherwise bigger than you are in every way. And a glass of cold water—what is that? Life or $2.35, with a plastic bottle thrown in for free. A bear? Bloody death or a good five months of fifteen-dollar admission fees, do the math. One good salmon behind glass in a refrigerated case is twenty dollars times twenty pounds, do the math, four hundred dollars, and a fish head buried in the garden. Oh, the trading that goes on, the choices, the risks and benefits. What will you give for love, what will you give for pride, what will you give for spite, this for that, and who can say that a man is good or bad depending on what he wants in trade?

LATER THAT AFTERNOON, Nora shoved up the bill of her baseball cap, leaned back in Lillian's chair, and stared at the bell on the ceiling. Afternoon light reflecting from the channel wavered on the plywood, then broke and bounced in the wake of a passing skiff. When Nora squinted her eyes shut, pink waves danced on her eyelids. She squinted harder. Yellow balls rose from the water and floated off the top of her eyeballs.

"More coffee?" Lillian asked.

Nora winced, then shoved her cup across the bar toward Lillian's apron. She watched her hand pour coffee into a cloud of steam. That was a surprisingly noisy operation, because Lillian was wearing a dozen hoop bracelets that caught and clanked in the folds of her wrist.

"Pretty bracelets, Lilly."

"You could wear jewelry," Lillian ventured. "Soften you up a little. Win you a man." Lillian felt bad about the expression on Nora's face. Her cheeks tightened up and went glassy, and it was hard to know if she was pissed or blue, but maybe she was both. Oh well. Nora was one of Lillian's Improvement Projects, and her IPs were always grateful for her straight talk in the end. All the same, Lillian walked over to the shelf and brought back a little pecan pie in a cellophane wrapper.

"Free," she said.

Nora poked at the wrapper with her spoon. She took a deep breath and changed the subject. "So what have you heard about the new Bear Palace?"

"Axel's on it. In this morning, giving orders to Howard."

"Damn that Axel," Nora said. "Why can't he take a break now and then? He's got the water project on the Kis'utch, and now he's going to set up a bear pit. What drives that man?"

Lillian opened her mouth to answer, but Nora plowed on.

"And why does it have to be me who stops him? I don't want this job. I didn't volunteer. I gave this work up after the last time. I'm retired. Isn't there somebody else in this town? I want to be the one who just minds her own business. I want to play my piano in the woods. That's all I want."

Nora looked up to see what Lillian thought of the whole mess. But Lillian was busy. She had a lit cigarette between two fingers, and she was pulling off her bracelets one by one, which required a great deal of squeezing and pulling of flesh and a final delicacy when the hoop passed over the cigarette and dented the line of rising smoke.

The door opened with so much violence that it banged against the wall. There, silhouetted against the blinding light, stood little Tommy McIver, his legs braced like a miniature gunslinger.

"Well, aren't we the little cliché," Lillian said.

Tommy ran across the room and grabbed Lillian around the hips. Lifting her cigarette in two fingers, she placed her palm against his forehead and pushed him away, somehow not catching his hair on fire.

"My mom's coming home. My dad has a job at the Bear Shelter and my mom's coming home.

"And listen to this. My dad's going to be a carpenter for Axel. I mean, Mr. Hagerman. My dad's going to build a Bear Shelter in the tank at the old cannery site. There'll be brown bears and you can watch them close up and even feed them. And a refreshment stand. My dad says I'll get in free, because he's the carpenter for the Bear Shelter.

"Tell everybody," he ordered Lillian, but he needn't have bothered.

Then he was gone, and the cigarette smoke swirled in the yellow light of the open door.

"KENNY, HOW'M I gonna trap a bear?" Tommy hovered a safe distance in front of Kenny, who was sitting in his wheelchair in the morning sun by the library door, cleaning his fingernails with a pocketknife. He was wearing a new hat he'd made of dried fish skin. He'd sewn the isinglass panels together with red embroidery floss, herringbone stitch, a nice touch. Ranger sat by Kenny's left wheel.

"Don't bother me, midget-boy. I got diggin' and grubbin' to do. Like I said. Look it up on the internet. They got two computers hooked up right here in the library. Learn to use 'em. Artofmanliness.com—everything you need to know to be a man. Now go away."

Tommy took a single step backward.

"Do you think a man-trap? I could dig this humungous hole and cover it with sticks and leaves. And the bear would walk by, sniff, sniff, and *whooomph*, down in the hole it goes." Tommy said *whooomph* so emphatically he jumped into the air.

"And then up out of the hole the bear comes in one giant leap and bites off your butt." A big grin spread over Kenny's face, lifting the braids in his beard. He growled suddenly and swiped a hand at Tommy, who leapt backward and teetered at the edge of the boardwalk.

Then Kenny's grin went slack. "How do you trap a bear? If it's this year's cub—no bigger than a bucket—all you need is a dog kennel and a can of sweetened condensed milk, the kind with the cow on the label. Don't make a mistake and get evaporated milk. Open the can and put it in the kennel and your only problem is that the bear won't leave the sweet milk unless you pick up the kennel and shake the cub out like the last Pringle in the can.

"How do you trap a baby hummingbird? With a pot of pansies behind the window. The baby will zippity right toward the flowers, crash into the window, and fall stunned in your hand. You can spring a trap for a crab with no more than a salmon tail on a string. A crab will grab hold with such ungodly stubbornness that you can pull it a hundred feet to the surface. Be ready with a net, because most crabs will let go when they start to see sunlight. But there are crabs who will never let go, ever, even when you swing them over the stove and lower them into boiling water.

"All you have to do is figure out what a thing wants, and then dangle it in front of him. Then he's yours."

Kenny considered. Then he made another swipe at Tommy.

"Kid, I hope you survive long enough to grow a brain. How about you go get me a squirrel instead," he said. "Twenty-five cents for the hide and I'll teach you to skin it."

"Get it how?"

"Like I taught you. Sit real still in a tree and when it comes by, clobber it with a two-by-four."

"Really?" Tommy eyes were big.

"Cripes," Kenny said. He reached under his poncho and pulled out a slingshot. "How old are you?"

"Six." Tommy held up one hand and a thumb.

"Plenty old."

By the time the librarian arrived with her son, Kenny had Tommy shooting pebbles at the *O* on the *Ocean Dreamer*'s transom. Couldn't hit the *O*, but he scored a lot of hits on the sailboat's hull.

"You are an evil influence on the children of this town," the librarian said. She was smiling, but she didn't let go of her own little kid.

Ten o'clock on the button, and here came Nora and Chum.

"We have a date, Nora and me," Kenny muttered experimentally. "Every Tuesday and Thursday, 10 a.m., at the library. A date." Then he started to shout, "*Above all, don't lie to yourself. The man who lies to himself loses all respect for himself and for others. And having no respect, he ceases to love.*"

"Shut up, Kenny," Nora said, and smacked his new fish-skin hat. "You do a bad imitation of a nut."

"Dostoyevsky was not a nut."

"Fine."

Chum flounced in front of Ranger, flopping like a marionette with the string tied to its rump. It was hard for old Ranger to keep his dignity. He hauled himself to his feet and started to maul Chum's face. Nora pulled off her boots and they all crowded into the library, two big wheels and two little wheels and two dogs and Kenny and Nora. Tommy stayed put and pinched another pebble into the slingshot.

The place hardly qualified as a library, more like a used bookstore, because nobody ever returned the books they borrowed. Random times, whenever they felt like it, people brought in a plastic grocery sack of whatever books they didn't want anymore, so it worked out. Books were stacked all the way to the ceiling, some on shelves, some just stacked. It was tricky for Kenny to make the sharp turns in such close quarters, with the librarian shouting out avalanche warnings and his USA flag catching on the photo books. But the library had computers and an internet connection, and that's what Nora went after. Kenny too.

Nora was studying up on Alaska things. Marine charts and the rules of navigation. Coho salmon, and then it was marbled murrelets. She wrote natural history pamphlets for the ferries—that was her job. Tourists could take the pamphlets from racks midship and learn things. So every week Nora was taking notes about some species, preferably something about to go extinct. Kenny thought she'd be depressed, but she got all excited about it.

"Did you know that marbled murrelets are shaped like such Milk Duds that they have to fly at forty miles an hour or they fall out of the sky?" she asked Kenny.

She did that. They'd be sitting across from each other at the computer table, quietly doing their work, and then she'd look up, and it was, "Did you know that a marbled murrelet flies from Snettisham to the Geicke Glacier, picks up a fish, flies it back to its nestling, does it again, twice a day, sixty miles each way?"

Kenny thought of himself as up on the animals, at least the dead ones, but he'd never heard of what she told him. Kenny never said "too stupid to live" or "yes" or "no" or "wow." He just grunted and went back to whatever website he was studying. Each marvel—she called them *marvels*—made her grin wider, and each one ground Kenny down, knowing that another marvel was going to be gone before he was a goner himself. Mostly he pretended to ignore her, even though he watched her from under the itchy edge of his cap.

But that day, Kenny saw Nora looking at him when she thought he wasn't watching. He was studying an internet site that showed how to skin a squirrel by turning it inside out over a post—you sort of prop up the body on the post, cut it just right, give a steady pull down on the hide, and get it skinned in one motion. Kenny wondered how mountain men ever figured things out before the internet. But Nora wasn't looking at the video that Kenny was studying or listening to him mutter. She was looking at him.

Kenny watched her looking. She had gold eyes. Maybe they were brown, but in that light, they were gold as a dogshark.

The librarian was hanging around, so Nora held her fire.

"What are you studying today?" she asked, but not like she cared.

"The life cycle of squirrels," Kenny said, then he looked away because he didn't want to encourage her.

Finally, the librarian's kid started to whine that he was hungry. The librarian propped the BACK SOON sign against her coffee mug and left. Kenny thought, here it comes, and sure enough. Nora reached across the table and put her hands on top of his hands, sort of grabbed the back of Kenny's fingerless gloves. He wished she wouldn't do that. He wished she wouldn't look so hard at him. He wished she'd be afraid of him, like everybody else. He shifted his hat down closer to his eyebrows.

"Har," he said.

"We've got to do something!" she said.

"We," Kenny said. It was the only coherent word he could come up with. What the hell was she thinking? They hadn't done anything that needed anything done about it.

"Tommy told me that Axel has hired Tick to build a bear pit," she said in her earnest voice. Kenny muttered something and shrugged his shoulders to keep his back from tightening up.

"Selling refreshments and charging admission to see bears caged in the cistern at the old cannery beach. It's the latest 'Good River Products Rural Economic Development Plan.' Logs, fish, water, now bears. That man Axel never rests. What have you heard about this one?"

Kenny hadn't heard anything about it. Nobody ever told him anything. But he didn't believe in caging things. Better to kill a problem bear than put it in a cage and make it a tourist attraction. Some things are worse than dying. Put something in a cage, and it's the people outside who turn into wild animals, taunting it and poking it with sticks and peeing on it.

On the video, a man's hands in rubber gloves placed the little naked squirrel on a table next to its inside-out skin.

First thing a bear would do, Kenny knew, was try to tear apart the cage, bringing it everything he had. Claws, teeth, brute strength. And when that didn't work, he'd turn his teeth on his own body, scratching and clawing. Then he'd slump down and curse day and night, curse himself for being so goddamn stupid to walk into a trap. Then curse the men with guns. Then he'd curse God. After a couple days of that, he'd be suddenly terrified of God, and he'd shake and cry out and *apologize*, trying to con a deal. But then a little kid would wing a rock at him. That's when he would lose all faith in God.

Nora was squeezing his hands, watching his face.

Kenny yanked his hands away. He rubbed them on his pants.

"Get Tommy to tell you more," Kenny said.

"That's all he knows."

"Get Tick fired up."

The video went back to the beginning. The rubber gloves moved a small knife around the squirrel's shoulders, slicing here and there, just right. The gloves put down the knife. They gripped the hide on both sides and started to pull.

Nora grimaced. "Tick's got his hands full. He can't help us."

A person who already looks sort of like a grunion should not grimace, Kenny decided, but all he said was, "Not 'help us.' Help *you*."

Kenny looked hard at Nora.

"What is it about you, Nora? Why can't you let it go? The world is fucked. So you came to Good River Harbor. Smart move. Low clouds and constant rain will cheer you up. Yessiree, what you need are twenty hours of darkness and exactly forty-six neighbors—six drunks, seven gossips, thirty-three crack shots, and a cat. If this doesn't make you forget about the world's troubles, nothing can. What did this town do to deserve you anyway, Nora Montgomery, Mary Poppins's evil twin, floating into town in her yellow raincoat whenever we need somebody to fuck things up."

Kenny leered, scrunching up one eye. "Joke," he said. "Har."

Nora's eyes flashed into fire, like propane rings. But soon it was water, not fire, that shimmered there. She closed her eyes and dropped her forehead onto the table. "Yeah. What is it about you, Nora?" she repeated.

While the gloved hands pulled the squirrel skin off the little body again, and then again, Kenny flailed himself. Truly stupid. Deeply, irredeemably stupid. An accursed man, of an accursed species, on a doomed planet. He reached over and lifted Nora's head, awkwardly, by the chin.

"I'm sorry, I'm really sorry. I'd help you. But I don't have a dog in this fight," he said.

"I think you do," said Nora.

≈

KENNY RETRIEVED a fish head he'd been saving in a five-gallon pail on his front gangway. Nora would be a lot happier person if she'd stop hoping so much. He raised his head and shouted, "*Glittering hope beckons many men to their undoing.*" Ranger yowled. A hopeful raven flapped off the railing. A passing tourist grabbed her husband's arm and pressed to the far side of the boardwalk. "Euripides," he yelled. The woman threw him a sick smile. The fish head's smile looked equally sick. "It means, like, pessimists don't go off on risky missions," he muttered at the woman, rolling toward her, trying to explain. The woman scurried away.

He poked a wire through the fish's eyeball and out its toothy jaw, twisted the ends together and wired it to the center of his crab ring. Once he'd tied the line to his porch rail, he lowered it into the tide until he felt it thud on the mud. Then he went inside.

Kenny lived in one room on pilings over the water, there next to the Bath 'n' Bar. He slept on a cot raised two feet off the floor, above the cold air. His only light was a kerosene lamp. His only heat was a woodstove. The roof leaked at a joist, but he rigged up a string that directed water from the leak into a plastic bucket, so it kept his blankets dry for the most part.

The place was adequate, a little damp, dim in the corners. He'd strung a line over the woodstove and got some clothespins, for drying gloves and plastic bags. He had a shelf for the kitchen, which was a washbasin, propane gas burner, and a bottle of the blue dish detergent that decorates every cabin in Alaska. The log walls of the cabin were wallpapered with animal skins, stretched and drying. Field mice. Pine squirrels.

Kenny's important possessions, however, were on the table. He had the full skeleton of a little brown bat. A rock scallop with a kelp holdfast attached. A beaver's front tooth, which was orange. A jar of feathers. A fossil trilobite.

This pleased Kenny, that he had everything he needed and absolutely nothing else. He knew everyone he needed to know and absolutely no one else. He said what he needed to say and nothing more. He knew how to do what he needed to do. He did nothing more than that. Everything he did, he did the way he always did it, and he was proud of that. He smelled like the house, and the house smelled like him—propane and fish. He lived alone. He didn't hope for anything or any fate he didn't already have.

He thought that might be his only virtue.

The bat skeleton could hope that one dark night, its bones would grow stringy muscles under black leather wings, and it would leap away toward the moon. The tooth could hope for a beaver. The feather might hope for a raven's wing. The holdfast could beat itself up with regret, knowing it should have put its roots down on something steadier than a scallop. The trilobite could hope and maybe even pray, "Dear God, in your infinite mercy, let me evolve." It could pray that its exoskeleton would soften like wet leather and pulse long enough at the edge of the sea-marsh that some day—yes!—it would become something—anything—alive and wondering.

Fine. Hope it, for all the good it does. Kenny was done with that.

In low light and gathering blackflies, Kenny pulled on his mouse hat and rolled out onto the porch. There must have been a northwest wind, because he could hear—faint and far away—the stumble-plink of Nora's pitiful piano playing, all the way over at Green Cove. He tossed a galvanized bucket into the bay, jerked it a couple of times to sink it, and hauled up seawater. He put the bucket on the burner, flicked a lighter and stepped back. Blue flames shot up the edges of the bucket and settled into a roaring yellow ring. This is the beauty of propane: You can count on propane to light when you turn the knob on and go off when you turn the knob off. That's one difference between propane and hope.

You've got to know when to turn the hope down so low it flicks green and pops off.

He reached over the railing to catch the line on his crab trap. Putting his back into it, he hauled the rope over the roller mounted on the rail. From the weight, he knew before the ring broke the surface that he'd caught a couple already. He levered the trap over the railing. Dungeness, big as dinner plates. The female he threw out first, reaching behind the pinchers to grab the rear of the carapace. She could try to pinch him, and she did, but he knew that the real danger is never from the ones you're grabbing, but from the ones you're not. He pulled out two nice males. These were the old guys, wider than the span of his hand, with barnacles on their carapaces. He laid them on their backs on the railing, where they gasped and bubbled and flexed their muscles, closing their claws on air. They were hoping, that's for sure.

"Hope doesn't do any good, can do a lot of harm," Kenny mumbled at the crabs, "all that random snapping at air. It's sad, that's what it is, all that trying. Try to stay away from sad trying."

He picked up one of the doomed crabs, wrapping one hand around each of its big claws. Fact was, when he had the crab, the crab couldn't get him. He hooked the side of the crab's carapace on the deck railing and pulled hard. There was a loud, crunching crack. The whole back pulled off and fell into the sea, spilling yellow fat. Now the crab really started hoping, and it's surprising how strong a crab is, how you have to hold on tight, because he's arm-wrestling you. Kenny centered the crab's body along the angle of the rail and pressed hard on both sides. The crab cracked into two halves. It went limp, claws and legs suddenly long. The gills lay in beautiful array along the back, like ivory feathers. When Kenny scraped them off and shook the crab over the water, the gills floated away like gulls flying.

Kenny held half a crab in each hand. He scolded the half that had the eyes still attached. "I know you don't have the brains to really hope. You probably don't even try. That's even sadder, to snap and struggle like you're trying but your brains are gone."

The crab's blue eyes had clouded yellow, like a foggy dawn. Kenny's crabs were always dead when they went into the boiling water. This was why he cleaned them first, so they didn't try to crawl out. That kind of scrabbling he couldn't stand.

When the crabs in the bucket flushed bright red, he pulled them out with tongs and dipped them in cold water. They steamed on the railing, cooling—red claws rigid, white muscles of the body in cartilage crisp and brittle as tracing paper.

"God damn it, Ranger," he said dejectedly. "Why do you want me to take these crabs to Nora?" Ranger dropped his nose to the ground and sprang up barking. "All right. But we're not going to stay. Just give her the crabs, turn around, and come home. She scares me, that one, all that fierce hope. And you, dumb dog, you're the worst hoper of all."

July 11

HIGH TIDE		LOW TIDE	
12:52am	17.7ft	6:25am	-0.8ft
0:57pm	6.5ft	6:33pm	0.3ft

"My dad says you're pretty." Davy stole a glance at Meredith's jeans.

"My dad says you're trouble." She flipped her hair over her shoulder.

"My dad says, 'Kiss her, but don't tell your mother.'"

"If you did, my dad would break your neck. Simple as that. " She snapped her fingers. "He says if I spend any time with you, he'll kill *you* and he'll ruin your *dad* and he'll be very disappointed in *me*." Meredith giggled, and said it again in her dad's steel-shiny voice, "Very dis-appoin-ted."

For some reason, Davy thought this was hilarious, and he laughed until he had to lean over to catch his breath. Meredith grabbed him by the throat and shook him, like she was going to choke him to death. Her hands felt smooth and warm on his neck.

Davy reached out, gripped the timber above him, swung out like on a trapeze, chinned himself, and dropped back onto the sand. Not every guy is strong enough to do that. Meredith pretended she didn't see, but he knew she did.

This was probably the greatest place Davy had ever found. It's hard to get alone with your secret girlfriend in a town like Good River Harbor, and after that tragedy with the note in the clamshell, the only thing Davy could think of was bribing Curtis to pass a message. Davy said a dollar, but he'd made the mistake of bragging to Curtis that he had a twenty and a five, so it ended up costing Davy all the gas money, but he made Curtis give a money-back guarantee that he'd get the message delivered right, so that was worth it. The message told Meredith to meet Davy on the mudflat under the school right after supper and he would skiff her out to a secret place and show her a surprise.

Davy told his dad he wanted to take Meredith to the clam beach at the Kis'utch River, and could he have the skiff? He had no idea what Meredith told her mom and dad—a lie, whatever it was. Davy couldn't believe his luck when there she was, in her tight jeans and high boots, waiting for him like he'd told her.

He nosed the skiff in. She jumped aboard, pushing them off, and Davy scooted them around Green Point. On behind the point and the cove, there was an old wharf that used to be part of the cannery. It was a big square of planked deck up on cross-braced piers—a deck that might have been wide enough to hold a cabin, but there was nothing up there now but fireweed growing in the gull crap on deck. A storm took out the gangway that connected the wharf to land, so it was just sitting offshore rotting up on high pilings. Nobody went there but gulls. A wooden shelf ran between the timbers underneath the wharf, making a place where a couple of people could sit. But what made it so wonderful was the skirting around the edges of the deck that made kind of a wall, so people on the shelf could disappear if they wanted to—which was really something in a small, nosy town squished between the mountain and the sea.

It was just past low tide when they boated in under the stranded wharf, and the tide would be rising fast. It was going to be the night of the flood-tide of the pink-salmon moon. That's a powerful time, Davy's mom had told him, when the sun and the moon pull from the same side of the Earth. Good and bad things can happen then. Davy cut the engine and tipped it up, letting the skiff coast under the wharf. He tied the boat tight to a piling and held out his hand, very gallant.

Meredith said, "I can get out myself," and vaulted into six inches of water. Right away, she leaned over and started looking for cool things between the rocks, which made her jeans fit her even better. Davy found a sea cucumber. It was long and red with orange spikes, like a punk sausage. He held the cucumber up to Meredith's mouth and pretended it was giving her a kiss. She swatted him hard in the arm.

"Dipshit," she said. "That's the ass end."

He was rummaging around in the kelp, looking for a leather star, so he could rub the garlic smell on her nose, but the incoming tide was lapping at his boot tops. Time to climb.

He showed Meredith how she could put one foot in the angle where the bracing of the wharf is bolted to the piling, then hold on to the brace above her and sort of side-step diagonally up to the next angle on the other side.

"You have to watch your fingers at first, because the mussels and barnacles can slice them easy. Fold your sleeves over your hands," he told her.

The hardest part was almost at the top, where the bracing beams are coated with algae. For that part, Davy stayed under Meredith.

"I've got you," he said. If she slipped, he would put his hand on her pretty bottom to hold her steady.

After the slippery part, it was easy, and she climbed up the last brace, Davy right after her. Under the shelter of the deck and above the high-tide line, the planking was dry and flat. The planks that came down to sheath the wharf made a shadowy, whispery place, completely enclosed except for where storms had ripped away boards. There was a wide shelf there, and that's where Davy had a surprise for Meredith.

They crawled along the shelf, Davy going first to show the way.

"Look," he said, and pressed back against the wall so she could see past him. There were five mud cups stuck to the wall—barn swallow nests. A mother barn swallow sat in each nest, rustling her wings down over the nestlings. In each nest, a row of little round heads stuck out from under the flared shadow-blue wings of a mom. The nestling heads were gray and brown, almost shadows themselves, but when one opened its mouth, its maw was as yellow as a buttercup.

"One, two, three, four in that nest." The moms fluttered their wing feathers and shifted on the nest, but they sat tight, even though Meredith was only a few feet away. Every time a mom shifted her weight, all the yellow mouths in her nest sprang open. Meredith giggled.

"I can hear the babies peeping," Meredith whispered.

"The moms are blinking. They have white eyelids."

Meredith looked at Davy. "That's cool," she said. "This is a cool place."

The wind was picking up and the tide was rising, but it was dry and cozy in their hideaway. The sun, bouncing along the western mountaintops, shone in under the wharf. Waves were really barreling in, but even the spray couldn't touch them, up on the shelf with the birds. They sat side by side, swinging their legs over the ledge.

"Isn't this a cool place!" Davy said, because he couldn't think of anything else to say, now that he was alone with Meredith. Her hair was long and brown and her eyes were blue as heaven. She was wearing low-rider jeans and a hooded sweatshirt halfway unzipped down the front. Davy squirmed closer to see if there was anything under the sweatshirt. Meredith leaned away and started to talk.

"How'd you find this place?" The question was an ordinary one, but Davy smiled to himself. His dad told him that girls will start to talk when they're thinking about kissing.

"I do a lot of exploring," Davy decided to say, "because I'm going to get myself set up as a wilderness guide."

"In Good River?" She seemed sort of surprised, which surprised him, because where else would he do it?

"I guess."

"My dad wants me to go to college Outside, but I'll do what I want."

Davy sat forward. This might be a problem, because how can you have a girlfriend who doesn't even live in your town?

She looked at him sort of cross, so Davy pulled a joint from his shirt pocket. This was the first time Davy ever smoked a joint with anybody but stupid Curtis and he wasn't sure about good manners with a girl. Do you get it going and then share, or do you offer her first drag? And what if she's worried about germs?—Davy had a hard enough time getting one joint from Curtis, no chance for two.

Meredith looked at the joint. "Is that dope?"

He grinned and nodded. This was the risky part.

"I do dope all the time," Meredith said, and shot him a look through lowered lids. She took the joint between her fingers like a cigarette and put it between her lips. He flicked a lighter, held it out.

"You have to sort of suck to get the fire going," he offered helpfully.

A wave smacked against a piling, splashing water. The wind lifted into their hideout and flowed back out. That was going to be some tide.

She sucked and then blew the smoke out of her mouth.

"Kind of hold it in for a minute," he said.

"There's a lot of bird poop up here," Meredith said.

Davy took off his jacket, spread it on his lap, and gave it a pat. Meredith stayed where she was. It was worth a try. She took another drag. Her words came out in bubbles of smoke.

"My dad says you can get schistosomiasis from bird poop."

"My dad doesn't give a schisto-whatever."

Meredith laughed out a mouthful of smoke. The joint wasn't working very well, but she didn't notice. Davy pivoted on the timber in front of the shelf, rolled onto his stomach, and stretched his arms and legs into space like an airplane, holding himself there, even though it took every muscle he had. Now what do I do? he wondered. Do people just say, do you want to be my girlfriend?

"Boeing 737," he said.

"Doofus," Meredith said, and poked his leg with her boot.

Davy climbed back onto the shelf. She handed him the joint, cold as stone. "Is this how you hold your mouth to suck the smoke?" she asked. She made a face like a gorilla slurping worms.

"No, it's like this." Davy made his mouth into a kiss. Meredith reached her hands behind his head, drew him toward her, and planted a soft kiss on his lips. She drew back, looked into his astonished face, and laughed. Davy reached his hand behind her head, tangled his fingers in her long, soft hair, and pulled her close to him. The kiss was on her lips, then on her neck, then deep in the sweetness of the space behind the half-open zipper. He burrowed his face down into that darkness, kissing. Still holding the cold joint in one hand, he reached his arm around her, lifting the sweatshirt, and ran his hand over the warm smooth arch of her back.

"Is this how you hold your mouth?" she asked, crossing her eyes and sticking out her tongue. Davy surfaced.

"Is this how you hold your mouth?" she asked, putting her finger in one corner of her mouth and pulling. Davy laughed as well as a person can laugh who is smothering a silly little face in kisses. She pushed him gently away.

Davy sighed and smiled. He put the joint in his own mouth. Holding back his hair to keep from setting himself on fire, he lit the joint, inhaled a stream of smoke, then inserted the joint gently between her beautiful lips. He put his arm around her shoulders and settled back against the wharf. It was wonderful, the way her shoulder fit right under his arm and her head rested against his neck. They sat like that for a long time before he got up the nerve to put his hand on the swell of her sweatshirt. The hillocks under his hand were warm and sort of squishy. He closed his eyes. If the world ended right then, if lightning flashed from heaven and incinerated him at that moment, if he had a heart attack and croaked right there and then, he would die a happy man.

A flock of sanderlings blew in. They fluttered around, crying out in their little voices, then cozied up together on a span. They flicked water off their backs, and called *kwit kwit* until they were quiet. The sun settled down behind a mountain, which turned suddenly black. Meredith whispered to keep from scaring the birds.

"What time is it? My dad will kill me if I'm not home by dark." She looked down at the tide.

"I gotta get home too. My mom's coming on the morning ferry—she's probably already on board—and me and Tommy are supposed to clean the house before he goes to bed."

"How are we going to get out of here?"

The sanderlings startled and flew off, peeping.

Meredith pointed at the water that was slapping halfway up the pilings. Deep shadows pooled under the wharf. Davy could hardly see the skiff. But there it was, dimly green and ghostly underwater, bottom up. It slowly rotated around the bowline that he'd tied tight to the pilings, a knot now ten feet below the tide.

"Oh shit. What a stupid cheechako mistake."

DAVY WOULD HAVE given everything to start his life over. Or go back one day, just one. "Let me do one thing different in my whole life, just one thing. Just one clove hitch. Stupid. I'm stupid. If I have to be so stupid, why does it have to be now?"

"You're always stupid," Meredith yelled. "So what's new?"

He had to think harder than he had ever thought before. But it was like he could either breathe or he could think, not both, and his head was thinking so hard he could have passed out.

"Stupid. That's what."

The swallows were circling around their nests, crapping in the air, peeping like they thought they'd die. The tide was smacking on the pilings. It was a dark tide, like some live thing trying to climb onto the wharf. It got a rough handhold on the barnacles, heaved itself up, and fell off, grunting. It slid a dark hand behind them. It tried again. Darkness spread across the water.

"No. Not swimming to shore," he yelled at Meredith, as if she'd suggested it. Too far, too cold, too rough. "And what would we do on shore if we made it?" soaking wet, freezing, and the tide pushing them against the cliffs or into the dog-hair alder.

"STOP IT."

They stopped yelling and looked at each other, breathing hard.

Davy had brought her out here. He'd tied the boat short and sunk it. It was his job to get her home before her dad figured them out.

"Just let me think," he said quietly.

She pulled her hood over her head and zipped her jacket, tucked up her legs, and huddled back in the corner with her eyes closed. Davy thought she was going to yell at him again, but she didn't.

"Okay," she said instead. "Let's see you think."

"Okay," he said. "Okay."

First thing is, we're safe, he told himself firmly. The tide is not going to come up more than another seven feet. The worse that could happen is that we have to spend the night on this shelf. High tide will be at midnight tonight. Low tide will be at six in the morning. We could wait it out, then muck it to shore at low tide and hike home on the beach. We would be coming down the boardwalk just after our dads finished eating breakfast. Just after my mom got off the ferry.

The horror of this made his head swim. Nobody would be eating breakfast in Good River Harbor tomorrow. Nobody would be meeting the ferry. Another hour and the grown-ups would be asking around, figuring out that Meredith wasn't wherever it was she said she would be, and he wasn't clamming, and the skiff wasn't at the slip, and wherever Meredith was, he probably was too. They'd launch every boat into the darkness, looking for them, scared they were dead. When they found them, they would kill them.

"I'm going to dive down and cut the line."

"No, you're not," she said without opening her eyes. "That water is fifty-six degrees. You know that."

He checked his belt for his knife. A sharpening stone would have been a help, but that's the way it was. He could dive ten feet.

"You can't dive that deep."

"I can. I have."

When he cut the line, the boat would bob to the surface. He was sure of this. He'd helped his dad put extra flotation in the stern this winter. The engine would be ruined already, soaked in all that saltwater. But his dad always kept oars tied into the boat, and once it was afloat, they could climb down, bail the boat, and row home. That would give him time to think about how to tell his dad about the engine.

Once he'd made up his mind, he saw things as clearly as watching a movie. Everything was dim around him, but he could see himself moving like an actor on the Technicolor screen, the colors that bright. He took off his jacket and T-shirt so he would have something warm to put on when he got out of the water. On the movie screen, his chest was as white as a halibut belly. He hoped Meredith still had her eyes closed, but he couldn't be sure. She was sitting up there in the balcony in the dark. He took off his boots, but left on his socks, so the barnacles didn't cut his feet. He wasn't sure about his jeans. Made sense to take them off, but there was Meredith right there, so he kept them on.

"It's dangerous," she said. "If you do this, it'll be the stupidest of all the stupid things you've ever done."

He sidled sideways down a diagonal brace. It shook under his weight. The tide heaved and grunted, slapping up, soaking his pants to the knees. His skin prickled up his crotch into his armpits. The black water reached up, grabbed at his legs, slipped off. A floating gas can rang against a piling. If he didn't get the boat off, the bells of the church in town would be gonging just like that, rousting people from their evening beers to search for two damn kids lost at sea, one of them so stupid they should drown him.

He took a huge breath, jumped feetfirst into the water, flailed to the surface, gasped as if he'd been kicked in the chest, took another breath, folded at the waist, and dove. His hand hit the keel. Kicking furiously, he followed it down to the bow and groped for the rope. The rope was humming, that tight. His hand gripped it, held it steady. He sawed against the fibers. A couple gave way. Damn this knife. How long can I saw without bursting? He doubled over, pushed off the hull, and rocketed back into birds screaming and dark water slapping.

Tread water, gulp air, and back down. This time or die. He smacked his head into the hull, he was pushing down so fast, and felt his way to the bow. With all the strength in his back, he slashed the full length of the knife against the rope. The rope flew apart. The boat reared up, caught him in the ribs, and cracked his shoulder against the piling. He saw the pain of it, a blue explosion, heard a snap. The boat lunged up. A wave grabbed it and tilted it into the tidal current. Davy leapt after it. That explosion again. His shoulder, on fire. The skiff turned bow for stern, then bucked away upside down in a mess of life jackets and buckets.

Waves dragged at Davy's jeans. He reached for the cross-timber. That flash of pain. With his good arm, he reached around a piling and hung on. Splinters dug into his skin. Every time a wave lifted him and dragged him under, barnacles sliced his chest. He scrabbled his legs against the post and grabbed again for the strut, but he couldn't pull up his weight with one arm. He must have weighed a thousand pounds.

"Shit, Meredith."

He felt the bounce of her steps on the strut, and her fist around his belt. As she dragged him up, he scrambled his feet onto the strut. Together they fumbled up the cross-timbers and heaved their bodies onto the shelf.

Sometime in the night, a humpback passed by. Davy heard its blow, like a chest dragged across a deck, then another blow, farther toward Good River Harbor. The dark water shone like it was polished. Now and then, a pod of porpoises leapt by, streaming wakes of bioluminescent sparks. Once a sanderling cried out in its sleep. When squalls blew through, the water rustled against the pilings, in and out, like breathing. Davy held as still as he could to keep his shoulder from catching fire. Salt stung his sliced chest.

When the church bell began to toll, far away and faint, Davy shuddered to keep from crying.

"Meredith," he whispered, but she was asleep.

Somehow his socks and jeans were hung to dry on a crossbeam. His T-shirt was wrapped around his feet. His jacket was wrapped around his legs. He and Meredith were sitting against the side planks. His naked back was against her bare chest, with her sweatshirt around both of them. Her breasts pressed hard into his back. He could sense the warm, slow rise and whistle of her breathing.

He breathed out when she breathed out, breathed in when she breathed in—the sea-wet air, the smell of birds, her hair warm on his neck. He did not hear the ferry churn by in the darkness. He did not hear the cries of the kittiwakes trailing off its stern.

PAN PAN. Pan pan. Pan pan. This is Coast Guard sector five, Ketchikan. Coast Guard sector five, Ketchikan. Time is two two three six. Two two three six. We have a report that a Lund skiff with a red stripe is overdue from Good River Harbor with zero two persons on board. Last seen leaving Good River Harbor, fifteen nautical miles northeast of the Bean Island buoy, at one nine three zero. All vessels are asked to keep a close lookout for signs of distress and render assistance if possible. If anyone has information about this vessel, please contact the Coast Guard, sixteen alpha. Out.

ELEVEN P.M. A tail wind was blowing, so it was cold at the stern of the ferry where Davy's mom had left her backpack. That's where Annie Klawon would sleep, but it was too soon for that. She wouldn't try to sleep until she was exhausted. She had found a dead spot at the bow, and this is where she stood, watching the ferry churn through the dark toward her family in Good River Harbor. Even out of the wind, the air was cold and thick with night-dampness and diesel fumes.

She cinched her hood tight, smiling to think of the fuss and flurry at the McIver household in Good River Harbor, as Tick and the boys cleaned the house. Her big Tick would be trundling fresh sheets back from Lillian's Bath 'n' Bar, probably for the first time since she'd left. Davy would have the broom, sweeping fish scales and hemlock needles out the door and off the deck to scatter on the tide. Tommy? Who knows what Tommy does when he's excited?—dance around, everything but sleep.

The ferry entered Muir's Passage. A chain rattled, a door clanged against metal, and a watchman walked to the bow. The watchman leaned over dark water that rolled under the hull. Navigational markers designate the channel, blinking green and red on a course angling through reefs. But nothing warns of the unexpected hazards—a log boom or gill net, a buoy escaped from its mooring or a boat dead in the water, the engine blown. Shuddering forward at barely ten knots, the ferry wove a drunkard's path through tidal currents and submerged shoals. The watchman suddenly straightened and spoke urgently into the intercom. A spotlight shot from the bridge and jabbed over the water, searching the bow, the forested shoreline, a rock reef. The light came to rest on a green buoy no more than fifty yards from the port bow. Male voices called back and forth. Then the spotlight winked out and the boat moved heavily to starboard away from a place foul with rocks.

Annie Klawon always sang a small prayer of thanksgiving when the ferry left the passage behind and nosed into the empty sea. Outside the passage, there are no horizons, no high bluffs to steer by, no sounds, no stars. Night clouds are indistinguishable from night ocean. The only indication of direction is rain, sluicing in from the west. But in the open sea, you won't stove in your keel on a reef or lurch in whirlpool tides. The open sea was where she was raised, and that's where she felt at home, safest with at least a hundred fathoms under her hull. Long-liners, that's what the Klawons were, pulling long fishing lines from big cylinders, a couple hundred hooks a line, hand baited with chunks of herring. When she was lucky, Annie Klawon's father told her to pilot the boat. That job was dry and warm enough. When she wasn't lucky, she was in the stern, unhooking fish as fast as the lines reeled in screeching, heaving the black cod into the tote, heaving the tomcod, the hake, the uglies, and the sharks overboard. That job was wet and cold and slippery on a shivering, slanting deck.

The watchman left his post. Annie Klawon left her post too and worked her way down the port deck, through the patch of light and laughter thrown from the bar, through yellow streaks from curtained cabins, into the empty dark at the stern. The deck was slick with splash. Her hair whipped across her eyes as she dragged a deck chair into the lee of the life jacket bin and pulled her sleeping bag from her pack. She stumbled backward and braced her legs on the suddenly pitching deck. The boat wallowed through the wake of a ship that had passed unseen long minutes ago. She felt behind her for the chair.

The night before she had dreamed that Tick had lost power in a troller in a gale. His long wet braid was blown across his face and rain was streaking down his slicker. He braced on the deck as wind turned the boat broadside to the waves and dark water poured over the rail. He struggled to start the engine, pulling out the choke, grinding the starter, leaping to check the fuel lines. Davy and Tommy clung to the rails as the world fell away, overwhelmed them, and fell away again. Rain plastered their hair to their faces, blinding them. Sideways to the waves, the lee rail rolled under, waves rose and broke over the weather deck. The figures of her family were cardboard cutouts dissolving in the wind and rain. She knew they were coming to find her. But she pitched past them in the storm, calling out.

Her father had told her that Tick would be taken by the sea. He hadn't said it in so many words, but he never did say things straight out. "If you marry him," is what her father had said, "sadness will come to you." Then he turned and went into his workshop. He had said all that he would ever say about Tick. She tried to imagine how Tick could make her sad. But the only cruel thing she could imagine that Tick could do was to die—that tall, beautiful, capable man with a beard impossibly golden red and hair as long as her father's hair, a braid straight down his back, but the color of dawn, not midnight. If Tick did anything to hurt her, it would be against his will and all his power. And the only force greater than he was, was the sea. That's how she had thought about it then. She had slammed out the door and spent the night with her Aunt Josephine.

She married Tick, but not in the way she wanted. All that winter, her mother crocheted blankets, piles of blankets to give away at her wedding. When Marjorie Klawon used up one ball of yarn, she tied in another and kept on crocheting. The blankets piled up—yellow and green, then green and red, then red and black, endlessly. All winter, Annie Klawon's father worked at his bench, making his tools. He carved the handle of a chisel from an alder limb and a mallet from maple. He would not make gifts for the people at the wedding. Instead, he would carve his only daughter a canoe as long as his arm and he would paint it red, green, black, so that his Annie Klawon would always have a way to come back to her father's house.

Day after day, he went into the forest, touching the trees as he passed through them, looking for the tree he needed. But one evening at the end of winter, her father did not come home, not even after dark, and when they looked for him with flashlights, they found him slumped against the base of a yellow cedar tree, cold as the night. So Annie Klawon and Tick were quietly married by the village priest, with only Aunt Josephine and Annie's sobbing mother as witnesses.

Why did she marry him? Annie married Tick because one day in Hollis, she was struggling with a wooden extension ladder that insisted on tangling in the alders between her family's house and her neighbor's shed. First the legs would snare on a branch, then the rope would wrap around a thicket, no matter how she aimed or tugged. A big man with huge hands came by and said, "Hey, let me help you with that. What's going on?"

"I locked myself out," Annie Klawon said.

The man picked up the ladder as if it weighed nothing. The ladder sprang free from the alders. He was wearing heavy weather gear, but not even the rubberized fabric could hide the expanse of his shoulders.

"Is that door up there unlocked?" The man pointed to the side door on her porch fifteen feet above the street.

"Yes," Annie said.

He lifted the ladder and set it against the porch railing. It was beautiful, how he lifted the ladder and set it against the porch railing. No grunting, no timid tugging to be sure the ladder wouldn't slip. Up he went and over the railing onto the porch. He must be a seaman, to be that graceful in the air. He disappeared through the side door, and before long, he came out the front, where Annie Klawon was standing, staring at him.

"There you go," he said. "But the front door wasn't locked."

Annie knew that. She had already climbed up to the side porch and let herself out the front door. She had been trying to return the neighbor's ladder when Tick came along.

"Wouldn't you love a man like that?" Annie had asked her Aunt Josephine, and Josephine had to agree that it's a good-hearted man who helps first and asks questions later.

"And wouldn't he be a good provider?"

"And isn't it a strong man who can lift an extension ladder out of alders?"

Annie wadded up her jacket for a pillow, tucked the garbage bag tightly around the foot of her sleeping bag, and burrowed in. She would have to be careful what she let herself think about, if she was to have any chance of getting to sleep. Lying on her back, looking into another squall, she began to call up her favorite memories. This is what she did each night in Seattle. After she sang her boys to sleep, she climbed into a cold cot and remembered herself to sleep. She remembered Tick with his legs stretched under the kitchen table and his stocking feet sticking out the other side. He's listening to marine forecasts as he torques pliers to crimp the wire on a fishing lure, or dismantles a spinning reel, every tiny screw laid out on a newspaper, or resolders the wires in the electric plug for the radio. She hears that spattering, and smells the acrid smoke. Sometimes she remembers snow falling past the window, snowflakes big and soft as mice. They appear as they enter the light cast from the kitchen window and then vanish, as if they existed only in that space of time. More often she remembered rain, shiny in the light from the lamps. Or a soft silver afternoon, sitting on the gravel beach at Good River Harbor, her legs braided into Tick's, her younger son, Tommy, climbing over the two of them as if they were logs, her older son, Davy, pitching stones into the sea.

Sometimes, she liked to remember putting Tommy to bed. She ducks under the top bunk and plants a kiss on Tommy's forehead. He reaches for her neck and pulls her to him and kisses her. Then he curls into a ball. She tucks the blankets around the curve of his narrow shoulders. She backs out of the room then, pulling the door closed. The lamplight from the room behind her narrows until only a yellow line draws the contours of her son. Then she sits on the floor by the bedroom door and she sings, always the same song, always the same ending line, "*Tefaay. Aliinghaku::n amsanaku::n. Tefaay.* Through this story, nice weather, clear and calm."

It's quiet in the house then. She knows they are all listening to her sing, Davy and Tick in the front room, Tommy in bed, she at the bedroom door. They listen to water lapping against pilings under the house, a harbor seal's sneeze, the E-flat whistle of wind in the rigging of trawlers at anchor, the Green Point buoy, its moan hushed by fog. She believes that if two people are aware of the same thing, they are somehow joined. When the moon is out in Seattle, or if the air smells of the sea, she looks at the moon or smells the air, thinking maybe her boys are watching out the window the same moon or smelling the same wind. Then she believes that they are together. This is why Annie Klawon tells her boys to pay attention to the rain, the wind. To listen for the voices of the birds.

In the night, kittiwakes circled the ferry. The big spotlight lit their white wings. She could hear their cries, *keit lay day*. But why the spotlight? It was unusual for a ferry to shine a spotlight in the open water past the narrows. A lost ship out there somewhere, or maybe a log raft got loose, or a fishing boat dead in the water. Turning her face suddenly to port, Annie listened closely. She sat up, listening even more intently, but she wasn't sure what she heard. She covered her head with her sleeping bag and closed her eyes.

Annie Klawon remembered what it would be like to come home. She would be at the railing at dawn when the ferry edged into the pilings at Good River Harbor. The ferry would pull into port, and then she would be back with Tick and Davy and Tommy. Gulls would rise from the fireweed that grew on the pilings. The bowman would throw the monkey fist underhand to the pier. The mooring lines would groan, winching the ferry tight against the pilings. Tommy would run down the ramp and wrap his arms around her waist. Davy and Tick would hold back, grinning, then reach their arms around her shoulders and take her pack. The pink salmon would be in. Salmonberries would be ripe and Swainson's thrushes will have fledged. The woods would be full of thrushes learning to sing and new sapsuckers learning to drill a straight row of holes. So many times she's come home. So many times she's left again.

How does it feel to come home? Some ways, it feels like danger, when every part of you is on alert—probing with your nose like a deer, inhaling warily to catch every change, listening as an act of will, willing your shoulders to remember the pressure of your oldest son's hug, willing your eyes to remember the vision of your young son's head, rumpled like a raven with its back to the wind. You have to force yourself to remember everything, knowing you will need to go over those details in your mind again and again. It feels like trying to memorize all the license plates in case you have to tell the police, and the details of every person's weight and height. You have to prepare for it all to be gone.

PAN PAN. *Pan pan. Pan pan. This is Coast Guard sector five, Ketchikan. Coast Guard sector five, Ketchikan. Time is zero zero three one. Zero zero three one. We have a report that a Lund skiff with a red stripe has been sighted. The skiff is capsized and drifting two miles north northeast of Green Point. Zero two persons are missing and unaccounted for. All vessels in the area are asked to keep a close lookout and render assistance if possible. Anyone having information about the persons aboard this vessel is asked to contact the Coast Guard, sixteen alpha. Out.*

ZERO ZERO THREE ONE. Thirty-one minutes past midnight. As Annie Klawon dozed on the ferry and her son slept in Meredith's arms, a wave surged onto the beach at the mouth of the Kis'utch River. It pushed a line of gravel, then rolled it down again, a great rush of stone on stone. Another wave spilled up the shingle, and this time, a tongue of saltwater crossed the bar. The mix of saltwater and fresh, that sizzle, that sudden shimmer, flooded to the knees of a great blue heron. He lifted one foot, then another, leaving splayed footprints in the mud. He eyed the star-gleam that lit the flanks of minnows. When the stars disappeared behind a squall, the minnows were lost to him. He stretched, lifting his wings. Tide rose around the heron's thin legs, curling into small whirlpools. The heron crouched, sprang, squawked, and scraped the air with his wings.

The high water probed into the roots of the sedges, flowing along voles' beaten-down paths, spreading through soft-bottomed saltmarsh. Black and slick, the water slid around the bend, past a bank topped with horsetails broken under the weight of bears. Geese, settled for the night on Jimmy Pete's weir, startled at the sound of water stealing up through the stones—a whisper, a click. Muttering, the geese pushed to their feet, paced the weir, shook rain off their tails. But the water continued to rise. A goose stalked to the pond and shoved off. Water poured over the weir. With great honking, the flock plowed into the air and dropped into the pool.

This was the flood-tide of the pink-salmon moon. Under the water, the rock yearned upward, as the sun and the moon pulled with their combined weight, and the Earth turned heavily on its axis. Every rock, every pebble, the heavy shoulders of bedrock lifted toward pale light that was just now flowing from the back of the squall. In each granite pore and crack between rocks, water rose. In each cavern, soft water rose. Rock and water, the whole mountain lifted its shoulders into the night. Rock creaked against stone slab, squeezing water upward; water deep inside the mountain lifted toward the distant moon. Stars poured blue light into crevasses in the snowfields and tugged on the ice, spilling water from pools on its pocked slick. Over the lip of the waterfall, meltwater dropped in vertical currents straight toward the heart of the Earth. Falling water caught the light of the stars and carried it, blue and bursting, to the bottom of the pool. There it rebounded, flying apart, spraying starlight on liverwort and maidenhair ferns. The night sounded the groan of the stiff Earth shifting, ancient stone against ancient bone.

Forest duff shifted and the trees themselves lifted heavily toward the starlight. An ancient Sitka spruce, in four hundred years grown heavy-bodied and twisted as a dragon, gradually released its grip on the soil. Its roots clawed for a long moment at the dirt, its branches convulsed, and it toppled into the river. Where it arced down, a cloud of golden needles floated in the night, a mist of starlit needles where the spruce branches had been. The first branches hit the water, flinging up fins of spray, a crackle like water on fire. Then, the top of the tree crashed into the far bank. The tree split its length, and its belly sank into the stream. Water piled against its body, then slid across, turning the rough trunk to beaten silver. Needles drifted down, swirled away. Underwater, blue bubbles traced current lines over and under the broken tree. Water drummed through branches, beating a dull rhythm onto the deeper grumble of the lifting Earth.

As moon and sun rode slowly through that moment, the Earth belled below the deep thrumming spruce, the squealing rock, the clatter of pebbles in water that fell down the flank of the moon-borne mountain. Salmon slid upstream.

≈≈≈

PAN PAN. Pan pan. Pan pan. This is Coast Guard sector five, Ketchikan. Coast Guard sector five, Ketchikan. Time is zero one three five. Zero one three five. We have a report that the vessel *Annie K* has a skiff under tow and is proceeding to Good River Harbor. Zero two persons are missing and unaccounted for. All vessels in the area are asked to keep a close lookout and render assistance. If anyone has information about the persons aboard this vessel, please contact the Coast Guard, sixteen alpha. Out.

≈≈≈

DAVY SWAM UP through dreams about bees, swam through bees scattered like points of light, but it was a single bee that chased him, buzzing with relentless fury. "Get away!" Davy sat up and then slumped back against Meredith as his shoulder shouted out and reality circled around him, more threatening than any bee. Shadows still filled the shelf under the wharf, but morning glare on the strand threw wavering light into the timbers. The tide had slipped out from under the wharf as the night slipped away, leaving a broad expanse of sand pocked with sea anemones, closed tight. There was no watery sound now, just the soft chirp of feeding nestlings and a buzz as insistent as bees.

"It's a skiff," Meredith said. "They've been coming past all night with spotlights. And look." She pointed at the beach. People were walking up and down the tideline, veering off to peer behind rocks and poke into piles of kelp, checking all the places a young body might have washed up in the night. One man was searching the fringe of alders where a bedraggled teenager might have stumbled, coughing and hypothermic, and fallen on his face.

"This is weird," she said softly. "I've heard that when you die, you leave your body and float up, and you can look down and see the sad people as they look at your corpse and take off your nightgown and wash your naked body. You can see your own naked body."

"Jesus Christ," Davy said. "We're not dead." He paused to consider. "Not yet." He considered further. "Let's see your naked body." But it was a lame joke and it wasn't going anywhere, and neither were they. "I think our best bet is to stay here forever. We could sneak down at night and get clams and sea urchins and eat them raw, and drink from the creek." He turned his head to give her a kiss, but it hurt like hell and he gave it up.

"Davy, look." Meredith whispered. She was pointing to a skiff. A man stood in the stern, scanning the sea with binoculars. "It's Dad."

He must have seen something, because he jerked around, revved the engine, and shot forward. Grabbing a boathook, he clambered to the bow and fished the object out of the water. An orange life jacket, dangling straps. He disentangled it from the hook and pressed it to his chest, holding it like a baby, that tight, that close to his body. Then he fell onto the seat, still cradling the life jacket as if he were sheltering it from a storm. The receding tide pulled him away from shore, but he didn't seem to notice, just held on to that jacket. Finally, he reached into his pack, fumbled with his handheld radio, and raised it to his mouth.

"So now everybody in the Harbor knows that when we went over, we didn't have life jackets on," Meredith breathed.

"Meredith, we didn't go over," Davy insisted, but even he was beginning to imagine a rogue wave, a boat unbalanced by two entangled teenagers, a tragedy, oh God, both of them drowned—two of only three teenagers in the town, fifteen years old and drowned in each other's arms, and only dumb Curtis left to inherit the school. "We are not dead." He glanced toward Axel's boat for reassurance, but found only a man slumped over an empty life jacket, alone in a skiff slipping out to sea.

Meredith looked at Davy. "Do you think you can climb down?" She zipped up her sweatshirt and reached for Davy's clothes.

Together, they managed to get one arm in his shirt, but that was the extent of it. They quit trying and just tied his shirt around his chest, pinning his bad arm to his ribs. Cold, stiff, torn by barnacles, with a dull ache in his shoulder and zinging pain whenever he moved—dragging on wet jeans was simply impossible, although they tried time and again in a space too cramped to stand. Finally, Meredith was able to work his socks over his feet and pull on his boots. "Guess you're going to walk home in your boots and underwear, Davy McIver," Meredith said, and for the first time that morning, began to giggle. But for Davy, giggling just plain hurt, and who could laugh who knew he would soon be dragging into town with his jeans wrapped around his butt like a loincloth?

"Going down is going to be easier than up," Meredith said. "I'll be under you, in case you slip." The barnacle scrapes on Davy's chest screamed as he slid over the edge, reaching with his feet for the beam. But what he was thinking was how ridiculous his legs must look from below, skinny white legs stuck in XtraTuf boots, dangling and groping around like an amputated octopus. Davy and Meredith were no more than halfway down the struts when they heard a shout. By the time they stood on the sand under the wharf, people were splashing toward them, yelling into radios, and by the time Davy and Meredith reached the shore, the church bell had begun to ring. The glad bronze song rolled down the sun-glazed beach, rebounded from the rocks, and filled the beach like light.

That's how they walked to town, through the light and church bells, holding hands, moving slowly because Davy's shoulder hurt and they had to stop often to tighten the knot that kept his jeans around his hips.

"WHERE ARE YOUR goddamn pants?"

Axel stood at the top of the ramp to the boardwalk.

"Leave him alone, Dad. He's hurt."

"He's going to be hurt before I get done with him. Meredith, get over here. As for you, McIver, if I ever see you with my daughter again, I'll kill you, you damned half-breed. Your father is fired fired fired and will never get a job in this town again. Meredith, get home and get a shower—wash off that kid's filth. Get out of my sight."

Meredith stared at her father. Then she straightened her shoulders, took Davy's face in her hands, and planted a kiss on his gaping mouth.

July 16

HIGH TIDE		LOW TIDE	
4:26am	17.7ft	10:42am	2.4ft
5:13pm	17.5ft	11:16pm	0.3ft

All the parts of Tick's outboard motor sat on a tarp on the front porch, stinking of WD-40. Annie Klawon didn't know how Tick thought he could get it going again after Davy sank it. Half the night soaking up saltwater, half the night under tow, it was already starting to rust. Tick was on his knees and elbows, with his face almost to the floor, crawling from bolt to spring, reducing everything to even smaller parts, rinsing them in fresh water, drying them, spraying them, blowing on them as if he could breathe life back into a sparkplug hole. He pulled the flywheel out of the bucket of fresh water, turned it in his big hands, and sat back on his heels. Here Annie was, not even a week back home, and if there was anything left that hadn't already fallen apart, Tick was busy dismantling it.

"It would have been a good job, building the Bear Shelter for Axel," he said. "The kind of thing I'm good at. It would have been all we needed."

She was so tired of hearing him say that. How many times before he gave it up?

"It would have been a good job," Annie Klawon said.

He didn't look at her or make any answer.

"It would have been a great job. But you're fired. It's not fair. It's not your fault. But that's how it is." She was tired of saying that too.

"Don't go back to Seattle, Annie Klawon. Stay home. We can put enough pieces together to keep going."

She used to be so proud of him, how smart he was about working with the pieces. He could do anything, and he would do anything for her. If the back fell off a chair? Why then, the chair was a stool. And if a leg fell off the stool, why, drill a hole in one end for a wrist loop and you've got yourself a fish-whacker. Cut off the other legs, sand smooth the finish on the seat and—hey—a breadboard! Annie has kneaded a lot of bread on the place smoothed by the seat of her pants. And then all those extra chair legs! Three of them! This unexpected wealth! Pile them with the broken-down bike pump and the cracked tote on the front porch.

A mason jar will hold canned salmon until its lip chips. Then sand down the chip and it's a drinking glass, up there on the shelf with the jelly jars and the beer stein that was a coffee mug until the handle broke off.

"Put enough pieces together? Put enough pieces together. See how you are? When will we have more than pieces?" She kept her voice low, so the boys couldn't hear. "There is so much broken in this family. For you people, broken is the best thing about life, a chance to make something new. You people can't wait for something to fall apart or wash up on the beach. Can't wait for the month to go by, so you can cut the picture of a collie off of March and tape it to the wall, where it will hang for . . . How long has that picture been there? Thirteen years?"

"You people?"

Annie Klawon turned and stumbled into the kitchen. Davy and Tommy looked up from the table. These *are* my people, she thought. This is my family, my home—all I have in the world, all I love. If I don't have them, I don't have anything. She sat down at the table to keep from falling, so afraid she could hardly breathe. Is this how families fall apart? Not that you don't have the pieces, but that you don't have the strength to hold them together anymore?

Is this the unhappiness her father knew would come to her? Not the sucking force of the dark sea, drawing her husband down and down, but the smashing force of the brilliant surf, knocking her family to its knees again and again, finally lifting it, dropping it, and shattering it on the rocks.

Tick came in, washed his hands, swiped at a towel, and sat down. She sat on the floor between his legs and rested her head on his knee. It was a rough brown Carhartt knee, stained with oil and fish. His hand was on her hair, heavy as a dead thing. For a long time, while the oven ticked and logs clunked apart in the woodstove, they sat there like that, not talking. Annie felt desperate to say something. The ferry back to Seattle would leave day after tomorrow, and they couldn't afford to waste any of this time together—they had so little. But what was there to say? They had done the math—how much she can earn, how much the family needs. Davy can sell a few hides to Kenny. Tick can keep them in salmon and venison. But now there was probably a new outboard motor. It had cost them almost seven hundred dollars to charter a seaplane to Ketchikan and get Davy's collarbone seen to. Where were they going to get seven hundred dollars, if she didn't go back to work?

There was no other way. She would be back in Seattle, and her boys would be here in Good River Harbor, and it would be only the light from the moon or the smell of the sea or remembered sadness that kept them together. She leaned back against Tick, feeling the bulk of her husband, looking up to find his eyes on her. He watched her like a dog watches a master who is putting on his coat, with that kind of cringing and hope. Annie couldn't see Davy's eyes under his hair, his head was bent so low. His shirt hung loosely over his bad arm, still taped tight to his ribs. Tommy was watching his mother with expectation in his eyes, as if he knew a surprise.

"Is it time to show her, Dad?" Tommy asked.

Tick nodded.

Tommy lifted a cardboard box from the closet floor and set it on the table.

"Open it," he demanded.

Annie Klawon tugged open the flaps. One at a time, she pulled out seven little birdhouses, no bigger than apples. Each one was different, each one made of what Tommy had found in the forest. One had walls of alder bark and a tiny roof shingled with bracts from a spruce cone. Another had cedar walls and a shredded cedar roof. One had a tiny post where an imagined wren could sit. There was one made of hemlock cones, glued together. She held each one, each little home her son had glued together from whatever he could find.

"They're Christmas tree decorations. I'm going to sell them," Tommy said. "I'll set up a little tree at the top of the docks. I'm going to make a lot of money, so you can stay home."

"Dear God." So this was going to be the glue that held the family together, a six-year-old kid, standing alone on the dock in damp jeans and a red sweater, black hair sticking out in tufts, holding a tiny birdhouse.

Who could refuse him money? Even pitiful is a commodity. Heck, Annie thought, let's sell that. Fighting back tears, she turned on Tick, but he was excited too, cupping a tiny house in his hand. If he were to close that hand, he could crush the little house back into pine bracts and kindling. But he didn't. He never would. He held his hand out so Annie could see all the shingles and shutters on the house. It was a big hand with a heavy, calloused palm, and the finger that reached over to touch the tiny stovepipe was gentle and hard as wood.

She turned away and crossed to the oven to check the salmon. Reaching into the heat, she pressed a finger into its flesh. Fish is perfectly cooked when it resists the pressure of your finger, exactly like the fin of skin between your thumb and forefinger when you make a fist.

PART TWO
DOG-SALMON TIDE

From the farthest reaches of the North Pacific, from cold Kamchatkan and Korean waters, the dog salmon find their ways to the mouth of the hemlock-shaded stream where they were hatched. They have grown thick as logs and fat, mottled like the sea-light and alder leaves on the bottom of the stream.

A female sweeps the silt off the gravel while a male swims alongside her. His jaw is elongated, his teeth sharp and protruding. Side by side, they fin and shiver. Already they are dying. Where the skin is torn, gray mold spreads. Their fins tatter. Sometime in the soft night, their bodies shudder and squirt—a stream of eggs, a cloud of milky sperm.

The high tide lifts their old bodies into the grasses where they lie every which way, dying and stinking, shimmering from the motion of maggots eating under their skin. Gulls come first, sinking their beaks into the eyes and anuses. Bears come. Eagles come, mink, river otters. Dead fish sink to the bottom of the creek, swaying in the tide as if they were swimming. But what they are doing is disappearing, the way all bodies disappear, eaten away from underneath by worms. In a few weeks, only a hooded jaw will remain on the gravel, or a spinal disk attached to ribs soaring like the wings of a gull.

August 10

HIGH TIDE		LOW TIDE	
0:58am	19.0ft	7:25am	-3.6ft
1:53pm	17.4ft	7:43pm	-0.3ft

Kenny shifted his back. If he slumped in his wheelchair at just the right angle, he could keep rain from spilling off his hat brim down his nose and into his beard braids. Three more hours until morning? He didn't know, didn't want to soak his arm to the elbow by checking his watch. Nothing worse than wet sleeves. Too dark anyway, no sign of light. Noise could make a man deaf, rain pounding on his poncho's hood, smacking on every leaf. Rainstorm had roared in like a floatplane landing. Rain in a dump is the worst, clanging on torn-up tin, ringing broken glass. Bad luck that it would be pouring rain, but what else did he expect? There is nothing to be done, he had told Nora. There is nothing I can do to stop Axel from getting his bear. Nothing will happen but what happens.

So there he was, sitting at the end of the dump road, at the edge of the dump. In dead dark. In driving rain. With his wheels sinking deeper and deeper in the mud. Not his favorite kind of place. But he'd patrolled in the dark before. And at least there would be no rats in a place scavenged by pine martens and bears.

Here is the brave hero, stupid and handsome, setting off with a shotgun to win the fair damselfish by . . . By what? By imbedding a slug in a beer can to scare away a bear? Something, anything to keep the bears out of Axel's trap. Goddamn. Nothing worse than a wet rear end.

He could have dealt with water falling down. But this water didn't just fall. Some force angrier than gravity drove it down. Rain came down so hard it slammed right back up again. The big devil's club leaves threw water in his face. Water ran down his neck, collected in a pool on his poncho. Dripped through onto his lap. Sleep might have been nice, but it was a bad idea. Made his head wobble. Then rain spilled off the hood of his poncho onto his face and he woke up dreaming he fell overboard.

Dark? There is nothing darker than night in a rainstorm, unless it is night in a rainstorm when you are expecting a brown bear. Kenny ran his finger along the barrel of the shotgun, hidden under the poncho. He couldn't see the edge of the dump, but he could smell it now and then, even in the slop of forest smells. Nora would ask him exactly how it smelled. So. Rain on cedar stumps and broken skunk cabbage leaves, rotten in duff like old bananas. Cold sweet Sitka spruce. Mint, unaccountably, or maybe it was stink currant, bruised. Generic salty intertidal. But also diesel fuel spilled from waste buckets and fetid garbage and crab shells gone to spoil and the sharp smell of aluminum cans against the dirt. The stink of men going bad. Kenny decided to breathe without smelling anything, breathe through his mouth.

He could give up, go home. Assuming he could get unstuck from the mud, he could roll down the dump road, up the ramp to the boardwalk, and onto his pier. Shake out his poncho, hang it by the door. That would be cold then, wind against wet clothes. Hurrying, he would roll into the cabin, his wheels throwing mud. The woodstove would be clanking and cooling. He would throw in some kindling and another couple of splits. There would be dry blankets heaped at the foot of his bed. He would wrap himself in a blanket, maybe two or three, not moving a muscle until the whole bed radiated heat. There are people who pitch and kick until their bed is warm. Kenny was not that kind.

Or he could have gone to Nora's. She would have been warm and sleepy when she heard the knock on the door, stretching under her blankets, the way a baby reaches out her arms, pressing her fists to her cheeks, arching her back and bringing her knees to her chest—but maybe not. Maybe she slept like Snow White, still and pale, with her hands folded on her breast. Or maybe she slept all splay-legged like a frog and when Kenny knocked on her door, she would leap up, blinking and popping. Maybe—surely—she sleeps with Chum, who would try to kill anybody knocking on the door at night. She would stumble to the door, dragged by her dog, the dog barking, her yelling at him, and she would open the door and there would be this man with dribbling chin-braids, dripping wet in a poncho long enough to conceal a shotgun.

Dreams. There was no going home. Kenny had promised Nora he'd make sure no bears got hurt. So it was better to be here, patrolling the dump in the night. That was his job. Hell of a job description.

Kenny raised binoculars through the opening at his neck and surveyed the dump. Army-issue night-vision binoculars—never know when you're going to need to see in the dark. Here was the perimeter of the dump, a circle of enormous trees. Their trunks glowed—that lurid green of night-vision glasses. When he followed the trunks up, there were the scattered green pixels of the forest canopy. Still higher, the sky was lumpy green, like algae at the outflow of the village drain. Shit. Rain down the back of his neck. He lowered the binocs to the dump.

The dump glowed just as green. He could make out bedsprings and the angle of an old green refrigerator, lying on its side. Across a distance of a hundred yards, there was a midden of beer bottles, shattered lumber, linoleum scraps. He focused closely on the bear trap wedged between a stand of alder and a twisted bicycle frame. The bear trap that the government trappers hauled up there was basically a big section of culvert mounted on a boat trailer. There were bars across the back end and a barred gate suspended over the front like the blade of a guillotine. It had been hell to pay, getting it up here. Axel's big-shot trappers brought it in on a USF&W barge, rolled it onto the dock, and then rousted out half the population to drag it up the hill and along the gravel path to the dump. They'd been smart enough to tie the tongue of the trailer onto an ATV. So that supported part of the weight. And they'd put Tick's younger one Tommy in the back, to balance it out. But that was a lot of pounds to pull up a hill. And it was only half the town that helped.

The other half went inside their houses and slammed their doors to rant or sulk or mutter on the radio—who knows. Kenny the Black-Hearted Knight, rolled up to the post office, lowered the American flag, and began calling out ruin, like Cassandra howling at the gates of Troy—a convincing enough portrayal of a madwoman to drive the tourists off the boardwalk and onto the dock.

Didn't matter what people thought, least of all Kenny. Axel had convinced the Feds that dump bears were problem bears that needed to be shut up in the Bear Shelter. So what, that he didn't convince everybody in town, didn't even try. He didn't need them. Didn't need to give a goddamn about what they were thinking. It's lucky the people were shut up in their houses and didn't see the big shots shoot a deer on the beach, cut off a haunch, and haul it up the hill to the trap. Left the deer three-legged on the gravel with ravens eating out its eyes and pecking its ass. The kid Davy was the one who scattered the ravens and dressed the deer. Damn the government trappers, setting the trap and going off to bed. They would probably be back bright and early in the morning, drinking Lillian's coffee in paper cups.

Rain drummed on the ground, pinged on the beer cans, patted on the leaves, sang on the glass. Rattled on the refrigerator. Kenny's chin sank to his chest. His eyes closed. A green bear stirred ice cubes with its great green paw and backhanded them off the ice floes. Radio waves cracked jagged ice calves off the Space Needle, they rattled into green seas, green seas, green seas. He swam hard, but green waves dragged him away from shore. The shadow of the wave. Follow me shall mercy and goodness? surely follow me? All the life of my days.

Not ice.

Glass.

Kenny jerked awake and peered into the darkness over the dump. Something new. Had he heard something new? He glassed the garbage dump. There. A big sow rummaging in the beer bottles. Massive side, humped back and lowered head, and maybe the shadow of a cub. Could that be? Damn the focus on these glasses. Yes, a cub. And maybe another? Nosing behind the refrigerator, a little bear with lighter shoulders. A sow with two cubs. Damnation.

The shape of the sow swayed heavily across the dump in his direction. The sow dropped onto her haunches, then rolled over, crunching glass. On her back, with her legs open like a shameless dog asking to be scratched, she lifted a beer bottle between two paws and put it to her jaws. The cubs hurried over, but she rolled onto her side, lifted her great weight, and made her way across broken glass, slowly, jingling and clanking, to the rim of forest. There she squatted on the moss and leaned her back against a hemlock. Then she was up again, lifting her snout to the air, moaning a warning to the cubs. She rose onto her hind legs, swaying, sniffing.

A dump must be a terrifying place for a bear, a place soaked with the metallic smell of humans. Cautiously now, she dropped down next to a stump. The cubs rustled up against her, nosing for a teat. That's how they stayed for a long time, the mother slouched against the tree, the little cubs snuggled onto her ample stomach, pushing against her legs with their back feet, climbing into her glistening fur and nursing while the rain let up and a silver-edged cloud opened for the moon.

Kenny sat perfectly still. Not frightened. He was far enough across the expanse of busted engines, and that was a timid bear. No, not frightened. Cold. Lonely. Okay, he was lonely. A mother bear quietly suckled her cubs—the universal trust of small babies sucking and humming. Behind a rusted boiler, he watched the bears, a lonely, cursed man with a gun across his knees.

If Axel's plan went off without a hitch, that mother bear and her cubs would be in the trap by morning. The trappers would trundle the loaded trap down the boardwalk to the barge, then off the barge at the newly planked dock and up to the old cistern—that Axel now called the "Bear Shelter."

Shoot. Now. Shoot a refrigerator or any damn thing. He waited and watched.

Kenny had called the Fish and Game guys at Ketchikan, left a profoundly profane message on their answering machine. But the guys called back to say that the dump was *federal* property, and the *federal* guys would decide if any of the *federal* bears were going into the water tank, and they would be grateful for the community's help—on a plan that is a model for using forest resources for economic development of rural communities. They've got grant money invested in this—habitat restoration funds—and they want the project to work. And then a couple of weeks later, here came the trappers in their green and gray jackets with all the badges on the sleeves.

Every now and then, the sow grunted and shifted her position, and then the cubs scrambled their paws against her side and pushed into the curve of her belly. Gradually, the sow slumped to the ground, wiggled her rump into the shelter of the rootball, curled around the cubs, and went to sleep. Rain shone on her hanks and reflected off the puddle on Kenny's lap. Dripping steadily from the trees, water plinked on the plastic lid of a broken five-gallon bucket.

Damn Axel to hell. Is there anything in this world that you can't buy and sell or just plain steal? A mother bear and her babies, for God's sake. But why not, when it seems like you can steal everything else or get the government to give it to you free. Trees. Fish. Water. Silence. Just gone. It is all unbearably gone. He waited and watched the sow bear. So comfortable, with her back against the tree. She slept. In the peace of the bears, Kenny slept.

Keening gulls. Smell of garbage. Yellow line of dawn. Metal clanking against metal. Kenny shouted out and threw up his arms. The trap slammed shut. The sow snarled and smashed her shoulder against the grate. Teeth clanged on metal. She huffed and snapped her jaws, slinging saliva through the bars, then launched herself against the corrugated metal. Gulls swirled over the dump, flapping long wings and screeching. The government trappers rose into view in their fresh uniforms, walking up the gravel road with coffee cups in their hands.

QUIETLY, SO HE didn't wake his boys, Tick rolled his great mass out of bed and shuffled onto the porch to piss over the rail. Yellow glassy water. Great blue herons stalking their own reflections. Orange buoy stranded in green sedges. Lap and flush of Kis'utch Falls across the channel. It was going to be a good day. Over the forest beyond town, ravens were up early, circling and yelling their heads off, but nobody was on the boardwalk at that time of the morning. Annie Klawon would want him to row her over to the huckleberry thicket, Tick thought, before he remembered that his wife was gone back to Seattle again. Damn that Annie Klawon.

He leaned back to zip up his fly. Most mornings, he would see her walking home from berrying with a yogurt bin hanging on a string around her neck and old-man's beard in her hair. Berrying was something Tick did not understand. You go out after a deer and you find one or it finds you and you raise your rifle and you shoot it. So that is that, and your family can eat for two weeks. But huckleberries—you pick one here and you pick one there, then you elbow a bear out of your way and you pick another one. All morning, and you might get enough for two pies that your family will eat in five minutes. Annie said it was peaceful, healing work. Tick said the easiest way to find peace was to put your feet up on a stool by the woodstove. And when it came to healing, he wasn't sick. That made Annie Klawon laugh, which was healing even for a man at the peak of his glory.

Tick went round to the back deck to set his crab pot. Crabs would feed his boys well tonight. He set the heavy crab pot on the deck, coiled the rope and tied the loose end to the railing. Then he went into the kitchen for his supply of old bread. The minute he pulled bread heels from the bottom of a plastic bag, gulls lifted off the water and swarmed in. He dropped a piece of bread onto the water. All the gulls swooped over, a screeching mob of clattering wings and scattered feathers. The first gull there gobbled down the bread and flapped off, trailing a couple of others. The rest of the gulls milled around under the deck, hollering their feeding call, the scream of the greedy and hopeful. Tick picked out the gull he wanted and held out the crab pot so it was right over the gull's head. He let the rope slide through his hand. The net pinned the gull to the water, and the heavy ring sank the pot to the bottom, carrying down the gull neat as a pin. Drowned seagull is the best crab bait there is. People say clams, but seagull out-crabs clams every time.

Tick poured a fresh cup of coffee and walked back to his front porch to wait for his boys to wake up. He'd give them another half hour and then roust them out of bed. He sat on the railing, hooked his heels over the bottom rail, and watched the town across the rim of his coffee cup. Gulls swarmed over the dump up the hill, but the boardwalk was still empty. Then Tick was back on his feet. A gunshot, close. Up the hill. What idiot would be shooting so near to town? He settled himself back on the rail, wondering. He listened closely. Nothing. Not even the lap of the tide. Then, a barrage of shots—one two shots three four. Ravens fled past, slashing the air.

Tick spun into his house, grabbed his rifle, and strode toward the gunfire.

He hadn't taken five steps before Axel's government trappers came running down the boardwalk. When they saw Tick, they dropped to a walk, humping along the boardwalk in their shirt-sleeves, as if they had important business—on most days, a cup of coffee and a shit, Tick figured, but not today. Something more on their minds today. They banged on Axel's door until he pulled it open. When he did, they practically fell inside. What the hell? Axel's at six in the morning?

Soon after, Kenny rolled around the corner with a big bundle in a poncho on his lap. A big kid and a little kid ran along behind him, the big one carrying a shotgun. Damned if they weren't Tick's own kids. What the hell were they doing out of bed? And armed?

Kenny went straight to his cabin, and the kids pushed in behind him. Two seconds later, the boys busted out of the cabin without the gun. Tommy ran up to Tick, with Davy right behind him.

Tick caught Tommy on the fly. "What the hell?"

"I found the baby bear and tried to save her, but they killed her."

Tommy grabbed Tick around the belly and burst out crying. Tick looked over at Davy.

"That's about right," Davy said.

"What the hell? Who killed her? What bear?"

"The government trappers Axel brought in to get a bear for the Bear Shelter. They killed her. A cub with silver shoulders."

Damn. Tick knew that Axel needed a bear for his pit. But not a dead bear. What the hell?

"Davy, you got some explaining."

Davy swallowed hard, his new Adam's apple working up and down.

"Really early. We were in bed, but we could hear the government trappers clanking around the woodstove at Axel's, Tommy and me. They clomped across the porch like they didn't care if they waked up the world. Tommy said we should follow them."

"Follow them," Tick said. "You followed Axel's government trappers."

Davy looked at his father out of the top of his eyes. He'd been acting nervy as a beaten dog, since he sunk Tick's boat. Tommy loosened himself from his father's arms and stood his ground.

"So we did that," Tommy said. "We followed them. We waited till they turned onto the dump road, and then I snuck along behind them, like a tracker. But not Davy. He just walked up the road because it was bendy enough they wouldn't have seen him probably. And so what if they did, Davy said. Can't a guy walk to the dump? Which I guess he can.

"We were almost to the dump. We heard a big bang."

"The door on the bear trap," Davy said. "We started running up to see. Kenny was yelling and motoring around, but he couldn't really get closer, and the men were yelling, and the bear was inside the trap, snarling and smashing into the metal. Gulls flew everywhere, so thick they beat their wings on our heads."

"It was scary," Tommy said. "Davy grabbed me and kept me back, but I could see almost down the bear's throat. She shook the bars with her jaws, and I heard her teeth break against the metal, and her nose was all pressed up, and she drooled long slobbers.

"We heard the man with the beard yell. A cub. A sow and a cub. We got a tuber, Larry."

"Two-fer. Two-fer." Davy corrected him. "Like two for the price of one."

"Yeah." Tommy caught at his breath. "The Larry guy yelled, 'far out,' and they high-fived."

"'Axel's gonna love this.' That's what the bearded guy yelled. God, Dad," Davy said. "They stood there drinking their coffee, slapping each other on the back, pretending to be calm even though they were about to shit."

"Real men, those government trappers," Tick said.

Davy studied his dad's face. "Well, they thought they were. They were all excited. The whole trap was rocking. I was ready to grab Tommy and run if it fell over. The sow was slamming and snarling. The cub had backed up into a corner of the trap. I don't think the trapper dudes knew me and Tommy were there, but Kenny did. He told us 'stay back,' which I already knew. The men were trying to figure out how to get the tongue of the trap attached to an ATV, and I had hold of Tommy, and we were staying back."

"That's good, Davy."

"I'm the one who found the other bear cub," Tommy said. "It was right by me, hiding behind a refrigerator. I found it because it was crying like a kitten. It was a little bear with a big baby head, and it was crying like a kitten. I'm the one found it. I showed Kenny and he saw it and hushed me, but it was too late. The trapper with the beard saw it too."

"What'd he do?" Tick guessed he knew how this story would end.

"He said, 'Ho,' real quiet, and he handed his coffee to the other guy without taking his eyes off the bear.

"'That's a beauty.' He was whispering. 'Look at those silver shoulders. Axel's tourists are going to love that.'"

"He never took his eyes off the cub," Davy said. "Even though the sow was about to tear the trap apart. He snuck around the frig. And then, I couldn't believe it. That trapper jumped for the bear. But he missed and smacked onto the ground. The cub ran up a tree. I told Tommy to shut up—he was laughing and cheering for the bear. The other man ran over, pulling his belt from its loops. I'm thinking, is that asshole going to lasso that cub with a leather belt?"

"Oh shit," Tick said. He turned to Davy. "Watch your language, son. Your mother doesn't want you to cuss."

Davy winced. "The bearded man waved away the lasso guy and ran to the tree. The sow was going nuts. God, the way a bear can roar! The gulls were going nuts too."

"They crapped on everything," Tommy said. "And the sow was crapping too. Crap all over."

"'Okay. We've got her treed. Where's the noose?'"

Tick laughed. Davy could do a pretty good imitation of a stone-ass government trapper, crouching down with pin eyes pointed to the bear.

"The Larry guy got a noose from the side of the trap. It was a long pole with wire in a ring at one end."

"What was Kenny doing?"

"Kenny was a stone wall. He said, 'That's enough. She'll come down when she's hungry. Leave her alone.'"

"'C'mon, baby,' the man said. 'Come to Daddy.' "Come to Daddy!" Davy squeaked again. He might make a pretty good asshole government trapper himself. "The guy reached up with the pole and tried to put the noose around the bear's neck."

"But I got loose from Davy, and I grabbed the back end of the pole and I'm pulling and yelling at him," Tommy said.

"Uh oh," Tick said, wondering what Axel would say about another one of Tick McIver's kids messing with him.

"Yeah. Tommy was wrestling the end of the pole and hollering, 'Leave it alone. It's not your bear!'" Davy laughed out loud. "Leave it alone," he said again in a high voice. "It's not your bear."

"Then! The man yelled, 'GET THE KID.' That scared me. The other man grabbed me and I started to fight him, because he was going to hurt the bear. Davy yelled, 'Let him go,' fiercer than I ever saw him. So the man let me go and Davy grabbed me and pulled me back. I would have fought that man. I would have punched him in the balls."

So now Tommy was talking as big as his old man. Annie was not going to like this.

"That's my boy, Tommy," Tick said. "So then what?"

"The man sneaked around and hiked himself up another tree, where he could reach the bear. Kenny didn't like it. He just bellowed, 'THAT'S ENOUGH. SHE'LL COME DOWN WHEN SHE'S READY.' Like he never heard Kenny, like Kenny never said a word, like Kenny didn't even exist, the man reached out the pole and slid the noose around the bear's neck."

"He pulled the noose."

"The cub jumped off the branch. The man held on to the pole with everything he had, and the cub swung out into space, hanging by its neck. Kenny said, 'Jeezus,' but that's all anybody said.

"Gulls were crying and shitting.

"After a while, the man let go of the pole and the cub fell onto the ground."

"It just thudded onto the ground."

"There were hemlock needles falling down, all yellow, like yellow rain."

Tick didn't say anything, watching his boys.

"I was telling Tommy we should go home. But before I could drag him off, he's scrabbling between the men to get to the bear cub."

Tommy buried his face in Tick's belly. Tick had to lean over to hear him. "The noose cut its neck and scraped the skin away. It made its head go all funny, off to the side. I saw the blood and muscle in its neck, Dad. One paw was twitching, like it was trying to get itself up. I knew it was going to die."

Tommy looked up at Tick.

"Kenny held me by the hand and put his other arm around me. I never knew Kenny could be nice like that. Davy came over and got me. Then, Dad? Kenny pointed his shotgun at the bear's head and pulled the trigger. I never heard a sound like that. One boom. One boom. The bear was dead. I knew that because her paw was still and Davy was crying."

"I wasn't crying."

"Never mind," Tick said. "What did the bastards do then?"

"Well, the bearded man said, 'I'd call that a DLP bear.'"

Defense of life or property. Damn them. They were going to say they killed the bear cub in self-defense.

"'Wouldn't you say so, Larry?'

"'I would certainly and officially say so. We'll need the skull and the hide. You got a knife, Larry?' The guy knew the rules. He knew they'd get away with it. He was all jolly, poking the cub with the toe of his boot.

"But Dad, listen to this. Kenny!

"Kenny said to the men, real low and quiet—'Take off your jackets.'

"They were like, 'WHAT?'

"'Listen here,' one man said. Kenny swung the gun his way and the man backed off."

"'Take off your Fish and Wildlife jackets. You don't deserve to wear them.'

"Kenny was sitting there with the shotgun at his shoulder, so they did, they took off their jackets. Kenny pointed the gun to a place in the dump. They put their coats there, watching Kenny all the time.

"Then Kenny shot their jackets. He shot their jackets, right there in the dump. The sleeves jumped up and down. He shot them again and again."

"Kenny said, real quiet, 'Get out of town.'

"The men walked away, sort of mean, like they wanted to go and they always do what they want. Kenny flicked on his safety and gave the gun to me.

"He took his poncho and spread it on his lap," Davy said. "I helped him roll the cub up like a baby in a blanket. He carried it to town. We followed him all the way home. Kenny will know what to do with a little dead bear."

"I should have got the noose away from the man with the beard. I could have maybe. I could have saved the cub maybe. I could have socked the man in the stomach."

Tick started to laugh, but the laughter got all tangled up in his throat.

"You did the best you could," he said, and roughed up Tommy's hair, as if it needed roughing up. "Sometimes that's enough."

Tick could say that. But the best you can do is never enough. He knew that as well as any man. Your best is never enough, but you do it anyway. Tick put his arms around his boys' shoulders. Davy's were almost as high as his own.

"Maybe I did the best I could," Tommy said. "But it wasn't enough."

They walked down the pier to their front porch.

"Stay here," Tick said to his boys. "And I mean it." He hung his rifle in its place, put a quart of diesel fuel and a lighter in his pack and headed out to the dump. He was going to burn a couple of shot-up government-issue uniforms into nothing but ashes and mud.

≋

"AW, TICK, YOU know there's nothing I can do with this cub," Kenny said, tugging on his braided beardlets. He rolled over to stare at the bear laid out on his kitchen table. "We gotta obey the law. We gotta skin it and send the hide and the paws and the head and all the paperwork to Juneau. Law's the law."

Tick smoothed the silver hair on the cub's shoulders. Ranger sniffed its back paw. Hair rose along his spine and he backed away, throwing a reproachful look at Kenny. Tick reached down to scratch between the dog's ears. It was dark in the cabin, except for stripes of morning light that slotted in where chinking mud had fallen from between the logs. The light threw stripes on Tick and Ranger.

"Har. You two look striped as convicts, standing there all stiff and guilty. Guess the law's already got you. Jean Valjean and his scruffy dog, Stupide." Kenny gaped at Tick and shouted.

"Ce n'est rien de mourir. C'est affreux de ne pas vivre."

Ranger padded across the room, put his chin on Kenny's knee, and whined. Kenny noodled a finger in front of the dog's nose.

"You skin out a cub, it's gonna look just like a toddler kid, shiny white skin and blood on its shoulders. Who's gonna eat that, whole family sits down, dad says who wants to gnaw on the baby's dimpled little leg? Organic, dump-raised baby. And why does everybody think I want to be left with the dead things? You think I'm a vulture on food stamps?"

"You skin it. I'm gonna cook it," Tick said. "I'm gonna cook it up with apricot jam and soy sauce, all pretty in a casserole dish and invite Axel over for dinner. You got a pretty casserole dish you can loan me?"

Kenny snickered. That was a lame joke. But it felt good to have some visitors in his house for once, even if one of them was dead.

"You want coffee?" Kenny said.

"Yeh."

Kenny ran his thumb around the rim of his mug, inspected it for drowned spiders, and poured in the coffee. "Sit down?" he said, but that was a joke too. Not a single chair in his cabin. Didn't need one himself, and nobody visited.

"Sure," Tick said, and propped himself up against the wall.

Tick didn't say anything then, just stood there. Kenny tried not to watch him. He was starting to not like this. He was thinking maybe Tick was looking at him or the squirrel skins tacked to the wall or his Marilyn Monroe poster. But it didn't seem like Tick was focusing on anything. He sort of slid down the wall and sat on the floor with his long legs bent at the knees, bringing the coffee mug up to his chin and looking in it, but not drinking any.

"What's wrong with the coffee? God, this business of visitors is making me nervy." Kenny pulled the coffeepot off the woodstove and looked inside, but there weren't any mice or anything floating in there, just the eggshells. He looked up slowly and met Tick's eyes.

"I know what you're thinking," Kenny said. "You're thinking I didn't save the bears. Went up to keep them out of the trap. Didn't do that. Went up to keep them from getting killed. Didn't do that. What a loser. I didn't want to scare them away, Tick. They were like Raphael's virgin and child, sitting there, and then BAM it's like the pietà, with the dead son sprawled across my lap." Kenny struck the table with his gloved fist. "Even if the bears fell asleep, did I have to? Falling asleep on watch? Lots of men have been shot for that. Shoot me, Tick."

The men were silent, the way men are silent.

"What's Nora going to think about this dead cub, and a sow and a cub in the tank?"

"She's not going to like it."

"Hell no, she's not going to like it. She's not going to like me either. Damn. Just when she was falling crazy in love with me." Kenny sniggered. "Yeah, I know. Bad joke."

Tick put a heavy hand on his friend's shoulder, then opened the door. He let in a yellow trapezoid of light. When Kenny spoke again, he spoke to Tick's bulky silhouette. Then to the suddenly dark room and the worried dog.

"That Nora," Kenny said quietly. "You know what she is? What she is, is wind across a fire. Wind across the fires of every person in this town. Whatever you have smoldering, she fans it. Lust. Anger. Ambition. Fear. Loneliness. Hope. What you think you have damped down, just the smallest spark of it left, what you spent all your life shoveling sand on, the wind picks up, the spark glows, a little flame flickers, looks like it might go out, leaps up, then it's a torch. And the hotter the fire burns, the stronger the wind grows, until the wind is a whirlwind and the fire is out of control.

"Loneliness on fire, that's a terrible, dangerous thing. Hope on fire— God save us from the beautiful smile of that wind. Long time ago, I gave up hoping that I could make a woman love me. These are dangerous times, Ranger. Be careful of fires you think are cold."

August 14

HIGH TIDE		LOW TIDE
4:10am	17.9ft	10:18am -1.8ft
4:40pm	18.3ft	10:51pm -0.9ft

Axel Hagerman, CEO, lay in bed with his eyes squeezed shut. It had been a rough week. For one thing, Kenny was parading around with a new bearskin cap. Axel couldn't stand looking at it, a big patch of bearskin like a tea cozy on Kenny's ugly head. Seemed like it was a living thing, the way the fur ruffled in the wind, glossy and catching the light. Whenever he passed Kenny on the boardwalk, that reflected light darted around Axel and touched him, as if the cap were haunting him. Sometimes it swirled in front of him and stopped him cold.

But that wasn't what was keeping him awake. Too much coffee? Maybe, but no. There was something wrong with the night. Axel shifted carefully on his pillow and looked out the window. Dark clouds scudded along, stained yellow by streetlights. The tide was low, but the sea seemed agitated, the way it shrugged and winced. There was enough wind to rock the day-sailors and jangle their halyards against the masts. No sound from the boardwalk, but Axel's mind would not shut up.

He did not like this night. He knew he should have been feeling good. He was juggling a couple of high-stakes projects, and he hadn't dropped any balls yet. The floating dock and the pavilion at the Bear Shelter were almost built. The replacement carpenter from Ketchikan worked almost as hard as damn Tick would have worked. Things looked real nice in the cistern, all according to the landscape plan Rebecca drew up. Hell, it was a genuine fake forest—well, a very small forest—but it had thimbleberries and fireweed. If he could get the sow and cub in there tomorrow—and there was no reason he couldn't—he could have tourists ringing the cash register in a week.

The water project was on schedule too. Axel grinned in the darkness. Could anyone but the amazing Axel Hagerman have pulled that off? He'd made a good decision to put Howard Fowler on that job. And that whole year of work on financing and permits was paying off. The bulldozers were taking down the alder over at the Kis'utch River, clearing the ground for the trailers that would hold the crew. The temporary landing was almost dredged out, so the barges were already getting in. Over at Jimmy Pete's weir, framing was going up for the dam. Axel expected to have concrete poured before the end of the month, the dam pretty well set up before the September storms.

It gave him a good feeling, the buzz of things getting done, men running around, following orders. When Axel heard a hammer ringing steel, an arc welder snapping, a bulldozer grinding through its gears, he felt okay. He felt good.

So what was so weird about this night?

He raised himself on an elbow again to double-check the dark. He could make out the yellow smudge of floodlights lighting up the construction site across the channel. It calmed him to know the bulldozer was sitting there by the river, with the supervisor's trailer alongside it. But the night was too melodramatic—dark clouds trimmed in gold galloped across the moon, engulfing it in darkness kicked up by the onrushing stampede. Ridiculous. Axel lay down and shut his eyes again.

He didn't like this at all. The trouble was, things were going great, then Kenny had gone and shot one of his bears. It didn't make any sense. Sure, Kenny hated the idea of the Bear Shelter. And yeah, he was a certified lunatic. But Kenny was the kind of guy who never did anything about anything, and here he was, going over the edge, shooting a bear cub just to spite him? It didn't make any sense.

Axel ran the scene again in his mind. His trappers get a sow and a cub in the trap, they find another cub, and Kenny shoots it dead. He had told the trappers they should bust Kenny's butt, but they acted like they were afraid of him. Afraid of Kenny's drooping shoulders? "No, no, let it go. We'll take care of things." They were all squirrelly, packing their duffels, practically shoving each other out of the way to climb on the floatplane. It didn't make any sense. None of it.

And then there was his own family. Meredith and Rebecca—his own daughter and his own wife—treated him like the enemy, when it was Tick's kid that got Meredith trapped by the tide. "You're mean to fire Davy's dad," Meredith had said. She had actually called him mean. To his face.

"Davy's dad didn't do anything wrong," she'd said. "Nobody did anything wrong. You're mean."

"No way I'm going to believe that you hot young kids spent the night watching a damn bluebird squat on an egg," Axel had told her. And there was no way Axel was going to believe that Tick McIver didn't know damn well what his kid was doing, grunting around his daughter.

I'm not mean, Axel said to himself. I'm the only one making any sense at all.

But Axel didn't like the feel of the night, not one bit, clouds moving too fast. Wires in the rigging singing like drowned seamen whistling in the storms. And Rebecca lying there with her back to him, her heart pulsing in her neck while she pretended to be asleep. "Vindictive," she had called him. Was he vindictive? Sounded like something a Roman soldier would be: vindictive.

Axel propped himself on one elbow and looked at Rebecca. She was still the prettiest girl in Good River Harbor—not very big, but pretty as a picture. Twenty years married, and she still had those soft freckled shoulders and slender back. He ran his hand around her neck and nuzzled her hair. Smooth and damp. She nudged his hand away with her shoulder.

"Give me something sweet, Mama Earth," he said. She liked that name sometimes, his beautiful gardener, coming to bed smelling so good. Geraniums, hemlock duff. He sniffed into her hair, and then his dick was aching, pressing against his pajamas.

"Tomato leaves?" he guessed—that warm smell, like hot sun.

"Leave me alone." That's what she said.

"Come on, be nice to me. I've had a hard day."

"Leave me alone." She said it again.

Axel rolled her onto her back. Her hair streamed over the pillow. One shoulder had fallen out of her nightgown. Axel reached down to give himself a little more room in his pajamas. He started in unbuttoning her nightgown. Her hands followed his, buttoning right back up again.

"Come on," he said, real nice, and he started over, unbuttoning those damn little buttons. She buttoned right back up, but the hell with that, Axel thought. Maybe a different week, she could have turned him away, but not this one. He grabbed hold of the nightgown and yanked it open, popping off whatever buttons didn't get with the program. Rebecca pulled her nightgown tight across her breasts, turned her back to Axel, and curled herself into a ball like a damn baby.

Axel kicked off his pajama bottoms. He didn't like it, how hard she made him work to get her nightgown up to her waist.

"Jesus!" Axel jerked away from Rebecca as if she were electrified. He sat straight up. The room filled with a tremendous roar. "What the hell?" The bellow came from the water. It echoed off the mountain, bellowed back. The roar rose to a squeal. From every quarter, the night trumpeted and screeched. The channel boomed with a sound like school buses falling off the dock.

It took Axel a long minute to figure it out.

"Feeding humpbacks," he said. White splashes and mighty snouts rose into the night air as the whales lunged and smacked the water. Holding her nightgown closed, Rebecca crossed to the window. Axel flopped back on the bed and only then realized that his heart was racing. Axel coughed, the only way he knew to settle his heart.

But then the noise was coming from right under the house, a roar like somebody starting up a motorcycle, that kind of loud. The house began to shake with the roaring and farting, the blue-smoke smell, the whole house vibrating as if it were going to fall off its pilings.

"Jesus," he said to Rebecca. She was still standing at the window, clutching her nightgown in both hands.

A windowpane cracked its length. A water glass walked off the nightstand and shattered, and still the world roared. Flat on his back, Axel spread his arms and legs and grabbed hold of the sheets. The noise puttered and then roared again. Do earthquakes make this kind of noise? Landslides? Tsunamis? The moon burst out from behind the clouds and sprayed shards of light into the room.

Meredith rushed through the door. "What is that? What is . . ." She stopped and stared.

Axel stared back at her. Slowly he reached out his hand and drew the sheet over his body. It draped there like a tent fly on a little pole. He cleared his throat. Meredith turned abruptly and fled. She lurched against the doorframe as the house shuddered.

The noise stopped as suddenly as it started. For a long minute, Axel lay sprawled on his back in a dark and a quiet that he did not like at all.

"I'll be back for you," he said to Rebecca. He pulled on his good work pants and went out the door.

MORNING DAWNED CLEAR, with variable winds.

Lillian shook the old coffee grounds into a five-gallon pail behind the bar. She was saving them for Rebecca to feed to her flowers, which in fact did grow like they were hopped up on caffeine. She poured a hillock of ground coffee into a fresh filter and fixed it into the machine. *My lord, what a morning, when the stars begin to fall.* Lillian was moving slowly this morning, trying to be easy on her hip. It had ached in the night, kept her from sleeping, which was not all bad, because she was awake when all the roaring started, and awake when the light flipped on at the Hagermans' house and Axel flew out the door, zipping his pants. Just like the blessed Mother, Lillian kept all these things and pondered them in her heart.

The door banged open and in rolled Kenny, resplendent in his new bearskin cap. Ranger trotted in after him. A cloud of damp air rolled in with them, and the smell of rising tide. Lillian closed her eyes and breathed. There is no better smell than coffee mixed with salt tide.

"Coffee, Lillian. Quick. I'm exhausted." Kenny stretched dramatically, which lifted his poncho like wings. "It's hard for a guy to get much sleep around here these days," he announced, and looked at Lillian sort of sly.

"Noisy night?" she said. She wasn't going to tell him anything. "Pickled egg today?"

"Roger on the egg, and roger on the noisy night." Kenny positively beamed. "Somebody sneaked under Axel's house with a chain saw last night and notched his piling. That's perfect." He spun his wheelchair in a tight circle. "One more cut and that woodsman would have felled the post and dropped the whole damn house into the drink. I bet Axel's ready to shit." Kenny hooked an arm over the back of his wheelchair and sat there grinning.

"Who did it, old woman?" he asked her.

Ah. "That's a reckless question."

Kenny laughed. Or belched. "A lot of people owe him one," he said.

Ah.

"It could wear a person out—gunshots in the morning, chainsaws all night, hammering all day."

He was right about the noise, Lillian knew. Of course, thirty years ago, the town was all noise, lumber and salmon—the highline squealing and diesel engines grinding, tugboats blasting their whistles. But it got real quiet, real quick, after the cannery closed and the workers moved on. Lillian could sit at the top of the ferry dock and all she would hear was a dog barking maybe, or somebody dropping a hammer on a deck, and ravens sometimes. For years, it was so quiet she could hear the river falling down the mountain across the way, day and night, rustling like that. People didn't say much to each other. Then Kenny rolled into town all grim and silent, hardly even talking to his dog.

But Axel had everything humming and clanking again. When Lillian looked across the channel, she saw bulldozers pushing up the landing on the Kis'utch flats. When she turned toward the southeast, there were hammers clonking that big cistern, men getting ready for the grand opening of the Bear shelter. Turned toward the northwest for some peace, and darned if Nora wasn't practicing the piano on her front porch—a buzz from the forest, like flies at the window.

"Yeah, it's a riot in Whoville," she said. "Nora especially, *dink, dink, dink*. You'd think, she hauled that piano all the way here, she'd know how to play it."

"Har," Kenny laughed again. The man was Merry Sunshine this morning, propping his Davy Crockett cap back on his head.

"Can't learn to play unless you play," he said. "It's like baby thrushes in the spring. Can't sing worth crap. Can't get the twist at the end of the song. So what do they do? They sing their pitiful songs until they learn. So it's pitiful. So we listen."

"'Für Elise,' a thousand times a day? The worse thing is, the parts she can't play, she plays over and over."

"That's the idea."

Lillian looked at Kenny with her head bent to the side. What demon has taken possession of this man's body? Kenny danced his wheelchair around the table to the window.

"Whoever notched Axel's pilings sure perked you up. And since when do you go on about baby thrushes in the spring?" Lillian frowned at him.

"You are very pretty when you glower," Kenny said. Lillian smoothed the front of her dress and adjusted her face. She did not want glower wrinkles.

"But hark! Here comes the lovely thrush herself." Kenny rolled himself closer to the door and pulled it open.

Nora had chopsticks in her hair, holding it all up in a knot. Her hair was so black it had turned coppery blue in that light, Lillian noticed. You never know, with hair that iridescent, what color it will throw back at you. Nora's arms were longer than the sleeves of her jacket, and when she walked into the bar, she threw her legs out in front of her, more like a heron than a thrush. Lillian thought she should talk to her about that, tell her how to walk like a lady.

Nora reached an arm around Lillian and drew her to her shoulder until Lillian's spine creaked. Lillian shrugged away. "Save that kind of hug for a funeral," she said. In this town, she thought, there was altogether too much hugging.

Nora dropped her arms and plopped into a chair beside Kenny. Chum nudged in between them and Ranger came over to squeeze in too. Kenny leaned over to scratch the dogs, although Lillian suspected it was Nora's knee he'd rather be scratching. You can't be in the bath and bar business as long as she's been without learning how to read people.

Nora reached over and tugged at Kenny's little beards. "Good work, whoever notched Axel's piling."

"Ho now, be cool, old Nora. I'm not saying Tick notched the piling under Axel's house. I'm not saying he didn't. I'm not saying I know who did it. Not saying I don't. But if I did do it, I'd be proud. And if *you* did it, you should be proud. Dangerous business, though. Nobody better say anything, because Axel will have the cops in here on the next flight, haul the suspect onto the backhaul in handcuffs. Willful destruction of property, reckless endangerment."

Nora spit out her breath. "Doesn't matter that he practically dropped a tree on my piano? Is that reckless? Is that endangerment? If that wasn't willful, then *nobody* has a will and we're all just flapping around, responding to the pain, like gaffed halibut. How come Tick and Axel can both do the same thing—notch a pole—and Tick's a criminal and Axel's not? I'm sick of this—all my life . . ."

She stopped herself.

"Hey, hey," Kenny said into the sudden silence. "I never said Tick notched his piling, and maybe he didn't. Understand? But whoever did, that's a crime. A perfect crime."

Kenny leaned back and laughed, lifting his little beards into the sunlight. "When I passed Axel's cabin and saw all the two-by's he's got nailed up to reinforce that piling, I about bust out laughing."

"Hunh," Nora snorted, but there was no energy in her. Without waiting for Kenny's shoulders to settle, she launched back in.

"Doesn't matter that Rebecca ran away from home last night?"

Lillian's head snapped around. "I don't believe it. Be careful what you say."

"Last night. She pounded on my door in the middle of the night. Barefoot. In her nightgown." Nora grabbed for Lillian's hand, but Lillian shook her loose. "She asked if she could stay with me, Lillian. Said she didn't feel safe with Axel anymore."

"Nothing, not even a dead codfish, is safe with Axel. So what's new?" Kenny did his best imitation of a dead cod, which was pretty good, complete with the cod's little chin-barb and frown.

For a long time, the only sound in Lillian's Bath 'n' Bar was the giggle-chortle of percolating coffee. Nora stared at the floor. With his index fingers, Kenny twirled his little beards. Lillian watched the coffee blurp. Steam filled the space between them.

Nora shook her head, as if she were in fact the cod, trying to throw off a treble hook.

"So, Kenny. I've been looking for you."

"Hey," he said, sort of surprised. "Looking for me?" But then he was back at it. "All that vibrating knock your piano out of tune again? Or did you lose out on some beauty sleep last night? Or have you been sawing logs?" Kenny apparently thought that was pretty funny, har har, but Nora apparently did not. She rocked back and forth with her hands rubbing her thighs. Chum nosed under her knees.

She was looking out across the water. Behind the dredge anchored off the mouth of the Kis'utch, a front loader ground over the flat, shoving broken trees into a pile. A couple of men in hard hats hammered at the plywood forms that would shape the concrete for the dam. There were snapping blue sparks over by the office trailer, and even in town, the smell of burning metal sharpened the air. Behind a thin line of smoke from a slash pile, the Kis'utch Mountains climbed up to the snowfields, and the river tumbled into the industrial site.

"The salmon," Nora said flatly. "And the bears," she said, as if she'd been making a list. She grabbed Kenny's arm.

"That cedar cistern is too small for any bear. It's cruel. Kenny, you can help the bears. You're a hero."

Kenny's eyes went wide.

"I'm not a hero," he said sorrowfully. Then he wobbled his head around and raised his voice to a shout. "I *am only a little soul carrying around a corpse.*"

He grinned expectantly at Nora. "That was Epictetus."

"Quit farting around, Kenny. I'm serious."

"Call in your Zeus, Epictetus," he yelled wildly. "Call in the southeast gale, flip the cottonwood leaves white-side up, throw the eagles into the air, bend the hemlocks, lift the water, and save my sorry soul from the serious lady."

Nora went on as if he hadn't said a word.

"I've been thinking about when Axel's men bring the trap down to the bear tank, line the doors up, and open the gate on the trap, what that'll be like for the mother bear, Kenny, thinking she's free, galloping out into the open, running smack into the far wall, what that'll be like when she figures out she's only traded a little trap for a bigger one. How will she figure it out? What'll it feel like when she does?"

Lillian looked over to Kenny for his smart-aleck answer, and it seemed for a while that he was trying to think of one. He grinned, but his mouth was working like he couldn't shape words.

Nora prompted him gently. "What will that feel like, trapped in that moldy pit?"

Kenny's grin faded. He jerked his arm away from Nora's hand, swiveled his chair, and backed away from her. Something terrible had come over him. Pushing with his arms, he crouched his back to get his weight over his bent legs and finally stood, crooked and off-angled under his poncho.

He stared at Nora. "It's evil to put a living thing in a cage," he whispered. "It destroys them."

"Yes," she said quietly. "I can imagine."

"No," he said flatly. "You can't."

Kenny closed his eyes as if the light hurt him. His legs began to tremble. He groped behind for the arms of his wheelchair. Nora moved quickly to help him, but Ranger jumped to his feet and barked sharply. Growling deep in his throat, he held Nora at bay until Kenny was able to lower himself into his chair and wheel away from her. Together, the man and his dog passed through the door into the bright light.

Lillian rested her back against the doorjamb and watched Kenny pump his arms to turn the wheels, his head bowed over. Ranger trotted along beside him, casting a few dark glances over his shoulder. When they reached the cabin, Kenny tugged the door open and pushed himself in. Ranger followed. The door shuddered against the frame as Kenny pulled it closed.

KENNY BACKED HIS chair against his door and sat with his eyes closed.

A hero.

No hero wants to be a hero.

He spat on the floor. All I know is a hero is afraid of the sound of rain, *tick tick* like rats scrabbling against tin. It's only rain coming. It's rain. Or claws on soft wood and teeth in a jaw narrow as needle-nose pliers, scraping teeth on bone. Day and night, the snapping and tapping. A hero is afraid of the dark too, because that's when sleep sneaks up and throws a hood over his head and forces mud into his mouth, stinking mud and stinging ants. And when his mind is thick and dark, defenseless, that's when sleep sends the child soldiers and long-dead grandmothers and cold fingers that walk across his neck and pinch and pinch. A hero wakes up screaming, with rats chewing his nipples. A hero squeezes rats with his bare hands until blood squirts out their noses. How many rats, marching through the dark, a fucking phalanx, falling back, ticking claws. Better awake in the dark than asleep. Better anything than asleep. A hero sleeps in mud and his dreams are pathetic. He is a little boy left out in a schoolyard when all the other children have gone in to their books and the doors are closed and locked and it is getting dark and no one hears him pounding on the door. A hero wakes up crying and wonders if he is dead.

"Ah, Ranger," Kenny sighed, nudging the dog with his foot. "Bark if I'm dead."

Ranger lifted his chin and barked sharply.

"Wrong answer," Kenny said, and closed his eyes again.

Ranger climbed to his feet and put a paw on Kenny's knee.

A hero makes the stupid, stupid mistake of believing in something. Anything. Love. Loyalty. Terrible mistake.

I don't have strength for all this and you too, Nora. I'm doing the best I can. Stay away from me. You don't know. Do you know? You don't know. You've been looking for me? Why? What do you want? And what about you? Why are you so afraid to do anything, Nora? What have you got to lose? Where do you come from, Nora? Why do you come to me?

Ranger whined and wagged his tail.

Kenny let his head fall back against the door. The room was quiet except for the scrabble of a gull on the roof. He heard its ridiculous feet slap the tin. Suddenly, Kenny pulled out his knife and spun across the room. He dug at the mud chinking between two logs until the point snapped off the blade. Then he dug with the broken blade until a section of chinking sprang out and clattered onto the floor. Ash and clinkers and clay. Prying at the edge of the opening, he popped out another piece. When a bar of light gleamed between the logs, he stuck his knife blade into the light and twisted. Soon he had cleared enough of the chinking to let the outside air flow in. He pressed his nose to the opening.

Woodsmoke, mildewed rope, maybe a trail of thyme and yeast, where a woman had walked by.

That's all he believed in. That and nothing more.

He liked being an end-of-the-roader, and wasn't this the end of the road, this broken-down shack at the last stop on the last ferry? He liked the name he'd chosen. He liked his ugly beard. He liked being crazy. Up until Nora came, he'd liked being alone, even though he'd thought a little sex would be a good thing now and then.

He reached one arm across his body to knead the muscles in his shoulder and settled back in his chair. The warmth from the stripe of light crept slowly, slowly up his face. Finally, he took a long breath and blew it out through a crooked grin.

Ranger ventured to let his tail slap back and forth on the floor.

Kenny threw Ranger a sly look.

"If I was going to be a hero, which I am not, as *you* know, Ranger, I would be a hero dog. Rin Tin Tin or somebody. A dog, yeah. Then Nora would ruffle up the hair on the back of my head. And hold my muzzle with both hands and kiss me on the nose. And slap me on my flanks and murmur goofy baby doggie words into my pricked-up ears. I'd rescue any kid for her then, capture any robber."

Ranger gave him a long, long look and flapped his tail experimentally. Kenny's shoulders dropped.

"Are you laughing at me, Ranger?"

Ranger's tail stopped abruptly.

Kenny leaned down to slap him on the butt. "Smart dog. We'll laugh last, Ranger. You and me." The tail started up again.

"But we're not in the hero business. I've learned my lesson. Har. Learned it the old-fashioned way."

Kenny gripped Ranger's lower jaw and looked him in the eye, smiling and fumbling his beards while he found the words. He nodded: Aeschylus. *He who learns must suffer. And even in our sleep, pain that cannot forget falls drop by drop upon the heart, and in our own despair, against our will, comes wisdom to us by the awful grace of God.*

Har.

He wrenched open his door and howled at the only person he could see, who was Lillian, watering her pansies. His terrible voice echoed over the boardwalk and into the dark spaces underneath. "*In our own despair, against our will, comes wisdom to us by the awful grace of God.*"

Lillian looked his way, smiled, and gave him a weary thumbs-up.

August 21

HIGH TIDE		LOW TIDE	
11:58am	13.1ft	5:21am	1.7ft
11:36pm	15.0ft	5:35pm	4.5ft

There's nothing a man does that lasts. Lillian knew this, if anybody did. A man makes his plans, plots it all out, builds his big buildings, thinks he's changed the world. But a few years go by and everything on his blueprints is decaying in a skunk-cabbage swale. Roofs cave in. Floods undermine the pilings. Down it goes. Alders grow over it, erasing every trace. Nothing lasts. When you have a choice between betting on a man and betting on an alder, always put your money on the tree. Only good thing about the human race is that nothing it does outlasts the alders.

This was Lillian's time for thinking, when the last paying customer had swayed out the door and pissed into the sea, and lapping water was the only sound to be heard in Good River Harbor. Lillian poured herself a glass of whiskey—not too much, not too little, not too expensive, but not the rotgut that Tick drinks. After she'd circumnavigated the room, snapping off lights, she waded through yellow rectangles thrown across the floor by streetlights on the boardwalk. Yellow beads glowed on the windows, gathered themselves into runnels, and rivered down the windowpane. She dug one shoe off with the other, sank into a chair and, grunting, lifted her feet onto the windowsill. Her ankles were swollen and her feet bulged around the shape of her shoes, the way a ball of dough only gradually releases the shape of the baker's fist. Lillian leaned over to knead the sorest of two sore knees.

A long day and a long night with a crowded bar and everybody giggling like kids about Axel's notched piling. Lillian sighed and raised the glass to her lips. Her lipstick left a kiss on the edge. She leaned forward, trying to see through the window, but all she could see was herself. It always surprised her, the fat old lady who peered at her from windows and mirrors, the soft round chin, as layered as a croissant, and the cheeks that drooped below her jawline. The old lady's eyes were bright blue, yes, but they floated in watery pink seas. The whole face was yellow-tinged and speckled, but that was surely the treachery of the window's reflection. Which is real—how you see yourself or how the vengeful mirror reveals you? She rubbed her chin, which more than one man had described as cute. It made her teeth feel tired and uprooted to think about that. Made her whole jaw ache. She washed the whiskey experimentally around her mouth.

One thing she knew, if you're a man getting old, don't look at an old salmon, growing that monstrosity of a jaw, teeth so big and jutted out he can't get his mouth shut. And if you're a woman getting old, for god's sake don't look at a salmon hen. Because there it is, the old thing dribbling red eggs even while her flesh is molding off her back, scratching dirt to make a redd, fraying her tail to a bloody stub. And the male squirting and leaving. Squirting and leaving—that's guaranteed.

Lillian stared across the dark channel to Axel's construction site. The yard lights illuminated the bottom of the rainsquall that was sliding down the mountain. As the storm descended, the lights over the equipment yard disappeared first. Then the lights in the office trailer dimmed out. A red pickup truck under a security light faded to pink and vanished.

Oh, there's a lesson in that for somebody like Nora, so upset about the dam and water project. Everything a man makes starts falling apart as soon as he pounds the last nail. That's the difference between Father Time and Mother Nature: He knocks things down, She grows things up. Lillian shook her head. Nora needs to know that Axel's not the first one to build on the tideflat at the base of the Kis'utch River, and he won't be the last. Used to be a whole town there. Lillian herself used to own a business in that town. Gone. Everything gone. She would tell Nora about that. Nora needed to know that. Put her mind at ease, settle her down.

Lillian sipped the whiskey in the dark and listened to the rain hit the window and gargle in the downspout.

"Sing for me, Lilly," the men would say. "Sing me a beautiful song. Do I have to get down on my knees?"

They did then. The men walked on their knees with their hands praying as if she were an angel, across the parlor to the base of the stairs where she waited for them. Men walked on their knees. "A song, then," she would say, curling her hand over a man's hair, stroking under his chin. She sang for them.

"*Summertime*."

The first words quieted them, the rough men. Even the snuffling dogs jerked to attention, sat back on their haunches, and stared. She sang slowly, as if this were the first time she had tasted the honey of the words. She sang with her eyes closed and her arms straight at her sides, her hands open and turned to the men. They thought she was an angel. She wore a white gown with feathers at the hem and let her hair fall over her shoulders. Golden curls down to her waist.

"*One of these mornings, you're gonna rise up singing. Then you'll spread your wings and you'll take to the sky*."

They cried then, the men. You don't know, when a man pays for a woman, if he wants his mama or his girl or an angel in a white dress.

"*Ain't nothing can harm you, with mama standin' by*."

That was back when timber crews worked the woods around Good River Harbor, yarding spruce logs down to the sea, penning them inside log booms and dragging them with tugboats to the mill. Back when choke setters and sawyers crowded the docks and each day crews moved higher and higher on the mountain. Back then, there was a little town at the mouth of the Kis'utch River, across the channel from Good River. The town fathers of Good River Harbor made Lillian run her business over there across the channel, over with the Indians and the clams and the stills. Her building backed up against the bank of Jimmy Pete's pond—a two-story frame shack propped by two-by-fours onto a ridge of boulders. On slow nights, Jimmy Pete would come and sit by her woodstove, drink her whiskey, and tell her how it used to be, about the Tlingit village and the songs.

I'll tell Nora my story, Lillian decided. I should think about how I might put it into words, what I might tell her. She needs to know. Axel's got the bulldozers over there now, pushing the rocks around, but those rocks have been pushed around before and will be pushed around again, and the trees grew up over the land and it was the bears' land again. That's what I'll tell her first.

The only man Lillian ever loved was John Shaddy. Oh, he had plans. Nineteen years old and he had plans. He was a Wisconsin boy, on his way north. If north was his direction, then north was Lillian's direction too. They hopped from logging camp to logging camp at every river along that wet green coast—Astoria, Aberdeen, Prince Rupert, Hydaburg, Wrangell, Juneau, Hoonah. John set chokers on giant trees. Lillian stood in clouds of horse flies and ground up venison for loggers' sausage. For four years, she cooked in logging camps—mosquito-plagued summer forests, bear-infested autumn forests, sea-rimmed winter forests, one after another.

John was a handsome man with a silky yellow beard and muscles so big in his arms he never could get them down to his side, walked around sort of spread out. At night, they tucked up tight under the blankets and made love and talked about their plan. They would go until they came to a place where two roads crossed and that's where they would stop. They would open a roadside inn with red-checked curtains and a sign held up by a carved bear. John would build the kitchen and the guest cottages, and Lillian would cook and sing for the customers.

In Hoonah, a yellow cedar rolled on John. Everybody knows how it happens. Choker setter on his knees reaches a cable under the log, the log gives way. Lillian's beloved John went whistling off to work with his buddies, and they carried his body home on a stretcher made of saplings and flannel shirts. He's buried there in the little cemetery grown up in alders, around the corner from Hoonah's ferry dock. So much for a man's plans. Lillian got on that ferry and rode from little town to rundown little town, until the end of the line, where she got off. Good River Harbor was the last stop.

Even back then, running her business, Lillian listened to the river. A sawyer's grunts were loud in one ear, but the river was louder in the other—that's a clean sound, water rushing always to another place. When the sawyer lifted his prickly chin, groaned, and called out to God, she imagined she was riding a log along the river, floating into a place with deep shadows and monkeyflowers blooming. By the time the river floated her to sea, the sawyer was pulling on his oily trousers. He flipped his suspenders up with his thumbs and let himself out the door, leaving a twenty-dollar bill on the bed. The next man came, the one who hauled deadheads from the river and sawed them into salty stovewood, the man with splinters in his hands and the smell of sweat and cedar in his beard. The machinist, with red hair between his legs—the one who kept the donkeys oiled and cranking. Then the harbormaster, with cold damp hands.

Lillian didn't know exactly how or when it happened, but just once, she conceived and bore a son. He was a beautiful child with a furze of hair so blond it might have been white. She named the baby John Shaddy, and she gave him away to a man and woman who lived on a seiner. They changed his name to Axel Hagerman, and that was that. That was a secret between her and that man and woman, nobody else, and that was that. That mistake is what it is, she had had to tell herself more than once. Grief is healing, so grieve. But regret is poison. No looking back.

After that, Lillian had walked upstream every morning to a shallow pond ringed with boulders. It was just a little pond, rushes and dragonflies, even in the rain. Sitting naked on a rock, she smeared herself with blue mud from the glacier, then washed it all away—the mud and the smell of the men.

In the summer of 1959, heavy rain fell on the snowfields. There'd been a lot of snow, and the rain melted it fast. Water rose in flood in the muskegs, then broke through the logjams and thundered all at once down the mountain. Lillian heard it coming and ran with the men to high ground. It wasn't the falling force of the water that destroyed everything, but its lift. Back-eddies rose into town and lifted every building—the mercantile, the hotel, the shacks where the loggers lived. The flood smashed into the log yard, rolling logs off the piles, turning them into ramrods that took down the walls. Wrecked everything and washed the wreckage away.

The flood lifted Lillian's shack and carried it downstream, upright and entire. She watched it go. It lodged against a rock, turned, and slowly came apart, boards springing up like herons. She watched it happen, nothing to be done about it. A curl of tar paper peeled off the wall and rolled under a wave. Her mattress rafted downriver. The bedspread swirled away. It was a lovely bedspread—red sateen. In an hour, nothing was left of her life but one of her shoes. She found it in the mud. Shiny patent leather, but the sole was gone.

Townsfolk salvaged the timbers of Lillian's shack, sawed them even and hammered them onto a log flattened by a chain saw. It made a good bridge over the Kis'utch until the next high water took it out.

"And what of you, Lillian?" she asked herself fondly.

"Me?" She downed the last of the whiskey and smiled at her reflection, which smiled back.

"I have spent the rest of my life washing the stains out of men's clothes and drowning men in booze." Her reflection leaned back its head and laughed.

"But I'll tell Nora about the flood. I'll do it tomorrow. That should cheer her up."

THE BEAR BOLTED out of the trap through the door into the cistern, then braced to a stop, swinging her great head and stumbling over her cub, he was that close to her rear legs. She raised her snout, swaying back and forth, then rounded back to the door just as it slammed shut. *Where is the smell of the other cub, the musk of milk and moss?* The slam brought her up short. She rose on her hind legs and stretched to full height, pawed the air and roared.

"Drop that bar across the door and chain it good."

The sow brought her head low, stiffened her front legs to raise her shoulders, and turned the full expanse of her shaggy flank toward the place where the shouts of men thudded into the wooden wall. She huffed and stamped, shaking her head, slinging saliva in long strings. Metal chains rapped metal. Moaning, the bear lunged along the side of the cistern, looking over her shoulder. The cub galloped along behind her.

This way, she extended the distance from the men, but even as she directed her course in a straight line, the wall turned her in, and in, and the farther she ran, the closer she came again to the smell of men and metal. She slowed, circled her cub, nudged him with her nose, then launched her weight against the door. A dull thud, shouts from men.

"She'll kill herself against that wall."

She reversed direction and quickened her pace, but the farther she ran in the curve of the cistern, the closer she came again to the smell of men. She smashed her shoulder into the door, then raised herself on back legs and let out a fearsome roar. Her claws tore against the wood.

"Stay back. Stay back," men shouted.

She turned and galloped back the way she'd come. Each time she ran into the smell of the place the men had been, she stopped so suddenly that her paws skidded in the gravel and dug holes into the dirt. Finally, at the farthest reach from the door, she slowed, gathered her cub under her flank, backed into a rank of transplanted alders, and crouched by the wall.

A hank of deer meat fell on the bear's hips. She lurched and spun around. *The smell of blood, the smell of men and metal.* She leapt from another thud, as a second chunk of meat dropped beside her. She backed from the meat, snarling. The cub sprinted away. *Iron-red blood smell, crushed bones, gun oil, the salty-sour smell of men.*

"She'll eat when she's hungry, I can money-back-guarantee you that."

Backing farther into the alders, into the crackle of branches and flutter of falling leaves, she lay down heavily, her eyes on the group of men leaning over the edge above her. Mewling, the cub followed her in, circled her, nudged at her belly. As the cub took shelter beside her, the sow growled, a long steady unbroken growl, the rasp of rising wind.

Ravens lined the rim of the tank, black against gray sky. They clonked and clattered, flapping strong wings to hop sideways, turning their heads to get a better look at the joints of deer. One raven spread its wings, hopped up, tilted, and dove. Flaring to arrest the dive, he landed with an extra hop next to the joint. He eyed the meat with one eye, then the other, hopped closer, looked in both directions, and stabbed at the meat with his hard beak. The bear watched, her head between her paws. A bald eagle soared overhead, banked sharply, then flew over again, lower this time, clattering. By the time the rain stopped, the birds had stripped the deer joints to clean white bones and only one raven remained, pecking between her toes, mumbling to herself. She flapped away as the men approached on the viewing platform.

"With the cub, we might want to raise the price. What's a cub worth? I mean, in the wild like this?"

"What do you think? Fifteen dollars a person? Twenty?"

"Are we charging by the person or by the hour or by the bear? And is it just the sight of the bears we're selling, or is it the whole scene—bears and eagles and mountains, a package deal?"

Exhausted, the bear slept with her chin in the mud, a wild dark empty sleep. Rain blew in at dusk, coursing off the bear's shoulders. She rolled to her feet and began to walk.

Broken rock, sulfurous mud, beach grass dead and decaying, gravel and gasoline. Sniffing under the door—the salt-air beach, driftwood rimed with shipworms, wave-windrowed kelp, broken clamshells, the body of a storm-drowned murre, hopping with beach fleas. She raked her claws against the door. Then she stalked around, around, around the cistern. *Off gravel onto broken rocks, slick with algae, then dirt and fireweed, back to the place of the bones, still there, shiny in the rain. Mud, fallen beach grass, gravel and gasoline, the place of the men, sea-smell, gravel, broken rocks. Algae-slicked mud, fireweed, bones, mud, beach grass, gravel and gasoline, the place of the men, sea-smell, gravel, broken rocks, mud, the place of the meat, mud, beach grass, gravel and gasoline, the smell of men and tide rising among blue mussels.* She did not find her second cub. There was no smell of her in this place. What *there was: not her smell.*

From time to time, the bear raised herself against the wall, reaching with her front paws, raking deep scratches as she scrabbled for purchase. Along the wall she paced, then lifted to scratch claws on cedar, and sank down and paced some more, and up again. She sniffed the ground. Then suddenly, she began to dig. Dirt and gravel flew past her face. A young alder toppled against her shoulder. Mud spattered the wall as water drained into the hole. Then her claws raked against the wooden floor. *Again no way out. Even under the earth: no way out.* Finally, the bear squatted in the hole, her haunches in mud, her chin resting on her front paws. Sometimes she turned a paw over and licked the bloody torn spaces between the claws, the flakes of wood and embedded stones. But as dark closed in, she sat without moving. Her cub nudged her hard in the flank, and she rolled over to let him drink what he could suck.

Remember. Spruce tips, arnica, cedar stumps crumbling into the place of the balsamroots. High meadow laced with the burrows of mountain voles, tubes of excavated dirt lying where melting snow had laid them.

Remember. Nests *of newborn mice. Fresh deer kills, slippery with ravens and marten. Clear trout-flecked water under banks of moss. Under the highest, oldest spruces, the place of the huckleberries. Two cubs, musky and suckling.* On a small wind, each remembered smell.

BY THE TIME he found the perfect tree, Davy's back was soaked with sweat and his neck itched from all the duff and moss that stuck to it. It had been a steep climb up behind the big old cistern, alders in there, bent over by avalanches, and the spongy stumps of felled spruce, hard enough to climb over with two good arms, really tricky if you don't quite trust the other one yet. And he couldn't trust the carpet of moss that covered the ground under his feet. Wherever a log had rotted out or a bear had undermined a stump, the carpet gave way, sinking him to his knees.

The tree he found was exactly what he needed. It was a western hemlock with limbs like a ladder, maybe the only hemlock left among the alder. He climbed one-handed to a place where nobody could see him, but he could see out between the branches, right down onto the viewing platform over the Bear Shelter. Davy didn't want Axel or anybody to know he was anywhere near the cistern, but man, he wanted to see Meredith. Even just see her. He had it figured she would visit the bears sometime that afternoon, and even if he had to wait half the day, that was okay with Davy.

For the best view, he needed to be just a little higher. He pulled himself to the next branch, and then he had to stop to think this over, because somebody had been in the tree before him. There was a plank set just right across the branches to make a steady seat. The plank hadn't been there long—no hemlock needles dusted it, no cobwebs or spiders, no tiny hemlock cones. It was like a deer stand, but who would hunt for deer right next to the old cannery site, when you can get a deer on Green Point whenever you want? More like somebody wanted to get a free look at the bears in the cistern, cheat Axel out of twenty-four bucks.

Davy hauled himself onto the plank. This would be a great place if you wanted to shoot a picture of the bears. Almost below him and off at a little angle, the sow was sitting in a hole she must have dug. She didn't move, so maybe she was asleep. Her cub was tucked up beside her, sitting in a mud puddle. She'd torn out a whole bunch of fireweed. It must have been a bad scene when they put her in the cistern. But nothing was happening now. Davy leaned against the trunk, settling himself for a long wait.

A carpenter he didn't know was hammering siding onto a kiosk. It made Davy sick, knowing that if he hadn't got Meredith stranded, big Tick would have been the carpenter pounding those nails. Each hand-built detail of the Bear Shelter—the ramps and platforms—flooded him with shame. Davy's dad hadn't driven the screws in the gangway that spanned the distance from the dock to the pavilion. He hadn't pounded in the footers that held the Bear Shelter pavilion onto the rocky shelf beside the cistern, or figured out how to build the observation platform so it wouldn't blow away. Like everything else, the observation platform got built without Davy's dad.

The carpenter crossed the pavilion to get another one-by-four. Somehow it all was happening without big Tick McIver, which made Davy's mouth go dry, at this evidence that the world could go on without Tick McIver, that anything good could happen without his dad. And that his very own screwup had taken his father completely out of this world. He felt like a lonesome murderer sitting in a goddamn tree. He squinted his eyes and tried to summon a picture of Meredith.

Approaching on the trail from town, a small woman in a red sweater climbed the ramp to the Bear Shelter pavilion and paused to look around. Her hair was tied up in a bandana, but Davy knew it was Meredith's mom. Rebecca Hagerman. He would know her from any distance—one, because she was so small, but also because of the way she walked, which was courteously, stepping lightly, nodding her head, as if she were friends with the bushes. She crossed the pavilion to the door in the cistern where they'd loaded in the bears. She stopped there, and maybe she was listening for the bears, but it couldn't have been only that, because she threw a quick look at the carpenter's back and then she moved in close to the bar that was levered across the door and fingered the lock. Finally, she climbed the path to the observation platform and looked over the rim at the bears.

Davy pulled himself out on the limb to see her more clearly. It was odd, the little squeaks she made, like a mew gull. It took him a couple of beats to realize she was crying. Davy had sunk so low, he hadn't thought a guy could feel any worse, but this was worse, all right, a mother crying.

Rebecca Hagerman straightened suddenly and pulled back from the edge. Davy pulled back too, because here came Curtis and a couple of kids he knew, jiving across the pavilion and bounding up the path to the observation deck.

Curtis leaned over the railing and dropped something on the bear. It hit the branch over her head and bounced onto the mud. Probably just luck, Davy figured, that the next thing he dropped bounced off her snout. The bear shook her big head.

"Does anybody have any more pennies?"

Davy ground his teeth. That stupid Curtis.

The bear hauled to her feet, shook her shoulders, huffed, and turned sideways to the voices. She drew her shoulders high, lowered her head, swaying it back and forth. Hair stood up along her neck. A stream of watery crap plopped onto the fallen alder leaves.

"Boy, if I ever came on a bear displaying like that, I'd be shitting my pants too," Davy muttered. "That's a pissed-off bear." Another penny bonked against the wall behind her and she backed away.

"Quit it, you dipshit."

It was Meredith.

She looked beautiful, climbing the path. She had on her gray hooded sweatshirt, open halfway like she does. Her jeans were shiny and stuck tight to her legs. She ignored her mother and leaned over the bears.

"I brought her huckleberries," Meredith said. Her voice was beautiful. And wasn't it just like Meredith, Davy marveled, to think of something nice like that?

"I brought her huckleberries," Curtis whined in a sick-sweet voice, and Davy could have popped him one. But Meredith whacked Curtis in the arm and he laid off. Meredith poured the huckleberries over the edge. Huckleberries bounced off the bear's head and fell in the mud between her paws. The sow moved away. But the cub nosed around in the huckleberries. Then he rolled on them, rubbing his back in the dirt.

"Huckleberries are to eat, you silly bear," Meredith said. She draped her arms over the railing. After a while Curtis and the others got bored and left, but Meredith stayed there, watching the bears. Davy thought she looked sad, the way she stared out, and maybe it was because of the bears. But maybe she missed him. Davy knew she didn't think it was fair that her dad fired his dad, because her mom told his mom so. Her mom had cried and cried about Meredith gone missing. But in the end, she said Davy did the best he could and they weren't drowned and that's what counted. And she said that was just mean to fire Davy's dad—even though it's good, she said, to keep Davy and Meredith apart for a while, to let things simmer down. Davy wondered what that meant, to let things simmer down. Maybe Meredith told her mom that things were pretty hot between them.

Davy cupped his hands to his mouth and gave his secret raven cry. "Gaaaa. Gaaa." Meredith turned around and looked up the mountainside. There were lots of real ravens around, cawing away, so Davy thought he'd better do it again. Meredith looked straight at him then. She ducked her head and waved her hands in front of her face, as if she were brushing away flies.

It might have been a warning. Then Davy was afraid, but he didn't know what of.

He stayed in the tree for a long time. Finally, Axel came and Meredith went home, although Rebecca stayed on, leaning over the bears in her bandana and her flowered skirt. By then it was getting toward dusk, and Davy thought if he didn't get home himself pretty soon, his dad would report him missing again, and then he'd be dead again.

He'd climbed down the tree and was backing down the mountainside through the alders, slipping on the branches, when he heard somebody bushwhacking up toward him. It was probably a person, because a bear would make more noise than that, and a deer wouldn't make so much. He slid down behind a stump. The branches kept cracking in his direction. If it was a person, it was a big person. And it was coming at him. Davy pressed the side of his face into the rotten stump and gathered his arms close to his body. If the person kept coming, this would be no hiding place at all. The footsteps tromped past him and then paused.

"Dad!" Davy said, and stood straight up.

Tick jumped and spun all in one motion, swinging the muzzle of a rifle toward Davy.

"Jeezus, Dad," Davy yelled, and dropped on his face in the duff.

Nothing happened. A jay cried an alarm call and nothing happened.

Davy lifted his head.

There stood Tick with his beard flowing over a camo jacket, his mouth open and his Marlin .444 hanging from his hand.

"What the hell you doing? God, Davy, I could of shot you, popping up from behind a stump like a goddam shooting gallery." Big as he was, Tick was shaking. "Don't you ever, ever, ever surprise a man with a gun. Whoa, if I'da shot you point-blank with a rifle this big, you'd be nothing but red mist." Tick closed his eyes.

"Yeah, but Dad, what are you doing up here with that gun?"

"Thought I'd . . ." Tick was stumped.

"What could you shoot from up here?"

"Thought I'd get us a deer liver for supper," Tick finally said.

"Yeah. Deer liver.

"But that would be a lot of trouble, wouldn't it?"

Tick shook his head again, as if to clear it, and then he had to sit down, right there in the ferns. Davy sat beside him, leaning against his dad.

"I guess let's us two go home and open a can of ravioli," Tick said finally. "That would be a better idea.

"Yeah," Tick said again, almost to himself.

"That would be a better idea."

August 22

HIGH TIDE		LOW TIDE	
		6:07am	0.9ft
12:39pm	13.9ft	6:21pm	3.6ft

Howard Fowler—formerly Howard Fowler, surveyor, but recently promoted to Howard Fowler, director of communications for Good River Products, Inc.—stood at his office window. He still couldn't believe how quickly Axel had promoted him. "I need new blood on my team," Axel had said, and Howard understood how this could be, since Axel had sort of bled out a lot of former employees. "I need a good mind on my team," Axel had said, and Howard could understand that too, being proud of his good mind and his wife always telling him that he was too smart to be just a surveyor. "You have a good rapport with the community, Howard," Axel had said. Now that was hard for Howard to understand, considering that the last time Howard talked much with any of them, he had his pants around his ankles on Lillian's bar. But he did understand that Axel had a public relations problem, and he was happy to help out, happy with the new salary, happy with his office.

This was the first real office he'd ever had, so even though it was just a construction trailer, he kept his computer desk tidy, his business cards squared up, his tie neatly knotted, and his office philodendron looking good. He reached over to pick a dead leaf off the potted plant. Because the trailer sat right there in the construction site at the river, Howard always knew whether the water project was on schedule and who was working hard, who was screwing up, and what was going to need explaining.

Howard glanced out the window each time he heard an outboard motor. Unfortunately, his Time Management Seminar hadn't told him what you do when you've got a meeting scheduled for 8 a.m. and all the people you're supposed to be meeting with are hanging around at the top of a wharf a hundred yards across the water, scratching dogs, shooting the breeze, gazing out to sea—doing everything but checking their watches.

He'd come to the site early, set up the PowerPoint presentation, put on the coffee. Axel was trusting him to do a good job with this meeting, which was a lot of trust in a surveyor who was promoted to communications director only last month. Axel had sent Howard up to Anchorage the week before to take some workshops, hone his people skills, get his confidence all ramped up—because confidence is everything—but he was feeling a little skittish. All the same, he'd learned that *Communications = community + relations*. That was his first PowerPoint slide.

Howard understood that Axel had a lot riding on this. He hadn't objected when the townies demanded a tour of the Kis'utch River construction site. Told Howard, set it up. Don't volunteer more information than you need to, make everybody sign a waiver, in case they trip over a clamshell and sue him. So that was fine—a good chance to get the town lined up behind the project. Howard didn't tell Axel that his own wife was the first one to sign up for the tour, which was just weird. He thought there might be quite a communications issue in that household.

Howard looked across the channel. No progress on that front. He toggled over to email. Twenty-four new messages. He searched for anything from home. If it weren't for Jennifer's emails, he wouldn't last a week in this town.

> **Taylor's playschool is putting on The Three Little Pigs, and she's going to be the middle-sized pig. She's got a little rubber pig nose with an elastic string. She loves it. Won't take it off, even to sleep. She's so cute, you should see her. I'm sewing a curly tail onto her pink pajamas.**

Howard chuckled. He lived on Jennifer's emails, breathed them in. I *can just see* it, he typed, Taylor asleep in her new big-person bed, cheeks all pink, arms thrown out, the little pig nose squashed into the blanket. Howard hoped Jennifer tiptoed in and took the nose off before Taylor suffocated.

> **She's been practicing her line. She's only got one: "Oh no, bad wolf, don't blow my house down."**

Last time Howard talked to his little girl on the phone, he told her he'd seen a real wolf from the floatplane, but Taylor said, "Oh, Daddy, that's just in movies." Whatever. Real or animated—it didn't matter. He would protect his daughter from wolves and winds and anything else that might blow down her house.

He checked out the window. Odd, how on a perfectly clear morning, a strip of fog hovered over the river at shoulder height. One end of the fogbank lifted slowly and floated there, reared up like a sea snake. But here the townspeople came, finally. They were all piled into Tick's workboat, standing in the bow. Howard picked up binoculars. Seven or eight of them, looking cheery enough. Better go down to the landing and help with the boat, he decided, because they do that here, run over to haul around each other's anchors. If they see you in the library, they might not even say hello. But come toward land in a boat, especially if the wind is blowing, they run over to keep your skiff from scraping on the gravel or bumping into a piling. As Howard watched from the beach, Tick lowered his bow and they all walked off like some Committee of Inspections.

First off the bow was Axel's wife, Rebecca, no taller than Howard's armpit. He had met her before. When she smiled to say hello, her cheeks crinkled up into her eye sockets. How she could smile and see at the same time, Howard could not figure. He remembered that her hair was long and brown, but she had it all bound up in a bandana for the tour—not exactly dress-for-success. Her head nodded reflexively, as if everything was yes. He shook Rebecca's hand firmly, covering the handshake with his left hand and looking her square in the place her eyes were buried—the way they taught him in Interpersonal Communication: Five Minutes to a Trusting Relationship.

Nora next. Yellow raincoat, jeans, some sort of tool stuck in her back pocket—socket wrench? But what's she been twisting? That woman made Howard nervous. So friendly and everything—she had her hand over his before he could put his over hers. But she was intense, always looking around, always thinking something, and Howard never could figure out whether she was beautiful or just bizarre. Her face changed fast as the weather. She could flash a smile that would make puddles steam and disappear. Other times, the puddle would shrink into the ground if it knew what was good for it. She looked Howard straight in the eye, just as he was looking her straight in the eye, a game of chicken, and then they both flinched.

"Welcome to corporate headquarters," Howard said, and smiled the rueful little smile he had been practicing, sweeping his hand toward his

Airstream. "Things are just getting going. We threw up that wharf just to get stuff in. Next time you come out, it'll be more impressive."

Couple more people. The postmaster with his arms crossed on his chest. The man and woman who lived on the schooner *Fairwinds*, wearing matching red bowling jackets, for God's sake, with FAIRWINDS stitched across the back. A random kid with black hair. Last one off the boat was Tick McIver, with his orange beard swinging off his face. He slung a long leg over the gunwale. He was carrying the anchor up the beach, which saved Howard the trouble of deciding if he would shake the hand of the man who had humiliated him in the bar—after he'd sprung for Tick's drink.

They all crowded into the office. Howard called up the PowerPoint presentation he'd prepared.

"Been reading email messages from my wife. My daughter's going to be the pig in a play." The personal touch. Howard congratulated himself. "Thanks for coming over. I'd like to share our vision for this project. We at Good River Products are proud of our plans for the future well-being of the community."

No response. Rebecca was nodding at him, *yes, yes*. The rest of them stared out the window. He walked over to close the mini-blinds.

"So if you'll direct your attention to the screen? And you just interrupt me whenever you have a question." He ran the cursor up to start and pressed enter.

"Can we do this outside," Rebecca said. Was that a question or a statement?

"I have prepared a PowerPoint presentation."

"Such a beautiful day."

So much for the PowerPoint.

"Sure thing," he said. Howard remembered to press the sleep button on his laptop to keep from running out the battery and let them go out the door first.

They all crunched over the gravel to the clamflat, stretched out empty and gleaming at low tide.

"The wharf's just a temporary fix. We'll be dredging a channel here and putting in a boat basin for the barges and tankers. We're going to need rocky fill for the dock. The engineers say that if we remove the top-fill from that slope, we'll find readily accessible basalt. This can be quarried at recoverable cost, since the Forest Service has agreed to waive . . ."

Damned if that big guy Tick wasn't crouched down in the sand, digging wildly with his bare hands, scraping away a hole that was filling with water as fast as he dug. The kid was helping him. He straightened up, holding a bulging clam that looked sort of like a yam with a droopy penis sticking out of one end.

"This is a geoduck," Tick said. "It's a clam. Some people call them horseneck clams, but this thing doesn't look like a horse neck to me." He smirked. "Pretty good to eat. And maybe you wonder how a geoduck breathes, under the sand."

Howard nodded stupidly. Damn.

"See, it has this siphon. Looks just like a penis. It pushes that up through the sand. You seen that?"

Howard didn't know. When would he have? "Yes," he lied.

"You can dig geoducks at low tide." Rebecca spoke up, all excited. "Just bring over a skiff with a couple of garden shovels and a couple of kids, and in less than an hour, you can have as many as you can eat. You got to skin that penis thing. Put it in boiling water for forty-five seconds and then the skin will just peel right off. Slice it crossways, pound it good with a mallet, and fry it up. Squeeze in some lemon and throw in some butter and half a clove of garlic and let them sizzle a bit."

Do these men think of nothing but sex and the women only of food? And who would eat such a thing, skinned or not? Howard's mind flashed to the beef Wellington Jennifer made for their anniversaries. A special meal, candlelight, sex.

Focus. Focus on your outcomes, Howard reminded himself.

"The kids will have good jobs over here before the year is out. They'll be too busy raking in the dough to think about digging up clams." That was good. Howard chuckled. Keep it light. Talk about the good of the children, but don't get too personal. He tried not to look at Nora, but whenever he did, she was looking straight back at him.

"Over here." Howard turned and walked them through wet grasses to the weir on the old Indian allotment the company had leased. "This was a coup, by the way, how Axel smooth-talked the Indian bureaucrats on that lease." Almost as brilliant as getting the environmental impact statement done before the salmon came back to the river. Howard chuckled, but before he had taken five steps toward the weir, his pant legs were soaked to the knee. He should have insisted on the PowerPoint.

Carpenters had finished nailing up plywood forms for the concrete pour. "This will be the front wall of the collection pond, built right here across where the river is now. We'll dig to bedrock, then build up about twenty feet above grade, rock and concrete, make a nice sturdy reservoir. The river will fill up to about here." Howard put his hand up under his chin to show the depth, only realizing from their stares that his gesture looked a lot like he was slitting his own throat.

He pulled out a handkerchief. "Excuse me." He blew his nose, because what else was he going to do?

"Pipes will carry the water about three hundred feet to the dock. We'll take the water in tankers to a bottling plant in Japan, ship it back to California to sell. *Glacier Water from Good River Harbor*. Quite a vision."

Howard smiled in the general direction of the townies. But that damn Tick was digging into a bear poop with a stick.

"Blueberries," he said. "Rock crabs. But mostly salmon. This time of year, the bears eat mostly the brains, leave the rest for the gulls." He picked up a gooey bone splinter for everyone to admire.

Howard rushed on with his planned speech. "If you're interested, the Environmental Impact Studies are all on file in the office, including the seismic reports on the quarry, and the restrictions on the covenants for the allotment land." Howard knew he was jabbering, but what was he supposed to do? "You'll find that the papers are all in good order. Axel worked on that for a full year before we even came on site, in close coordination with the congressional delegation."

Rebecca looked up sharply, showing her eyes. "Axel's been working on this for a year?" Rebecca shot a glance at Nora, and Howard was glad he wasn't between them to intercept that one. He'd be collateral damage, that's for sure. He thought of Jennifer, and how much luckier he was than Axel. Rebecca just might be a house on fire.

As if Howard hadn't said a word of any interest whatsoever, Tick kept right on talking about the salmon.

"The seals will eat the stomachs, biting big gashes in their sides. And sometimes, bears will stand here and bite out the salmons' humps while they're swimming upstream."

"The covenants on the allotment land . . ." Howard said, because it was all he could think of to say. Suddenly, Tick was nudging him.

"It's important for you to know what salmon do," Tick said, with a level of sternness Howard had not seen before.

Howard ran a hand over his mouth. What was he doing there, manager of communications, standing in muck, being lectured by the prince of defecation?

"Oh, we'll take care of Mother Earth," Howard said. "This entire area will be a nature reserve. There will be no hunting of bears or deer, no fishing for salmon, no clamming. Total protection. Total. Very enviro. Don't you worry."

Howard beamed his warmest smile toward Rebecca. "Anyway, Mother Earth is a tough old gal."

Rebecca looked away, staring out to sea. "If the Earth were your mother," she said in her sweet little girl voice, "she would grab you in one rocky hand and hold you underwater until you no longer bubbled."

≈≈≈

HOW QUICKLY THAT had gone sour. Howard loosened his tie and leaned back in his new Naugahyde chair. He knew there was nothing Tick or Nora or any of them could do to stop the water plant. That wasn't the issue. Axel had covered all his bases; you could count on the front office of Good River Products. So why did he feel so shitty? Honestly? He wanted them to be grateful—for the project, for all the trouble Axel and he and Good River Products were going to, to develop the channel. That was it. He wanted them to like him. He wanted them to understand he was on their side. Good River Products was doing it *for them*.

"I'm not a monster," Howard said to his potted philodendron. "My little girl doesn't think I'm so bad." In the evenings, when he's home, she settles into his lap with a book, all cuddled tight in pink footie pajamas. He reaches around her with both arms and takes her little fuzzy feet in his hands, and brings her up into a little ball that fits exactly in his lap. Nothing in his life makes him happier than that—that he can provide the people he loves with that kind of shelter and safety. And with this new job, this new income, it will be even better. When he gets home, she will crawl into his lap with her little piggy nose on its elastic string, and he will gather her in his arms, lean over her, and say, "Little Piggy, Daddy will never, ever, let anyone blow your house down. That's why Daddy works so hard," he will tell her, "that's why I have to be away so much, so we have enough money to build a house out of the strongest bricks in the world."

Howard's eyes fogged up, but he shook it off.

"For how good you Good River Harbor people are with your hands, you are surprisingly dim when it comes to business." This was what he should have said when Tick was going on about fish. "You could have it all—that's what you don't understand. You can mine the mountains and the seas and the rivers, and the Earth will just keep growing more trees, growing more fish, and do any of you think the rain will stop falling? That's the miracle of water: It falls from the sky! It melts from the glaciers! It's yours for the taking, world without end, amen."

That's exactly what Good River Products was doing, taking it. *Transforming the unused resources of the Earth into wealth—for everybody*: PowerPoint slide seven. The more money there is, the more money there is to share around. Give Good River Products a couple more years, and this channel will be swimming in money. And this was just the beginning, selling the water. If those people were smarter, they could figure out how to sell the goddamn air.

Howard clicked the email icon, looking for a message from home. Nothing new.

Sometimes he was as frightened of wolves as any of the three little pigs, even though he would never tell Taylor. Frightened of brown-skinned people in the cities, poor and rude. Of cancer. Of getting old and sick. Of radical environmentalists taking control of the government. Of the weather, so violent. Of not being able to give Taylor what she wants, of having her unhappy. In a dangerous world, you need money, because money is the only thing that gives you the power to protect yourself and the people you love. His PowerPoint presentation had a nice section on this, the benefit to the families. Instead he got Tick's clam penises.

Oh well. When he got home, he would read to Taylor about "silver bells and cockleshells and pretty maids all in a row." He'd tell her that he has seen a cockleshell, all fat and chalky, dug right up out of the sand by one of his new friends. And he would be able to tell her stories about her teddy bear too. The way its nose pokes out its big round face. That makes it a brown bear, he would tell her. He would tell her that he's seen a real teddy bear's baby—saw it from a boat just last week—big head and button eyes and round, fuzzy ears sticking up above the grasses, the little bear swaying on its hind feet, its paws curled over its fat tummy. Right there, on the beach.

She would think he was making it up, but he would say, no, no, someday I'll take you there and you can see all this for yourself. She would giggle and snuggle into his lap, and his heart would almost break. How long would it be before he got to go home? All he wanted to do was go home.

WHEN THE TOUR of her husband's water project was over, Rebecca climbed back onto the *Annie K* for the trip back to town. She was glad she'd gone over to the dam site to see for herself what Axel had planned. She moved to the edge of the boat to watch as they approached town and the house that she designed and Axel built for their family. That was her home, her only place on Earth, before she fled to Nora's. She felt her whole body pulled toward it. What is that force that draws an animal so strongly back home? The Kis'utch River salmon swim to the Oregon coast or make a wide arc to the Russian Kamchatka Peninsula—two, three years, two thousand miles. Suddenly, all they want to do is go home. Even when the water from their river is diluted in the salt sea, they can smell it, some combination of hemlock roots, melted snow, rotting alder leaves, glacial till, and the bones of their mothers, the flesh of their fathers, the breath of the winters away. For miles, they home in on that smell, finally bursting upriver on the rising tide. They will create new life in the place they were born, or they will die trying. Some succeed. Some come all the way home, only to find that their home has been destroyed or denied to them. These die at the mouth of the river with their eggs still in them, or leak eggs into the mud, red and doomed on the gray glacial silt.

Not just salmon—hummingbirds, geese, frogs, sandhill cranes, humpback whales, songbirds, wounded soldiers, and children at the end of the day when the air turns suddenly cold and woodsmoke drifts over the tide. Suddenly all they want to do is be home.

She knows that, but who can explain it? And who can explain the desperation? Who understands why a salmon launches its body over the rocks of a waterfall again and again and again until it gets past or batters itself to pieces? Nothing but dying will stop a salmon from going home.

With the free edge of the bandana, Rebecca swiped at tears as the workboat took her toward the harbor. Then her shoulders straightened. So here is the greatest mystery. What kind of person would dam salmon from a river? What kind of person would cut the salmon off when they are moving most urgently, stop them just short of home after they have traveled a thousand miles to get there? Who could do that? Who could deny them? Hundreds of fish, struggling upstream? How could that ever be right, in what morally corrosive world? Dam a river, and salmon will throw their bodies against the dam until their faces are white with torn flesh. Then they will fin slowly in the cold tailwater, stinking and dying like drunks outside the door at the Greyhound station.

AFTER TICK SHOOK the last of the shrimp into a five-gallon pail, he stuffed a new tomcod into the bait cage on the shrimp trap and snapped shut the lid. Poking a fillet knife through the wires, he slashed at the cod's belly until it dripped intestines. He shoved the trap a little farther over the bow of the skiff, so the cod didn't bleed into the boat.

"Got to keep a boat clean so the bears don't come sniffing around," he told Nora. "They'll chew on your gas cans and hoses, just for fun."

With his boot, Tick shoved away a tote full of coiled rope. Then he checked the knots and tilted the trap into the water. "Stay free of the lines," he ordered. As the trap sank, the rope lifted in curls from the tote and disappeared underwater. Forty fathoms of lead line, and then the last of the line slid overboard and flipped the buoys out of the boat.

Tick picked up a shrimp that was flicking on the floor of the skiff. He hooked it on his fishing line and cast it out. "You catch your bait, then you use the bait to catch a mess of shrimp, then you use one of the shrimp to catch more bait, and you hope that in this whole process, you get something to eat." He put his rod in the holder, settled himself between the oars.

The day had been calm, but light winds were starting to crinkle the water and turn the whole channel to used tinfoil. Tick reached behind to start the engine, remembered he didn't have one, pulled on an oar to head them into the wind. He turned to watch Nora.

"No. Like this."

Tick let the oars rest on the oarlocks while he reached into the bucket of shrimp Nora had between her knees.

"Put your whole hand around the head. With a shrimp this big, you can't just hold it with your thumb and finger and your pinky in the air. See all those spines, that whole ridge of spines along the back? See that spear out the front? You don't want to give it any room to wiggle or it can poke a hole in you. You got it. Wrap your whole hand tight around it, like you're holding the handlebar on your bike. Same thing with the other hand—grab the tail. Now twist, like you're wringing out your undies."

Tick watched her face, because he knew what was going to happen next. The head end would twist off just fine. Then the beheaded shrimp would muscle around, flapping in her hand, surprisingly strong, like it's trying to get away. A shrimp has more sense in its ass than its head. But Nora just twisted the head off, heaved it overboard, dropped the tail in a ziplock bag, and reached for the next.

"One," she said. Tick had promised her four dozen shrimp if she would teach Tommy to play a song on the piano.

"What song?" she had said.

"Annie Klawon said any song. But Tommy wants 'Ninety-Nine Bottles of Beer on the Wall.' Both hands."

"Deal."

So the deal was done. After the official tour of the dam site, Nora had gone out with Tick in his little skiff to help pull up the trap. Tick put shrimp traps deep, at least thirty-five fathoms. But in fjord country, that's only a hundred yards offshore and that's a good thing, he thought, especially if your son sank your outboard and turned your skiff into a damn rowboat. It was embarrassing to row out from town, everybody watching. But everybody knew that Tick was still working on his Evinrude and expected it to be running any day. At least he'd got his winch back to working. All that lead line, he wasn't going to be hauling it in hand over hand.

Nora was twisting the heads off shrimp, tossing the heads overboard, counting the tails into the bag, hardly looking at what she was doing. All the time, she was watching Tick.

"What," Tick said.

She didn't say anything.

"You don't need to be thinking how'm I doing without a job. Everybody's thinking how'm I doing. I walk down the boardwalk, everybody says, how'm I doing. Order a beer, how'm I doing. Open the door, somebody's left a zucchini or a loaf of warm bread. No job. No wife. No outboard. Kid in trouble. Fine. I'm doing fine. Except for that look. That gives me the creeps.

"I'm fine," Tick said.

"Good." Nora said. "That makes one person in this town."

Then she let loose. Tick grinned and leaned his bulk away from her. For a lady who didn't say much of anything except nice, always smiling and hugging, she had a bunch of not-nice to say. The Bear Shelter was not fine with her. The water-collection dam on the Kis'utch was not fine. It was not fine, the way Axel treated Tick. Tick's grin faded back into his beard.

"Firing you because of what Davy did is not fair. Sins of the son visited on the father—on the whole family—which I don't think even God would do, even though God is mean mean mean and He definitely takes sides. If God and Axel got in a wrestling match to see who's meanest, they'd bite off each other's ears. So there's God saying, 'What? I can't hear you!' which at least gives Him an excuse for never answering."

Three more shrimp met their maker.

It was not fine the way Axel treated Tick about the Bear Shelter.

It was not fine the way nobody, not Kenny, not even the bear, and definitely not Nora Montgomery was standing up to Axel.

"I'm tired of ignoring Axel's bulldozers. I've tried. I've tried picking berries. I've tried reading a romance novel. I've tried teaching my dog to dance. But all the time, the roar of those bulldozers drown out the river while the salmon circle in muddy water, and I'm sick of it."

Tick was glad he wasn't a shrimp, the way she was tearing off their heads. He was glad he wasn't Axel. Or Kenny. He was pretty sure the only reason she wasn't laying into old Tick McIver himself was because she thought he notched Axel's piling, which maybe he did and maybe he didn't, but whoever did, did a good thing.

"Every place I've lived, people came and wrecked, cutting the old growth, strip-mining the ore, filling marshes for subdivisions. That's not making a living. That's vandalism. That's theft. That's murder—except that people call it enterprise. They didn't have to. If they'd thought about it, they could have found a gentler way to make a living on the land. But no, they wrecked every place I've lived. Why? Because no one stopped them. What did I do? Nothing. I trucked my piano to the next place. So they came and wrecked that. Finally, I got sick of it. You have to do something after a while, don't you?"

She studied a big shrimp loaded with eggs. "Good luck," she said, and tossed it overboard.

"What we need is an act of God."

"Not quite sure whose side God is on, Nora," Tick said, surprised by this whole conversation.

"An act of God, like a lightning strike. Or a flood!

"Here's the thing, Tick. Lillian told me that once there used to be a whole town across the channel, on the clamflat at the base of the Kis'utch River. Right where Axel's dam and the water exportation dock are going in. Lillian had a business where the construction office is now. There was a huge flood—warm rain on the muskegs and snowfields—and the Kis'utch thundered down and wiped it all out. The whole town. Wiped it off the face of the Earth."

Tick knew that this was true.

Nora lifted her head from the shrimp bucket and stared across the channel at the Kis'utch clamflat. "That's all I'm hoping for now. A huge flood to tear out the construction site. Pray for rain. Forty days and forty nights. C'mon, God!"

She cupped her hands around her mouth and shouted to the sky. "A flood, God! Another big flood. No, not a *rug*, you stupid. A *flood*."

"Hell," Tick said. "You want a flood, why don't you ask *me*?"

She stopped yanking off heads and stared at him.

"What."

"You teach Tommy to play some songs Annie will like, I'll make you all the floods you want. Something good. Nashville."

"What are you talking about?"

"Meet Tick McIver, splash dam maker."

"What."

"Making floods is one of the things I used to do. I made a good living. I built splash dams. The timber company falls some trees up high, drags them over to dam up a stream at the top of a hill. Rain comes, the dam makes a reservoir. You load the reservoir with floating logs from the cut. When the reservoir is full of water and chock-full of logs, you lever out the key log in the splash dam. Bam, the dam gives way. The whole thing—water, logs, the whole pond—comes screaming down the hill. Look out below! When the tidal wave settles, you got your logs delivered right to your dock."

Nora didn't say anything. But she was starting to show some mercy to the shrimp. She weighed a small one in her hand, then threw it overboard.

"That's a beautiful thing," she said, "that shrimp floating down." Tick looked over the side—long pink antennas waving thank you, God, blue bobble eyes, spidery legs, stripy pink scales. One lucky shrimp. Unless something ate it on the way down. It had a long way to go.

"How much would it be for one splash dam, a big one, just above the Kis'utch Falls?"

Tick looked up at the ridge where the river broke through the granite and fell to the clamflat. Any shithead could build a splash dam up there. He'd built dams in lots worse places than that. Above the falls, the Kis'utch ran through a narrow gorge, so the dam could be small and tight—hard work, but could be done in a couple of days. There's plenty of muskeg in the basin behind the gorge, so the water would have room to build up.

Lots of water up there, draining steep snowfields. The waterfall was so noisy, nobody would hear chain saws. A flood is an act of God—who can blame God? Who can handcuff the Holy Ghost? The more Tick thought about it, the more he thought he might be able to drive a good deal.

"That would cost you four songs," Tick said. "But right and left hands on both songs. Not just the tune. Chords too. Why not?"

Nora raised her face to the clouds. The swell rocked the boat, sent waves of light across her face. Shrimp tails flicked and popped in the bucket. Tick reeled in his line, found nothing on his hook, cast out again.

Nora sucked in a great breath. "Okay, so I'll tell you why not."

Tick looked into her face and leaned away. "Ah. Maybe you shouldn't tell me, Nora."

Nora plunged on. "Last place I lived, Weyerschafft decided they'd log the hills up the river behind my house. Cut them to stumps, three-hundred-year-old trees. What's a person to do, when every day you watch trucks rumble down the hill and across a little wooden bridge right in front of your house, carrying the giant corpses, red bark chipped off, scarred, blue numbers spray-painted on their butt ends?

"I had a jerry can of lawn mower gas. I had a lighter. I had all night. What more did I need?"

Nora pulled on her ponytail. Broken light from the sea scattered across her face.

"When the truckers hauled up to the creek the next morning, the bridge was still smoldering. I didn't know they would be that angry, so then I was really scared. Before the Feds could figure out who did it, my friends helped me load my piano on the ferry and I just took off, figuring I'd go until the ferry stopped going, and then I would get off. I'd stop making trouble. Model citizen. That piano would be my anchor. I'd get it tangled up there in the rocks until nothing could wash me loose, and that is where I would stay. Then I would have to mind my own business. I would have to keep my mouth shut."

Tick started to hum and play his fingers over his knees.

"No, Tick, you bastard. I can't do anything. I don't dare make any more trouble. They've got a warrant out on me. Arson. Mandatory four-year sentence for using fire to destroy federal property. They'll find me out. I got my piano holding me down, and I can't even play it." She looked up at Tick. "But I *can* play it, Tick. I can play it beautifully. But if I did, they'd be on me—the Feds. Better mark of identification than a tattoo. So I teach kids to play with three fingers.

"This is my home now. All I want is to mind my own business."

"You don't seem real good at minding your own business."

Nora took a halfhearted swing at his chin. "It's hard," she protested, but gave it up.

"You're a good man, Tick McIver. It's really too bad I'm reformed. But I'll teach Tommy the songs anyway."

The tip of his rod bounced. He grabbed it, pulled it up sharp. Started reeling. The thing fought him for a while, then it was all dead weight. A bad sign.

"Rockfish," he said. "Halibut fight all the way. Rockfish die halfway up. Pulling them up from forty fathoms gives them a hell of a case of the bends. Eyes bulge out of the sockets. Bladder pops out their mouth." He held it out to show her. It was a bright red fish with quills standing up on its back and a white thing sticking out its mouth like a swollen tongue. Tick laid it in the bait bucket. There would be rockfish for supper at the McIver house that night.

Tick expected Nora to be gazing into the fish's googly eyes, saying "isn't that wonderful," but she didn't even look. She was all business, twisting shrimp. The wind had laid down, and the water was flat and shiny as glass, except where shrimp heads hit the water, eyes all big and surprised. Toward the horizon rose seven columns of mist, the exhalation of feeding whales. The channel reflected the whole Kis'utch Range upside down.

"Good place," Tick said.

"It's like we're floating in our boat on the top of the mountain," Nora said, "up there with the snowfields, all bent and wavy. You'd think it's a perfect reflection, but the blue is more blue than really, the green is greener, like the reflected world is made of stained glass with light coming through. Like church. Good place for an act of God."

Tick squinted into the water. Nora was right. When a flock of white gulls settled onto the channel, another flock flew upside down to meet it. Each gull sat on the rump of an upside-down one. Whiter than white. But all the gulls lifted off, just like that, screeching, and swam toward a ruckus on the water a boat's length away. Great bubbles the size of washtubs blurped up and burst. "Hang on!" Tick grabbed the oars, spun the boat, and stroked away with all the strength in his back. Nora ducked under the thunder of a terrible roar.

The sea in their wake bulged and broke apart and up rose the humpback whales, with all the majesty of their great size. Their open mouths were caverns, dimly lit and terrible, engulfing fish and sea. Nora threw her head back to see them, they were that high. They fell back between thunderous walls of waves. Water poured from their baleen. Tick's oars grabbed immense bites of water as he rowed. Waves rebounding from the whales' crusted flanks lifted his stern and pushed his boat away. The whales slammed their tails, stunning the herring, then leapt on them, openmouthed, and swallowed them down. Nora crouched in the boat, hanging on, squinting, while sunlight dove deep into the sea, bubbled up, slammed down again, rebounded in violent arcs. Gulls swarmed and screeched.

Then came again the roar of the feeding whales and Tick's answering halloo. "I told you this was a good place," he shouted. Broken herring finned away from the echo into the ambush of the whales.

Tick rested on his oars. Grinning, Nora rested her back against the stern. A whale rested beside them on the glaze of the sea, lifted by the calming water of its own wake. It blew a great breath. Sunlight silvered the spray. There were many whales. They all sucked bright day into their lungs, blew it out with the sound of a rock slide. Then there was silence except for the whispers of murrelets and the flicks of the fins of wounded fish, fluttering in small circles. Already, the sun had melted the rough water, skinning it with silver. Gulls swayed on the swell, and even the sacrilegious gulls were silent.

A whale folded its back, slowly unfolded, and levered its flukes into the air. The tail stood like a black jib, streaming water, then sank as the whale dove to a seam below the reach of the sun. Water slipped into the space the whale had pressed on the sea. One by one, other whales raised their flukes and dove. The gulls, still silent, waited still. They knew that in their own time, the whales would begin the hunt again. The water rose and fell in meditative breath.

August 24

HIGH TIDE		LOW TIDE	
0:59am	16.2ft	7:20pm	-0.3ft
1:43pm	15.4ft	7:33pm	1.9ft

Just before midnight, a bulge of sea rolls smoothly past Good River Harbor. It's the flood tide of the dog-salmon moon, the highest tide of the month. On its dark currents, it carries a lost gill net, drifting unmoored. These are the dangerous nets, detached from human intention. A dog salmon nudges into the net. Her head slides through the mesh, but her body is too wide to pass. She backs away. The net snags her gill plates. The fibers dig into the feathery red tissue, deeper as the salmon tugs to get away. She curls her body and snaps it straight, yanking at the net until her blood pinkens the sea. There she hangs by her head, caught by gill plates bright and round as the moon, cratered with the moon's shadowed seas. More salmon nudge into the net, flashing silver as they struggle to escape. A school of salmon weaves through the kelp forest, approaching the net, wary in the night. Salmon and salmon and salmon nose into the net that seizes them more tightly the more they flail. The nets bulge and recoil. Silver tails swirl.

Tasting blood, a salmon shark sways close to the net, singing his rough flank against the fibers. He snatches off a thrashing tail, snatches another. But then he veers and noses into the net. He catches first a tooth, then pushing forward, catches another. The shark whips his head from side to side, savaging the net, driving the falling scales into silver swirls. He vomits salmon tails and trailing intestines that sink through the currents. A gray cod snaps up the falling pieces and pushes into the net, where she finds her own death. Heavy now with the dead, the net slowly sinks until it settles, swaying on the floor of the sea.

A hermit crab reaches tentatively for torn flesh. Dungeness crab move in, scuttling sideways. A small sculpin thrusts its spiked head into the red tissues and spins, tearing off flesh. The water is cloudy with sea-fleas and shrimp eating the soft meat under the silver skin, nibbling around the bones, a cloud of eating. Hear the tick of small teeth, the click of small claws. Spot-shrimp stalk in on spidery legs, following their orange prows. Long antennae reach toward the dying and the dead. Bubbles pop from shrimps' mouths and stream toward the moon. When the banquet is finished, there is no flesh, only skeletons and strips of white skin, swaying.

Without the heavy flesh, the net rises again on its floats. Listen now. Skeletons with silver skirts ride the ghost net, hissing. Strips of skin swirl. Plated heads grin. The ghost net floats past the town on great tidal currents, gathering bones.

THE GHOST NET slipped under the *Annie K*, which was tied up at the brand-new dock at the Bear Shelter. Tick sat on his bow under the dog-salmon moon—a full moon pale and pockmarked. He studied the joinery where the pilings met the planking. He could of done a hell of a lot better work. But never mind that, like Annie Klawon said, that's gone, and the moon really did look like a dog salmon's belly. Yep, he decided, with the same rim of pink where the curve fell away and the same shadowy spots and rays. White clouds floated across the night sky. Their reflections rose and fell, stretched and shrank on the swell. Tick sat on his life jacket locker, leaned back against the cockpit window, and watched moonlight move over the waters. If it weren't for the windshield wiper gouging his back, the bow would make a great reclining chair. The boat swayed on a long swell that made the ropes creak on the cleats—more than likely a wake from a ship too far away to see. He clasped his hands across his great beard.

There was no place Tick would rather be than on the bow of his boat, tied to a dock on calm seas on a God-glorious night like this. The dock was so new it still smelled of sawdust and creosote. Even if Tick wasn't the man who dropped his piney pants on the floor after every good day's work, glad to hear the thud of money in his pocket, he admired a guy who could pull off a project like this. Axel had brought in a lot of men and moved fast—crappy work, but done on deadline. The dock was plenty big enough for the eco-tour boats that would put in there and send passengers up the ramp to the pavilion. *Pavilion.* Tick guffawed. That's what Axel was calling the wooden platform they'd built on the shelf of cliff next to the cistern. Passengers would pay their money and crowd in under the Good River Harbor Bear Shelter sign. Tromping across the pavilion past the refreshment stand, they would climb the path around the back of the cistern to the observation deck. That's where they would lean over and watch the bears in the pit below.

Except for the security lamp over the door where they'd prodded the bears into the tank, only moonlight lit up the site. New-cut plywood shone under the moon and even the old water tank gleamed like an oil slick. In the morning, kids and their folks in brand-new Bear Shelter sweatshirts would lean over the edge, throwing salmon heads to caged bears. The sow and cub would shy into the ditch they'd dug behind a thimbleberry bush and lie still. Camera flashes would bounce off the rain-shine on their pelts. Tick pulled at his beard and considered.

He'd seen the posters stapled to walls all over town. GRAND OPENING, 10 A.M. FREE ADMISSION FOR GOOD RIVER HARBORITES, FIRST HOUR ONLY. THEN TWENTY-FOUR BUCKS, KIDS HALF PRICE. When Axel set his mind to something, he got it done. Tick rearranged his back against the *Annie K*'s windshield and snapped open another beer.

He would think about calm seas, Tick decided. He would think about the moon. He would think about the pull of that moon, like a silver seiner hauling up the highest tide of the month. He wouldn't think about Axel or his dead bear. Instead, he would think of dog salmon charging upstream to their spawning beds. He would think about Annie Klawon, dreaming in Seattle. He wished she were here beside him, right here, leaning against the windshield, tucked under Tick's arm. He could smell her hair even now, the black strands tangling in his orange beard. Cedar. Kelp, maybe.

"Don't think about the bad things," she would say. What do you notice about this night? What is true of this exact moment in time? She would have talked about the smells. She would have talked about the way a high tide has no smell, like a special kind of olfactory silence, every smell hidden and hushed.

"High pressure in the gulf will linger through tomorrow. Tonight, winds calm. Light winds becoming south ten point zero knots by morning. Seas two feet or less, mainly west swell. Pressure thirty-three and steady. Tomorrow, light winds becoming west ten point zero knots in the afternoon. Seas two feet or less. Visibility ten miles."

Tick grinned. The steady low voice on the marine radio was so precise, so sure. Annie Klawon was afraid of the prideful forecasts—"As if anybody really can know what the wind will bring, let alone calibrate the future to the tenth of a knot," she had whispered. But the radio told a comforting story, bringing order out of the watery chaos, safe seas, the blessing of calm winds. Tick wouldn't have been surprised to hear that solemn voice just come out and say it straight: "The moon will make its face to shine upon you and be gracious unto you, both now and forevermore. This is NOAA Weather Service WXJ twenty-five, on one six two point four two five megahertz. Update at 6 a.m."

Tick had been glad to help when Kenny asked for a ride to the Bear Shelter dock. He knew how hard it would have been for Kenny to get down the boardwalk stairs, along the town trail, and up to the pavilion in that little wheelchair. Kenny was stuck between town and the dump, unless somebody delivered him somewhere else. And even then, the boat had to be a drop-bow or have a pretty good gangway. Kenny told Tick he wanted to go at midnight, to catch the high tide. At low tides, the gangway from the floating dock to the pavilion would be too steep. But on this night of the dog-salmon moon, the tide had lifted the floating dock so high the gangway was almost flat. Tick had lowered the bow, and Kenny pushed off onto the dock and on up the gangway to the pavilion.

Tick squinted up the platform. He could see Kenny hunched by the door to the cistern, a sharp silhouette under the security lamp. A strange and wonderful man, Kenny. Sort of a self-appointed scientist, studying all the animals. An old-fashioned natural philosopher, Nora said he was. That means he likes animals best when they're dead or at least on their way to extinction. Nora said that Kenny had been studying the life cycles of squirrels. But he's been reading about bats lately, she said, coming to the library early to be there when it opened and staying all morning. Bats and man! Fruit-eating bats! Rare bats of the world!

When he'd asked Tick for a ride, Kenny said he was looking for one of those rare bats, thinking its range might extend this far north. He thought that if it was around, it might be attracted to insects coming to the bright light over the door to the bear tank. He was excited on the run over, leaning forward in his wheelchair, talking away, happily mourning the loss of bat habitat and cussing out white-nose fungus.

Tick tried to remember exactly what Kenny had said on the ride out. "White-nose fungus hits a cave, next thing you know, it's dead bats lying a foot deep on the floor." He might as well have been talking about the coronation of the queen, he was so keyed up. He had printed out a page from a website that described the bat he was headed out to look for. He'd unfolded the paper and waved it in Tick's face, but it was too dark in the boat to make it out.

So there Tick was, sitting on his boat in the middle of the night, waiting for a weird guy to get tired of waiting for a bat that might or might not even exist in Good River Harbor. Made sense to him. How could it not?—it was a warm, sweet night and bats are as good a reason as any to stay out late.

He scanned the moonlight for flying mammals. If Kenny wanted to see his bat, he should move into the darkness, instead of sitting there right under the security light. And he should be quiet. But all of a sudden, he was making a lot of noise. Tick sat up. He squinted into the distance, trying to make it out. But he was too far away to see anything more than Kenny's lumpy silhouette. The sound coming from that direction was scratchy, like a big grasshopper's up-and-down song.

It sounded like somebody fiddling away on a busted violin.

It sounded like someone sawing away on a chain.

"No," Tick shouted. The word hit the side of the cistern and slammed back in his face. Kenny looked up. Tick leapt from the boat and sprinted up the gangway.

"Don't!"

Kenny turned back to sawing, faster then. Tick heard the chains fall away even before he got to the welcome sign—a rattle and a heavy clank.

"Don't do it."

Tick pounded past the sign, past the refreshment stand, leaping over their shadows black as holes in the planking. He could see Kenny lean forward and pull open the door to the pit. Not too late to slam the door shut. Not too. Late. Slam the door. Damn it, running in slow motion. If only he hadn't worn boots. Damn these boots. Now, almost, another step and then leap for the door.

A small shape ran into the light and disappeared in the shadow of Kenny's wheelchair.

"No."

A black mass hurtled out the door. Kenny's shadow tangled in the darkness of the bears. The whole dark mass cartwheeled off the pavilion. Tick dove, trying to grab a wheel. The wheelchair fell, tipped sideways, disappeared into black space. A terrible crack and rattle of metal on rock, clatter of bears fleeing over gravel, snap of breaking branches through the forest, and then nothing but the slowly settling echoes.

"Mother of God," Tick whispered, but then he was screaming. "Kenny!"

Tick ran down the gangway and skidded down the pilings to the rocky strand below the cliff. He couldn't hear anything but blood in his ears. He couldn't see Kenny. He ran across the rocks, slipped on the rocks, fell on the rocks, damn those rocks.

The security light threw Tick's big shadow across Kenny's poncho. Tick leaned out of the light, but oh God. Blood was running from Kenny's mouth. The bones of his skull dear God. All busted on the rocks, brains oh God. His twisted neck. The security light in his startled eye.

Do something. What do you do? Tick's howl echoed against the mountain. Tick pressed his fists against his mouth to quiet himself and fell onto the rocks beside Kenny, but dear God. There was nothing to do.

So quiet. A single wheel still turning.

Tick ran up the steps to the pavilion, grabbed a two-by-four from a lumber pile and slammed it against the interpretive sign. THE KINSHIP OF LIFE smashed and toppled. Tick swung again. The glass on the USE CAUTION AROUND BEARS display blew to bits. The two-by-four levered out of his hands and thudded against the cedar tank.

"Damn that Kenny." Tick leaned over and vomited, cradling one hand in the other.

When he could breathe again, he wiped his mouth on his sleeve and closed his eyes. The door to the cistern. He should close the door to the cistern. He crept to the opening. Not a sound came from inside. Not a breath of wind. Not a killdeer's call. The air smelled dank. He stared at moisture beading on the sawed link of chain. Starlight trickled down a link, paused, then grew into a drop as round as an eye. The drop gave way and rivered to the next link. Another drop formed and fell away. Already Kenny's eyes would be wet with dew.

Tick walked into the cistern. Its mounds of dirt lay cold and white under the moon, as cold and white as snowbanks. He stepped out between the pale trunks of dead alders. In the puddles of their shadows, they held all the loneliness of the world. He stood, quiet and empty. He stood. In the quiet of that white night, he heard moonlight drip down the cedar walls.

There were bats, he slowly realized, lots of them. Kenny had been right. The moon cast their shadows over the ashen mounds. One darted toward Tick, then at the last minute veered away. Another sailed past his ear. He felt the bats more than saw them—breath on his forehead. He could see the shadows of big moths too. A whisper and a moth disappeared.

"Kenny, Kenny, if you had told me the truth, I could have helped you do it right. I could still catch a bat for you, Kenny, if you ever really cared about bats. If I lift my hand into the air at just the right time, like a catcher's mitt, I could grab a bat out of the night. I could hold it in my fist and bring it to you. You could extend its wing, and we would see through the membrane and touch the claw at its elbow. We would look into its face." Dear God a horrid face. Eyes afraid and bleeding, and the face pushed all to the side.

The black shadows of the alder limbs were perfectly still on the cistern walls.

Tick turned and ran to the door. He needed to tell people. He needed to tell Nora. He needed to tell Lillian. She would know what to do. He couldn't wait until morning to tell them. In the morning, Meredith would come to open up the ticket booth. There would be a line of people waiting. They would be disappointed that the bears were gone.

The cistern's door squeaked as Tick slumped against it and slid to his haunches. The pale wing of a moth drifted through the light and settled on the planks. One wing fell, bitten off at the base, then another. They fluttered down, soft as ashes. Tick lifted his hand to catch one, but his reaching pushed it away.

Nora was still awake, working at her plywood desk in the light of a kerosene lamp. For many minutes, Tick stood outside the window and watched her. The smell of that kerosene—dark and musky—and the mewling of the Green Point buoy, they confused him. Marine charts were spread over the desk. She held one finger at a place on a chart. With the other hand, she typed with one finger. The keys ticked, tick-tocked. She looked happy. Suddenly afraid for her, Tick fled and ran instead to Lillian's and pounded on her door.

Soon enough the church bell began to ring, sounding the alarm. People flew from their front doors. In the storm of rising shouts and running feet, banging doors and outboard motors, Tick stood on the boardwalk, as unmoving as a piling in a flood tide. He stared over the inlet. While he watched, the hemlock trees slowly rose to touch the bottom of the moon.

THE MOON HAD set and Orion was high in the sky when Nora got back to her cabin. Chum nosed in and Nora stumbled after him. With shaking hands, she lit the kerosene lamp on her writing table. It dropped a pool of yellow light on the paragraphs she had been writing. Where did that world go, this orderly, predictable world she had been describing?

> "RED RIGHT RETURN" IS THE PRINCIPAL RULE OF NAVIGATION. THAT MEANS THAT AS YOU ARE COMING INTO PORT, YOU KEEP THE RED NAVIGATION MARKERS ON YOUR STARBOARD, OR RIGHT, SIDE. THE GREEN MARKERS STAY ALWAYS TO PORT. IF YOU ARE HEADING HOME BETWEEN THE RED AND THE GREEN LIGHTS, YOU ARE SAFE FROM SHOALS.
>
> IN NARROW CHANNELS, THERE ARE SOMETIMES RANGE-MARKERS TO HELP MARINERS NAVIGATE THE DANGEROUS PASSAGES. RANGE-MARKERS ARE WHITE MARKERS—ONE NEAR, ONE FARTHER AWAY.

If you steer a course in such a way that the white markers are lined up, seeming to merge into one, you will avoid the shoals.

Crying out, she tore the page from the typewriter and crumpled it against her chest. Chum barked sharply. "Oh, Chum." She fell on her bed. Chum nosed at her face. She pulled the dog over her like a rug and trapped him in her arms. He lay still, barely breathing. "Oh dear God. Kenny, oh dear Kenny."

"Come back," she whispered. Chum whined and struggled to escape. She held him, whispering urgently. *It's dangerous. You can't be sure. You can't trust the bottom of the ocean not to heave up in shoals. It does that, it heaves up a shoal and the ocean breaks against it. Your boat will be lost. You think buoys don't come loose from their moorings. But they do. Buoys come loose from their moorings and float into the wrong places and you follow them, you trust them, and they take you onto the shoals. You think the numbers on the chart will keep you safe, even on a dangerous sea, foul with rocks. But maybe there is no chart. Maybe you believe in it, but it doesn't exist. Maybe there are only the sea and the rocks and the wind. Or maybe there is a chart but it's made up or wrong, and how would you know? A blinking light can be near or far, you just can't tell. Light bends. It gets lost in the fog. How can you find your way? And sometimes you think it's a lighthouse but it's a star behind a wave. You think you're on the right course but it's wrong, and how do you know until you hear the terrible crying and waves smacking rocks? You have to keep going, or you lose steerageway. Even if you don't know where you're going, you have to keep going or the seas will turn you broadside. You have to keep going, even in the dark, you have to steer by the foghorn, but how can you trust the moaning sea? Can you steer by shame? Kenny. Oh, Kenny, what have I done? What have I done to you?*

Chum howled, but the sea was silent.

PART THREE
COHO TIDE

Oncorhynchus kisutch, the coho salmon, squirts her eggs at the head of a riffle in the small tributary of the river. Cold water flows through the dark spaces between grains of gravel where the eggs have come to rest—a hundred red beads among the gray stones, sparks of life in the dark. Over time, months and months, the red fades, and each globe takes on the shape of a tiny fish with a yolk sack on its belly. More translucent than stray light, smaller than a spruce needle, it shivers there in the interstices of the stones, absorbing the nutrients it carries in its sack. When it is fully a fish, grown to the size of a hemlock needle, it wriggles up through stones into the moving water.

How it comes to be, that the onrushing, taut-muscled ferocity of a coho salmon grows from a sliver of light in water-washed darkness, who can say? But there it is, leaping at the end of a whistling line, a hook in its jaw, and a silver flasher twisting light. Listen to the thud as its heavy flank strikes the wave.

August 28

HIGH TIDE		LOW TIDE	
3:13am	16.2ft	9:19am	0.1ft
3:32pm	16.6ft	9:39pm	0.7ft

Howard watched out the little window of his room over the library. A strange guy lets a bear loose and gets his skull broken for his trouble. So what do the people do? They make a casserole. The guy's dead, so they put water on to boil and dump in noodles. It's like it's the only thing they know how to do. A whole parade of women wearing hot mitts carries casseroles over to Kenny's house, their men in tow. So who's going to eat all that salmon loaf and potato salad? Do they think about that? It's not like Kenny's hungry, for God's sake. Or like he has a grieving wife and kids sitting on his couch, crying over family pictures.

The women bucked up against Kenny's front door, which was closed up tight. They could have let themselves in. Kenny had put a super-duper new padlock on the door, but then—to make sure of the point—he'd told everyone that the combination was K.E.E.P., as in KEEP OUT. So people respected that. You could see each one of them thinking—Nobody home. Hmmm. Well, we'll eat this ourselves. No place to sit on Kenny's gangway. No dishes or silverware. When the women realized this, they sent the kids back for forks and plastic chairs. Soon, people were lined up along the boardwalk to Kenny's, eating from paper plates filled with casserole. Men looked around, then went home and came back with six-packs. The postmaster came by with an accordion in a suitcase and it was a party, there on the dock, in silvery light under low clouds.

Howard knew this wasn't his party. But being alone wasn't much of a party either. He pulled on his jacket and walked over to Lillian's. He was the only customer in the whole place. He sat by the window, nursing a cup of coffee, knowing he should check in with Axel. Lillian bustled around, swiping at red eyes with the edge of her apron. She closed down the popcorn machine, piled up a platter of hot dogs, pulled down the shades. The whole place was submerged in darkness.

When Lillian opened the door, Howard turned his head against the glare of light. She stood there, silhouetted with her hot dogs. "If you have another cup, leave the money on the counter," Lillian said, and left. Howard dropped his forehead onto his crossed arms and closed his eyes.

That was exactly what he would do, sit there alone, have another cup of coffee, listen to "Good Night, Irene" from the accordion outside and "Yellow Submarine" from the jukebox inside, all the time thinking he really should stop by Axel's, let him know the breaking news.

He had called Jennifer in the middle of the night last night, as soon as he heard about Kenny. He woke her up, and she was frightened until she learned that he had called, as people do, to tell her that someone else had died.

"Kenny," she had said, wondering. "Did you know him? Was he a friend?"

"No. I didn't really know him. Nora was his friend. Tick McIver." He paused. "Maybe Lillian."

"He must have been a good man," Jennifer said.

"No. I wouldn't say that."

There was a long pause. He heard Taylor crying in the background. The phone would have frightened her too.

"Listen. Jennifer. I'm sorry I called. I don't know why I called. I just thought you should know. I thought I should pass along the news, so you would know."

"No. No, you should always call, any time day or night, I like to hear your voice and know you're okay. You okay?"

He had been okay, until she asked. Then he really wasn't.

"Yeah. Fine." He had to get this call over with. "You go back to bed. I love you. Tell Taylor I love her too." That's when he started to weep, holding his hand over the phone.

"I love you too. And I'm sorry about your friend."

He'd hung up without saying good-bye.

What was the matter with him, calling his wife in the middle of the night? He walked over to Lillian's coffeepot and poured himself another cup of lukewarm coffee. Maybe that was it. Maybe when people cry because someone's dead, they're crying because they'll be dead too someday, and they cry out of terror and pity for the people who love them. That's what, maybe. Maybe he called Jennifer to say that he was still alive, but someday he would be dead, and he was sorry about that, really, really sorry that he would have to leave her alone and really, really sorry for Taylor, to be making it alone in the world without a father, and who would keep her safe? Maybe all he wanted was for Jennifer to say, "Howard. Howard, *you're* alive. You called me, so *you* can't be dead," and maybe that's what she was telling him, and maybe he cried with relief, about that fact, that he was alive. Briny night, full moon, taut seas, dead guy shining in the rocks—that's when *you would* call the one *you* love more than anyone else in the world and tell her that *you* are alive. And why wouldn't that fact make *you* cry? Close *your* eyes and weep with gratitude and relief.

Howard went behind the bar, helped himself to a splash of whiskey for his coffee, and laid three dollars on the counter. He *really* should get over to Axel's. But it was comfortable behind the bar, with a little warm steam and the rattle of a clothes dryer coming from the door of the laundry.

Howard had had only one real conversation with Kenny, and that—he realized with a start—was behind that very bar. Lillian was washing the floor. It was afternoon, and the sun was warming up the wet wood and raising the stink of Lysol. She'd put all the chairs up on the tables, so Kenny had rolled behind the bar to drink his cup of coffee. His hair was still wet—from a shower, Howard had guessed. Howard poured himself a cup of coffee, and because there was nowhere else to sit, he pulled a chair alongside Kenny.

"Mind?"

Grunt.

That was the extent of the conversation for a long time. Lillian went on shoving and lapping at the water with a long mop, humming away, *there is a balm in Gilead*, her hair protected by a plastic accordion rain hat.

Out of the blue, Kenny looked out the window and said, "So, surveyor-person, what do *you* think of Good River Harbor, now *you've* got it all measured up?"

Howard was not going to say *anything* remotely offensive. He was not comfortable with this man.

"Beautiful place. Friendly people. Different from any other place I've been."

How could Kenny have taken offense at any of that, Howard wondered. He was bewildered and sort of offended himself by the face Kenny was making, like he smelled a garlic pickle. But it turned out Kenny was just thinking.

"I've thought a lot about what makes it different," he said, and Howard had about fallen out of his chair. Who was this man and was this the start of a conversation? He couldn't be sure, because Kenny was clearly directing his remarks to some ghost outside the window.

"Don't mean a damn thing, our lives," Kenny said. "How hard we try, whether we suffer or don't. We're not part of any plan."

Howard didn't take the bait Kenny was clearly dangling in his face.

"You know Sisyphus?"

Howard might have and might have not, so he said, "Sure."

"Condemned."

Howard flinched when Kenny pulled a knife out of a sheath on his belt and started scraping at a pile of candle wax on the bar.

"Condemned. Zeus made him push a huge rock up a hill each day, when all it did was roll back down again each night. Slowly up each day, fast down each night. He had to keep doing it, but it didn't mean a damn thing."

The story was starting to come back to Howard, vaguely and from the distant past. But the last thing he expected was a philosophy lesson from a guy with a Buck knife and a mouse-skin hat, although it made sense later, of course. Out of the corner of his eye, Howard saw Lillian straighten up and lean on her mop, listening.

"Everybody in the world has his own rock. Big fucking lichen-crusted rocks in this town. And everybody's got his shoulder to that rock, shoving it up the mountain. After a while, people get pretty attached to their rocks, think they're the greatest. But here's the difference."

Kenny was working more and more intensely on the wax, pushing the blade of his knife with his thumb.

"Every time the people in this town get their rocks to the top of the mountain," he said, "they sit down and look at the view. Har." Kenny clearly thought that was pretty funny. His shoulders shook like an engine starting up. "That glacier valley over there, that arm of the sea. And some of the people, some of them even climb up on their rocks and sing a song." He poked the point of his knife toward Lillian. "Yep. Music. That's the mistake Sisyphus made. While he was on top of the mountain, sitting beside his rock, catching his breath, he should of stood up and let out a song. Should of sung loud, so Zeus could hear him. I *go to the hills for the sound of music!* Wouldn't that have made Zeus rage?

"Har.

"Probably would have aimed a lightning bolt right between Sisyphus's ugly eyes."

Then maybe he was laughing or maybe he was hawking, but the conversation was clearly over. Kenny had winked broadly at the ghost out the window, drained his cup, and rolled out, still laughing.

≈≈≈

WHEN HOWARD FINALLY got over to Axel's, Axel was sitting alone at his dining room table, making to-do lists. He poured Howard a glass of wine. He poured himself one too, which kind of surprised Howard, who thought he was strictly a coffee kind of guy.

"You'd think Kenny was some kind of *hero*, instead of a criminal, the way those people are *acting*," Axel said. "Who's stopping by my house to say they're sorry about the losses to the business?—bears gone, picnic pavilion wrecked, grand opening canceled. We're going to have to act fast, or this whole Bear Shelter business is going to sink like a stone. You're the community relations guy. Get in touch with the press. Seattle. Juneau. Anchorage. Tell them about how he snuck in at midnight and cut the chain. Tell them about how he had a lookout in a boat at the harbor. Tell them about how he vandalized the *interpretive displays*. Tell them we're, um, looking into a conspiracy, how somebody practically *felled my house*, how they had the piling notched before I scared them away. They'll ask about what we're going to do next. Tell them that we are going to keep our commitment to provide shelter for imperiled bears. Axel Hagerman is not going to be intimidated by a gang of *eco-terrorists*."

Oh boy. Howard thought maybe he'd wait until the next morning to write the release, to give Axel time for second thoughts.

"What are the lawyers saying?"

"No real liability issues on our part," Howard said. "Easy case to defend. Harm caused in pursuit of an illegal activity is presumptive evidence of contributory negligence. Nobody to blame but himself. You can sue his estate for damages, but that's an empty pocket."

"Good. Sue him. We'll get the house at least, and we can tear that down, sell the pier for somebody else to build on. What else have you been doing, Howard, for community relations?"

Howard cringed. Axel was either going to like this or hate it, but you don't need a special seminar to understand that it's important to project an image of caring.

"I issued a statement expressing Good River Products's condolences to the town for the loss of a friend and neighbor. Pinned it to the bulletin board at the post office."

Axel looked up sharply. "Neighbor maybe. Friend? Not so much."

"I told Nora that as an expression of sympathy, we would cover funeral expenses, fly the body out for cremation, fly the ashes back for burial."

"Umm. What'd she say?"

"No thanks."

"No *thanks*? That's two thousand bucks, easy."

"A long time ago, Kenny told Lillian he wanted to be burned on a big funeral pyre on the beach, so that's what they're going to do. They got his body wrapped in a tarp and cooling on ice down with the salmon in the hold of a seiner tied up at the dock. Tomorrow they're going to burn him."

Axel glared at Howard.

"Report them to the police and to the Environmental Protection Agency. That's a crime and an air-quality issue. And it's *sick*."

"Too late. Nora already called around and got the permits."

Axel went to the window. The setting sun glared on the glass. "I'll Fly Away"—banjo-accordion duet—leaked in under the closed door.

"If they invite me to their pig roast," Axel said, "tell them I am otherwise engaged."

Howard felt sorry for Axel. The thing was, nobody would invite him to the funeral. It's sad, Howard thought, how people don't like the man who does them favors. Quickest way to lose a friend is to give him a job or give him a promotion he doesn't deserve. Tells him who's boss. Makes a guy feel bested. Howard suspected that the only reason people tolerated his own presence is because they pulled down his pants in the bar and then turned his PowerPoint presentation into a discursus on clam penises and bear poop. They showed him who's boss, so he's okay. The other thing is, you don't like the man you fear. These people suck up to Axel when he's on top of the world, but any sign of weakness, they're on him like weasels. He'd had a run of bad luck, and already they were saying it was his fault that Kenny was dead. If it weren't for Axel, they were saying, Kenny would still be alive and farting among us. And that's not all that the people were saying. Axel didn't know the worst.

Howard reached for Axel's glass and poured him another drink. Can you fire a community relations man for bringing bad news? He was sure Axel would. And maybe Howard didn't care. Right now, he wanted to be home. That was all. He knew that's not how a corporate executive is supposed to feel, but that's the way it was. Somebody dies, a normal guy wants to be home.

"So," Howard said.

Axel looked at him with narrowed eyes. "So. What?"

"They found a congressional Medal of Honor in his things."

"Kenny? The guy with the mouse-tail hat? The dead guy?"

"Yep. The crippled guy. When they found the medal, Nora went to the internet and looked it up. Put in the name of the medal and the date and up popped the whole story. Took her two seconds to find it, and people are saying she already knew. Born in Chicago, 1947. Real name is William Kenniston. Dartmouth grad. Philosophy. He was an Army Ranger, a prisoner of war in Vietnam. Kenniston. I actually think I remember reading about this, decades ago. He had a horrible time of it. When the Viet Cong captured him, they put him in a cage. To fit him in, they bent his legs until they splintered. They left him in the cage in the center of the village.

People cursed him, poked him with sticks between the bars, urinated on him. Seven weeks he endured this, and then the Viet Cong abandoned the village. They just left him and ran. Rats were a plague, chewing on him. He survived on rainwater another week until Special Forces found him."

Axel let his breath out real slow, sucked in his wine. "He was a strange man. Not much use for people."

"Yeah, well. That might explain it."

Axel went out the side door onto his deck. Howard followed him out. It was getting toward dusk. Howard knew that at home, Jennifer would be tucking Taylor into bed. First Teddy B. Bear. Jennifer tucks the blankets up under his floppy arms. Then Taylor. Jennifer smooths the hair back from Taylor's forehead and kisses her.

A thick fog had moved in over the harbor. Across the channel, the yard light at the site was just a faint glow. The signal at the end of the pier blinked a big pillow of light. Howard could barely make out the green light at the end of the breakwall. The only person on the dock was Tick McIver, wobbling on his long legs toward the fish-cleaning table. Still, the music played on at Kenny's party and laughter sank into the fog.

"Call the press," Axel said slowly. "Tell them that Good River Products expresses its sorrow and sympathy at the death of an American hero, and the . . ." He paused. Howard could tell he was making this up as he went along.

". . . and the particular tragedy of Kenny What . . . What's the guy's name? Kenniston . . . that would lead a man who defended his country so . . ."

"So courageously," Howard said.

Axel threw him a look. ". . . so effectively, to engage in acts that are deeply harmful to the American way of doing business. Uh, make that the American way of life."

Axel cranked open another bottle of wine and poured himself a glass.

"Are you sure you want another glass, Axel . . . ?" When Alex didn't answer, Howard took out his notebook, and got it down while it was fresh in his mind. It's true, Kenny did Axel some real damage. Kenny did mean to let those bears go. You can't accumulate capital if you can't prevent theft, and that was a theft. Before he put the notebook back in his pocket,

Howard flipped to the front cover, where he'd pasted last year's Christmas portrait of his family. There were Jennifer and Howard, smiling, and Taylor in a red velvet dress. Howard stared out over the railing on Axel's porch.

"Axel!" he said suddenly. "Where are Rebecca's flowers?"

There was nothing there. The deck had been heaped with flowers—flowers in pots on the railings, flowers in planters on the stairs, flowers hanging from the rafters and climbing up the posts from planters under the house. Used to be, a man had to claw his way through Rebecca's vines and leaves out there, like George of the Jungle. But the deck was clean and empty. Howard leaned over the rail to look under the deck. Not a flowerpot, not a pile of dirt.

"When she left, she took the wheelbarrow too," Axel said, and turned away.

TICK PUSHED BETWEEN the flocks of people at Kenny's and teetered in front of the fish-cleaning station, which the women had commandeered for a table. Leaning forward slowly, carefully, he studied the empty, encrusted casserole dishes and half-empty liquor bottles. He lifted a half gallon of Jim Beam up to where the sun would have been, if fog hadn't flopped over Good River Harbor and settled itself like a nesting gull. The sun wasn't going to tell him how much whiskey was left in there. He sloshed the bottle. Good enough. So he stuck it into his shirt and aimed toward the harbor. He picked a halting path between conversations.

"Kenny sure bunged up Axel's bear-o-rama."

"Somebody's in deep shit, but I can't figure out who."

Tick spun off the bear-o-rama person and ran right into the next.

"Think Tick knew?"

"Why'd Kenny smash up the place?"

Tick looked hard in the face of the person who asked. "I don't know," he said, and wandered off, shaking his head sorrowfully.

"I'da taken a gun."

"I'm gonna hunt down that sow and kill her good."

Tick stopped to stare. Kill her? Who?

"Where's Axel?"

"What's Axel saying?"

Pushing the whiskey bottle deeper into his shirt, Tick looked wildly around for Axel. He was nowhere to be seen, but he could be anywhere, and nobody much could be seen in this fog.

"What's that Kenny got for brains?"

At this, Tick stopped for a long pull on the bottle, because in fact, Kenny didn't have *anything* for brains. His brains were scattered on the beach, getting pinched up by gulls that probably thought God had sent them a special blessing. Tick flinched as a banjo sprang into action.

"*I'll fly away, oh Lordy. I'll fly away.*" The music shoved Tick toward the harbor. "*When I die, hallelujah by and by, I'll fly away.*" That Lillian sure did sing like an angel, and the accordion player was Gabriel himself.

The anchor lights on the masts in the harbor swayed. Tick grabbed a light pole and hung on. Fog made the lights into fuzzy yellow balls. So thick the fog erased the edge of the docks too, and Tick stumbled between the disembodied bows of boats that rested against the dock.

"*To a land where joy shall never end, I'll fly away.*"

The dock suddenly stopped, and Tick slammed on the brakes, unsure where the planks had gone. Nothing in front of him but a patch of gray velvet sea and a five-gallon bucket on a post at the end of the planking. He swayed and burped as a bilious wave lifted his shoulders. He grabbed for a piling, but he was wobbling so violently it took two tries to get hold. As he reached for the bucket, he completely forgot why, turned it over and lowered himself to sitting.

"Flying apart," he whispered, wondering. "Everything's flying. Apart." There was no answering explanation from the rising tide. "Seen this kind of thing when the planks pop off an old dory. Soon's one pops, another one goes. Dangerous. Axel's dangerous. I'm scaring myself too, the shit-head ideas I get."

He fumbled with his suspenders, trying to release the whiskey bottle.

"Why'd you have to go be a hero, Kenny? Makes the rest of us look like losers. And if you had to be a hero, why'd you have to go get yourself killed? Come on back, Kenny. Drinks on me. Come over to my place. Annie Klawon's gone off. Boys dancing at your party. Place all to ourselves."

Still there was no response, but the fog began to turn lavender as evening came on and the tide sank under the dock.

"Found the bottle of tequila in your woodpile. That's gone by now. Thought you wouldn't mind. We're missing a good wake, you and me, people singing in the fog. Real thick out here on the docks too. Can't hardly find my own mouth."

There was silence on the docks, then, and vague music on the fog.

"Holy shit, Kenny. You under there?"

The reply was a nasty growl and the crunch of teeth crushing bone.

Tick rolled off the bucket onto all fours and pressed his eye to the space between the planks. The dock shifted under his weight. The sudden movement made his head spin.

"Kenny?"

A heavy body bashed into the planking and growled again. Tick jerked back. It smelled hellish down there, like rotting fish. He swung his head toward a great splash and ruckus at the edge of the dock. From the folds of the tide, the pallid carcass of a halibut slowly rose and, with a great growling and smacking, slid onto the float under the planking of the dock.

Tick put his eye to the crack again. In the dim light, the halibut skeleton's grinning head, its smashed eye, the knobby spine and stiletto ribs—they all passed by like a film reel, and Tick found himself eyeball to eyeball with a river otter. It snarled.

Tick jumped back. "Do that again, I'll piss my pants."

He sat back on his haunches and gripped the spinning planks. How could he shoot that otter without blasting a hole in the float and sinking the dock? Before long, the line of thought dissolved into the fog. Tick fumbled for the bottle and found it safely next to the bucket.

"Sure is a pile of people over on your gangway." He took a slug, for Kenny.

"Pretty dark in your cabin.

"Nora was there. All by herself. Leaning on the wall. Her face was white as a flounder. Shivering like a dying flounder too. You know that, Kenny, how it shivers down its fins when you run a knife down its line?"

Tick waited to see if Kenny had anything to say about that. The river otter moaned. Water hummed along the planking of the boats. The tide was running hard.

"'This is all my fault,' that's what old Nora said, but she was a liar. I said it was all my fault, and oh then she was pissed.

"'You did the best you could,' she said. 'Even if it wasn't good enough to save him, it was still the best you could do and how could you know what Kenny was up to, even if I could have figured it out if I wasn't such an *idiot*, and even if you had figured out what Kenny was doing, how would you know what the bear was going to do . . .

"'If I wasn't such a coward.' That's what she said, Kenny. 'A slinking coward.' She kind of choked then, Kenny. 'That Kenny was a good one. He was a prince. And look what I've done.'

"A prince, Kenny. She called you a prince." Tick's sudden laughter collapsed into sobs. "If it was anybody's fault, it was Axel's for putting the bear in the tank and for using a cheap chain on the lock.

"God's truth. If Axel wasn't such a cheapskate, you'd still be here, Kenny, stinkin' up the boardwalk, that's what I told Nora, negligent homicide, that's Axel, cuff him and fly him out of here. Ask me, you took a bullet for Axel. Bear should have went for Axel. But you won't see Axel saying thank you any time soon. That's what I was saying."

The first of the sunset was seeping out of the fog and spreading across the water. On the sinking tide, seas pulsed against the pilings, slow and steady and dark red as a heartbeat. As if each impact bruised the sea, the Green Point buoy moaned again and again and moaned again. Tick rolled onto his back and groaned.

"Oh God, I'm sorry, Kenny. You know it was my fault. Coulda shot the sow and cub that afternoon, I was ready to, had it all set up. Knew you wouldn't like that, but that's not why I didn't. You know why I didn't shoot 'em? Chicken. That's what I was. Davy shows up, that was just an excuse to go home. Didn't want to go to jail, boys sent off to Seattle. You'd've told me, 'aahh go on, shithead. Shoot 'em. Put 'em out of their misery.' But it's different when there's us two thinking up crazy things.

"Crazy things.

"Yeah."

The otter went back to chewing.

"That was a good one, you and me, notching Axel's cabin." Tick's chest guffawed, but his throat closed against the laughter. "Yeh. Good one. You got the ideas and the balls. I got the chain saw, no ideas, no cojones. A perfect team, Laurel and Hardy, that's us. Now I guess it's just Laurel. Or Hardy.

"Crap.

"Up at your cabin, I rummaged in your woodpile until I found your stash, hah hah knew that's where it would be, poured Nora a stiff one. She wouldn't take it, so I drank it myself. To be friendly. It was awful quiet, Nora just standing there in your cabin with her eyes closed sometimes and sometimes open, sort of staring, party going on outside.

"'There's lasagna,' I said, and even stupid me, I knew that was a stupid thing to say to old Nora, who was just standing there. Standing . . . that's all.

"'We're going to give him a good fire.' Nora said that. Out of the blue. I said, 'What?' She said, 'You can help,' so I said okay." Tick rubbed his eyes, saltwater on his hands. "Shit. My job? Getting dry firewood from everybody and loading it onto the *Annie K.* Then I guess we'll load you on too, unless you want to ride out to the bonfire beach in the seiner."

For a long time, Tick lay stiff on his back under the cold hand of the fog and waited for Kenny to make up his mind. As if they were uncomfortable, the boats in the harbor shifted and the lines creaked.

"Don't want you too froze, or you'll just smolder."

"No more cold iron shackles for my feet."

Tick lurched up straight, then quickly laid back down, gripping the edge of the dock. The sound came from another world. His head reeled.

"What's that? What, Kenny?"

But it was the music up on the boardwalk, and the accordion solo trickling down through the fog and an electric guitar joining in, *bwaa.* Tick sucked on the bottle and settled back down.

"So listen, damn you, Kenny.

"Nora must've loved you something else, Kenny, cuz she's furious that you went and died. 'We need him.' She said that. 'The world needs Kenny. What a waste! What a *terr-i-ble* waste.' Like you were toothpaste or something, all squoze out for nothing.

"Aw, sorry about your brains, Kenny."

Tick wished the otters would quit their chewing. All that smacking and the fog sinking and the night falling until there was only a narrow crawl space between the fog and the bones.

"And I was getting nervous, up there in your cabin, because there came Lillian, and all your buddies huddling in the dark was starting to look like a freaking committee meeting. Freaking. Committee. What we gonna do first? What we gonna do next? Couldn't figure out why Nora was acting like I was in on something. Did everybody know I notched Axel's piling? Did they know about the Marlin .444, how I was gonna put the bears out of their misery? I was getting out of there, and somebody knocks on your door.

"It's Rebecca Hagerman, peeking into the dark.

"Ah shit, I'm thinking. I am so busted.

"But what's the crime in being the friend of a dead guy? I'm tired of thinking, am I doing somethin' Axel won't like? Screw it. I was drinking a dead guy's tequila, and in walks the wife of the guy who probably killed him—I mean, yessiree, if you think about it. Is she gonna arrest me? She looks around, kind of letting her eyes get used to the light . . . I guess squinty is what she always is, kind of checking out who's there and who isn't, nodding yes yes. But she's crying, Kenny. That little nose is red as a bug. She says, 'I brought Kenny a petunia,' and damned if she didn't. A purple petunia in a little green pot. Nora grabs her in a big hug and says Kenny would be so glad to have the petunia, and I thought yessirreebob. Kenny would be so glad to have a petunia, so he could pee in the pot at night and wouldn't have to go out and pee over the side. He'd pee until the poor petunia keeled over and died. Then he'd throw it overboard."

Pee. Tick rolled to his knees and stumped like a penitent to the edge of the dock. He leaned his forehead against the bow of a Boston Whaler and fumbled with his fly. Where he pissed into the bay, tiny jellyfish flickered like candlelight. Had he been in this place before? He had, maybe a long time before. He struggled to remember. He knew the sound of the wine pouring into the chalice and the pressure on his knees, and he knew the hand on his head and the smell of candles burning. He knew the sound of a hundred people trying to be quiet. It was the rustle of water when the tide had fallen and stilled.

"How can you stand it, Kenny, to lose this? How can you stand it, losing night tides and wet docks? What's it like when it all disappears? Just, suck, gone.

"Ah man, I'm going to lose it all. Lost you. Lost my fishing trawler a long time ago. Lost my job. Lost my nerve. I'm going to lose Annie Klawon. Then I'm sure to lose my boys, Tommy crying for his mom in the night. How pitiful is that? Davy coming home smelling of dope and not saying where he was at, and why should he say anything to a shithead father can't hold anything together?"

Hand over hand on the light pole, Tick raised himself to standing. He rebounded from bow to bow along the dock, until he got to the edge of the falling tide under the dripping cross-timbers of the town, to the hidden places only vaguely revealed, the rotten bases of the pilings, the gaping holes in the mud where soft things retreated. The slow slug of waves, the *tick tick* of barnacles. Fog opened in front of him as he stumbled along, and fog closed behind him, the way music will do, or water. Not night, not day, not alive, not dead, the fog absorbed everything, digested it into something vague and formless and yellow—the air and the soft mud, the stinking shame that emanated from every step Tick took, the deflated kelp, the vague yellow shame of the world.

August 30

HIGH TIDE		LOW TIDE	
4:19am	14.8ft	10:22am	1.9ft
4:33pm	16.1ft	10:51pm	1.3ft

"Here, get your hands off me."

Tick had Lillian under the arms and was about to hoist her from the wharf onto the deck of the *Annie K*. Great God almighty, if he would just leave her alone, she could climb on board under her own power. It had been a while since she'd got herself in and out of a boat, and her knees didn't work like they used to, but that was no reason to treat a lady like a crate of pigs. Besides, why would a woman want to hang on to a man when there was a perfectly trustworthy railing right there in front of her? She stuck her good slacks into her boots, tugged down her hat, held on to the railing, and hauled herself onto the boat.

"See?" she said to Tick, and poked him sharp with her elbow. He'd been standing by, hanging on to Lillian's raincoat as she hauled, the way a longshoreman holds the rope to guide a pallet that's being on-loaded by a crane—sort of off to the side and ready to jump if she gave way.

Once Lillian and Tick were on board, Tick pulled the *Annie K* next to the salmon seiner where they were keeping Kenny on ice. He and the fishermen went into the fish-hold and brought him out. Kenny was rolled up in a blue tarp, tight as a burrito, so with a couple of guys holding the tarp at one end, and a couple holding the other, they didn't have any trouble slinging him onto the *Annie K*. Kenny was plenty cold. The breath of the guys fogged when they leaned over to set him down by the wheelhouse.

The *Annie K* was a heck of a hearse, that old rattletrap boat with greasy rags thrown in the corners and splinters and moss-bark all over the deck. But Kenny couldn't have asked for a more beautiful funeral-parade route. It'd been misting all morning, but as the *Annie K* left the harbor, the sun came out, and every fleck of rain glittered.

Lillian looked over the stern. The people of Good River Harbor had turned out to honor Kenny's last journey. They stood bunched up on the ferry dock, reflected upside down on the water. All of them were turned on their heads—the men and women who stood silently on the dock to watch the *Annie K* leave, the children riding bikes past green, pink, blue houses, the postal clerk by the flag at half-mast. As the *Annie K*'s wake rolled under the town, the town and all its people stretched and narrowed, stretched and narrowed, then slowly rocked themselves together again. When a stray cloud drifted over the town, the reflected figures shivered under light rain.

The *Annie K* rounded Green Point and motored along the shore, past Nora's cove, past the headland, then along alder shores. The sun paraded in and out among the clouds, sending down rays like roaming spotlights, pointing to the spruce forest, then the clear-cut hill. A layer of low clouds bisected the mountains, so the mountaintops floated up there like green and white balloons.

"Don't you be grumbling, Kenny," Lillian said to the blue tarp. "I'm tired of hearing you complain that the sun spoils your complexion. Shut up and enjoy it just for once."

"HAR!" Tick yelled from the wheelhouse, making her jump.

Propping her hip against the rail, Lillian buttoned up her raincoat, tightened the knot on her belt, and pushed her hat down tighter. She had chosen the hat because it looked good with her eyes. It was a cloche she had knitted herself from yarn she unraveled from a blue sweater. She pulled a couple of curls down over her forehead. Then she stood braced in the bow beside Kenny, watching the coves and headlands go by.

Lillian had dressed up in honor of the fact that she was the preacher and the choir for the day. Nora and Tick had appointed her. They needed a preacher, they said, to say some holy words over Kenny's ashes and they needed a choir to sing a hymn. Lillian thought that was appropriate. She had been doing laundry for twenty years, washing men's dirty clothes. How much harder could it be to clean up their snotty, soot-stained souls? Absolution might even be easier than washing Carhartt overalls, which takes some muscle, getting them out of the washer, all soaked. But who knows? It might have been smart to start off her soul-cleaning business with somebody easier than Kenny was going to be.

Poor old Kenny. Lillian pulled her eyes away from the blue tarp. On the day he died, Kenny and Ranger had rolled into the bar, just as they did every Friday morning at ten. Ranger sniffed at the door to the laundry, rolled his eyes, and lay down with his chin on his paws. Evidently, he did not approve of what was about to happen. Kenny shoved a dollar in the can, helped himself to a clean towel and bar of soap from the shelves, chose a hunting magazine from the slanting pile, and shut himself into the laundry and shower room. After a while, Lillian heard the hot water clank on, and after many more than the five minutes he had paid for, she heard it clank off. Then a lot of scuffling, and three out of four quarters dropped into the coin receptacle on the washing machine. She heard Kenny pound on the washing machine the way he always did, trying to make the fourth quarter fall.

"Just jiggle it," Lillian had yelled. It pained her now to know that those would be the last words she said to him.

There had been no response, but the washing machine rattled violently on its screw feet. Water poured into the machine, and Lillian went back to her accounts as the machine sprayed and spun. She knew that Kenny would be sitting in the steamy laundry room, white and naked and skinny as a tomcod, reading about rifles. Naked as a tomcod before the eyes of God, while the machine washed every item of clothing he had been wearing, which is about every item of clothing he owned—with the notable exception of his hats. The machine spun and squealed and finally clanked to a stop. Then dimes dropped into place and the dryer bumped and thumped.

There is no place in the Bible—Lillian knew, because she had looked. There is no place in the Bible where Jesus or the Apostles or anybody says, please God, tighten the screws and oil the bearings on my soul. Nobody says, glue these splayed soul-joints and clamp them tight. Oh no. When people's souls need attending to, what they need is a good washing. *Dear God, wash my soul clean from sin.* Water is holy, and the person who runs the Laundromat is doing the Lord's work, even though the carpenter got first billing. Lillian didn't have much use for God, or vice versa, she guessed, but it mattered to her that Kenny was clean when he died. She hoped that when she died, she would be fresh out of the shower and that she would have had time to arrange her hair into curls pretty enough to please the angels.

Tick nudged the *Annie K* into the beach, jumped out, and dragged his anchor up the strand. He'd chosen a wide gravel beach encircled by a forest, a good distance and downwind from town. Nora had her little team working hard. She was splitting wood, bareheaded in her yellow raincoat, her hair stringy and stuck to her back. She had already split an enormous pile of kindling, and she was still going at it. Tick had been in and out of town with the *Annie K* all day, collecting the firewood people donated—milled wood ends, broken shipping pallets, quartered rounds of hemlock and spruce. It was three miles out of town and a mountain of firewood, so that was a lot of hauling. Lillian ran a practiced eye over the stovewood. Two, three cords, maybe more. This was going to be some fire. A small woman with her hair tied up in a red bandana was kneeling in the gravel, hammering together a sort of lattice platform from poles cut from alders.

Rebecca Hagerman, Axel's sweetie, Lillian said to herself. I'd heard she defected.

Rebecca looked like she'd been crying. Her nose was always unattractively pink, but it wasn't usually *that* pink. She was smiling over her work now, and her head was bobbing, even though hitting a nail square on the head was apparently a work in progress. Lillian wondered what Axel thought about his wife working with Kenny's funeral crew. She guessed Axel didn't know what Rebecca was doing, partly because she'd moved over to Nora's, but mostly because he had decided not to care. That was one of the talents Axel had developed early, a talent that other people had to work all their lives to perfect—without even breaking a sweat, he could decide not to care.

Now that the guest of honor had arrived in his blue tarp and the clergy-and-choir was present, everybody was there who was invited. Lillian turned her head away as Tick leaned down to unwrap Kenny from the tarp. When she heard the familiar thunder of a tarp being shaken, she turned back. Nora was folding the blue tarp as carefully as if it were a soldier's flag, and Kenny's body lay on the gravel, wrapped head to toe in his camouflage poncho. Two ravens marched over and stood by like an honor guard.

"Let's get to work," Tick ordered, and the ravens lifted off and soared to the edge of the clearing. First, they built the structure that would hold the body, setting a platform on thick green poles. Tick and Nora struggled to get Kenny up there without unrolling him. The platform was head height, and the last thing they wanted was to roll him out onto the beach, half thawed. Once he was safely loaded, they stuck the pinwheel and the little American flag from his wheelchair into a chink in the wood near him. Nora had brought along the hat he'd made from the bear cub with silver shoulders. Crying quietly, she tucked it under his head.

Tick brought over a bucket for Lillian to sit on, bless his heart, get the weight off her feet while she watched. They built four big piles of kindling near the corners of the platform. Then they loaded on the firewood, stacking it under the platform in a teepee higher than Tick's shoulders. People had picked out good wood, nothing punky or wet, and that's one thing you can say about the people in Good River Harbor, they have good judgment in firewood. Tick had held back probably another half-cord to feed the fire if they needed to. He ran around the pyre, getting things set up just right, pouring a slug of diesel fuel at the corners. Then he went back to the *Annie K* and brought out four propane torches.

Tick gave out the torches and made one last check. Then he sent Nora around to one pile of kindling, and Lillian and Rebecca to the others. He looked over to Lillian to see if the preacher was ready to issue the call to prayer.

The preacher stood up and smoothed the front of her raincoat.

"Light him," she said.

They all knelt down and set their propane torches to the kindling. It struck Lillian to the heart, to see Kenny's friends down on their knees like that, bent over like they were sinners, not arsonists. Starting at that moment, she missed old pickle-face, missed him hard and bad, like she would miss the sour pleasure of coffee in the morning if it died and went to hell. White smoke rose from the four corners of the pyre. Everyone backed away to watch it catch. Before long, smoke was sliding up the side of the firewood, and then flames licked up through the pile. Yellow smoke seeped through the platform and curled around the edges. Soon Lillian could hardly see the poncho in the haze. If they can't get a fire hotter than this, she fretted, they should have brined and smoked him.

A new wind sucked the fire into the center. Suddenly, the pyre erupted in flame. Smoke rose straight up. The loose edge of the poncho flapped violently. The stars and stripes waved. The pinwheel spun madly. Flames shot up twenty feet. The edge of the poncho blackened and melted onto the pole. Lillian backed away. The pyre was all on fire now, burning like a torch. Kenny sizzled. Everyone backed even farther away, pressing toward the cool forest behind them. Ashes shot into the sky. The air above the flames was clear and shimmering, the fire was that hot.

One of the poles on the platform burned through and dropped a corner of the platform deeper into the fire. Sparks and cinders flew straight up. A scrap of poncho, seared at the edges, sailed toward the sky. The fire roared and snapped. Each time it fell into itself, Tick ran toward the fire, threw on another log, and raced away before he melted his raincoat. Above his orange beard, his face was bright red. Another pole burned through, sending up a shower of sparks. The noise of that fire was terrifying as a train in a tunnel. The heat of it backed them against the trees. They all shifted out of the smoke.

A shotgun went off, so near that Lillian almost crinked her neck, flinching. Then another blast. She grabbed hold of Nora and cranked around. There was Tick, the gun to his shoulder, shooting into the air. He shot it off again. He stopped to reload.

"Twenty-one gun salute," he said somberly. "Eighteen to go." He fired them all off, three at a time, stopping to reload, sending buckshot into the ocean, into the trees, into the fire, *blam, blam, blam*. Lillian's ears rang from the shotgun blasts and the roar of the fire.

She couldn't see anything of Kenny. Her eyes were watering from flame and shimmering mountains—yellow flames, orange flames, sometimes a feather of blue, a burst of black smoke, a spiral of white, then the silver air and the flames. Who knows how long the fire burned? After a while, Tick stopped throwing on logs. He joined the others on boulders at the edge of the beach and watched the fire settle into itself. A wind came up from the northwest and the fire came to life again. Flames raced up and down the logs. Gray smoke blew over the water. Then the fire settled itself into a flickering burn. Evening came on, with yellow streaks behind the mountains. The cold started to flow from the forest. The fire felt good. They moved a little closer—to the fire, to each other, to Kenny's warm ashes.

The tide began to rise. The leading edge fingered under the fire. White ash lifted on the curl, a sheen of ashes that swayed and spread across the water. A river of ashes seeped out on the current, flowing across the ocean and vanishing in the slick of last light. The tide lifted burning embers and drifted them away, smoking and sparkling yellow. The fire whistled and whispered as water rose under it, and smoke bubbled up and burst. Lillian realized it was time to sanctify the moment.

She settled her cloche and curls, stood up, and made her way over the gravel to the upwind edge of the fire. She waited until Tick paid attention.

"Dearly Beloved," she said. Everybody was looking at her. Nora put her arm around Rebecca. Tick straightened his shoulders. Out of her coat pocket, Lillian pulled a bottle of the best brandy behind her bar. She uncorked the bottle, moved as close as she could to the fire, and slowly began to pour. Beautiful blue flames licked over the log—blue as moonlit midnight, blue as muskeg lakes, blue as crab eyes. As she poured, Lillian looked toward heaven and began to sing.

"*Sunset and evening star,*" she sang.

"Stop!"

Lillian was so startled she tweaked her bad knee. Tick had already started toward her. He cradled the bottle in his big hands and looked at the label. "You *drink* the host," he said soberly. "You don't pour it on the ground."

He had wrecked Lillian's holy moment, after she had practiced it, the gestures and the silken tone. But she was feeling dry herself. So they drank the brandy. They sat by the fire, like people would sit around any campfire, and passed the bottle as the tide crept in and floated the ashes away. The brandy opened Lillian's throat. After a while, she stood up, lifted her arms the way she'd practiced, closed her eyes, and began again to sing.

Sunset and evening star, and one clear call for me,
And may there be no moaning of the bar, when I put out to sea.

When I put out to sea, when I put out to sea.
And may there be no moaning of the bar, when I put out to sea.

But such a tide as moving seems asleep, too full for sound and foam,
When that which drew from out the boundless deep, turns again home.

Turns again home, turns again home,
When that which drew from out the boundless deep, turns again home.

Lillian waited a long moment, then lowered herself onto her five-gallon pail. She lit a cigarette. The only sounds then were the snap of the fire and the whisper of water and ash.

"Damn that Kenny. Damn him to hell." Tick was blubbering, so he could only croak out the words. He has a way of turning the mood, Lillian could say that for him.

"Hellfire's going to be an anticlimax," Rebecca said softly.

Lillian figured it was time to exert some ecclesiastical authority. "No more talk of hellfire. The only sins Kenny committed were pigheadedness, grumpiness . . ." She stopped to think. ". . . and corrupting the youth. None of these are mortal sins, last time I looked."

"Shitheadedness. And lusting in his heart," Tick choked. "And lying to his friends," he added, with some degree of resentment.

"He was kind to dogs," Nora pointed out.

"That will turn the argument for St. Peter," Lillian decreed. "That and the fact that he had more courage than all of us put together. And he died playing what he thought was a good trick on the world." She ground out the cigarette with her boot on the sand.

So the issue of salvation was settled. Lillian nodded to Nora, who had prepared the benediction. Lillian had chosen her because she was the only writer among them and she would work hard on it and say something good. Nora pulled a piece of paper out of her raincoat pocket and unfolded it in the light of the flashlight Tick held.

"You're free, Kenny. So, go. Float into snaggle-top spruce trees and settle on the shoulders of disappointed ravens. Rise on the upslope winds to the snowfields. Dust the blue ice and bog orchids. Spread your ashy wing across the water. Drift with the torn kelp. Sift slowly down in the dim saltwater, past bulging yellow eyes watching. Suck into the gullet of a great ugly sculpin, and stick to the tube feet of the blood-red star. Rise again with the roaring whales. And when the salmon come, go home with them. Go home to the place where they die. That is the place where life begins again."

Nora refolded the paper and pushed it into the embers. It caught and flared. Kenny's friends murmured.

"Roger that."

Lillian wasn't expecting to be touched, but that part about going home? That did it for her. This time, she didn't mind when Nora wrapped her long arms around her and dragged her damp hair over Lillian's face.

Night covered the cove like a raven's wing, and still they sat. Tide fluttered in. Lifted, the *Annie K* nosed into shore. Tick picked his way through the dark to pull in slack rope. When he lifted the painter from the water, it trailed a skirt of sparks. Tick threw down a loop of rope, drawing an answering loop of sparks that flashed and popped so sharply they almost crackled.

"You in hell after all, Kenny?" Tick hefted a rock and tossed it in the drink. In the place it disappeared, a splash rose like a circlet of flame.

He tossed in another stone. Small creatures in the sea—bioluminescent algae, dinoflagellates, jellyfish—flashed blue, flashed white. Nora waded in. Small sparkling lives swirled around her feet. Rebecca held Lillian's hand and led her into the water. That's how it ended, Kenny's funeral. Silhouetted black against a black night, four friends slowly, sedately, danced in the tidal swash and the flash of small lives. Ashes stuck to their boots.

September 9

HIGH TIDE		LOW TIDE	
1:35am	19.3ft	7:47 am	-3.0ft
2:07pm	19.2ft	8:11 pm	-2.6ft

So it was decided. That quickly. On an early morning walk in the intertidal to hunt for sea cucumbers. On a day of scattered clouds and minus tides, with a skiff running down the channel and an eagle watching the kelp beds for crabs. By two people standing ankle-deep in water beside a log polished silver by winter storms, it was decided. Is this how it happens, as routinely as day turns to night?

All the week before Kenny died, Nora and Tick had been talking big, hanging out in her kitchen while Tommy practiced the piano and Rebecca washed old wine bottles for salmonberry wine. But all their talk had been hypothetical, a silly joke they shared.

"If we wanted to wash away the plywood framing for the dam, we would need just the right flood—not too big, not too little. We would be trying to save the salmon, not wreck the place." Nora.

"We could time it to a flood-tide, water rising up, water crashing down, yeehaw." Tick.

"We would have to figure out how nobody gets hurt. Just stuff, right? Just the dam." Rebecca had walked over, drying her hands, and they all three solemnly shook on that.

It was just fun, a charade, nothing real. They laughed, their uproarious little committee.

Then Kenny died. That was real.

On the beach, Nora leaned over to pick up the empty carapace of a crab. The outer surface of the shell was ruddy and knobby. But inside was luminous, opalescent, lavender.

"Look at this, Tick," she said. "You tell me why this is so beautiful in its hidden places. What's the use of that, what's the survival value in that, to be beautiful inside, where no one will ever see until it's dead and gone?" It made her think of Kenny, but that was no surprise. Everything made her think of Kenny. "Kenny told me about that philosophical problem, called it the Problem of Unnecessary Beauty."

Tick took the crab shell in his big hand. "Yeah. The guy was full of philosophical problems."

"Do you remember that night at Lillian's when Kenny told us the story of Abraham from the Bible?" Nora went on.

Tick snorted.

"God said to Abraham, 'I command you to kill your son, your only son, the one whom you love—Isaac,' Kenny said. 'Take him to the mountain, tie him to an altar, pile sticks around him, slit his throat, and set him on fire.' So being a man of faith and obedience, Abraham did what God said. But just when he was bending to cut his son's throat, an angel appeared. She told Abraham to let Isaac go and sacrifice a ram instead. Which he did.

"'So was Abraham a good man or a bad man?' Kenny demanded. He drew his knife then, right there in Lillian's bar, and held it to his own throat.

"'Jeezus, Kenny,' everybody was yelling. 'Put the knife away.'

"'HAR,' Kenny said, and drove the blade into the table."

Nora settled herself on a driftwood log with her knees to her chin and her arms wrapped around them. Abraham was a good person, wasn't he? She had asked Kenny, but he wouldn't say. It's a good person, who does what she thinks is right, even if she loses what she loves the very most. Even if she wrecks her chance for a normal life? Even if she destroys stuff. Isn't that true? Is that true? Or is that just stubborn and stupid? Her eyes were huge and bright with yellow light reflected from a glaze on the sea at the Green Point buoy. She inhaled the smell of the cove—hemlocks and salt-crusted algae. God, she loved this place.

"Shit, shit, shit, shit, shit," she said. "Here I go again. I guess we really are going to make that flood. This one's for you, Kenny." And because Kenny couldn't answer, Nora answered for him, not shouting as Kenny would have done, but murmuring quiet as the tide. "*When you were called, did you answer, or not? Perhaps softly and in a whisper?*"

"Kierkegaard," she told Tick, and grinned. Tick grunted, and sat down so hard he lifted Nora's end of the log. Chum barked sharply, then jumped off the log to snuffle under a coil of kelp.

"That splash dam has to go in this week, before the rains start to fall on the old snowfields," Nora said. She looked hard at Tick. "You all in?"

He rubbed his forehead with his beard. "I'm in. I'm stupid, but I'm in. For one damn time, I'm putting myself in charge. All my years in the Harbor, I tried to keep my tools oiled, my propane tanks full, my pantry stocked," Tick said. "Didn't always get it done, but I knew I had to try. That's what you do when you know it's all going to end. You keep your chain saw sharpened, and you stay alert, because you know you won't get much warning. Then, sure enough, it's over and that's that. Don't know how many times my life has ended, Axel laying me off, Annie Klawon heading back to Seattle. Five? Six? And each time, I think how in the name of the ever-lovin' God am I going to get my life started up again, but I got to. I just do."

Nora closed her eyes. Didn't she know it?

Tick whapped her solidly on the back. "But this is no end, old Nora. For once, we got ourselves a beginning." He looked around. "Where are the trumpets? Shouldn't there be trumpets? Gonna make a world that doesn't have to end all the time, used up and shut down.

"I can build a splash dam across that little opening in a day, maybe two. That might be bragging, but close enough. I know how to fix the dam up with a key log, so it only takes one person on a pry pole to break it open." Tick stopped. "Who's gonna be on that pry pole?"

Nora took a deep breath. "That would be me," she said.

There were no trumpets, just young ravens yakking, kelp blades swashing in a falling tide, and a single thrush whistling. That was it.

From the curve of ancient logs that rims the cove on the far side of the point, they could see the lines on the beach that mark each level of the receding tide—a row of clean gravel, then the line of green eelgrass laid down by the ebb tide, then a windrow of white clamshells, then a band at the edge of the water—broad brown blades of kelp. Past that, there was clear sand in shallow water.

Nora leaned back and rubbed her eyes. "Those five tide lines are laid out like the lines of a musical score," she said, pointing to the lines of shells and seaweed on the beach. Tick looked up. Five lines there were, and sea stars clinging like quarter notes to the places they had landed when the tide went out. Chum's footprints ran in and out of the lines. A black raven stood in the eelgrass strip and pecked at a clam.

"It is all so ordered and inevitable—as if God were trying to find the language to tell us something. Or to make us feel something, some emotion. If only we could learn to read that music. The notes are written right there on the gravel. There is a divine score. The universe is a madrigal, and it's beautiful and true and complicated, all the parts moving together in these changing relations through time, and we're all part of it—I just know this, that we're part of the music—but we can't quite figure it out, no matter how hard we try, *and we do* try, but we play our parts wrong and what could have been so beautiful is ugly and mean. It's so sad."

"Shut up, Nora." Tick flipped up his beard to cover his eyes.

"We're all trying to find that resonance, the hum in our bodies that tells us we are exactly in tune with the planet, and sometimes we do—enough to make us long for it every day. We tune ourselves too high this way, too low that way. We come so close, but that's the worst dissonance, to be close and get it wrong. Don't you think that when even a five-year-old kid can hear when harmony goes sour and change his fingers until he knows it's right, *just from the sound of* it, that the rest of us could figure it out? You have to try something, and listen. Why is that so hard for us?"

Tick covered his ears. Nora lifted her head. She listened more intently than she had listened in her life. Under the slow pulse of the sea on stones, under the mutter and squeak of unseen lives in the kelp, she heard the rush of her own heart, not beating against a wall—the way it always had—but flooding, as a wave pours down the beach.

She squared her shoulders and stood up to retrieve the bucket. Tick stood up too, and they walked down to the water, where they would find the sea cucumbers they were hunting.

"Okay, so we should get started. Who knows how long it will take for the reservoirs to fill. And the first salmon are already staging at the mouth of the river."

They skidded along the slippery edge of the bay, trying to put their boots on the rough grip of gravel. Eelgrass is slippery, and kelp blades are even worse.

“It’s time.” Nora nodded. “I dreamed the salmon’s dream again last night. It was dark and it was raining. I was trying to get home. But everything stopped me. I couldn’t find shoes. I looked everywhere, in my file cabinets and suitcases. Just tore them apart. And all the time I was looking for my shoes, I knew I only had ten minutes before the bus left. I ran to the bus, in snow, in the dark. Snow now. I don’t know if I found my shoes. The last people were getting on and they looked back at me and frantically waved me in, but I had forgotten my suitcase, and when I went back to the house, it was locked, and when I ran back, the bus driver said, ‘Where to?’ I didn’t know. It was written on my ticket and I couldn’t find my ticket because it was in my coat, but the coat was in the closet and I went back home and I was pounding on the door of my apartment, but how could that be, because I was home, but I had to get home. I couldn’t and I had to.”

She had told Tick about the salmon dream several times before. She believed that salmon have the same dream as she does, and swallows, and college students, and every homesick goose, all trying to get home, all feeling that panic when you have to go home and everything conspires against you. She thinks this is the dream of the world. “We’re all one big dream of going home,” she said, “and it’s a nightmare.”

Water lapped at their boots, reminding them that they were supposed to be gathering dinner. Still they stood there. Chum waded out and then looked back, waiting for them. The tide was rising. It straightened the kelp and pulled at the fur on Chum’s belly.

“I’ll check the tide tables and set the date,” Nora said.

She couldn’t believe the words were coming out of her mouth. She felt like someone else, maybe someone she used to be.

“And Tick, I’m going to talk to Axel one more time. We have to give him a chance to do the right thing.”

“How many chances does a dick get in one lifetime?”

“One more.”

SO THAT WAS that. Nora checked her watch. "I need to be careful of the time. I want to get back to tuning that poor piano before Tommy comes for his lesson. God, Tick, it's hard to keep things tuned up in this place. It's not like you can get every tone right in itself, they have to be right in relation to each other. That's the tough part. Constant struggle. Then the weather changes."

They waded in the tide up to their boot tops, stumbling over rocks hidden by kelp. Under the kelp were all the sea cucumbers they would ever want. For a good dinner, they needed five of the astonishing things—short, fat phallic echinoderms with orange spikes poking out every which way and a crayon-red body. In the water, they're fat. But when Tick draped a sea cucumber over his hand and lifted it out of the water, it stretched to twice its length on both ends and rolled away, a stretchy pouch of water almost too insubstantial to hold. Tick pushed his sleeve back up, reached into the sea, and pulled up another sea cucumber. Nora offered the pail.

As they hiked up the trail from the cove, they heard Tommy playing Nora's piano. Chum ran ahead, barking. Nora had told Tommy to chord with his left hand and play the melody with his right. He had mastered the melody, but the chords were coming more slowly, so it was an oddly limping song he played, with long pauses when it was time to switch chords. He sang along, accompanying himself, patiently waiting for the chord to change before he picked up the next phrase. Nora laughed. It felt good, almost like a fairy tale, to walk with a big woodsman from the moss-fragrant forest into a clearing where a little boy was playing the piano rather badly on the front porch of a log cabin. How can a life like this last forever?

Rebecca was sitting on the porch next to Tommy, sorting leaves from a bucket of red huckleberries, nodding her head in time with the music. Nora went straight to Tommy, rubbing his head and praising his song. Then she leaned over his back to watch him play. That's how they went through "Motorcycle Cops." Tommy was racing through it as well as he could, asking when they would get to "Jingle Bells," and what would be the song after that?

It seemed like a good thing, this trade—a flood for a song, a song for a flood—the power of water for the beauty of music, the beauty of water for the power of music.

"Dashing through the snow, in a one-horse open sleigh."

Nora was playing the song, with Tommy on her lap and his hands on hers. Tick pulled a plank from Nora's lumber pile and leaned it against the porch. He drove a nail all the way through the board. Reaching into the bucket, he pulled out a sea cucumber and impaled one end on the nail.

"O'er the fields we go, laughing all the way."

The sea cucumber hung there on its stake, getting longer and longer, stretched by the weight of the water collecting at its aft end. Tick snipped its skin at the bottom. The water drained out. With a fillet knife, he slit the sea cucumber stem to stern and opened it. There were the five long, white muscles that they were going to eat. Sliding the knife under one end of each muscle, he stripped them off, one and then another. Then he slit each muscle lengthwise, ending up with ten strips of meat and a limp sack of skin.

"What fun it is to laugh and sing a sleighing song tonight."

While Nora and Tommy worked over the chords, practicing the switch from C to G, Rebecca turned on the propane tank and went inside to cook. While the oil heated in the skillet, Rebecca dredged the sea cucumber strips in flour, salt, and pepper. She cooked them fast, until they were golden. They ate them with their fingers, the four of them, sitting on the planks of the front porch in the gleam of the day. The sea cucumbers were salty and good.

Hold on to this memory, Nora reminded herself. Let it settle into your mind, the sweetness of this point in time. Step back and see it from a distance. Try different angles, front view, rear. Chew slowly, and hold the taste on your tongue. You will look back on this very day and wonder what happened, and you will need to remember the sound and the taste of it, and this crazy, awful thing, that you will give up this home, what you love the best, so the salmon can find their way home.

"Which do you think my mom would like better," Tommy asked. "'Go Tell Aunt Rhody' or 'Angels Watchin' Over Me'? The dead gray goose maybe, or angels? Nora says I get to choose."

Rebecca reached around his shoulders and pulled him close. Her eyes disappeared in her smile.

"May it be angels," she said.

≈≈≈

AFTER SHE MOVED out of Axel's house, Rebecca had trudged up and down the boardwalk, nodding yes yes, pushing wheelbarrows full of plants from her house to the bear pit, a load of tomatoes just turning red and then back again for Shasta daisies and back for lilies, and back for petunias and zucchini. She planted them every which way in the bear pit, sticking them in piles of dirt as if she didn't care if they lived or died, until her house was stripped bare and the bear pit looked like a community garden planted by a committee of zombies.

But Rebecca had come alive while she lived with Nora. She had laughed like a schoolgirl while she stuffed a rotten salmon into a sculpin's mouth. Tick thought it was a silly trick, risky and useless, but she said, no, it was almost perfect and the only thing better would be if it was a bear's paw. And then she laughed and laughed, until she started to cry. Nora went over and hugged her, and Rebecca put her little face into Nora's shoulder and sobbed. Sobbing still, she went back to the sink and started in again twisting a knife into the sculpin's jaw, trying to work it big enough to take in the salmon's tail. She swiped at her tears with the back of her wrist, because her hands were disgusting. At midnight, she had snuck down the boardwalk and dropped the fish in Axel's boot.

Nora laughed as she pulled out her tuning lever and opened the piano. Rebecca came out and sat cross-legged on the porch beside her.

"How's the Axel Improvement Project coming?" Nora asked as she bent to her work.

"How's the piano tuning?" Rebecca replied. "About the same constant struggle?"

"You said that right," Nora said, as she turned and tuned, turned and tuned, stopping only to wave away blackflies.

To tune a piano, it isn't enough to get each string to sing out, loud and true. It has to sing in relation to the other strings. You turn, tiny turns, tiny turns, to get middle C right. But each tone has three strings. So you mute two of them with narrow rubber pads. You have to be able to make them silent; it's the silence that allows you to hear that glorious moment when the middle C vibrates with the middle tone of all things, the center of time, the hum of tide through a sea urchin's spines, the golden mean that is the exact middle between two extremes, the way courage exactly cuts the difference between recklessness and cowardice. You find that center if you listen when everything else is quiet. Then you bring those other two strings into the shimmer of that tone. It is a shimmer—you feel it in your body, you feel it with a surety that this is the way the world was meant to be.

Okay, so that's what you do first. It's hard to explain, it's complicated—imagine finding that center, how that feels. Then D has to be right in relation to C. Tiny, tiny. Right turn, tighten, sharp. Left turn, loosen, flat. Tiny change. And E has to be right in relation to D and C, all the way up to the next C, and that gives you the temperament. Well, that's just the start. But it's good, because now you have the reference, that's what you need, the eight true tones.

Now you find the octaves, matching D to D and E to E, you find the miracle, the notes that are the same and not the same—an identity so obvious in your ear that even monkeys can hear it, even babies. And what you hear is the pulse of melded frequency, one frequency and another that is double it, or half. You have seen this if you have seen a wave overlap a wave that is rolling to shore, a convergence like a zipper, the sides of a zipper converging as they race along the shore, until there is one wave, a wave so clear and blue you can see light through it, and sometimes the dark form of a harbor seal. Convergences, all the way up the piano, all the way down. Tiny turns. Tiny changes.

It takes hours. And then the day darkens and the sky descends and the piano breathes wetter, cooler air, or the sun flashes between clouds. The world is as new as if it had been created at that moment, and that is the world in which the piano now has to resound. You keep the tuning lever always in your pocket, the way other people always carry a pocketknife, or pliers or a Bible.

Nora gave the piano an affectionate pat, packed up her tools, and went into the house. Rebecca stayed for a few more minutes on the porch. She smelled her hands and smiled.

"THAT'S IT," AXEL said. "That is entirely enough."

Notching his piling, wrecking his bear shelter pavilion, stealing his bears—fine. Just fine. But the rotten salmon in his boot, that was going too far. The fish was so far gone that it was just a mass of slime and maggots, barely held together by moldy skin, pocked and fuzzy. That was disrespectful. That was taunting him. That was poking him in the eye with a stick. And that was something he couldn't stand, being poked in the eye with a stick.

It would have made more sense for him to wash his boot out on the deck, where he could use the hose. But Axel was determined that no one—not one person—would have the satisfaction of seeing him scrubbing. So after Meredith left for his office, he put the boot in the kitchen sink, half filled it with hot water and poured in a good slug of bleach. Then he pulled on rubber gloves, grabbed a scrub brush, and went to work. It's not easy, scrubbing fish slime out of a boot. You have to reach all the way to the toe, and that's a tight fit. And where the brush doesn't fit, you have to sort of scratch with your fingers. He scratched and scrubbed, then held the boot closed at the top and shook it, sloshing the water around. When he had rinsed it, which he had to do quickly because bleach eats neoprene, he leaned down and gave a test smell. He threw the boot against the sink so hard it jumped out like it had a foot in it, kicking water onto the floor.

"Now we're playing for keeps," he said to the boot, as he pulled it out of the sink. He cranked the heat up so high under the teakettle that it rattled and buzzed. He would go after the smell and the slime with boiling water and just hope he didn't melt the damn boot.

Axel could have believed it was just kids playing a joke, maybe one of Meredith's friends, stuffing a huge dog salmon into his boot on the porch. The salmon might have washed up on the beach, stinking, with its stomach bitten out by a bear, and some kids might have found it and thought, hey that's cool, and they could have carried it up on the boardwalk and thought, hey that would be fun, let's stick the fish in this boot. But why his boot, when every single person on the boardwalk left his boots by the front door? They had probably ninety boots to choose from, and it would take some guts to choose the boot of Axel Hagerman.

No. This wasn't a joke.

Axel poured in the boiling water, careful that the boot didn't bend over and empty a load of scalding water onto his socks.

When he was young—he didn't remember how young, but just starting school—somebody stole his lunch box, took his lunch, and replaced it with a bear's paw. People find bear paws sometimes. Dogs bring them in from hunters' gut piles. He would never forget opening his lunch box, hungry for the sandwich that would be there, and finding instead that paw. A big furry hand that ended abruptly in a trail of tendons and broken bone. A bear paw is a terrible thing—not the claws so much, even though they're scary—but the monstrous puffy black pads. They are rough as sandpaper, and thick as moose hide, which makes sense, and you think it's one thing to be slashed by claws, clean and neat, but what a bear could do to your face with the roughness of the pads! Take your cheeks down to bone. Axel shook the paw into the tide and sat on a rock under the school all during lunch period, so no one could see that he didn't have anything to eat.

That was the worst part of it, that he didn't have anything to eat, and if he had gone home, Mrs. Hagerman would have said, "Do you think halibut sandwiches grow on trees? Go back and find the person eating it and take it back." She would have been right, because there wasn't extra bread on that seiner, and you can't make halibut out of thin air. So he didn't tell anybody how hungry he was, and one good thing he can remember is that he didn't cry then. Not one sniffle. He wanted to throw away the lunch box too, and tell Mrs. Hagerman he accidently dropped it and the tide carried it away, but he wasn't a liar and that was the other good thing.

When school was over and all the kids and the teacher had gone home, he took the lunch box into the school bathroom, locked the door, and washed it and washed it until it smelled like raw metal. That's when he cried, but that was okay.

Axel poured the boiling water out of his boot and went back to scrubbing and scratching. And here's the part that got him. Whoever put the fish in his boot took the trouble to catch a sculpin, pry open the sculpin's mouth, and stuff in the whole tail of that salmon. It looked like the little fish was swallowing the big one. This was a message. Axel knew a message when he saw one. A small ugly thing has got you gutless creature by the tail.

That's what they were saying. This was not a joke. This was a threat. That takes some guts, to threaten Axel Hagerman. He smelled again at the boot and went back to scrubbing.

He never learned who stuck the bear paw into his lunch box, even though he watched people carefully to see who was laughing at him. But he would find out who left him that dead fish.

Who are my enemies? He ran names through his mind, making a list. Who's jealous of me? Who have I fired lately? Who hates my projects? Who loved Kenny? Who have I outmaneuvered? Who have I ruined or driven out of town?

It turned out to be a long list. Axel crossed the kitchen and locked the back door. First thing, he needed to protect himself and his family. This was a blood threat. He needed a security guard. Somebody local, with his ear to the ground. He ran the names of possible hires through his mind. It was pretty much the same list as the enemies list.

War games can wear a man down. If you keep looking over your shoulder to see if somebody's going to stab you in the back, you can't look forward, can't get anything done. He knew he needed to outsource that job, get somebody to watch his back. Rebecca said his work was making him brutal, but that was a woman speaking. He had to remember to take everything she said with a grain of salt. "Brutal" she had said—actually, more than once. That was hardly fair.

"A rapist," she had said when he got back home the night somebody notched his pilings. "You can rape the mountainsides. You can rape the channel. You can rape the whole beautiful town. But you will not rape me."

Axel slumped into a kitchen chair and looked around. He could hardly recognize his own kitchen without windowsills messy with pansies and counters buried under egg cartons spilling dirt and whatever sprouts. You can't rape a mountainside. That is illogical. He would have told her that, except it would have been a waste of time, trying to reason with a woman. Rape is where you say, I'm going to take something that you don't want to give me, and I'm going to take it whether you want me to or not. It's sort of like armed robbery. But the mountainside doesn't say no, I have a headache, or no, you can't have these trees. The mountainside doesn't say a damn thing. A mountain doesn't think like a mountain or anything else. It's a pile of dirt, for God's sake. Limestone and dirt. Granite. And when you take the trees, they grow back and the mountainside has its damn trees, even more than it had before, and more deer than it ever saw under the closed canopy. Besides which, if the mountainside loved you, which let us presume for the sake of argument it *said* it did and *promised to forever*, it would *give* you the trees. It would want you to have whatever you wanted. You can't rape someone, if they really love you.

Axel stood up, tucked in his shirttail, and put on his dress shoes. Let it go. There is no reasoning with her. He shouldn't have torn off the buttons on her nightgown. That wasn't nice. He knew better. That wasn't who he was. But she should know that wasn't who he was. She should know him better than that. He was sorry, but she should know he was sorry.

And then, after Kenny got himself dead, she called him a killer. But was he a killer? She was throwing her clothes into Meredith's old red wagon, and he was trying to tell her. He was *sorry* Kenny was dead, he would *never* have killed him. He didn't do it. He didn't do anything. All he was trying to do was run a business, and is that a crime? "Where are you going?" he'd asked her. "I'm going where I'm safe." But she was safe with him. What's he supposed to do? He was trying every way he knew how to do what he was supposed to do, which is make her happy and keep her safe. He was trying every way he knew how. She should know, he was trying every way. All he wanted was for her to be safe and happy. All he wanted.

He sat at his kitchen table, put his face in his hands.

All he wanted was for his girls to be safe and happy. He was trying as hard as he could. And wouldn't they love him for that, how hard he tried?

He wiped the dishcloth around the sink, wrung it out, blotted his face, and hung the cloth over the faucet. He didn't need to wipe up the water on the floor. He'd already soaked it up in his socks. After he'd straightened the kitchen and locked the back door, Axel walked out onto his porch. He tugged at the front door to make sure it had locked behind him and made his way toward the office of Good River Products. Howard was sitting on the bench above the ferry dock, resting in the sun. Axel stood in front of him. That forced Howard to stand up. They walked together to the office without saying a word.

Once he'd closed the door to the office, Axel told Howard about the fish in his boot.

"We've got an enemy," Axel said, surprised at how good it felt to say *we*. "To protect ourselves and our work, we need to think this through very carefully." Axel studied Howard.

Howard was looking sharp in his brand-new Good River Products jacket. He clamped his hand over his mouth and closed his eyes. He bowed his head and shook it slowly back and forth.

"Ugly situation."

"Absolutely. Ugly.

"We need a security guard. Be best to have somebody from Good River Harbor, somebody the people trust. Who do we have?"

Howard sobered himself up and considered. He cocked his head and considered again. There was a lot of considering to do.

"Well," he finally said. "Tick McIver needs a steady job." He put his hand back over his mouth and kneaded his cheek.

"Oh for God's sake, Howard," Axel said. "Right, Howard. Exactly right. I'm going to hire the guy who probably hates me the most, hire the guy whose son sneaks around with my daughter, the best friend of the guy everybody thinks I killed. Hire this guy to protect me and figure out who's messing with me, when he's probably the one, and if he isn't, he knows who is. Tick McIver, security guard. Right."

There was silence in the Good River Products office then. On the roof, two young ravens hollered back and forth.

"Yikes," they said. "Yow."

But the two men just stared at each other across the desk.

"Howard, that might be the best idea you ever had."

"Put a guy on payroll, you own him."

"I tell him what to do, and if he doesn't do it, I fire him and his family doesn't eat. 'Find a way to put a stop to this vandalism,' I'll tell him, 'and you'll keep your job.' Won't that put him between a rock and a hard place."

"A very large rock and a very hard place."

"You go hire Tick, Howard. I don't want to talk to the guy. And put an engine on his half-drowned skiff. He might need it."

September 18

HIGH TIDE		LOW TIDE	
10:33am	12.4ft	3:45am	3.3ft
10:16pm	13.2ft	4:17pm	5.6ft

Axel sat on the edge of his desk so he could look down on Nora, who was perched on a folding chair backed against the wall of the Good River Products office. He poured himself a cup of coffee, gestured in Nora's direction with the pot.

"No thanks."

He set the pot down and took a thoughtful gulp.

"You're a pretty girl, Nora, and you live by your conscience, just like I do," he said. "I admire that. You speak your mind, and I admire that too. In a different world, we could be a team."

It was sort of sweet, really, the meeting she had called, Axel thought. Her first mistake was agreeing to meet him at his office. That shifted the balance of power right there, him sitting on his desk, her clinging to a chair like a robin about ready to fly out the window. Her second mistake was that she didn't have a bargaining position. She didn't hold a single card. Under those circumstances, Axel was moved to tell her the truth, and he did. He wanted her to understand that he was not a bad or stupid man.

"I'm sorry about blocking the salmon," he said. "I really am. I like to watch salmon spawning as much as the biggest eco-freak. If I thought I would be hurting salmon populations, I'd shut down. But my operation isn't going to hurt the population. It's not like there aren't other rivers and other spawning beds up and down the channel. No way we're going to run out of rivers. That's like saying Antarctica is going to run out of igloo ice."

Nora stared at him, openmouthed. That wasn't Nora's most becoming expression. Axel smiled. He hadn't really meant to throw her off-balance like that. She seemed to be thinking hard.

"That's good to know," she said. "So okay. The point is that there has to be some way to make a living off the land without wrecking it. There has to be some way to take what the land gives us, and give back what it needs to be even healthier—the way the salmon do, that way. Our job—you and me, working together—is to imagine how to do that."

"Salmon give back by dying," Axel said. "You volunteering?"

Ooh, that was nasty. Axel tried again.

"Nah, just joking. Tell me what you have in mind." He really was trying, but he did not get that Nora Montgomery.

"Okay, so here's an idea." Nora pulled at her ponytail, and Axel had the impression that she was really trying too, in her muddled way. "You go ahead and put a small dam on the river. You pull water out winter and summer. But when the silver salmon come in to spawn in the fall, you leave the water in the river, open the dam, and let them swim upstream. In the spring, you open the dam again, to let the fingerlings run out to sea."

Axel let the room refill with silence before he answered.

"That puts me at half capacity," he said.

"Which is more than you need to make a living," she said.

"I don't want to make a living." Axel gazed at her over the rim of his cup. "I plan to make a killing." He leaned back and chuckled. But when he saw her face, he froze.

"You've already made one killing," she said quietly.

"Now that's uncalled for."

"Unless you count the bear cub, and that makes two."

"Now that's enough." Axel stood up.

"Of course, if you count the salmon . . ."

"That is *the end of this discussion.*"

"That is the beginning," she said. She stood up, which forced Axel to look up to her.

"Is that a threat, because if it is . . ."

"It is not," said Nora. "It's a warning."

Axel threw his hands up in mock dismay.

"It took God a whole week to make this world," Nora said. "He likes it, said lots of times that it was good, and it was good, and it was good. If I came to work every day and plotted how to wreck God's good world, I'd be keeping my eye out for lightning strikes. Earthquakes."

She walked out the door, not even bothering to close it behind her.

"Fire and brimstone." She threw that one over her shoulder, and something in her voice made Axel follow her out and watch her stride down the pier.

As soon as he closed the door, he slammed his cup on his desk. Coffee sloshed on his blotter.

"The beginning," he repeated. "The beginning of what?"

He crossed to the window.

Calm seas. Flat calm all the way across the channel. A few squalls out toward the narrows, but nothing that would reach him there. God on his side. Axel fell into his chair, then abruptly returned to the window. A day this calm makes me think maybe life is playing me for a *sucker*, he thought, pulling away from my punches to *throw me off-balance*. Wouldn't that be something. Sun coming out. Water calm. Nora weak as a wienie. Muhammad Ali ducking so fast, George Foreman falls on his face.

As he stared at the water, a black knife blade rose out of the channel, sliced a long gash through the surface, and sank. The wound slowly closed. Then another black knife blade, closer than the first, cut a long incision through water that winced and ran. Water shrank away as another knife rose slowly up and began to slice the surface. Gulls screamed. They swarmed to feed in the open wounds. And then there were five black blades, each as tall as a man, cutting the channel into strips. They veered suddenly in Axel's direction, and he fell back from the window.

Dropping into his chair, he forced a laugh.

He'd seen killer whales a thousand times before. They always appeared like that, those dorsal fins like scimitars sticking out of the water, and the rest of the great beast hidden, the way an army of cavalrymen thrust their swords over their horses' heads until they seem to be a sea of swords advancing. Nothing to be frightened of, unless you're a coho salmon, and then you're good as dead.

Axel went back to the window. There was nothing there, just the sea as flat as silver plate. Gulls floated, as if nothing had happened. The reflection of the mountains stood still, *as if nothing had happened*. The perfect peace of the calm sea. If Axel hadn't just seen them, he would never know there were huge black beasts circling their prey twenty fathoms down.

Suddenly restless, he walked out his gangway, gripping the deck rail, and looked toward the boardwalk. Somebody had a marine radio on at the other end of town. Axel could hear the urgent pattern of a man's voice. From down at the dock, a hammer echoed against a metal hull. Tommy mangled a song on the piano out at Nora's. Beyond that, there was only the quiet of the channel, and the purr of the Kis'utch waterfall.

How is this possible, that the sea can calm so quickly and completely? Events could engulf a man's hopes and plans—the way water closes the gap where a man has fallen through, the way the present closes over the past, the way death closes over life—and leave no trace at all.

Axel walked quickly back to his office, shut down his computer, turned off the lights, locked the door, and turned toward home. The head of a harbor seal rose from the calm sea. With red-rimmed eyes, the seal stared at Axel's retreating back. When Axel turned the corner to his house, the seal sank out of sight.

Who does she think she is, telling *me* what God does and does not like. God likes a man who loves his daughter and his wife so much that he spends his whole life providing for them. Who does she think she is? Who is she? Who . . . is . . . Nora Montgomery?

Axel swerved one hundred eighty degrees off course and bustled back to his office.

He opened the computer and then set about pacing around the desk while the machine took its sweet time to wake up.

Finally, *dink*.

He plopped into his chair and went to work, pudgy white fingers poking keys, reaching like inchworms for the letters, enter, search, scroll, enter. If she is planning some fire-and-brimstone thing, she'll have done it before, someplace else. Outstanding warrants. Pacific Coast? Washington? Oregon? Getting closer. No, dead end. Try this. Eco-terrorist. Federal. Closer. Closer, closer, no. Woman. Closer. Bingo. Logging action. That would be her.

She burned up a goddamned bridge.

Well, well, well. A bridge to a logging site. The face in the photo was hard to mistake. Forty-five minutes of searching and he was sure enough. Axel's white face puffed into a smile. He reached for the phone.

≋

"HELLO, BELLINGHAM D.A.? . . .

"Axel Hagerman, Good River Harbor . . .

"Yeah. Good River Harbor . . .

"Alaska. Doesn't matter where it is. Listen . . .

"No. Southeast. Listen . . .

"I don't know your stupid brother-in-law. Do you know how big Alaska is? Listen . . .

"For God's sake, will you listen to me? I've got your fugitive.

"Yeah! Now you listening?

"No, not the rapist, Goddamn it." Axel threw his pen at his desk.

"The eco-terrorist. The woman who burned down the bridge to keep the logging trucks from hauling out the Nooksack timber sale.

"Nooksack. Arson . . .

"Yeah, I'll wait."

. . .

"Yeah, that's the one. About five years ago.

"No, not blond. Her hair is so black you can hardly believe . . .

"Yeah, okay, blond. I'll be damned.

"Concert pianist? Hell, no. She can't play the piano any better than a five-year-old kid. Come on. Focus!

"Right! That's the one. I'd say five foot ten or eleven. I don't know. She's thin. Thirty? Thirty-five—I don't know. Eyes like a . . .

"Yeah. Fish! That's the one. How soon can you get a deputy up here, slap some cuffs on her, and get her out of my sight forever?

"No. She's not a flight risk. She's gotta stay right here, at least until the next piano tide.

"Piano tide. Right.

"Oh, for God's sake, because she has a piano with her, and you can't move a piano without a good high tide.

"Jesus Christ. Trust me on this. You can't move a piano until the tide lifts . . . Forget it.

"Look, just come and get her. I guarantee she'll be here.

"What do you mean, low priority?

Axel plucked at the top of his head.

"You Bellingham granolas soft on terrorism?

"You'd come and get her tonight if you knew she had another crime planned, I betcha.

"No, I don't have hard proof of another crime. Which *side are you guys on?*

"Okay. You guys just sit in the office down there, coddling criminals. I'm going to set a trap for this little lady. Catch her red-handed. I'll be back in touch."

Axel thoughtfully pushed the off button and walked to the window to scan for the killer whales. He, Axel Hagerman, father of one, husband of another, president and CEO of Good River Products, enemy of eco-terrorists, had a sudden new interest in killer whales.

"ALLOW TO REMAIN on hair for twenty minutes, then rinse thoroughly." Lillian squinted at the Lady Clairol box to be sure of the timing. Did she get all her roots? She checked in the mirror. What a sight, hair dye glooped all over her scalp, and the dry hair sticking out in stiff curls.

"You look like a Brillo pad that just scraped a stew pot," she chided herself fondly. But it would be worth it. She loved the brightness of the new color they called "autumn auburn." Lillian was quite sure that she was the only woman in Good River Harbor who took the trouble to keep her hair looking young. She could name half a dozen women who didn't need to look so old, if they just took a little trouble. In fact, she could do this for them, start up a little color salon, if she got tired of the bar.

She shook out the plastic bag that came in the Clairol box and put it on like a shower cap over her hair, clipping it in place with a clothespin. Now she would get a fresh cup of coffee and wait. It was cozy in the bar with the rain pouring down outside.

And wouldn't you know. The door to the bar scraped open.

"I'm closed," Lillian yelled. She darted into the laundry room and cracked the door.

"That's okay." It was Nora with a couple of others. "We just want a cup of coffee," Nora called out. The people dragged their chairs up to a table, and one of them rustled around behind the bar, clinking cups and pouring coffee. "Anybody want cream and sugar?"

Apparently so. There was more rummaging and then Nora called out, "Lilly, where do you keep the cream?"

"There's a quart of milk in the beer cooler," Lillian yelled back, wondering how she was going to get her cup of coffee without showing her head.

"Leave the money on the counter." First things first.

"And pour me a cup and leave it inside the door to the laundry. Sugar. No cream."

It was warm in the bathhouse. Lillian settled her chair by the door and sipped the best coffee in any harbor bar in Southeast. She paid attention to the amenities that made a bar more than just a place to pour down drinks. She pulled an old *National Geographic* off the shelf. Gorillas.

Nora clumped back to the table with their coffee and they started in on the weather, which was not much to talk about—clouds sitting down on the mountains, rain showers blowing through now and then. Lillian knew Nora's voice. And Howard Fowler's. But it took her a minute to figure out the third voice. Rebecca Hagerman—this was a voice Lillian didn't hear much in the bar. Turned out to be kind of a committee meeting. Lillian drew her chair closer to the door.

"There's been too much trouble in this town," Nora was saying.

Lillian swallowed hard to keep from laughing out loud. Nora should know. She was about ninety-nine percent of the trouble herself.

"People taking sides. People getting hurt."

Yeah, getting killed must hurt, Lillian thought. Poor old Kenny.

"Well, I agree it's time for reconciliation." That was Rebecca.

Howard was not saying anything.

"Time for people to come together to celebrate the values we all share—a healthy community, people helping people, making music together, making a life in this beautiful place."

Lillian smothered another laugh. Were they reading off a script?

"Let's have a community potluck," Nora chimed in. "Everybody comes—the people in the town, Axel's employees out at the Kis'utch water plant site, Axel, everybody. Food, games, music."

"The values we all share." Lillian harrumphed in a fair imitation of Kenny. If he were hiding back there by the washing machine, he'd be bent over laughing. "*The values we all share*. Let me count the things we value," he would say. "Dead fish. Foster's beer. And then there's, um, BIG dead fish. Um, LOTS of beer."

"And fireworks," Nora was saying.

"We get to know each other, eat and drink and dance and laugh together. It will be a healing time. The potluck will go down in history as the time when Good River Harbor came together again into a community."

"What do you need from Good River Products?" Howard said. It was the first thing he said, and Lillian thought it didn't sound like a very friendly response. What's the matter with him? You'd think he'd jump at this. It sounds like the end of the resistance to everything Axel's doing. He's the public relations guy; he ought to be encouraging that.

"I'll bring down my popcorn machine," Lillian hollered out, to set a good example, "and set up coolers of beer. Take a beer, put a dollar in the slot in the can."

There was a startled silence.

"That's great, Lilly," Nora yelled.

"See what I mean, Howard," Rebecca said. "Everyone pitching in."

"The only thing we need from Good River Products is buy-in, or co-sponsorship, or whatever, so we're doing this as partners," Nora said, "to get everybody involved. Get your employees to put their names on the sign-up sheets for setup and cleanup, running the games. Get them to come to the potluck. There can't be a single person left at the construction site. No one. Not even the night security man. That's the whole point. If you can empty out that place, get everybody to the potluck, that's all we need from you. That's essential. We'll turn out the townspeople."

Howard apparently was considering. He's a good man, that Howard, Lillian thought. Solid family man.

"I imagine Axel will want to leave a security man on site."

"Oh, the big spoilsport," Rebecca said. "Tell Axel not to spoil the fun. Let everybody come." Lillian was surprised by what Howard said next.

"We can do this. Maybe Good River Products can supply the fireworks. We're shipping in explosives for the quarry, probably be easy enough to get somebody to put a show's worth of skyrockets and aerial shells on the barge.

"And we got a new man on site, Mike Sorenson. Do you know him? He's a great guy. From Forks, Washington coast. And he plays the banjo like God would, if He gave up trumpets."

Rebecca nodded yes yes. "Mike Sorensen joins the band. We're going to need dancing music. Let's get some lists started."

Back in the laundry room, Lillian grinned at her reflection in the mirror—dancing music.

So then it was down to work. Nora wanted the party to be on the coho tide, the highest tide of the month, "to honor the natural world." Howard didn't see a problem with that. In fact, that could be a nice phrase for the press release. Coho Day. They'd need to round up blue tarps in case it was raining. Howard thought he could put a man on that.

"I'll need to check everything with Axel," he said. "Um. Unless you want to, Rebecca."

She shook her head, yes yes, but what she said was, "No, no. You go ahead." Didn't sound like Rebecca wanted to talk to Axel about anything. They made a list of the lists they'd need.

That was Lillian's twenty minutes, so she went back and rinsed out her hair. It looked pretty good, a lot lighter than mahogany, with nice reddish overtones. She towel-dried her hair, fluffed up the curls, tied on a fresh apron, and went into the bar to make more coffee.

"You're looking especially pretty today, Lilly," Nora said.

"A person can try," Lillian said, hoping Nora would get the point.

By this time, they must have had the plans all laid, because Howard was sitting back with his stocking feet on a chair. He's educable. First time he was here, he didn't know enough to take off his boots. He was telling Nora and Rebecca about his kid and his wife.

"Jennifer told Taylor I live in the movies with the whales and the bear cubs, so she wants to come to visit. I'd like that more than anything in the world, because if they could just see this place, they'd love it, and they'd never want to leave. It's not good for a man to live in one place, and his family to live in another. I mean, I can do it, because it's my work, but I think about my girls all the time. I asked Jennifer before to come, but she said, 'If I wanted to go to a place without hot water or indoor plumbing, I could go to India.' That sort of hurt, but I told her it's not like that, it's beautiful and you can always heat the water and Lillian has hot-water showers. But now I'm thinking, invite them for the Coho Day party. Let them see what a real community is. Maybe Taylor could ride Tommy's bike, when he's not using it."

Howard was talking on and on about his kid while Nora made supportive noises and Rebecca looked sad. Pretty soon he was pulling out a photo of them all at Christmas. Poor guy. Lonely is his middle name. Howard Lonely Fowler, surveyor. Howard Pitiful Lonely Fowler. Howard Pitifully Hopeful Fowler. Lillian hoped his family came to town for the potluck. She hoped they liked it here. They'd probably add a little class to the place. Just as long as they didn't think they could take Kenny's cabin and fix it up. The town wasn't through remembering Kenny.

Lillian shook the coffee grounds into the compost bucket and added fresh to the pot. While water gurgled up through, she walked out the front door with the compost. A cold, gray day, sort of blustery, rain pouring down like Noah's flood. Standing under her eaves, she deadheaded the pansies, throwing the spent flowers into the sea. The nasturtiums were still blooming, but the plants were getting leggier and leggier. Summer was about done with. She gave each plant a shot of coffee grounds, thinking it might perk them up.

≈≈≈

HOWARD SAT ON the ferry-dock bench beside Tommy McIver. He reached over and patted down the crest of black hair that always riffled up from the back of Tommy's head. Tommy was wearing a T-shirt and jeans tucked into one boot and hanging over the other.

"You warm enough, Tommy?" Howard asked. Just because it wasn't raining at that particular moment didn't mean it was warm.

"Sort of cold," Tommy said, and skooched over until his side pressed into Howard's. Howard reached out his jacket and enclosed Tommy in its flap like a mother bird. They sat there together, absorbing each other's warmth, watching a seiner back out of the harbor in a cloud of gulls and diesel exhaust. It thrilled Howard, honestly, how much Tommy seemed to trust him and seek him out. Maybe Tommy knew that Howard was a father and thought that fathers can always be trusted, or maybe Tommy sensed somehow that Howard was as lonely as he was. "He's a half-breed kid," Axel had told Howard, "but still, he's smart and friendly—in an annoying sort of way."

"He's a kid," Howard had said back, "and he misses his mother." Sometimes Howard surprised himself, and this time, he had clearly surprised Axel. Howard reached down and tucked Tommy's errant pant leg into his boot.

"I'm going to piano lessons," Tommy confided, showing Howard his lesson book. "I already know how to play one song, and I'm learning another one."

"What song can you play?"

"'Ninety-Nine Bottles of Beer on the Wall.' Now Nora's teaching me 'Motorcycle Cops on Guard.'"

"Well, let's hear it," Howard said.

Tommy unfolded a cardboard representation of two octaves of piano keys and set it on his lap. Howard reached over, turned it right side up, and steadied it. With his hands on the drawings of the keys, Tommy moved his fingers up and down as if he were playing. Middle, pointer, thumb, pointer, middle, middle, middle. He sang at the top of his lungs.

Motorcycle cops on guard,
Chase the cars that speed.
Every driver must watch out,
Traffic laws to heed.
Stop on red and go on green,
That's the safest way.
Motorcycle cops on guard.
Laws we must obey.

"That's pretty good," Howard said. "Nora must be a good teacher." He wasn't sure how much the movement of Tommy's left hand had to do with the song, but the melody hand seemed right there.

"I practice on this," he said, "but it's more fun to play on a real piano."

"Tommy, what does that mean?" Howard ventured to ask. "Stop on red and go on green?"

Tommy looked surprised. He thought for a long time. "Some places, like if you go to Seattle where my mom is, there's red squares and green squares, like in a game," he said. "If you get on a red square, you have to stop."

"You are one very smart kid," Howard said.

"Yes," said Tommy, as he folded up his paper piano and gathered his lesson book. "I'm going to learn three more songs, plus my two, that's five songs that I can play for my mom when she comes home." He worked that out on his fingers to be sure. "It's going to make her really happy. 'Jingle Bells' is next. My dad's trading Nora for lessons." Tommy smiled up into Howard's face, as if this was the most wonderful thing in the world.

"That's the most wonderful thing in the world," Howard said, because it was. "What's Nora get in the deal?"

Tommy considered. "The first song, she traded for four dozen dead shrimp. I don't know about the next," he said. Then he was off, down the boardwalk toward Nora's.

Howard leaned back on the bench. He knew that before long, he would hear the broken notes of "Motorcycle Cops" vaguely and endlessly from the forest at the edge of town. He hoped Tommy's mom would come home soon. He really did. He hoped she liked the songs. And whatever Nora got in the deal, Howard hoped it was exactly what she wished for.

Howard pulled his pocketknife and a small block of maple from his jacket pocket. He was carving a baby bear for Taylor. He pressed the knife into the wood, using his thumb to guide the angle. It was hard for him to imagine that his Jennifer would want to move here from Bellevue, give up her friends and committees. But he'd been thinking about it more and more, especially if he kept getting promoted. He was already associate project manager, as well as community relations specialist. They could buy Kenny's cabin from Axel, raze it, and build a two-story log house with lots of windows framing that million-dollar view. Jennifer would like Rebecca. Maybe she'd like Nora—that was a harder call. Taylor could go to school over the tideflats with the twelve other kids. She could look out the window and see bears rolling boulders to find crabs on the beach, and then she'd believe him about what it's like to live in Good River Harbor. Jennifer had told Taylor that her father was living in the Discovery Channel, and sometimes he felt that he was, out there with the starfish and the whales.

He stretched out his legs in the dim sunlight and looked up and down the boardwalk—a sweet, soft, silver day. Fireweed had blown to seed, leaning out over the tide. When Jennifer and Taylor came to visit, he hoped it was a day like this. The sun had brought everybody out. Mrs. Chambers wobbled by on her bicycle, coming from Lillian's bathhouse with her hair wrapped in a towel like a turban. The postmaster was practicing the guitar, sitting in the doorway of the post office. Down the way, Jeanne and Dave Berkowski and all three of their grown kids were sitting on stacks of lumber, leaning over cigarettes in the sun. The ravens were plonking and belling, gulls muttering. Dogs flopped on the boardwalk as if they'd sprung leaks. It surprised Howard how much he felt at home.

Things were even settling down at Good River Products. Axel had a lead on a new bear, a young male that was nosing around the dump at a hunting lodge out of Eagle Cove. "That bear's either headed for a bullet or salvation at the shelter," Axel said. The guy was starting to believe his own propaganda. Now *that* was the sign of an effective communications person. Axel had pulled a couple of men from the water-bottling job to do the repairs to the Bear Shelter pavilion and the cedar cistern. No need to root out the flowers Rebecca planted there, he told Howard. Let the bears do that job. What a guy.

A column of smoke rose from the slash pile at the construction site across the channel. Mike had his bulldozer moving rock fill across the riverbed. Howard could see it backing and pushing, trailing black smoke, hear him shift gears. The water-selling project was still on schedule. And what gratified him most, as community relations specialist, was that all the muttering in town about freeing the bears or saving the river for the salmon seemed to have died down, now that Kenny was dead and gone. That sure knocked the stuffing out of Nora and Tick. They didn't say much to each other, at least not when Howard was around them. And Nora seemed on edge and somehow thinner, although she was thin to start with. Now that Rebecca was boarding with her, Nora seemed to be doing a lot less agitating and a lot more of what the women in Good River Harbor like to do—berrying and making jam and collecting everybody's old wine bottles, setting up to brew black currant wine. And now the potluck, the party that would celebrate a new start.

Boats creaked on a low swell in the harbor. The spars and masts swayed. Ordinarily, Howard would need to be out at the work site. But Axel hadn't called him in yet, so he wasn't in any hurry. Through half-closed eyes, he watched Tick paddle a canoe from behind Green Point. Crossing the inlet, he nosed into the bank at the far edge of the clamflat, pulled out a chain saw and a peavey, then hauled the canoe onshore and hid it behind the rocks.

REBECCA AND TICK scrambled like bears toward the Kis'utch Ridge, holding on to roots and pawing over rotted logs and head-high ferns. Tick carried a chain saw and a peavey that would lever logs around. Rebecca carried an axe, using it as an awkward alpenstock. Her foot slid off a root that skidded her down a muddy chute. Reaching to stop her slide, she grabbed the stinging spines of a devil's club, snatched her hand away, and grabbed for the rootball of a lady fern. It came loose from the duff, spraying hemlock needles that stuck to her cheeks and hair. She came to rest, lodged against a stump.

"You bust anything, Mrs. Hagerman?" Tick looked back over his shoulder.

Ever since Kenny's funeral bonfire, Tick had been Rebecca's friend, crazy as that was, Tick and Axel's wife. Maybe she had been a little bit drunk on Lillian's brandy, or maybe funerals are the sort of occasion when you want to clear the air, not let your sins linger around you for everybody to smell, like cigarette smoke in your clothes. For whatever reason, Rebecca had walked over to where Tick sat on a log watching the last flames flutter in the coals. She perched next to him. When he inched away from her, she inched after him, until it was stay put or fall off the butt end. She remembered the hellfire smell of that moment, probably spruce smoke and dioxin from Kenny's plastic poncho.

"I'm really sorry, Tick," she had said. "I'm sorry about how rotten Axel has been to you. Giving you really crummy jobs and then laying you off all the time, so you're always struggling, and you're always depending on him. And I'm sorry that all I've done is try to make that look pretty, decorate it all up and pretend that's the way the world was meant to be. That makes me even worse than Axel. How can I make it up to you and all the other broken men?" Thinking about it later, she decided there was in fact a bit of brandy in that question.

"Here's to me and all the other broken men," Tick had said quietly. For a long time, he rubbed his thumb against the palm of his other hand, stroking his life line. What he said next was like a blessing, the cool of holy water on Rebecca's forehead.

"You're not the stink-bait in that pot, Mrs. Hagerman," he said.

Rebecca had looked at him closely then, maybe for the first time, certainly for the first time in the golden light of brandy. His cheeks were pink under his orange beard and his eyes an astonishing blue. His shoulders were broad and his hands were huge and capable. She wondered what it would be like to be touched by those hands, what those hands would feel like on her hair, on the back of her neck.

"I'm not sure," she said back. "I haven't done anything to check Axel. He was rotten to fire you for what Davy did—and Meredith. They were in it together. And if he hadn't put a bear in the cedar cistern, it couldn't have charged out and killed Kenny." She had known she was babbling, but it pressed on her, that she was the only one who could move Axel off course, and she hadn't.

"Aach," Tick said. "We'll fix up Axel, we broken men. You ever see a halibut corpse after the sea-fleas and bent-back shrimp get done with it?"

She hadn't.

"It's a skeleton as spidery and white and clean as the day it was born."

Tick stopped climbing and looked back down the mountainside. He called again. "You okay, Mrs. Hagerman?"

"Nothing broken," she answered. "Everything covered with mud."

"Well, then, get a load off," he said.

She grabbed her hair in a fist and stuffed it down the back of her raincoat. She retied her long skirt in a knot at her waist and started up the slope again. She could not have been wetter. Clouds dropped rain. Thimbleberry leaves and sword ferns batted rain into her face. The waterfall drenched the air with fine fern-scented rain. But every step gained up the mountain made her feel lighter on her feet and clearer in her mind. The air was sweet in ways she had forgotten, broken bracken ferns, and when she crawled under the trunk of a giant tree that had fallen across the slope, she caught her breath at the fragrance of decaying cedar and hemlock boughs broken by snow. Tick had disappeared above her, but it was easy to follow the trail of gouged dirt he left in his wake. Every once in a while, he yahooed, and Rebecca yahooed back, not knowing if he was calling out to frighten bears from the track, or to make sure she was still following along.

Before long, Rebecca scrambled over the shoulder of the ridge and found herself on the easy walking of a rock ledge. Then suddenly, they were at the place Nora had said she would recognize by its beauty—a place where the Kis'utch quieted in a tarn before it pushed through a narrow rock opening and plunged off the mountain. She would help Tick build a splash dam here.

Their little act of God team had been careful not to attract attention. They never let anyone see all three of them talking together, and Rebecca was careful not to be more than just polite to Tick in public. That morning, she had wandered through town with a berry bucket, chatting with her neighbors, then turned conspicuously into the forest. Once she was out of sight, she cut downhill back to Nora's house. Nora called Tick on the marine radio, saying she was cutting firewood and needed help with a chain saw that was acting up. Since everyone in town eavesdrops on radio chatter, no one was surprised when Tick walked up the boardwalk with his chain saw and turned toward Green Point. Hidden from town by the point, Rebecca crossed the channel in Nora's yellow kayak. Tick followed in her canoe.

The rainclouds scattered. On the ridge, Rebecca stood with her face to the breeze, taking in the sudden space of it, the vast sky falling onto the rocks. The morning sun flared on muskeg ponds that reflected spruce copses and mountaintops. Between the bogs and rocky outcrops, plants grew low and springy, forced by the winds to hunker down, forced by the frost to spread every leaf flat to the rays of the sun, and who knows what forced them to bear fruit? But every plant, the mountain blueberry, the bog cranberry, the kinnikinnick, was flush with berries. Every berry held a drop of dew, and every drop of dew held the sun in its slipping grip.

When Rebecca looked down toward Good River Harbor, she saw only clouds heaped like pearls. She knew that somewhere under there, neighbors rewired radios or corrected children's spelling, looking up only to grumble at the foul weather. They seemed far away and unreal, as if, when Rebecca stopped imagining them, they would all dissolve into the drizzle, hallooing as they lost color and faded away. She pitied them, that under the fog they had no idea there was a heavenly blue sky just a hundred feet straight up.

Her heart beat in her ears, and whether it was the altitude or the astonishment of being in this place, she did not know. What would Axel say if he knew she was going to help blow out his project? The likely answer made her catch her breath. What would he think of her if he could see her here, standing on a mountain ridge with an axe in her hand?

On a fallen log, a pine squirrel squeaked an alarm call and leapt for cover.

I wish he could see me now, she thought, with mud in my hair. I am strong in ways he never could imagine. I have friends who trust me. I have hard work that I believe in. I do what I think is right. Who is brave enough to rip the nightgown off such a woman?

Rebecca stood on a boulder, spread her arms, and turned like a prayer wheel. Around and around she turned. Every turn was a prayer for the chance for a new beginning. Her boot slipped off the boulder and she had to throw herself into the grasses to keep from rolling an ankle. She sat in the blueberries, laughing.

"You okay, Mrs. Hagerman? Jeezus. You looked like Julie Andrews dancing up there on that rock, except you got mud on your pinafore.

"*The hills fill my heart with the sound of music.*"

Singing in an appalling falsetto, Tick pinched out his pant legs like an apron and pranced around. Rebecca giggled and then she was singing too, and she was spinning again.

"*My heart wants to sing every song it hears. My heart wants to beat like the wings of the birds that rise, from the lake to the trees.*"

Tick laughed and went back to work. His chain saw sang against a hemlock. His voice roared along with the saw. "*Like a lark who is learning to pray.*"

Rebecca dropped onto the rock and studied her hands.

"Listen to me, Axel," she whispered. "I will send you trials. I will not sleep in your house. I will cram dead fish into your boots. I will strip you of art and flowers. I will wash away your dam. I will make you afraid. I will take away one thing after another until you figure out what you can live without, and what you can't. And then you'll know how to love your family."

She raised her head.

"It's glorious up here, Axel. Why have we never seen this meadow?"

That small cirque held all the beauty and sorrow of autumn, a few yellow leaves on wind-stunted willows, cottontop grass, horsetails beaded with rain, the seedpods of wild iris and penstemon. The stream passed under moss pillows and spilled through cascades of hanging bells gone to seed. There behind the ridge, Rebecca couldn't hear heavy equipment moving rock. When Tick turned off the chain saw, the silence was a holiness she almost remembered—water flowing onto rock and the stillness of the mountain. The words she wanted to say to Axel tumbled through her mind.

We'll come back here when it's over, Axel. You'll sit beside me and never once think about how you could market the meadow. You'll think about how beautiful it is, and how strong I am, and how blessed you are, to be in this place with the woman you love. We'll tell the story of the flood God sent into the valley to save your soul.

We will make love then. It will be awkward, our rubber raincoats squeaking and sticking together. We will laugh and tug at the endless layers. "Is there no end to this tugging and pulling?" you will moan. "Is there any way to pull off a boot but to hop and yank?" But then our clothes will be in a pile on the blueberries and we will stand naked in our woolen socks. You will stroke my hair away from my cheeks and hold my face in your hands, using your thumbs to wipe the dew from my eyelashes, and you will say—maybe you mumble this into my hair—you will say, "We can find a better way, Rebecca. There has to be a better way." And we will make love in the thin air, with the valley dropping out from below us, and the ache of grief will expand in your heart—every mortal loneliness, every broken plan, the terrible danger to every child—until your heart bursts. And when you lay back in the blueberry bushes with my body melted into yours, you will be sobbing. I will stroke your face and shush you.

The pine squirrel chirred. Rebecca jumped and then laughed at herself. She sure could spin a story, weepy enough to make even herself cry. Ought to be a romance writer. Make some money. Rebecca blew her nose, and then she went to work. She hooked her axe over a branch and dragged the tree to a growing pile at the opening in the rocks.

≈≈≈

"I DON'T GET it, Ranger," Davy whispered. "I really don't get it. Mrs. Hagerman climbing to the Kis'utch Ridge with my dad? Why isn't she picking berries and making wine with Nora? What are they doing, dragging those little trees over by the creek? My dad does lots of weird things. But this is weirdest. Dad and Mrs. Hagerman? Cutting down trees and piling them by a creek? Is it going to be some kind of garden hut?"

Ranger evidently didn't get it either. He kept close to Davy and whined.

Davy grabbed his muzzle and whispered in his ear. "Better be quiet, Ranger. Last thing I need is for them to know I've followed them." He actually didn't really follow them. He'd been sort of keeping an eye on Mrs. Hagerman lately, weekends and after school and such, making sure she was safe, thinking he'd show Axel he was responsible after all. Meredith's mom didn't always make good decisions. Like who would go berry-picking without a bear spray? When Davy saw her heading out like that, unprotected, he got his dad's rifle and called Ranger to follow him, and they walked into the forest behind her, keeping their distance. In case she needed help. Ranger was the world's best dog, and once he understood that Davy had inherited him from Kenny, he heeled close and minded. He was brave, and he would let Davy know if there was a bear around, and then Davy would feel sorry for that bear.

But the thing is, Mrs. Hagerman didn't go into the huckleberry patch behind the post office. She started that way, but then she circled around through the forest and came out at Nora's. Davy and Ranger almost got found out then, because Chum came bouncing into the bushes where they were hiding. Nobody even noticed. That proved Davy's point: Something could be following Mrs. Hagerman, and she wouldn't even know it.

Davy couldn't hear what was happening at Nora's. They were talking real quiet. Since when does Nora talk quiet? She's always yahoo this and yahoo that. Davy was thinking, this is so weird. And then Nora went back in the house, and Davy crept around to the bay, where he could watch Mrs. Hagerman paddle her kayak across the channel. She didn't have a float coat or anything.

Ranger and Davy snuck back to the dock and got his dad's skiff. That was a pain, having to row that old thing, but close to town, he didn't want the noise of the outboard motor Howard had loaned them. Once he'd rowed past Green Point, he started up the engine and crossed the channel.

A kayak and a canoe were hidden in the trees at the far edge of the clamflat. Two boats. That threw him. And two sets of boot prints, one big and one little, going up the mountain. He took a different route, so they wouldn't see Ranger's tracks or his. It wasn't easy, climbing up roots with a gun, but Davy could do it, even with his shoulder only just healing, and it wasn't far. When he heard voices, he dropped behind a rock and peered over. The first person he saw was Mrs. Hagerman. The second person was his dad.

A pine squirrel chirred in alarm.

"Sit," he whispered urgently to Ranger. "Stay." The commands clearly bewildered Ranger, but he did as he was told.

Davy watched Rebecca and Tick for a long time, but they didn't do anything, like kiss or anything. They just hollered and sang to each other and pranced around and joked and felled sapling alder, like they were best friends. Are they best friends? And who is Julie Andrews? And why does she go to the hills? What do they need to build, way up there?

Finally, Davy signaled Ranger and they crept away, so he could get the skiff tied up at the harbor before his dad came in from pretending he was helping overhaul a chain saw. Why would he do that?

By the time his dad came striding up the boardwalk from Nora's, carrying an empty jerry can, Davy and Ranger were hanging out on their front porch. Davy looked carefully at the sawdust on his dad's pants and the mud on his boots. Tick looked carefully at Davy.

"Well. Took all afternoon, but we finally got Nora's chain saw going. Gummed-up carburetor. Had to take the whole thing apart." Ranger wandered up and sniffed Tick's boots.

Davy didn't know what to say, so he didn't say anything.

I should ask my dad about what I saw, he thought. But then he'd know I was spying. I would tell Meredith if she would ever hang out with me at school, always running off with the girls, giggling. She's smart and she would know what's up. I wouldn't ever tell Tommy anything. He'd just blab. Maybe Howard Fowler—he's a nice man who knows things. Maybe I should ask him. Probably everybody knows about this but me. But it might be a mystery. Maybe I've discovered a dangerous secret and I shouldn't tell a soul. Just Ranger and me, protecting Meredith's mom's secret. I better keep my eyes open.

ANNIE KLAWON CHECKED her watch. Almost eight o'clock in Seattle and still Tick and the boys hadn't called. They almost never called on time, but a half hour made Annie wonder. Every Friday, she got off the bus from work and walked to University and Fourteenth. There was a pay phone in a booth next to the coffee shop on the corner, and some plastic chairs where she could sit under the awning and be sheltered from the rain while she waited. At exactly seven thirty Alaska time, Tick was supposed to gather the boys at Lillian's and call the Seattle pay phone.

Sometimes, there would already be someone on the phone when Annie got there. Worse, sometimes a person would walk up just at 7:28 and punch in a number. Then Annie would pace, trying not to listen, while some balding professor argued endlessly and unkindly with his wife over whether it should be Italian or domestic Parmesan cheese he picks up on the way home, or a high school girl explained in pained detail what a dork her mother was, what a complete jerk, to yank her cell phone, which she didn't have a right to do, and that's stealing, and as soon as she ended this conversation, she would call the police and report her mother, who was a thief. Worse yet, some people spoke gently to their lovers—"Tell me how you will love me"—as Annie ground her hands into her ears.

But today, there was no one on the phone and still the phone did not ring. Rain was falling hard. Already the day had turned dark. In the glare from shop windows, red leaves ran like rafts down the gutters. The yellow lines of the coffee shop's neon signs reflected in the windshields of parked cars. She turned her back to escape cigarette smoke that seeped from the noses of teenagers at the next table. Diesel fumes sank into a blue pool behind the Fourteenth Street bus. Annie caught the scent of woodsmoke from someone's chimney, and then the wind picked up, sending leaves spiraling, and she could smell the lively air of the sea.

At home in Good River Harbor, summer is over when the berries of the mountain ash turn bright red and the wind swings around from the southeast and the salmon come home. Coho salmon push up the Kis'utch River to the pool with the lavender bubbles. Highbush cranberries are ripe. Annie used to hike to clear-cuts with her cousins to gather the berries in five-gallon buckets. She gathered stink currants too. Every house would have a jug of stink currant wine fermenting behind the woodstove.

Eight fifteen.

When they call, she thought, it will be like always. She will talk to Davy first, who will answer all her questions in the same flat voice—he's great, his shoulder is great, things are going great. No, no news, no new clients for his guiding business. No, Dad couldn't get the outboard to run yet, but almost. Then Tommy will get on the line and talk and talk as if he were sitting on her lap—telling her about the playing-card clicker he made for his bike and singing "Jingle Bells," right on the phone. Tick will be last. He'll say he's doing fine and the kids are doing fine, the same old song, and then he will say, "Come home, Annie Klawon. I miss you. The boys miss you. We can make a living here."

If Tick didn't call in five more minutes, she would call Lillian's phone, but that would be a last resort because then she would have to pay for the call.

She went into the coffee shop and poured herself a glass of water. The air in there was hot and steamy. Water ran across the floor from umbrellas propped by the front door. Parents in three-hundred-dollar rain parkas leaned over their children at the counter, buying them a paper cup of cocoa on their way home from daycare on a rainy day. Annie brought the news section of yesterday's *Seattle Times* outside and tried to read it, but how can you read when you don't know where your boys are?

She dug for change and called Lillian's bar. It was Lillian who answered.

"Annie Klawon! It's good to hear your voice. All's well in Seattle?"

Just hearing Lillian's voice made her crazy with worry. "Where's Tick, Lilly?"

"I don't know."

"Where's Davy?"

"I wish I could help, Annie, but I don't know. Last I saw, Tick was over at Nora's with a jerry can of chain saw gas. I'm guessing he's cutting trees."

"At Nora's?"

"Yeah. He *was*. I don't know where he is now. I don't know about Davy. Haven't seen him today. Tommy's riding his bike up and down the boardwalk, happy as a clam. You shouldn't worry. Everything's going fine for them. Tick's been smoking salmon."

When the silver salmon come into the channel, skiffs troll slowly past the town. People pull in three, four coho, as many as will fit in the propane smoker on their back porch. While they brine the fillets, they soak alder chips in fresh water. Then they light the propane, put the pan of wood chips on the burner, load in the fillets, and soon the smell of warm salmon fills the air. It's smoky, sweet, and salty. When the salmon smoke sifts through the hemlocks and sinks onto the intertidal stones, there is no more beautiful smell in all the world.

"Have the sandhill cranes been flying?"

"Just a few, so far. I heard them bugling last night."

Annie Klawon had missed seeing the cranes last fall and the fall before that, sandhill cranes tangling their lines as they staged to fly south. They kettle into the sky before dawn, circling up and up, gargling like wet trumpets. She would not be there to hear them this year. She would not be there to lie in bed next to Tick, to hear him breathe, to hear rain on the cedar shakes, hear the sea rising under the house, hear the sandhill cranes flying home. She would not be there to know the woodbox was full and sweet salmon were smoking and the children were safely sleeping—to be warm under the quilt, to be slowly aware of coming light, to think of the first cup of coffee with Tick and a second cup with friends.

"Anything you want me to tell Tick?" Lillian was saying. She waited.

"Annie Klawon?"

There was a long silence on the phone.

Father, send me a carved canoe. Raven on the bow, beaver on the stern. Send me a canoe with a flying hull that will cut the waves and curl their froth into long gray feathers. Send it, Father, on the wind that lifts the cranes. Here is the sadness you told me would come.

"Annie, is there anything you want me to tell Tick?" Lillian's voice was a little softer than the first time she asked.

"Tell Tick I'm coming home. I'm coming home to stay."

If Lillian hesitated, Annie did not notice.

"That's a good thing, Annie Klawon," she said. "That's a really good thing."

September 20

HIGH TIDE		LOW TIDE	
12:03am	14.2ft	5:36am	2.0ft
11:58pm	15.0ft	5:58pm	3.4ft

Meredith stuck her head out her front door. "Shut up!" she yelled to Tommy and slammed the door shut. The kid was driving her crazy, riding his bike up and down the boardwalk in pouring rain, singing at the top of his lungs.

"All *day, all night, angels watching over me, my lord.* All *day, all night, angels watching over me."*

Every time he got to the end of the boardwalk, he screeched his bike to a stop and no matter where he was in the angel song, he yelled out, "*Stop on red.*" Then he yelled, "Go on *green,*" and off he sped. "*When at night I go to sleep, angels watching over me.*"

Tourists thought that kid was cute. It made Meredith want to puke. They held up their cameras and shot videos while he went speeding by in his red sweater with his bed-hair sticking up. They gave him a dollar the next time he came by, and then he was singing and riding his bike and eating an ice cream bar he bought from Lillian. Tourists probably read in a guidebook that they should tip Indians if they're going to take their picture.

Tommy pedaled by again, this time practicing his syncopation, hitting the brakes on the short notes and stuttering through the song. "WATCH in' O *ver* ME."

Meredith opened the door again. "Shut up!" she shouted, and found herself looking straight into the broad face of Lillian Shaddy. Lillian was standing there in her Seattle raincoat, with a couple of damp curls sticking out under a blue cloche hat. She had pinned a corsage of yellow silk carnations to the collar of her coat, where they sagged under a load of rain. She had hot mitts on both hands, and she was holding out a pot.

"Hello, Meredith," she said. "I thought with your mother gone off, you and your father might like some salmon chowder." She paused, then added confidentially, "and a lady does not shout."

Of course a lady doesn't shout, Meredith thought, confused, but what does a lady do when somebody shows up at her door in hot mitts? Clearly something was expected of her, but this was a new problem for a house where very few people knocked on the door and the ones who did weren't coming to give her something.

"Thank you." Meredith said. Was that all you did? "Would you like to come in?"

That's what her mother would say, Meredith knew, but it wasn't what she wanted to say. She groaned when Lillian bustled right in the door and crossed to the kitchen to put the pot on the stove.

Lillian stood expectantly, dripping on the kitchen floor. Now what?

"Would you like a cup of tea?"

Lillian smiled encouragingly, as if Meredith had got her lines right in play practice, and she crossed the room to hang her coat on a hook by the door. The old woman tugged her sweater closed across her belly and held it tight. Meredith didn't like tea, and she didn't like talking to old people, especially not fat old women wearing lipstick, and she didn't like talking to strangers, which Lillian practically was, even though she'd seen her every day of her life, and she didn't like people telling her whether to shout or not, and she had no idea how she was going to get Lillian out the door again. But when Lillian sat down, put the cup to her pink lips, and asked, "How are things for you?" Meredith found that all she wanted to do was tell somebody, anybody, how things were for her, which was totally crappy.

"All I'm allowed to do in this town is go to school in the week, and look out the window on the weekend, and all I can see is this stupid kid and the broken-down cabin of a dead man. I'm practically a prisoner in this house. I wanted to move out to Nora's with my mom, but she's like, 'Oops, nope, no room, sorry—you're best off with your dad.' Work at the office, helping Howard Fowler all day Saturdays. Call about this bear, call about that bear, type up a news release about the new bear. And then I have to stay home all night. I only see Davy McIver out the window. I'm sick of him, too. He's started carrying a rifle through town and sort of swinging his shoulders like he's a big shot. Tourists take pictures of him, too, probably, going, 'Oooh wilderness, must be bears nearby. Even the half-witted teenagers are armed.'"

Lillian nodded, which made Meredith feel somehow good, that there was another human being who knew how pathetic her life was.

"Can you believe I listen to the marine radio for entertainment at night? How pitiful is that? Sometimes I get to watch a video on the computer at the office, but mostly it's just, 'Coast Guard sector Juneau, Coast Guard sector Juneau, vessel calling mayday please state your position.' Like you're going to be reading your GPS while you're sinking. Five eight glub. Then Nora calls on the radio—'Tick, come out to help me start my chain saw.' If Tick would just stay home, maybe his kid Tommy would have something else to do than disturb the peace. Teach him to change the sparkplug on a chain saw.

"My mom might think about coming home sometimes too, instead of all the time living with Nora. She even went to that funeral, where they barbecued Kenny on the beach. That was so gross. Came back smelling like greasy smoke and talking about redemption. 'Mom, you are gross,' I said. Dad was mad she went, but she said, 'From now on, I guess I will decide what I do.' Oooo. Sassy. Thought he was going to yell, but he seemed too tired."

Whoa. Maybe she shouldn't be telling Lillian all this, but Lillian didn't seem all that interested. Just went over and poured more hot water in her cup like she lived here.

"It's grim around here, dad's all grim, no flowers. Mom even took down the paintings in the house. Never said anything, just took them all down one day and stacked them in the corner. 'Not my room,' I said, and she said, 'Okay.' Maybe I will go to that boarding school in Sitka. Might be a cheerier prison than this one.

"'Be glad you have a job,' my dad says. 'You're not a prisoner. You're an employee, and you're better off than your friends, who are just hanging around being useless. And besides, you'll want to do well in school.' Like that's supposed to cheer me up."

Meredith stopped talking long enough to make sure Lillian understood how definitely not cheery that was. Lillian gave a twisty smile, then turned toward the door, where Tommy's song was going by again.

"All *day, all night, angels watching over me, my lord.*"

Even in the house, there was no refuge from Tommy. The song swelled and faded like a train whistle. Meredith ran to the door, pulled it open and yelled.

"ALL DAY, ALL NIGHT, DEVIL CHASE ME OFF THE DOCK, MY LORD."

She knew she shouldn't have done that, not right after Lillian told her not to shout. But that would be good—she could see it so clearly in her mind's eye. *Stop on red!!! but he doesn't, and he and his dipshit bike and his ice cream bar just sail off the end of the wharf and disappear forever, nothing on the water but a glob of vanilla.* Meredith laughed out loud.

She saw Lillian grinning across the table—not at her, but at something farther away. The feeling was strong enough that Meredith looked over her shoulder to see what was making Lillian seem so soft and glad, but there was nothing there.

"I like you," Lillian said suddenly, as if she'd just decided. "You're funny. And you're pretty.

"You remind me of me when I was a girl."

Meredith stared in horror. No way. Could that be right? Had this town turned her, Meredith Hagerman, into somebody who would turn into Lillian? Things were even worse than she thought. She pulled at her hair, determined never to cut it, but maybe she was truly doomed.

"Well," Lillian said. "I didn't mean to stay. Thank you for the conversation and thank you for the tea." She picked up her mug. "And Meredith? You might think about tucking your hair into a ribbon so people can see your pretty eyes." Her chair made an obscene grunt as she pushed away from the table.

Meredith stood at the door and watched Lillian walk up their gangway on feet that seemed too small for the job. At the intersection with the boardwalk, she stopped and lit a cigarette. Lillian was probably crazy, that's all. That happens to old people, they get crazy and imagine crazy things. She turned to put away the tea mugs before her father got home and figured out she'd had company, and he would never in the world believe her if she said it was Lillian. And then she'd be in worse trouble than since Davy messed up so bad and got them both in deep shit—not like Davy didn't try to do the right thing and there's nothing wrong with that, but what a mess, and what a wienie.

And now this stupid mystery.

The day before, Meredith had opened her desk at school. There was a clamshell with a string sticking out. When she pulled on the string, out came one of Davy's stupid notes.

Dear Meredith, I have uncovered a mystery. It is about your mom and my dad. Meet me on the rocks under the school on the day of the potluck. I'll be there with my dad's skiff. Meet me exactly when the men go down to the dock to set off the fireworks—that way, nobody will hear the outboard. Wear boots and rain overalls. Your (very) good friend, Davy

Meredith snorted. Just because we spent the night together half dressed under the wharf, do we have to be very good friends?

She read the note again.

So what's he talking about, his dad and my mom? Not likely. And what's the mystery? The trouble is that Davy always tells the truth. So something's up. I already know my mom's not acting normal—Mrs. Barbecue Hagerman. Mrs. Black-Swamp-Gooseberry-Jam Hagerman. Mrs. Hum-All-the-Time-and-Don't-Even-Bother-to-Comb-My-Hair Hagerman. I don't know what's up. I just wish it wasn't Davy who's going to tell me.

≋

AXEL SAT DOWN at his desk, pulled out a piece of paper, and began to think. What did he know about Nora's next crime?

It would be arson. *ARSON*, he wrote on the paper. Everything fit. All the bottles Nora had been collecting for salmonberry wine? For all that bottle-gathering, he hadn't been seeing much berry-picking. And all the chain saw gas Tick had been carrying over to her place? For all that gas-carrying, he hadn't been hearing much tree-cutting. Molotov cocktails, for sure, and enough gas to soak the place. Hell, she practically confessed—be careful of fire and brimstone, she said. Axel had no idea what brimstone was, but he sure knew what she meant by fire. And then, arson seemed to be her MO, judging from her burning down that bridge.

The target would be the water-bottling site on the Kis'utch. *KIS'UTCH RIVER CONSTRUCTION SITE,* he wrote. Axel didn't have any doubt about this either. Nothing much happening at the Bear Shelter, and she'd already hit that. Nothing at all happening at the logging sites. No, it was the construction going on over at the Kis'utch River. She hated that as much as she loved the sloppy salmon. She practically confessed that too—coming with her plan to close down for the salmon half the time. She didn't get half, so she was going after it all.

The date? It would be during the potluck. *POTLUCK: OCT. 1.* This was a no-brainer too. God, either Axel was one very smart detective, or she was a dumb, dumb criminal. And that she was not. At first, he'd thought the potluck idea was jim-dandy. Hah—a jim-dandy way to empty out the site, so she wouldn't get caught and she wouldn't kill anybody. She might be an arsonist, but she wasn't a murderer.

But when? She would choose her time carefully. A smart arsonist would throw firebombs when the fireworks were blasting away. Nobody would know the difference. They would ooh and ahh at the spectacle, never figuring it out until the buildings were in flames and the trucks were exploding. Hah, Axel thought. Maybe he should go into crime, he was so good at planning it.

The co-conspirators? Axel stopped to think about this. He leaned back and crossed his feet on his desk. He felt good. Okay.

Number one? Tick. Big orange-beard himself. *TICK?* he wrote. Tick was an interesting problem. He was Axel's security guard and needed that job. That argued against his being a co-conspirator. He was in love with Annie Klawon and he doted on his boys. That argued against him. But he was an idiot and a horse's ass. That was a point in favor.

Number two? Kenny. Well, sure, Kenny was dead, but he might be the brains behind the whole thing. Axel made a note on the paper: *THINK LIKE KENNY.* Then he thought better of it, and crossed it off.

Anybody else?

Rebecca had been living at Nora's. She could be indoctrinated, like those women with Charles Manson, twisting their sweet souls to the dark side. *REBECCA?????* But no, she would be afraid of a plan like this. He crossed her name off the list, then went back and wrote a heart next to it, to make up for drawing a line through her name.

Axel walked over to the window. Rain tingled on the harbor. It watered down the bright paint on the sailboats and seiners and softened the spruce trees on the far side. Frayed ends of clouds draped over the mountains and dragged in the wind channels. Axel felt tingly too, that same shimmer. He wished he could tell Rebecca what a genius he was.

Now. What about Howard? No point in spoiling Howard's fun now. He was so excited about Jennifer and Taylor coming, he wasn't thinking straight anyway. Axel decided that at the very last minute, maybe fifteen minutes before the guys went down to light off the fireworks, he would tap Howard on the shoulder, tell him to corral Tick and get his ass over to the construction site. They would be there to greet Nora when she arrived. He would loan Howard his revolver, in case Nora got ugly. That would impress little Taylor—that first night in town, her dad corners a criminal.

Axel sat in his chair, folded his paper into a small square and tucked it in his "to do" file. Wind must have been picking up. The Green Point buoy moaned.

BEST TICK COULD figure, lining up the post office flagpole with the Kis'utch River, he had about two hundred thirty feet under his hull. There ought to be at least five big halibut down in that hole, sitting there looking stunned. Which they always do, being fish. You'd think pretty soon one of them would want to bite a nice fresh herring with a hook stuck through its spine. Up and down, up and down, Tick lifted his rod and dropped it—bump the sinker on the bottom, lift it five feet, bump it, lift it. "Come on, sweetheart. Look at that herring, swimming up there, sinking, twisting onto its back, flashing its belly. That's one sick puppy, easy pickings. You tired of busted-up herring? I got a bucket of octopus tentacles I can feed you."

Tick needed a freezer full of halibut, and a smoker full of salmon too, before Annie Klawon got home. It might have been smarter to trade his splash dam for venison instead of songs, he thought, if Nora could've shot a deer without popping her dog one. Got himself kind of behind the old eight ball, making a dam instead of going after fish. Didn't exactly expect Annie Klawon to come home so soon. She said she was lonely for the smell of smoking salmon. That puts a man in a hard place, it does. "Yeah," Tick said when he called her back on Lillian's phone, "that's the world's best smell," and sucked deep, like he could smell salmon, and about choked.

"Come on, sweetheart. Don't just nibble." Ah. That hard sharp tug, and Tick tugged back, and then it was like being hooked to a Chevrolet. Pull up, crank away, pull up, crank away, lose ground when she makes a run for it. Pull up, crank away. Two hundred feet of line he had to bring in. This was a honey of a fish, dragging him out to sea. Crank, pull. Pull, crank. Finally he got her almost up, but when she saw the skiff, she took a run straight down, stripping line off his reel. "Son of a bitch." The reel handle spun around, cracking into his thumb. He grabbed the whole thing and started cranking again.

"I don't need a free bath," Tick had told Lillian.

But she said, "Yes you do, and so do your boys. I'm not going to have Annie Klawon come home to this."

Nora said, "Take this jam. You don't want Annie Klawon to come home to this."

Rebecca'd been over, dusting and sweeping. "So Annie Klawon doesn't have to come home to this."

Davy said, "Dad. What. Is. Going. On!"

"What Rebecca is doing is called 'dusting' and 'sweeping.'"

"Cripes," Davy said. "Why is Rebecca doing mom's job?"

That boy scared Tick, he had so much to learn about women. "Son," Tick had said, "Go out and get us a deer."

"I guess I will," Davy said, kind of sad, and took the rifle and off he went.

So Tick had been running around after halibut. He'd been thinking he could trade some for silvers. And Nora had promised to help him cut and haul wood, fill the woodshed. By the time Annie Klawon got there, she was going to think she landed in a movie set. Wilderness cabin, with strong, handsome husband with a freshly combed beard. Fine husband in a clean shirt, and two strong, handsome, clean children, one of 'em singing "Jingle Bells." There would be a clean oilcloth on the table and thimbleberry jam on the shelf. And all the empty whiskey bottles would be sunken in the clean blue sea.

Finally, the halibut was coming in. When Tick got it close to the boat, he gaffed it and dragged it up. But he clubbed it good before he hauled it in. Too many fishermen have been knocked out of their boats by a pissed-off halibut. Tick wouldn't pull the halibut into the boat until its eyes were crossed.

"My mistake was, I thought I didn't have anything to lose," he said to the fish.

What a jerk. And now I've got myself in a fix, where I really could lose everything—Annie Klawon, my boys, my new job, my cabin—just to save some salmon spawning beds. Or just to piss on my boss. Maybe that's what I'm doing. Or just to yuck it up with people I want to be my friends. Or to keep my promise to Nora, because wouldn't she twist my tail if I didn't. I don't know why I'm going to flood out Axel. "Forty-eight shrimp tails for one song," I said, and that was a good deal. "A splash dam for four more songs." Now when I hear Tommy sing and poke his fingers against that paper piano, I am so afraid I almost vomit. "Jingle Bells" puts me in a cold sweat. "Angels Watching Over Me" will be the end of the line.

The dam was holding. Rain was coming down hard on the old snow. The reservoir was filling fast. Their only weather worry now was that there would be more rain than they needed, more flood than they wanted. But there was nothing to do about that. God ran the rain-machine.

The potluck promised to be a foot-thumper. Tommy would play the cardboard piano and sing for his mother. Annie Klawon would laugh and cry and put her arms around Tick, about crushing him, and say, "It feels so good to be home. I'm never going to leave again. We'll make it work somehow." Tick's ear would be so full of her tears, he'd have to shake them out so he didn't go deaf, and he would love her so much he would almost turn inside out. But shit. When the finale of the fireworks finally went off, and that dam went, busting out Axel's water plant, Tick would lose it all.

Nora had said, "No, really. Everybody will think it's a natural event. Rain happens. Floods happen. Just ask Lillian"—which Nora had been doing, every time she caught Lillian in public. "Raining hard, isn't it, Lilly," she said. "Tell us about the flood that washed out Jimmy Pete's townsite in the fifties."

But Tick said, "Fat chance. Axel doesn't believe in natural events. He'll get some goons out here and they'll haul our asses off to jail. The guy's a dog's dick, but he's not dumb. All he has to do when that flood hits is look around on the ridge and see the new cuts."

"People don't make floods," Nora had said back. "Even Axel knows we don't have that kind of power."

"But we do. We can make that water rear up and roar."

Tick put his head in his great hands. I gotta tell Annie Klawon how much I love her. I gotta tell her what I'm thinking of doing, and make her understand that it's all a mistake, and I'm sorry, and I didn't know what I had to lose. But I'm more afraid of that than dying. I'm his security officer—I could go to Axel, tell him everything, stop the show, cancel the party, take out the splash dam when everything's froze.

But then wouldn't dead old Kenny haunt me, *har har* all night long, "Eunuch," he'd call me. "Chicken-shit. *Har.*" I would have a job, be working for Axel, and I'd be ducking like a crazy man with a ghost chasing him around, hitting him over the head with a two-by-four. *Har.* But I would have a job, and I would have a family, instead of going crazy in jail for ten years and then wandering the streets in Seattle, muttering like a drunk. But I'm no snitch. I might be a horse's ass, but I'm no snitch.

Back down to the bottom with another dead herring. Bump down, haul up. Bump down, haul up.

September 29

HIGH TIDE		LOW TIDE	
4:44am	14.2ft	10:37am	3.6ft
4:41pm	16.2ft	11:45pm	0.8ft

Coho Day was promising to be one of Good River Harbor's finest days—fair, so far, with just a little breeze. The ferry was only a few hours away. Howard checked his reflection in the post office window to make sure he hadn't missed a spot shaving. He wished there had been a way to get a haircut, but at least he was clean—two dollars' worth of clean in Lillian's bathhouse. He stretched his back and smoothed down the tie under his Good River Products jacket. He thought maybe he was broader in the shoulders than he had been when he came to town. He walked back to check the window again. Honestly, if other people were feeling the same high excitement he felt, the whole town was ready to explode. The little bear he'd carved for Taylor was in one pocket. In the other pocket was his present for Jennifer—an alder bracelet, two circlets he'd carved from the same piece of wood, entwined and inseparable. It made him feel shy, how hard he had worked on it and how much he hoped she would like it. Hard to believe that Jennifer and Taylor were on the ferry at that very moment, watching the mountains slide by, looking out for Green Point and their first glimpse of Good River Harbor. He had emailed Jennifer to keep an eye out for spouting whales and bears pacing at the mouths of the rivers. Taylor would be telling her teddy bear to look, pressing his plastic nose to the steamy window.

Annie Klawon, big Tick's wife, was on the ferry too, coming home. Home for good, Tick said. Tick had Tommy and Davy down in his skiff, bailing and sponging, shining up the Evinrude Axel had loaned him, while he walked back and forth on the dock, retying the bowline, retying the stern, coiling his lines. Then he'd had his boys down at Lillian's while Howard was there, scrubbing them up. It had been quite a man's meeting. And Tick was all scrubbed up too, his beard as smooth as if it had been steam-ironed. Lillian had made sure of that, sending him back into the shower with some hair conditioner. In their hungry waiting, Tick and Howard and the pacing bears could be brothers. Is there any more primal joy, any satisfaction more deeply seated in a man's soul, than his family safe and together?

The town's brass band was warming up. On this occasion, it would be a banjo, a penny whistle, and the accordion. They riffed all over each other and ran up and down the scales, *Alleluia the great storm is over / tis a gift / when the saints / and may the circle / all the live-long day / the Lord loves his own and your mother is here.*

It was as raucous as any orchestra converging on A. The band would be first on the dock to greet the ferry. Everybody knew the band was playing to honor Annie Klawon and to kick off the Coho Days celebration, but Taylor would think it was great, like she was the queen.

Howard had done everything he needed to do for the party. The potato salad he voted for won first prize, and who could resist a patriotic salad with the eggs dyed red and the potatoes blue? Mike and Sherm, Axel's men, had finished stringing blue tarps over the boardwalk, tight as fore-sails. It was a glorious, flag-snapping, high-clouds day, so they probably wouldn't need the tarps for shelter, but it never hurts, the way the weather changes. That was a piece of good luck—that Jennifer's first view of Good River Harbor would be on a sunny day. There would be time enough for her to get used to rain.

Axel splayed himself over the top of a ladder, stapling the wires of Christmas tree lights to posts. The colors would be pretty at night, reflected on the water. Howard had to hand it to Axel. He had come around on this party, which took more . . . what would you call it? . . . *good sportsmanship* than Howard thought the guy had. Axel gestured to Meredith, probably telling her to hurry up and untangle the Christmas lights, which Axel should know is a job you can't hurry. The guy seemed beside himself with excitement.

Tick steered a two-wheel cart full of beer down from Lillian's. At the corner, he veered and ran the cart into the railing to avoid running over Tommy on his bike. Tommy was singing, as usual: "All I *ever need is a song in my heart, food in my belly, love in my family.* All I *ever need . . .*"

"Stop. Wait." Tick beckoned Tommy back. "What? Sing that again. Did Nora teach you that?"

"*All I ever need is a song in my heart*," and there was Tick, staring at Tommy with shining eyes and mouthing the words to the song. A glorious day indeed.

The ravens were lining up on the railings, hopping sideways, yawping, getting ready for the potluck. Mike and Sherm were hooking up propane for the grills. Nora had insisted that the Good River Products guys sign up for practically every committee, putting the site security guards on cleanup. That was fair enough, and Howard made sure they did. He put himself on the committee to judge the potato salad contest, but he didn't sign himself up for cleanup duty, which Nora thought was fine when he explained. He wanted to be able to take Taylor back to his little room and tuck her into the bed he'd made her from a fish box. Whether he could do that without crying, he didn't know, it had been that long.

Everything was ready for Tommy's concert. Axel's workmen brought out a table and taped on Tommy's cardboard keyboard so it wouldn't blow away. They got him a chair with a booster seat so he could reach the keys that Nora had drawn on. Tommy could sing while he moved his fingers, and Nora and Annie Klawon would probably be the only ones watching his hands. But still Nora had spent a full day tuning her piano, who knows why—that seemed to be her work in life, trying to get that piano to come into harmony with itself.

"Here is where I want to spend the rest of my life," Howard whispered to the post office window, and he was only a little surprised to hear himself say it. If he were the mayor of the village, he would appoint a special committee with only one job—to sit around in Lillian's, drink skunky beer, and imagine how you can live in a place without wrecking it. Now and then, the committee might have to pull the pants off a stranger. But other than that, thinking's easy work.

Imagine how to make a living—literally, a living. Imagine how to fish a channel without fishing it out. Imagine how to log the mountains without logging them over. Imagine how to make a potato salad so good it wins first prize, and then give it away, every bite. On Sisyphus's boulder wobbling in desperate balance at the top of a steep mountain, imagine how to sing in harmony. Just like Kenny said.

"What does she look like?"

Howard turned and there was Lillian, resplendent in her plaid Seattle raincoat, with a yellow nasturtium pinned in her hair. Despite himself, Howard reached his arms around her and pressed her bosom into his belt buckle. Could he hope that she would be part of his family too, an entrepreneur just like he was, a grandmother who would brush his daughter's hair back from her face and tell her to stand up straight?

"Why does everybody think they can hug me, just because I have a flower in my hair?" Lillian said. She pulled away and tugged down her raincoat, fore and aft. "I hardly made it down the boardwalk without getting my back disjointed."

Howard laughed. But when he considered how to describe Jennifer, he was so moved, he could hardly speak.

"She will have short blond hair. It will be wavy and unruly, because of the marine air. For the first few days in Good River Harbor, she will be wearing pink lipstick and jeans with the crease pressed in. She will be smiling. She will have a little girl by the hand."

AXEL PULLED DOWN the front of his GR Products jacket, straightened his shoulders, and again walked the perimeter of the dock where the party was gearing up. Past the banjo player, practicing his licks. Past the accordion in its suitcase. Past Tick, who opened a bag of ice and poured it into a cooler. Axel's body was already buzzing, all senses on full alert, and the scritch of the falling ice made his spine shudder. He rolled his shoulders and turned away. But he stopped then and raised his head. He heard a sound he had not heard before in Good River Harbor, like ice, but like music. Was it coming from the cooler, or from the forest? He bent his head toward the sound. Then he strode down the ramp to Nora's trail. The music rang clearer, the closer he came. He slowed his pace. A few yards short of the opening in the woods, he slid behind a cedar and peered out. There was the bleeding stump of the old hemlock he'd felled. There was the pile of firewood he'd expected. There was Chum, snoozing like a schmuck. And there was Nora, seated with her back to him, playing her piano like a pro. Her hands dashed up and down the keyboard. The piano bounced with the force of her playing. The floorboards buzzed. The woods filled with music.

Axel grinned a slow smile. Final evidence; she was a concert pianist. The felon was almost in his grasp. One move against his construction site, and she was caught. His armpits prickled with pleasure.

Axel slid back behind the tree. The music—she moved her fingers and the very air sang. Single notes fell, fell, fell, while above them, small pops fluttered off descending scales. There was a sudden crash of chords, then another, and then it all fell apart and trickled down, whatever it was, this music. No sooner down than the music shot up again. It was like rain, it was like fire, it was like a thousand glass birds flying together from a cave, beating their wings so fast, so close, that when they smashed their wings together in flight, they made the sound of breaking glass, tinkling down, broken. Then up up, the shards of light, colliding, and falling in a cascade of music, all those silver feathers of music, falling in the sun. It was a revelation. It was a miracle, that music, the music that burst from the piano and filled the clearing with a clarity so sparkling that the trees might have been encased in ice.

When her hands were finally still, Nora leaned over the keyboard while the last vibrations shivered toward the sea. Axel exhaled. The wind shifted. Suddenly, Chum jumped to his feet as if he had been stuck with a stick and began to growl. Axel dropped to the ground behind a fallen log and pushed his face into the moldering dirt.

"What is it, Chum?" Nora leaned over to pat him, but his fur bristled under her hand. She grabbed his collar. "So. We have company." Judging from Chum's revulsion, it was either a bear or it was Axel.

"Hi, Axel," she sang out.

Axel held his breath. Wet moss was soaking his elbow and the length of his leg. A broken skunk cabbage was stinking up his jacket. He hadn't anticipated that crime-stoppers would get so dirty.

"Debussy. 'Feux d'Artifice.' Fireworks," Nora called out. "Now I'll play a piece just for you, and then you go back to town. I have work to do."

Work to do! Axel's heart raced.

"The piece I will play for you is 'Fantasie,' by Robert Schumann," Nora announced.

Axel crouched lower. A mushroom squashed on his cheek.

As Nora began to play, Axel crawled away from the clearing and walked slowly up the forest path through the saddest, loneliest music he had ever heard. He emerged into the looping twang of banjos tuning up and resumed his patrol. He did not hear the last notes of the piece she played. He did not see what she did next.

IT ISN'T EASY to steer an old upright piano, each wheel rust-stuck sideways. Nora retrieved a hammer from the kitchen and whacked at each of the wheels until she got them pointed sort of straight. She put her shoulder to the side of the piano, braced her boots, and pushed. She had to cut her anchor line somehow and leave Good River Harbor, she knew this. She had to leave, and the piano had to let her go.

The piano creaked across the porch, veering to starboard. Nora smacked the front wheels back into line, aiming them for the plywood boards she'd set up as a ramp. She could have used some help—one to push and one to steer—but all help was gone. Finally, over the uneven boards, Nora muscled the piano to the edge of the ramp. The tide was out, and the water beyond the yellow rock-wrack, beyond the blue mussel beds, past the eelgrass, was calm. Across the channel, a line of clouds cut the mountains in half—shadowy spruce and hemlock by the water, patchy snowfields above the clouds.

Nora leaned into the side of the piano and pushed. Once the advancing wheels dropped off the porch, the piano rumbled down the ramp under its own weight, lurching from side to side as the plywood sagged and popped. Nora stood back and watched it go. It lunged off the ramp onto smooth granite and picked up speed, rolling toward the drop where the high tide had undercut the shore. The starboard wheel struck a rock. The piano cartwheeled onto the tideflat, smacked into the mud, and fell on its back.

The cabinet split diagonally, and all two hundred strings rang at once. A flock of gulls startled up, mewling. Ravens clonked in the spruce. Two eagles lifted, clattering the way they do, like stone on steel. Nora shook her head. Wouldn't you know. The universe starts with a single bell tone across the water, and this is how it ends—everything in creation crying out in one terrible chord.

Nora listened until the last of the piano's music faded away. Then she forced herself to turn her back on it. Behind the cabin, there was a bunch of punky firewood and rotted planks on a busted-up shipping pallet. She loaded up the wheelbarrow and hauled all the firewood down to the piano, then the planks and even the pallet. With the slats and scrap spruce, she built a pyramid against the piano. She rearranged a couple of sticks until she got it just right. Then she poured kerosene onto the pile. Closing her eyes against the sting of fumes, the sting of tears, she waited for the kerosene to soak in. When she held a match to a fir slat, a blue flame spread like water across the wood.

Kerosene starts slow, but once it gets going, even in wet wood, it burns hot. Before long, the fire was sucking air and roaring. The piano disappeared under oily smoke. Nora backed away from the heat. She pulled off her cap and wiped her forehead with the back of her hand. A few strands of damp hair stuck to her cheeks. Ashes flew at her like mosquitoes. She put a hand over her mouth, as if closing off her face would keep the smoke away.

Ravens swooped in on the rising air. Always, there are ravens at a fire, pacing, pacing, angry at the wait. With an oar, Nora shoveled embers to keep the fire tight, but then the oar began to smoke and she had to stir it in the sea.

The flames were so hot they turned the air above the fire to the trembling clarity of fresh water on salt. Through that air, snowfields shook on the mountains across the channel. Nora leaned on the oar and traced the ridgeline with wet and squinty eyes. Up there—that's where Nora would take hold of the prypole. She would feel its roughness in her hands, smell the sap still in it, feel its weight. She would wedge it against the fulcrum Tick had chosen. It was a worthy fulcrum, the resistance that would change everything—a granite boulder matted with green liverwort and specked with the orange lichen that marked a deer mouse's tiny river of pee. For a week, she had rehearsed how she would grip the pole with two hands, brace her legs against a ledge, and pull with all her strength. The lever would groan against the boulder and pop out the bottom logs. The whole barrier would twist apart then, and the force of all that water falling down the mountain would tear out Axel's dam. The salmon would be free to come home again. Nora closed her eyes. What would that be like, to be finally coming home?

The top of the fire let loose and crashed into the heart of it. Ravens hopped back. There was an eruption of sparks, then flames flared pink and green. Nora heard a muffled plink, a treble string breaking. Another plink.

"That blessed fire is playing my piano." Nora's hands were shaking. She tightened her grip on the oar. Single notes broke free, throwing sparks. Nora raised her head and listened to it play.

As afternoon came on, the tide leaked under the pyre and lifted the smoking coals. Nora sat on a log with the oar beside her and wept, while the tide pushed a current line of charcoal and ashes across the cove. Slowly, the cove filled almost to the top of Nora's boots. From wood smoldering under the tide, bubbles the size of ping-pong balls bobbed to the surface. For a time, they floated there, domes on the scum. When they finally popped, they let loose puffs of gray smoke.

The tide. It was time for the party. She put a gallon of drinking water in the front hatch of her kayak. In the back, just a blanket, a tarp, a loaf of bread, dog food. She tied the kayak to a root on the bank. At high tide, she would find it there, floating. Double-checking the knot, she whistled for Chum and turned to go. When she looked back, there were gray bubbles puttering up from the piano fire—smoke backfiring in random bursts from the sea, puffing smoke alongside a frond of bullwhip kelp.

"DIDN'T YOUR MOTHER teach you to give your seat to a lady?" Lillian said loudly. Half a dozen kids popped up and scuttled out of her way, ducking in and out of their dancing parents and coming to rest in a covey by the post office wall. Lillian eased herself onto a suddenly empty folding chair. The Coho Day festivities were still in full swing, but there is a limit to how much waltzing a lady can ask of any given set of knees. Axel's workmen were handsome, and they knew how to dance. Lillian had thought her feet would never be waltzing again. Probably wouldn't be waltzing tomorrow. But that banjo player really spiked up the music in the rest of the band, and why should she sit still when so many people wanted to dance with her?

All through the party, Axel stood off to the side by the post office gangway and scanned the crowd, like a secret service agent. Every time she danced by, Lillian could see him, standing alone and watching. Finally, she made up her mind. When the band began to play a waltz, she went over and stood in front of him.

"Will you dance with a woman who is old enough to be your mother?" she asked Axel. He glared at her. Lillian smoothed down her raincoat and said it again. "Will you dance with me?" He lifted one hand and put it at the center of her back. He took her hand in his other. She put her hand on his shoulder. It was the first time she had touched him in forty-seven years. His shoulder felt firm under her hand, and his hand, clinging to hers, was warm and damp. He smelled as musty as a newborn baby. Lillian felt an ancient ache in her breasts. And so they danced. Not like Fred and Ginger, but they danced. And all the time they danced, Axel said not a word. But his head bounced around, watching.

Meredith had walked up and down the potluck line, giving away grilled shrimp as fast as the postman could cook them. She is a pretty girl, Lillian thought. She'd been pretty from the day she was born. All she needed now was a grandmother to teach her about . . . oh, there was so much a grandmother could teach Meredith. Like, for example, rubber boots are not dancing shoes.

Howard had followed Meredith up and down the line, introducing his wife and little girl, as if the party was his wedding reception, and maybe that's how he felt, that kind of happiness. His wife was a pretty woman too. If she stayed, it wouldn't be long before she let her hair grow out to dark roots and traded her sandals for muckers. Annie Klawon was back, and if her spine isn't out of joint from being hugged so hard by so many people, she's a strong woman. She was home, and that was good and natural and the way the world ought to be.

It was moving and generous, Lillian thought, how his friends stuck close to Tick all afternoon. Who knows, maybe they'd all signed up for the Tick Committee. Whenever he opened a beer, took a swallow, and set the can down next to him, the can mysteriously disappeared and there would be Rebecca, pouring a beer into the sea. Or somebody else would say, we need you over here, Tick, and poor thirsty Tick would be scrubbing a grill or emptying the trash while his beer can bobbed on the tide. And here would be Rebecca, offering him a Coke. It might have seemed strange, that kind of solicitude, except this was Annie Klawon's first night in, and her friends probably thought she'd prefer him sober. And Tick—he was as nervy as Lillian had ever seen him, tripping over chairs, looking over the deck rail to check the tide.

The tables were cluttered with empty casserole dishes crusted with noodles, and a rim of frosting was all that was left of the giant cake. The town dogs nosed around underneath, licking between the planks of the boardwalk. That was disgusting, those long pink tongues.

"Get away," Lillian said, flipping her hand at the dogs. Half a dozen more kids edged off.

Lillian had to admit that Tommy's recital was the highlight of the party. It went off without a hitch. People clapped as he began When At Night I Go to Sleep, and their faces softened as Tommy pounded along through I *pray the lord my soul to keep.* When he paused to let his left hand catch up to his right, every single person in Good River Harbor, toddlers to grandfathers, mouthed the next words, and if it was a prompt or a blessing, who could say? *Angels watching over me.*

When the applause died down, Nora called out to Lillian for a song.

"A song," Tick shouted. Lillian took off her raincoat and walked to the front of the crowd. She had worn her purple dress with the lilacs on the bodice, just for this occasion. People started shouting requests. But Nora wanted "Amazing Grace," and that's what Lillian decided to sing. For the first verse, Lillian's solo voice rang the mountains. Then other voices joined in. It's a miracle really, Lillian believed, people singing in harmony, all those different voices singing different tones, and all the voices sounding together the slow, resonant chords.

"*I once was lost, but now I'm found.*"

"Yes, Lilly," Tick said soberly. "Yes. A good and true song."

Lillian looked toward Nora, hoping she had liked the song, but Nora had melted back into the crowd.

As dusk turned toward darkness, the men began to rustle around to prepare the fireworks. People shifted chairs, pointing them at the channel. Blankets appeared from houses. The kids set their bikes aside and gathered cross-legged on the blankets. Sensing the climax of the evening, Lillian walked up the boardwalk to the bar. Of all the occasions in this town, this was the one that truly called for the gallon of good whiskey she'd been keeping under her bed. She did not know what she was saving it for, if she wasn't saving it for this town, this night.

It was a long haul up the stairs for those old legs. Lillian sat on her bed with her arms on her knees and caught her breath. From her upstairs window, she could see the dock and all the way down the channel across Green Point to the Kis'utch clamflats. A beautiful party, she thought to herself, and then inhaled sharply as she saw Davy drop into his skiff and row silently under the town.

"Uh-oh," Lillian exhaled, as she scanned the crowd for Meredith and did not find her.

A bartender can sweep her eyes over a situation and know precisely when something's not right—when a fight is about to start, or a woman is about to rag on her man. That silenced skiff and their disappearing teenagers were not right. The solicitude for Tick was not right. The list of committees was not right. "Amazing Grace" was suddenly terrifying. In fact, something was off about the whole party.

Lillian stuck her head out the window to get a better angle as Axel walked over to Howard. Poor, decent Howard was shaking his head no, gesturing to his wife and daughter, no no. No. But Axel spoke to him urgently and at some length. Finally, Howard nodded, walked over to Tick, who was just settling his big bulk on a blanket. Howard tapped Tick on the shoulder, said something. Tick also began to point and protest, his beard flapping no. He pushed Howard away with his shoulder. But Howard gestured toward Axel, said something more, and Tick finally let himself be steered toward the harbor, where the two men disappeared in the direction of the Good River Products skiff.

What in God's name?

Forgetting the whiskey, Lillian swept to the head of the stairs and hobbled back to the party as fast as her old legs would go.

"THIS BETTER BE good, Davy McIver. If my dad finds us together, you and I are both dead meat."

Davy didn't know if it was good or not, this miserable mystery. Maybe it *was* good. Maybe his dad and Meredith's mom were up to something sneaky and important, something Axel would want to know about. That was the thing. Davy really could make good decisions. Axel had called him irresponsible, right there in front of his mom and dad. But wouldn't it be irresponsible if he learned an important secret and didn't tell? Or maybe the secret wasn't anything. Maybe Rebecca wanted help getting alpine plants or something. Raising a false alarm was completely irresponsible.

Axel's right, Davy decided. I am a complete jerk.

"Because if he finds out that we're together, I'm on the next ferry to Sitka, signed up for boarding school. That's what he said."

Davy didn't know that. This just got worse and worse. He wished he had never gone up that mountain, tracking Rebecca Hagerman. And if he had, he wished he had never left that note for Meredith. He should have been able to figure this out himself.

"Which might be fine with me, to get away from a dweeb like you."

Davy's head sank down between his shoulders. So why did she meet me here? Why is she sitting in the bow of my dad's boat, smiling while she beats me down? I'm beat down plenty already. For the first time since I sunk the boat, my family is happy. My mom is home. When I gave her a hug on the ferry dock, it felt good, her head on my shoulder, I'm that tall. "Have you grown another foot?" she said. "Just an inch," I said, but she was teasing me. We hung around together. Then I had to sneak away. My mom's home three hours, and I'm sneaking away to wreck it all. Just to show off for Meredith, that's what it is. Meredith, who calls me a dweeb.

It was dark and cramped, floating under the school. Their heads practically hit the stringers, and the tide was still rising. Davy wished the guys would get on with the fireworks.

When he had rowed out to the school to pick up Meredith, there had been plenty of room to sneak along under the houses. Not anymore. This was going to be a huge tide. Eighteen feet. He planned to get away from town as soon as he heard the first boom from the first fireworks. He figured, that way nobody would hear the engine noise, and if they did hear it, nobody would pay attention because the fireworks would be so cool, and if they did pay attention, they couldn't see the boat in the dark.

Davy would speed across the channel. He would tie the boat by the main channel of the Kis'utch River, where nobody would see the skiff. Then quick up to the ridge by flashlight to see what Meredith's mom and Tick had built with those downed trees, whatever it was. Maybe a hideout, he was starting to think, but what would Rebecca and Tick do in a hideout, except hunt. Or maybe kiss—a disgusting thought. He shoved it aside. Once he and Meredith had found the hideout or whatever, they would slide quick down the hillside, and nobody would know they'd been gone. Except if they solved the mystery. Then they would be heroes. Or maybe the mystery would be so terrible that they would have to keep the secret their whole lives, just Meredith and Davy forever, sharing a terrible secret.

"The trouble with you, Davy, is that you don't think things through."

"Oh for crying out loud, Meredith. Thinking things through is what I'm trying to do. Why do you think I asked you to come with me? To think things through. And what help are you? I think just fine except when you're around, and then I can't think at all. Forget it. Just forget it. Everything about this plan is nuts. Especially me."

There was silence between them.

"Okay," he said finally. "I'll row you to the beach at the end of the boardwalk, and you can get out and walk back to the party. Forget this ever happened. Forget everything. Maybe I'll see you around sometime."

If he lived to be a thousand years old, Davy would never understand women. His dad had told him that this is something a man simply cannot do. Meredith brushed back her bangs with her hand and looked at him with those big soft eyes. They were filling with tears.

"Are you breaking up with me?" she asked in a little voice.

There was a sizzling noise and a deafening report. Pink and yellow fountains of light sprayed into the night. Smoke twirled down from the first explosion, and then each twirl exploded, sharp as a hammer on gunpowder. The reports echoed in the cavern under the school. Meredith covered her ears. Thunder bounced back and forth between the mountains behind the town and the mountains across the channel. The skyrocket was followed by a burst of pink light that grew and grew until it turned yellow and fizzled away.

Davy yanked the starter cord. The motor caught.

"Dear God, let this be the right decision. Just once, let it be right."

He nosed the skiff out from under the school, pointed it at the waterfall, and gunned it.

THE BANJO PLAYER signaled to the fireworks crew and laid down another mighty lick. The postmaster touched a flame to a wick. The flame sizzled into the heart of the rocket. An aerial shell burst into pink and yellow bloom against the dark clouds. Its petals disintegrated into burning stars that arced toward the sea. A matching starburst rose from the black water. They met in a shower of sparks. Twists of smoke sizzled out of the center of the bloom. They detonated with a blast of white light and a sharp report. Annie Klawon reached over to cover Tommy's ears.

"Ooooh," he shouted, and shook his head free.

Three more balls of light arced almost to the top of the ridge. Three bursts of blue sparks lit up the whole clamflat. Clearly visible beside their skiff drawn up on the beach at the industrial site, Tick and Howard faced each other, opening and closing their mouths and shaking their heads violently as they flashed blue and green under the fireworks. Tick looked up the mountain, pointed, began to talk again. By now, he had Howard by the shirtfront and was yelling at him.

A skyrocket sizzled up and exploded into a fountain of rosy sparks that blew apart into more fountains—blue, pink, yellow. Ribbons of light crisscrossed the sky. Across the channel, Tick and Howard ducked their heads under the barrage. Pink waves rolled up on shore at their feet. At the harbor, the crowd exhaled excitement.

Annie Klawon stood up abruptly. She grabbed hold of Rebecca.

"What's going on?

"Tick!" Annie cried out.

Tommy clutched his mom and began to whimper.

A deep-throated rumble rolled across the channel and slowly engulfed the crowd in its black shudder. Under the construction lights across the channel, Tick looked up, grabbed Howard by the front of his shirt, and began to pull at him. He gestured wildly toward the waterfall. Howard resisted his pull, bracing his boots into the mud, and gestured as wildly toward the construction site. For a moment, they pulled apart and faced each other, the way wrestlers lean in, at that moment before the lunge. Then Tick lifted Howard into the air and slung him over his shoulder. With Howard's long legs teetering behind him like two-by-fours, Tick ran hard away from the river and scrambled up a rocky slope. The air flashed yellow and another skyrocket rocked the channel.

Through the thunder, a dark vee cut across a pink pool of light. Annie Klawon peered through the crowd. The vee was the wake of a boat, a small boat, a skiff, their skiff, with a person in the bow and, in the stern, another person, a person who surely was her son, her son who was steering straight toward the mouth of the Kis'utch River.

In the yellow glare of Axel's construction floodlights, a black paw of water reached over the ridge above the dam site. The flood crouched there, gathering its strength. Logs spun in the gleam of the advancing edge. Then the flood clawed through the last rocks and bounded down the mountainside. With great leaps from ledge to ledge, it batted away the rootballs of ferns and tore out young alders.

"Flash flood," Annie Klawon shouted. "No, Davy. No."

Tangled with ferns and alders in the advancing flood, a log tumbled and thumped in the torrent, caught a cut end, somersaulted, dove underwater, and leapt up again, spraying a skyrocket's orange glare. In a final black sluice, the flood smashed onto the alder flat. It crouched again and bounded toward the industrial site.

"Meredith." Rebecca's voice was more a breath than a whisper. In the chaos of the great roar, the construction lights blacked out. Darkness rolled with the echoing thunder over the channel.

On the wharf, people grabbed up children and walked slowly backward, as they knew to do in the face of a great beast. The last pink sparks flashed out. All color sank under the black waves.

"Light," Annie Klawon shouted. "We need light."

Every member of the fireworks team touched a lighter to a fuse. A skyrocket shot up and sprayed the air with silver flowers. A blue chrysanthemum blew itself to smithereens. Silver confetti streaked across the sky, laying down orange contrails. The flood itself became a fire, throwing pink sparks and shooting off reflected flares of blue and orange. A foaming orange wave smashed into the dam's plywood forms. Boards jumped into the air and dove back into the suddenly blue face of the flood. Trailing sparks, an arm of water swept the Airstream trailer off its blocks. The corporate headquarters of Good River Products, Inc. careened down a torrent of jittering colors. Roman candles crackled into the sky. Thunder rocked from mountain to mountain, shot through with reports from multibreak shells. With stars burning in its teeth, the flood advanced toward the incoming tide. When flood and tide collided, their contrary forces threw up a giant wave that roared toward the town, carrying logs and gas cans, boards and hellfire.

Davy's skiff slowed as the breaker rushed toward them. Then the engine roared, and Davy turned the boat so hard it raised a curtain of water. But the flood was faster than the engine. It caught the transom in one hard slap, and flipped the skiff. Two dark forms catapulted into the wave.

"Please," whispered Annie Klawon. She sprinted for the harbor.

She stood at the slip where their skiff should have been, but of course, it was gone. She ran for the Good River Products boat and did not find it there. Racing up the dock, she jumped into the *Annie K.*

"CUT THE LINES," Annie Klawon yelled to Axel, as he pounded down the dock. He smashed the firebox, grabbed the axe, slashed the bowline with a single blow, and dashed back to cut the stern. He leapt into the front-loader as

Annie kicked it into reverse. With one hand on the wheel and her head out the side window, Annie shoved it to forward, pointed her bow straight toward the giant wave that was careening into the tide, and gunned it. Smashing into the flood, the *Annie K*'s bow reared up, hung on the crest of the wave. Then the bow smacked down hard between walls of water, rocked and settled, and they were in the recoiling water behind the wave, moving like an icebreaker through the wreckage. Thunder rolled away and darkness fell around them as the last of the fireworks winked out. All Annie heard was the engine grinding and boards banging against the hull. All she could see were flashes of phosphorescence from the startled sea creatures themselves. She could not see her son. She could not find Meredith.

"The spotlight. Get the spotlight," she yelled.

Axel grabbed the handle and flipped the switch. A spear of light shot wildly over the seas. Floating plywood, five-gallon bucket, curl of kelp, corrugated metal roofing, sharp as knives. Back and forth the light swept, until it bounced off Davy and Meredith, found them again, and rested like a hand on their shining hair. Their heads rose and fell on the swash of the flood. Davy had one arm around Meredith and the other around a bobbing gas can. She flailed at entangling kelp and kicked away a desk drawer.

"Tie a line on that life ring," Annie called. "Heave it out and stand by to release the pins." So slowly, so carefully, through bucking lumber and floating lines, she fought to bring the boat close to Meredith and Davy. In the slapping, slopping chaos of the flood and tide, logs struck the bow, knocking the boat from its course.

"Grab the boat hook and get that crap out of the way," Annie shouted.

Axel poked at the logs to make a space, and suddenly there they were, Davy and Meredith, grabbing for the life ring.

"Release the pins." The apron clanked to the water.

Kneeling, Axel got hold of Davy's jacket but the jacket slipped from his grasp as Davy shoved Meredith to the edge of the apron.

"Get your leg up. Get your leg over," Davy shouted.

With Axel pulling and Davy pushing, Meredith rolled onto the boat and turned to haul in Davy. They lay panting on the deck. Blood trickled from Meredith's forehead. As Annie Klawon turned the boat and maneuvered through debris to the dock, Axel drew the children into the shelter of the pilothouse and pressed them both to his chest. This is how they rode to shore, in this awkward embrace.

Holding woolen blankets, hands reached down from the dock, and soon Davy was stripped of his wet clothes and engulfed in a blanket, bundled with Annie to share the warmth of a mother's body. Axel helped Meredith climb from the bow and soon she too was wrapped close to her mother's life-saving warmth, which everyone in Good River Harbor knew was the best thing for people who almost drowned, and for their mothers too. Stumbling in the blankets, Davy and Meredith let their mothers lead them home to their woodstoves and heaped quilts.

The rest of the mothers gathered their children and made their ways up the boardwalk to their homes, the spotlights of their headlamps bobbing before them like jellyfish in a dark sea. Shadows of their dogs wandered behind. Then it was quiet on the wharf, just a few people slowly putting away chairs or coiling strings of lights. Mike Sorensen snapped shut the latches on his banjo case, said goodnight to Lillian, to Axel, and turned to the work of his Cleanup Committee. Suddenly came a great hollering and hallooing from across the channel.

"Hey, you suckers. What about us? Me and my friend Howard need a ride home." *Home, home,* echoed the channel. There Tick and Howard stood, at the top of a rocky slope above the splintered construction site. Tick was waving an orange highway cone as if it were a megaphone. Howard flapped a yellow safety vest.

Mike Sorenson put down his banjo, hopped into his skiff, and took off toward the clamflat. When the skiff nosed into the sand, Tick and Howard were standing together, each with his long arm draped over the other's shoulders.

They could not have seen that, not so far down the beach, a gyre of dark shapes circled in the deep water at the mouth of the Kis'utch. The circle flashed now and then when a salmon turned its side to the starlit night. As the flood-tide held, shimmering, at its peak, a ribbon of salmon unspooled from the spiral and turned toward home. Crossing the bar, each fish pushed a gleaming bow-wave upstream.

Back on the silent wharf, Axel sat down heavily on a bench, dropped his head in his hands, and began to shiver. Lillian, uncertain, sat down beside him. Then, because he was shivering, she took off her raincoat and arranged it over his shoulders. In her new purple dress, she sat tight beside him with her arm around his back. Because she was his mother and he was her son, she sheltered him as well as she could from the wind, which was just beginning to rise, the way the wind will sometimes rise when the tide begins to turn.

The black water of the channel shook under the small wind, then settled. All the stars in heaven reflected onto the water. The constellations swam there, the animals and ancient heroes, lifted and bent by the slow current of the tide. Far down the night-black channel, just where the tide turns past Bean Point, a kayak's silver wake moved slowly through the Great Bear, heading for Orion.

CODA

As the tide drained from the cove at Nora's cabin, a flock of crows banked sharply and dropped onto the circle of blackened mud where scorched rock-wrack still held on to the stones. They stalked stiff-legged across the soot, pecking experimentally at a bent, gray screw, a scrap of burnt leather, a charred timber. One tugged at a wire, hopping backward. When an eagle set its wings and carved over the cove, the crows lifted as one being, circled squawking, then settled again, jostling for space, tripping over the debris. Bolts with the nuts fused on them had fallen onto the cast-iron plate of the piano. They lay across a curve of tuning pins and busted-up wires, unsprung and brittle. In the mud some feet away was the brass pedal that sustains the sound.

ACKNOWLEDGMENTS

Over so many years, so many people have helped with *Piano Tide* in so many ways. Such good friends and family members—I hold you in my heart and thank you for your genius, your generosity, and your faith in a process that seemed to have no end. Deep gratitude to all of you:

To the people who read and responded to early drafts, John Calderazzo, Brook Elgie, Charles Goodrich, Kim Heacox, John Keeble, Hank Lentfer, Nancy Lord, Carol Mason, Erin Moore, Frank Moore, Jonathan Moore, and Vicki Wisenbaugh.

To all the remarkably generous and capable people who welcomed our family into their Southeast Alaska communities and homes, told us stories, taught us new skills and words, took us to sea and poetry readings, laughed and fished and feasted with us—all those friends on the VHF radio and the trails and the ferries. I will not name you, to save you any possible grief. You know who you are; I hope you know how much I love and admire you.

To concert pianist Rachelle McCabe, salmon ecologist Jonathan Moore, then-teenager Zachary Wisenbaugh, architect Erin Moore, naturalist Frank Moore, and all the other experts who shared their expertise—from how to tune a piano to how to swear like a teenager. To Richard A. Zagars, the incomparable Juneau artist who gave me the gift of his painting for the book cover. To Portland writer Brian Doyle, who grins at the mysterious chiming of our novels; we are born, he says, of the same "salt and song."

To my characters. Philosophy professor than I am, I had originally invented each one to embody a different theory of environmental ethics. But they soon told me that they had minds of their own, and free will.

They would do and think what they damned well pleased, which was way more complicated than I could ever learn—although they would try to teach me.

To Southeast Alaska, its denizens and its tides—the trumpeting whales, hidden coves, ticking barnacles—on every scale, in every weather, an astonishment of beauty and thriving.

For early sustenance and inspiration, thanks to the Wrangell Mountain Center, Fishtrap Writers' Residency on the Imnaha River, Playa, and the Spring Creek Project.

To those who have given always good advice, good will, and support in publishing, Laura Blake Peterson, Carol Mason, and Jack Shoemaker.

To my family, exceptional people who fill me with ideas, stories, love, and laughter. And especially to my truly wonderful husband, Frank. With his strong hands, deep intelligence, and generous love, Frank has built the foundation under every one of our shared dreams, including this one. Love and gratitude to you, dear Frank. Forever.